THE INTEL MICROPROCESSORS

8086/8088, 80186, 80286, 80386, and 80486
Third Edition

THE INTEL MICROPROCESSORS

8086/8088, 80186, 80286, 80386, and 80486 Architecture, Programming, and Interfacing
Third Edition

BARRY B. BREY
DeVRY Institute of Technology

Merrill, an imprint of
Macmillan Publishing Company
New York

Maxwell Macmillan Canada
Toronto

Maxwell Macmillan International
New York   Oxford   Singapore   Sydney

Editor: David Garza
Production Supervisor: bookworks
Production Manager: Aliza Greenblatt
Text Designer: Debra A. Fargo
Cover Designer: Robert Freese
Illustrations: Academy Art Works, Inc.

This book was set in Times Roman by Carlisle, and printed and bound by R.R. Donnelley & Sons.

Macmillan Publishing Company
866 Third Avenue, New York, New York 10022

Macmillan Publishing Company is
part of the Maxwell Communication
Group of Companies.

Maxwell Macmillan Canada, Inc.
1200 Eglinton Avenue East
Suite 200
Don Mills, Ontario M3C 3N1

Library of Congress Cataloging-in-Publication Data

Brey, Barry B.
     The Intel microprocessors : 8086/8088, 80186, 80286, 80386, and
80486 : architecture, programming, and interfacing / Barry B. Brey.
— 3rd ed.
          p.   cm.
     Includes bibliographical references and index.
ISBN 0-02-314250-2
     1. Intel 8086 (Microprocessor)   2. Intel 8088 (Microprocessor)
  3. Intel 80xxx series microprocessors.   I. Title.
QA76.8.I292B75 1994
004. 165—dc20
                                                                      90-21801
                                                                      CIP

Printing: 1 2 3 4 5 6 7   Year: 4 5 6 7 8 9 0

MERRILL'S INTERNATIONAL SERIES IN ENGINEERING TECHNOLOGY

Zanger & Zanger, *Fiber Optics: Communication and Other Applications*, 0-675-20944-7

Microcomputer Servicing

Adamson, *Microcomputer Repair*, 0-02-300825-3

Asser, Stigliano, & Bahrenburg, *Microcomputer Servicing: Practical Systems and Troubleshooting, 2nd Edition*, 0-02-304241-9

Asser, Stigliano, & Bahrenburg, *Microcomputer Theory and Servicing, 2nd Edition*, 0-02-304231-1

Programming

Adamson, *Applied Pascal for Technology*, 0-675-20771-1

Adamson, *Structured BASIC Applied to Technology, 2nd Edition*, 0-02-300827-X

Adamson, *Structured C for Technology*, 0-675-20993-5

Adamson, *Structured C for Technology (with disk)*, 0-675-21289-8

Nashelsky & Boylestad, *BASIC Applied to Circuit Analysis*, 0-675-20161-6

Instrumentation and Measurement

Berlin & Getz, *Principles of Electronic Instrumentation and Measurement*, 0-675-20449-6

Buchla & McLachlan, *Applied Electronic Instrumentation and Measurement*, 0-675-21162-X

Gillies, *Instrumentation and Measurements for Electronic Technicians, 2nd Edition*, 0-02-343051-6

Transform Analysis

Kulathinal, *Transform Analysis and Electronic Networks with Applications*, 0-675-20765-7

Biomedical Equipment Technology

Aston, *Principles of Biomedical Instrumentation and Measurement*, 0-675-20943-9

Mathematics

Monaco, *Essential Mathematics for Electronics Technicians*, 0-675-21172-7

Davis, *Technical Mathematics*, 0-675-20338-4

Davis, *Technical Mathematics with Calculus*, 0-675-20965-X

INDUSTRIAL ELECTRONICS/INDUSTRIAL TECHNOLOGY

Bateson, *Introduction to Control System Technology, 4th Edition*, 0-02-306463-3

Fuller, *Robotics: Introduction, Programming, and Projects*, 0-675-21078-X

Goetsch, *Industrial Safety and Health: In the Age of High Technology*, 0-02-344207-7

Goetsch, *Industrial Supervision: In the Age of High Technology*, 0-675-22137-4

Geotsch, *Introduction to Total Quality: Quality, Productivity, and Competitiveness*, 0-02-344221-2

Horath, *Computer Numerical Control Programming of Machines*, 0-02-357201-9

Hubert, *Electric Machines: Theory, Operation, Applications, Adjustment, and Control*, 0-675-20765-7

Humphries, *Motors and Controls*, 0-675-20235-3

Hutchins, *Introduction to Quality: Management, Assurance, and Control*, 0-675-20896-3

Laviana, *Basic Computer Numerical Control Programming*, 0-675-21298-7

Pond, *Fundamentals of Statistical Quality Control*

Reis, *Electronic Project Design and Fabrication, 2nd Edition*, 0-02-399230-1

Rosenblatt & Friedman, *Direct and Alternating Current Machinery, 2nd Edition*, 0-675-20160-8

Smith, *Statistical Process Control and Quality Improvement*, 0-675-21160-3

Webb, *Programmable Logic Controllers: Principles and Applications, 2nd Edition*, 0-02-424970-X

Webb & Greshock, *Industrial Control Electronics, 2nd Edition*, 0-02-424864-9

MECHANICAL/CIVIL TECHNOLOGY

Dalton, *The Technology of Metallurgy*, 0-02-326900-6

Keyser, *Materials Science in Engineering, 4th Edition*, 0-675-20401-1

Kokernak, *Fluid Power Technology*, 0-02-305705-X

Kraut, *Fluid Mechanics for Technicians*, 0-675-21330-4

Mott, *Applied Fluid Mechanics, 4th Edition*, 0-02-384231-8

Mott, *Machine Elements in Mechanical Design, 2nd Edition*, 0-675-22289-3

Rolle, *Thermodynamics and Heat Power, 4th Edition*, 0-02-403201-8

Spiegel & Limbrunner, *Applied Statics and Strength of Materials, 2nd Edition*, 0-02-414961-6

Spiegel & Limbrunner, *Applied Strength of Materials*, 0-02-414970-5

Wolansky & Akers, *Modern Hydraulics: The Basics at Work*, 0-675-20987-0

Wolf, *Statics and Strength of Materials: A Parallel Approach to Understanding Structures*, 0-675-20622-7

DRAFTING TECHNOLOGY

Cooper, *Introduction to VersaCAD*, 0-675-21164-6

Ethier, *AutoCAD in 3 Dimensions*, 0-02-334232-3

Goetsch & Rickman, *Computer-Aided Drafting with AutoCAD*, 0-675-20915-3

Kirkpatrick & Kirkpatrick, *AutoCAD for Interior Design and Space Planning*, 0-02-364455-9

Kirkpatrick, *The AutoCAD Book: Drawing, Modeling, and Applications, 2nd Edition*, 0-675-22288-5

Kirkpatrick, *The AutoCAD Book: Drawing, Modeling, and Applications, Including Release 12, 3rd Edition*, 0-02-364440-0

Lamit & Lloyd, *Drafting for Electronics, 2nd Edition*, 0-02-367342-7

Lamit & Paige, *Computer-Aided Design and Drafting*, 0-675-20475-5

Maruggi, *Technical Graphics: Electronics Worktext, 2nd Edition*, 0-675-21378-9

Maruggi, *The Technology of Drafting*, 0-675-20762-2

Sell, *Basic Technical Drawing*, 0-675-21001-1

TECHNICAL WRITING

Croft, *Getting a Job: Resume Writing, Job Application Letters, and Interview Strategies*, 0-675-20917-X

Panares, *A Handbook of English for Technical Students*, 0-675-20650-2

Pfeiffer, *Proposal Writing: The Art of Friendly Persuausion*, 0-675-20988-9

Pfeiffer, *Technical Writing: A Practical Approach, 2nd Edition*, 0-02-395111-7

Roze, *Technical Communications: The Practical Craft, 2nd Edition*, 0-02-404171-8

Weisman, *Basic Technical Writing, 6th Edition*, 0-675-21256-1

This text is dedicated to my loving wife, Sheila, whose patience and understanding have made this endeavor possible.

PREFACE

This text is written for the student in a course of study that requires a thorough knowledge of programming and interfacing of the Intel family of microprocessors. It is a very practical reference text for anyone interested in all programming and interfacing aspects of this important microprocessor family. Today, anyone functioning or striving to function in a field of study that uses computers must understand assembly language programming and interfacing. Intel microprocessors have gained wide applications in many areas of electronics, communications, control systems, and particularly in desktop computer systems.

ORGANIZATION AND COVERAGE

In order to cultivate a comprehensive approach to learning, each chapter of the text begins with a set of objectives that briefly define the contents of the chapter. This is followed by the body of the chapter, which includes many programming applications that illustrate the main topics of the chapter. At the end of each chapter, a numerical summary, which doubles as a study guide, reviews the information presented in the chapter. Finally, questions and problems are provided to promote practice and mental exercise with the concepts presented in the chapter.

This text contains many example programs, using the Microsoft Macro Assembler program, which provide an opportunity to learn how to program the Intel family of microprocessors. Operation of the programming environment includes the linker, library, macros, DOS function, and BIOS functions.

Also provided is a thorough description of each family member, memory systems, and various I/O systems that include: disk memory, ADC and DAC, USARTs, PIAs, timers, keyboard/display controllers, arithmetic coprocessors, and video display systems. Through these systems, a practical approach to microprocessor interfacing is learned.

APPROACH

Because the Intel family of microprocessors is quite diverse, this text initially concentrates on real mode programming, which is compatible with all versions of the Intel family of microprocessors. Instructions for each family member, which includes the 80386 and 80486, are compared and contrasted with the 8086/8088 microprocessor. This entire series of microprocessors is very similar, which allows more advanced versions to be learned once the basic 8086/8088 is understood.

In addition to fully explaining the programming and operation of the microprocessor, this text also explains the programming and operation of the numeric coprocessor (8087/80287/80387/80486/7). The numeric coprocessor functions in a system to provide access to floating-point calculations that are important in applications such as control systems, video graphics, and computer aided design (CAD). The numeric coprocessor allows a program to access complex arithmetic operations that are otherwise difficult to achieve with normal microprocessor programming.

Also described are the pinouts and function of the 8086–80486 microprocessors. Interfacing is first developed using the 8088/8086 with some of the more common peripheral components. After learning the basics, a more advanced emphasis is placed on the 80186/80188, 80386, and 80486 microprocessors. Coverage of the 80286, because of its similarity to the 8086 and 80386, is minimized so the 80386 and 80486 can be covered in complete detail.

Through this approach, the operation of the microprocessor and programming with the advanced family members, along with interfacing all family members, provides a working and practical background on the Intel family of microprocessors. On completion of a course of study based on this text, you should be able to:

1. Develop control software to control an application interface to the 8086/8088, 80186/80188, 80286, 80386, or 80486 microprocessor. Generally, the software developed will also function on all versions of the microprocessor. This software also includes DOS-based applications.
2. Program using DOS function calls to control the keyboard, video display system, and disk memory in assembly language.
3. Use the BIOS functions to control the keyboard, display, and various other components in the computer system.
4. Develop software that uses interrupt hooks and hot keys to gain access to terminate and stay resident software.
5. Program the numeric coprocessor (80287/80387) to solve complex equations.
6. Explain the differences between the family members and highlight the features of each member.
7. Describe and use real and protected mode operation of the 80286, 80386, and 80486 microprocessors.
8. Interface memory and I/O systems to the microprocessor.
9. Provide a detailed and comprehensive comparison of all family members, their software, and hardware interface.
10. Explain the operation of disk and video systems.

CONTENT OVERVIEW

Chapter 1 introduces the Intel family of microprocessors with an emphasis on the microprocessor-based computer system. This first chapter serves to introduce the microprocessor, its history, its operation, and the methods used to store data in a microprocessor-based system. It also explores the programming model of the microprocessor and system architecture. Both real and protected mode operation are explained in this introductory chapter. Once an understanding of the basic machine is grasped, chapters 2–5 explain how each instruction functions with the Intel family of microprocessors. As instructions are explained, simple applications are presented to illustrate the operation of the instructions and develop basic programming concepts.

Once the basis for programming is developed, chapter 6 provides applications using the assembler program. These applications include programming using DOS and BIOS function calls. Disk files are explained as well as keyboard and video operation on a personal computer system. This chapter provides the tools required to develop virtually any program on a personal computer system. It also introduces the concept of interrupt hooks and hot keys.

Chapter 7 introduces the 8086/8088 family as a basis for learning basic memory and I/O interfacing that follow in later chapters. This chapter shows the buffered system as well as the system timing.

Chapter 8 provides complete detail on memory interface using both integrated decoders and programmable logic devices. Parity is illustrated as well as dynamic memory systems. The 8-, 16- and 32-bit memory systems are provided so the 8086–80486 microprocessors can be interfaced to memory.

Chapter 9 provides a detailed look at basic I/I interfacing that includes PIAs, timers, keyboard/display interfaces, USARTs, and ADC/DAC. It also describes the interface of both DC and stepper motors.

Once these basic I/O components and their interface to the microprocessor are understood, chapters 10 and 11 provide detail on advanced I/O techniques that include interrupts and direct memory access (DMA). Applications include a printer interface, real-time clock, disk memory, and video systems.

Chapter 12 details the operation and programming for the 8087–80387 family of arithmetic coprocessors. Today, few applications function efficiently without the power of the arithmetic coprocessor.

Chapters 13 and 14 provide detail on the advanced 80186/80188–80486 microprocessors. In these chapters we explore the differences between the 8086/8088 and their enhancements and features. Cache memory as well as interleaved and burst memory are described with the 80386 and 80486 microprocessors. Also described are memory management and memory paging.

Appendices are included to enhance the application of the text. These include:

A. A complete listing of the DOS INT 21H function calls. This appendix also details the use of the assembler program and many of the BIOS function calls including BIOS function call INT 10H.

    B. Complete listing of all 8086/8088/80286/80386/80486 instructions including many example instructions and machine coding in hexadecimal as well as clock timing information.

    C. A compact list of all the instructions that change the flag bits.

    D. Detailed pinouts of the personal computer bus standards so they can be interfaced to additional hardware systems.

    E. Answers for the even-numbered questions and problems.

B. B. B.

CONTENTS

3   DATA MOVEMENT INSTRUCTIONS   73

4   ARITHMETIC AND LOGIC INSTRUCTIONS   116

5   PROGRAM CONTROL INSTRUCTIONS   154

10   INTERRUPTS   412

11   DIRECT MEMORY ACCESS AND DMA-CONTROLLED I/O   452

12   THE FAMILY OF ARITHMETIC COPROCESSORS   511

CHAPTER 1

Introduction
to the Microprocessor

INTRODUCTION

This chapter introduces the Intel family of microprocessors. This important family of microprocessors, which includes the 8086, 8088, 80186, 80286, 80386, and 80486, evolved from the early 4- and 8-bit microprocessors. In this chapter, we describe the architecture and the memory structure of the microprocessor and introduce the instruction set of the Intel family of microprocessors.

Also presented are the formats used by the microprocessor for data storage. These formats include binary integers stored as signed and unsigned numbers in bytes, words, and double words; BCD data, floating-point data, and ASCII data.

CHAPTER OBJECTIVES

Upon completion of this chapter, you will be able to:

1. Describe the evolution of the microprocessor.
2. Explain the internal operation of the microprocessor detailing the function of the pipeline, queue, and various internal structures.
3. Detail the structure of the memory and microprocessor's internal register array.
4. Define the terms memory segment address and offset address.
5. Calculate the effective address for the next program step using the contents of the instruction pointer (IP) and code segment (CS) registers.
6. Show how data are stored in the memory for the following integer and unsigned data types: byte, word, and double word.
7. Define real and protected mode operation as it applies to more advanced family members.
8. Provide an overview of the Intel family instruction set.

1–1   THE EVOLUTION OF THE MICROPROCESSOR

Before we discuss modern microprocessors, we must first understand what brought these devices to the forefront. History shows us that the ancient Babylonians first began using the *abacus* (a primitive calculator made of beads) in about 500 B.C. This simple calculating machine eventually sparked humankind into the development of calculating machinery that used gears and wheels (Blaise Pascal in 1642). Refinements continued with the giant computing machines of the 1940s and 1950s constructed with relays and vacuum tubes. Next the transistor and solid-state electronics were used to build the mighty computers of the 1960s. Finally, the advent of the integrated circuit led to the development of the microprocessor and microprocessor-based computer system.

The 4-Bit Microprocessor

In 1971, Intel Corporation and the creative talents of Marcian E. Hoff released the world's first microprocessor—the 4004, a 4-bit microprocessor. This integrated, programmable controller on a chip was meager by today's standards, because it only addressed 4,096 4-bit memory locations. The 4004 contained an instruction set that offered only 45 different instructions. As a result, the 4004 could be used only in limited applications such as early video games and small microprocessor-based controllers. When more sophisticated applications emerged for the microprocessor, the 4004 proved inadequate.

The 8-Bit Microprocessor

Later in 1971, realizing that the microprocessor was a commercially viable product, Intel Corporation released the 8008—the first 8-bit microprocessor. The expanded memory size (16K × 8) and additional instructions (a total of 48) in this new microprocessor provided the opportunity for many more advanced applications. (*1K* is equal to 1,024 and a *byte* is an 8-bit number).

As engineers developed more demanding uses for the microprocessor, the still relatively small memory and instruction set of the 8008 soon limited its usefulness. Thus, in 1973, the Intel Corporation introduced the 8080—the first of the modern 8-bit microprocessors. Soon other companies began releasing their own versions of the 4- and 8-bit microprocessors. Table 1–1 lists many of these early microprocessors.

But what was special about the 8080? Not only did it address more memory and execute more instructions, but it executed instructions ten times faster than the 8008. An

TABLE 1–1 Early 8-bit microprocessors

Manufacturer	Part Number
Fairchild	F-8
Intel	8080
MOS Technology	6502
Motorola	MC6800
National Semiconductor	IMP-8
Rockwell International	PPS-8

addition that took 20 μs on an 8008-based system took only 2.0 μs on an 8080-based system. Also, the 8080 was transistor-transistor logic (TTL) compatible, which meant it could be easily interfaced to standard TTL logic components. All these advantages ushered in the era of the 8080, and the ever expanding era of the *microprocessor.*

A newer version of the 8080, the 8085, was introduced by Intel Corporation in 1977. Only slightly more advanced than the 8080, the 8085 addresses the same amount of memory, executes about the same number of instructions, and adds in 1.3 μs instead of 2.0 μs. The main advantages of the 8085 are its built-in clock generator and system controller, which were external components in the 8080-based system. Intel alone has sold well over 100 million copies of the 8085 microprocessor. Other companies, such as NEC, AMD, Toshiba, and Hitachi, also manufacture a licensed version of the 8085 microprocessor. These features have made the 8085 one of Intel's most popular microprocessors.

The 16-Bit Microprocessor

In 1978, Intel Corporation released the 8086 microprocessor and about a year later, the 8088. Both devices are 16-bit microprocessors that execute instructions in as little as 400 ns, a vast improvement over the execution speed of the 8085. The 8086 and 8088 are also capable of addressing a 1M byte (8-bit wide) or a 512K word (16-bit wide) memory. The higher execution speeds and larger memory sizes allow the 8086 and 8088 to replace smaller minicomputers in many applications.

One important need that spurred the evolution of the 16-bit microprocessor is hardware multiplication and division. These functions are not available on most of the 8-bit microprocessors, with the exception of the Motorola MC6809, which can multiply, but not divide. But the 16-bit microprocessor evolved for other reasons as well. It provides a larger addressable memory space than the 8-bit microprocessor, allowing it to perform some very sophisticated operations that just didn't fit into 64K bytes of memory. The 8086 and 8088 have a large number of internal registers, which are accessible in 200 ns compared to the 800 ns it takes to reach a register on an 8-bit microprocessor. These additional registers allow software to be written far more efficiently. Finally, software application programs (data-based management systems, spreadsheets, word processors, and spelling checkers) began to require more than the 64K bytes of memory available on the 8-bit microprocessor. The time was ripe for the 16-bit microprocessor.

Evolution of the 16-bit microprocessor did not end with the 8086 and 8088; it continued with the introduction of the 80186, a highly integrated version of the 8086. The 80186 is today one of Intel's more popular 16-bit microprocessors. The 80186 is used in many control system applications, but not as the main microprocessor in personal computer systems. If the 80186 is found in a personal computer, it is on a plug-in daughter board that may control a hard disk memory system or a communications interface.

The last 16-bit microprocessor developed by Intel is the 80286, an improved version of the 8086 that contains a memory-management unit and addresses a 16M byte memory instead of a 1M byte memory. The clock speed of the 80286 also increased to 16 MHz on the latest version produced by Intel. The basic version of the 8086 and 8088 executed up to 2.5 MIPs (*millions of instructions per second*), while the basic version of the 80286 executes up to 8 MIPs.

TABLE 1–2   Intel microprocessors

Part Number	Data Bus Width	Memory Size
8048	8	2K internal
8051	8	8K internal
8085A	8	64K
8086	16	1M
8088	8	1M
8096	16	8K internal
80186	16	1M
80188	8	1M
80286	16	16M
80386DX	32	4G
80386SL	16	32M
80386SX	16	16M
80486DX	32	4G
80486SX	32	4G
Pentium*	32/64	4G

*   Pentium is a registered trademark of Intel Corporation.

The 32-Bit Microprocessor

The most recent version of the microprocessor is the 32-bit microprocessor (see Table 1–2 for a list of all Intel microprocessors). Intel currently produces two main versions: the 80386 and 80486. The 80386 was the first 32-bit microprocessor produced by Intel. The main advantage of this device is a much higher clock frequency (33 MHz for the 80386 and 66 MHz for the double-clocked version of the 80486) and a much larger memory space (4G bytes).

The 80486 microprocessor basically contains an improved 80386, an arithmetic co-processor (for the DX version of the 80486), and an 8K byte internal cache memory. The 80386 executes many instructions in 2 clocks, while the 80486 executes many instructions in 1 clock. These improvements combined with a 66 MHz clock (80486DX2) allow instructions to execute at 54 MIPs according to Intel Corporation. This compares to the 8085, released 12 years prior to the 80486, that executes instructions at the rate of about 0.5 MIPs. These speed improvements will continue with newer versions of the 32-bit microprocessor as they become available. The next generation (Pentium) promises speeds of 100 MIPs.

1–2   BASIC MICROPROCESSOR ARCHITECTURE

Efficient programming and interfacing require a clear understanding of the basic architecture of the Intel family of microprocessors and microprocessor-based computer systems. This section provides a detailed description of the basic architecture of these microprocessors.

Basic Internal Architecture

Like early microprocessors, modern microprocessors fetch instructions from the memory, but they do it in an entirely new way. Modern microprocessors are structured so they contain many internal processing units that each perform a specific task. (Note that each of these processing units is actually a special-purpose microprocessor.) This means that the modern microprocessor can often process several instructions simultaneously at various stages of execution. This ability is often called *pipelining*.

Figure 1–1(a) illustrates the normal operation of an 8085, which is typical of most 8-bit microprocessors. Notice that an instruction is fetched from the memory by a memory-read operation. Next, while the 8085 executes the instruction, the memory system is idle. The Intel family of microprocessors, beginning with the 8086 and 8088, make use of this idle memory time by prefetching the next instruction while executing the current one. This accelerates the overall execution of a program.

Figure 1–1(b) illustrates the sequence of events for the 80486 microprocessor. Notice that the bus is almost always busy. Notice also that the 80486 contains more then one internal unit. Each unit is designed to function in the *pipe* with instructions at various phases of execution.

The BIU (bus interface unit) is responsible for fetching instructions and for reading or writing data between the microprocessor and the memory. The output of the BIU connects to an 8K byte cache memory that stores the most recent data and instructions. The output of the cache feeds a prefetcher (queue) that holds 32 bytes of instructions. This means that the microprocessor can hold 32 bytes of unexecuted

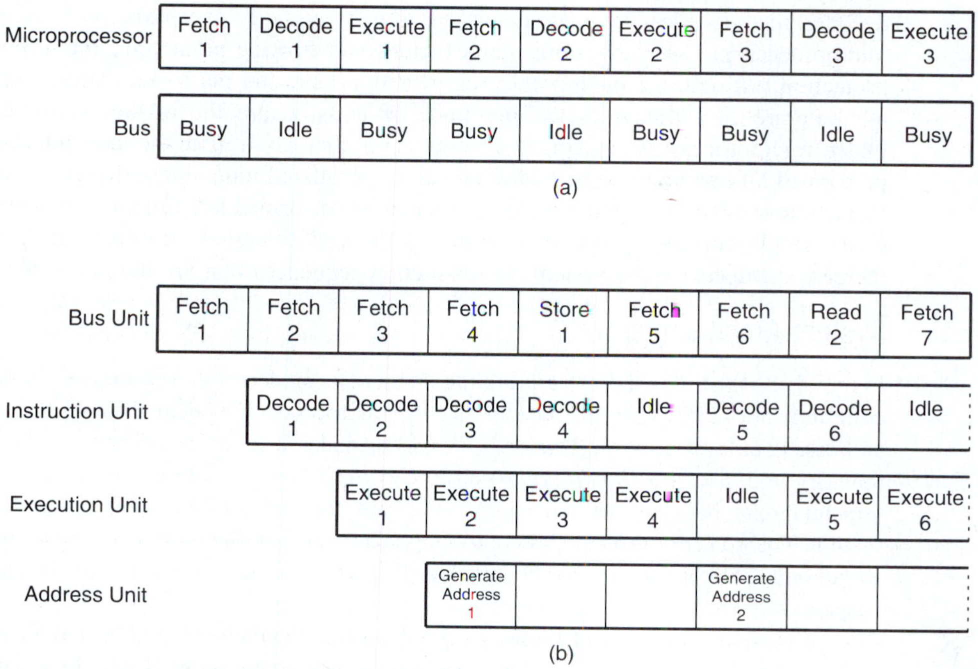

Microprocessor	Fetch 1	Decode 1	Execute 1	Fetch 2	Decode 2	Execute 2	Fetch 3	Decode 3	Execute 3
Bus	Busy	Idle	Busy	Busy	Idle	Busy	Busy	Idle	Busy

(a)

Bus Unit	Fetch 1	Fetch 2	Fetch 3	Fetch 4	Store 1	Fetch 5	Fetch 6	Read 2	Fetch 7
Instruction Unit		Decode 1	Decode 2	Decode 3	Decode 4	Idle	Decode 5	Decode 6	Idle
Execution Unit			Execute 1	Execute 2	Execute 3	Execute 4	Idle	Execute 5	Execute 6
Address Unit				Generate Address 1			Generate Address 2		

(b)

FIGURE 1–1 (a) The operation of an early microprocessor such as the 8085A, and (b) the operation of the 80486 pipelined microprocessor.

i486™ Microprocessor Pipelined 32-Bit Microarchitecture

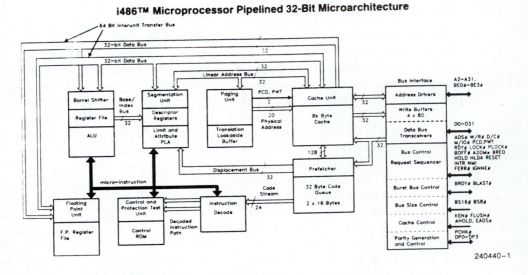

iRMX, iRMK, 386, 387, 486, i486 are trademarks of Intel Corporation.
MS-DOS is a registered trademark of Microsoft Corporation.
**OS/2™ is a trademark of Microsoft Corporation.
***UNIX™ is a trademark of AT&T.

FIGURE 1–2   The internal structure of the 80486 microprocessor. (Courtesy of Intel Corporation)

instructions in the prefetcher. Connected to the output of the prefetcher is an instruction decoder that decodes the instructions for use by various execution units within the microprocessor. These execution units include the floating-point unit, the control and protection test unit, the paging unit, segmentation unit, and the barrel shifter and ALU.

Figure 1–2 illustrates the multitude of units within the 80486 microprocessor. Older microprocessors contained a single unit that controlled the bus interface and performed all operations. The 80486 contains specialized units that individually perform these functions so more than one operation can be performed at a time. In the future more than a single microprocessor, such as the 80486, will be contained in one unit to further increase the speed of the system for instruction sequences that are not dependent.

System Architecture

Figure 1-3 illustrates the system architectures of a modern microprocessor. Notice that communications between the system and the microprocessor occur through three buses: address, data, and control. The *address bus* provides a memory address to the system memory and also I/O (*input/output*) addresses to the system I/O devices. The *data bus* transfers data between the microprocessor and the memory and I/O attached to the system. The *control bus* provides control signals that cause the memory or I/O to perform a read or a write operation. The control signals that cause memory or I/O reads and writes vary slightly from one family member to the next.

A close examination of Figure 1–3 reveals that the data bus widths and address bus widths vary from one version of the microprocessor to the next. Table 1–3 lists these

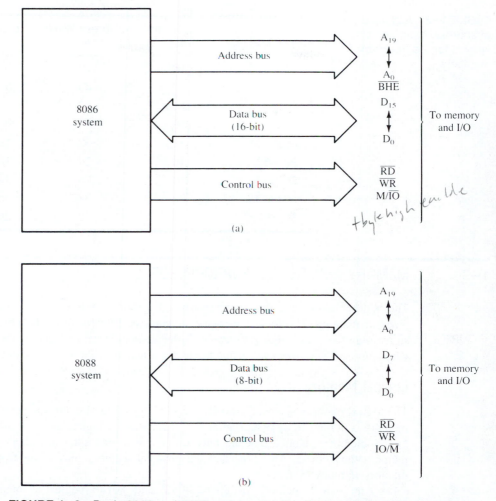

FIGURE 1-3 Basic 8086 and 8088 systems. (a) The 8086 system, illustrating the 16-bit data bus, the 20-bit address bus, and the control bus. (b) The 8088 system, illustrating the 8-bit data bus, the 20-bit address bus, and the control bus.

variations for comparison and also the clock speed when the microprocessor was first released. After each microprocessor was initially released, higher clock frequency versions became available.

The data bus width determines how many bytes are transferred between the microprocessor and memory at a time, while the address bus width determines how much memory is addressed by each microprocessor. Generally, the wider the data bus width the faster a microprocessor becomes. The next few generations of microprocessor and microprocessor-based computers will contain data bus widths of 64 and possibly 128 bits.

TABLE 1–3 A comparison of address, data, and clock speeds for the Intel family members

Microprocessor	Data Width (bits)	Address Width its	Clock (MHz)
8086	16	20	5
8088	8	20	5
80186	16	20	6
80286	16	24	8
80386DX	32	32	16
80386SX	16	24	16
80386SL	16	25	16
80486DX	32	32	25
80486SX	32	32	20

1–3   MEMORY AND THE MICROPROCESSOR

The address space in a microprocessor-based system is referenced as either logical or physical memory. The logical memory structure is different from the physical memory structure in most cases. *Logical memory* is the memory system as seen by the programmer, while *physical memory* is the actual hardware structure of the memory system.

Logical Memory

The logical memory space is basically the same for all Intel microprocessors. The logical memory is numbered by byte. Figure 1–4 illustrates the logical memory map for all Intel family members. Notice that the only difference is that some members contain more memory than others. Also note that the physical memory may differ from the logical memory in many systems.

The logical memory of 8086, 8088, and 80186 begins at memory location 00000H and extends to location FFFFFH. This range of addresses specifies the 1M byte of memory available in these systems. The logical memory of the 80286 and 80386SX begins at memory location 000000H and extends to location FFFFFFH for a total of 16M bytes of memory. The 80386SL contains 32M bytes of memory beginning at location 0000000H and ending with location 1FFFFFFH. Finally, the 80386DX, 80486SX, and 80486DX contain memory beginning at location 00000000H and ending at location FFFFFFFFH for a total of 4G bytes of memory (*1G = 1,024M and 1M = 1,024K*).

When these microprocessors address a 16-bit word of memory, two consecutive bytes are accessed. For example, the word at location 00122H is stored at bytes 00122H and 00123H with the least significant byte stored in location 00122H. If a 32-bit double word is accessed, four consecutive bytes contain the double word. For example, the double word stored at location 00120H is stored at bytes 00120H, 00121H, 00122H, and 00123H with the least significant byte stored at 00120H and the most significant byte at location 00123H.

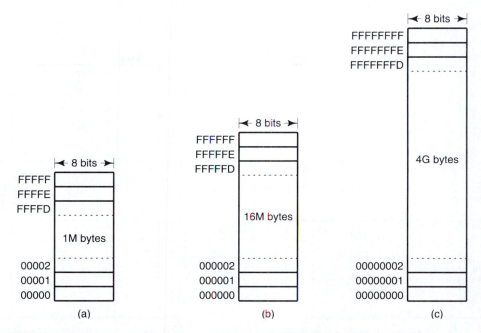

FIGURE 1–4   The logical memory map of the (a) 8086/8088/80186; (b) 80286/80386DX; and (c) 80386DX and 80486 microprocessors.

Physical Memory

The physical memories of the Intel family members differ in width. The 8088 memory is 8 bits wide; the 8086, 80186, 80286, and 80386SX memories are 16 bits wide; and the 80386DX and 80486 memories are 32 bits wide. For programming there is no difference in memory width, because the logical memory is always 8 bits wide—but, as you can see in Figure 1–5, there is a difference for the hardware designer.

Memory is organized in memory banks on all versions of the microprocessor except the 8088, which contains only one memory bank. A *memory bank* is an 8-bit wide section of the memory. The 16-bit microprocessors contain two memory banks to form a 16-bit wide section of memory that is addressed as bytes or words. The 32-bit microprocessors contain four memory banks that are addressed as bytes, words, or double words.

Memory in the Personal Computer

Any study of the Intel family requires an understanding of the memory structure of the personal computer. Because the personal computer was originally based on the 8088 microprocessor, its main memory is considered to be 1M bytes in length. This main memory is often called *real memory*. Memory expansion was never allowed until LIM (Lotus-Intel-Microsoft) developed a standard for an *expanded memory system* (EMS).

The expanded memory was placed in an unused *page frame* (64K bytes) located between read-only memory (ROM) BIOS (Basic I/O System) areas in the system. Through this 64K byte page frame, the LIM standard allows access to an unlimited

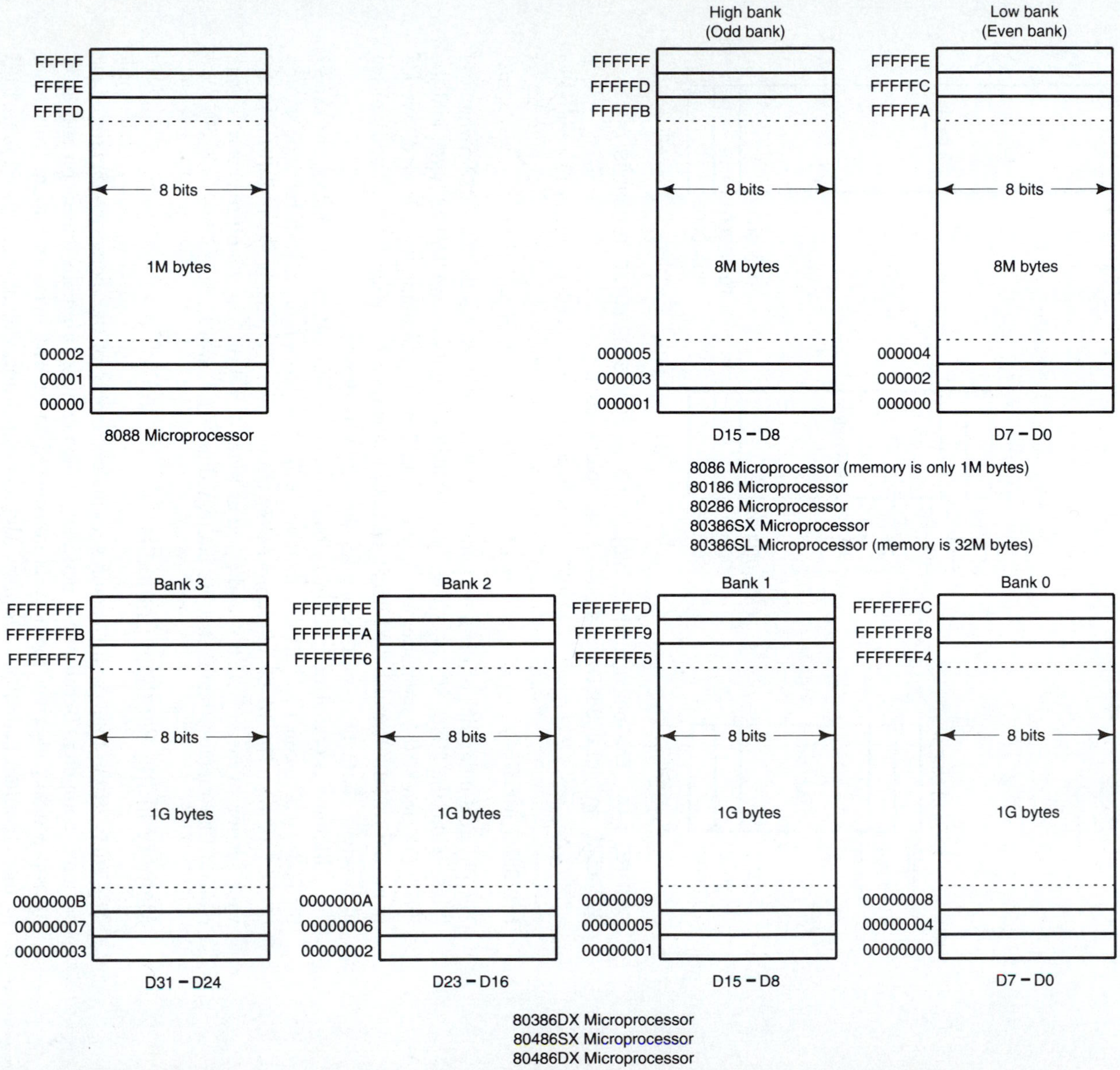

Low bank (Even bank)

FFFFFE
FFFFFC
FFFFFA

8 bits

8M bytes

000004
000002
000000

D7 – D0

High bank (Odd bank)

FFFFFF
FFFFFD
FFFFFB

8 bits

8M bytes

000005
000003
000001

D15 – D8

8086 Microprocessor (memory is only 1M bytes)
80186 Microprocessor
80286 Microprocessor
80386SX Microprocessor
80386SL Microprocessor (memory is 32M bytes)

8088 Microprocessor

FFFFF
FFFFE
FFFFD

8 bits

1M bytes

00002
00001
00000

Bank 0

FFFFFFFC
FFFFFFF8
FFFFFFF4

8 bits

1G bytes

00000008
00000004
00000000

D7 – D0

Bank 1

FFFFFFFD
FFFFFFF9
FFFFFFF5

8 bits

1G bytes

00000009
00000005
00000001

D15 – D8

Bank 2

FFFFFFFE
FFFFFFFA
FFFFFFF6

8 bits

1G bytes

0000000A
00000006
00000002

D23 – D16

Bank 3

FFFFFFFF
FFFFFFFB
FFFFFFF7

8 bits

1G bytes

0000000B
00000007
00000003

D31 – D24

80386DX Microprocessor
80486SX Microprocessor
80486DX Microprocessor

FIGURE 1–5 The physical memory systems of the 8086–80486 microprocessor family.

10

FIGURE 1-6 The memory map for a personal computer system.

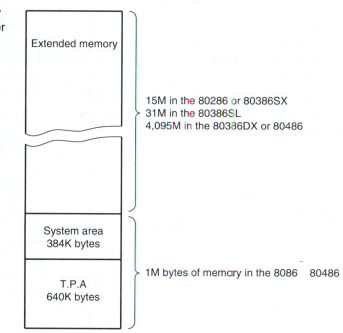

Extended memory

15M in the 80286 or 80386SX
31M in the 80386SL
4,095M in the 80386DX or 80486

System area
384K bytes

1M bytes of memory in the 8086   80486

T.P.A
640K bytes

number of 64K byte expanded memory pages, albeit slowly accessed memory pages. The expanded memory system became obsolete with the advent of the 80286 and newer microprocessors, although it is still supported for older 8086- and 8088-based systems.

With the 80286, 80386, and 80486 we are able to address memory above the first 1M byte. This additional memory, called the *extended memory system* (XMS), contains an additional 15M bytes in the 80286 and 80386SX system and 4,095M bytes in the 80386DX and 80486 systems. The XMS system has replaced the EMS system of earlier personal computers.

Figure 1-6 shows a memory map of a personal computer with memory labeled by areas. The first 640K bytes of the memory system in all personal computers is called the *transient program area* (TPA). The TPA contains RAM (*read/write*) memory to store software applications, the operating system, and various programs that control I/O devices. Stored after the TPA is the system area that contains various BIOS (*basic I/O system*) memory for controlling the system, video display RAM for storing video images, and open areas that can be used for an EMS page frame, and installable options for the computer system. Above this first 1M byte memory area we have the extended memory system that contains disk caching programs, and other segments of data as defined by the operating system.

1-4   THE PROGRAMMING MODEL

Programming requires a clear understanding of the internal register structure of the Intel family of microprocessors. This section illustrates the register structure of the microprocessor and explains how memory is addressed through segment registers and offset addresses.

Figure 1–7 illustrates the internal register array of the microprocessor. This array applies to all versions of the microprocessor. Note that the shaded areas are only available on the 80386 and 80486 microprocessors. The internal program visible register array consists of three groups of registers: general-purpose registers, pointer and index

FIGURE 1–7 The internal register array (programming model) of all versions of the microprocessor.

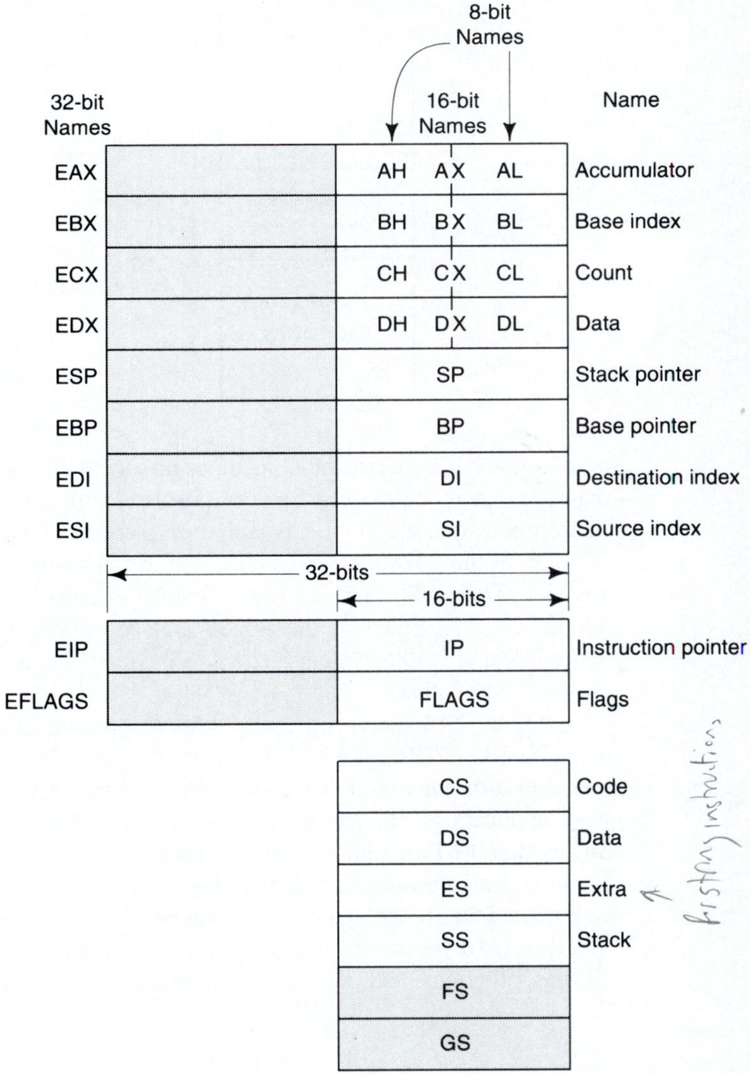

Notes:
1. The shaded areas are not available to the 8086, 8088, or 80286 microprocessors.
2. No special names are given to the FS and GS registers.

registers, and segment registers. In addition to these groupings, there is also a flag register that indicates conditions about the operation of the arithmetic and logic unit (ALU).

General-Purpose Registers

The *general-purpose registers* are used in any manner that the programmer wishes. Each general-purpose register is addressable as 32-bit registers (EAX, EBX, ECX, and EDX), as 16-bit registers (AX, BX, CX, and DX), or as 8-bit registers (AH, AL, BH, BL, CH, CL, DH, and DL). Note that only the 80386 and 80486 contain the 32-bit register set. Some of the instructions explained in later chapters also use the general-purpose registers for specific tasks. For this reason, each is also given a name (Accumulator, Base, Count, and Data). In assembly language, the general-purpose register is always referred to by the two-letter or three-letter combination. For example, the accumulator is referred to as EAX, AX, AH, or AL.

The primary functions of the general-purpose registers include:

AX (*Accumulator*)—often holds the temporary result after an arithmetic and logic operation. Also addressed as EAX, AH, or AL.

BX (*Base*)—often holds the base (offset) address of data located in the memory and also the base address of a table of data referenced by the translate instruction (XLAT). Also addressed as EBX, BH, or BL.

CX (*Count*)—contains the count for certain instructions such as shift count (CL) for shifts and rotates the number of bytes (CX) operated upon by the repeated string operations, and a counter (CX or ECX) with the LOOP instruction. Also addressed as ECX, CH, or CL.

DX (*Data*)—is a general-purpose register that also holds the most significant part of the product after a 16- or 32-bit multiplication, the most significant part of the dividend before a division, and the I/O port number for a variable I/O instruction. Also addressed as EDX, DH, or DL.

Pointer and Index Registers

Although the pointer and index registers are also general purpose in nature, they are more often used to index or point to the memory location holding the operand data for many instructions. These registers are 16-bit on the 8086, 8088, 80186, and 80286, and 32-bit on the 80386 and 80486 microprocessors.

The pointer and index registers include:

SP (*Stack Pointer*)—used to address data in a LIFO (last-in, first-out) stack memory. This occurs most often when the PUSH and POP instructions are executed or when a subroutine is CALLed or RETurned from in a program. This register is also the 32-bit ESP register.

BP (*Base Pointer*)—is a general-purpose pointer often used to address an array of data in the stack memory. This register is also the 32-bit EBP register.

SI (*Source Index*)—used to address source data indirectly for use with the string instructions. This register is also the 32-bit ESI register.

DI (*Destination Index*)—normally used to address destination data indirectly for use with the string instructions. This register is also the 32-bit EDI register.

IP (*Instruction Pointer*)—always used to address the next instruction executed by the microprocessor. The actual location of the next instruction is formed by adding the contents of IP to CS × 10H, as described in the next section. This register is also the 32-bit register EIP.

Data are often indirectly addressed through four of these five 16-bit registers, but never by an instruction pointer.

The Flag Register

The *flags* indicate the condition of the microprocessor as well as control its operation. Figure 1-8 shows the flag registers of all versions of the 8086–80486 microprocessors. Note that the flags are upward compatible from the 8086/8088 to the 80486 microprocessor. The 8086–80286 contain a FLAG register (16 bits) and the 80386–80486 contain an EFLAG register (32-bit extended flag register).

The flag bits change after many arithmetic and logic instructions execute. Some of the flags are also used to control features found in the microprocessor. Following is a list of each flag bit with a brief description of its function. As instructions are introduced in subsequent chapters, additional detail on the flag bits is provided.

C (*carry*)—indicates a carry after addition or a borrow after subtraction. The carry flag also indicates error conditions in some programs and procedures.

P (*parity*)—is a logic 0 for odd parity and a logic 1 for even parity. Parity is a count of ones in a number expressed as even or odd. For example, if a number contains 3 binary one bits, it has odd parity. If a number contains zero one bits, it is considered to have even parity.

A (*auxiliary carry*)—holds a carry after addition or a borrow after subtraction between bits positions 3 and 4 of the result. This highly specialized flag bit is tested by the DAA and DAS instructions to adjust the value of AL after a BCD addition or subtraction. Otherwise, the A flag bit is not used by the microprocessor.

Z (*zero*)—indicates that the result of an arithmetic or logic operation is zero. If Z = 1, the result is zero, and if Z = 0, the result is not zero.

S (*sign*)—indicates arithmetic sign of the result after an addition or subtraction. If S = 1, the sign is set or negative, and if S = 0, the sign is cleared or positive. Note that the value of the most significant bit position is placed into the sign-bit for any instruction that affects the flags.

T (*trap*)—when the trap flag is set, it enables trapping through the on-chip debugging feature. More detail of this debugging feature is provided later in the text.

I (*interrupt*)—controls the operation of the INTR (interrupt request) input pin. If I = 1, the INTR pin is enabled, and if I = 0, the INTR pin is disabled. The state of the I flag bit is controlled by the STI (set I flag) and CLI (clear I flag) instructions.

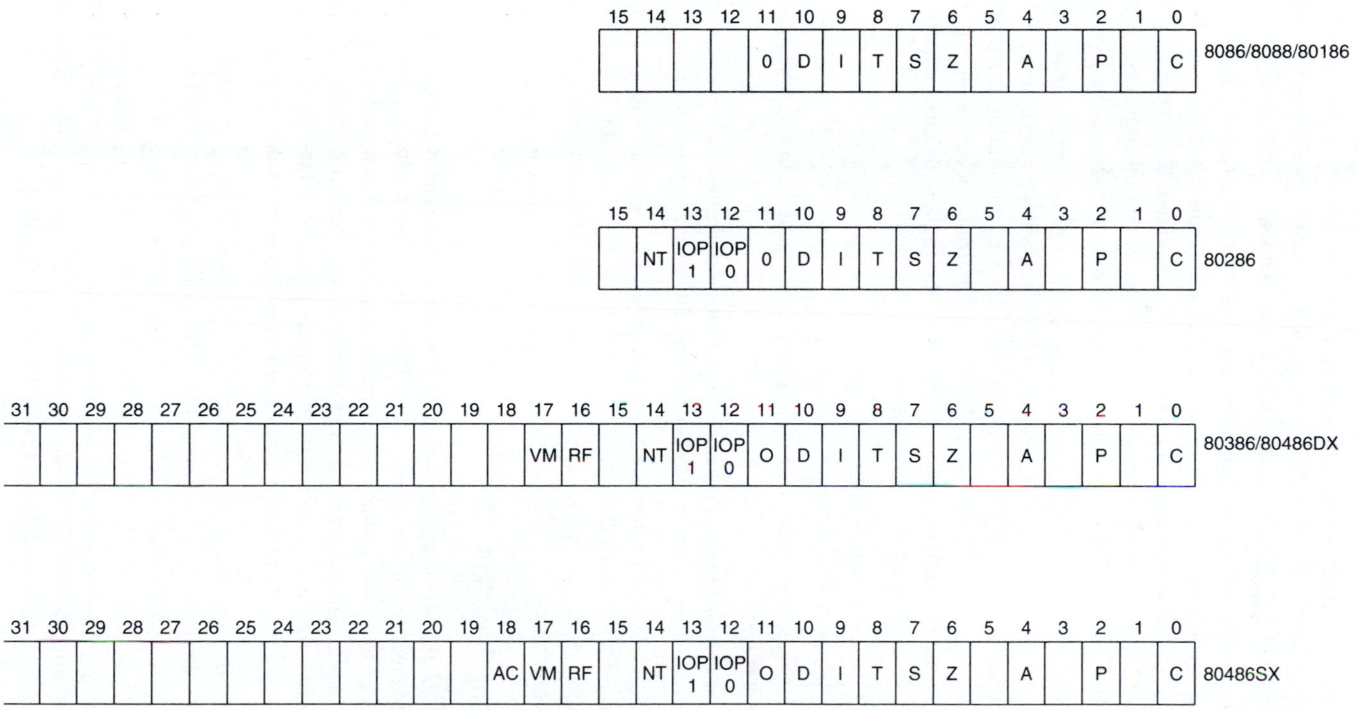

8086/8088/80186

15	14	13	12	11	10	9	8	7	6	5	4	3	2	1	0
				O	D	I	T	S	Z		A		P		C

80286

15	14	13	12	11	10	9	8	7	6	5	4	3	2	1	0
	NT	IOP 1	IOP 0	O	D	I	T	S	Z		A		P		C

80386/80486DX

31	30	29	28	27	26	25	24	23	22	21	20	19	18	17	16	15	14	13	12	11	10	9	8	7	6	5	4	3	2	1	0
														VM	RF		NT	IOP 1	IOP 0	O	D	I	T	S	Z		A		P		C

80486SX

31	30	29	28	27	26	25	24	23	22	21	20	19	18	17	16	15	14	13	12	11	10	9	8	7	6	5	4	3	2	1	0
												AC	VM	RF		NT	IOP 1	IOP 0	O	D	I	T	S	Z		A		P		C

Note: The blank bits are reserved for future use and must not be defined.

FIGURE 1–8 The flag registers of all family members. Note how they are all upward compatible.

D (*direction*)—controls the selection of increment or decrement for the DI and/or SI registers during string instructions. If D = 1, the registers are automatically decremented and if D = 0, the registers are automatically incremented. The D flag is set with the STD (set direction) and cleared with the CLD (clear direction) instructions.

O (*overflow*)—is a condition that occurs when signed numbers are added or subtracted. An overflow indicates that the result has exceeded the capacity of the machine. For example, if a 7FH (+ 127) is added to a 01H (+ 1), the result is 80H (− 128). This result represents an overflow condition indicated by the overflow flag for signed addition. For unsigned operations, we ignore the overflow flag.

IOPL (*input/output privilege level*)—used in protected mode operation to select the privilege level for I/O devices. If the current privilege level is higher or more trusted than the IOPL, then I/O executes without hindrance. If the IOPL is lower than the current privilege level, an interrupt occurs causing execution to be suspended. Note that an IOPL of 00 is the highest or most trusted and an IOPL of 11 is the lowest or least trusted.

NT (*nested task*)—indicates that the current task is nested within another task in protected mode operation. This flag is set when the task is nested by software.

RF (*resume*)—used with debugging to control resuming execution after the next instruction.

VM (*virtual mode*)—selects virtual mode operation in a protected mode system. A virtual mode system allows multiple DOS memory partitions.

AC (*alignment check*)—if a word or double word is addressed on a nonword or non-double word boundary, this flag bit is set. Only the 80486SX microprocessor contains the alignment check bit that is primarily used with its companion numeric coprocessor.

Segment Registers

Additional registers, called *segment registers,* generate memory addresses along with other registers in the microprocessor. There are either 4 or 6 segment registers in various versions of the 8086–80486 microprocessors. A segment register functions differently in the real mode when compared to protected-mode operation of the microprocessor. Detail on their function in real and protected mode is provided later in this chapter. Following is a list of each segment register along with its function in the system:

CS (*code*)—the code segment is a section of memory that holds programs and procedures used by programs. The code segment register defines the starting address of the section of memory-holding code. In real mode operation it defines the start of a 64K byte section of memory and in protected mode it selects a descriptor that describes the starting address and length of a section of memory-holding code. The code segment is limited to 64K bytes in length in the 8088–80286 and 4G bytes in the 80386/80486.

DS (*data*)—the data segment is a section of memory that contains most data used by a program. Data are accessed in the data segment by an offset address or the contents of other registers that hold the offset address.

ES (*extra*)—the extra segment is an additional data segment that is used by some of the string instructions.

SS (*stack*)—the stack segment defines the area of memory used for the stack. The location of the current entry point in the stack segment is determined by the stack pointer register. The BP register also addresses data within the stack segment.

FS and GS—these supplemental segment registers are available in the 80386 and 80486 microprocessors to allow two additional memory segments for access by programs.

1–5   REAL MODE MEMORY ADDRESSING

The 80286–80486 microprocessors operate in either the real or protected mode. The 8086, 8088, and 80186 only operate in the real mode. This section of the text details the operation of the microprocessor in the real mode. Real mode operation allows the microprocessor to only address the first 1M byte of memory space even if it is an 80486 microprocessor. Both the MSDOS or PCDOS operating systems assume that the microprocessor is operated in the real mode at all times. Real mode operation allows application software written for the 8086 and 8088, which only contain 1M byte of memory, to function with the 80286, 80386, and 80486 microprocessors. In all cases, each of these microprocessors begins operation in the real mode by default whenever power is applied or if the microprocessor is reset.

Segments and Offsets

A segment address and an offset address generate a memory address in the real mode. All real mode memory addresses consist of a segment address plus an offset address. The *segment address,* located within one of the segment registers, defines the beginning address of any 64K byte memory segment. The *offset address* selects a location within the 64K byte memory segment. Figure 1–9 shows how the segment plus offset addressing scheme selects a memory location. This illustration shows a memory segment that begins at location 10000H and ends at location 1FFFFH—64K bytes in length. It also shows how an offset, sometimes called a *displacement,* of F000H selects memory location 1F000H in the memory system. Note that the offset address or displacement is the distance *above* the start of the segment.

The segment register in Figure 1–9 contains a 1000H yet it addresses a starting segment location of 10000H. In the real mode, each segment register is internally appended with a *0H* on its rightmost end to form a 20-bit memory address allowing it to access the start of the segment at almost any location within the first 1M byte of memory. For example, if a segment register contains a 1200H, it addresses a 64K byte memory segment beginning at location 12000H. Likewise, if a segment register contains a 1201H, it addresses a memory segment beginning at location 12010H. Because of the internally appended 0H, segments can begin at any 16-byte boundary in the memory system. We often call this 16-byte boundary a *paragraph* of memory.

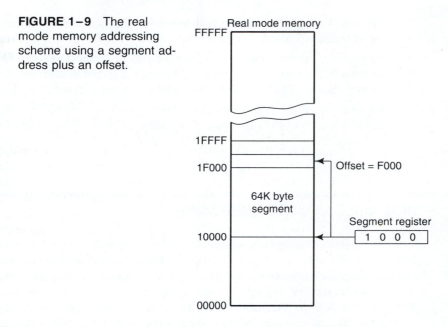

FIGURE 1–9 The real mode memory addressing scheme using a segment address plus an offset.

Because a real mode segment of memory is 64K in length, once the beginning address is known, the ending address is found by adding an FFFFH to the starting address. For example, if a segment register contains 3000H, the first address of the segment is 30000H and the last address is 30000H + FFFFH or 3FFFFH. Table 1–4 shows several examples of segment register contents and the starting and ending addresses of the memory segments selected by each segment address.

The offset address is added to the start of the segment to select a memory location in the memory segment. For example, if the segment address is 1000H and the offset address is 2000H, the microprocessor selects or addresses memory location 12000H. The segment and offset address is sometimes written as *1000:2000* for a segment address of 1000H with an offset of 2000H.

Default Segment and Offset Registers

The microprocessor has a set of rules that apply whenever memory is addressed. These rules, which apply in both the real or protected mode, define the segment register and offset register combination used by certain addressing modes. For example, the code segment register is always used with the instruction pointer to address the next instruction

TABLE 1–4 Example segment addresses

Segment Register	Starting Address	Ending Address
2000H	20000H	2FFFFH
2100H	21000H	30FFFH
AB00H	AB000H	BAFFFH
1234H	12340H	2233FH

in a program. This combination is CS:IP or CS:EIP depending on the microprocessor and mode of operation. The code segment register defines the start of the code segment and the instruction pointer points to the next instruction within the code segment executed by the microprocessor. For example, if CS = 1400H and IP/EIP = 1200H, the microprocessor fetches its next instruction from memory location 14000H + 1200H or 15200H.

Another default is the stack. Stack data are referenced through the stack segment at the memory location addressed by either the stack pointer (SP/ESP) or the base pointer (BP/EBP). These combinations are referred to as SS:SP (SS:ESP) or SS:BP (SS:EBP). For example, if SS = 2000H and BP/EBP = 3000H, the microprocessor addresses location 23000H for a stack segment memory location addressed by the BP/EBP register. Note that in real mode, only the rightmost 16 bits of the extended register addresses a location within the memory segment. Never place a number larger than FFFFH into an offset register if the microprocessor is operated in the real mode. Addressing memory above the 100000H (or 10FFEFH if HIMEM.SYS is installed) in real mode will cause the microprocessor to interrupt the program and indicate an error.

Other defaults are shown in Table 1–5 for addressing memory using the 8086–80286 microprocessor. Table 1–6 shows the defaults assumed in the 80386 and 80486 microprocessors. Note that the 80386 and 80486 microprocessors have a far greater selection of segment/offset address combinations than the 8086–80286 microprocessors.

The 8086–80286 allow four memory segments and the 80386 and 80486 allow 6 memory segments. Figure 1–10 shows a system that contains 4 memory segments. Note that a memory segment can touch or even overlap if 64K bytes of memory are not required for a segment. Think of segments as windows that can be moved over any area of memory to access data or code.

Suppose that an application program requires 1000H bytes of memory for its code, 190H bytes of memory for its data, and 200H bytes of memory for its stack. This

TABLE 1–5 8086–80286 default segment and offset addresses

Segment	Offset
CS	IP
SS	SP or BP
DS	BX, DI, SI, or a 16-bit number
ES	DI for string instructions

TABLE 1–6 80386 and 80486 default segment and offset addresses

Segment	Offset
CS	EIP
SS	ESP or EBP
DS	EAX, EBX, ECX, EDX, EDI, ESI, an 8-bit number, or 32-bit number
ES	EDI for string instructions
FS	no default
GS	no default

FIGURE 1-10 An example
memory system illustrating
four memory segments.

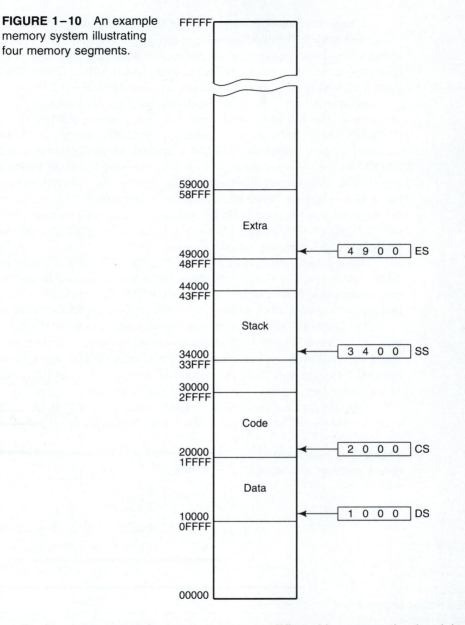

application does not require an extra segment. When this program is placed in the memory system by DOS, it is loaded in the TPA at the first available area of memory above the drivers and other TPA programs. Figure 1–11 shows how this application is stored in the memory system. The segments show an overlap because the amount of data in them does not require 64K bytes of memory. The side view of the segments clearly shows the overlap and how segments can be slid to any area of memory. Fortunately for us, DOS calculates and assigns segment addresses. This is explained in a later chapter that details the operation of the assembler, BIOS, and DOS for an assembly language program.

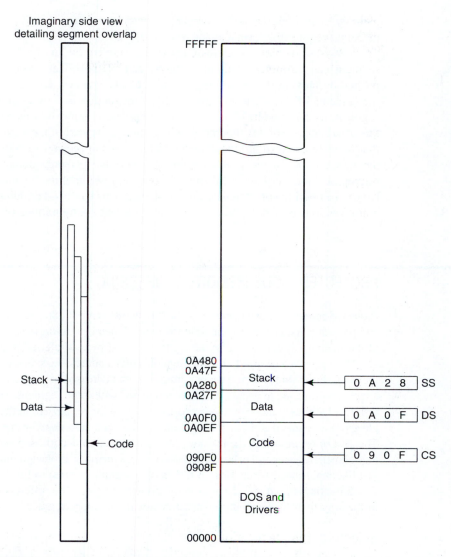

FIGURE 1-11 The memory map of an application illustrating the segments and segment overlaps.

Segment and Offset Addressing Allows Relocation

The segment and offset addressing scheme seems unduly complicated. It is complicated, but it also affords an advantage to the system. This complicated scheme of segment plus offset addressing allows programs to be relocated in the memory system. A *relocatable program* is one that can be placed into any area of memory and executed without change. *Relocatable data* are data that can be placed in any area of memory and used without any change to the program. The segment and offset addressing scheme allows both programs and data to be relocated without changing a thing in a program or data. This is perfect for use in a general-purpose computer system where not all machines contain the same memory areas. The personal computer memory structure is different from machine to machine, requiring relocatable software and data.

Because memory is addressed within a segment by an offset address, the memory segment can be moved without changing any of the offset addresses. This is accomplished by moving the entire program, as a block, to a new area and then changing only the contents of the segment registers. If an instruction is 4 bytes above the start of the segment, its offset address is 4. If the entire program is moved to a new area of memory, this offset address of 4 still points to 4 bytes above the start of the segment. The only thing that must be changed are the contents of the segment register to address the program in the new area of memory. Relocation has made the personal computer based on Intel microprocessors very powerful and very common. Without this feature, a program would have to be rewritten or altered before it is moved. This would take additional time or require many versions of a program for the many different configurations of computer systems.

1–6   PROTECTED MODE MEMORY ADDRESSING

Protected mode memory addressing (80286, 80386, and 80486 only) allows access to data and programs located *above* the first 1M byte of memory. Addressing this extended section of the memory system (memory above the first 1M byte is referred to as *extended memory* or *XMS*) requires a change to the segment plus offset addressing scheme used with real mode memory addressing. When data and programs are addressed in extended memory, the offset address is still used to access information located within the segment. The segment address, discussed with real mode memory addressing, is no longer present in the protected mode. In place of the segment address, the segment register contains a *selector* that selects a *descriptor*. The *descriptor* describes the memory segment's location, length, and access rights. Because the segment register and offset address still access memory, protected mode instructions look just like real mode instructions. In fact, most programs written to function in the real mode will function without any changes in the protected mode. The difference between modes is in the way that the segment register accesses the memory segment.

Selectors and Descriptors

The *selector,* located in the segment register, selects one of 8,192 descriptors from a table of descriptors. The *descriptor* describes the location, length, and access rights of a segment of memory. Indirectly, the segment register still selects a memory segment, but not directly as in the real mode.

There are two descriptor tables used with the segment registers: one contains global descriptors and the other contains local descriptors. The *global descriptors* contains segments that apply to all programs, while the *local descriptors* are usually unique to an application. Each descriptor table contains 8,192 descriptors so a total of 16,384 descriptors are available at any time. Because the descriptor describes a memory segment, this allows up to 16,384 memory segments to be described for each application.

Figure 1–12 shows the format of a descriptor for the 80286 and 80386/80486 microprocessors. Note that each descriptor is 8 bytes in length so the global and local descriptor tables are each a maximum of 64K bytes in length. Descriptors for the 80286

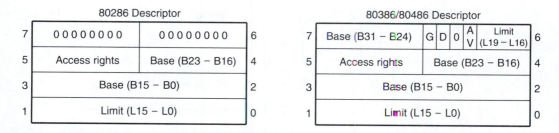

FIGURE 1–12 The descriptor formats for the 80286 and 80386/80486 microprocessors.

and the 80386/80486 differ slightly, but the 80286 descriptor is upward compatible with the 80386 and 80486 microprocessors.

The base address portion of the descriptor is used to indicate the starting location of the memory segment. For the 80286 microprocessor, the base address is a 24-bit address so segments can begin at any of its 16M bytes of memory. The 80386/80486 uses a 32-bit base address that allows segments to begin at any of its 4G byte memory locations. Notice how the 80286 descriptor's base address is upward compatible to the 80386/80486 descriptor.

The segment limit contains the last offset address found in a segment. For example, if a segment begins at memory location F00000H and ends at location F000FFH, the base address is F00000H and the limit is FFH. For the 80286 microprocessor, the base address is F00000H and the limit is 00FFH. For the 80386/80486 microprocessors, the base address is 00F00000H and the limit is 000FFH. Notice the limit for the 80286 is a 16-bit limit and the limit for the 80386/80486 is 20 bits. The 80286 accesses memory segments that are from 1 byte to 64K bytes in length. The 80386/80486 accesses memory segments that are from 1 byte to 1M byte or from 4K byte to 4G bytes in length.

There is another feature found in the 80386/80486 descriptor that is not found in the 80286 descriptor: the G bit or *granularity* bit. If G = 0, the limit specifies a segment limit of from 1 to 1M bytes in length. If G = 1, the value of the limit is multiplied by 4K bytes. If G = 1, the limit can be any multiple of 4K bytes. This allows a segment length of 4K bytes to 4G bytes in steps of 4K bytes. The reason that the segment length is 64K bytes in the 80286 is that the offset address is always 16 bits, while the offset address in the protected mode operation of the 80386/80486 is 32 bits. This 32-bit offset address allows segment lengths of 4G bytes, and the 16-bit offset address allows segment lengths of 64K bytes.

The AV bit in the 80386/80486 descriptor is used by the operating system and indicates that the segment is available (AV = 1) or not available (AV = 0). The D bit indicates how the 80386/80486 instructions access register and memory data in the protected mode. If D = 0, the 80386/80486 assumes that the instructions are 16-bit instructions compatible with the 8086–80286 microprocessors. This means that the instructions use 16-bit offset addresses and 16-bit registers. This mode is often called the *16-bit instruction mode*. If D = 1, the 80386/80486 assumes that the instructions are 32-bit instructions. The *32-bit instruction mode* assumes all offset addresses are 32 bits as well as all registers. The MSDOS or PCDOS operating system requires that the instructions are always used in the 16-bit instruction mode. More detail on these modes and their application to the instruction set appears in Chapters 3 and 4.

The access rights byte (see Figure 1–13) controls access to the memory segment. This byte describes how the segment functions in the system. Notice how complete the

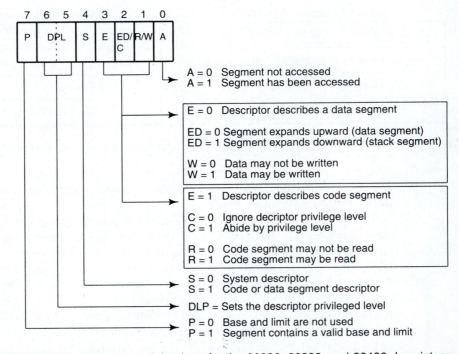

FIGURE 1–13 The access rights byte for the 80286, 80386, and 80486 descriptors.

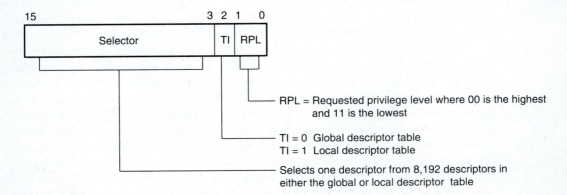

FIGURE 1–14 The contents of a segment register during protected mode operation of the 80286, 80386, or 80486 microprocessor.

control is over the segment. If the segment is a data segment, the direction of growth can be specified. If the segment grows beyond its limit, the microprocessor's program is interrupted. You can even specify if a data segment can be written or is write-protected. The code segment is also controlled in a similar fashion and can have reading inhibited.

Descriptors are chosen from the descriptor table by the segment register. Figure 1–14 shows how the segment register functions in the protected mode system. The segment register contains a 13-bit selector field, a table selector bit, and a requested privilege level field. The 13-bit selector chooses one of the 8,192 descriptors from the descriptor table. The TI bit selects either the global descriptor table (TI = 0) or the local descriptor table (TI = 1). The requested privilege level (RPL) requests the access privilege level to a memory segment. The highest privilege level is 00 and the lowest is 11. If the requested privilege level matches or is higher in priority than the privilege level set by the access rights byte, access is granted. For example, if the requested privilege level is 10 and the access rights byte sets the segment privilege level at 11, access is granted because 10 is a higher priority privilege level than 11. Privilege levels are used in multiuser environments.

Figure 1–15 shows how the segment register, containing a selector, chooses a descriptor from the global descriptor table. The entry in the global descriptor table selects a segment in the memory system. In this illustration DS contains 0008H, which accesses the descriptor number 1 from the global descriptor table using a requested privilege level of 00. Descriptor number 1 contains an 80286 descriptor that defines the base address as 100000H with a segment limit of 00FFH. This means that a value of 0008H loaded into DS causes the microprocessor to use memory locations 100000H–1000FFH for the data segment with this example descriptor table.

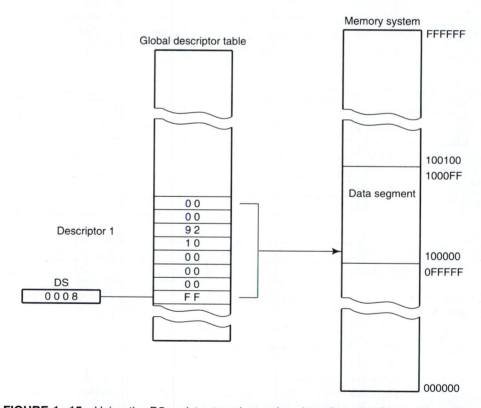

FIGURE 1–15 Using the D5 register to select a descriptor from the Global Descriptor Table. In this example, the D5 register accesses memory locations 100000H–10000FFH as a data segment.

Program-Invisible Registers

The global and local descriptor tables are found in the memory system. In order to access and specify the address of these tables, the 80286, 80386, and 80486 contain program-invisible registers. The *program-invisible* registers are not directly addressed by normal software, so we give them this name. Some of these registers are accessed by the system software. Figure 1–16 illustrates the program-invisible registers as they appear in the 80286, 80386, and 80486 microprocessors. These registers control the microprocessor when operated in the protected mode.

Each of the segment registers contains a program-invisible portion used in the protected mode. This is a cache memory that is loaded with the base address, limit, and access rights each time the number is changed in the segment register. When a new segment number is placed in a segment register, the microprocessor accesses a descriptor table and loads the descriptor into the program-invisible cache portion of the segment register. It is held there and used to access the memory segment until the segment number is again changed. This allows the microprocessor to repeatedly access a memory segment without referring back to the descriptor table for each access.

The GDTR (*global descriptor table register*) and IDTR (*interrupt descriptor table register*) contain the base address of the descriptor table and its limit. The limit of each descriptor table is 16 bits in the 80286, 80386, and 80486 microprocessors because the maximum table length is 64K bytes. When protected mode operation is desired, the address of the global descriptor table and its limit are loaded into the GDTR. Before using protected mode,

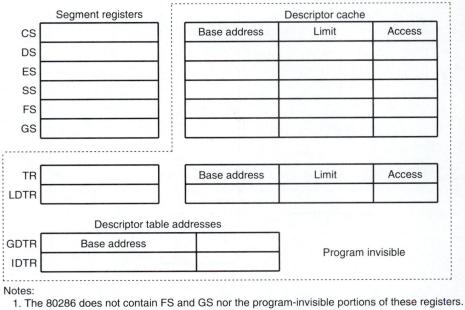

Notes:
1. The 80286 does not contain FS and GS nor the program-invisible portions of these registers.
2. The 80286 contains a base address that is 24 bits and a limit that is 16 bits.
3. The 80386 and 80486 contain a base address that is 32 bits and a limit that is 20 bits.
4. The access rights are 8 bits in the 80286 and 12 bits in the 80386 and 80486.

FIGURE 1–16   The program-invisible register within the 80286, 80386, and 80486 microprocessor.

the interrupt descriptor table and the IDTR must also be initialized. More detail is provided on protected mode operation in Chapter 14 in this text. Chapter 14 provides a complete coverage of the 80386 and 80486 microprocessors and their protected mode operation. At this point, the programming and additional description of these registers are impossible.

The location of the local descriptor table is selected from the global descriptor table. One of the global descriptors is set up to address the local descriptor table. To access the local descriptor table, the LDTR (*local descriptor table register*) is loaded with a selector just as a segment register is loaded with a selector. This selector accesses the global descriptor table and loads the base address, limit, and access rights of the local descriptor table into the cache portion of the LDTR.

The *task register* (TR) accesses a descriptor that defines a task. A task is most often a procedure or application program. The descriptor for the procedure or application program is stored in the global descriptor table so access can be controlled through the privilege levels.

1-7   DATA FORMATS

Successful programming also depends on a clear understanding of data formats. In this section, we describe the common data formats used with the 8086–80486 family of microprocessors. Data are presented as: ASCII, BCD, 8-bit (byte) signed and unsigned integers, 16-bit (word) signed and unsigned integers, 32-bit (double-word) signed and unsigned integers, and both short and long real numbers (or floating-point numbers).

ASCII Data

ASCII (*American Standard Code for Information Interchange*) data (see Table 1–7) are normally used to represent alphanumeric character in the memory of a computer system. The ASCII code is a 7-bit code with the eighth and most significant bit used to hold parity in some systems. If the ASCII data are used with a printer, the most significant bit is a 0 for alphanumeric printing and a logic 1 for graphics character printing.

The ASCII control characters are also listed in Table 1–7 along with a brief description of the function of each code. If control codes are entered on the keyboard, the control key is held down, followed by an @ for a 00, an a for an 01, a b for an 02, and so forth.

TABLE 1–7   The ASCII code

	X0	X1	X2	X3	X4	X5	X6	X7	X8	X9	XA	XB	XC	XD	XE	XF
First																
0X	NUL	SOH	STX	ETX	EOT	ENQ	ACK	BEL	BS	HT	LF	VT	FF	CR	SO	SI
1X	DLE	DC1	DC2	DC3	DC4	NAK	SYN	ETB	CAN	EM	SUB	ESC	FS	GS	RS	US
2X	SP	!	"	#	$	%	&	'	(	)	*	+	,	-	.	/
3X	0	1	2	3	4	5	6	7	8	9	:	;	<	=	>	?
4X	@	A	B	C	D	E	F	G	H	I	J	K	L	M	N	O
5X	P	Q	R	S	T	U	V	W	X	Y	Z	[	u	]	^	_
6X	`	a	b	c	d	e	f	g	h	i	j	k	l	m	n	o
7X	p	q	r	s	t	u	v	w	x	y	z	{			}	~	:::

Second

In most personal computers an additional set of characters exist in the ASCII code called extended ASCII characters. This set of extended characters (see Table 1–8) will always be displayed on the video display, but may or may not print correctly. The only printer that will print these correctly is the IBM pro-printer or a printer that emulates the pro-printer.

BCD

Binary-coded decimal (BCD) information is stored in either packed or unpacked forms in the memory. Packed BCD occurs when two BCD digits are stored per memory byte, unpacked BCD when one BCD digit is stored per byte. With BCD data, the valid 4-bit binary codes are 0000 (0)– 1001 (9). Table 1–9 lists several decimal numbers displayed in both packed and unpacked BCD formats.

BYTE

Byte data are stored in two forms: unsigned and signed integers. Figure 1-17 illustrates both the unsigned- and the signed-integer bytewide formats. Notice that the only difference between the signed and unsigned forms is the weight of the leftmost bit position. In the signed form, the leftmost bit is negative, and in the unsigned form, it is

TABLE 1–8   The extended ASCII code

							Second									
	XO	X1	X2	X3	X4	X5	X6	X7	X8	X9	XA	XB	XC	XD	XE	XF
First																
8X																
9X																
AX	á	í	ó	ú	ñ	Ñ	a	o	¿	⌐	¬	½	¼	¡	«	»
BX	▦	▦	▦	│	┤	╡	╢	╖	╕	╣	║	╗	╝	╜	╛	┐
CX	└	┴	┬	├	─	┼	╞	╟	╚	╔	╩	╦	╠	═	╬	╧
DX	╨	╤	╥	╙	╘	╒	╓	╫	╪	┘	┌	█	▄	▌	▐	▀
EX	α	β	Γ	π	Σ	σ	μ	τ	Φ	Θ	Ω	δ	∞	φ	ε	∩
FX	≡	±	≥	≤	⌠	⌡	÷	≈	°	•	·	√	η	^{2}	■	

TABLE 1–9   Packed and unpacked BCD data

Number	Packed	Unpacked
23	00100011	00000010 00000011
237	00000010 00110111	00000010 00000011 00000111
612	00000110 00010010	00000110 00000001 00000010
1,234	00010010 00110100	00000001 00000010 00000011 00000100

FIGURE 1–17 8-bit integers. (a) An unsigned 8-bit integer. (b) A signed 8-bit integer.

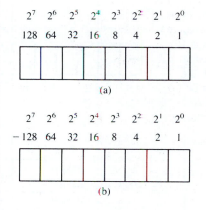

positive or unsigned. For example, an 80H is equal to an unsigned value of 128 and a signed value of −128. An 81H is equal to an unsigned value of 129 or a signed value of −127.

Even though negative signed numbers are represented with the leftmost bit of −128, they are stored in two's complement form. This method of evaluating a signed number (leftmost bit of −128) is much easier than the act of two's complementing the number to determine its value, especially in the world of calculators that are designed for programmers. If you desire you may use the two's complement to convert a negative number to a positive number to determine its value. The two's complement of a number is formed by inverting each bit, then by adding a one to the result.

Word

A word (16 bits) is formed with 2 bytes of data. The least significant byte is always stored in the lowest numbered memory location, and the most significant byte in the highest. Figure 1–18(a) illustrates the weights of each bit position in a word of data, and Figure 1–18(b) illustrates how a 1234H is stored in the memory. The only difference between a signed and an unsigned number is the leftmost bit position. In the signed number its weight is negative, and in the unsigned number it has no sign. Again, this leftmost bit is the same as for byte data except that its positional value is different.

Double Words

The double-word format is used to store 32-bit numbers (4 bytes) that are the product after multiplication or the dividend before a division. Double words are also used by the 80386 and 80486 for most operations because these newer microprocessors operate on 32-bit data as well as 8- and 16-bit data. Figure 1–19 illustrates the binary weights and memory storage formats for a double word. In addition to storing data, the double-word format is also used for storing addresses in the memory. Figure 1–20 illustrates the form used to store an address in a double word. Notice that the offset address is stored in the two lowest memory locations and that the segment address is stored in the two highest memory locations.

FIGURE 1–18 16-bit Integers. (a) The binary weights of each bit position in a 16-bit word of data. Recall that if the number is signed, the weight of the leftmost bit position is negative. (b) A 1234H stored in the memory beginning at location at 10000H.

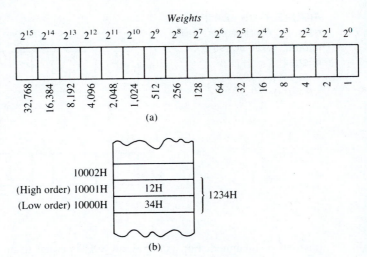

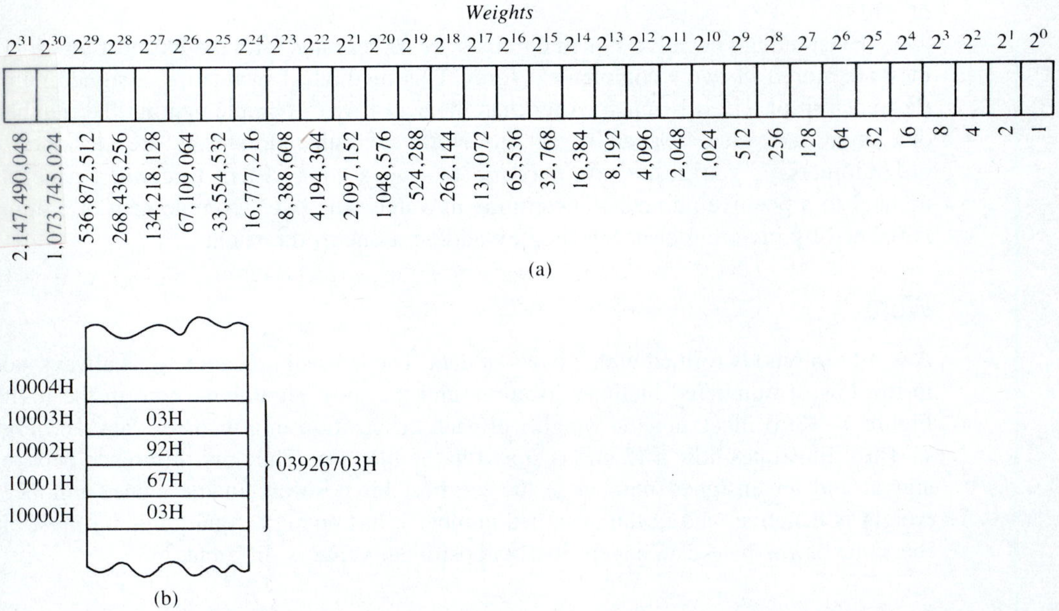

FIGURE 1–19 32-bit Integers. (a) The binary weights of each bit position in a 32-bit double word of data. (b) A 03926703H stored in the memory beginning at location 10000H.

Real Numbers

Because the 8086/8088 family is used with many high-level languages and also some very sophisticated control systems, real numbers are often encountered. A *real number* or, as it is often called, a *floating-point number*, is composed of two parts: a *mantissa* and an *exponent*. Figure 1–21 depicts both the 4- and 8-byte forms of the real number as it is stored in the microprocessor memory system. This is the same form as specified

FIGURE 1–20 An example memory map illustrating how memory address 11300H is stored in the memory. The segment number is 1100H and the offset address is 0300H. Notice that the offset address is stored first, followed by the segment address.

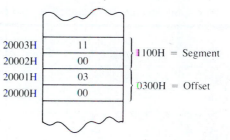

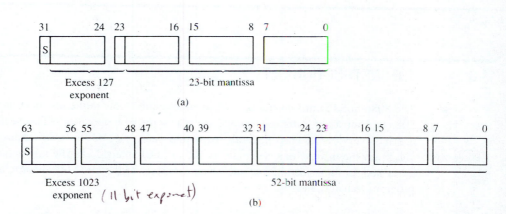

FIGURE 1–21 Real or floating-point data storage. (a) The 4-byte short form of a real number. (b) The 8-byte long form of a real number.

by the IEEE standard, IEEE-754, version 10.0. Figure 1–21(a) illustrates the single-precision form that contains an 8-bit exponent, a 24-bit mantissa (fraction), and a sign bit.

Simple arithmetic indicates that it should take a 33-bit number to store all these data. Not true—the 24-bit mantissa contains an implied (*hidden*) 1 bit that allows the mantissa to be stored in 23 bits instead of 24 bits. The hidden bit is the first bit of the normalized real number. When a number is normalized, it is adjusted so that its value is at least 1, but less than 2. For example, if a 12 is converted to binary (1100) and normalized, the result is a 1.1×2^3. Table 1–10 illustrates the short-form version of this number and other example numbers converted to floating-point format.

The exponent is stored as a *biased exponent*. With the short-form real number, the bias is 127 (7FH); with the long-form real number, it is 1,023 (3FFH). In the previous example, there is an exponent of 2^3, represented as a biased exponent of 127 + 3 or 130 (82H) in short form and 1,023 + 3 or 1,026 (402H) in long form. There are two exceptions to these rules: (1) if the number is 0.0, then the real number is stored with an exponent, sign, and mantissa of 0, and (2) if the number is too large to be held in the real number format, the exponent, sign, and mantissa are stored as ones.

TABLE 1–10   Short-form real number notation (single-precision)

Decimal	Binary	Normalized	Sign	Biased Exponent	Mantissa
+12	1100	1.1×2^3	0	10000010	1000000 00000000 00000000
–12	1100	-1.1×2^3	1	10000010	1000000 00000000 00000000
+100	1100100	1.1001×2^6	0	10000101	1001000 00000000 00000000
–1.75	1.11	-1.11×2^0	1	01111111	1100000 00000000 00000000
0.25	0.01	1.0×2^{-2}	0	01111101	0000000 00000000 00000000
0.0	0.0	0.0	0	00000000	0000000 00000000 00000000

1–8   THE INSTRUCTION SET

The 8086/8088 family instruction set includes equivalents to the instructions found in the 8085 or almost any 8-bit microprocessor plus some new operations. This section provides a brief overview of each general instruction category and the instructions themselves. Usage for the instructions is explained further in Chapters 2–5. The instruction categories described in this section include: data transfer, arithmetic, bit manipulation, string, program transfer, and processor control.

Data Transfer

The 8086–80486 family instruction set includes data transfer instructions that move bytes, words, or double words of data between memory and registers as well as between the accumulator and the I/O ports. Only the 80386 and 80486 are capable of double-word transfers. Table 1–11 lists these instructions and also briefly notes the operating characteristics of each.

Arithmetic

The 8086–80486 family is capable of adding, subtracting, multiplying, and dividing data as bytes, words, or double words. Note that double-word operations only apply to the 80386 and 80486 microprocessors. The system adds and subtracts by using signed or unsigned data and BCD or ASCII data. It multiplies and divides signed, unsigned, or ASCII numbers. Table 1–12 lists the arithmetic instructions found in the 8086–80486 family of microprocessors.

Bit Manipulation

Binary bit manipulation instructions are used to control data down to the bit level in the 8086–80486 family of microprocessors. These instructions include logic operations, shifts, and rotates. A brief description of each instruction and its symbolic opcode appears in Table 1–13

TABLE 1-11 Data transfer instructions

Opcode	Function
IN	Inputs data to accumulator from an I/O device
LAHF	Moves flags to AH
LEA	Loads effective address
LDS	Loads DS and 16-bit register with 32-bit memory data
LES	Loads ES and 16-bit register with 32-bit memory data
**LFS	Loads FS and 16-bit register with 32-bit memory data
**LGS	Loads GS and 16-bit register with 32-bit memory data
**LSS	Loads SS and 16-bit register with 32-bit memory data
MOV	Moves byte, word, or double word
OUT	Outputs data from the accumulator to an I/O device
POP	Pops a word from the stack
*POPA	Pops all word registers from the stack
**POPAD	Pops all double-word registers from the stack
**POPD	Pops a double word from the stack
POPF	Pops the flags from the stack
**POPFD	Pops the extended flags from the stack
PUSH	Pushes word onto stack
*PUSHA	Pushes all word registers onto stack
**PUSHAD	Pushes all double-word registers onto stack
**PUSHD	Pushes double word onto stack
PUSHF	Pushes flags onto stack
**PUSHFD	Pushes extended flags onto the stack
SAHF	Moves AH to flags
XCHG	Exchanges bytes, words, or double words
XLAT	Translates AL into entry from a lookup table

Notes: * = instructions that are new to the 80186 through the 80486 and ** = instructions that are new to the 80386 and 80486.

String Instructions

The string instructions are used to manipulate strings of data in the memory. Each string is composed either of bytes or words and is up to 64K bytes in length. The string instructions use the SI and/or DI registers to address the data and the CX register to count the number of bytes or words operated upon. String instructions occur once unless they are prefixed with the REP, REPE/REPZ, or REPN/REPNZ prefix. If a string instruction is thus prefixed, it is repeated up to the number of times contained in the count register—CX. Table 1-14 lists the string operations available in the 8086-80486 family of microprocessors.

Program Transfer

Program transfer instructions include jump, CALL, and return instructions familiar in the 8085. Also listed are some additional instructions that form *loops*. Table 1-15 lists the program transfer instructions.

TABLE 1–12 Arithmetic
instructions

Opcode	Function
AAA	Adjusts the result after an ASCII addition
AAD	Adjusts before ASCII division
AAM	Adjusts result of an ASCII multiplication
AAS	Adjusts the result after an ASCII subtraction
ADD	Adds data between register or memory and a register
ADC	Adds data with the carry flag bit
CBW	Converts byte to word
*CDQ	Converts double word to quad word
CMP	Compares data
CWD	Converts word to double word
DAA	Decimal adjusts AL after a BCD addition
DAS	Decimal adjusts AL after a BCD subtraction
DEC	Subtracts one
DIV	Unsigned division
IDIV	Signed division
IMUL	Signed multiplication
INC	Adds one
*MOVSX	Move and sign-extend data
*MOVZX	Move and zero-extend data
MUL	Unsigned multiplication
NEG	Changes the sign (negate)
SBB	Subtracts with borrow
SUB	Subtracts data between registers or memory and a register

Note: * = these instructions appear only in the 80386 and 80486 microprocessors.

Processor Control

The processor control instructions enable and disable interrupts, modify the flag bits, and synchronize external events. In the 80286, 80386, and 80486 these instructions control the operation of the system in the protected mode. See Table 1–16 for a listing of the processor control instructions.

TABLE 1–13 Bit manipulation instructions

Opcode	Function
AND	Logical AND
*BSF	Bit scan forward
*BSR	Bit scan reverse
*BT	Bit test instruction
*BTC	Bit test and complement
*BTR	Bit test and reset
*BTS	Bit test and set
NOT	Inversion (one's complement)
OR	Logical OR
SAR	Shift arithmetic right
SHL/SAL	Shift left
**SHLD	Shift left double-precision
SHR	Shift logical right
**SHRD	Shift right double-precision
RCL	Rotate left with carry
ROL	Rotate left
RCR	Rotate right with carry
ROR	Rotate right
TEST	Logical AND operation, but only flags change
XOR	Logical Exclusive-OR

Note: * = only on the 80386 and 80486 microprocessor and ** = only on the 80486 microprocessor.

TABLE 1–14 String instructions

Opcode	Function
CMPS	Memory-to-memory comparison
*INS	Inputs data from I/O to memory
LODS	Loads the accumulator
MOVS	Memory-to-memory move
*OUTS	Outputs memory data to I/O
SCAS	Memory-to-accumulator comparison
STOS	Stores the accumulator

Note: * = these instructions function on the 80186 through the 80486 microprocessors.

TABLE 1–15 Program transfer instructions

Opcode	Function
*BOUND	Tests boundary
CALL	Calls a procedure (subroutine)
*ENTER	Enter procedure
INT	Interrupt
INT 3	Type 3 interrupt
INTO	Interrupt on an overflow
IRET	Return from an interrupt
*IRETD	Return from an interrupt
JA	Jump if above
JAE	Jump if above or equal
JB	Jump if below
JBE	Jump if below or equal
JC	Jump if carry
JE/JZ	Jump if equal/jump if zero
JG	Jump if greater than
JGE	Jump if greater than or equal
JL	Jump if less than
JLE	Jump if less than or equal
JMP	Jumps to another part of a program
JNC	Jump if no carry
JNE/JNZ	Jump if not equal/jump if not zero
JNO	Jump if no overflow
JNP	Jump if no parity (odd)
JNS	Jump if no sign (positive)
JO	Jump if overflow
JP	Jump if parity (even)
JS	Jump if sign (negative)
*LEAVE	Leave procedure
LOOP	Loops CX times
*LOOPD	Loops ECX times
LOOPE	Loop while equal (CX = count)
*LOOPED	Loop while equal (EXC = count)
LOOPNE	Loop while not equal (CX = count)
*LOOPNED	Loop while not equal (ECX = count)
JCXZ	Jump if CX is zero
*JECZX	Jump if ECX = 0
RET	Returns from a procedure (subroutine)

Note: * = only on the 80386 and 80486 microprocessors.

TABLE 1-16 Processor control instructions

Opcode	Function
ARPL	Adjusts requested privilege level
CLC	Clear carry flag
CLD	Select auto-increment mode
CLI	Disable INTR pin
CMC	Complement carry flag
CTS	Clears task-switched flag
ESC	Instruction for coprocessor
HLT	Halt until reset of interrupt
LAR	Loads access rights
LGDT	Loads global descriptor table register
LIDT	Loads interrupt descriptor table register
LLDT	Loads local descriptor table register
LMSW	Loads machine status register (80286 only)
LOCK	Controls the $\overline{\text{LOCK}}$ pin on the 8086/8088
LSL	Loads segment limit
LTR	Loads task register
NOP	Performs no operation
SGDT	Stores global descriptor table register
SIDT	Stores interrupt descriptor table register
SLDT	Stores local descriptor table register
SMSW	Stores machine status register (80286 only)
STC	Set carry flag
STD	Select auto-decrement mode
STI	Enable INTR pin
STR	Store task register
VERR	Verifies read access
VERW	Verifies write access
WAIT	Waits for the $\overline{\text{TEST}}$ pin = 0

1-9   SUMMARY

1. The life of the 4-bit microprocessor was limited because of its inferior speed, instruction set, and memory size.
2. The 8-bit microprocessor solved many of the problems encountered with the 4-bit microprocessors until recent times. Recently, microprocessor-based systems have begun replacing minicomputers in many applications that require 16-bit data widths, additional instructions, and much more memory than the 8-bit microprocessors provided.
3. The 32-bit microprocessor is becoming more popular because of its increased execution speed, enhanced instruction set, and vast amount of addressable memory.

4. A change in the internal organization of the 16- and 32-bit microprocessors has made their use of the buses connected to the memory more efficient. The prefetch queue, which prefetches instructions while the memory is idle, allows more efficient use of the memory system. This queue keeps the pipeline filled so the microprocessor executes software at a higher speed than possible without a queue.

5. Logical memory is the memory system viewed by the programmer; physical memory is the actual structure of the memory viewed by the hardware designer. The 8088 logical and physical memory maps are identical, while the other family members' logical and physical maps differ. The 8086, 80186, 80286, and 80386SX physical memory is constructed of two separate bytewide banks of memory, while the 80386DX and 80486 contain a physical memory constructed with four bytewide memory banks.

6. The programming models of the 8086, 8088, 80186, and 80286 microprocessors are identical. The programming models of the 80386 and 80486 are almost identical with the earlier family members except most of the registers are extended to 32-bit registers. All family members contain general-purpose registers, index and pointer registers, segment registers, and a flag register.

7. The general-purpose registers are used as four 32-bit registers (EAX, EBX, ECX, and EDX), four 16-bit registers (AX, BX, CX, and DX), or as eight 8-bit registers (AH, AL, BH, BL, CH, CL, DH, and DL). Note that only the 80386 and 80486 contain extended 32-bit registers.

8. There are five pointer and index registers (SP, BP, IP, SI, and DI) available to the programmer. In the 80386 and 80486 microprocessors we also have extended versions of these five registers (ESP, EBP, EIP, ESI, and EDI).

9. Segment registers hold the 16-bit segment number that is appended on the rightmost side by a 0000_2 to form a 20-bit address when the microprocessor operates in the real mode. This allows the microprocessor to address 64K bytes of memory per segment. The four memory segments available to the programmer are the code, data, stack, and extra segments. On the 80386 and 80486 microprocessors there are two addition segments labeled FS and GS.

10. All real mode memory addresses are created (effective address) by using a segment register to address a 64K-byte segment of the memory plus an offset. The offset is a 16-bit number that is added to the segment address to form the actual memory address.

11. The flag or status word contains 8085-like flags (rightmost 8 bits) plus additional flags. Some of the new flags are used to control the interrupts (1), select the direction (D) of the auto-increment/auto-decrement feature in string instructions, sense an overflow (O), and control the single-instruction mode of operation (T).

12. Memory above the first 1M byte in the 80286, 80386, and 80486 are accessible whenever the microprocessor is operated in the protected mode. Protected mode operation treats the contents of the segment register as a selector. The selector chooses a descriptor, which describes the memory segment, from a descriptor table.

13. Data formats consist of bytes (8 bits), words (16 bits), and double words (32 bits).

14. Real numbers are expressed in either 32-bit (short) or 64-bit (long) formats using the IEEE-754 standard. We often call the short form a single-precision floating-point number and the long form a double-precision floating-point number.

15. The microprocessor instruction set includes instructions that allow data transfer, arithmetic, bit manipulation, string operations, program transfer, and processor control.

1-10   QUESTIONS AND PROBLEMS

1. What were some of the problems of the early 4-bit microprocessors?
2. List a few applications for the early 4-bit microprocessors.
3. What improvements in microprocessor technology led to the advent of the 8-bit microprocessor?
4. Compare the execution speeds of the 4-, 8-, 16-, and 32-bit microprocessors.
5. How much memory does the 8086 microprocessor address?
6. How much memory does the 80386 microprocessor address?
7. Explain why the 80486 is faster than some of the earlier microprocessors.
8. What is the pipeline? Why does it allow the microprocessor to execute software more efficiently?
9. What three buses are connected to the memory and I/O of the microprocessor?
10. Both the 8086 and 8088 microprocessors address _____ bytes of memory.
11. The 80286 microprocessor addresses _____ bytes of memory.
12. The 80386 addresses memory that is physically _____ bytes in width.
13. Logical memory is numbered from _____ to _____ in the 8086 microprocessor.
14. A word requires _____ bytes of memory.
15. A double word requires _____ bytes of memory.
16. What are the differences between the 8088 logical and physical memory maps?
17. What are the differences between the 80486 logical and physical memory maps?
18. A bank of memory is capable of storing _____ bytes in the microprocessor memory system.
19. What is the EMS in a personal computer and where is it located?
20. The extended memory system begins at memory location _____.
21. How much memory is found in the TPA in a computer system?
22. How many 8-bit general-purpose registers are available in the 8086/8088 microprocessor family? What are their names?
23. How many 16-bit general-purpose registers are available in the 8086/8088 family of microprocessors? What are their names?
24. How many 32-bit general-purpose registers are available to the 80386 microprocessor? What are their names?
25. Why is the CX register called the count register?
26. Why is the DX register called the data register?
27. List the five pointer and index registers and explain their normal function.
28. Segment registers are used to address a 64K-byte block of memory in the real mode. How is this possible when a segment register is only 16 bits wide and the memory address is 20 bits wide?
29. What segment registers are added to the 80386 and 80486 microprocessors?
30. May memory segments overlap? If so, what is the minimum number of overlapped bytes other than 0?
31. If IP = 1000H and CS = 2000H, then the actual real mode address of the next instruction is at memory location _____ .
32. If SS = 1234H and SP = 0100H, the current address of the stack is _____ .
33. What two pointers use the stack segment register to address memory?

34. The string source (SI) is located in the _____ segment, and the string destination (DI) is located in the _____ segment for string instructions.

35. How many of the 16 flag bits of the 8086 actually contain information?

36. List and describe the function of each of the 8085-like flag bits.

37. What is the purpose of the 80386 IOPL flag bit?

38. Explain where the D flag bit is used and what it is used for.

39. What is an overflow?

40. A byte = _____ bits, a word = _____ bits, and a double word = _____ bits.

41. Signed and unsigned numbers are bytes, words, and double words. (TRUE/FALSE)

42. Show how a 1234H is stored in a word and a double word if both the word and double word begin at memory address 10000H.

43. Show how memory address 1000:1234 is stored in a double word that begins at address 04000H.

44. What register holds the selector in the protected mode system?

45. What mode of operation must be used to access memory above the first 1M byte in the 80386 microprocessor?

46. Convert the following numbers into 16-bit signed binary numbers:
    a. − 105
    b. + 302
    c. − 12
    d. + 134
    e. − 1003

47. Convert the following 8-bit binary numbers into both signed and unsigned decimal values:
    a. 10000000
    b. 00101011
    c. 11011011
    d. 00111111
    e. 10001111

48. Convert the following decimal numbers to IEEE-754 short-form real numbers:
    a. + 10
    b. − 11
    c. + 101.125
    d. − 65.0625
    e. + 300.09375

CHAPTER 2

Addressing Modes

INTRODUCTION

Efficient software development for the 8086–80486 requires a complete familiarity with the addressing modes employed by each instruction. In this chapter, we use the MOV (*move data*) instruction to describe the data-addressing modes. The MOV instruction transfers bytes or words of data between registers or between registers and memory in the 8086–80286 and bytes, words, or double words in the 80386 and 80486 microprocessors. In describing the program memory-addressing modes, we use the call and jump instructions that modify the flow of the program.

The data-addressing modes include: register, immediate, direct, register indirect, base-plus-index, register relative, and base relative-plus-index in the 8086–80286 microprocessor. The 80386 and 80486 microprocessors also include a scaled-index mode of addressing memory data. The program memory-addressing modes include: program-relative, direct, and indirect. The operation of the stack memory is explained so that PUSH and POP instructions are understood.

CHAPTER OBJECTIVES

1. Explain the operation of each data-addressing mode.
2. Use the data-addressing modes to form assembly language statements.
3. Explain the operation of each program memory-addressing mode.
4. Use the program memory-addressing modes to form assembly and machine language statements.
5. Select the appropriate addressing mode to accomplish a given task.
6. Detail the difference between address memory data using real mode and protected mode operation in the 80386 and 80486 microprocessors.
7. Describe the sequence of events that places data onto the stack or removes data from the stack.

2–1   DATA-ADDRESSING MODES

Because the MOV instruction is a simple and flexible 8086–80486 instruction, it provides the basis for an explanation of the data-addressing modes. Figure 2–1 illustrates the MOV instruction and defines the direction of data flow. The source is to the right and the destination is to the left, next to the opcode MOV. (An *opcode* or *operation code* tells the microprocessor which operation to perform.) The direction of flow is at first awkward, because we naturally assume things move from left to right, where here they move from right to left. Notice that a comma *always* separates the destination from source in an instruction.

In Figure 2–1, the MOV AX,BX instruction transfers the word contents of the source register (BX) into the destination register (AX). The source *never* changes, but the destination *usually* changes.[1] It may help to remember that a MOV instruction makes a *copy* of the source data and transfers this copy to the destination.

Figure 2–2 shows all variations of the data-addressing modes using the MOV instruction. This illustration helps show how each data-addressing mode is formulated with the MOV instruction and also serves as a reference. Note that these are the same data-addressing modes found with all 8086–80486 microprocessors except for the scaled-index addressing mode. Scaled-index addressing is only found in the 80386 and 80486 microprocessors. The 8086–80486 data-addressing modes are:

1. *Register Addressing*—transfers a byte or word from the source register or memory location to the destination register or memory location. (Example: The MOV CX,DX instruction copies the word-sized contents of register DX into register CX.) In the 80386/80486 microprocessor, a double word can be transferred from the source register or memory location to the destination register or memory location. (Example: The MOV ECX,EDX instruction copies the double-word-sized contents of register EDX into register ECX.)
2. *Immediate Addressing*—transfers an immediate byte or word of data into the destination register or memory location. (Example: The MOV AL,22H instruction copies the byte-sized 22H into register AL.) In the 80386/80486 microprocessor, a double word of immediate data can be transferred into a register or memory location. (Example: The MOV EBX,12345678H instruction copies double-word-sized data 12345678H into the 32-bit wide register EBX.)

FIGURE 2–1 The MOV AB,BX instruction illustrating how the source is copied into the destination.

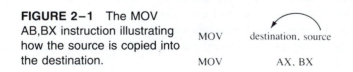

MOV   destination, source

MOV   AX, BX

---

[1]The exceptions are the CMP and TEST instructions that never change the destination. These instructions are described in later chapters.

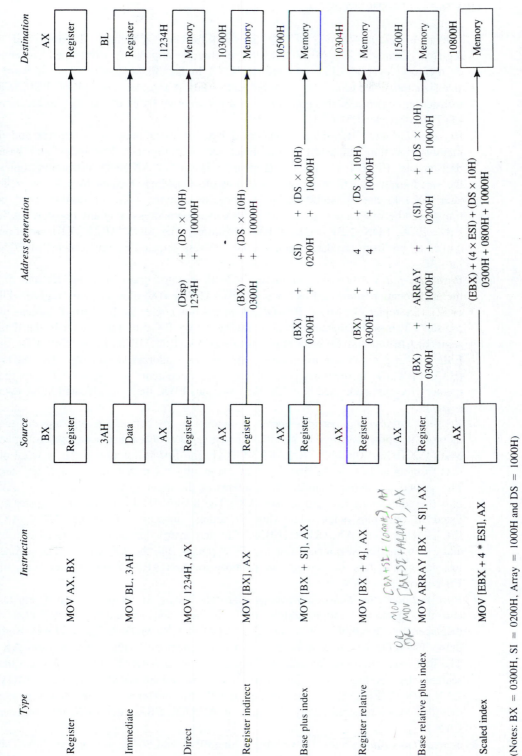

FIGURE 2–2

The page contents (from the figure):

Type	Instruction	Source	Address generation	Destination
Register	MOV AX, BX	BX — Register		AX — Register
Immediate	MOV BL, 3AH	3AH — Data		BL — Register
Direct	MOV 1234H, AX	AX — Register	(Disp) + (DS × 10H) 1234H + 10000H	11234H — Memory
Register indirect	MOV [BX], AX	AX — Register	(BX) + (DS × 10H) 0300H + 10000H	10300H — Memory
Base plus index	MOV [BX + SI], AX	AX — Register	(BX) + (SI) + (DS × 10H) 0300H + 0200H + 10000H	10500H — Memory
Register relative	MOV [BX + 4], AX	AX — Register	(BX) + 4 + (DS × 10H) 0300H + 4 + 10000H	10304H — Memory
Base relative plus index	MOV ARRAY [BX + SI], AX	AX — Register	ARRAY + (SI) + (DS × 10H) 1000H + 0200H + 10000H	11500H — Memory
Scaled index	MOV [EBX + 4 * ESI], AX	AX	(EBX) + (4 × ESI) + (DS × 10H) 0300H + 0800H + 10000H	10800H — Memory

Handwritten notes near "Register relative":
OL MOV [BX+SI + (0000)], AX
OL MOV [BX+SI +ARRAY], AX

(Notes: BX = 0300H, SI = 0200H, Array = 1000H and DS = 1000H)

43

3. *Direct Addressing*—moves a byte or word between a memory location and a register. (Example: The MOV CX,LIST instruction copies the word-sized contents of memory location LIST into register CX.) In the 80386/80486 a double-word-sized memory location can also be addressed. (Example: The MOV ESI,LIST instruction copies a 32-bit number from 4 consecutive bytes of memory at location LIST into register ESI.)

4. *Register Indirect Addressing*—transfers a byte or word between a register and a memory location addressed by an index or base register. The index and base registers are BP, BX, DI, and SI. (Example: The MOV AX,[BX] instruction copies the word-sized data from the data segment offset address located by BX into register AX.) In the 80386/80486 microprocessor a byte, word, or double word is transferred between a register and a memory location addressed by any register: EAX, EBX, ECX, EDX, EBP, EDI, or ESI. (Example: The MOV AL,[ECX] instruction copies a byte from the data segment offset address selected by the contents of ECX into AL.)

5. *Base-Plus-Index Addressing*—transfers a byte or word between a register and the memory location addressed by a base register (BP or BX) plus an index register (DI or SI). (Example: The MOV [BX+DI],CL instruction copies the byte-sized contents of register CL into the memory location addressed by BX plus DI located in the data segment.) In the 80386/80486 any registers (EAX, EBX, ECX, EDX, EBP, EDI, or ESI) may be combined to generate the memory address. (Example: The MOV [EAX+EBX],CL instruction copies the byte-sized contents of register CL into the memory location addressed by EAX, the base, plus EBX, the index, located in the data segment.)

6. *Register Relative Addressing*—moves a byte or word between a register and the memory location addressed by an index or base register plus a displacement.(Example: MOV AX,[BX+4] or MOV AX,ARRAY[BX]. The first instruction copies a word of data from an address in the data segment, formed by BX plus 4, into the AX register. The second instruction transfers the contents of the memory location in an ARRAY plus the contents of BX into register AX.) The 80386/80486 can use any register as listed in base-plus-index addressing to address memory. (Example: MOV AX, [ECX+4] or MOV AX,ARRAY[EBX]. The first instruction copies a word from an address in the data segment, formed by ECX plus 4, into the AX register. The second instruction transfers the contents of memory location ARRAY plus the contents of EBX into register AX.)

7. *Base Relative-Plus-Index Addressing*—transfers a byte or word between a register and the memory location addressed by a base and an index register plus a displacement. (Example: MOV AX,ARRAY[BX+DI] or MOV AX,[BX+DI+4]. Both these instructions copy a word of data from a memory location into register AX. The first instruction uses an address formed by adding ARRAY, BX, and DI and the second by adding BX, DI, and 4.) (An 80386/80486 example: MOV EAX,ARRAY[EBX+ECX] that copies the 32-bit contents of the data segment memory location accessed by the sum of ARRAY, EBX, and ECX into register EAX.)

8. *Scaled-Index Addressing*—is available to the 80386 and 80486 microprocessors. The second register of the pair of registers, the index, is modified by the scale factor 2X,

4X, or 8X to generate the operand memory address. (Example: The MOV AL,[EAX+4*EBX] instruction copies the byte-sized contents of the data segment memory location addressed by EAX plus 4 times EBX into the AL register.) Scaling is used to access word (2X), double word (4X), or quad word (8X) memory array data. Note that a scaling factor of 1X also exists, but it normally is implied and does not appear in the instruction. The MOV AL,[EBX+ECX] is an example where the scaling factor is a one. Alternately, we could use MOV AL,[EBX+1*ECX].

2-2   REGISTER ADDRESSING

Register addressing is easy to understand once the many registers inside the 8086–80486 are learned. The 8086–80286 contain the following 8-bit registers used with register addressing: AH, AL, BH, BL, CH, CL, DH, and DL. They also contain the following 16-bit registers: AX, BX, CX, DX, SP, BP, SI, and DI. In the 80386/80486, the additional extended 32-bit registers are: EAX, EBX, ECX, EDX, ESP, EBP, EDI, and ESI. Some MOV instructions and the PUSH and POP instructions use the 16-bit segment registers (CS, ES, DS, SS, FS, and GS) for register addressing. It is important that instructions use registers that are of uniform size. *Never* mix an 8-bit register with a 16-bit register, an 8-bit register with a 32-bit register, or a 16-bit register with a 32-bit register because this is not allowed by the 8086–80486 instruction set. This is even true when a MOV AX,AL or a MOV EAX,AL instruction may seem to make sense. Of course the MOV AX,AL and MOV EAX,AL instructions are *not* allowed because the registers are of different sizes.

Table 2–1 shows various versions of register MOV instructions. It is impossible to show all variations because there are so many possible combinations. For example,

TABLE 2–1 Examples of the Register-Addressed Instructions

Assembly Language	Operation
MOV AL,BL	Copies BL into AL
MOV CH,CL	Copies CL into CH
MOV AX,CX	Copies CX into AX
MOV SP,BP	Copies BP into SP
MOV DS,AX	Copies AX into DS
MOV DI,SI	Copies SI into DI
MOV BX,ES	Copies ES into BX
MOV ECX,EBX	Copies EBX into ECX
MOV ESP,EDX	Copies EDX into ESP
MOV ES,DS	Not allowed (segment-to-segment)
MOV BL,BX	Not allowed (mixed sizes)
MOV CS,AX	Not allowed (the code segment register may not be used as a destination register)

FIGURE 2–3 The effect of executing the MOV BX,CX instruction at the point just before the BX register changes. Note that the 1234H is copied from the CX register and is about to enter the BX register. Once 1234H enters the BX register, the 76AFH currently in BX is lost.

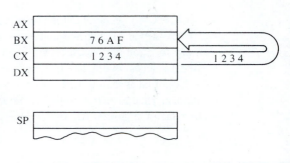

just the 8-bit subset of the MOV instruction has 64 different variations. About the only type of register MOV instruction not allowed, is a segment register to segment register MOV instruction. Also note that the code segment register may not be changed by a MOV instruction. The reason is that the address of the next instruction is found in both IP/EIP and CS. If only CS is changed, the address of the next instruction is unpredictable.

Figure 2–3 shows the function of the MOV BX,CX instruction. Note that the source register does not change, but the destination does. This instruction moves a 1234H from register CX into register BX. This data transfer erases the old contents (76AFH) of register BX, but the contents of CX remain unchanged. The contents of the destination register or destination memory location changes for all instructions except the CMP and TEST instructions.

2–3   IMMEDIATE ADDRESSING

Another data-addressing mode is immediate addressing. The term *immediate* implies that the data immediately follow the hexadecimal opcode in the memory. Immediate addressing operates on a byte or word of data. In the 80386/80486 microprocessor immediate addressing also operates on double-word data. The MOV immediate instruction transfers a copy of the immediate data into a register or a memory location. Figure 2–4 shows the operation of a MOV EAX,13456H instruction. This instruction copies the 13456H from the instruction, located in the memory, into register EAX. As with the MOV instruction illustrated in Figure 2–3, the source data overwrites the destination data.

In symbolic assembly language, the symbol # precedes immediate data in a few 8086–80486 assemblers.[2] The MOV AX,#3456H instruction is an example of immediate data. Most assemblers do not use the # symbol, but represent immediate data as in the MOV AX,3456H instruction. In this text we do not use the # symbol for immediate data.

---

[2]This is true in the assembler provided for an HP64100 logic development system manufactured by Hewlett-Packard, Inc.

FIGURE 2-4 The effect of executing a MOV AX,3456H instruction. Here the data, which follow the opcode B8, are moved from the memory into the AX register. The operation is shown at the point just before register AX changes.

The Intel, MASM,[3] and TASM[4] assemblers do not use the # symbol for immediate data, but an assembler for the HP64000 logic development system does.

The symbolic assembler portrays immediate data in many ways. The letter H appends hexadecimal data. If hexadecimal data begins with a letter, we start it with a 0. For example, to represent an F2H, we use 0F2H in assembly language. Decimal data is represented, as is, and requires no special codes or adjustments. An example is the 100 decimal in the MOV AL,100 instruction. An ASCII coded character or characters may be depicted in the immediate form if the ASCII data are enclosed in apostrophes. An example is the MOV BH,'A' instruction, which moves an ASCII-coded A (41H) into register BH. Be careful to use apostrophes (') to surround ASCII data and not single quotation marks ('). Binary data are represented if the binary number is followed by the letter B or the letter Y. Table 2-2 shows many different MOV instructions that apply immediate data.

TABLE 2-2 Examples of immediate addressing using the MOV instruction

Assembly Language	Operation
MOV BL,44	Moves a 44 decimal (2CH) into BL
MOV AX,44H	Moves a 44 hexadecimal into AX
MOV SI,0	Moves a 0000H into SI
MOV CH,100	Moves a 100 (64H) into CH
MOV AL,'A'	Moves an ASCII A (41H) into AL
MOV AX,'AB'	Moves an ASCII BA* (4241H) into AX
MOV CL,11001110B	Moves a binary 11001110 into CL
MOV EBX,12340000H	Moves a 12340000H into EBX
MOV ESI,12	Moves a 12 decimal into ESI
MOV EAX,100Y	Moves a 100 binary into EAX

Note: This is not an error; the ASCII characters are stored as a BA, so care should be exercised when using a word-sized pair of ASCII characters.

---

[3]The MASM (macro assembler) is an assembler program from Microsoft Corporation.
[4]The TASM (turbo assembler) is an assembler program from Borland Corporation.

2-4   DIRECT DATA ADDRESSING

Most instructions can use the direct data addressing mode. Direct data addressing is applied to many instructions in a typical program. There are two basic forms of direct data addressing: (1) direct addressing that only applies to a MOV between a memory location and AL, AX, or EAX; and (2) displacement addressing for almost any instruction in the 8086–80486 instruction set. In either case the address is formed by adding the displacement to the default data segment address or an alternate segment address.

Direct Addressing

Direct addressing is only allowed with a MOV instruction that transfers data between a memory location, located within the data segment, and the AL (8-bit), AX (16-bit), or EAX (32-bit) register. This instruction is always a 3-byte long instruction.

The MOV AL,DATA instruction, as represented by most assemblers, transfers a copy of the byte stored at memory location DATA (1234H), within the data segment, into the AL register. Memory location DATA is a *symbolic memory location.* Many assemblers represent this instruction as a MOV AL,[1234H].[5] The [1234H] is an *absolute memory location* that is not always allowed by all assembler programs. Figure 2–5 shows how this instruction transfers a copy of the byte-sized contents of memory location 11234H into AL. We form the effective address by adding 1234H (the offset address) to 10000H (the data segment address) in a system operating in the real mode.

Table 2–3 lists three direct addressed instructions. These instructions often appear in programs, so Intel decided to make them special 3-byte long instructions. All other instructions that move data from a memory location to a register, called displacement addressed instructions, require 4 or more bytes of memory for storage in a program.

Displacement Addressing

Displacement addressing is almost identical to direct addressing except the instruction is 4 bytes wide instead of 3. In the 80386/80486, this instruction can be 6 bytes wide if a

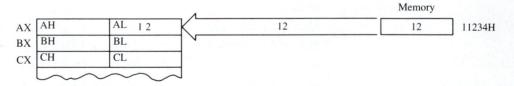

FIGURE 2–5   The effect of executing the MOV AL,[1234H] instruction if DS = 1000H. Here the AL register is shown after the data (12) have destroyed the previous contents of register AL.

---

[5]This form may be used with MASM, but most often appears when a program is entered or listed by DEBUG, a debugging tool provided with the disk operating system.

TABLE 2-3 The four possible direct addressed instructions using AX and AL

Assembly Language	Operation
MOV AL,NUMBER	Copies the byte contents of memory address NUMBER located in the data segment into AL
MOV AX,COW	Copies the word contents of memory address COW in the data segment into AX
*MOV EAX,WATER	Copies the double-word contents of memory WATER located in the data segment into EAX
MOV NEWS,AL	Copies AL into memory location NEWS in the data segment
MOV THERE,AX	Copies AX into memory location THERE in the data segment
*MOV HOME,EAX	Copies EAX into data segment memory location HOME

Note: The 80386/80486 microprocessor will at times use more than 3 bytes of memory for the 32-bit move between EAX and memory.

32-bit displacement is specified. This type of direct data addressing is much more flexible because most 8086/80486 instructions use it.

Figure 2-6 shows the operation of the MOV CL,[2000H] instruction. This instruction operates in the same manner as the MOV AL,[1234H] instruction of Figure 2-5. The difference only becomes apparent upon examination of the assembled versions of these two instructions. The MOV AL,[1234H] instruction is 3 bytes in length and the MOV CL,[2000H] instruction is 4 bytes, as illustrated in Example 2-1.

EXAMPLE 2-1

```
0000 A0 1234          MOV   AL,[1234H]
0003 8A 0E 2000       MOV   CL,[2000H]
```

Table 2-4 lists some MOV displacement forms of direct addressing. Not all forms are listed because there are many MOV instructions of this type. Please notice that the segment registers can be stored or loaded from memory.

Register Indirect Addressing

Register indirect addressing allows data to be addressed at any memory location through any of the following 8086-80486 registers: BP, BX, DI, and SI. For example, if register BX contains a 1000H and the MOV AX,[BX] instruction executes, the word contents of

FIGURE 2-6 The effect of executing the MOV CL,[2000H] instruction if DS = 1000H. Here the CL register is shown after the data (8A) have destroyed the previous contents of CL.

TABLE 2–4 Examples of direct data addressing using a displacement

Assembly Language	Operation
MOV CH,DOG	Copies the contents of memory location DOG from the data segment to register CH. The actual offset address of DOG is calculated by the assembler
MOV CH,[1000H]	*Copies the contents of memory location 1000H from the data segment into register CH
MOV ES,DATA6	Copies the word-sized contents of data segment memory location DATA6 into ES
MOV DATA,BP	BP is copied into memory location DATA within the data segment
MOV NUMBER,SP	SP is copied into memory location NUMBER within the data segment
MOV DATA1,EAX	EAX is copied into memory location DATA1 within the data segment
MOV EDI,SUM1	Copies the contents of memory location SUM1 from the data segment into register EDI

Note: This form of addressing is seldom used with most assemblers because we don't often address an actual numeric offset address.

data segment memory offset address 1000H is copied into register AX. If the microprocessor is operated in the real mode and DS = 0100H, this instruction addresses the word stored at memory bytes 2000H and 2001H and transfers it into register AX (see Figure 2–7). Note that the contents of 2000H are moved into AL and the contents of 2001H are moved into AH. The [ ] symbols denote indirect addressing in assembly language. In addition to using the BP, BX, DI, and SI registers to indirectly address memory, the 80386 and 80486 microprocessors allow register indirect addressing using any extended register except ESP. Some typical instructions using indirect addressing appear in Table 2–5.

When using register indirect addressing or any other addressing mode that uses BX, DI, or SI to address memory, these registers address data in the data segment. If register BP addresses memory, it uses the stack segment. These are considered the default settings for these four index and base registers. For the 80386 and 80486, EBP addresses memory, by default, in the stack segment while EAX, EBX, ECX, EDX, EDI, and ESI address memory in the data segment by default. When using a 32-bit register to address memory in the real mode, the contents of the 32-bit register must never exceed 0000FFFFH. In the protected mode, any value can be used in a 32-bit register used to indirectly address memory. An example 80386/80486 instruction is MOV EAX,[EBX]. This instruction takes the double-word-sized number stored at the data segment offset address indicated by EBX and copies it into EAX.

In some cases, indirect addressing requires that the size of the data are specified with the special assembler directive BYTE PTR, WORD PTR, or DWORD PTR. These directives indicate the size of the memory data addressed by the memory pointer (PTR).

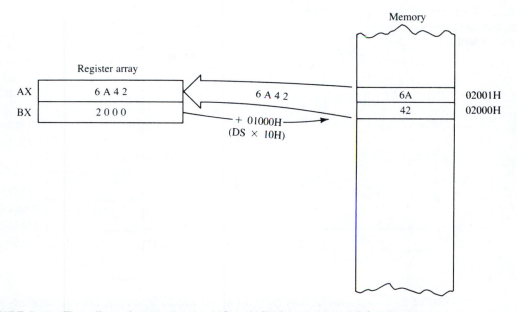

FIGURE 2–7   The effect of executing the MOV AX,[BX] instruction if DS = 0100H and BX = 1000H. Here the AX register is shown after the data (6A42H) have destroyed the previous contents of AX.

TABLE 2–5   Example instructions using register indirect addressing

Assembly Language	Operation
MOV CX,[BX]	A word from the memory location address by BX within the data segment moves into register CX
MOV [BP],DL	A byte is copied from register DL into the memory location addressed by BP within the stack segment
MOV [DI],BH	A byte is copied from register BH into the memory location addressed by DI within the data segment
MOV [DI],[BX]	Memory-to-memory moves are not allowed except with string instructions
MOV DI,[DI]	This instruction is not allowed because the register used to indirectly address memory may not be changed by the instruction.
MOV AL,[EDX]	A byte is copied into AL from the data segment memory location addressed by EDX
MOV ECX,[EBX]	A double word is copied into ECX from the data segment memory location addressed by EBX

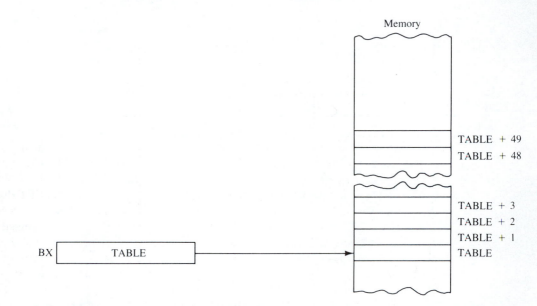

FIGURE 2–8   An array of data (TABLE) containing 50 bytes that are indirectly addressed through the BX register.

For example, the MOV AL,[DI] instruction is clearly a byte-sized move instruction, but the MOV [DI],10H instruction is vague. Does the MOV [DI],10H instruction address a byte, word, or double-word-sized memory location? We can't determine the size and neither can the assembler. The instruction MOV BYTE PTR [DI],10H clearly shows that the location addressed by DI is a byte-sized memory location. Likewise, the MOV DWORD PTR [DI],10H clearly shows the memory location as double-word-sized. The BYTE PTR, WORD PTR, and DWORD PTR directives are only used with instructions that address a memory location through a pointer or index register with immediate data and for a few other instructions that are covered in subsequent chapters.

Indirect addressing often allows a program to refer to tabular data located in the memory system. For example, suppose that you must create a table of information that contains 50 samples taken from a digital voltmeter. Figure 2–8 shows the table and the BX register used to address each location in the table sequentially. To address the table, you must load the starting location of the table into the BX register with a MOV immediate instruction. After initializing the starting address of the table, you then use register indirect addressing to store the 50 samples sequentially.

EXAMPLE 2–2

```
        ;instructions that read 50 bytes of data from DATA_PORT
        ;and stores them in a TABLE.
        ;
0000 BB 0000 R    MOV    BX BX,OFFSET TABLE    ;address TABLE
0003 B9 0032      MOV    CX,50                 ;load counter
```

```
0006            AGAIN:

0006 E4 2A        IN    AL,DATA_PORT        ;read
0008 88 07        MOV   [BX],AL             ;save data
000A 43           INC   BX                  ;address next
000B E2 F9        LOOP  AGAIN
```

The instruction sequence shown in Example 2–2 loads register BX with the starting address of the table and initializes the count, located in register CX, to 50. The OFFSET directive tells the assembler to load BX with the offset address of memory location TABLE and not the contents of TABLE. For example, the MOV BX,DATA instruction copies the contents of memory location DATA into BX while the MOV BX,OFFSET DATA instruction copies the address of DATA into BX. When the OFFSET directive is used with the MOV instruction, the assembler calculates the address and then uses a move immediate instruction to load the address into the specified 16-bit register.

Once the counter and pointer are initialized, a repeat-until CX = 0 loop executes. Here data are input (IN) from the voltmeter and then stored in the memory location indirectly addressed by register BX. Next, BX increments (*adds one*) to the next table locations and finally the LOOP instruction repeats the LOOP 50 times. The LOOP instruction decrements (*subtracts one*) the counter (CX) and if CX is not zero, LOOP jumps to memory location AGAIN. If CX becomes zero, no jump occurs and the sequence of instructions ends.

2–5 BASE-PLUS-INDEX ADDRESSING

Base-plus-index addressing is similar to indirect addressing because it indirectly addresses memory data. In the 8086–80286, this type of addressing uses one base register (BP or BX) *plus* one index register (DI or SI) to indirectly address memory. Often the base register holds the beginning location of a memory array, while the index register holds the relative position of an element in a byte-sized array. Remember that whenever BP addresses memory data, both the stack segment register and BP generate the effective address.

In the 80386/80486, this type of addressing allows the combination of any two 32-bit extended registers except ESP. For example, the MOV DL,[EAX+EBX] instruction is an example of using EAX (base) plus EBX (index) to address data segment data. If the EBP register is used, the data are located in the stack segment.

Locating Data with Base-Plus-Index Addressing

Figure 2–9 shows how data are addressed by the MOV DX,[BX+DI] instruction when the microprocessor operates in the real mode. In this example, BX = 1000H, DI = 0010H, and DS = 0100H, which translate into memory address 02010H. This instruction transfers a copy of the word from location 02010H (DL) and 02011H (DH) into the DX register. Table 2–6 lists some instructions used for base-plus-index addressing. Note that the Intel

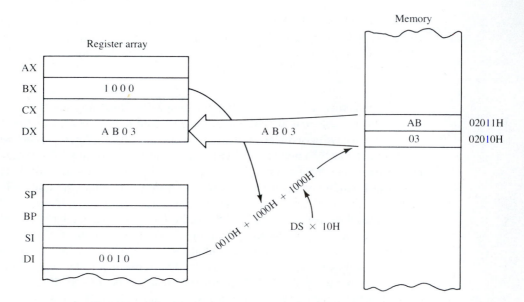

FIGURE 2-9   An example showing how the base-plus-index mode of addressing functions for the MOV DX,[BX + DI] instruction. Notice that memory address 02010H is referenced by this instruction because DS (0100H), BX (1000H), and DI (0010H) are summed to generate this address.

TABLE 2-6   Examples of base-plus-index addressing

Assembly Language	Operation
MOV CX,[BX+DI]	The word contents of the memory location addressed by BX plus DI within the data segment are copied into register CX
MOV CH,[BP+SI]	The byte contents of the memory location addressed by BP plus SI within the stack segment are copied into register CH
MOV [BX+SI],SP	The word contents of SP is stored in the data segment at the location addressed by BX plus SI
MOV [BP+DI],CX	The word contents of CX is stored in the stack segment at the memory location addressed by BP plus DI
MOV CL,[EDX+EDI]	The byte contents of the data segment memory location addressed by EDX plus EDI is copied into register CL
MOV [EAX+EBX],ECX	The double-word contents of ECX is copied into the data segment memory location addressed by EAX plus EBX

assembler and the CPM-86[6] operating system require that this addressing mode appear as [BX][DI] instead of [BX+DI]. The MOV DX,[BX+DI] instruction is MOV DX,[BX] [DI] for a program written for the Intel assembler. This text uses the first form in all example programs because it is more common.

Locating Array Data Using Base-Plus-Index Addressing

A major use of the base-plus-index addressing mode is to address elements in a memory array. Suppose we address the elements in an array located in the data segment at memory location ARRAY. To accomplish this, register BX (base) is loaded with the beginning address of the array and register DI (index) is loaded with the element number. Figure 2–10 shows the use of BX and DI to access an element in an array of data.

EXAMPLE 2–3

```
        ;using the base-plus-index addressing mode

0000 BB 0032 R      MOV     BX,OFFSET ARRAY  ;address ARRAY
0003 BF 0010        MOV     DI,10H           ;address element 10H
0006 8A 01          MOV     AL,[BX+DI]       ;get data
0008 BF 0020        MOV     DI,20H           ;address element
000B 88 01          MOV     [BX+DI],AL       ;save data
```

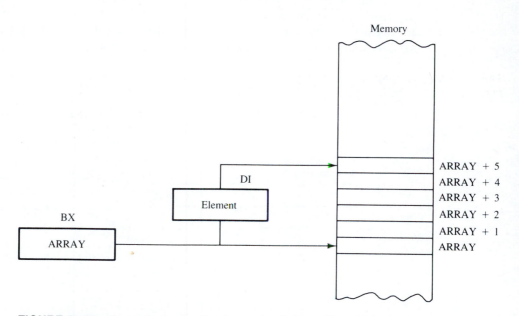

FIGURE 2–10 An example showing base-plus-index addressing. Here an element (DI) of an array of data (BX) is accessed.

---

[6]CPM-86 and DR DOS version 6.0 are operating systems produced by Digital Research Corporation.

A short program listed in Example 2–3 moves array element 10H into array element 20H. Notice that the array element number, loaded into the DI register, selects the array element.

2–6   REGISTER RELATIVE ADDRESSING

Register relative addressing is similar to base-plus-index addressing and displacement addressing discussed earlier. In register relative addressing, the data in a segment of memory are addressed by adding a displacement to the contents of a base or an index register (BP, BX, DI, or SI). Figure 2–11 shows the operation of the MOV AX,[BX+1000H] instruction. In this example, BX = 0100H and DS = 0200H so the address generated is the sum of DS x 10H, BX, and the displacement of 1000H, which is 03100H. Remember that BX, DI, or SI address the data segment and BP addresses the stack segment. In the 80386/80486 the displacement can be a 32-bit number and the register can be any 32-bit register except the ESP register. Remember that the size of a real mode segment is 64K bytes in length. Table 2–7 lists a few instructions that use register relative addressing.

A displacement is a number added to the register within the [ ], as in the MOV AL,[DI+2] instruction, or it is subtracted from the register, as in MOV AL,[SI-1]. A displacement is also an offset address appended to the front of the [ ] as in MOV AL,DATA[DI]. Both forms of displacements can appear simultaneously as in the MOV

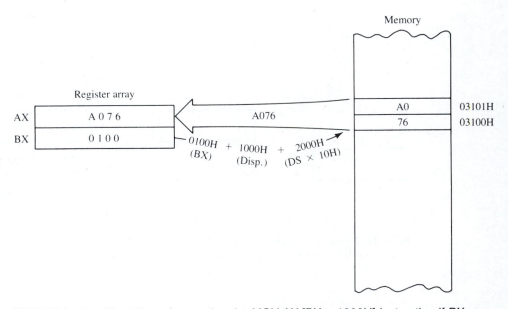

FIGURE 2–11   The effect of executing the MOV AX,[BX + 1000H] instruction if BX = 0100H and DS = 0200H.

TABLE 2–7 Examples of register relative addressing

Assembly Language	Operation
MOV AX,[DI+100H]	The word contents of the data segment memory location addressed by DI plus 100H is copied into register AX
MOV ARRAY[SI],BL	The byte contents of BL is copied into the data segment at the location addressed by ARRAY plus SI
MOV LIST[SI+2],CL	The byte contents of CL is copied into the data segment at the location addressed by the sum of LIST, SI, and 2
MOV DI,SETS[BX]	DI is loaded from the data segment location addressed by SETS plus BX
MOV DI,[EAX+100H]	The word-sized contents of the data segment memory location addressed by EAX plus 100H is transferred into DI
MOV ARRAY[EBX],AL	AL is copied into the data segment memory location address by ARRAY plus EBX

AL,DATA[DI+3] instruction. In all cases, both forms of the displacement add to the base or base and index register within the [ ]. In the 8086–80286 microprocessor the value of the displacement is limited to a 16-bit signed number or ± 32K and in the 80386/80486 a 32-bit displacement is allowed.

Addressing Array Data with Register Relative

It is possible to address array data with register relative addressing much as one does with base-plus-index addressing. In Figure 2–12, we illustrate register relative addressing with the same example we used for base-plus-index addressing. This shows how the displacement ARRAY adds to index register DI to generate a reference to an array element.

Example 2–4 shows how this new addressing mode can transfer the contents of array element 10H into array element 20H. Notice the similarity between this example and Example 2–3. The main difference is that in Example 2–4 we do not use register BX to address memory area ARRAY; instead we use ARRAY as a displacement to accomplish the same task.

EXAMPLE 2–4

```
        ;using register relative addressing

0000 BF 0010        MOV  DI,10H          ;address element 10H
0003 8A 85 0300 R   MOV  AL,ARRAY[DI]    ;get data
0007 BF 0020        MOV  DI,20H          ;address element 20H
000A 88 85 0300 R   MOV  ARRAY[DI],AL    ;save data
```

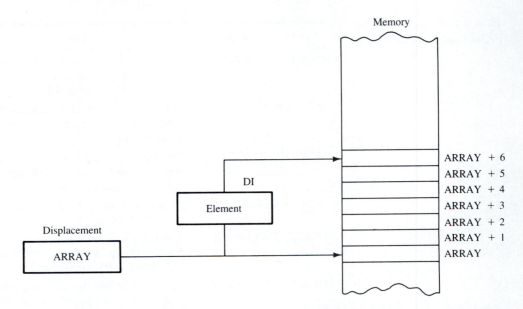

FIGURE 2–12 Register relative addressing used to address an element of ARRAY. The displacement addresses the start of the array, and the contents of DI (the element) selects an element of the array.

2–7   BASE RELATIVE-PLUS-INDEX ADDRESSING

The base relative-plus-index addressing mode is similar to the base-plus-index addressing mode, but adds a displacement besides using a base register and an index register to form the memory address. This type of addressing mode often addresses a two-dimensional array of memory data.

Addressing Data with Base Relative-Plus-Index

Base relative-plus-index addressing is the least-used addressing mode. Figure 2–13 shows how data are references if the instruction executed by the microprocessor is a MOV AX,[BX+SI+100H]. The displacement of 100H adds to BX and SI to form the offset address within the data segment. Registers BX = 0020H, SI = 0010H, and DS = 1000H, so the effective address for this instruction is 10130H—the sum of these registers plus a displacement of 100H. This addressing mode is too complex for frequent use in a program. Some typical instructions using base relative-plus-index addressing appear in Table 2–8. Note that with the 80386/80486 microprocessor, the effective address is generated by the sum of two 32-bit registers plus a 32-bit displacement.

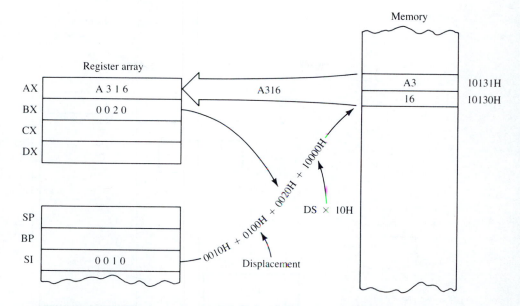

FIGURE 2-13 An example of base relative-plus-index addressing is illustrated with the MOV,100H[BX + SI] instruction. This instruction moves data from memory to the AX register. The memory address is the sum of DS × 10H, 100H, BX, and SI.

TABLE 2-8 Example base relative-plus-index instructions

Assembly Language	Operation
MOV DH,[BX+DI+20H]	DH is loaded from the data segment location addressed by the sum of BX, DI, and 20H
MOV AX,FILE[BX+DI]	AX is loaded from the data segment location addressed by the sum of FILE, BX, and DI
MOV LIST[BP+DI],CL	CL is stored at the stack segment location addressed by the sum of LIST, BP, and DI
MOV LIST[BP+SI+4],DH	DH is stored at the stack segment location addressed by the sum of LIST, BP, SI, and 4
MOV AL,FILE[EBX+ECX+2]	AL is loaded from the data segment memory location address by the sum of FILE, EBX, ECX, and 2

Addressing Arrays with Base Relative-Plus-Index

Suppose that a file of many records exists in memory and each record contains many elements. This displacement addresses the file, the base register addresses a record, and the index register addresses an element of a record. Figure 2-14 illustrates this very complex form of addressing.

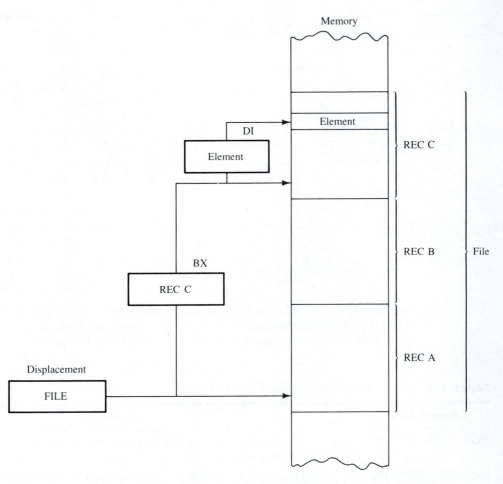

FIGURE 2–14 Base relative-plus-index addressing used to address a FILE that contains multiple records (REC); each record contains many elements.

Example 2–5 provides a program that copies element 0 of record A into element 2 of record C using the base relative-plus-index mode of addressing.

EXAMPLE 2–5

```
;using the base-plus-indexed addressing mode

0009 BB 0364 R      MOV  BX,OFFSET RECA    ;address record A
0003 BF 000         MOV  DI,0              ;address element 0
0006 8A 81 04F4 R   MOV  AL,FILE[BX+DI]    ;get data
000A BB 042C R      MOV  BX,OFFSET RECC    ;address record C
000D BF 0002        MOV  DI,2              ;address element 2
0010 88 81 04F4 R   MOV  FILE[BX+DI],AL    ;save data
```

2–8 SCALED-INDEX ADDRESSING

Scaled-index addressing is the last type of data-addressing mode discussed. This data-addressing mode is unique to the 80386 and 80486 microprocessors. Scaled-index addressing uses two 32-bit registers (a base register and an index register) to access memory. The second register (index) is multiplied by a scaling factor. The scaling factor is 1X, 2X, 4X, or 8X. A scaling factor of 1X is implied and need not be included in the assembly language instruction (MOV AL,[EBX+ECX]). A scaling factor of 2X addresses word-sized memory arrays, a scaling factor of 4X addresses double-word-sized memory arrays, and a scaling factor of 8X is used with quad word-sized memory arrays.

An example instruction is MOV AX,[EDI+2*ECX]. This instruction uses a scaling factor of 2X, which multiplies the contents of ECX by 2 before adding it to the EDI register to form the memory address. If ECX contains a 00000000H, memory element 0 is addressed, if ECX contains a 00000001H, memory element 1 is accessed and so forth. The scaling factor scales the index (ECX) by a 2 for a word-sized memory array. There are an extremely large number of scaled-index addressed register combinations. Refer to Table 2–9 for some examples of scaled-index addressing.

Example 2–6 shows a sequence of instructions that uses scaled-index addressing to access a word-sized array of data called LIST. Note that the offset address of LIST is loaded into register EBX with the MOV EBX,OFFSET LIST instruction. Once EBX addresses array LIST, the elements (located in ECX) of 2, 4, and 7 of this wordwide array are added using a scaling factor of 2 to access the elements.

TABLE 2–9 Examples of instructions that use scaled-index addressing

Assembly Language	Operation
MOV EAX,[EBX+4*ECX]	Register EAX is loaded from the data segment memory location addressed by the sum of EBX plus 4 times ECX
MOV [EAX+2*EBX],CX	Register CX is copied into the data segment memory location addressed by EAX plus 2 times EBX
MOV AX,[EBP+2*EDI+100H]	Register AX is loaded from the stack segment memory location addressed by EBP plus 2 times EDI plus 100H
MOV LIST[EAX+2*EBX+10H],DX	Register DX is copied to the data segment memory location addressed by LIST plus EAX plus 2 times EBX plus 10H

EXAMPLE 2-6

```
                        ;sequence of instructions that sum word-sized elements of LIST
                        ;
0000 66| BB 00000000       MOV   EBX,0
0006 BB 0000 R             MOV   BX,OFFSET LIST        ;address array LIST

0009 66| B9 00000002       MOV   ECX,2                 ;address element 2
000F 67& 8B 04 4B          MOV   AX,[EBX+2*ECX]        ;get element 2

0013 B1 04                 MOV   CL,4                  ;address element 4
0015 67& 03 04 4B          ADD   AX,[EBX+2*ECX]        ;add element 4

0019 B1 07                 MOV   CL,7                  ;address element 7
001B 67& 03 04 4B          ADD   AX,[EBX+2*ECX]        ;add element 7
```

2-9   PROGRAM MEMORY-ADDRESSING MODES

Program memory-addressing modes, used with the JMP and CALL instructions, consist of three distinct forms: direct, relative, and indirect. This section introduces these three addressing forms, using the JMP instruction to illustrate their operation.

Direct Program Memory Addressing

Direct program memory addressing was used by most early microprocessors for all jumps and calls. Direct program memory addressing is also used in high-level languages as GOTO and GOSUB instructions. The 8086–80486 can use this form of addressing, but doesn't use it nearly as often as relative and indirect program addressing.

The instructions for direct program memory addressing store the address with the opcode. For example, if a program jumps to memory location 10000H for the next instruction, the address (10000H) is stored following the opcode in the memory. Figure 2–15 shows the direct *intersegment* JMP instruction and the four bytes required to store the address 10000H. A JMP 10000H instruction loads CS with 1000H and IP with 0000H to jump to memory location 10000H for the next instruction. (An *intersegment* jump is a jump to any memory location within the memory system.) We often call the direct jump a *far* jump because it can jump to any memory location for the next instruction. In the real mode, a far jump accesses any location in the first

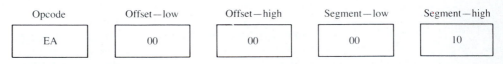

Opcode	Offset—low	Offset—high	Segment—low	Segment—high
EA	00	00	00	10

FIGURE 2-15   The 5-byte machine language instruction for a JMP [10000H] instruction. The opcode is followed by the offset address (0000H) and then the code segment address (1000H).

1M byte of memory by changing both CS and IP. In protected mode operation, the far jump accesses a new code segment descriptor from the descriptor table allowing it to access any memory location in an 80286—80486 microprocessor's 4G byte memory system.

The only other instruction that uses direct program addressing is the intersegment CALL instruction. Usually, the name of a memory address, called a *label,* refers to the location that is called or jumped to instead of the actual numeric address. When using a label with the CALL or JMP instruction, most assemblers select the best form of program addressing.

Relative Program Memory Addressing

Relative program memory addressing is not available in many early microprocessors, but it is available to the 8086–80486 microprocessor. The term *relative* means "relative to the instruction pointer (IP)." For example, if a JMP instruction skips the next 2 bytes of memory, the address in relation to the instruction pointer is a 2 that adds to the instruction pointer. This develops the address of the next program instruction. An example of the relative JMP instruction is shown in Figure 2–16. Notice that the JMP instruction is a 1-byte instruction with a 1-byte or a 2-byte displacement that adds to the instruction pointer. A 1-byte displacement is used in *short* jumps and a 2-byte displacement is used with *near* jumps and calls. Both types are considered intrasegment jumps. (An *intrasegment* jump is a jump anywhere within the current code segment.) In the 80386/80486 microprocessor the displacement can also be a 32-bit value allowing the 80386/80486 to use relative addressing to jump to any location within its 4G byte code segment.

Relative JMP and CALL instructions contain either an 8-bit or a 16-bit signed displacement that allows a forward memory reference or a reverse memory reference. (The 80386/80486 can have a 32-bit displacement.) All assemblers automatically calculate the distance of the displacement and select the proper 1-, 2- or 4-byte form. If the distance is too far for a 2-byte displacement in an 8086—80286 microprocessor, some assemblers use the direct jump. An 8-bit displacement (*short*) has a value between +127 and −128, while a 16-bit displacement (*near*) has a value between ±32K. In the 80386/80486, a 32-bit displacement allows a range of ±2G bytes.

Indirect Program Memory Addressing

The 8086–80486 allow several forms of program indirect memory addressing for the JMP and CALL instruction. Table 2–10 lists some acceptable program indirect jump

FIGURE 2–16   A JMP [2] instruction, which will skip over the next two bytes in the program. In this example, the program continues at location 10004H.

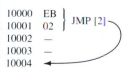

TABLE 2–10 Examples of program indirect addressing

Assembly Language	Operation
JMP AX	Jump to the location addressed by AX in the current code segment
JMP CX	Jump to the location addressed by CX in the current code segment
JMP [BX]	Jump to the current code segment location to the address stored at the data segment location plus BX
JMP [DI+2]	Jump to the current code segment location to the address stored at the data segment location plus DI + 2
JMP TABLE[BX]	Jump to the current code segment location addressed by the contents of TABLE plus BX
JMP ECX	Jump to the current code segment location addressed by ECX

instructions, which can use any 16-bit register (AX, BX, CX, DX, SP, BP, DI, or SI), any relative register ([BP], [BX], [DI], or [SI]), and any relative register with a displacement. In the 80386/80486, an extended register also can hold the address or indirect address of a relative JMP or CALL. For example, the 80386/80486 can use a JMP EAX to jump to the location addressed by register EAX.

If a 16-bit register holds the address of a JMP instruction, the jump is near. For example, if the BX register contains a 1000H and a JMP BX instruction executes, the microprocessor jumps to offset address 1000H in the current code segment.

If a relative register holds the address, the jump is also considered an indirect jump. For example, a JMP [BX] refers to memory location within the data segment at the offset address contained in BX. At this offset address is a 16-bit number that is used as the offset address in the intrasegment jump.

Figure 2–17 shows a jump table that is stored beginning at memory location TABLE. This jump table is referenced by the short program of Example 2–7. In this example, the BX register is loaded with a 4, so when it combines in the JMP TABLE[BX] instruction with TABLE, the effective address is the contents of the second entry in the jump table.

FIGURE 2–17 A jump table that is used to allow the program to select different jump addresses for different values in the BX register.

```
TABLE   DW   LOC0  ⎫   Addresses of four
        DW   LOC1  ⎪   different programs.
        DW   LOC2  ⎬  (Each address is a 2-byte
        DW   LOC3  ⎭         offset.)
```

EXAMPLE 2–7

```
                              ;using indirect addressing for a jump
                              ;
0000 BB 0004                  MOV   BX,4           ;address LOC2
0003 FF A7 23A1 R             JMP   TABLE[BX]      ;jump to LOC2
```

2–10   STACK MEMORY ADDRESSING

The stack is an important part of the memory system in all microprocessors. It holds data temporarily and stores return addresses for procedures or subroutines. The stack memory is a *LIFO* (last-in, first-out) memory in the 8086–80486 microprocessor. Data are placed onto the stack with a PUSH instruction and removed with a POP instruction. The CALL instruction uses the stack to hold the return address for procedures and a RET (return) instruction to remove the return address from the stack.

The stack memory is maintained by two registers: the *stack pointer* (SP or ESP) and the *stack segment register* (SS). Whenever a word of data is pushed onto the stack [see Figure 2–18(a)], the high-order 8 bits are placed in the location addressed by SP - 1. The low-order 8 bits are placed in the location addressed by SP - 2. The SP is then decremented by 2 so the next word of data is stored in the next available stack memory location. The SP/ESP register always points to an area of memory located within the stack segment. The SP/ESP register adds to SS x 10H to form the stack memory address in the real mode. With protected mode operation, the SS register holds a selector that accesses a descriptor for the base address of the stack segment.

Whenever word data are popped from the stack [see Figure 2–18(b)], the low-order 8 bits are removed from the location addressed by SP. The high-order 8 bits are removed from the location addressed by SP + 1. The SP register is then incremented by 2. Table 2–11 lists some of the PUSH and POP instructions available in the 8086–80486 microprocessor. Note that PUSH and POP always store or retrieve *words* of data—never bytes—in the 8086–80286 microprocessor. The 80386/80486 allow words or double words to be transferred to and from the stack. Data may be pushed onto the stack from any 16-bit register or segment register and in the 80386/80486 any 32-bit extended register. Data may be popped off the stack into any 16-bit register or any segment register except CS. The reason that we may not pop data from the stack into CS is that this only changes part of the address of the next instruction.

The PUSHA and POPA instructions either push or pop all of the registers, except the segment registers, on the stack. These instructions are not available on the early 8086/8088 microprocessor. The push immediate instruction is also new to the 80286–80486 microprocessor. Note the examples in Table 2–11 that show the order of the registers transferred by the PUSHA and POPA instructions. The 80386/80486 also allows extended registers to be pushed or popped.

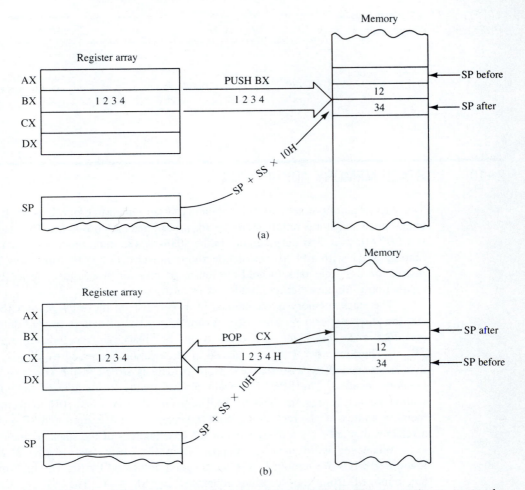

FIGURE 2–18 The PUSH and POP instructions. (a) PUSH BX places the contents of the BX register onto the stack addressed by the SP + SS × 10H. (b) POP CX removes data from the stack at the location addressed by SP + SS × 10H and places the data into the CX register.

TABLE 2–11 Example
PUSH and POP instructions

Assembly Language	Operation
POPF	Removes a word from the stack and places it into the flags
POPFD	Removes a double word from the stack and places it into the EFLAGS
PUSHF	Stores a copy of the flag word on the stack
PUSHFD	Stores a copy of the EFLAGS on the stack
PUSH AX	Stores a copy of AX on the stack
POP BX	Removes a word from the stack and places it into BX
PUSH DS	Stores a copy of DS on the stack
PUSH 1234H	Stores a 1234H on the stack
POP CS	Illegal instruction
PUSH [BX]	Stores a copy of the word contents of the memory location addressed by BX in the data segment on the stack
PUSHA	Stores a copy of registers AX, CX, DX, BX, SP, BP, DI, and SI on the stack
PUSHAD	Stores a copy of registers EAX, ECX, EDX, EBX, ESP, EBP, EDI, and ESI on the stack
POPA	Removes data from the stack and places it into SI, DI, BP, SP, BX, DX, CX, and AX
POPAD	Removes data from the stack and places it into ESI, EDI, EBP, ESP, EBX, EDX, ECX, and EAX
POP EAX	Removes data from the stack and places it into EAX
PUSH EDI	Stores a copy of EDI onto the stack

2–11 SUMMARY

1. The data-addressing modes include: register, immediate, direct, register indirect, base-plus index, register relative, and base relative-plus-index addressing. In the 80386/80486 microprocessor an additional addressing mode called scaled-index addressing exists.

2. The program memory-addressing modes include: direct, relative, and indirect addressing.

3. Table 2–12 lists all real mode data-addressing modes available to the 8086–80486 microprocessor. In the protected mode, the function of the segment register is to address a descriptor that contains the base address of the memory segment.

TABLE 2–12 8086–80486 real mode data-addressing modes

Assembly Language	Address generation
MOV AL,BL	8-bit register addressing
MOV DI,BP	16-bit register addressing
MOV DS,BX	Segment register addressing
MOV AL,LIST	(DS × 10H) + LIST
MOV CH,DATA1	(DS × 10H) + DATA1
MOV DS,DATA2	(DS × 10H) + DATA2
MOV AL,12	Immediate data of 12 decimal
MOV AL,[BP]	(SS × 10H) + BP
MOV AL,[BX]	(DS × 10H) + BX
MOV AL,[DI]	(DS × 10H) + DI
MOV AL,[SI]	(DS × 10H) + SI
MOV AL,[BP+2]	(SS × 10H) + BP + 2
MOV AL,[BX–4]	(DS × 10H) + BX – 4
MOV AL,[DI+1000H]	(DS × 10H) + DI + 1000H
MOV AL,[SI+300H]	(DS × 10H) + SI + 0300H
MOV AL,LIST[BP]	(SS × 10H) + BP + LIST
MOV AL,LIST[BX]	(DS × 10H) + BX + LIST
MOV AL,LIST[DI]	(DS × 10H) + DI + LIST
MOV AL,LIST[SI]	(DS × 10H) + SI + LIST
MOV AL,LIST[BP+2]	(SS × 10H) + BP + LIST + 2
MOV AL,LIST[BX–6]	(DS × 10H) + BX + LIST – 6
MOV AL,LIST[DI+100H]	(DS × 10H) + DI + LIST + 100H
MOV AL,LIST[SI+20H]	(DS × 10H) + SI + LIST + 20H
MOV AL,[BP+DI]	(SS × 10H) + BP + DI
MOV AL,[BP+SI]	(SS × 10H) + BP + SI
MOV AL,[BX+DI]	(DS × 10H) + BX + DI
MOV AL,[BX+SI]	(DS × 10H) + BX + SI
MOV AL,[BP+DI+2]	(SS × 10H) + BP + DI + 2
MOV AL,[BP+SI–4]	(SS × 10H) + BP + SI – 4
MOV AL,[BX+DI+30H]	(DS × 10H) + BX + DI + 30H
MOV AL,[BX+SI+10H]	(DS × 10H) + BX + SI + 10H
MOV AL,LIST[BP+DI]	(SS × 10H) + BP + DI + LIST
MOV AL,LIST[BP+SI]	(SS × 10H) + BP + SI + LIST
MOV AL,LIST[BX+DI]	(DS × 10H) + BX + DI + LIST
MOV AL,LIST[BX+SI]	(DS × 10H) + BX + SI + LIST
MOV AL,LIST[BP+DI+2]	(SS × 10H) + BP + DI + LIST + 2
MOV AL,LIST[BP+SI–7]	(SS × 10H) + BP + SI + LIST – 7
MOV AL,LIST[BX+DI–10H]	(DS × 10H) + BX + DI + LIST – 10H
MOV AL,LIST[BX+SI+1AFH]	(DS × 10H) + BX + SI + LIST + 1AFH

4. The 80386 and 80486 microprocessors have additional addressing modes that allow the extended registers EAX, EBX, ECX, EDX, EBP, EDI, and ESI to address memory. These addressing modes are too numerous to list in tabular form, but in general any of these registers function in the same way as those listed in Table 2–12. For example, the MOV AL,TABLE[EBX+2*ECX+10H] is a valid addressing mode for the 80386/80486 microprocessor.

5. The MOV instruction copies the contents of the source operand into the destination operand. The source never changes for any instruction.

6. Register addressing specifies any 8-bit register (AH, AL, BH, BL, CH, CL, DH, or DL) or any 16-bit register (AX, BX, CX, DX, SP, BP, SI, or DI). The segment registers (CS, DS, ES, or SS) are also addressable for moving data between a segment register and a 16-bit register/memory location or for PUSH and POP. In the 80386/80486 microprocessor, the extended registers also are used for register addressing and consist of: EAX, EBX, ECX, EDX, ESP, EBP, EDI, and ESI. Also available to the 80386/80486 are the FS and GS segment registers.

7. The MOV instruction that uses immediate addressing transfers the byte or word, immediately following the opcode, into a register or a memory location. Immediate addressing manipulates constant data in a program. In the 80386/80486 a double-word immediate data may also be loaded into a 32-bit register or memory location.

8. Direct addressing occurs in two forms in the microprocessor: (1) direct addressing and (2) displacement addressing. Both forms of addressing are identical except direct addressing is used to transfer data between either AX or AL and memory, while displacement addressing is used with any register-memory transfer. Direct addressing requires 3 bytes of memory, while displacement addressing requires 4 bytes.

9. Register indirect addressing allows data to be addressed at the memory location pointed to by either a base (BP and BX) or index register (DI and SI). In the 80386/80486, extended register EAX, EBX, ECX, EDX, EBP, EDI, and ESI are used to address memory data.

10. Base-plus-index addressing often addresses data in an array. The memory address for this mode is formed by adding a base register, index register, and the contents of a segment register times 10H. In the 80386/80486 the base and index registers may be any 32-bit register except EIP and ESP.

11. Register relative addressing uses either a base or index register plus a displacement to access memory data.

12. Base relative-plus-index addressing is useful for addressing a two-dimensional memory array. The address is formed by adding a base register, an index register, displacement, and the contents of a segment register times 10H.

13. Scaled-index addressing is unique to the 80386/80486 microprocessor. The second of two registers (index) is scaled by a factor of 2X, 4X, or 8X to access words, double words, or quad words in memory arrays.

14. Direct program memory addressing is allowed with the JMP and CALL instructions to any location in the memory system. With this addressing mode, the offset address and segment address are stored with the instruction.

15. Relative program addressing allows a JMP or CALL instruction to branch forward or backward in the current code segment by ±32K bytes. In the 80386/80486 the 32-bit

displacement allows a branch to any location in the current code segment using a displacement value of ±2G bytes.

16. Indirect program addressing allows the JMP or CALL instructions to address another portion of the program or subroutine indirectly through a register or memory location.

17. The PUSH and POP instructions transfer a word between the stack and a register or memory location. A PUSH immediate instruction is available to place immediate data on the stack. The PUSHA and POPA instructions transfer AX, CX, DX, BX, BP, SP, SI, and DI between the stack and these registers. In the 80386/80486, the extended register and extended flags can also be transferred between registers and the stack. A PUSHFD stores the EFLAGS, while a PUSHF stores the FLAGS.

2-12   QUESTIONS AND PROBLEMS

1. What do the following MOV instructions accomplish?
   (a) MOV AX,BX
   (b) MOV BX,AX
   (c) MOV BL,CH
   (d) MOV ESP,EBP
   (e) MOV AX,CS
2. List the 8-bit registers that are used for register addressing.
3. List the 16-bit registers that are used for register addressing.
4. List the 32-bit registers that are used for register addressing in the 80386 and 80486 microprocessors.
5. List the 16-bit segment registers used with register addressing by MOV, PUSH, and POP.
6. What is wrong with the MOV BL,CX instruction?
7. What is wrong with the MOV DS,SS instruction?
8. Select an instruction for each of the following tasks:
   (a) copy EBX into EDX
   (b) copy BL into CL
   (c) copy SI into BX
   (d) copy DS into AX
   (e) copy AL into AH
9. Select an instruction for each of the following tasks:
   (a) move a 12H into AL
   (b) move a 123AH into AX
   (c) move a 0CDH into CL
   (d) move a 1000H into SI
   (e) move a 1200A2H into EBX
10. What special symbol is sometimes used to denote immediate data?
11. What is a displacement? How does it determine the memory address in a MOV [2000H],AL instruction?
12. What do the symbols [ ] indicate?
13. What does the address 2000:3000 indicate?

14. Suppose that DS = 0200H, BX = 0300H, and DI = 400H. Determine the memory address accessed by each of the following instructions assuming real mode operation:
    (a) MOV AL,[1234H]
    (b) MOV EAX,[BX]
    (c) MOV [DI],AL
15. What is wrong with a MOV [BX],[DI] instruction?
16. Choose an instruction that requires BYTE PTR.
17. Choose an instruction that requires WORD PTR.
18. Choose an instruction that requires DWORD PTR.
19. Explain the difference between the MOV BX,DATA instruction and the MOV BX,OFFSET DATA instruction.
20. Given that DS = 1000H, SS = 2000H, BP = 1000H, and DI = 0100H, determine the memory address accessed by each of the following assuming real mode operation:
    (a) MOV AL,[BP+DI]
    (b) MOV CX,[DI]
    (c) MOV EDX,[BP]
21. Given that DS = 1200H, BX = 0100H, and SI = 0250H, determine the address accessed by each of the following instructions assuming real mode operation:
    (a) MOV [100H],DL
    (b) MOV [SI+100H],EAX
    (c) MOV DL,[BX+100H]
22. Given that DS = 1100H, BX = 0200H, LIST = 0250H, and SI = 0500H, determine the address accessed by each of the following instructions assuming real mode operation:
    (a) MOV LIST[SI],EDX
    (b) MOV CL,LIST[BX+SI]
    (c) MOV CH,[BX+SI]
23. Given that DS = 1300H, SS = 1400H, BP = 1500H, and SI = 0100H, determine the address accessed by each of the following instructions assuming real mode operation:
    (a) MOV EAX,[BP+200H]
    (b) MOV AL,[BP+SI-200H]
    (c) MOV AL,[SI-0100H]
24. Which base register addresses data in the stack segment?
25. Given that EAX = 00001000H, EBX = 00002000H, and DS = 0010H, determine the addresses accessed by the following instructions assuming real mode operation:
    (a) MOV ECX,[EAX+EBX]
    (b) MOV [EAX+2*EBX],CL
    (c) MOV DH,[EBX+4*EAX+1000H]
26. List all three program memory-addressing modes.
27. How many bytes of memory store a far direct jump instruction? What is stored in each of the bytes?
28. What is the difference between an intersegment and intrasegment jump?
29. If a near jump uses a signed 16-bit displacement, how can it jump to any memory location within the current code segment?
30. What is a far jump?

31. If a JMP instruction is stored at memory location 100H within the current code segment, it cannot be a _____ jump if it is jumping to memory location 200H within the current code segment.

32. Show which JMP instruction assembles (short, near, or far) if the JMP THERE instruction is stored at memory address 10000H and the address of THERE is:
    (a) 10020H
    (b) 11000H
    (c) 0FFFEH
    (d) 30000H

33. Form a JMP instruction that jumps to the address pointed to by the BX register.

34. Select a JMP instruction that jumps to the location stored in memory at location table. Assume that it is a near JMP.

35. How many bytes are stored on the stack by PUSH instructions?

36. Explain how the PUSH [DI] instruction functions.

37. What registers and in what order are they placed on the stack by the PUSHA instruction?

38. What does the 80386/80486 instruction PUSHAD accomplish?

CHAPTER 3

Data Movement Instructions

INTRODUCTION

In this chapter, we explain the 8086–80486 data movement instructions. The data movement instructions include: MOV, MOVSX, MOVZX, PUSH, POP, BSWAP, XCHG, XLAT, IN, OUT, LEA, LDS, LES, LFS, LGS, LSS, LAHF, SAHF, and the string instructions: MOVS, LODS, STOS, INS, and OUTS. We present data movement instructions first because they are used more often and are easy to understand.

The microprocessor requires an assembler program, which generates machine language, because machine language instructions are too complex to generate by hand. This chapter describes the assembly language syntax and some of its directives. (This text assumes that the user is developing software on an IBM personal computer or clone using the Microsoft MACRO assembler (MASM), Intel Assembler (ASM), Borland Turbo assembler (TASM), or similar software. This text presents information that functions with the Microsoft MASM assembler, but most programs function without change using other assemblers. Appendix A explains the Microsoft assembler and provides detail on the linker program.)

CHAPTER OBJECTIVES

1. Explain the operation of each data movement instruction with applicable addressing modes.
2. Explain the purposes of the assembly language pseudo-operations and key words such as: ALIGN, ASSUME, DB, DD, DW, END, ENDS, ENDP, EQU, OFFSET, ORG, PROC, PTR, USE16, USE32, and SEGMENT.
3. Given a specific data movement task, select the appropriate assembly language instructions to accomplish it.
4. Given a hexadecimal machine language instruction, determine the symbolic opcode, source, destination, and addressing mode.
5. Use the assembler to set up a data segment, stack segment, and a code segment.

6. Show how to set up a procedure using PROC and ENDP.
7. Explain the difference between memory models and full segment definitions for the MASM assembler.

3–1   MOV REVISITED

We used the MOV instruction in Chapter 2 to explain the diverse 8086–80486 addressing modes. In this chapter, we use MOV to introduce the machine language instructions available to the programmer for various addressing modes and instructions. Machine code is introduced because it may occasionally be necessary to interpret machine language programs generated by an assembler. Interpretation of the machine's language allows debugging or modification at the machine language level. We also show how to convert between machine and assembly language instructions using Appendix B.

Machine Language

Machine language is the native binary code that the microprocessor understands and uses as the instructions that control its operation. Machine language instructions, for the 8086–80486, vary in length from 1 to as many as 13 bytes. Although machine language appears complex, there is order to this microprocessor's machine language. There are over 20,000 variations of machine language instructions for the 8086–80486 microprocessor, which means there is no complete list of these variations. Because of this, some binary bits in a machine language instruction are given, and the remainder must be determined for each variation of the instruction.

Instructions for the 8086–80286 are 16-bit mode instructions that take the form found in Figure 3–1(a). These 16-bit mode instructions are compatible with the 80386 and 80486 microprocessor if they are set to use 16-bit mode instruction formats. The 80386/80486 assumes that all instructions are 16-bit mode instructions when the machine is operated in the real mode. In the protected mode, the upper byte of the 80386/80486 descriptor contains the D bit that selects either the 16- or 32-bit instruction mode. The

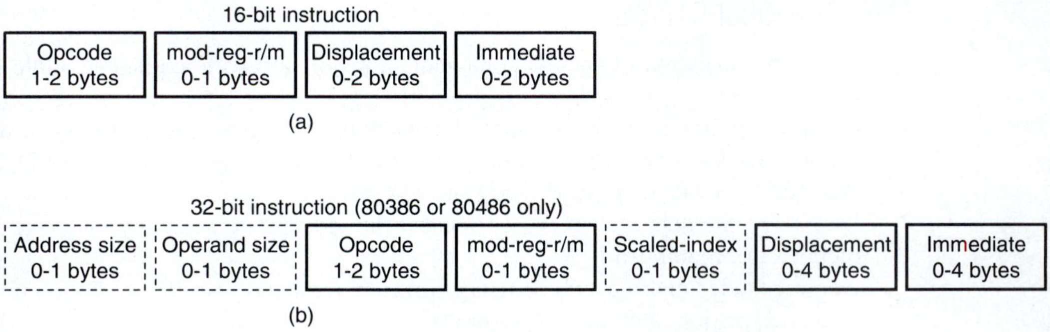

16-bit instruction

Opcode 1-2 bytes	mod-reg-r/m 0-1 bytes	Displacement 0-2 bytes	Immediate 0-2 bytes

(a)

32-bit instruction (80386 or 80486 only)

Address size 0-1 bytes	Operand size 0-1 bytes	Opcode 1-2 bytes	mod-reg-r/m 0-1 bytes	Scaled-index 0-1 bytes	Displacement 0-4 bytes	Immediate 0-4 bytes

(b)

FIGURE 3–1   The formats of the 8086–80486 instructions. (a) The 16-bit form and the (b) the 32-bit form.

80386 and 80486 also use 32-bit mode instructions in the form shown in Figure 3–1(b). These instructions can occur in the 16-bit instruction mode, by the use of prefixes.

The first 2 bytes of the 32-bit instruction mode format are called override prefixes because they are not always present. The first modifies the size of the address used by the instruction and the second modifies the register size. If the 80386/80486 is operating as a 16-bit instruction mode machine (real or protected mode) and a 32-bit register is used, the operand size prefix (66H) is appended to the front of the instruction. If the 80386/80486 is operating as a 32-bit instruction mode machine (protected mode only) and a 32-bit register is used, the operand size prefix is not present. If a 16-bit register appears in an instruction, in the 32-bit instruction mode, the register size prefix is present to select a 16-bit register. The address size prefix is used in a similar fashion as explained later. The prefixes toggle the size of the register and operand from 16-bit to 32-bit or 32-bit to 16-bit for the prefixed instruction.

The Opcode. The *opcode* selects the operation (addition, subtraction, move, etc.) performed by the microprocessor. The opcode is either one or two bytes in length for machine language instructions. Figure 3–2 illustrates the general form of the first opcode byte of many, but not all, machine language instructions. Here the first 6 bits, of the first byte, are the binary opcode. The remaining 2 bits indicate the *direction* (D) of the data flow and whether the data are a *byte* or a *word* (W). In the 80386/80486, double words and words are both specified when W = 1. The instruction mode and operand size prefix select whether W represents a word or a double word in the 80386/80486 microprocessor.

If the D-bit = 1, data flow to the register (REG) field from the R/M field in the next byte of the instruction. If the D-bit = 0, data flow to the R/M field from the REG field. If the W-bit = 1, the data size is a word/double word, and if the W-bit = 0, data size is a byte. The W-bit appears in most instructions while the D-bit mainly appears with the MOV and a few other instructions. Refer to Figure 3–3 for the binary bit pattern of the second opcode byte (reg-mod-r/m) of many instructions. This illustration shows the location of the REG (*register*), R/M (*register/memory*), and MOD (*mode*) fields.

MOD Field. The *MOD field* specifies the addressing mode (MOD) for the selected instruction. The MOD field selects the type of addressing and whether a displacement is present with the selected type. Table 3–1 lists the operand forms available to the MOD field for 16-bit instruction mode in the 8086–80486 microprocessors. If the MOD field contains a 11 it selects the register addressing mode. Register addressing uses the R/M field to specify a register instead of a memory location. If the MOD field contains a 00, 01, or 10, the R/M field selects one of the data memory-addressing modes. When MOD selects a memory-addressing mode, it indicates that the addressing mode contains no displacement (00), an 8-bit sign-extended displacement (01), or a 16-bit displacement (10). The MOV AL,[DI] instruction is an example that uses no displacement, a MOV

FIGURE 3–2 Byte 1 of many machine language instructions, illustrating the position of the opcode, D, and W.

Opcode

FIGURE 3–3 Byte 2 of many machine language instructions, illustrating the position of the MOD, REG, and R/M fields.

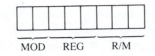

MOD   REG   R/M

TABLE 3–1 MOD field specifications for the 16-bit instruction mode

MOD	Function
00	No displacement
01	8-bit sign-extended displacement
10	16-bit displacement
11	R/M is a register

AL,[DI+2] instruction uses an 8-bit displacement (+2), and a MOV AL,[DI+1000] instruction uses a 16-bit displacement (+1000).

All 8-bit displacements are sign-extended into 16-bit displacements when the microprocessor executes the instruction. If the 8-bit displacement is 00H–7FH (positive), it is sign-extended to 0000H–007FH before adding to a segment address. If the 8-bit displacement is 80H–FFH (negative), it is sign-extended to FF80H–FFFFH. To sign-extend a number, its sign-bit is copied to the next higher-order byte, which generates a 00H or an FFH in the higher-order byte.

In the 80386/80486 microprocessor, the MOD field may be the same as Table 3–1 or, if the instruction mode is 32 bits, it is as appears in Table 3–2. The MOD field is interpreted as selected by the address override prefix or the operating mode of the microprocessor. This change in the interpretation of the MOD field and instruction supports the numerous additional addressing modes allowed in the 80386/80486 microprocessor. The main difference is when the MOD field is a 10. This causes the 16-bit displacement to become a 32-bit displacement to allow any protected mode memory location (4G bytes) to be accessed. The 80386/80486 only allows an 8- or 32-bit displacement when operated in the 32-bit instruction mode.

Register Assignments.   Table 3–3 lists the register assignments for the REG field and the R/M field (MOD = 11). This table contains three lists of register assignments: one is used when the W-bit = 0 (bytes), and the other two are when the W-bit = 1 (words or double words). Note that double-word registers are only available to the 80386/80486.

Suppose that a 2-byte instruction, 8BECH, appears in a machine language program. Because neither a 66H (operand size override prefix) nor 67H (register size override

TABLE 3–2 MOD field specifications for 32-bit instruction mode (80386/80486 only)

MOD	Function
00	No displacement
01	8-bit sign-extended displacement
10	32-bit displacement
11	R/M is a register

TABLE 3-3 REG and R/M (when MOD = 11) assignments

Code	W = 0 (Byte)	W = 1 (Word)	W = 1 (Double Word)
000	AL	AX	EAX
001	CL	CX	ECX
010	DL	DX	EDX
011	BL	BX	EBX
100	AH	SP	ESP
101	CH	BP	EBP
110	DH	SI	ESI
111	BH	DI	EDI

prefix) appears as the first byte, the first byte is the opcode. Assuming that the microprocessor is operated in 16-bit instruction mode, this instruction is converted to binary and placed in the instruction format of bytes 1 and 2 as illustrated in Figure 3–4. The opcode is 100010. If you refer to Appendix B, which lists the machine language instructions, you will find that this is the opcode for a MOV instruction. Also notice that both the D- and W-bits are a logic 1, which means that a word moves into the register specified in the REG field. The REG field contains a 101, indicating register BP, so the MOV instruction moves data into register BP. Because the MOD field contains a 11, the R/M field also indicates a register. Here, R/M = 100 (SP), therefore this instruction moves data from SP into BP and is written in symbolic form as a MOV BP,SP instruction.

Suppose that a 668BE8H instruction appears in an 80386/80486 operated in the 16-bit instruction mode. The first byte (66H) is the operand-size override prefix which selects 32-bit operands for the 16-bit instruction mode. The remainder of the instruction indicates that the opcode is that of the MOV with a source operand of EAX and a destination operand of EBP. This instruction is a MOV EBP,EAX. The same instruction becomes a MOV BP,AX instruction in the 80386/80486 microprocessor if it is operating in the 32-bit instruction mode. Luckily the assembler program keeps track of the operand- and address-size prefixes.

R/M Memory Addressing. If the MOD field contains a 00, 01, or 10, the R/M field takes on a new meaning. Table 3–4 lists the memory-addressing modes for the R/M field when MOD is a 00, 01, or 10 for the 16-bit instruction mode.

All of the 16-bit addressing modes presented in Chapter 2 appear in Table 3–4. The displacement, discussed in Chapter 2, is defined by the MOD field. If MOD = 00

FIGURE 3-4 The 8BEC instruction placed in the byte 1 and 2 formats of Figures 3–1 and 3–2. This machine language instruction is decoded as the symbolic instruction MOV BP,SP.

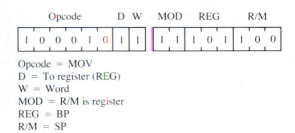

Opcode = MOV
D = To register (REG)
W = Word
MOD = R/M is register
REG = BP
R/M = SP

TABLE 3–4 The 16-bit R/M memory-addressing modes

Code	Function
000	DS:[BX+SI]
001	DS:[BX+DI]
010	SS:[BP+SI]
011	SS:[BP+DI]
100	DS:[SI]
101	DS:[DI]
110	SS:[BP]*
111	DS:[BX]

*Note: See text under Special Addressing Mode.

and R/M = 101, the addressing mode is [DI]. If MOD = 01 or 10, the addressing mode is [DI + 33H] or LIST [DI + 22H] for the 16-bit instruction mode. This example uses LIST, 33H, and 22H as arbitrary values for the displacement.

Figure 3–5 illustrates the machine language version of the 16-bit instruction MOV DL,[DI] or instruction (8A15H). This instruction is 2 bytes long and has an opcode 100010, D = 1 (*to REG from R/M*), W = 0 (*byte*), MOD = 00 (*no displacement*), REG = 010 (*DL*) and R/M = 101 (*[DI]*). If the instruction changes to MOV DL,[DI + 1], the MOD field changes to 01, for an 8-bit displacement, but the first 2 bytes of the instruction otherwise remain the same. The instruction now becomes 8A5501H instead of 8A15H. Notice that the 8-bit displacement appends to the first 2 bytes of the instruction to form a 3-byte instruction instead of 2 bytes. If the instruction is again changed to a MOV DL,[DI+1000H], the machine language form becomes an 8A750010H. Here the 16-bit displacement of 1000H (coded as 0010H) appends the opcode.

Special Addressing Mode. There is a special addressing mode (for 16-bit instructions) that does not appear in Tables 3–3, 3–4, or 3–5 that occurs whenever memory data are referenced by only the displacement mode of addressing for 16-bit instructions. Examples are the MOV [1000H],DL and MOV NUMB,DL instructions. The first instruction moves the contents of register DL into data segment memory location 1000H. The second instruction moves register DL into symbolic data segment memory location NUMB.

FIGURE 3–5 A MOV DL,[DI] instruction coded into binary machine language.

Opcode						D	W	MOD		REG		R/M		
1	0	0	0	1	0	1	0	0	0	0	1	0	1	0	1

Opcode = MOV
D = To register (REG)
W = Byte
MOD = No displacement
REG = DL
RIM = [DI]

FIGURE 3-6 A MOV[1000H],DL instruction coded into binary machine language. Note that two additional bytes are required for the displacement of 1000H.

Opcode	D	W	MOD	REG	R/M
1 0 0 0 1 0	0	0	0 0	0 1 0	1 1 0

Byte 1   Byte 2

Displacement—low	Displacement—high
0 0 0 0 0 0 0 0	0 0 0 1 0 0 0 0

Byte 3   Byte 4

Whenever an instruction has only a displacement, the MOD field is always a 00 and the R/M field is always a 110. This combination normally shows that the instruction contains no displacement and uses addressing mode [BP]. You cannot actually use addressing mode [BP] without a displacement in machine language. The assembler takes care of this by using an 8-bit displacement (MOD = 01) of 00H whenever the [BP] addressing mode appears in an instruction. This means that the [BP] addressing mode assembles as a [BP + 0] even though we use [BP].

Figure 3-6 shows the binary bit pattern required to encode the MOV [1000H],DL instruction in machine language. If the individual translating this symbolic instruction into machine language does not know about the special addressing mode, it would incorrectly translate to a MOV [BP],DL instruction. Figure 3-7 shows the actual form of the MOV [BP],DL instruction. Notice that this is a 3-byte instruction with a displacement of 00H.

32-Bit Addressing Modes. The 32-bit addressing modes found in the 80386/80486 microprocessor are obtained by running these machines in the 32-bit instruction mode or in the 16-bit instruction mode using the address-size prefix 67H. Table 3-5 shows the coding for R/M used to specify the 32-bit addressing modes. Notice that when R/M = 100, an additional byte appears in the instruction called a *scaled-index byte*. The scaled-index byte indicates the additional forms of scaled-index addressing that do not appear in Table 3-5. The scaled-index byte is mainly used when two registers are added to specify the memory address in an instruction.

Figure 3-8 shows the format of the *scaled-index byte* as selected by a value of 100 in the R/M field of an instruction when the 80386/80486 uses a 32-bit address. The

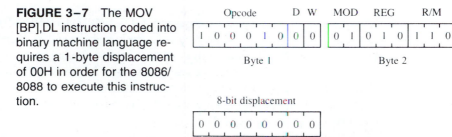

FIGURE 3-7 The MOV [BP],DL instruction coded into binary machine language requires a 1-byte displacement of 00H in order for the 8086/8088 to execute this instruction.

Opcode	D	W	MOD	REG	R/M
1 0 0 0 1 0	0	0	0 1	0 1 0	1 1 0

Byte 1   Byte 2

8-bit displacement
0 0 0 0 0 0 0 0

Byte 3

TABLE 3–5 32-bit addressing modes selected by R/M

Code	Function
000	DS:[EAX]
001	DS:[ECX]
010	DS:[EDX]
011	DS:[EBX]
100	Uses scaled-index byte
101	SS:[EBP]*
110	DS:[ESI]
111	DS:[EDI]

Note: If the MOD bits are 00 this
addressing mode uses a 32-bit displacement without register EBP. This
is similar to the special addressing
mode for the 16-bit instruction mode.

FIGURE 3–8 The scaled
index byte of some 32-bit
addressing modes.

s s
00 = × 1
01 = × 2
10 = × 4
11 = × 8

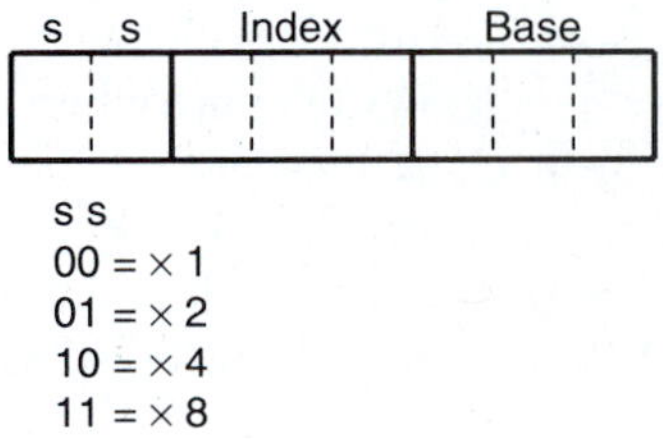

leftmost 2 bits select a scaling factor (multiplier) of 1X, 2X, 4X, or 8X. Note that a scaling factor of 1X is implicit if none is used in an instruction that contains two 32-bit indirect address registers. The index and base fields both contain register numbers as indicated in Table 3–3 for 32-bit registers.

The instruction MOV EAX,[EBX+4*ECX] is encoded as 67668B048BH. Notice that both the address size (67H) and register size (66H) override prefixes appear for this instruction. This means that the instruction is 67668B048BH when operated with the 80386/80486 in the 16-bit instruction mode. If the 80386/80486 is operated in the 32-bit instruction mode, both prefixes disappear so the instruction becomes an 8B048BH instruction. The use of the prefixes depends on the mode of operation for the 80386 and 80486 microprocessors.

An Immediate Instruction.   Suppose we choose the MOV WORD PTR [BX+1000H],1234H instruction as an example of a 16-bit instruction using immediate addressing. This instruction moves a 1234H into the word-sized memory location addressed by the sum of 1000H, BX, and DS × 10H. This 6-byte instruction uses 2 bytes for the opcode, D, W, MOD, REG, and R/M fields. Two of the 6 bytes are the data of 1234H. Two of the 6 bytes are the displacement of 1000H. Figure 3–9 shows the binary bit pattern for each byte of this instruction.

This instruction, in symbolic form, includes WORD PTR. The WORD PTR directive indicates to the assembler that the instruction uses a word-sized memory pointer.

FIGURE 3–9 A MOV word PTR[BX + 1000H], 1234H instruction converted into binary machine language requires 6 bytes of memory: 2 for the instruction, 2 for the displacement of 1000H, and 2 for the immediate data of 1234H.

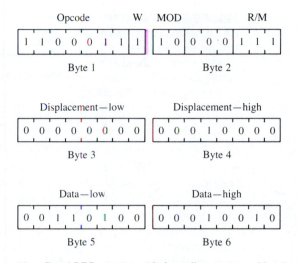

Opcode	W	MOD	R/M
1 1 0 0 0 1 1	1	1 0 0 0 0	1 1 1

Byte 1   Byte 2

Displacement—low   Displacement—high

| 0 0 0 0 0 0 0 0 | 0 0 0 1 0 0 0 0 |

Byte 3   Byte 4

Data—low   Data—high

| 0 0 1 1 0 1 0 0 | 0 0 0 1 0 0 1 0 |

Byte 5   Byte 6

Note: D and REG are not used in immediate memory addressing.

If the instruction moves a byte of immediate data, then BYTE PTR replaces WORD PTR in the instruction. Likewise, if the instruction uses a double word of immediate data, the DWORD PTR directive replaces BYTE PTR. Most instructions that refer to memory through a pointer do not need the BYTE PTR, WORD PTR, or DWORD PTR directives. These are only necessary when it is not clear if the operation is a byte or a word. The MOV [BX],AL instruction is clearly a byte move, while the MOV [BX],1 instruction is not exact and could therefore be a byte-, word-, or double word-sized move. Here the instruction must be coded as MOV BYTE PTR [BX],1, MOV WORD PTR [BX],1, or MOV DWORD PTR [BX],1. If not, the assembler flags it as an error because it cannot determine the intent of this instruction.

Segment MOV Instructions. If the contents of a segment register are moved by the MOV, PUSH, or POP instruction, a special set of register bits (REG field) selects the segment register (see Table 3–6).

TABLE 3–6 Segment register selection bits

Code	Segment Register
000	ES
001	CS*
010	SS
011	DS
100	FS
101	GS

Note: MOV CS,?? and POP CS are not allowed by the microprocessor. The FS and GS segments are only available to the 80386/80486 microprocessor.

FIGURE 3–10 A MOV BX,CS instruction converted into binary machine language. Here the REG is encoded as the CS register and R/M is encoded as the BX register.

Opcode	MOD	REG	R/M
1 0 0 0 1 1 0 0	1 1	0 0 1	0 1 1

Note: W and D are not present in this instruction.

Figure 3–10 shows a MOV BX,CS instruction converted to binary. The opcode for this type of MOV instruction is different for the prior MOV instructions. Segment registers can be moved between any 16-bit register or 16-bit memory location. For example, the MOV [DI],DS instruction stores the contents of DS into the memory location addressed by DI in the data segment.

Although this has not provided complete coverage of machine language coding, it should give you a good start in machine language programming. Remember that a program written in symbolic assembly language (assembly language) is rarely assembled by hand into binary machine language. An *assembler* converts symbolic assembly language into machine language. With the microprocessor and its over 20,000 instruction variations, let us hope that an assembler is available for the conversion, because the process is very time-consuming, although not impossible.

3–2   **PUSH/POP**

The PUSH and POP instructions are important instructions that store and retrieve data from the LIFO (last-in, first-out) stack memory. The 8086–80486 microprocessor has six forms of the PUSH and POP instructions: register, memory, immediate, segment register, flags, and all registers. The PUSH and POP immediate and the PUSHA and POPA (all registers) forms are not available in the earlier 8086/8088 microprocessor, but are available to the 80286, 80386, and 80486.

Register addressing allows the contents of any 16-bit register to be transferred to or from the stack. In the 80386/80486, the 32-bit extended registers and flags (EFLAGS) can also be pushed or popped from the stack. Memory addressing stores the contents of a 16-bit memory location (32 bits in the 80386/80486) on the stack or stack data into a memory location. Immediate addressing allows immediate data to be pushed onto the stack, but not popped off the stack. Segment register addressing allows the contents of any segment register to be pushed onto the stack or removed from the stack (CS may be pushed, but data from the stack may never be popped into CS). The flags may be pushed or popped from that stack and the contents of all the registers may be pushed or popped.

Push

The 8086–80286 PUSH instruction always transfers *2 bytes* of data to the stack and the 80386/80486 transfers 2 or 4 bytes depending on the register or size of the memory location. The source of the data may be any internal 16-bit/32-bit register, immediate data, any segment register, or any 2 bytes of memory data. There is also a PUSHA instruction that copies the contents of the internal register set, except the segment registers, to the stack. The PUSHA (*push all*) instruction copies the registers to the stack in the following order: AX, CX, DX, BX, SP, BP, SI, and DI. The value of SP pushed to the stack is whatever it was before the PUSHA instruction executes. The PUSHF (*push flags*) instruction copies the contents of the flag register to the stack. The PUSHAD and POPAD instructions push and pop the contents of the 32-bit register set found in the 80386 and 80486 microprocessors.

Whenever data are pushed onto the stack, the first (most significant) data byte moves into the stack segment memory location addressed by SP − 1. The second (least significant) data byte moves into the stack segment memory location addressed by SP − 2. After the data are stored by a PUSH, the contents of the SP register decrement by 2. The same is true for a double-word push except 4 bytes are moved to the stack memory (most significant byte first), then the stack pointer decrements by 4. Figure 3–11 shows the operation of the PUSH AX instruction. This instruction copies the contents of AX onto the stack where address SS:[SP − 1] = AH, SS:[SP − 2] = AL, and afterwards SP = SP − 2.

The PUSHA instruction pushes all the internal 16-bit registers onto the stack as illustrated in Figure 3–12. This instruction requires 16 bytes of stack memory space to store all eight 16-bit registers. After all registers are pushed, the contents of the SP register are decremented by 16. The PUSHA instruction is very useful when the entire register set (*microprocessor environment*) of the 80286–80486 must be saved during a task.

The PUSH immediate data instruction has two different opcodes, but in both cases a 16-bit immediate number moves onto the stack or if PUSHD is used, a 32-bit

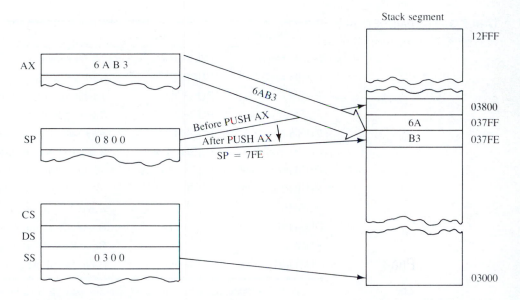

FIGURE 3–11 The effect of a PUSH AX instruction on the SP register and stack memory locations 037FFH and 037FEH.

FIGURE 3–12

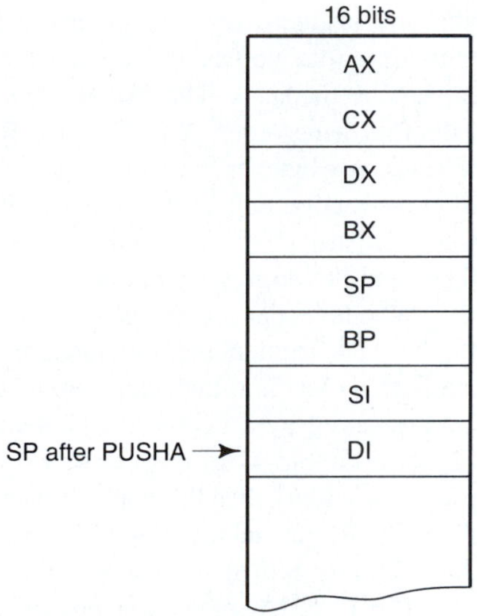

16 bits

| AX |
| CX |
| DX |
| BX |
| SP |
| BP |
| SI |
| DI |

SP after PUSHA ⟶ (points to DI)

immediate datum are pushed. If the value of the immediate data are 00H–FFH, the opcode is a 6AH and if the data are 0100H–FFFFH, the opcode is 68H. The PUSH 8 instruction assembles as a 6A08H and the PUSH 1000H instruction assembles as 680010H.

Table 3–7 lists the forms of the PUSH instruction that include PUSHA and PUSHF. Notice how the instruction set is used to specify different data sizes with the assembler.

TABLE 3–7 The PUSH instructions

Symbolic	Example	Note
PUSH reg16	PUSH BX	16-bit register
PUSH reg32	PUSH EAX	32-bit register
PUSH mem16	PUSH [BX]	16-bit addressing mode
PUSH mem32	PUSH [EAX]	32-bit addressing mode
PUSH seg	PUSH DS	Any segment register
PUSH imm8	PUSH 12H	8-bit immediate data
PUSHW imm16	PUSHW 1000H	16-bit immediate data
PUSHD imm32	PUSHD 20	32-bit immediate data
PUSHA	PUSHA	Save 16-bit registers
PUSHAD	PUSHAD	Save 32-bit registers
PUSHF	PUSHF	Save 16-bit flag register
PUSHFD	PUSHFD	Save 32-bit flag register

Note: The 80386/80486 is required to operate with 32-bit addresses, registers, and immediate data.

POP

The POP instruction performs the inverse operation of a PUSH instruction. The POP instruction removes data from the stack and places them into the target 16-bit register, segment register, or a 16-bit memory location. In the 80386/80486 a POP can also remove 32-bit data from the stack and use a 32-bit address. The POP instruction is not available as an immediate POP. The POPF (*pop flags*) instruction removes a 16-bit number from the stack and places it into the flag register, and the POPFD removes a 32-bit number from the stack and places it into the extended flag register. The POPA (*pop all*) instruction removes 16 bytes of data from the stack and places them into the following registers in the order shown: DI, SI, BP, SP, BX, DX, CX, and AX. This is the reverse order from the way they are placed on the stack by the PUSHA instruction. In the 80386/80486 a POPAD instruction reloads the 32-bit registers from the stack.

Suppose that a POP BX instruction executes. The first byte of data removed from the stack (the memory location addressed by SP in the stack segment) moves into register BL. The second byte is removed from stack segment memory location SP + 1, and placed into register BH. After both bytes are removed from the stack, the SP register increments by 2. Figure 3–13 shows how the POP BX instruction removes data from the stack and places them into register BX.

The opcodes used for the POP instruction, and all its variations, appear in Table 3–8. Note that a POP CS instruction is not a valid instruction in the 80286 instruction set. If we allow a POP CS instruction to execute, only a portion of the address (CS) of the next instruction changes. This makes the POP CS instruction unpredictable and therefore not allowed.

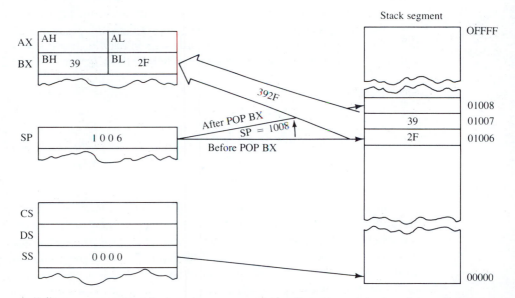

FIGURE 3–13 POP BX removes 2 bytes of data from the stack segment and places them into the BX register.

TABLE 3–8   The POP instructions

Symbolic	Example	Note
POP reg16	POP DI	16-bit register
POP reg32	POP EBX	32-bit register
POP mem16	POP WORD PTR[DI+2]	16-bit memory address
POP mem32	POP DATA3	32-bit memory address
POP seg	POP GS	Any segment register
POPA	POPA	16-bit registers
POPAD	POPAD	32-bit registers
POPF	POPF	16-bit flag register
POPFD	POPFD	32-bit extended flag register

Note: The 80386/80486 is required to operate with 32-bit addresses and registers.

Initializing the Stack

When the stack area is initialized, we load both the stack segment register (SS) and the stack pointer (SP) register. It is normal to designate an area of memory as the stack segment by loading SS with the bottom location of the stack segment.

For example, if the stack segment resides in memory locations 10000H–1FFFFH, we load SS with a 1000H. (Recall that we append the rightmost end of the stack segment register with a 0H for real mode addressing.) To start the stack at the top of this 64K byte stack segment, the stack pointer (SP) is loaded with a 0000H. Figure 3–14 shows how this value causes data to be pushed onto the top of the stack segment with a PUSH CX instruction. Remember that all segments are *cyclic* in nature—that is, the top location of a segment is *contiguous* with the bottom location of the segment.

EXAMPLE 3–1

```
0000                    STACK_SEG    SEGMENT STACK

0000   0100[                 DW   100H DUP (?)
              ????
                   ]
0200                    STACK_SEG    ENDS
```

In assembly language, a stack segment is set up as illustrated in Example 3–1. The first statement identifies the start of the stack segment and the last statement identifies the end of the stack segment. The assembler and linker program places the correct stack segment address in SS and the length of the segment (top of the stack) into SP. There is no need to load these registers in your program unless you wish to change the initial values for some reason.

An alternative method for defining the stack segment is used with one of the memory models for the MASM assembler only (refer to Appendix A). Other assemblers do not use models, or if they do, they are not exactly the same as with MASM. Here (see

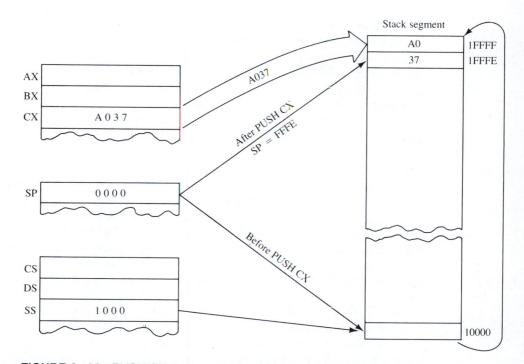

FIGURE 3–14 PUSH CX illustrating the cyclic nature of the stack segment. Notice that SP starts at 0000H and, after being decremented, ends up at FFFEH.

Example 3–2) the .STACK statement, followed by the number of *bytes* allocated to the stack, defines the stack area. This is identical to Example 3–1. The .STACK statement also initializes both SS and SP.

If the stack is not specified using either method, a warning will appear when the program is linked. The warning may be ignored if the stack size is 128 bytes or less. The system automatically assigns (through DOS) a 128-byte section of memory to the stack. This memory section is located in the program segment prefix, which is appended to the beginning of each program file. If you use more memory for the stack, you will erase information in the PSP that is critical to the operation of your program and the computer.

EXAMPLE 3–2

```
.MODEL SMALL
.STACK 200H        ;set stack size
```

3–3

LOAD-EFFECTIVE ADDRESS

There are several load-effective address (LEA) instructions in the 8086–80486 microprocessor instruction set. The LEA instruction loads any 16-bit register with the address as determined by the addressing mode selected for the instruction. The LDS and LES variations load any 16-bit register with the offset address retrieved from a memory location and then load either DS or ES with a segment address retrieved from memory. In the 80386 and 80486 microprocessor LFS, LGS, and LSS are added to the instruction set and a 32-bit register can be selected to receive a 32-bit offset from memory. Table 3–9 lists the load-effective address instructions.

LEA

The LEA instruction loads a 16-bit register with the offset address of the data specified by the operand. As the first example in Table 3–9 shows, the operand address NUMB is loaded into register AX, not the contents of address NUMB.

By comparing LEA with MOV, we observe the following effect: LEA BX,[DI] loads the offset address specified by [DI] (contents of DI) into the BX register; MOV BX,[DI] loads the data stored at the memory location addressed by [DI] into register BX.

Earlier in the text, we presented several examples using the OFFSET pseudo-operation. The *OFFSET directive* performs the same function as an LEA instruction if the operand is a displacement. For example, the MOV BX,OFFSET LIST performs the same function as LEA BX,LIST. Both instructions load the offset address of memory location LIST into the BX register.

But why is the LEA instruction available if the OFFSET directive accomplishes the same task? First, OFFSET only functions with simple operands such as LIST. It may not be used for an operand such as [DI], LIST [SI], etc. The OFFSET directive is more efficient than the LEA instruction for simple operands. It takes the microprocessor longer to execute LEA BX,LIST than MOV BX,OFFSET LIST. The 80286, for example, requires 3 clocks to execute the LEA BX,LIST instruction and only 2 clocks to execute MOV BX,OFFSET LIST. The reason that the MOV BX,OFFSET LIST instruction executes faster is because the assembler calculates the offset address of LIST, while with the LEA instruction, the microprocessor does the calculation as it executes the instruction. The MOV BX,OFFSET LIST instruction is actually assembled as a move immediate instruction and is more efficient.

TABLE 3–9   The load-effective address instructions

Symbolic	Function
LEA AX,NUMB	AX is loaded with the address of NUMB
LEA EAX,NUMB	EAX is loaded with the address of NUMB
LDS DI,LIST	DI and DS are loaded with the address stored at LIST
LDS EDI,LIST	EDI and DS are loaded with the address stored at LIST
LES BX,CAT	BX and ES are loaded with the address stored at CAT
LFS DI,DATA1	DI and FS are loaded with the address stored at DATA1
LGS SI,DATA5	SI and GS are loaded with the address stored at DATA5
LSS SP,MEM	SP and SS are loaded with the address stored at MEM

Suppose that the microprocessor executes an LEA BX,[DI] instruction and DI contains a 1000H. Because DI contains the offset address, the microprocessor transfers a copy of DI into BX. A MOV BX,DI instruction performs this task in less time and is often preferred to the LEA BX,[DI] instruction.

Another example is LEA SI,[BX + DI]. This instruction adds BX to DI and stores the sum in the SI register. The sum generated is a modulo-64K sum. If BX = 1000H and DI = 2000H, the offset address moved into SI is 3000H. If BX = 1000H and DI = FF00H, the offset address is 0F00H. Notice that the second result is a modulo-64K sum. (A *modulo-64K sum* drops any carry out of the 16-bit result.)

LDS, LES, LFS, LGS, and LSS

The LDS, LES, LFS, LGS, and LSS instructions load any 16-bit or 32-bit register with an offset address and the DS, ES, FS, GS, or SS segment register with a segment address. These instructions use any of the memory-addressing modes to access a 32-bit or 48-bit section of memory that contains both the segment and offset address. These instructions may not use the register-addressing mode (MOD = 11). Note that the LFS, LGS, and LSS instructions are only available on 80386 and 80486 microprocessors, as are the 32-bit registers.

Figure 3–15 illustrates an example LDS BX,[DI] instruction. This instruction transfers the 32-bit number, addressed by DI in the data segment, into the BX and DS

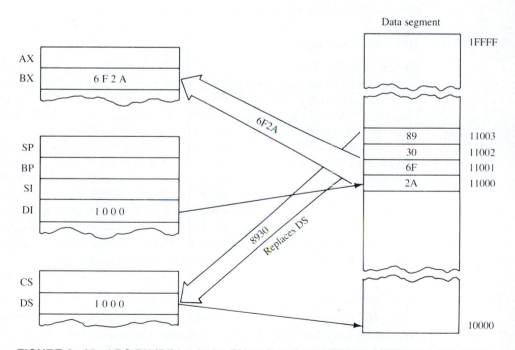

FIGURE 3–15 LDS BX,[DI] loads the BX register from locations 11000H and 11001H and the DS register from locations 11002H and 11003H. This instruction will change the data segment from 10000H–1FFFFH to 89300H–992FFH.

registers. The LDS, LES, LFS, LGS, and LSS instructions obtain a new far address from memory. The offset address appears first, followed by the segment address. This format is used for storing all 32-bit memory addresses.

A far address can be stored in memory by the assembler. For example, the ADDR DD FAR PTR FROG instruction stores the offset and segment address (*far address*) of FROG in 32 bits of memory at location ADDR. The DD directive tells the assembler to store a *double word* (32-bit number) in memory address ADDR.

In the 80386/80486, an LDS EBX,[DI] instruction loads EBX from the 4-byte section of memory addressed by DI in the data segment. Following this 4-byte offset is a word that is loaded to the DS register. Notice that instead of addressing a 32-bit section of memory, the 80386/80486 addresses a 48-bit section of the memory whenever a 32-bit offset address is loaded to a 32-bit register.

3-4 STRING DATA TRANSFERS

There are five string data transfer instructions—LODS, STOS, MOVS, INS, and OUTS. Each string instruction allows data transfers that are either a single byte, word, or double word, or if repeated, a block of bytes, words, or double words. Before the string instructions are presented, the operation of the D flag-bit (*direction*), DI, and SI must be understood as they apply to the string instructions.

The Direction Flag

The direction flag (D) selects auto-increment (D = 0) or auto-decrement (D = 1) operation for the DI and SI registers during string operations. The direction flag is only used with the string instructions. The CLD instruction *clears* the D flag (D = 0) and the STD instruction *sets* it (D = 1). Therefore, the CLD instruction selects the auto-increment mode (D = 0) and STD selects the auto-decrement mode (D = 1).

Whenever a string instruction transfers a byte, the contents of DI and/or SI increment or decrement by 1. If a word is transferred, the contents of DI and/or SI increment or decrement by 2. Double-word transfers cause DI and/or SI to increment or decrement by 4. Only the actual registers used by the string instruction increment or decrement. For example, the STOSB instruction uses the DI register to address a memory location. When STOSB executes, only DI increments or decrements without affecting SI. The same is true of the LODSB instruction, which uses the SI register to address memory data. LODSB only increments/decrements SI without affecting DI.

DI and SI

During the execution of a string instruction, memory accesses occur through either or both the DI and SI registers. The DI offset address accesses data in the extra segment for all string instructions that use it. The SI offset address accesses data, by default, in the data segment. The segment assignment of SI may be changed with a segment override prefix as described later in this chapter. The DI segment assignment is *always* in the extra segment when a string instruction executes. This assignment cannot be changed. The reason that one pointer addresses data in the extra segment and the other in the data segment is so the MOVS instruction can move 64K bytes of data from one segment of memory to another.

LODS

The LODS instruction loads AL, AX, or EAX with data stored at the data segment offset address indexed by the SI register. (Note that only the 80386 and 80486 can use EAX.) After loading AL with a byte, AX with a word, or EAX with a double word, the contents of SI increment, if D = 0, or decrement, if D = 1. A 1 is added to or subtracted from SI for a byte-sized LODS, a 2 is added or subtracted for a word-sized LODS, and a 4 is added or subtracted for a double-word-sized LODS.

Table 3-10 lists the permissible forms of the LODS instruction. The LODSB (*loads a byte*) instruction causes a byte to be loaded into AL, the LODSW (*loads a word*) instruction causes a word to be loaded into AX, and the LODSD (*loads a double-word*) instruction causes a double word to be loaded into EAX. Although rare, as an alternative to LODSB, LODSW, and LODSD the LODS instruction may be followed by a byte-, word- or double-word-sized operand to select a byte, word, or double word transfer. Operands are often defined as bytes with DB, as words with DW, and as double words with DD. The DB pseudo-operation *defines byte(s)*, the DW pseudo-operation *defines word(s)*, and the DD pseudo-operation *defines double word(s)*.

Figure 3-16 shows the effect of executing the LODSW instruction if the D flag = 0, SI = 1000H, and DS = 1000H. Here a 16-bit number, stored at memory locations 11000H and 11001H, moves into AX. Because D = 0, and this is a word transfer, the contents of SI increment by 2 *after* AX loads with memory data.

STOS

The STOS instruction stores AL, AX, or EAX at the extra segment memory location addressed by the DI register. (Note only the 80386/80486 uses EAX and double words.) Table 3-11 lists all forms of the STOS instruction. As with LODS, a STOS instruction may be appended with a B, W, or D for a byte, word, or double-word transfers. The STOSB (*stores a byte*) instruction stores the byte in AL at the extra segment memory

TABLE 3-10 Forms of the LODS instruction

Symbolic	Function
LODSB	AL = [SI]; SI = SI ± 1
LODSW	AX = [SI]; SI = SI ± 2
LODSD	EAX = [SI]; SI = SI ± 4
LODS LIST	AL = [SI]; SI = SI ± 1 (if LIST is a byte)
LODS DATA1	AX = [SI]; SI = SI ± 2 (if DATA1 is a word)
LODS DATA4	EAX = [SI]; SI = SI ± 4 (if DATA4 is a double word)

Note: SI addresses data in the data segment by default for LODS and only the 80386/80486 uses double words.

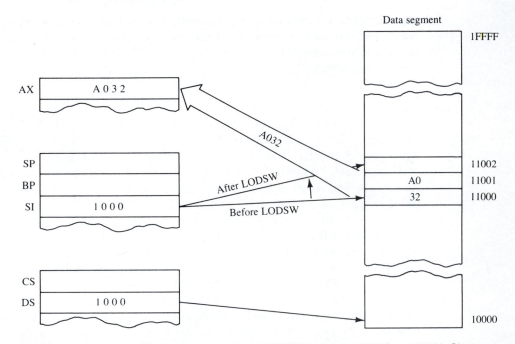

FIGURE 3–16   The effect of executing the LODSW instruction if DS = 1000H, SI = 1000H, D = 0, 11000H = 32, and 11001H = A0.

TABLE 3–11   Forms of the STOS instruction

Symbolic	Function
STOSB	[DI] = AL; DI = DI ± 1
STOSW	[DI] = AX; DI = DI ± 2
STOSD	[DI] = EAX; DI = DI ± 4
STOS LIST	[DI] = AL; DI = DI ± 1 (if LIST is a byte)
STOS DATA1	[DI] = AX; DI = DI ± 2 (if DATA1 is a word)
STOS DATA4	[DI] = EAX; DI = DI ± 4 (if DATA4 is a double word)

Note: DI addresses data in the extra segment and double words are used by the 80386 or 80486 microprocessor.

location addressed by DI. The STOSW (*stores a word*) instruction stores AX in the extra segment memory location addressed by DI. A double word is stored in the extra segment location addressed by DI with the STOSD (*stores a double-word*) instruction. After the byte (AL), word (AX), or double word (EAX) is stored, the contents of DI increments or decrements.

STOS with a REP.   The *repeat prefix* (REP) may be added to any string data transfer instruction except the LODS instruction. The REP prefix causes CX to decrement by 1 each time the string instruction executes. After CX decrements, the string instruction repeats. If CX reaches a value of 0, the instruction terminates and the program continues with the next sequential instruction. Thus, if CX is loaded with a 100, and a REP STOSB instruction executes, the microprocessor automatically repeats the STOSB instruction 100 times. Since the DI register is automatically incremented or decremented after each datum is stored, this instruction stores the contents of AL in a block of memory instead of a single byte of memory.

Suppose that 10 bytes of data, in an area of memory (BUFFER), must be cleared to 00H. This task is accomplished with a series of STOSB instructions (10 of them) or with one STOSB prefixed by a REP, if CX is a 10. The program listed in Example 3–3 clears memory area BUFFER.

EXAMPLE 3–3

```
        ;clearing a block of memory using STOS

0000 C4 3E 05BC R    LES   DI,BUFFER      ;get buffer address
0004 B9 000A         MOV   CX,10          ;load counter
0007 FC              CLD                  ;select auto-increment
0008 B0 00           MOV   AL,0           ;clear AL
000A F3/ AA          REP   STOSB          ;clear buffer
```

This short sequence of instructions addresses location BUFFER using the MOV DI,OFFSET BUFFER instruction. Though BUFFER is in the extra segment, the assembler still uses an offset address to address the memory. Notice how the REP prefix precedes the STOSB instruction in both assembly language and hexadecimal machine language. In machine language, the F3H is the REP prefix and AAH is the STOSB opcode.

A faster method of clearing this 10-byte buffer is to use the STOSW instruction with a count of 5. Example 3–4 illustrates the same task as Example 3–3 except the count changes to a 5 and the STOSW instruction repeats instead of the STOSB instruction. Also, register AX is cleared instead of register AL.

EXAMPLE 3–4

```
        ;using STOSW to clear a buffer

0000 C4 3E 05BC R    LES   DI,BUFFER      ;get buffer address
0004 B9 0005         MOV   CX,5           ;load counter
0007 FC              CLD                  ;select auto-increment
0008 B8 0000         MOV   AX,0           ;clear AX
000B F3/ AB          REP   STOSW          ;clear buffer
```

MOVS

The most useful string data transfer instruction is the MOVS instruction because it transfers data from one memory location to another. This is the only *memory-to-memory* transfer allowed in the 8086–80486 microprocessor. The MOVS instruction transfers a byte, word, or double word from the data segment location addressed by SI to the extra segment location addressed by DI. As with the other string instructions, the pointers then increment or decrement as dictated by the direction flag. Table 3–12 lists all the permissible forms of the MOVS instruction. Note that only the source operand (SI),

TABLE 3–12   Forms of the MOVS instruction

Symbolic	Function
MOVSB	[DI] = [SI]; DI = DI ± 1; SI = SI ± 1 (byte transferred)
MOVSW	[DI] = [SI]; DI = DI ± 2; SI = SI ± 2 (word transferred)
MOVSD	[DI] = [SI]; DI = DI ± 4; SI = SI ± 4 (double word transferred)
MOVS BYTE1,BYTE2	[DI] = [SI]; DI = DI ± 1; SI = SI ± 1 (if BYTE1 and BYTE2 are bytes)
MOVS WORD1,WORD2	[DI] = [SI]; DI = DI ± 2; SI = SI ± 2 (if WORD1 and WORD2 are words)
MOVS DWORD1,DWORD2	[DI] = [SI]; DI = DI ± 4; SI = SI ± 4 (if DWORD1 and DWORD2 are double words)

located in the data segment, may be overridden so another segment may be used. The destination operand (DI) must always be located in the extra segment.

Suppose that the contents of a 100-byte array must be transferred to another 100-byte array. The repeated MOVSB (*moves a byte*) instruction is ideal for this task, as illustrated in Example 3–5.

EXAMPLE 3–5

```
      ;using the MOVS instruction

0000 C4 3E 05C0 R    LES   DI,LIST1   ;addressLIST1
0004 C5 36 05C4 R    LDS   SI,LIST2   ;address LIST2
0008 FC              CLD              ;clear direction
0009 B9 0064         MOV   CX,100     ;load counter
000C F3/ A4          REP   MOVSB      ;transfer 100 bytes
```

INS

The INS (*input string*) instruction (not available on the 8086/8088 microprocessor) transfers a byte, word, or double word of data from an I/O device into the extra segment memory location addressed by the DI register. The *I/O address* is contained in the DX register. This instruction is useful for inputting a block of data from an external I/O device directly into the memory. One application transfers data from a disk drive to memory. Disk drives are often considered and interfaced as I/O devices in a computer system.

As with the prior string instructions, there are two basic forms of the INS. The INSB instruction inputs data from an 8-bit I/O device and stores it in the byte-sized memory location indexed by SI. The INSW instruction inputs 16-bit I/O data and stores them in a word-sized memory location. The INSD instruction inputs a double word. These instructions can be repeated using the REP prefix. This allows an entire block of input data to be stored in the memory from an I/O device. Table 3–13 lists the various forms of the INS instruction.

TABLE 3–13 Forms of the INS instruction

Symbolic	Function
INSB	[DI] = [DX]; DI = DI ± 1 (byte transferred)
INSW	[DI] = [DX]; DI = DI ± 2 (word transferred)
INSD	[DI] = [DX]; DI = DI ± 4 (double word transferred)
INS LIST	[DI] = [DX]; DI = DI ± 1 (if LIST is a byte)
INS DATA1	[DI] = [DX]; DI = DI ± 2 (if DATA1 is a word)
INS DATA4	[DI] = [DX]; DI = DI ± 4 (if DATA4 is a double word)

Note: [DX] indicates that DX contains the I/O device address. These instructions are not available on the 8086/8088 microprocessor and only the 80386/80486 use double words.

Example 3–6 shows a short program that inputs 50 bytes from an I/O device whose address is 03ACH and stores the data in memory array LISTS. This software assumes that data are available from the I/O device at all times. Otherwise, the software must check to see if the I/O device is ready to transfer data precluding the use of a REP prefix.

EXAMPLE 3–6

```
                        ;using REP INSB to input data to a memory array
                        ;
0000 BF 0000 R                  MOV   DI,OFFSET LISTS        ;address array
0003 BA 03AC                    MOV   DX,3ACH               ;address I/O
0006 FC                         CLD                          ;auto-increment
0007 B9 0032                    MOV   CX,50                  ;load count
000A F3/6C                      REP   INSB                   ;input data
```

OUTS

The OUTS (*output string*) instruction (not available on the 8086/8088 microprocessor) transfers a byte, word, or double word of data from the data segment memory location address by SI to an I/O device. The I/O device is addressed by the DX register as it was with the INS instruction. Table 3–14 shows the variations available for the OUTS instruction.

Example 3–7 shows a short program that transfers data from a memory array to an I/O device. This software assumes that the I/O device is always ready for data.

EXAMPLE 3–7

```
                        ;using REP OUTS to output data from a memory array
                        ;
0000 BE 0064 R                  MOV   SI,OFFSET ARRAY        ;address array
0003 BA 03AC                    MOV   DX,3ACH               ;address I/O
0006 FC                         CLD                          ;auto-increment
0007 B9 0064                    MOV   CX,100                 ;load count
000A F3/6E                      REP   OUTSB
```

TABLE 3–14 Forms of the OUTS instruction

Symbolic	Function
OUTSB	[DX] = [SI]; SI = SI ± 1 (byte transferred)
OUTSW	[DX] = [SI]; SI = SI ± 2 (word transferred)
OUTSD	[DX] = [SI]; SI = SI ± 4 (double word transferred)
OUTS LIST	[DX] = [SI]; SI = SI ± 1 (if LIST is a byte)
OUTS DATA1	[DX] = [SI]; SI = SI ± 2 (if DATA1 is a word)
OUTS DATA4	[DX] = [SI]; SI = SI ± 4 (if DATA4 is a double word)

Note: [DX] indicates that DX contains the I/O device address. These instructions are not available on the 8086/8088 microprocessor and only the 80386/80486 use double words.

3–5   MISCELLANEOUS DATA TRANSFER INSTRUCTIONS

Don't be fooled by the term "miscellaneous"; these instructions are used in programs. The data transfer instructions detailed in this section are: XCHG, LAHF, SAHF, XLAT, IN, OUT, BSWAP, MOVSX, and MOVZX. Because the miscellaneous instructions are not used as often as a MOV instruction, they have been grouped together and represented in this section.

XCHG

The exchange instruction (XCHG) exchanges the contents of a register with the contents of any other register or memory location. The XCHG instruction cannot exchange segment registers or memory-to-memory data. Exchanges are byte-, word-, or double-word-sized (80386/80486 only) and use any addressing mode discussed in Chapter 2 except immediate addressing. Table 3–15 shows the forms available for the XCHG instruction.

The XCHG instruction, using the 16-bit AX register with another 16-bit register, is the most efficient exchange. This instruction occupies one byte of memory. Other XCHG instructions require two or more bytes of memory depending on the addressing mode selected.

TABLE 3–15 Forms of the XCHG instruction

Symbolic	Note
XCHG reg,reg	Exchanges byte, word, or double-word registers
XCHG reg,mem	Exchanges byte, word, or double-word memory data with register data

Note: Only the 80386/80486 use double-word data.

When using a memory-addressing mode and the assembler, it doesn't matter which operand addresses memory. The XCHG AL,[DI] instruction is identical to the XCHG [DI],AL instruction as far as the assembler is concerned.

If the 80386/80486 microprocessor is available, the XCHG instruction can exchange double-word data. For example, the XCHG EAX,EBX instruction exchanges the contents of the EAX register with the EBX register.

LAHF and SAHF

The LAHF and SAHF instructions are seldom used because they were designed as *bridge* instructions. These instructions allowed 8085 (an early 8-bit microprocessor) software to be translated into 8086 software by a translation program. Because any software that required translation was probably completed many years ago, these instructions have little application today. The LAHF instruction transfers the rightmost 8 bits of the flag register into the AH register. The SAHF instruction transfers the AH register into the rightmost 8 bits of the flag register.

XLAT

The XLAT (*translate*) instruction converts the contents of the AL register into a number stored in a memory table. This instruction performs the direct table lookup technique often used to convert one code to another. An XLAT instruction first adds the contents of AL to BX to form a memory address within the data segment. It then copies the contents of this address into AL. This is the only instruction that adds an 8-bit number to a 16-bit number.

Suppose that a 7-segment LED display lookup table is stored in memory at address TABLE. The XLAT instruction then translates the BCD number in AL to a 7-segment code in AL. Example 3–8 provides a short program that converts from a BCD code to 7-segment code. Figure 3–17 shows the operation of this example program if TABLE = 1000H, DS = 1000H, and the initial value of AL = 05H (a 5 BCD). After the translation, AL = 6DH.

EXAMPLE 3–8

```
        ;using XLAT to convert from BCD to 7-segment code

0012 BB 000 R  MOV  BX,OFFSET TABLE   ;address lookup table
0015 D7        XLAT
```

IN and OUT

Table 3–16 lists the forms of the IN and OUT instructions, which perform I/O operations. Notice that the contents of AL, AX, or EAX *only* are transferred between the I/O device and the microprocessor. An IN instruction transfers data from an external I/O device to AL, AX, or EAX, and an OUT transfers data from AL, AX, or EAX to an external I/O device. (Note only the 80386/80486 contain EAX.)

Two forms of I/O device (*port*) address exist for IN and OUT: fixed-port and variable-port. Fixed-port addressing allows data transfer between AL, AX, or EAX using an 8-bit I/O port address. It is called *fixed-port addressing* because the port number

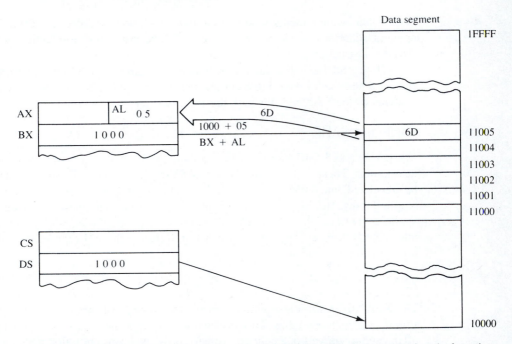

FIGURE 3–17 The effect of executing the XLAT instruction at the point just before the 6DH from memory location 11005H is gated into the AL register.

TABLE 3–16 IN and OUT instructions

Symbolic	Function
IN AL,p8	8-bit data are input to AL from port p8
IN AX,p8	16-bit data are input to AX from port p8
IN EAX,p8	32-bit data are input to EAX from port p8
IN AL,DX	8-bit data are input to AL from port DX
IN AX,DX	16-bit data are input to AX from port DX
IN EAX,DX	32-bit data are input to EAX from port DX
OUT p8,AL	8-bit data are sent to port p8 from AL
OUT p8,AX	16-bit data are sent to port p8 from AX
OUT p8,EAX	32-bit data are sent to port p8 from EAX
OUT DX,AL	8-bit data are sent to port DX from AL
OUT DX,AX	16-bit data are sent to port DX from AX
OUT DX,EAX	32-bit data are sent to port DX from EAX

Notes: p8 = an 8-bit I/O port number and DX = the 16-bit port address held in DX.

follows the instruction's opcode. Often instructions are stored in a ROM. A fixed-port instruction stored in a ROM has its port number permanently fixed because of the nature of read-only memory.

The port address appears on the address bus during an I/O operation. For the 8-bit fixed-port I/O instructions, the 8-bit port address is zero extended into a 16-bit address. For example, if the IN AL,6AH instruction executes, data from I/O address 6AH is input to AL. The address appears as a 16-bit 006AH on pins A0–A15 of the address bus. Address bus bits A16–A19 (8086/8088), A16–A23 (80286/80386SX), A16–A24 (80386SL/80386SLC), or A16–A32 (80386/80486) are undefined for an IN or OUT instruction.

Variable-port addressing allows data transfers between AL, AX, or EAX and a 16-bit port address. It is called *variable-port addressing* because the I/O port number is stored in register DX, which can be changed (*varied*) during the execution of a program. The 16-bit I/O port address appears on the address bus pin connections A0–A15. The IBM PC uses a 16-bit port address to access its I/O space. The I/O space for a PC is located at I/O port 0000H–03FFH. Some plug-in adapter cards may use I/O addresses above 03FFH.

Figure 3–18 illustrates the execution of the OUT 19H,AX instruction, which transfers the contents of AX to I/O port 19H. Notice that the I/O port number appears as a 0019H on the 16-bit address bus and that the data from AX appears on the 16-bit data bus of the 8086, 80286, 80386SX, or 80386SL/80386SLC microprocessor. The system control signal, IOWC (I/O write control), is a logic zero to enable the I/O device.

MOVSX and MOVZX

The MOVSX (move and sign-extend) and MOVZX (move and zero-extend) instructions are found in the 80386 and 80486 instruction sets. These instructions move data and at the same time either sign- or zero-extend it. Table 3–17 illustrates these instructions with several examples of each.

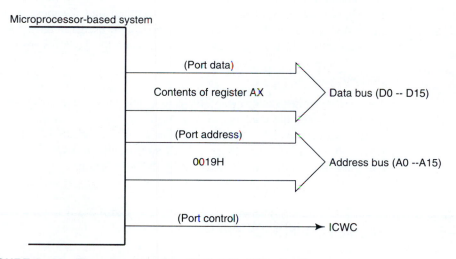

FIGURE 3–18 The execution of an OUT 19H, AX instruction.

TABLE 3–17   The MOVSX and MOVZX instructions

Symbolic	Example	Note
MOVSX reg,reg	MOVSX CX,BL	Converts the 8-bit contents of BL into a 16-bit number in CX by sign-extension
	MOVSX ECX,AX	Converts the 16-bit contents of AX into a 32-bit number in ECX by sign-extension
MOVSX reg,mem	MOVSX BX,DATA	Converts the 8-bit contents of DATA into a 16-bit number in BX by sign-extension
	MOVSX EAX,[EDI]	Converts the 16-bit contents of the data segment memory location addressed by EDI into a 32-bit number in EAX by sign-extension
MOVZX reg,reg	MOVZX DX,AL	Converts the 8-bit contents of AL into a 16-bit number in DX by zero-extension
	MOVZX EBP,DI	Converts the 16-bit contents of DI into a 32-bit number in EBP by zero-extension
MOVZX reg,mem	MOVZX DX,DATA1	Converts the 8-bit contents of DATA1 into a 16-bit number in DX by zero-extension
MOVZX reg,mem	MOVZX EAX,DATA2	Converts the 16-bit contents of DATA2 into a 32-bit number in EAX by zero-extension

When a number is zero-extended, the most significant part fills with zeros. For example, if an 8-bit 34H is zero-extended into a 16-bit number, it becomes 0034H. Zero-extension is often used to convert unsigned 8- or 16-bit numbers into unsigned 16- or 32-bit numbers using the MOVZX instruction.

A number is sign-extended when its sign-bit is copied into the most significant part. For example, if an 8-bit 84H is sign-extended into a 16-bit number, it becomes FF84H. The sign-bit of an 84H is a one, which is copied into the most significant part of the sign-extended result. Sign-extension is most often used to convert 8- or 16-bit signed numbers into 16- or 32-bit signed numbers using the MOVSX instruction.

BSWAP

The byte swap instruction (BSWAP) is available only in the 80486 microprocessor. This instruction takes the contents of any 32-bit register and swaps the first byte with the fourth and the second with the third. For example, the BSWAP EAX instruction with EAX = 00112233H swaps bytes in EAX so it results in EAX = 33221100H. Notice that the order of all four bytes is reversed by this instruction.

3–6   SEGMENT OVERRIDE PREFIX

The segment override prefix, which may be added to almost any 8086–80486 instruction in any memory-addressing mode, allows the programmer to deviate from the

TABLE 3–18 Instructions that include segment override prefixes

Symbolic	Segment Accessed	Normal Segment
MOV AX,DS:[BP]	Data segment	Stack segment
MOV AX,ES:[BP]	Extra segment	Stack segment
MOV AX,SS:[DI]	Stack segment	Data segment
MOV AX,CS:[SI]	Code segment	Data segment
MOV AX,ES:LIST	Extra segment	Data segment
LODS ES:DATA	Data segment	Extra segment
MOV EAX,FS:DATA2	FS segment	Data segment
MOV BL,GS:[ECX]	GS segment	Data segment

Note: Only the 80386 and 80486 allow the use of the FS and GS segments.

default segment. The segment override prefix is an additional byte that appends the front of an instruction to select an alternate segment register. About the only instructions that cannot be prefixed are the jump and call instructions that must use the code segment register for address generation. The segment override is also used to select the FS and GS segments in the 80386–80486 microprocessor.

An example, the MOV AX,[DI] instruction, accesses data within the data segment by default. If required by a program, this can be changed by prefixing the instruction. Suppose that the data are in the extra segment instead of the data segment. This instruction addresses the extra segment if changed to MOV AX,ES:[DI].

Table 3–18 shows some altered instructions that address different memory segments than normal. Each time we prefix an instruction with a segment override prefix, the instruction becomes one byte longer. Although this is no serious change to the length of the instruction, it does add to its execution time. Usually, we limit the use of the segment override prefix and remain in the default segments to write shorter and more efficient software.

3–7   ASSEMBLER DETAILS

The assembler[1] for the 8086–80486 microprocessor can be used in two ways. This section of the text presents both methods and explains how to organize a program's memory space using the assembler. It also explains the purpose and use of some of the more important directives used with this assembler. Appendix A provides additional detail about the assembler.

Directives

Before the format of an assembly language program is discussed, some details about the directives (pseudo-operations) that control the assembler must be learned. Some common assembly language directives appear in Table 3–19. Directives indicate how an operand

---

[1]The assembler used in this text is the Microsoft macro assembler, called MASM.

TABLE 3–19 Common assembler directives

Directive	Function
.286	Selects the 80286 instruction set
.286P	Selects the protected mode 80286 instruction set
.386	Selects the 80386 instruction set
.386P	Selects the protected mode 80386 instruction set
.486	Selects the 80486 instruction set
.486P	Selects the 80486 protected mode instruction set
.287	Selects the 80287 numeric coprocessor
.387	Selects the 80387 numeric coprocessor
ALIGN 2	Starts the data in a segment at word or double-word boundaries
ASSUME	Indicates the names of each segment to the assembler; it does not load the segment registers
AT	Indicates what physical segment address is used with the SEGMENT statement
BYTE	Indicates a byte-sized operand as in BYTE PTR or THIS BYTE
DB	Defines byte(s) (8 bits)
DD	Defines double word(s) (32 bits)
DQ	Defines quad word(s) (64 bits)
DT	Defines 10 bytes (80 bits)
DUP	Generates duplicates of characters or numbers
DW	Defines word(s) (16 bits)
DWORD	Indicates a double word-sized operand as in THIS DWORD
END	Indicates the end of the program
ENDM	Indicates the end of a macro sequence
ENDP	Indicates the end of a procedure
ENDS	Indicates the end of a segment
EQU	Equates data to a label
FAR	Specifies a far address as in JMP FAR PTR LISTS
MACRO	Defines the name, parameters, and start of a macro
NEAR	Specifies a near address as in JMP NEAR PTR HELP
OFFSET	Specifies an offset address
ORG	Sets the origin within a segment
PROC	Defines the beginning of a procedure
PTR	Indicates a memory pointer
SEGMENT	Defines the start of a memory segment
STACK	Indicates that a segment is a stack segment
STRUC	Defines the start of a data structure
THIS	Used with EQU to set a label to a byte, word, or double word
USES	A MASM version 6.0 directive that automatically saves registers used by a procedure
USE16	Directs the assembler to use the 16-bit instruction mode and data sizes for the 80386 and 80486 microprocessors
USE32	Directs the assembler to use the 32-bit instruction mode and data sizes for the 80386 and 80486 microprocessors
WORD	Acts as a word operand as in WORD PTR or THIS WORD

Note: Most of these directives function with most versions of the assembler.

or section of a program is to be processed by the assembler. Some directives generate and store information in the memory, while others do not. The DB (define byte) directive stores bytes of data in the memory, while the BYTE PTR directive never stores data. The BYTE PTR directive indicates the size of the data references by a pointer or index register.

Note that the assembler by default accepts only 8086/8088 instructions unless the software is preceded by the .286 or .286P directive or one of the other microprocessor selection switches. The .286 directive tells the assembler to use the 80286 instruction set in the real mode, while the .286P directive tells the assembler to use the 80286 protected mode instruction set.

Storing Data in a Memory Segment. The DB (define byte), DW (define word), and DD (define double-word) directives are most often used with the 8086–80486 to define and store memory data. If a numeric coprocessor is present in the system, the DQ (define quad-word) and DT (define ten bytes) directives are also common. These directives use the label to identify a memory location and the directive to indicate the size of the location.

EXAMPLE 3-9

```
                         using DB, DW, and DD
                         ;
0000                     LIST_SEG       SEGMENT

0000 01 02 03            DATA_ONE       DB        1,2,3        ;define bytes
0003 45                                 DB        45H          ;hexadecimal
0004 41                                 DB        'A'          ;ASCII
0005 F0                                 DB        11110000B    ;binary
0006 000C 000D           DATA_TWO       DW        12,13        ;define words
000A 0200                               DW        LIST1        ;symbolic
000C 2345                               DW        2345H        ;hexadecimal
000E 00000300            DATA_THREE     DD        300H         ;hexadecimal
0012 4007DF3B                           DD        2.123        ;real
0016 544269E1                           DD        3.34E+12     ;real
001A 00                  LISTA          DB        ?            ;reserve 1 byte
001B 000A[               LISTB          DB        10 DUP (?)   ;reserve 10 bytes
             ??
                ]
0025 00                                 ALIGN     2            ;set word boundary

0026 0100[               LISTC          DW        100H DUP (0)
         0000
                ]
0226 0016[               LIST_NINE      DD        22 DUP (?)
         ????????
                ]

0027E 0064[              SIXES          DB        100 DUP (6)
         06
                ]

02E2                     LIST_SEG       ENDS
                                        END
```

Example 3–9 shows a memory segment that contains various forms of data definition directives. The first statement indicates the start of the segment and its symbolic name. The last statement of the segment contains the ENDS directive that indicates the end of the segment. The name of the segment (LIST_SEG) can be anything that the programmer desires to call it.

This example shows various forms of data storage for bytes at DATA_ONE. More than one byte can be defined on a line in binary, hexadecimal, decimal, or ASCII code. The DATA_TWO label shows how to store various forms of word data. Double words are stored at DATA_THREE and they include floating-point, single-precision real numbers.

Memory can be reserved for use in the future by using a ? as an operand for a DB, DW, or DD directive. When a ? is used in place of a numeric or ASCII value, the assembler sets aside a location and does not initialize it to any value. The DUP (duplicate) directive creates an array as shown in several ways in Example 3–9. A 10 DUP (?) reserves 10 locations of memory, but stores no specific value in any of the 10 locations. If a number appears within the () part of the DUP statement, the assembler initializes the reserved section of memory with data.

The ALIGN directive, used in this example, makes sure that the memory arrays are stored on word boundaries. An ALIGN 2 places data on word boundaries for the microprocessor and an ALIGN 4 places them on double-word boundaries for an 80386 or 80486 and double-word data. It is important that word-sized data are placed at word boundaries and double-word-sized data at double-word boundaries. If not, the microprocessor spends more time than necessary accessing these data types. A word stored at an odd-numbered memory location takes twice as long to access as a word stored on an even-numbered memory location.

EQU and THIS.   The equate directive (EQU) equates a numeric, ASCII, or label to another label. Equates make a program clearer and simplify debugging. Example 3–10 shows several equate statements and a few instructions that show how they function in a program.

EXAMPLE 3–10

```
                    ;using equate
                    ;
= 000A              TEN      EQU   10
= 0009              NINE     EQU   9

0000 B0 0A                   MOV   AL,TEN
0002 04 09                   ADD   AL,NINE
```

The THIS directive always appears as THIS BYTE, THIS WORD, or THIS DWORD. In certain cases, data must be referred to as both a byte and a word. The assembler can only assign either a byte or a word address to a label. To assign a byte label to a word, we use the software listed in Example 3–11.

EXAMPLE 3–11

```
                    ;using THIS and ORG
                    ;
0000                DATA_SEG         SEGMENT

0100                         ORG     100H

= 0100              DATA1    EQU     THIS BYTE
```

```
0100 0000                 DATA2    DW    ?

0102                      DATA_SEG  ENDS

0000                      CODE_SEG  SEGMENT 'CODE'

                          ASSUME CS:CODE_SEG,DS:DATA_SEG

0000 8A 1E 0100 R              MOV   BL,DATA1
0004 A1 0100 R                 MOV   AX,DATA2
0007 8A 3E 0101 R              MOV   BH,DATA1+1

000B                      CODE_SEG  ENDS
```

This example also illustrates how the ORG (origin) statement changes the starting address of the data in the data segment to location 100H. The ASSUME statement tells the assembler what names have been chosen for the code, data, extra, and stack segments. Without the assume statement, the assembler assumes nothing and uses a prefix on all instructions that address memory data.

PROC and ENDP. The PROC and ENDP directives indicate the start and end of a procedure (*subroutine*). These directives force structure because the procedure is clearly defined. Both directives require a label to indicate the name of the subroutine. The PROC directive, which indicates the start of a procedure, must also be followed with either NEAR or FAR. A NEAR procedure is one that resides in the same code segment as the program. A FAR procedure may reside at any location in the memory system. We often call NEAR procedures *local,* and FAR procedures *global.* The term global denotes a procedure that can be used by any program, while local defines a procedure that is only used by the current program.

EXAMPLE 3–12

```
                ;procedure that adds BX, CX, and DX with the sum
                ;stored in AX
                ;
0000            ADDEM      PROC   FAR

0000 03 D9                 ADD    BX,CX
0002 03 DA                 ADD    BX,DX
0004 8B C3                 MOV    AX,BX
0006 CB                    RET

0007            ADDEM      ENDP
```

Example 3–12 shows a procedure that adds BX, CX, and DX and stores the sum in register AX. Although this procedure is short, and may not be that useful, it does illustrate how to use the PROC and ENDP directives to delineate the procedure.

If version 6.0 of the Microsoft MASM assembler program is available, the PROC directive can specify and automatically save any registers used within the procedure. The USES statement indicates what registers are used by the procedure so the assembler can automatically save them before the procedure begins and restore before the procedure ends with the RET instruction. For example, the ADDS PROC USES AX BX CX statement automatically pushes AX, BX, and CX on the stack before the procedure begins and pops them from the stack before the RET instruction executes at the end of the procedure. Example 3–13 illustrates a procedure written using MASM 6.0 that shows the USES statement. Note that the registers in the list are not separated by commas and the PUSH and POP instructions are not displayed in the procedure listing. The USES statement does not appear elsewhere in this text so compatibility with MASM version 5.10 can be maintained.

EXAMPLE 3–13

```
                    ;procedure that includes the USES directive to save
                    ;BX, CX, and DX on the stack.
                    ;
0000                ADDS        PROC NEAR USES BX CX DX

0003 03 D8                      ADD    BX,AX
0005 03 CB                      ADD    CX,BX
0007 03 D1                      ADD    DX,CX
0009 8B C2                      MOV    AX,DX
                                RET

000F                ADDS        ENDP
```

Memory Organization

The assembler uses two basic formats for developing software. One method uses models and the other uses full segment definitions. Memory models, as presented in this section, are unique to the MASM assembler program. The TASM assembler also uses memory models, but they differ from the MASM models. The full segment definitions are common to most assemblers, including the *Intel assembler,* and most often used for software development. The models are easier to use, but the full segment definitions offer better control over the assembly language task and are recommended and used in other places in this text. We use full segments because they apply to all assemblers, where models do not.

Models.   There are many models that can be used with the MASM assembler from tiny to huge. Appendix A contains a table that lists all the models available for use with the assembler. To designate a model, we use the .MODEL statement followed by the size of the memory system. The tiny model requires that all software and data fit into one 64K byte memory segment and be useful for small programs. The small model requires that only one data segment is used with one code segment for a total of 128K bytes of memory. Other models are available up to the huge model.

EXAMPLE 3–14

```
                         .MODEL SMALL

                         .STACK 100H         ;define stack

                         .DATA               ;define data

0000 0064[       LISTA    DB      100 DUP (?)
          ??
            ]

0064 0064[       LISTB    DB      100 DUP (?)
          ??
```

```
                                 ]

                                        .CODE                ;define code

0000 B8-R            HERE:        MOV   AX,@DATA             ;load ES, DS
0003 8E C0                        MOV   EX,AX
0005 8E D8                        MOV   DS,AX

0007 FC                           CLD                        ;move data
0008 BE 0000 R                    MOV   SI,OFFSET LISTA
000B BF 0064 R                    MOV   DI,OFFSET LISTB
000E B9 0064                      MOV   CX,100
0011 F3/A4                        REP MOVSB

0013                              .EXIT 0                    ;exit to DOS

                                  END   HERE
```

Example 3–14 illustrates how the .MODEL statement defines the parameters of a short program that copies the contents of a 100-byte block of memory (LISTA) into a second 100-byte block of memory (LISTB).

EXAMPLE 3–15

```
0000                   STACK_SEG      SEGMENT STACK

0000 0100[                          DW       100H DUP (?)
          ????
            ]

0200                   STACK_SEG      ENDS

0000                   DATA_SEG       SEGMENT 'DATA'

0000 0064[                  LISTA DB    100 DUP (?)
          ??
            ]

0064 0064[                  LISTB DB    100 DUP (?)
          ??

            ]

00C8                   DATA_SEG       ENDS

0000                   CODE_SEG       SEGMENT 'CODE'

                              ASSUME CS:CODE_SEG,DS:DATA_SEG,SS:STACK_SEG

0000                          MAIN  PROC    FAR

0000 B8-R                            MOV   AX,DATA_SEG    ;load DS and ES
0003 8E C0                           MOV   ES,AX
0005 8E D8                           MOV   DS,AX

0007 FC                              CLD                    ;move data
0008 BE 0000 R                       MOV   SI,OFFSET LISTA
000B BF 0064 R                       MOV   DI,OFFSET LISTB
000E B9 0064                         MOV   CX,100
```

```
0011 F3/A4                         REP  MOVSB

0013 B4 4C                         MOV   AH,4CH        ;exit to DOS
0015 CD 21                         INT   21H

0017                          MAIN ENDP

0017                  CODE_SEG     ENDS

                                   END   MAIN
```

Full Segment Definitions.   Example 3–15 illustrates the same program using full segment definitions. This program appears longer but more structured than the model method of setting up a program. The first segment defined is the STACK_SEG that is clearly delineated with the SEGMENT and ENDS directives. Within these directives a DW 100 DUP (?) sets aside 100H words for the stack segment. Because the word STACK appears next to SEGMENT, the assembler and linker automatically load both the stack segment register (SS) and stack pointer (SP).

Next the data are defined in the DATA_SEG. Here two arrays of data appear as LISTA and LISTB. Each array contains 100 bytes of space for the program. The names of the segments in this program can be changed to any name. We include the group name 'DATA' so the Microsoft program CODEVIEW can be effectively used to debug this software. If the group name is not placed in a program, CODEVIEW can still be used to debug a program, but the program will not be debugged in symbolic form. Other group names such as 'STACK,' 'CODE,' and so forth are listed in Appendix A.

The CODE_SEG is organized as a far procedure because most software is procedure oriented. Before the program begins, the code segment contains the ASSUME statement. The ASSUME statement tells the assembler and linker the name used for the code segment (CS) is CODE_SEG; it also tells the assembler and linker that the data segment is DATA_SEG and the stack segment is STACK_SEG. Also notice we include the group name 'CODE' for the code segment. Other group names appear in Appendix A with the models.

After the program loads both the extra segment register and data segment register with the location of the data segment, it transfers 100 bytes from LISTA to LISTB. Following this is a sequence of two instructions that return control back to DOS (the disk operating system).

The last statement in the program is END MAIN. The END statement indicates the end of the program and the location of the first instruction executed. Here we want the machine to execute the main procedure so a label follows the END directive. In a file that is linked to another file, there is no label on the END directive.

In the 80386/80486 microprocessor an additional directive is found attached to the code segment. The USE16 or USE32 directive tells the assembler to use 16- or 32-bit instruction modes for the microprocessor. Software developed for the DOS environment must use the USE16 directive for the 80386/80486 program to function correctly. In fact, any program designed to execute in the real mode must include the USE16 directive. Example 3–16 shows how the same software listed in Example 3–15 is formed for the 80386/80486 microprocessor.

EXAMPLE 3-16

```
                           .386                                        ;select the 80386
0000                       STACK_SEG      SEGMENT STACK

0000 0100[                                DW        100H DUP (?)
          ????
             ]

0200                       STACK_SEG      ENDS

0000                       DATA_SEG       SEGMENT 'DATA'

0000 0064[                        LISTA DB      100 DUP (?)
          ??
             ]

0064 0064[                        LISTB DB      100 DUP (?)
          ??
             ]

00C8          DATA_SEG               ENDS

0000          CODE_SEG               SEGMENT USE16'CODE'

                            ASSUME CS:CODE_SEG,DS:DATA_SEG,SS:STACK_SEG

0000                        MAIN PROC       FAR

0000 B8--R                     MOV       AX,DATA_SEG    ;load DS and ES
0003 8E C0                     MOV       ES,AX
0005 8E D8                     MOV       DS,AX

0007 FC                        CLD                        ;move data
0008 BE 0000 R                 MOV       SI,OFFSET LISTA
000B BF 0064 R                 MOV       DI,OFFSET LISTB
000E B9 0064                   MOV       CX,100
0011 F3/A4                     REP MOVSB

0013 B4 4C                     MOV       AH,4CH       ;exit to DOS
0015 CD 21                     INT       21H

0017                        MAIN  ENDP

0017          CODE_SEG      ENDS

                            END       MAIN
```

A Sample Program

EXAMPLE 3-17

```
          ;program that reads a key and displays key
          ;an @ key ends the program
          ;
0000      CODE_SEG     SEGMENT 'CODE'

                ASSUME  CS:CODE_SEG
```

```
0000                      MAIN   PROC   FAR

0000 B4 06                       MOV    AH,6        ;read key
0002 B2 FF                       MOV    DL,0FFH
0004 CD 21                       INT    21H
0006 74 F8                       JE     MAIN        ;if no key

0008 3C 40                       CMP    AL,'@'      ;test for @
000A 74 08                       JE     MAIN1       ;if @

000C B4 06                       MOV    AH,6        ;display key
000E 8A D0                       MOV    DL,AL
0010 CD 21                       INT    21H
0012 EB EC                       JMP    MAIN        ;repeat
0014           MAIN1:
0014 B4 4C                       MOV    AH,4CH      ;exit to DOS
0016 CD 21                       INT    21H

0018                      MAIN   ENDP

0018          CODE_SEG    ENDS

                          END    MAIN
```

Example 3–17 provides a sample program that reads a character from the keyboard and displays it on the CRT screen. Although this program is trivial, it does illustrate a complete workable program that functions on any personal computer using DOS from the earliest 8088-based system to the latest 80486-based system. This program also illustrates the use of a few DOS function calls. Appendix A lists the DOS function calls with their parameters. The BIOS function calls allow the use of the keyboard, printer, disk drives, and everything else that is available in your computer system.

This example program uses only a code segment because there is no data. A stack segment should appear, but has been left out because DOS automatically allocates a 256-byte stack for all programs. The only time that the stack is used in this example is for the INT 21H instructions that call a procedure in DOS. Note that when this program is linked, the linker signals that no stack segment is present. This warning may be ignored in this example because the stack is less than 256 bytes.

The program uses DOS functions 06H and 4CH. The function number is placed in AH before the INT 21H instruction executes. The 06H function reads the keyboard if DL = 0FFH or displays the ASCII contents of DL if it is not 0FFH. Upon close examination, the first section of the program moves a 06H into AH and a 0FFH into DL so a key is read from the keyboard. The INT 21H tests the keyboard and if no key is typed, it returns equal. The JE instruction tests the equal condition and jumps to MAIN if no key is typed.

When a key is typed, the program continues to the next step. This step compares the contents of AL with an @ symbol. Upon return from the INT 21H, the ASCII character of the typed key is found in AL. In this program if we type an @ symbol, the program ends. If we do not type an @ symbol, the program continues by displaying the character typed on the keyboard with the next INT 21H instruction.

The second INT 21H instruction moves the ASCII character into DL so it can be displayed on the CRT screen. After displaying the character a JMP executes. This causes the program to continue at MAIN where it repeats reading a key.

If the @ symbol is typed, the program continues at MAIN1 where it executes the DOS function code number 4CH. This causes the program to return to the DOS prompt (A>) so the computer can be used for other tasks.

More information about the assembler and its application appears in Appendix A and in the next several chapters. The Appendix provides a complete overview of the assembler, linker, and DOS functions. It also provides a list of the BIOS (*basic I/O system*) functions. The information provided in the following chapters clarifies how to use the assembler for certain tasks at different levels of the text.

3-8 SUMMARY

1. Data movement instructions transfer data between registers, a register and memory, a register and the stack, memory and the stack, the accumulator and I/O, and the flags and the stack.

2. Data movement instructions include: MOV, PUSH, POP, XCHG, XLAT, IN, OUT, LEA, LSD, LES, LAHF, SAHF, and the string instructions: LODS, STOS, MOVS, INS, and OUTS.

3. The first byte of an instruction contains the opcode, which specifies the operation performed by the microprocessor. The opcode may be preceded by an override prefix in some forms of instructions.

4. The D bit, located in many instructions, selects the direction of data flow. If D = 1, the data flow from the REG field to the R/M field of the instruction. If D = 1, the data flow from the R/M field to the REG field.

5. The W-bit, found in most instructions, selects the size of the data transfer. If W = 0, the data are byte-sized and if W = 1, the data are word-sized. In the 80386/80486 microprocessor W = 1 can also specify a 32-bit register.

6. MOD selects the addressing mode of operation for a machine language instruction's R/M field. If MOD = 00, there is no displacement, if a 01, an 8-bit sign-extended displacement appears, if 10, a 16-bit displacement occurs, and if a 11, a register is used instead of a memory location. In the 80386/80486 the MOD bits also specify a 32-bit displacement.

7. A 3-bit binary register code specifies the REG and R/M fields when the MOD = 11. The 8-bit registers are: AH, AL, BH, BL, CH, CL, DH, and DL, and the 16-bit registers are: AX, BX, CX, DX, SP, BP, DI, and SI. The 32-bit registers are EAX, EBX, ECX, EDX, ESP, EBP, EDI, and ESI.

8. When the R/M field depicts a memory mode, a 3-bit code selects one of the following modes: [BX+DI], [BX+SI], [BP+DI], [BP+SI], [BX], [BP], [DI], or [SI] for 16-bit instruction in the 8086–80486. In the 80386/80486 the R/M field specifies: EAX, EBX, ECX, EDX, EBP, EDI, and ESI or one of the scaled-index modes of addressing memory data. If the scaled-index mode is selected (R/M = 100) an additional byte (scaled-index byte) is added to the instruction to specify the base register, index register, and the scaling factor.

9. All memory-addressing modes, by default, address data in the data segment unless BP addresses memory. The BP register addresses data in the stack segment.

10. The segment registers may be addressed only by the MOV, PUSH, or POP instruction. The MOV instruction may transfer a segment register to a 16-bit register or vice versa. We do not allow the MOV CS,reg or POP CS instruction.

11. Data are transferred between a register or a memory location and the stack by the PUSH and POP instructions. Variations of these instructions allow immediate data to be pushed onto the stack, the flags to be transferred between the stack, and all the 16-bit registers can be transferred between the stack and the registers. When data are transferred to the stack, two bytes (8086–80286) always move with the least significant byte placed at the SP location - 1 byte and the most significant byte placed at the SP location - 2 bytes. After placing the data on the stack, SP decrements by 2. In the 80386/80486, 4 bytes of data from a memory location or register may also be transferred to the stack.

12. Opcodes that transfer data between the stack and the flags are PUSHF and POPF. Opcodes that transfer all the 16-bit registers between the stack and the registers are PUSHA and POPA. In the 80386/80486 a PUSHFD and POPFD transfer the contents of the EFLAGS.

13. LEA, LDS, and LES instructions load a register or registers with an effective address. The LEA instruction loads any 16-bit register with an effective address, while LDS and LES load any 16-bit register and either DS or ES with the effective address. In the 80386/80486 additional instructions include: LFS, LGS, and LSS that load a 16-bit register and FS, GS, or SS.

14. String data transfer instructions use either or both DI and SI to address memory. The DI offset address is located in the extra segment and the SI offset address is located in the data segment.

15. The direction flag (D) chooses the auto-increment or auto-decrement mode of operation for DI and SI for string instructions. If we clear D with the CLD instruction, we select the auto-increment mode, and if we set D with STD, we select the auto-decrement mode. Either or both DI and SI increment/decrement by 1 for a byte operation and by 2 for a word operation.

16. LODS loads AL, AX, or EAX with data from the memory location addressed by SI, STOS stores AL, AX, or EAX in the memory location addressed by DI, and MOVS transfer a byte or a word from the memory location addressed by SI into the location addressed by DI.

17. INS inputs data from an I/O device addressed by DX and stores it in the memory location addressed by DI and OUTS outputs the contents of the memory location addressed by SI and sends it to the I/O device addressed by DX.

18. The REP prefix may be attached to any string instruction to repeat it. The REP prefix repeats the string instruction the number of times found in register CX.

19. Translate (XLAT) converts the data in AL into a number stored at the memory location address by BX plus AL.

20. IN and OUT transfer data between AL, AX, or EAX and an external I/O device. The address of the I/O device is either stored with the instruction (fixed-port) or in register DX (variable-port).

21. The segment override prefix selects a different segment register for a memory location than the default segment. For example, the MOV AX,[BX] instruction uses the data segment, but the MOV AX,ES:[BX] instruction uses the extra segment because of the ES: prefix. The segment override prefix is the only way that the FS and GS segments are addressed in the 80386/80486 microprocessor.

22. The MOVZX (move and zero-extend) and MOVSX (move and sign-extend) instruction found in the 80386/80486 microprocessor increase the size of a byte to a word or a word to a double word. The zero-extend version increases the size of the number by inserting leading zeros. The sign-extend version increases the size of the number by copying the sign-bit into the more significant bits of the number.

23. Assembler directives DB (define byte), DW (define word), DD (define double word), and DUP (duplicate) store data in the memory system.

24. The EQU (equate) directive allows data or labels to be equated to labels.

25. The SEGMENT directive identifies the start of a memory segment and ENDS identifies the end of a segment.

26. The ASSUME directive tells the assembler what segment names you have assigned to CS, DS, ES, and SS. In the 80386/80486 it also indicates the segment name for FS and GS.

27. The PROC and ENDP directives indicate the start and end of a procedure.

28. Memory models can be used to shorten the program slightly, but they are more difficult to use for larger programs and programming in general. Memory models are not compatible with all assembler programs.

3-9 QUESTIONS AND PROBLEMS

1. The first byte of an instruction is the _____ unless it contains an override prefix.

2. Describe the purpose of the D- and W-bits found in some machine language instructions.

3. The MOD field, in a machine language instruction, specifies what information?

4. If the register field (REG) of an instruction contains a 010 and W = 0, what register is selected assuming that the instruction is a 16-bit mode instruction?

5. How are the 32-bit registers selected for the 80386/80486 microprocessor?

6. What memory-addressing mode is specified by R/M = 001 with MOD = 00 for a 16-bit instruction?

7. Identify the default segment register assigned to:
   (a) SP
   (b) BX
   (c) DI
   (d) BP
   (e) SI

8. Convert an 8B07H from machine language to assembly language.

9. Convert an 8B1E004CH from machine language to assembly language.

10. If a MOV SI,[BX+2] instruction appears in a program, what is its machine language equivalent?

11. If a MOV ESI,[EAX] instruction appears in a program for the 80386/80486 microprocessor operated in the 16-bit instruction mode, what is its machine language equivalent?

12. What is wrong with a MOV CS,AX instruction?

13. PUSH and POP always transfer a _____-bit number between the stack and a register or memory location in the 8086–80286 microprocessor.

14. What segment register may not be popped from the stack?

15. What registers move onto the stack with the PUSHA instruction?

16. What registers move onto the stack for a PUSHAD instruction?

17. Describe the operation of each of the following instructions:
    (a) PUSH AX
    (b) POP ESI
    (c) PUSH [BX]
    (d) PUSHFD
    (e) POP DS
    (f) PUSH 4

18. Explain what happens when the PUSH BX instruction executes. Make sure to show where BH and BL are stored. (Assume that SP = 0100H and SS = 0200H.)

19. Repeat question 18 for the PUSH EAX instruction.

20. The 16-bit POP instruction (except for POPA) increments SP by _____ .

21. What values appear in SP and SS if the stack pointer addresses memory location 02200H?

22. Compare the operation of a MOV DI,NUMB instruction with an LEA DI,NUMB instruction.

23. What is the difference between an LEA SI,NUMB instruction and a MOV SI,OFFSET NUMB instruction?

24. Which is more efficient, a MOV with an OFFSET or an LEA instruction?

25. Describe how the LDS BX,NUMB instruction operates.

26. What is the difference between the LDS and LSS instructions?

27. Develop a sequence of instructions that moves the contents of data segment memory locations NUMB and NUMB+1 into BX, DX, and SI.

28. What is the purpose of the direction flag?

29. Which instructions set and clear the direction flag?

30. The string instructions use DI and SI to address memory data in which memory segments?

31. Explain the operation of the LODSB instruction.

32. Explain the operation of the STOSW instruction.

33. Explain the operation of the OUTSB instruction.

34. What does the REP prefix accomplish and what type of instruction is it used with?

35. Develop a sequence of instructions that copy 12 bytes of data from an area of memory addressed by SOURCE into an area of memory addressed by DEST.

36. Where is the I/O address (port number) stored for an INSB instruction?

37. Select an assembly language instruction that exchanges the contents of the EBX register with the ESI register.

38. Would the LAHF and SAHF instructions normally appear in software?
39. Explain how the XLAT instruction transforms the contents of the AL register.
40. Write a short program that uses the XLAT instruction to convert the BCD numbers 0-9 into ASCII-coded numbers 30H-39H. Store the ASCII-coded data into a TABLE.
41. Explain what the IN AL,12H instruction accomplishes.
42. Explain how the OUT DX,AX instruction operates.
43. What is a segment override prefix?
44. Select an instruction that moves a byte of data from the memory location addressed by the BX register, in the extra segment, into the AH register.
45. Develop a sequence of instructions that exchanges the contents of AX with BX, ECX with EDX, and SI with DI.
46. What is an assembly language directive?
47. Describe the purpose of the following assembly language directives: DB, DW, and DD.
48. Select an assembly language directive that reserves 30 bytes of memory for array LIST1.
49. Describe the purpose of the EQU directive.
50. What is the purpose of the .386 directive?
51. What is the purpose of the .MODEL directive?
52. If the start of a segment is identified with .DATA, what type of memory organization is in effect?
53. If the SEGMENT directive identifies the start of a segment, what type of memory organization is in effect?
54. What does the INT 21H accomplish if AH contains a 4CH?
55. What directives indicate the start and end of a procedure?
56. Explain the purpose of the USES statement as it applies to a procedure with version 6.0 of MASM.
57. Develop a near procedure that stores AL into four consecutive memory locations, within the data segment, as addressed by the DI register.
58. Develop a far procedure that copies word-sized memory location CS:DATA1 into AX, BX, CX, DX, and SI.

CHAPTER 4

Arithmetic and Logic Instructions

INTRODUCTION

In this chapter, we examine the arithmetic and logic instructions found in the 8086–80486 instruction set. Arithmetic instructions include: addition, subtraction, multiplication, division, comparison, negation, incrementation, and decrementation. Logic instructions include: AND, OR, Exclusive-OR, NOT, shifts, rotates, and the logical compare (TEST). Also presented are the 80386/80486 instructions: SHRD, SHLD, bit tests, and bit scans.

We also will introduce string comparison instructions, which are used for scanning tabular data and for comparing sections of memory. Both tasks perform efficiently with the string scan and string compare instructions.

If you are already familiar with an 8-bit microprocessor, you will recognize that the 8086–80486 instruction set is superior. Even if this is your first microprocessor, you will quickly learn that the microprocessor possesses a powerful and easy-to-use set of arithmetic and logic instructions.

CHAPTER OBJECTIVES

1. Use the arithmetic and logic instructions to accomplish simple binary, BCD, and ASCII arithmetic.
2. Use AND, OR, and Exclusive-OR to accomplish binary bit manipulation.
3. Use the shift and rotate instructions.
4. Explain the operation of the 80386/80486 double-precision shift, bit test, and bit scan instructions.
5. Check the contents of a table for a match with the string instructions.

4-1 ADDITION, SUBTRACTION, AND COMPARISON

The bulk of the arithmetic instructions found in any microprocessor includes addition, subtraction, and comparison. The 8086-80486 microprocessor is no different. In this section we illustrate and define these instructions. We also show their use in manipulating register and memory data.

Addition

Addition takes many forms in the 8086-80486 microprocessor. This section details the use of the ADD instruction for 8-, 16-, and 32-bit binary addition. Another form of addition, called *add-with-carry,* is introduced with the ADC instruction. The ADC instruction allows additions of nearly any width. Finally increment (INC), a special type of addition, is presented. In section 4-3 we examine other forms of addition, such as BCD and ASCII.

Table 4-1 illustrates the addressing modes available to the ADD instruction. (The addressing modes include almost all those mentioned in Chapter 2.) Since there are over 1,000 variations of the ADD instruction in the instruction set, it is impossible to list all of them in this table. The only types of addition not allowed are memory-to-memory and segment register. The segment registers can only be moved, pushed, or popped. Note that as with all other instructions, the 32-bit registers are only available to the 80386/80486 microprocessor.

Register Addition. Example 4-1 shows a simple program that uses register addition to add several registers. In this example, we add contents of AX, BX, CX, and DX to form a 16-bit sum that is stored in the AX register.

EXAMPLE 4-1

```
0000 03 C3          ADD     AX,BX
0002 03 C1          ADD     AX,CX
0004 03 C2          ADD     AX,DX
```

Whenever most arithmetic and logic instructions execute, the contents of the flag register changes. The flags show the result of the arithmetic operation. Any ADD instruction modifies the contents of the sign, zero, carry, auxiliary carry, parity, and overflow flags. (Note that flag bits never change for most of the data transfer instructions presented in Chapter 3.)

Immediate Addition. Immediate addition is used whenever constant or known data are added. An 8-bit immediate addition appears in Example 4-2. In this example, we first load DL with 12H using an immediate move instruction. Next we add a 33H to the 12H in DL using an immediate addition. After the addition, the sum (45H) moves into register DL and the flags change as follows:

$$Z = 0 \text{ (result not zero)}$$
$$C = 0 \text{ (no carry)}$$

TABLE 4–1   Addition instructions

Instruction	Comment
ADD AL,BL	AL = AL + BL
ADD CX,DI	CX = CX + DI
ADD EBP,EAX	EBP = EBP + EAX
ADD CL,44H	CL = CL + 44H
ADD BX,35AFH	BX = BX + 35AFH
ADD EDX,12345H	EDX = EBX + 00012345H
ADD [BX],AL	AL adds to contents of the data segment offset location addressed by BX and the result is stored in the same memory location
ADD CL,[BP]	The contents of the stack segment offset location addressed by BP adds to CL and the result is stored in CL
ADD AL,[EBX]	The contents of the data segment offset location addresses by EBX adds to AL and the result is stored in AL
ADD BX,[SI + 2]	The word-sized contents of the data segment location addressed by SI plus 2 adds to BX and the result is stored in the same memory location
ADD CL,TEMP	The contents of data segment location TEMP adds to CL with the result stored in CL
ADD BX,TEMP[DI]	The word-sized contents of the data segment location addressed by TEMP plus DI adds to BX and the result is stored in the same memory location
ADD [BX + DI],DL	The data segment memory byte addressed by BX + DI is the sum of that byte plus DL
ADD BYTE PTR [DI],3	Add a 3 to the contents of the byte-sized memory location addressed by DI within the data segment
ADD BX,[EAX+2*ECX]	The data segment memory word address by the sum of 2 times ECX and EAX adds to BX

$$A = 0 \text{ (no half-carry)}$$
$$S = 0 \text{ (result positive)}$$
$$P = 0 \text{ (odd parity)}$$
$$O = 0 \text{ (no overflow)}$$

EXAMPLE 4–2

```
0006 B2 12        MOV    DL,12H
0008 80 C2 33     ADD    DL,33H
```

Memory-to-Register Addition.   Suppose an application requires that memory data is added to the AL register. Example 4–3 shows an example that adds 2 consecutive bytes of memory data, stored at the data segment offset locations NUMB and NUMB+1, to the AL register.

EXAMPLE 4–3

```
0000 BF 0000 R          MOV   DI,OFFSET NUMB    ;address NUMB
0003 B0 00              MOV   AL,0              ;clear sum
0005 02 05              ADD   AL,[DI]           ;add NUMB
0007 02 45 01           ADD   AL,[DI+1]         ;add NUMB+1
```

The sequence of instructions first loads the contents of the destination index register (DI) with offset address NUMB. The DI register, used in this example, addresses data in the data segment beginning at memory location NUMB. Next the ADD AL,[DI] instruction adds the contents of memory location NUMB to AL. This occurs because DI addresses memory location NUMB, and the instruction adds its contents to AL. Finally, the ADD AL,[DI+1] instruction adds the contents of memory location NUMB+1 to the AL register. After both ADD instructions execute, the result appears in the AL register as the sum of NUMB plus NUMB+1.

Array Addition. Memory arrays are lists of memory data. Suppose that an array of data (ARRAY) contains 10 bytes numbered from element 0 through element 9. Example 4–4 shows a program that adds the contents of array elements 3, 5, and 7. (The program and the array elements it adds are chosen to demonstrate the use of some of the addressing modes for the microprocessor.)

EXAMPLE 4–4

```
0000 B0 00              MOV   AL,0              ;clear sum
0002 BE 0003            MOV   SI,3              ;address element 3
0005 02 84 0002 R       ADD   AL,ARRAY[SI]      ;add element 3
0009 02 84 0004 R       ADD   AL,ARRAY[SI+2]    ;add element 5
000D 02 84 0006 R       ADD   AL,ARRAY[SI+4]    ;add element 7
```

This example first clears AL to zero so it can be used to accumulate the sum. Next we load register SI with a 3 to initially address array element 3. The ADD AL,ARRAY-[SI] instruction adds the contents of array element 3 to the sum in AL. The instructions that follow add array elements 5 and 7 to the sum in AL using a 3 in SI plus a displacement of 2 to address element 5 and a displacement of 4 to address element 7.

Suppose that an array of data contains 16-bit numbers that add to form a 16-bit sum in register AX. Example 4–5 shows a short sequence of instructions, written for the 80386/80486 microprocessor, that uses scaled-index addressing to add elements 3, 5, and 7 of an area of memory called ARRAY. In this example, we load EBX with the address ARRAY, and ECX holds the array element number.

EXAMPLE 4–5

```
0000 66| BB 00000000 R   MOV   EBX,OFFSET ARRAY   ;address ARRAY
0006 66| B9 00000003     MOV   ECX,3              ;address element 3
000C 67& 8B 04 4B        MOV   AX,[EBX+2*ECX]     ;get element 3
0010 66| B9 00000005     MOV   ECX,5              ;address element 5
0016 67& 03 04 4B        ADD   AX,[EBX+2*ECX]     ;add element 5
001A 66| B9 00000007     MOV   ECX,7              ;address element 7
0020 67& 03 04 4B        ADD   AX,[EBX+2*ECX]     ;add element 7
```

Increment Addition. Increment addition (INC) adds 1 to a register or a memory location. The INC instruction can add 1 to any register or memory location except a segment register.

Table 4–2 illustrates some of the possible forms of the increment instruction available to the 8086–80486 microprocessor. As with other instructions presented thus far, it is impossible to show all variations of the INC instruction because of the large number available.

With indirect memory increments, the size of the data must be described using the BYTE PTR, WORD PTR, or DWORD PTR directives. The reason is that the assembler program cannot determine if, for example, the INC [DI] instruction is a byte-, word-, or double-word-sized increment. The INC BYTE PTR [DI] instruction clearly indicates byte-sized memory data, the INC WORD PTR [DI] instruction unquestionably indicates a word-sized memory data, and the INC DWORD PTR [DI] instruction increments double-word-sized data.

EXAMPLE 4–6

```
0000 BF 0000 R          MOV   DI,OFFSET NUMB    ; address NUMB
0003 B0 00              MOV   AL,0              ; clear sum
0005 02 05              ADD   AL,[DI]           ; add NUMB
0007 47                 INC   DI                ; address NUMB+1
0008 02 05              ADD   AL,[DI]           ; address NUMB+1
```

Example 4–6 shows how the program of Example 4–3 is modified to use the increment instruction for addressing NUMB and NUMB+1. Here, an INC DI instruction changes the contents of register DI from offset address NUMB to offset address NUMB+1. Both programs of Examples 4–3 and 4–6 add the contents of NUMB and NUMB+1. The difference between these programs is the way that this data's address is formed through the contents of the DI register using the increment instruction.

Increment instructions affect the flag bits as do most other arithmetic and logic operations. The difference is that increment instructions do not affect the carry flag bit. Carry is not affected because we often use the increment instruction in programs that depend on the contents of the carry flag.

Addition with Carry.   An addition-with-carry instruction (ADC) adds the bit in the carry flag (C) to the operand data. This instruction mainly appears in software that adds

TABLE 4–2   Increment instructions

Instruction	Comment
INC BL	BL = BL + 1
INC SP	SP = SP + 1
INC EAX	EAX = EAX + 1
INC BYTE PTR [BX]	The byte contents of the memory location addressed by BX in the data segment increment
INC WORD PTR [SI]	The word contents of the memory location addressed by SI in the data segment increment
INC DWORD PTR [ECX]	The double word contents of the data segment memory location addressed by ECX is increment
INC DATA1	The contents of DATA1 increment

numbers that are wider than 16 bits in the 8086–80286 or wider than 32 bits in the 80386/80486 microprocessor.

Table 4–3 lists several add-with-carry instructions with comments that explain their operation. Like the ADD instruction, ADC affects the flags after the addition.

Suppose that we write a program for the 8086–80286 that adds the 32-bit number in BX and AX to the 32-bit number in DX and CX. Figure 4–1 illustrates this addition so the placement and function of carry flag can be understood. This addition cannot be performed without adding the carry flag bit because the 8086–80286 only adds 8- or 16-bit numbers. Example 4–7 shows how the addition occurs with a program. Here the contents of registers AX and CX add to form the least significant 16 bits of the sum. This addition may or may not generate a carry. A carry appears in the carry flag if the sum is greater than FFFFH. Because it is impossible to predict a carry, the most significant 16 bits of this addition are added with the carry flag using the ADC instruction. The ADC instruction adds the one or zero in the carry flag to the most significant 16 bits of the result. This program adds BX—AX to DX—CX with the sum appearing in BX—AX.

EXAMPLE 4–7

```
0000 03 C1            ADD   AX,CX
0002 13 DA            ADC   BX,DX
```

Suppose the same program is rewritten for the 80386/80486 microprocessor, but modified to add two 64-bit numbers. The changes required are the use of the extended registers to hold the data and modifications of the instructions for the 80386/80486 microprocessor. These changes are shown in Example 4–8, which adds two 64-bit numbers.

TABLE 4–3 Add-with-carry instructions

Instruction	Comment
ADC AL,AH	AL = AL + AH + carry
ADC CX,BX	CX = CX + BX + carry
ADC EBX,EDX	EBX = EBX + EDX + carry
ADC [BX],DH	The byte contents of the memory location in the data segment address by BX are summed with DH and carry, the result is stored in memory
ADC BX,[BP + 2]	BX and the word contents of the memory location in the stack segment addressed by BP are summed with carry and the result is stored in BX
ADC ECX,[EBX]	ECX and the double-word contents of the memory location in the data segment addressed by EBX are summed with carry and the result is stored in ECX

Note: Only the 80386/80486 use 32-bit registers and addressing modes.

FIGURE 4-1 Addition-with-carry showing how the carry flag (C) links the two 16-bit additions into one 32-bit addition.

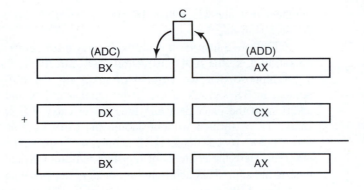

EXAMPLE 4-8

```
0000 66: 03 C1          ADD   EAX,ECX
0003 66: 13 DA          ADC   EBX,EDX
```

Exchange and Add for the 80486 Microprocessor.   A new type of addition appears in the 80486 instruction set called exchange and add (XADD). The XADD instruction adds the source to the destination and stores the sum in the destination just as any addition. The difference is that after the addition takes place, the original value of the destination is copied into the source operand. This is one of the few instructions that change the source.

For example, if BL = 12H and DL = 02H, and the XADD BL,DL instruction executes, the BL register contains the sum of 14H and DL becomes 12H. The sum of 14H is generated and the original destination of 12H replaces the source. This instruction functions with any register size and any memory operand just as the normal ADD instruction.

Subtraction

Many forms of subtraction (SUB) appear in the 8086–80486 instruction set. These forms use any addressing mode with 8-, 16-, or 32-bit data. A special form of subtraction (decrement) subtracts a 1 from any register or memory location. Section 4–5 shows how BCD and ASCII data subtract. As with addition, numbers that are wider than 16 bits or 32 bits must occasionally be subtracted. The subtract-with-borrow instruction (SBB) performs this type of subtraction.

Table 4–4 lists many addressing modes allowed with the subtract instruction (SUB). There are well over 1,000 possible subtraction instructions, far too many to list. About the only types of subtraction not allowed are memory-to-memory and segment register subtractions. Like other arithmetic instructions, the subtract instruction affects the flag bits.

Register Subtraction.   Example 4–9 shows a program that performs register subtraction. This example subtracts the 16-bit contents of registers CX and DX from the contents of register BX. After each subtraction, the microprocessor modifies the contents of the flag register. The flags change for most arithmetic and logic operations.

TABLE 4–4 Subtraction instructions

Instruction	Comment
SUB CL,BL	CL = CL – BL
SUB AX,SP	AX = AX – SP
SUB ECX,EBP	ECX = ECX – EBP
SUB DH,6FH	DH = DH – 6FH
SUB AX,0CCCCH	AX = AX – 0CCCCH
SUB EAX,23456H	EAX = EAX – 00023456H
SUB [DI],CH	CH subtracts from the byte contents of the data segment memory location addressed by DI
SUB CH,[BP]	The byte contents of the stack segment memory location addressed by BP subtracts from CH
SUB AH,TEMP	The byte contents of the data segment memory location TEMP subtracts from AH
SUB DI,TEMP[BX]	The word contents of the data segment memory location addressed by TEMP plus BX subtracts from DI
SUB ECX,DATA1	The double-word contents of the data segment memory location address as DATA1 subtracts from ECX

Note: Only the 80386/80486 use 32-bit registers and addressing modes.

EXAMPLE 4–9

```
0000 2B D9              SUB   BX,CX
0002 2B DA              SUB   BX,DX
```

Immediate Subtraction. As with addition, the microprocessor also allows immediate operands for the subtraction of constant data. Example 4–10 presents a short program that subtracts a 44H from a 22H. Here, we first load the 22H into CH using an immediate move instruction. Next, the SUB instruction, using immediate data 44H, subtracts a 44H from the 22H. After the subtraction, the difference (DEH) moves into the CH register. The flags change as follows for this subtraction:

$$Z = 0 \text{ (result not zero)}$$
$$C = 1 \text{ (borrow)}$$
$$A = 1 \text{ (half-borrow)}$$
$$S = 1 \text{ (result negative)}$$
$$P = 1 \text{ (even parity)}$$
$$O = 0 \text{ (no overflow)}$$

EXAMPLE 4–10

```
0000 B5 22              MOV   CH,22H
0002 80 ED 44           SUB   CH,44H
```

Both carry flags (C and A) hold borrows after a subtraction instead of carries, as after an addition. Notice in this example there is no overflow. This example subtracted a 44H (+ 68) from a 22H (+ 34) resulting in a DEH (− 34). Because the correct 8-bit signed result is a −34, there is no overflow in this example. An 8-bit overflow only occurs if the signed result is greater than +127 or less than −128.

Decrement Subtraction.   Decrement subtraction (DEC) subtracts a 1 from a register or the contents of a memory location. Table 4−5 lists some decrement instructions that illustrate register and memory decrements.

The decrement indirect memory data instructions require BYTE PTR, WORD PTR, or DWORD PTR because the assembler cannot distinguish a byte from a word when an index register addresses memory. For example, DEC [SI] is vague, because the assembler cannot determine if the location addressed by SI is a byte or a word. Using DEC BYTE PTR [SI], DEC WORD PTR [DI], or DEC DWORD PTR [SI] reveals the size of the data.

Subtract with Borrow.   A subtraction-with-borrow (SBB) instruction functions as a regular subtraction, except the carry flag (C), which holds the borrow, also subtracts from the difference. The most common use for this instruction is for subtractions that are wider than 16 bits in the 8086−80286 microprocessor or wider than 32 bits in the 80386/80486. Wide subtractions require that borrows propagate through the subtraction just as wide additions propagated the carry.

Table 4−6 lists many SBB instructions with comments that define their operation. Like the SUB instruction, SBB affects the flags. Notice that the subtract from memory immediate instruction in this table requires a BYTE PTR, WORD PTR, or DWORD PTR directive.

When the 32-bit number held in BX and AX is subtracted from the 32-bit number held in SI and DI, the carry flag propagates the borrow between the two 16-bit subtractions required to perform this operation in an 8086−80486 microprocessor. Figure 4−2 shows how the borrow propagates through the carry flag (C) for this task.

TABLE 4−5   Decrement instructions

Instruction	Comment
DEC BH	BH = BH − 1
DEC SP	SP = SP − 1
DEC ECX	ECX = ECX − 1
DEC BYTE PTR [DI]	The byte contents of the data segment memory location addressed by DI decrements
DEC WORD PTR [BP]	The word contents of the stack segment memory location addressed by BP decrements
DEC DWORD PTR [EBX]	The double-word contents of the data segment memory location addressed by EBX decrements
DEC NUMB	Decrements the contents of data segment memory location NUMB. The way that NUMB is defined determines whether this is a byte or word decrement.

Note: Only the 80386/80486 use 32-bit registers and addressing modes.

TABLE 4–6 Subtract-with-borrow instructions

Instruction	Comment
SBB AH,AL	AH = AH – AL – carry
SBB AX,BX	AX = AX – BX – carry
SBB EAX,EBX	EAX = EAX – EBX – carry
SBB CL,3	CL = CL – 3 – carry
SBB BYTE PTR [DI],3	3 and carry subtract from the byte contents of the data segment memory location addressed by DI
SBB [DI],AL	AL and carry subtract from the byte contents of the data segment memory location addressed by DI
SBB DI,[BP + 2]	The word contents of the stack segment memory location addressed by BP plus 2 and carry subtract from DI
SBB AL,[EBX+ECX]	The byte contents of the data segment memory location address by the sum of EBX and ECX and carry subtract from AL

Note: Only the 80386/80486 use 32-bit registers and addressing modes.

FIGURE 4–2 Subtraction-with-borrow showing how the carry flag (C) propagates the borrow.

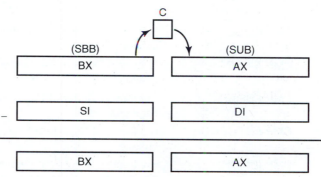

Example 4–11 shows how this subtraction is performed by a program. With wide subtraction, the least significant 16- or 32-bit data are subtracted with the SUB instruction. All subsequent and more significant data are subtracted using the SBB instruction. The example uses the SUB instruction to subtract DI from AX then SBB to subtract-with-borrow SI from BX.

EXAMPLE 4–11

```
0004 2B C7              SUB   AX,DI
0006 1B DE              SBB   BX,SI
```

Comparison

The comparison instruction (CMP) is a subtraction that only changes the flag bits. A comparison is useful for checking the entire contents of a register or a memory location against another value. A CMP is normally followed by a conditional jump instruction, which tests the condition of the flag bits.

Table 4–7 lists a variety of comparison instructions that use the same addressing modes as the addition and subtraction instructions already presented. Similarly, the only disallowed forms of compare are memory-to-memory and segment register compares.

EXAMPLE 4–12

```
0000 3C 10          CMP  AL,10H  ;compare with 10H
0002 73 1C          JAE  SUBER   ;if 10H or above
```

Example 4–12 shows a comparison followed by a conditional jump instruction. In this example, the contents of AL are compared with a 10H. Conditional jump instructions that often follow the compare are: JA (jump above) or JB (jump below). If the JA follows the compare, the jump occurs if the value in AL is above 10H. If the JB follows the compare, the jump occurs if the value in AL is below 10H. In this example, the JAE instruction follows the compare. This instruction causes the program to continue at

TABLE 4–7   Comparison instructions

Instruction	Comment
CMP CL,BL	Subtracts BL from CL; neither BL nor CL change, but the flags change
CMP AX,SP	Subtracts SP from AX; neither AX nor SP change, but the flags change
CMP EBP,ESI	Subtracts ESI from EBP; neither EBP nor ESI change, but the flags change
CMP AX,0CCCCH	Subtracts 0CCCCH from AX; AX does not change, but the flags change
CMP [DI],CH	Subtracts CH from the byte contents of the data segment memory location addressed by DI; neither CH nor memory changes, but the flags change
CMP CL,[BP]	Subtracts the byte contents of the stack segment memory location addressed by BP from CL; neither CL nor memory change, but the flags change
CMP AH,TEMP	Subtracts the byte contents of data segment memory location TEMP from AH; neither AH nor memory change, but the flags change
CMP DI,TEMP [BX]	Subtracts the word contents of the data segment memory location addressed by TEMP plus BX from DI; neither DI nor memory change, but the flags change
CMP AL,[EDI+ESI]	Subtracts the byte contents of the data segment memory location addressed by the sum of EDI and ESI; neither AL nor memory change, but the flags change

Note: Only the 80386/80486 use 32-bit registers and addressing modes.

memory location SUBER if the value in AL is 10H or above. There is also a JBE (jump below or equal) instruction that could follow the compare to jump if the outcome is below or equal to 10H. Chapter 5 provides more detail on the compare instruction and conditional jump instructions.

Compare and Exchange. The compare and exchange instruction (CMPXCHG) found only in the 80486 instruction set compares the destination operand with the accumulator. If they are equal, the source operand is copied into the destination. If they are not equal, the destination operand is copied into the accumulator. This instruction functions with 8-, 16-, or 32-bit data.

The CMPXCHG CX,DX instruction is an example of the compare and exchange instruction. This instruction first compares the contents of CX with AX. If CX equals AX, DX is copied into AX. If CX is not equal to AX, CX is copied into AX. This instruction also compares AL with 8-bit data and EAX with 32-bit data if the operands are either 8- or 32-bit.

4-2 MULTIPLICATION AND DIVISION

Only the more modern microprocessors, such as the 80486, 80386, 80286, or earlier 8086/8088, contain multiplication and division instructions. Earlier 8-bit microprocessors could not multiply or divide directly. They required a program that multiplied or divided using a series of shifts and additions or subtractions. Because microprocessor manufacturers were aware of this inadequacy, they incorporated multiplication and division instructions into the instruction sets of the newer microprocessors.

Multiplication

Multiplication is performed on bytes, words, or double words and can be signed integer (IMUL) or unsigned (MUL). Note that only the 80386/80486 can multiply 32-bit double words. The product after a multiplication is always a double-width product. If we multiply two 8-bit numbers, they generate a 16-bit product; if we multiply two 16-bit numbers, they generate a 32-bit product; and if we multiply two 32-bit numbers, a 64-bit product is generated.

Some flag bits (O and C) change when the multiply instruction executes, and produce predictable outcomes. The other flags also change, but their results are unpredictable and therefore are unused. In an 8-bit multiplication, if the most significant 8 bits of the result are 0, both C and O flag bits equal 0. These flag bits show that the result is 8 bits wide or 16 bits wide. In a 16-bit multiplication, if the most significant 16 bits of the product are 0, both C and O clear to 0. In a 32-bit multiplication, both C and O indicate that the most significant 32 bits of the product are zero.

8-bit Multiplication. With 8-bit multiplication, whether signed or unsigned, the multiplicand is always in the AL register. The multiplier can be any 8-bit register or any memory location. Immediate multiplication is not allowed unless the special signed immediate multiplication instruction, discussed later in this section, appears in a program. The multiplication instruction contains one operand because it always multiplies the operand times the contents of register AL. An example is the MUL BL instruction, which multiplies the unsigned contents of AL by the unsigned contents of BL. After the multiplication, the unsigned product is placed in AX—a double-width product. Table 4–8 illustrates some 8-bit multiplication instructions.

Suppose that BL and CL each contain two 8-bit unsigned numbers and these numbers must be multiplied to form a 16-bit product stored in DX. This procedure cannot be accomplished by a single instruction because we can only multiply a number times the AL register for an 8-bit multiplication. Example 4–13 shows a short program that generates: DX = BL x CL. This example loads registers BL and CL with example data 5 and 10. The product, a 50, moves into DX from AX after the multiplication by the MOV DX,AX instruction.

EXAMPLE 4–13

```
0000 B3 05          MOV   BL,5    ;load data
0002 B1 0A          MOV   CL,10
0004 8A C1          MOV   AL,CL   ;position data
0006 F6 E3          MUL   BL      ;multiply
0008 8B D0          MOV   DX,AX   ;position product
```

For signed multiplication, the product is in true binary form, if positive, and in two's complement form, if negative. These are the same forms used to store all positive and negative signed numbers used by the microprocessor. If the program of Example 4–13 multiplies two signed numbers, only the MUL instruction is changed to IMUL.

16-Bit Multiplication.   Word multiplication is very similar to byte multiplication. The difference is that AX contains the multiplicand instead of AL and the product appears in DX—AX instead of AX. The DX register always contains the most significant 16 bits of the product and AX the least significant 16 bits. As with 8-bit multiplication, the choice of the multiplier is up to the programmer. Table 4–9 shows several different 16-bit multiplication instructions.

TABLE 4–8   8-bit multiplication instructions

Instruction	Comment
MUL CL	AL is multiplied by CL; this unsigned multiplication leaves the product in AX
IMUL DH	AL is multiplied by DH; this signed multiplication leaves the product in AX
IMUL BYTE PTR [BX]	AL is multiplied by the byte contents of the data segment memory location addressed by BX; this unsigned multiplication leaves the product in AX
MUL TEMP	AL is multiplied by the contents of the data segment memory location TEMP; if temp is defined as an 8-bit number, the unsigned product is found in AX

TABLE 4-9 16-bit multiplication instructions

Instruction	Comment
MUL CX	AX is multiplied by CX; the unsigned product is found in DX—AX
IMUL DI	AX is multiplied by DI; the signed product is found in DX—AX
MUL WORD PTR [SI]	AX is multiplied by the word contents of the data segment memory location addressed by SI; the unsigned product is found in DX—AX

Immediate 16-Bit Multiplication. The 8086/8088 microprocessor could not perform immediate multiplication, but the 80286, 80386, and 80486 can by using a special version of the multiply instruction. Immediate multiplication must be signed multiplication and the instruction format is different because it contains three operands. The first operand is the 16-bit destination register, the second operand is a register or memory location that contains the 16-bit multiplicand, and the third operand is either an 8-bit or 16-bit immediate data used as the multiplier.

The IMUL CX,DX,12H instruction multiplies 12H times DX and leaves a *16-bit* signed product in CX. If the immediate data are 8 bits, they sign-extend into a 16-bit number before the multiplication occurs. Another example is IMUL BX,NUMBER,1000H, which multiplies NUMBER times 1000H and leaves the product in BX. Both the destination and multiplicand must be 16-bit numbers. Although this is immediate multiplication, the restrictions placed on it limit its utility, especially the fact that it is a signed multiplication and the product is 16 bits wide.

32-Bit Multiplication. In the 80386 and 80486 microprocessors, 32-bit multiplication is allowed because these microprocessors contain 32-bit registers. As with 8- and 16-bit multiplication, we can multiply signed or unsigned numbers using the IMUL and MUL instructions. With 32-bit multiplication, the contents of EAX are multiplied by the operand specified with the instruction. The product (64 bits wide) is found in EDX and EAX where EAX contains the least-significant 32 bits of the product. Table 4-10 lists some of the 32-bit multiplication instructions found in the 80386/80486 instruction set.

TABLE 4-10 32-bit multiplication instructions

Instruction	Comment
MUL ECX	EAX is multiplied by ECX; the unsigned product is found in EDX—EAX
IMUL EDI	EAX is multiplied by EDI; the signed product is found in EDX—EAX
MUL DWORD PTR[ECX]	EAX is multiplied by the double-word contents of the data segment memory location addressed by ECX; the unsigned product is found in EDX—EAX

Division

Like multiplication, division occurs on 8- or 16-bit numbers in the 8086–80486 and also 32-bit numbers in the 80386/80486. These numbers are signed (IDIV) or unsigned (DIV) integers. The dividend is always a double-width dividend that is divided by the operand. This means that an 8-bit division divides a 16-bit number by an 8-bit number, a 16-bit division divides a 32-bit number by a 16-bit number, and a 32-bit division divides a 64-bit number by a 32-bit number. There is no immediate division instruction available to any 8086–80486 microprocessor.

None of the flag bits change predictably for a division. A division can result in two different types of errors. One of these is an attempt to divide by zero and the other is a divide overflow. A divide overflow occurs when a small number divides into a large number. For example, suppose that AX = 3,000 and that we divide it by 2. Because the quotient for an 8-bit division appears in AL, the result of 1,500 causes a divide overflow because the 1,500 does not fit into AL. In both cases the microprocessor generates an interrupt if a divide error occurs. The divide-error-interrupt and all other interrupts for the microprocessor are explained in Chapter 5.

8-Bit Division.   An 8-bit division uses the AX register to store the dividend that is divided by the contents of any 8-bit register or memory location. The quotient moves into AL after the division with AH containing a whole number remainder. For a signed division, the quotient is positive or negative, but the remainder is *always* a positive integer. For example, if AX = 0010H (+ 16) and BL = FDH (− 3) and the IDIV BL instruction executes, AX = 01FBH. This represents a quotient of − 5 (AL) with a remainder of 1 (AH). Table 4–11 lists some of the 8-bit division instructions.

With 8-bit division, the numbers are usually 8 bits wide. This means that one of them, the dividend, must be converted to a 16-bit wide number in AX. This is accomplished differently for signed and unsigned numbers. For the unsigned number, the most significant 8 bits must be cleared to zero (*zero-extended*). The MOVZX instruction described in Chapter 3 can be used to zero-extend a number in the 80386/80486 microprocessor. For the signed number, the least significant 8 bits are sign-extended into the most significant 8 bits. In the microprocessor a special instruction exists that sign-extends AL into AH, or converts an 8-bit signed number in AL into a 16-bit signed number in AX. The CBW

TABLE 4–11   8-bit division instructions

Instruction	Comment
DIV CL	AX is divided by CL; the unsigned quotient is in AL and the remainder is in AH
IDIV BL	AX is divided by BL; the signed quotient is in AL and the remainder is in AH
DIV BYTE PTR [BP]	AX is divided by the byte contents of the stack segment memory location addressed by BP; the unsigned quotient is in AL and the remainder is in AH

(*convert byte to word*) instruction performs this conversion. In the 80386/80486 microprocessor a MOVSX instruction (see Chapter 4) can sign-extend a number.

EXAMPLE 4–14

```
0000 A0 0000 R          MOV   AL,NUMB        ; get NUMB
0003 B4 00              MOV   AH,0           ; zero-extend
0005 F6 36 0002 R       DIV   NUMB1          ; divide by NUMB1
0009 A2 0003 R          MOV   ANSQ,AL        ; save quotient
000C 88 26 0004 R       MOV   ANSR,AH        ; save remainder
```

Example 4–14 illustrates a short program that divides the unsigned byte contents of memory location NUMB by the unsigned contents of memory location NUMB1. Here we store the quotient in location ANSQ and the remainder in location ANSR. Notice how the contents of location NUMB are retrieved from memory and then zero-extended to form a 16-bit unsigned number for the dividend.

EXAMPLE 4–15

```
0000 A0 0000 R          MOV   AL,NUMB        ; get NUMB
0003 98                 CBW                  ; sign-extend
0004 F6 3E 0002 R       IDIV  NUMB1          ; divide by NUMB1
0008 A2 0003 R          MOV   ANSQ,AL        ; save quotient
000B 88 26 0004 R       MOV   ANSR,AH        ; save remainder
```

Example 4–15 shows the same basic program except that the numbers are signed numbers. This means that instead of zero-extending AL into AH, we sign-extend it using the CBW instruction.

16-Bit Division. Sixteen-bit division is similar to 8-bit division except that instead of dividing into AX we divide into DX—AX, a 32-bit dividend. The quotient appears in AX and the remainder in DX after a 16-bit division. Table 4–12 lists some of the 16-bit division instructions.

As with 8-bit division, numbers must often be converted to the proper form for the dividend. If we start with a 16-bit unsigned number in AX, then DX must be cleared to 0. In the 80386/80486 the number is zero-extended using the MOVZX instruction. If AX is a 16-bit signed number, the CWD (*convert word to double word*) instruction

TABLE 4–12 16-bit division instructions

Instruction	Comment
DIV CX	DX—AX is divided by CX; the unsigned quotient is in AX and the remainder is in DX
IDIV SI	DX—AX is divided by SI; the signed quotient is in AX and the remainder is in DX
DIV NUMB	DX—AX is divided by the word contents of the data segment memory location NUMB; the unsigned quotient is in AX and the remainder is in DX

sign-extends it into a signed 32-bit number. If the 80386/80486 microprocessor is available, the MOVSX instruction can also be used to sign-extend a number.

EXAMPLE 4–16

```
0000 B8 FF9C              MOV   AX,-100            ; load-100
0003 B9 0009              MOV   CX,9               ; load+9
0006 99                   CWD                      ; sign-extend
0007 F7 F9                IDIV  CX
```

Example 4–16 shows the division of two 16-bit signed numbers. Here a –100 in AX is divided by a + 9 in CX. The CWD instruction converts the –100 in AX to a –100 in DX—AX before the division. After the division, the results appear in DX—AX as a quotient of –11 in AX and a remainder of 1 in DX.

32-Bit Division. The 80386/80486 microprocessor performs 32-bit division on signed or unsigned numbers. The 64-bit contents of EDX—EAX are divided by the operand specified by the instruction leaving a 32-bit quotient in EAX and a 32-bit remainder in EDX. Other than the size of the registers, this instruction functions in the same manner as the 8- and 16-bit divisions. Table 4–13 shows some example 32-bit division instructions. The convert double-word-to-quad word instruction (CDQ) is used before a signed division to convert the 32-bit contents of EAX into a 64-bit signed number in EDX—EAX.

The Remainder. What do we do with the remainder after a division? There are a few possible choices. We could use the remainder to round the result or we could drop the remainder to truncate the result. If the division is unsigned, rounding requires that remainder is compared with half the divisor to decide whether to round up the quotient. We could also convert the remainder to a fractional remainder.

EXAMPLE 4–17

```
0000 F6 F3               DIV  BL               ;divide
0002 02 E4               ADD  AH,AH            ;double remainder
0004 3A E3               CMP  AH,BL            ;test for rounding
```

TABLE 4–13   32-bit division instructions

Instruction	Comment
DIV ECX	EDX—EAX is divided by ECX; the unsigned quotient is in EAX and the remainder is in EDX
DIV DATA2	EDX—EAX is divided by the double-word contents of the data segment memory location DATA2; the unsigned quotient is in EAX and the remainder is in EDX
IDIV DWORD PTR [EDI]	EDX—EAX is divided by the double-word contents of the data segment memory location addressed by EDI; the signed quotient is in EAX and the remainder is in EDX

```
0006 72 02                    JB    NEXT
0008 FE C0                    INC   AL                        ;round
000A              NEXT:
```

Example 4–17 shows a sequence of instructions that divide AX by BL and round the result. This program doubles the remainder before comparing it with BL to decide whether or not to round the quotient. Here, an INC instruction rounds the contents of AL after the compare.

Suppose that we need a fractional remainder instead of an integer remainder. A fractional remainder is obtained by saving the quotient. Next the AL register is cleared to zero. The number remaining in AX is now divided by the original operand to generate a fractional remainder.

EXAMPLE 4–18

```
0000 B8 000D                  MOV   AX,13              ; load 13
0003 B3 02                    MOV   BL,2               ; load 2
0005 F6 F3                    DIV   BL                 ; 13/2
0007 A2 0003 R                MOV   ANSQ,AL            ; save quotient
000A B0 00                    MOV   AL,0               ; clear AL
000C F6 F3                    DIV   BL                 ; generate remainder
000E A2 0004 R                MOV   ANSR,AL            ; save remainder
```

Example 4–18 shows how a 13 is divided by a 2. The 8-bit quotient is saved in memory location ANSQ and then AL is cleared. Next the contents of AX are again divided by 2 to generate a fractional remainder. After the division, the AL register equals an 80H. This is a 10000000_2. If the binary point (radix) is placed before the leftmost bit of AL, we have a fractional remainder of 0.10000000_2 or 0.5 decimal. The remainder is saved in memory location ANSR in this example.

4–3   BCD AND ASCII ARITHMETIC

The 8086–80486 microprocessor allows arithmetic manipulation of both binary-coded decimal (BCD) and American Standard Code for Information Interchange (ASCII) data. This is accomplished by instructions that adjust the numbers for BCD and ASCII arithmetic.

The BCD operations occur in systems such as point-of-sales terminals (cash registers) and other systems that seldom require arithmetic. The ASCII operations are performed on ASCII data used by some programs. In most cases today, we rarely use BCD or ASCII arithmetic.

BCD Arithmetic

Two arithmetic techniques operate with BCD data: addition and subtraction. The instruction set provides two instructions that correct the result of a BCD addition and a BCD subtraction. The DAA (*decimal adjust after addition*) instruction follows BCD addition and DAS (*decimal adjust after subtraction*) follows BCD subtraction. Both instructions correct the result of the addition or subtraction so it is a BCD number.

For BCD data, the numbers always appear in the packed BCD form and are stored as two BCD digits per byte. The adjust instructions only function with the AL register after BCD addition and subtraction.

DAA Instruction.   The DAA instruction follows the ADD or ADC instruction to adjust the result into a BCD result. Suppose that DX and BX each contain 4-digit packed BCD numbers. Example 4–19 provides a short sample program that adds the BCD numbers in DX and BX and stores the result in CX.

EXAMPLE 4–19

```
0000 BA 1234        MOV   DX,1234H        ;load 1,234
0003 BB 3099        MOV   BB 3099H        ;load 3,099
0006 8A C3          MOV   AL,BL           ;sum BL with DL
0008 02 C2          ADD   AL,DL
000A 27             DAA                   ;adjust
000B 8A C8          MOV   CL,AL           ;answer to CL
000D 8A C7          MOV   AL,BH           ;sum BH with DH and CF
000F 12 C6          ADC   AL,DH
0011 27             DAA                   ;adjust
0012 8A E8          MOV   CH,AL           ;answer to CH
```

Because the DAA instruction only functions with the AL register, this addition must occur 8 bits at a time. After adding the BL and DL registers, the result is adjusted with a DAA instruction before being stored in CL. Next, we add BH and DH registers with carry and the result again is adjusted with DAA before being stored in CH. In this example, a 1,234 adds to a 3,099 to generate a sum of 4,333 that moves into CX after the addition. Note that 1234 BCD is the same as 1234H.

DAS Instruction.   The DAS instruction functions as does the DAA instruction except it follows a subtraction instead of an addition. Example 4–20 is basically the same as Example 4–19 except that it subtracts instead of adds DX and BX. The main difference in these programs is that the DAA instructions change to DAS and the ADD and ADC instructions change to SUB and SBB instructions.

EXAMPLE 4–20

```
0000 BA 1234        MOV   DX,1234H        ;load 1,234
0003 BB 3099        MOV   BX,3099H        ;load 3,099
0006 8A C3          MOV   AL,BL           ;subtract DL from BL
0008 2A C2          SUB   AL,DL
000A 2F             DAS                   ;adjust
000B 8A C8          MOV   CL,AL           ;answer to CL
000D 8A C7          MOV   AL,BH           ;subtract DH and CF from BH
000F 1A C6          SBB   AL,DH
0011 2F             DAS                   ;adjust
0012 8A E8          MOV   CH,AL           ;answer to CH
```

ASCII Arithmetic

The ASCII arithmetic instructions function with ASCII-coded numbers. These numbers range in value from 30H to 39H for the numbers 0–9. There are four instructions used with ASCII arithmetic operations: AAA (*ASCII adjust after addition*), AAD (*ASCII adjust before division*), AAM (*ASCII adjust after multiplication*), and AAS (*ASCII adjust after subtraction*). These instructions use register AX as the source and as the destination.

AAA Instruction. The addition of two 1-digit ASCII-coded numbers will not result in any useful data. For example, if we add a 31H and 39H, the result is a 6AH. This ASCII addition (1 + 9) should produce a 2-digit ASCII result equivalent to a 10 decimal, which is a 31H and a 30H in ASCII code. If we execute the AAA instruction after this addition, the AX register will contain a 0100H. Although this is not ASCII code, it can be converted to ASCII code by adding 3030H, which generates 3130H. The AAA instruction clears AH if the result is less than 10 and adds a 1 to AH if the result is greater than 10.

EXAMPLE 4–21

```
0000 B8 0031          MOV   AX,31H          ; load ASCII 1
0003 04 39            ADD   AL,39H          ; add ASCII 9
0005 37               AAA                   ; adjust
0006 05 3030          ADD   AX,3030H        ; answer to ASCII
```

Example 4–21 shows how this ASCII addition functions in the microprocessor. Please note that we clear AH before the addition by using the MOV AX,31H instruction. The operand of 0031H places a 00H in AH and a 31H into AL.

AAD Instruction. Unlike all the other adjust instructions, the AAD instruction appears before a division. The AAD instruction requires that the AX register contains a 2-digit unpacked BCD number (not ASCII) before executing. After adjusting the AX register with AAD, it is divided by an unpacked BCD number to generate a single-digit result in AL with any remainder in AH.

EXAMPLE 4–22

```
0000 B3 09            MOV   BL,9            ; load divisor
0002 B8 0702          MOV   AX,0702H        ; load dividend
0005 D5 0A            AAD                   ; adjust
0007 F6 F3            DIV   BL
```

Example 4–22 illustrates how a 72 in unpacked BCD is divided by 9 to produce a quotient of 8. The 0702H loaded into the AX register is adjusted by the AAD instruction to 0048H. Notice that this converts a 2-digit unpacked BCD number into a binary number so it can be divided with the binary division instruction (DIV). The AAD instruction converts the unpacked BCD numbers between 00 and 99 into binary.

AAM Instruction. The AAM instruction follows the multiplication instruction after multiplying two 1-digit unpacked BCD numbers. Example 4–23 shows a short program that multiplies a 5 times a 5. The result after the multiplication is 0018H in the AX register. After adjusting the result with the AAM instruction, AX contains a 0205H. This is an unpacked BCD result of 25. If 3030H adds to 0205H, this becomes an ASCII result of 3235H.

EXAMPLE 4–23

```
0000 B0 05                MOV    AL,5          ; load multiplicand
0002 B1 05                MOV    CL,5          ; load multiplier
0004 F6 E1                MUL    CL
0006 D4 0A                AAM                  ; adjust
```

One side benefit of the AAM instruction is that AAM will convert from binary to unpacked BCD. If a binary number between 0000H and 0063H appears in the AX register, the AAM instruction converts it to BCD. For example, if AX contains a 0060H before AAM, it will contain a 0906H after AAM executes. This is the unpacked BCD equivalent to a 96. If 3030H is added to 0906H, we have just changed the result to ASCII.

EXAMPLE 4–24

```
0000 33 D2                XOR    DX,DX         ; clear DX register
0002 B9 0064              MOV    CX,100        ; divide DX—AX by 100
0005 F7 F1                DIV    CX            ; AX=quotient DX=remainder
0007 D4 0A                AAM                  ; convert quotient to BCD
0009 05 3030              ADD    AX,3030H      ; convert to ASCII
000C 92                   XCHG   AX,DX         ; repeat for remainder
000D D4 0A                AAM
000F 05 3030              ADD    AX,3030H
```

Example 4–24 shows how the 16-bit binary contents of AX is converted to a 4-digit ASCII character string by using division and the AAM instruction. Note that this works for numbers between 0 and 9,999. First DX is cleared and then DX—AX is divided by a 100. For example, if AX = 245 after the division, AX = 2 and DX = 45. These separate halves are converted to BCD using AAM and then a 3030H is added to convert to ASCII code.

AAS Instruction.   Like other ASCII adjust instructions, AAS adjusts the AX register after an ASCII subtraction. For example, suppose that a 35H subtracts from a 39H. The result will be a 04H, which requires no correction. Here AAS will modify neither AH or AL. On the other hand, if 38H subtracts from 37H, then AL will equal 09H and the number in AH will decrement by 1. This decrement allows multiple-digit ASCII numbers to be subtracted from each other.

4–4   BASIC LOGIC INSTRUCTIONS

The basic logic instructions include AND, OR, Exclusive-OR, and NOT. Another logic instruction is TEST, which is explained in this section of the text because the operation of the TEST instruction is a special form of the AND instruction. Also explained is the NEG instruction, which is similar to the NOT instruction.

Logic operations provide binary bit control in *low-level software*. The logic instructions allow bits to be set, cleared, or complemented. Low-level software appears in machine language or assembly language form and often controls the I/O devices in a system. All logic instructions affect the flag bits. Logic operations always clear the carry and overflow flags, while the other flags change to reflect the condition of the result.

When binary data are manipulated in a register or a memory location, the rightmost bit position is always numbered bit 0. Bit position numbers increase from bit 0 toward the left to bit 7 for a byte and to bit 15 for a word. A double word (32 bits) uses bit position 31 as its leftmost bit.

AND

The AND operation performs logical multiplication as illustrated by the truth table in Figure 4–3. Here two bits, A and B, are ANDed to produce the result X. As indicated by the truth table, X is a logic 1 only when both A and B are logic 1's. For all other input combinations of A and B, X is a logic 0. It is important to remember that 0 AND anything is always 0 and 1 AND 1 is always a 1.

The AND instruction often replaces discrete AND gates if the speed required is not too great. With the 8086–80486 microprocessor, the AND instruction often executes in about a microsecond. So if the circuit that the AND instruction replaces operates at a slower speed than a microsecond, the AND instruction is a logical replacement. This replacement saves a considerable amount of money. A single AND gate integrated circuit (7408) costs approximately 40¢, while it costs less than 1/100¢ to store the AND instruction in a read-only memory.

The AND operation also clears bits of a binary number. The task of clearing a bit in a binary number is called **masking.** Figure 4–4 illustrates the process of masking. Notice that the leftmost four bits clear to 0, because 0 AND anything is 0. The bit positions ANDed with 1's do not change. This occurs because if a 1 ANDs with a 1, a 1 results, and if a 1 ANDs with a 0, a 0 results.

FIGURE 4–3 The truth table demonstrating the AND operation (logical multiplication).

A	·	B	=	X
0		0		0
0		1		0
1		0		0
1		1		1

FIGURE 4–4 Here a mask (0000 1111) is ANDed with an unknown number. Notice how the leftmost 4 bits are masked off (cleared) to 0.

	XXXX	XXXX	(Unknown pattern)
·	0000	1111	(Mask pattern)
	0000	XXXX	(Result)

The AND instruction uses any addressing mode except memory-to-memory and segment register addressing. Refer to Table 4–14 for a list of some AND instructions and a comment about their operation.

EXAMPLE 4–25

```
0000 BB 3135          MOV  BX,3135H          ; load ASCII
0003 81 E3 0F0F       AND  BX,0F0FH          ; mask BX
```

An ASCII coded number can be converted to BCD by using the AND instruction to mask off the leftmost 4 binary bit positions. This converts the ASCII 30H to 39H to 0–9. Example 4–25 shows a short program that converts the ASCII contents of BX into BCD. The AND instruction in this example converts 2 digits from ASCII to BCD simultaneously.

OR

The OR operation performs logical addition and is often called the *Inclusive-OR function.* The OR function generates a 1 out if any inputs are 1. A 0 appears at the output only when all inputs are 0. The truth table for the OR function appears in Figure 4–5. Here the inputs, A and B, OR together to produce the X output. It is important to remember that 1 ORed with anything yields a 1.

The OR instruction often replaces discrete OR gates. This results in a considerable savings, because a quad, 2-input OR gate (7432) costs about 40¢, while an OR instruction costs less than 1/100¢ to store in a read-only memory.

Figure 4–6 shows how the OR gate sets (1) any bit of a binary number. Here an unknown number (XXXX XXXX) ORs with a 0000 1111 to produce a result of XXXX

TABLE 4–14   AND Instruction

Instruction	Comment
AND AL,BL	AL = AL AND BL
AND CX,DX	CX = CX AND DX
AND ECX,EDI	ECX = ECX AND EDI
AND CL,33H	CL = CL AND 33H
AND DI,4FFFH	DI = DI AND 4FFFH
AND ESI,34H	ESI = ESI AND 00000034H
AND AX,[DI]	AX is ANDed with the word contents of the data segment memory location addressed by DI; the result moves into AX
AND ARRAY [SI],AL	The byte contents of the data segment memory location addressed by ARRAY plus SI is ANDed to AL; the result moves to memory
AND [EAX],CL	The byte contents of CL is ANDed with the byte contents of the data segment memory location addressed by register EAX; the result moves to memory

FIGURE 4-5 The truth table illustrating the OR operation (logical addition). Note that a + sign is used to indicate the OR operation.

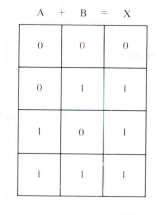

A	+	B	=	X
0		0		0
0		1		1
1		0		1
1		1		1

FIGURE 4-6 A test pattern (0000 1111) is ORed with an unknown number to illustrate how the OR operation is used to selectively set bits.

```
  XXXX   XXXX    (Unknown pattern)
+ 0000   1111    (Test pattern)
  XXXX   1111    (Result)
```

1111. The rightmost four bits set, while the leftmost four bits remain unchanged. The OR operation sets any bit and the AND operation clears any bit.

The OR instruction uses any of the addressing modes allowed to any other instruction except segment register addressing. Table 4–15 illustrates several example OR instructions with comments about their operation.

EXAMPLE 4-26

```
0000 B0 05              MOV   AL,5              ; load data
0002 B3 07              MOV   BL,7
0004 F6 E3              MUL   BL
```

TABLE 4-15 OR instructions

Instruction	Comment
OR AH,BL	AH = AH OR BL
OR SI,DX	SI = SI OR DX
OR EAX,EBX	EAX = EAX OR EBX
OR DH,0A3H	DH = DH OR 0A3H
OR SP,990DH	SP = SP OR 990DH
OR EBP,10	EBP = EBP OR 0000000AH
OR DX,[BX]	DX is ORed with the word contents of the data segment memory location addressed by BX
OR DATES [DI + 2],AL	The data segment memory location address by DATES plus DI plus 2 is ORed with AL

```
0006 D4 0A                    AAM                      ; adjust
0008 0D 3030                  OR    AX,3030H           ; to ASCII
```

Suppose we multiply two BCD numbers and adjust them with the AAM instruction. The result appears in AX as a 2-digit unpacked BCD number. Example 4–26 illustrates this multiplication and shows how to change the result into a 2-digit ASCII-coded number using the OR instruction. Here, OR AX,3030H converts the 0305H found in AX to 3335H. The OR operation can be replaced with an ADD AX,3030H to obtain the same results.

Exclusive-OR

The Exclusive-OR instruction (XOR) differs from Inclusive-OR (OR). The difference is that a 1,1 condition of the OR function produces a 1, while the 1,1 condition of the Exclusive-OR operation produces a 0. The Exclusive-OR operation excludes this condition, while the Inclusive-OR includes it.

Figure 4–7 shows the truth table of the Exclusive-OR function. (Compare this with Figure 4–5 to appreciate the difference between these two OR functions.) If the inputs of the Exclusive-OR function are both 0 or both 1, the output is 0. If the inputs are different, the output is a 1. Because of this, the Exclusive-OR is sometimes called a *comparator*.

The XOR instruction uses any addressing mode except segment register addressing. Table 4–16 lists various forms of the exclusive-OR instruction with comments about their operation.

As with the AND and OR functions, Exclusive-OR also replaces discrete logic circuitry. The 7486 quad, 2-input Exclusive-OR gate is replaced by one XOR instruction. The 7486 costs about 40¢, while the instruction costs less than 1/100¢ to store in the memory. Replacing just a single 7486 saves a considerable amount of money, especially if we build many systems.

The Exclusive-OR instruction is useful if some bits of a register or memory location must be inverted. This instruction allows part of a number to be inverted or complemented. Figure 4–8 shows how just part of an unknown quantity can be inverted by

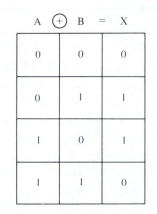

FIGURE 4–7   The truth table for the Exclusive-OR function. Notice that the % sign is used to indicate an Exlusive-OR operation.

TABLE 4-16 Exclusive-OR instructions

Instruction	Comment
XOR CH,DL	CH = CH XOR DL
XOR SI,BX	SI = SI XOR BX
XOR EBX,EDI	EBX = EBX XOR EDI
XOR CH,0EEH	CH = CH XOR 0EEH
XOR DI,00DDH	DI = DI XOR 00DDH
XOR ESI,100	ESI = ESI XOR 00000064H
XOR DX,[SI]	DX is XORed with the word contents of the data segment memory location addressed by SI; the result is left in DX
XOR DATES[DI + 2],AL	The byte contents of the data segment memory location addressed by DATES plus DI plus 2 are XORed with AL; the result is left in memory

FIGURE 4-8 A test pattern (0000 1111) Exclusive-ORed with an unknown quanitity produced inversion in the bit positions where the test pattern contains logic 1.

$$
\begin{array}{ll}
\text{XXXX} \quad \text{XXXX} & \text{(Unknown pattern)} \\
(+)\ 0000 \quad 1111 & \text{(Test pattern)} \\
\hline
\text{XXXX} \quad \overline{\text{XXXX}} & \text{(Result)}
\end{array}
$$

XOR. Notice that when a 1 Exclusive-ORs with X, the result is $\overline{X}$. If a 0 Exclusive-ORs with X, the result is X.

Suppose that the leftmost 10 bits of the BX register must be inverted without changing the rightmost 6 bits. The XOR BX,0FFC0H instruction accomplishes this task. The AND instruction clears (0) bits, the OR instruction sets (1) bits, and the Exclusive-OR instruction inverts bits. These three instructions allow a program to gain complete control over any bit, stored in any register or memory location. These logical operations are ideal for control system applications where equipment must be turned on (1), turned off (0), and toggled from on-to-off or off-to-on.

Test and Bit Test Instructions

The TEST instruction performs the AND operation. The difference is that the AND instruction changes the destination operand, while the TEST instruction does not. A TEST only affects the condition of the flag register, which indicates the result of the test. The TEST instruction uses the same addressing modes as the AND instruction. Table 4-17 illustrates some forms of the TEST instruction with comments about the operation of each form.

The TEST instruction functions in the same manner as a CMP instruction. The difference is that the TEST instruction normally tests a single bit, while the CMP instruction tests the entire byte or word. The zero flag (Z) is a logic 1 (indicating a zero result) if the bit under test is a zero, and Z = 0 (indicating a nonzero result) if the bit under test is not zero.

TABLE 4–17   TEST instructions

Instruction	Comment
TEST DL,DH	DL is ANDed with DH; neither DL nor DH change; only the flags change
TEST CX,BX	CX is ANDed with BX; neither CX nor BX change; only the flags change
TEST EDX,ECX	EDX is ANDed with ECX; neither EDX nor ECX change; only the flags change
TEST AH,4	AH is ANDed with 4; AH does not change; only the flags change
TEST EAX,256	EAX is ANDed with 256; EAX does not change; only the flags change

Usually the TEST instruction is followed by either the JZ (*jump zero*) or JNZ (*jump not zero*) instruction. The destination operand is normally tested against immediate data. The value of immediate data is 1, to test the rightmost bit position, 2 to test the next bit, 4 for the next and so on.

Example 4–27 lists a short program that tests the rightmost and leftmost bit positions of the AL register. Here, 1 selects the rightmost bit and 128 selects the leftmost bit. The JNZ instruction follows each test to jump to different memory locations depending on the outcome of the tests. The JNZ instruction jumps to the operand address (RIGHT or LEFT in the example) if the bit under test is not zero.

EXAMPLE 4–27

```
000   A8 01          TEST   AL,1          ;test right bit
0002  75 1C          JNZ    RIGHT         ;if set
0004  A8 80          TEST   AL,128        ;test left bit
0006  75 38          JNZ    LEFT          ;if set
```

The 80386/80486 microprocessors contain additional test instructions that test bit positions. Table 4–18 lists the four bit test instructions available to these microprocessors.

TABLE 4–18   Bit test instructions.

Instruction	Comment
BT	Test a bit in the destination operand specified by the source operand
BTC	Test and complement a bit in the destination operand specified by the source operand
BTR	Test and reset a bit in the destination operand specified by the source operand
BTS	Test and set a bit in the destination operand specified by the source operand

TABLE 4–19   NOT and NEG instructions

Instruction	Comment
NOT CH	CH is one's complemented
NEG CH	CH is two's complemented
NEG AX	AX is two's complemented
NOT EBX	EBX is one's complemented
NEG ECX	ECX is two's complemented
NOT TEMP	The contents of the data segment memory location addressed by TEMP are one's complemented. The size of TEMP is determined by how TEMP is defined
NOT BYTE PTR [BX]	The byte contents of the data segment memory location addresses by BX are one's complemented

All four forms of the bit test instruction test the bit position in the destination operand selected by the source-operand. For example, the BT AX,4 instruction tests bit position 4 in AX. The result of the test is located in the carry flag bit. If bit position 4 is a 1, carry is set, and if bit position 4 is a zero, carry is cleared.

The remaining three bit test instructions also place the bit under test into the carry flag, and afterwards, change the bit under test. The BTC AX,4 instruction complements bit position 4 after testing it, the BTR AX,4 instruction clears it (0) after the test, and the BTS AX,4 instruction sets it (1) after the test.

NOT and NEG

Logical inversion or *one's complement* (NOT) and arithmetic sign inversion or *two's complement* (NEG) are the last two logic functions presented except for shift and rotate in the next section of the text. These are two of the few instructions that contain only one operand. Table 4–19 lists some variations of the NOT and NEG instructions. As with most other instructions, NOT and NEG can use any addressing mode except segment register addressing.

The NOT instruction inverts all bits of a byte or word. The NEG instruction two's complements a number, which means that the arithmetic sign of a signed number changes from positive to negative or negative to positive. The NOT function is considered logical and the NEG function is considered an arithmetic operation.

4–5   SHIFTS AND ROTATES

Shift and rotate instructions manipulate binary numbers at the binary bit level, as did the AND, OR, Exclusive-OR, and NOT instructions. Shifts and rotates find their most common application in low-level software used to control I/O devices. The 8086–80486 microprocessor contains a complete set of shift and rotate instructions used to shift or rotate any memory data or register.

Shifts

Shift instructions position or move numbers to the left or right within a register or memory location. They also perform simple arithmetic such as multiplication by powers of 2^{+n} (*left shift*) and division by powers of 2^{-n} (*right shift*). The 80286 instruction set contains four different shift instructions: two are *logical shifts* and two are *arithmetic shifts*. All four shift operations appear in Figure 4–9.

Notice in Figure 4–9 there are two different right shifts and two different left shifts. The logical shifts move a 0 into the rightmost bit position for a logical left shift and a 0 into the leftmost bit position for a logical right shift. There are also two arithmetic shifts. The arithmetic and logical left shifts are identical. The arithmetic and logical right shifts are different because the arithmetic right shift copies the sign-bit through the number while the logical right shift copies a 0 through the number.

Logical shift operations function with unsigned numbers and arithmetic shifts function with signed numbers. Logical shifts multiply or divide unsigned data, and arithmetic shifts multiply or divide signed data. A shift left always multiplies by 2 for each bit position shifted, and a shift right always divides by 2 for each bit position shifted.

Table 4–20 illustrates some addressing modes allowed for the various shift instructions. There are two different forms of shifts that allow any register (except the

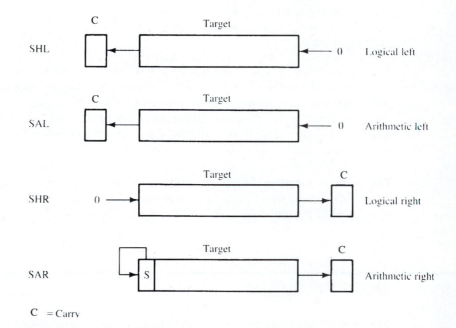

FIGURE 4–9 The four shift operations available in the 8086/8088 instruction set. Note that the target is any 8- or 16-bit register or memory location except the segment register.

TABLE 4–20 Shift instructions

Instruction	Comment
SHL AX,1	Logically shift AX left one place
SHR BX,12	Logically shift BX right 12 places
SHR ECX,10	Logically shift ECX right 10 places
SAL DATA1,CL	Arithmetically shift DATA1, in the data segment, left the number of places contained in CL
SAR SI,2	Arithmetically shift SI right 2 places
SAR EDX,14	Arithmetically shift EDX right 14 places

Note: The 8086/8088 microprocessor allows an immediate shift count of 1 only.

segment register) or memory location to be shifted. One mode uses an immediate shift count, and the other uses register CL to hold the shift count. Note that CL must hold the shift count. When CL is the shift count, it does not change when the shift instruction executes. Note that the shift count is a modulo-32 count. This means that a shift count of 33 will shift the data one place (33 / 32 = remainder of 1).

EXAMPLE 4–28

```
0000 C1 E2 0E                 SHL   DX,14

                        or

0003 B1 0E                    MOV   CL,14
0005 D3 E2                    SHL   DX,CL
```

Example 4–28 shows how the DX register shifts left 14 places in two different ways. The first method uses an immediate shift count of 14. The second method loads a 14 into CL and then uses CL as the shift count. Both instructions shift the contents of the DX register logically to the left 14 binary bit positions or places.

EXAMPLE 4–29

```
                  ;multiply AX by 10 (1010)
                  ;
0000 D1 E0                SHL   AX,1      ; AX times 2
0002 8B D8                MOV   BX,AX
0004 C1 E0 02             SHL   AX,2      ; AX times 8
0007 03 C3                ADD   AX,BX     ; 10 × AX
                  ;
                  ;multiply AX by 18 (10010)
                  ;
0009 D1 E0                SHL   AX,1      ; AX times 2
000B 8B D8                MOV   BX,AX
000D C1 E0 03             SHL   AX,3      ; AX times 16
0010 03 D8                ADD   BX,AX
```

Suppose that the contents of AX must be multiplied by 10, as in Example 4–29. This can be done in two ways: by the MUL instruction or by shifts and additions. A number is doubled when it shifts left one binary place. When a number is doubled, then added to the number times 8, the result is 10 times the number. The number 10 decimal is 1010 in binary. A logic 1 appears in both the 2's and 8's positions. If 2 times the number adds to 8 times the number, the result is 10 times the number. Using this technique, a program can be written to multiply by any constant. This technique often executes faster than the multiply instruction.

Double-Precision Shifts (80386/80486 Only).   The 80386/80486 contain two double-precision shifts SHLD (shift left) and SHRD (shift right). Each of these instructions contains 3 operands instead of the 2 found with the other shift instructions. Both instructions function with two 16- or 32-bit registers or with one 16- or 32-bit memory location and a register.

The SHRD AX,BX,12 instruction is an example of the double-precision shift right instruction. This instruction logically shifts AX right by 12-bit positions. The rightmost 12 bits of BX shift into the leftmost 12 bits of AX. The contents of BX remain unchanged by this instruction. The shift count can be an immediate count as in this example or can be found in register CL as with other shift instructions.

The SHLD EBX,ECX,16 instruction shifts EBX left. The leftmost 16 bits of ECX fill the rightmost 16 bits of EBX after the shift. As before, the contents of ECX, the second operand, remain unchanged. This instruction as well as SHRD affect the flag bits.

Rotates

Rotate instructions position binary data by rotating the information in a register or memory location either from one end to another or through the carry flag. They are often used to shift or position numbers that are wider than 16 bits in the 8086–80286 microprocessor or wider than 32 bits in the 80386/80486. The four rotate instructions available appear in Figure 4–10.

Numbers rotate through a register and a memory location and the C flag (carry) or through a register and memory location only. With either type of rotate instruction, the programmer can use either a left or a right rotate. Addressing modes used with rotate are the same as used with the shifts. A rotate count can be immediate or located in register CL. Table 4–21 lists some of the possible rotate instructions. If CL is used for a rotate count, it does not change. As with shifts, the count in CL is a modulo-32 count.

EXAMPLE 4–30

```
0000  D1 E0              SHL    AX,1
0002  D1 D3              RCL    BX,1
0004  D1 D2              RCL    DX,1
```

Rotates are often used to shift wide numbers to the left or right. The program listed in Example 4–30 shifts the 48-bit number in registers DX, BX, and AX left one binary place. Notice that the least significant 16 bits (AX) shift left first. This moves its leftmost bit of AX into the C flag bit. Next the rotate BX instruction rotates C into BX and its leftmost bit moves into C. The last instruction rotates C into DX and the shift is complete.

FIGURE 4–10 The four rotate operations available in the 8086/8088 instruction set. Note that both the RCL and RCR instructions have data rotated through C (carry) and ROL and ROR rotate data only through the target.

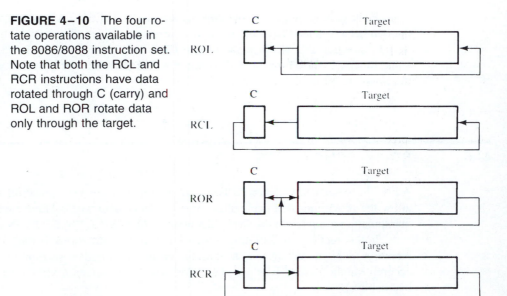

TABLE 4–21 Rotate instructions

Instruction	Comment
ROL SI,4	SI rotates left 4 places
RCL BL,6	BL rotates left through carry 6 places
ROL ECX,18	ECX rotates left 18 places
RCR AH,CL	AH rotates right through carry the number of places contained in CL
ROR WORD PTR [BP],2	The word contents of the stack segment memory location addressed by BP rotates right 2 places

Note: The 8086/8088 microprocessor can only use an immediate rotate count or 1.

Bit Scan Instructions

Although the bit scan instructions don't shift or rotate a number, they do scan through a number searching for a one bit. Because this is accomplished within the microprocessor by shifting the number, bit scan instructions are included in this section of the text.

The bit scan instructions BSF (bit scan forward) and BSR (bit scan reverse) are only available in the 80386/80486 microprocessor. Both forms scan through a number searching for the first 1-bit encountered. The BSF instruction scans the number from the rightmost bit toward the left, and BSR scans the number from the leftmost bit toward the right. If a 1-bit is encountered by either bit scan instruction, the zero flag is set and the bit position of the 1-bit is placed into the destination operand. If no 1-bit is encountered (i.e., the number contains all zeros), the zero flag is cleared. This means that the result is not-zero if no 1-bit is encountered.

For example, if EAX = 60000000H and the BSF EBX,EAX instruction executes, the number is scanned from the rightmost bit toward the left. The first 1-bit encountered is at bit position 29, which is placed into EBX and the zero flag bit is set. If the same value for EAX is used for the BSR instruction, the EBX register is loaded with a 30 and the zero flag bit is set.

4-6   STRING COMPARISONS

As we have seen in Chapter 3, the string instructions are very powerful because they allow the programmer to manipulate large blocks of data with relative ease. Block data manipulation occurs with the string instructions: MOVS, LODS, STOS, INS, and OUTS.

In this section, we will discuss additional string instructions that allow a section of memory to be tested against a constant or against another section of memory. To accomplish these tasks we use the SCAS (*string scan*) or CMPS (*string compare*) instructions.

SCAS

The string scan instruction (SCAS) compares the AL register with a byte block of memory, the AX register with a word block of memory, or the EAX register (80386/80486 only) with a double-word block of memory. The SCAS instruction subtracts memory from AL, AX, or EAX without affecting either the register or the memory location. The opcode used for byte comparison is *SCASB,* the opcode used for the word comparison is *SCASW,* and the opcode used for a double-word comparison is *SCASD.* In all cases the contents of the memory location addressed by DI, in the extra segment, is compared with AL, AX, or EAX. Recall that this default segment cannot be changed with a segment override prefix.

Like the other string instructions, SCAS instructions use the direction flag (D) to select either auto-increment or auto-decrement operation for DI. They also repeat if prefixed by a *conditional* repeat prefix.

EXAMPLE 4-31

```
0000 BF 0011 R          MOV    DI,OFFSET BLOCK   ; address data
0003 FC                 CLD                      ; auto-increment
0004 B9 0064            MOV    CX,100            ; load counter
0007 32 C0              XOR    AL,AL             ; clear AL
0009 F2/AE              REPNE  SCASB             ; search
```

Suppose a section of memory is 100 bytes in length and begins at location BLOCK. This section of memory must be tested to see if any location contains a 00H. The program in Example 4-31 shows how to search this part of memory for a 00H using the SCASB instruction. In this example, the SCASB instruction is prefixed with an REPNE (*repeat while not equal*). The REPNE prefix causes the SCASB instruction to repeat until *either* the CX register reaches 0, or until an equal condition exists as the outcome of the SCASB instruction's comparison. Another conditional repeat prefix is REPE (*repeat while equal*). With either repeat prefix, the contents of CX decrements without affecting the flag bits. The SCASB instruction changes the flags.

Suppose you must develop a program that skips ASCII-coded spaces in a memory array. This task appears in the procedure listed in Example 4–32. This procedure assumes that the DI register already addresses the ASCII coded character string, and that the length of the string is 256 bytes or less. Because this program is to skip spaces (20H), the REPE (repeat while equal) prefix is used with a SCASB instruction. The SCASB instruction repeats the comparison, searching for a 20H, as long as an equal condition exists.

EXAMPLE 4–32

```
0000                    SKIP    ·PROC   FAR

0000 FC                         CLD                 ; auto-increment
0001 B9 0100                    MOV     CX,256      ; counter
0004 B0 20                      MOV     AL,20H      ; get space
0006 F3/AE                      REPE SCASB          ; search
0008 CB                         RET

0009                    SKIP    ENDP
```

CMPS

The *compare strings* instruction (CMPS) always compares two sections of memory data as bytes (CMPSB), words (CMPSW), or double words (CMPSD). Note that only the 80386/80486 can use double words. The contents of the data segment location addressed by SI is compared with the contents of the extra segment location addressed by DI. The CMPS instruction increments or decrements both SI and DI. The CMPS instruction is normally used with either the REPE or REPNE prefix. Alternates to these prefixes are REPZ (repeat while zero) and REPNZ (repeat while not zero), but usually we use REPE or REPNE.

EXAMPLE 4–33

```
0000                    MATCH   PROC    FAR

0000 BE 0075 R                  MOV     SI,OFFSET LINE   ; address LINE
0003 BF 007F R                  MOV     DI,OFFSET TABLE  ; address TABLE
0006 FC                         CLD                      ; auto-increment
0007 B9 000A                    MOV     CX,10            ; counter
000A F3/A6                      REPE    CMPSB            ; search
000C CB                         RET

000D                    MATCH   ENDP
```

Example 4–33 illustrates a short procedure that compares two sections of memory searching for a match. The CMPSB instruction is prefixed with a REPE. This causes the search to continue as long as an equal condition exists. When the CX register becomes 0, or an unequal condition exists, the CMPSB instruction stops execution. If CX is zero or the flags indicate an equal condition, the two strings match. If CX is not zero or the flags indicate a not-equal condition, the strings do not match.

4–7   SUMMARY

1. Addition (ADD) can be 8-, 16-, or 32-bit. The ADD instruction allows any addressing mode except segment register addressing. All flags change when the ADD instruction executes. A different type of addition, add-with-carry (ADC), adds two operands and the contents of C. The 80486 microprocessor has an additional instruction (XADD) that combines addition with an exchange.

2. The increment instruction (INC) adds 1 to a byte, word, or double word of register or memory data. The INC instruction affects all the flag bits except the carry flag. The BYTE PTR, WORD PTR, and DWORD PTR directives appear with the INC instruction when the contents of a memory location are addressed by a pointer.

3. Subtraction (SUB) is a byte, word, or double word and is performed on a register or a memory location. The only form of addressing not allowed by the SUB instruction is segment register addressing. The subtract instruction affects all the flags and subtracts carry if the SBB form is used.

4. The decrement (DEC) instruction subtracts one from the contents of a register or a memory location. The only addressing modes not allowed with DEC are immediate or segment register addressing. The DEC instruction does not affect the carry flag and is often used with BYTE PTR, WORD PTR, or DWORD PTR.

5. The compare (CMP) instruction is a special form of subtraction that does not store the difference; instead the flags change to reflect the difference. Compare is used to compare an entire byte or word located in any register (except segment) or memory location. An additional compare instruction (CMPXCHG) is a combination of compare and exchange instructions in the 80486 microprocessor.

6. Multiplication is byte, word, or double word and can be signed (IMUL) or unsigned (MUL). The 8-bit multiplication always multiplies register AL by an operand with the product found in AX. The 16-bit multiplication always multiplies register AX by an operand with the product found in DX—AX. The 32-bit multiply always multiplies register EAX by an operand with the product found in EDX—EAX. A special IMUL immediate instruction exists on the 80286–80486 that contains three operands. For example, the IMUL BX,CX,3 instruction multiplies CX by 3 and leaves the product in BX.

7. Division is byte, word, or double word and can be signed (IDIV) or unsigned (DIV). For an 8-bit division, the AX register divides by the operand, after which the quotient appears in AL and remainder in AH. In the 16-bit division, the DX—AX register divides by the operand, after which the AX register contains the quotient and DX the remainder. In the 32-bit division, the EDX—EAX register is divided by the operand, after which the EAX register contains the quotient and the EDX register the remainder.

8. BCD data add or subtract in packed form by adjusting the result of the addition with DAA or the subtraction with DAS. ASCII data are added, subtracted, multiplied, or divided when the operations are adjusted with AAA, AAS, AAM, and AAD.

9. The AAM instruction has an interesting added feature that allows it to convert a binary number into unpacked BCD. This instruction converts a binary number between 00H–63H into unpacked BCD in AX.

10. The AND, OR, and Exclusive-OR instructions perform logic functions on a byte, word, or double word stored in a register or memory location. All flags change with these instructions with carry (C) and overflow (O) cleared.

11. The TEST instruction performs the AND operation, but the logical product is lost. This instruction changes the flag bits to indicate the outcome of the test.

12. The NOT and NEG instructions perform logical inversion and arithmetic inversion. The NOT instruction one's complements an operand and the NEG instruction two's complements an operand.

13. There are 8 different shift and rotate instructions. Each of these instructions shifts or rotates a byte, word, or double-word register or memory data. These instructions have two operands—the first is the location of the data shifted or rotated, and the second is an immediate shift or rotate count or CL. If the second operand is CL, the CL register holds the shift or rotate count. In the 80386/80486 microprocessor, two additional double-precision shift (SHRD and SHLD) instructions exist.

14. The scan string (SCAS) instruction compares AL, AX, or EAX with the contents of the extra segment memory location addressed by DI.

15. The string compare (CMPS) instruction compares the byte, word, or double-word contents of two sections of memory. One section is addressed by DI, in the extra segment, and the other by SI, in the data segment.

16. The SCAS and CMPS instructions repeat with the REPE or REPNE prefixes. The REPE prefix repeats the string instruction while an equal condition exists and the REPNE repeats the string instruction while a not-equal condition exists.

4–8   QUESTIONS AND PROBLEMS

1. Select an ADD instruction that will:
   (a) add BX to AX
   (b) add 12H to AL
   (c) add EDI and EBP
   (d) add 22H to CX
   (e) add the data addressed by SI to AL
   (f) add CX to the data stored at memory location FROG

2. What is wrong with the ADD ECX,AX instruction?

3. Is it possible to add CX to DS with the ADD instruction?

4. If AX = 1001H and DX = 20FFH, list the sum and the contents of each flag register bit after the ADD AX,DX instruction executes.

5. Develop a short sequence of instructions that adds AL, BL, CL, DL, and AH. Save the sum in the DH register.

6. Develop a short sequence of instructions that adds AX, BX, CX, DX, and SP. Save the sum in the DI register.

7. Develop a short sequence of instructions that adds ECX, EDX, and ESI. Save the sum in the EDI register.

8. Select an instruction that adds BX to DX and that also adds the contents of the carry flag (C) to the result.

9. Choose an instruction that adds a 1 to the contents of the SP register.
10. What is wrong with the INC [BX] instruction?
11. Select a SUB instruction that will:
    (a) subtract BX from CX
    (b) subtract 0EEH from DH
    (c) subtract DI from SI
    (d) subtract 3322H from EBP
    (e) subtract the data address by SI from CH
    (f) subtract the data stored 10 words after the location addressed by SI from DX
    (g) subtract AL from memory location FROG
12. If DL = 0F3H and BH = 72H, list the difference after BH subtracts from DL and show the contents of the flag register bits.
13. Write a short sequence of instructions that subtracts the numbers in DI, SI, and BP from the AX register. Store the difference in register BX.
14. Choose an instruction that subtracts 1 from register EBX.
15. Explain what the SBB [DI − 4],DX instruction accomplishes.
16. Explain the difference between a SUB and a CMP instruction.
17. When two 8-bit numbers multiply, in which register is the product found?
18. When two 16-bit numbers multiply, in which two registers is the product found? Show which register contains the most and least significant portions of the product.
19. When two numbers multiply, what happens to the O and C flag bits?
20. Where is the product stored for a MUL EDI instruction?
21. What is the difference between the IMUL and MUL instructions?
22. Write a sequence of instructions that will cube the 8-bit number found in DL, assuming DL contains a 5 initially. Make sure your result is a 16-bit number.
23. Describe the operation of the IMUL BX,DX,100H instruction.
24. When 8-bit numbers divide, in which register is the dividend found?
25. When two 16-bit numbers divide, in which register is the quotient found?
26. What type of errors are detected during division?
27. Explain the difference between the IDIV and DIV instructions.
28. Where is the remainder found after an 8-bit division?
29. Write a short sequence of instructions that will divide the number in BL by the number in CL and then multiply the result by 2. The final answer must be a 16-bit number stored in the DX register.
30. What instructions are used with BCD arithmetic operations?
31. What instructions are used with ASCII arithmetic operations?
32. Explain how the AAM instruction converts from binary to BCD.
33. Develop a sequence of instructions that adds the 8-digit BCD number in AX and BX to the 8-digit BCD number in CX and DX. (AX and CX are the most significant registers. The result must be found in CX and DX after the addition.)
34. Select an AND instruction that will:
    (a) AND BX with DX and save the result in BX
    (b) AND 0EAH with DH
    (c) AND DI with BP and save the result in DI
    (d) AND 1122H with EAX
    (e) AND the data addressed by BP with CX and save the result in memory

    (f) AND the data stored in four words before the location addressed by SI with DX and save the result in DX

    (g) AND AL with memory location WHAT and save the result at location WHAT

35. Develop a short sequence of instructions that will clear the three leftmost bits of DH without changing DH and store the result in BH.

36. Select an OR instruction that will:

    (a) OR BL with AH and save the result in AH

    (b) OR 88H with ECX

    (c) OR DX with SI and save the result in SI

    (d) OR 1122H with BP

    (e) OR the data addressed by BX with CX and save the result in memory

    (f) OR the data stored 40 bytes after the location addressed by BP with AL and save the result in AL

    (g) OR AH with memory location WHEN and save the result in WHEN

37. Develop a short sequence of instructions that will set the rightmost five bits of DI without changing DI. Save the result in SI.

38. Select the XOR instruction that will:

    (a) XOR BH with AH and save the result in AH

    (b) XOR 99H with CL

    (c) XOR DX with DI and save the result in DX

    (d) XOR 1A23H with ESP

    (e) XOR the data addressed by EBX with DX and save the result in memory

    (f) XOR the data stored 30 words after the location addressed by BP with DI and save the result in DI

    (g) XOR DI with memory location WELL and save the result in DI

39. Develop a sequence of instructions that will set the rightmost four bits of AX, clear the leftmost three bits of AX, and invert bits 7, 8, and 9 of AX.

40. Describe the difference between AND and TEST.

41. Select an instruction that tests bit position 2 of register CH.

42. What is the difference between a NOT and a NEG?

43. Select the correct instruction to perform each of the following tasks:

    (a) shift DI right 3 places with zeros moved into the leftmost bit

    (b) move all bits in AL left one place making sure that a 0 moves into the rightmost bit position

    (c) rotate all the bits of AL left 3 places

    (d) rotate carry right one place through EDX

    (e) move the DH register right one place making sure that the sign of the result is the same as the sign of the original number

44. What does the SCASB instruction accomplish?

45. For string instructions, DI always addresses data in the _____ segment.

46. What is the purpose of the D flag bit?

47. Explain what the REPE prefix does.

48. What condition or conditions will terminate the repeated string instruction REPNE SCASB?

49. Describe what the CMPSB instruction accomplishes.

50. Develop a sequence of instructions that will scan through a 300H byte section of memory called LIST searching for a 66H.

CHAPTER 5

Program Control Instructions

INTRODUCTION

The program control instructions direct the flow of a program and allow the flow of the program to change. A change in flow often occurs after decisions, made with the CMP or TEST instruction, are followed by a conditional jump instruction. This chapter explains the program control instructions including jumps, calls, returns, interrupts, and machine control instructions.

CHAPTER OBJECTIVES

1. Use both conditional and unconditional jump instructions to control the flow of a program.
2. Use the call and return instructions to include procedures in the program structure.
3. Explain the operation of the interrupts and interrupt control instructions.
4. Use machine control instructions to modify the flag bits.
5. Use ENTER and LEAVE to enter and leave programming structures.

5–1 THE JUMP GROUP

The main type of program control instruction, the jump (JMP), allows the programmer to skip sections of a program and branch to any part of the memory for the next instruction. A conditional jump instruction allows the programmer to make decisions based on numerical tests. The results of these numerical tests are held in the flag bits, which are then tested by conditional jump instructions. Another instruction similar to the conditional jump, the conditional set, is explained with the conditional jump instructions.

In this section of the text, we cover all jump instructions and illustrate their use with sample programs. We also revisit the LOOP and conditional LOOP instructions, first presented in Chapter 2, because they are also forms of the jump instruction.

Unconditional Jump (JMP)

Three types of unconditional jump instructions (refer to Figure 5–1) are available in the microprocessor's instruction set: short jump, near jump, and far jump. The **short jump** is a 2-byte instruction that allows jumps or branches to memory locations within +127 and −128 bytes from the memory location following the jump. The 3-byte **near jump** allows a branch or jump within ±32K bytes (anywhere) from the instruction in the current code segment. Finally, the 5-byte **far jump** allows a jump to any memory location within the entire memory system. The short and near jumps are often called *intrasegment jumps* and the far jumps are often called *intersegment jumps*.

In the 80386/80486 microprocessor, the near jump is within ±2G if the machine is operated in the protected mode and ±32K bytes if operated in the real mode. The protected mode 80386/80486 jump uses either an 8- or 32-bit displacement that is not shown in Figure 5–1. The 80386/80486 far jump allows a jump to any location within the 4G byte address range of these microprocessors.

Short Jump.   Short jumps are called *relative jumps* because they can be moved anywhere in current code segment without a change. This is because a jump address is *not* stored with the opcode. Instead of a jump address, a distance or *displacement* follows the opcode. The short jump displacement is a *distance* represented by a 1-byte signed number whose value ranges between +127 and −128. The short jump instruction appears in Figure 5–2. When the microprocessor executes a short jump, the displacement sign-extends and adds to the instruction pointer (IP/EIP) to generate the jump address within the current

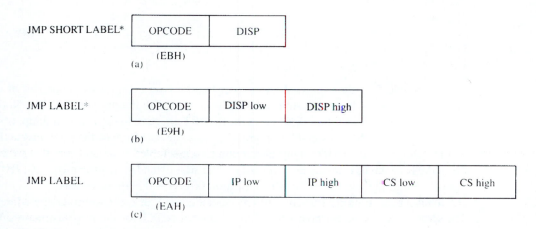

*Label in label field appears as LABEL:

FIGURE 5–1   The types of jump instruction. (a) short JMP (2 bytes), (b) near JMP (3 bytes), and (c) far JMP (5 bytes).

FIGURE 5–2 A short JMP to four memory locations beyond the address of the next instruction. (Note that this will skip the next 4 bytes of memory.)

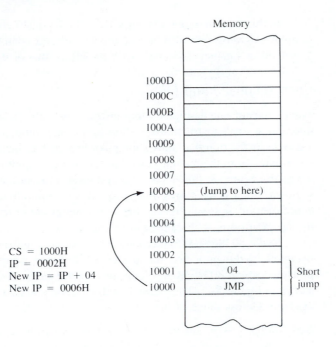

code segment. The short jump instruction branches to this new address for the next instruction in the program.

EXAMPLE 5–1

```
0000  33 DB                    XOR   BX,BX

0002  B8 0001       START:     MOV   AX,1
0005  03 C3                    ADD   AX,BX
0007  EB 17                    JMP   SHORT NEXT

0020  8B D8         NEXT:      MOV   BX,AX
0022  EB DE                    JMP   START
```

Example 5–1 shows how short jump instructions pass control from one part of the program to another. It also illustrates the use of a label with the jump instruction. Notice how one jump (JMP SHORT NEXT) uses the SHORT directive to force a short jump, while the other does not. Most assembler programs choose the best form of the jump instruction so the second (JMP START) jump instruction also assembles as a short jump. If we add the address of the next instruction (0009H) to the sign-extended displacement (0017H) of the first jump, the address of NEXT is location 0017H + 0009H or 0020H.

Whenever a jump instruction references an address, a *label* identifies the address. The JMP NEXT is an example which jumps to label NEXT for the next instruction. We never use an actual hexadecimal address with any jump instruction. The label NEXT must be followed by a colon (NEXT:) to allow an instruction to reference it for a jump. If a colon does not follow a label, you cannot jump to it. Note that the only time we ever use a colon after a label is when the label is used with a jump or call instruction.

Near Jump.   The near jump is similar to the short jump except the distance is farther. A near jump passes control to an instruction in the current code segment located within ±32K bytes from the near jump instruction or ±2G in the 80386/80486 operated in protected mode. The near jump is a 3-byte instruction that contains an opcode followed by a signed 16-bit displacement. In the 80386/80486 the displacement is 32 bits and the near jump is 5 bytes in length. The signed displacement adds to the instruction pointer (IP) to generate the jump address. Because the signed displacement is in the range of ±32K, a near jump can jump to *any* memory location within the current real mode code segment. The protected mode code segment in the 80386/80486 can be 4G bytes in length, so the 32-bit displacement allows a near jump to any location ±2G bytes. Figure 5–3 illustrates the operation of the real mode near jump instruction.

The near jump is also relocatable as was the short jump because it is also a *relative* jump. If the code segment moves to a new location in the memory, the distance between the jump instruction and the operand address remains the same. This allows a code segment to be relocated by moving it. This feature, with the relocatable data segments, makes the Intel family of microprocessors ideal for use in a general-purpose computer system. Software can be written and loaded anywhere in the memory and it functions without modification because of the relative jumps and relocatable data segments. This is true of very few other microprocessors.

EXAMPLE 5–2

```
0000 33 DB                    XOR   BX,BX

0002 B8 0001     START:       MOV   AX,1
0005 03 C3                    ADD   AX,BX
0007 E9 0200 R               JMP   NEXT

0200 8B D8       NEXT:        MOV   BX,AX
0202 E9 0002 R               JMP   START
```

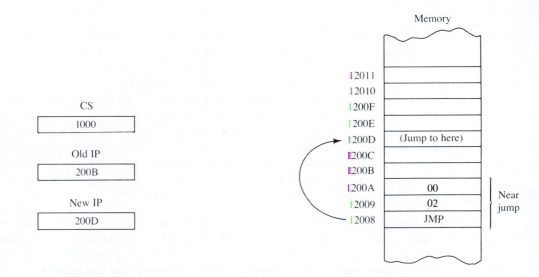

FIGURE 5–3   A near JMP that adds the displacement (0002H) to the contents of IP.

Example 5–2 shows the same basic program that appeared in Example 5–1, except the jump distance is greater. The first jump (JMP NEXT) passes control to the instruction at memory location 0200H within the code segment. Notice that the instruction assembles as an E9 0200 R. The letter R denotes the relocatable jump address of 0200H. The relocatable address of 0200H is for the assembler's internal use only. The actual machine language instruction assembles as an E9 F6 01, which *does not* appear in the assembler listing. The actual displacement is a 01F6H for this jump instruction. The assembler lists the actual jump address as 0200 R so the address is easier to interpret as we develop software. If we were to view the linked execution file in hexadecimal, we would see this jump has assembled as an E9 F6 01.

Far Jump.   Far jumps (see Figure 5–4) obtain a new segment and offset address to accomplish the jump. Bytes 2 and 3 of this 5-byte instruction contain the new offset address, and bytes 4 and 5 contain the new segment address. If the microprocessor (80286–80486) is operated in the protected mode, the segment address accesses a descriptor. The descriptor contains the base address of the far jump segment and the offset address, which is either 16 or 32 bits, contains the offset location within the new code segment.

EXAMPLE 5–3

```
                              EXTRN   UP:FAR

0000  33 DB               XOR     BX,BX

0002  B8 0001    START:   MOV     AX,1
0005  03 C3               ADD     AX,BX
0007  E9 0200 R           JMP     NEXT

0200  8B D8      NEXT:    MOV     BX,AX
0202  EA 0002--R          JMP     FAR PTR START

0207  EA 0000--E          JMP     UP
```

Example 5–3 lists a short program that uses a far jump instruction. The far jump instruction sometimes appears with the FAR PTR directive as illustrated. Another way to obtain a far jump is to define a label as a far label. A label is far only if it is external to the current code segment. The JMP UP instruction in the example references a far label. The label UP is defined as a far label by the EXTRN UP:FAR directive. External labels appear in programs that contain more than one program file.

When the program files are joined, the linker inserts the address for the UP label into the JMP UP instruction. It also inserts the segment address in the JMP START instruction. The segment address in JMP FAR PTR START is listed as—*R* for relocatable, and the segment address in JMP UP is listed as—*E* for external. In both cases, the—is filled in by the linker when it links or joins the program files.

Jumps with Register Operands.   The jump instruction also can specify a 16- or 32-bit register as an operand. This automatically sets up the instruction as an indirect jump. The address of the jump is in the register specified by the jump instruction. Unlike the displacement associated with the near jump, the contents of the register are transferred directly into the instruction pointer. It does not add to the instruction pointer as with the short and near jumps. The JMP AX instruction, for example, copies the contents of the

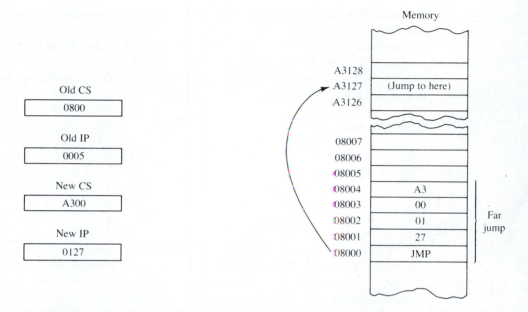

FIGURE 5-4 A far JMP that replaces the contents of both the CS and IP registers with the 4 bytes that follow the opcode.

AX register into the IP when the jump occurs. This allows a jump to any location within the current code segment. In the 80386/80486 a JMP EAX instruction also jumps to any location within the current code segment; the difference is that in protected mode the code segment can be 4G bytes in length, so a 32-bit offset address is needed.

EXAMPLE 5-4

```
0000 03 F6                    ADD   SI,SI              ;double SI
0002 81 C6 000B R             ADD   SI,OFFSET TABLE    ;add TABLE address
0006 2E: 8B 04                MOV   AX,CS:[SI]         ;get jump address
0009 FF E0                    JMP   AX

000B 1000 R        TABLE:     DW    ZERO
000D 2000 R                   DW    ONE
000F 3000 R                   DW    TWO
```

Example 5-4 shows how the JMP AX instruction accesses a jump table. This sequence of instructions assumes that SI contains a 0, 1, or 2. Because the jump table contains 16-bit offset addresses, the contents of SI double to 0, 2, or 4 so a 16-bit entry in the table can be accessed. Next the offset address of the start of the jump table adds to SI to reference a jump address. The MOV AX,CS:[SI] instruction fetches an address from the code segment jump table so the JMP AX instruction jumps to the location in the jump table.

This example fetches address ZERO if a 0 appears in SI. Once the address is fetched, the JMP AX instruction causes the program to branch to address ZERO. The same is true for an initial value of 1 and 2 in the SI register. These numbers access addresses ONE and TWO for their branch locations.

Indirect Jumps Using an Index.   The jump instruction also may use the [ ] form of addressing to directly access the jump table. The jump table can contain offset addresses for near indirect jumps or segment and offset addresses for far indirect jumps. The assembler assumes that the jump is near unless the FAR PTR directive indicates a far jump instruction. Here we repeat Example 5–4 in Example 5–5 using the JMP CS:[SI] instead of JMP AX. This reduces the length of the program.

EXAMPLE 5–5

```
0000 03 F6                        ADD   SI,SI              ;double SI
0002 81 C6 0009 R                 ADD   SI,OFFSET TABLE    ;add TABLE address
0006 2E: FF 24                    JMP   CS:[SI]

0009 1000 R           TABLE:      DW    ZERO
000B 2000 R                       DW    ONE
000D 3000 R                       DW    TWO
```

The mechanism used to access the jump table is identical with a normal memory reference. The JMP CS:[SI] instruction points to a jump address stored at code segment memory location addressed by SI. It jumps to the address stored in the memory at this location. Both the register and indirect index jump instructions usually address a 16-bit offset. This means that both types of jumps are near jumps. If a JMP FAR PTR [SI] instruction executes, the microprocessor assumes that the jump table contains double-word 32-bit addresses (IP and CS).

Conditional Jumps and Conditional Sets

Conditional jumps are always *short jumps* in the 8086–80286 microprocessors. This limits the range of the jump to within +127 bytes and −128 bytes from the location following the conditional jump. In the 80386/80486 conditional jumps are either short or near jumps. This allows a conditional jump to any location within the current code segment in the 80386/80486 microprocessor. Table 5–1 lists all the conditional jump instructions with their test conditions.

The conditional jump instructions test the following flag bits: sign (S), zero (Z), carry (C), parity (P), and overflow (O). If the condition under test is true, a branch to the label associated with the jump instruction occurs. If the condition is false, the next sequential step in the program executes.

The operation of most conditional jump instructions is straightforward because they often test just one flag bit, but some test more than one flag. Relative magnitude comparisons require more complicated conditional jump instructions that test more than one flag bit.

Because we use both signed and unsigned numbers, and the order of these numbers is different, there are two sets of magnitude comparison conditional jump instructions. Figure 5–5 shows the order of both signed and unsigned 8-bit numbers. The 16- and 32-bit numbers followed the same order as the 8-bit numbers except they are larger. Notice that an FFH is above the 00H in the set of unsigned numbers, but an FFH (−1) is less than 00H for signed numbers. Therefore, an unsigned FFH is *above* 00H, but a signed FFH is *less than* 00H.

[handwritten notes at top: "CMP A,B / A-B", "unsigned   C=1 then A<B", "signed   O=1 / S=?"]

TABLE 5-1 Conditional jump instructions

Instruction	Condition Tested	Comment
JA	C = 0 and Z = 0	Jump above
JAE	C = 0	Jump above or equal to
JB	C = 1	Jump below
JBE	C = 1 or Z = 1	Jump below or equal to
JC	C = 1	Jump carry set
JE or JZ	Z = 1	Jump equal to or jump zero
JG	Z = 0 and S = O	Jump greater than
JGE	S = O	Jump greater than or equal to
JL	S ≠ O	Jump less than
JLE	Z = 1 or S ≠ O	Jump less than or equal to
JNC	C = 0	Jump carry cleared
JNE or JNZ	Z = 0	Jump not equal to or jump not zero
JNO	O = 0	Jump no overflow
JNS	S = 0	Jump no sign
JNP/JPO	P = 0	Jump no parity/jump parity odd
JO	O = 1	Jump on overflow
JP/JPE	P = 1	Jump on parity/jump parity even
JS	S = 1	Jump on sign
JCXZ	CX = 0	Jump if CX = 0
JECXZ	ECX = 0	Jump if ECX = 0 (80386/80486 only)

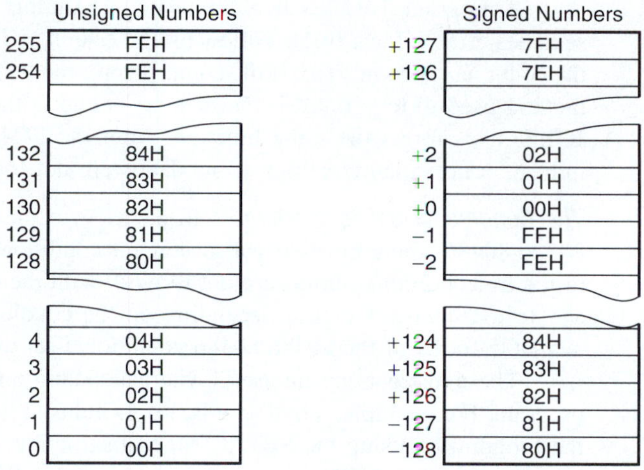

FIGURE 5-5 Signed and unsigned numbers follow different orders.

Unsigned Numbers		Signed Numbers	
255	FFH	+127	7FH
254	FEH	+126	7EH
132	84H	+2	02H
131	83H	+1	01H
130	82H	+0	00H
129	81H	−1	FFH
128	80H	−2	FEH
4	04H	+124	84H
3	03H	+125	83H
2	02H	+126	82H
1	01H	−127	81H
0	00H	−128	80H

When we compare signed numbers, we use JG, JE, JGE, JLE, JE, and JNE. The terms greater than and less than refer to signed numbers. When we compare unsigned numbers, we use JA, JB, JAE, JBE, JE, and JNE. The terms above and below refer to unsigned numbers.

The remaining conditional jumps test individual flag bits such as overflow and parity. Notice that JE has an alternative opcode JZ. All instructions have alternates, but many aren't used in programming because they don't make much sense. (The alternates appear in Appendix B with the instruction set listing.) For example, the JA instruction (jump above) has the alternative JNBE (jump not below or equal). A JA functions exactly as a JNBE, but JNBE sounds and is awkward when compared to JA.

The most radical of the conditional jump instructions are JCXZ (jump if CX = 0) and JECXZ (jump if ECX = 0). These are the only conditional jump instructions that do not test the flag bits. Instead, JCXZ directly tests the contents of the CX register without affecting the flag bits and JECXZ tests the contents of the ECX register. If CX = 0, a jump occurs, and if CX ≠ 0, no jump occurs. Likewise for the JECXZ instruction, if ECX = 0, a jump occurs and if CX ≠ 0, no jump occurs.

EXAMPLE 5–6

```
                          ;procedure that searches a table of 100 bytes
                          ;for a OAH
                          ;
0000                      SCAN      PROC    NEAR

0000 BE 0000 R                      MOV     SI,OFFSET TABLE        ;address TABLE
0003 B9 0064                        MOV     CX,100                 ;load count
0006 B0 0A                          MOV     AL,0AH                 ;load search data
0008 FC                             CLD
0009 F2/AE                          REPNE   SCASB
000B E3 23                          JCXZ    NOT_FOUND
000D C3                             RET

000E                      SCAN      ENDP
```

A program that uses JCXZ appears in Example 5–6. Here the SCASB instruction searches a table for a 0AH. Following the search, a JCXZ instruction tests CX to see if the count has become zero. If the count is zero, the 0AH is not found in the table. Another method used to test to see if the data are found is the JNE instruction. If JNE replaces JCXZ, it performs the same function. After the SCASB instruction executes, the flags indicate a not-equal condition if the data were not found in the table.

The Conditional Set Instructions.   In addition to the conditional jump instructions, the 80386/80486 microprocessors also contain conditional set instructions. The conditions tested by conditional jumps are put to work with the conditional set instructions that set a byte to either a 1 or a 0 depending on the condition under test. Table 5–2 lists the available forms of the 80386/80486 conditional set instructions.

These instructions are useful where a condition must be tested at a point later in the program. For example, a byte can be set to indicate that the carry is cleared at a point in the program by using the SETNC MEM instruction. This instruction places a 01H into memory location MEM if carry is cleared and a 00H into MEM if carry is set. The

TABLE 5-2 The conditional set instructions

Instruction	Condition Tested	Comment
SETB	C = 1	Set byte if below
SETAE	C = 0	Set byte if above or equal
SETBE	C = 1 or Z = 1	Set byte if below or equal
SETA	C = 0 and Z = 0	Set byte if above
SETE/SETZ	Z = 1	Set byte if equal/set byte if zero
SETNE/SETNZ	Z = 0	Set byte if not equal/set byte if not zero
SETL	S ≠ O	Set byte if less than
SETLE	Z = 1 or S ≠ O	Set byte if less than or equal
SETG	Z = 0 and S = O	Set byte if greater than
SETGE	S = O	Set byte if greater than or equal
SETS	S = 1	Set byte if sign (negative)
SETNS	S = 0	Set byte if no sign (positive)
SETC	C = 1	Set byte if carry
SETNC	C = 0	Set byte if no carry
SETO	O = 1	Set byte if overflow
SETNO	O = 0	Set byte if no overflow
SETP	P = 1	Set byte if parity (even)
SETNP	P = 0	Set byte if no parity (odd)

contents of MEM can be tested at any point later in the program to determine if carry is cleared at the point where the SETNC MEM instruction executed.

LOOP

The LOOP instruction is a combination of a decrement CX and a conditional jump. In the 8086–80286, LOOP decrements CX and if CX ≠ 0, it jumps to the address indicated by the label. If CX becomes a 0, the next sequential instruction executes. In the 80386/80486, LOOP decrements either CX or ECX depending on the instruction mode. If the 80386/80486 is operated in the 16-bit instruction mode, LOOP uses CX and if operated in the 32-bit instruction mode, LOOP uses ECX. This can be changed by the LOOPW (using CX) and LOOPD (using ECX) instructions in the 80386/80486 only.

EXAMPLE 5-7

```
                    ;procedure that adds word in BLOCK1 and BLOCK2
                    ;
0000                ADDS      PROC NEAR

0000 B9 0064                  MOV   CX,100          ;load count
0003 BE 0064 R                MOV   SI,OFFSET BLOCK1 ;address BLOCK1
0006 BF 0000 R                MOV   DI,OFFSET BLOCK2 ;address BLOCK2
```

```
0009                    AGAIN:
0009 AD                              LODSW              ;get BLOCK1 data
000A 26: 03 05                       ADD  AX,ES:[DI]    ;add BLOCK2 data
000D AB                              STOSW              ;store in BLOCK2
000E E2 F9                           LOOP AGAIN         ;repeat 100 times
0010 C3                              RET

0011            ADDS    ENDP
```

Example 5–7 shows how data in one block of memory (BLOCK1) adds to data in a second block of memory (BLOCK2) using LOOP to control how many numbers add. The LODSW and STOSW instructions access the data in BLOCK1 and BLOCK2. The ADD AX,ES:[DI] instruction accesses the data in BLOCK2 located in the extra segment. The only reason that BLOCK2 is in the extra segment is that DI addresses extra segment data for the STOSW instruction.

Conditional LOOPs. As with REP, the LOOP instruction also has conditional forms: LOOPE and LOOPNE. The LOOPE (loop while equal) instruction jumps if $CX \neq 0$ while an equal condition exists. It will exit the loop if the condition is not equal or if the CX register decrements to 0. The LOOPNE (loop while not equal) instruction jumps if $CX \neq 0$ while a not-equal condition exists. It will exit the loop if the condition is equal or if the CX register decrements to 0. In the 80386/80486 the conditional LOOP instruction can use either CX or ECX as the counter. The LOOPEW or LOOPED or LOOPNEW or LOOPNED override the instruction mode if needed.

As with the conditional repeat instructions, alternates exist for LOOPE and LOOPNE. The LOOPE instruction is the same as LOOPZ and the LOOPNE is the same as LOOPNZ. In most programs only the LOOPE and LOOPNE apply.

5–2   PROCEDURES

The procedure or *subroutine* is an important part of any computer system's architecture. A **procedure** is a group of instructions that usually performs one task. A procedure is a reusable section of the software that is stored in memory once, but used as often as necessary. This saves memory space and makes it easier to develop software. The only disadvantage of a procedure is that it takes the computer a small amount of time to link to the procedure and return from it. The CALL instruction links to the procedure and the RET instruction returns from the procedure.

The stack stores the return address whenever a procedure is called during the execution of a program. The CALL instruction pushes the address of the instruction following it on the stack. The RET instruction removes an address from the stack so the program returns to the instruction following the CALL.

EXAMPLE 5–8

```
0000                    SUMS    PROC    NEAR

0000 03 C3                      ADD     AX,BX
```

```
0002 03 C1                    ADD     AX,CX
0004 03 C2                    ADD     AX,DX
0006 C3                       RET

0007              SUMS        ENDP

0007              SUMS1       PROC    FAR

0007 03 C3                    ADD     AX,BX
0009 03 C1                    ADD     AX,CX
000B 03 C2                    ADD     AX,DX
000D CB                       RET

000E             SUMS1        ENDP
```

With the assembler, there are some finite rules for the storage of procedures. A procedure begins with the PROC directive and ends with the ENDP directive. Each directive appears with the name of the procedure. This structure makes it easy to locate the procedure in a program listing. The PROC directive is followed by the type of procedure: NEAR or FAR. Example 5–8 shows how the assembler requires the definition of both a near (intrasegment) and far (intersegment) procedure. In MASM version 6.0, the NEAR or FAR type can be followed by the USES statement. The USES statement allows any number of registers to be automatically pushed to the stack and popped from the stack within the procedure.

When we compare these two procedures, the only difference is the opcode of the return instruction. The near return instruction uses opcode C3H and the far return uses opcode CBH. A near return removes a 16-bit number from the stack and places it into the instruction pointer to return from the procedure in the current code segment. A far return removes 32 bits from the stack and places it into both IP and CS to return from the procedure to any memory location.

Most procedures that are to be used by all software (*global*) should be written as far procedures. Procedures that are used by a given task (*local*) are normally defined as near procedures.

CALL

The CALL instruction transfers the flow of the program to the procedure. The CALL instruction differs from the jump instruction because a CALL saves a return address on the stack. The return address returns control to the instruction that follows the CALL in a program when a RET instruction executes.

Near CALL.   The near CALL instruction is 3 bytes long with the first byte containing the opcode and the second and third bytes containing the displacement or distance of ±32K in the 8086–80286. This is identical to the form of the near jump instruction. The 80386/80486 uses a 32-bit displacement when operated in the protected mode to allow a distance of ±2G bytes. When the near CALL executes, it first places the offset address of the next instruction on the stack. The offset address of the next instruction appears in the instruction pointer (IP or EIP). After saving this return address, it then adds the displacement from bytes 2 and 3 to the IP to transfer control to the procedure. There is no short CALL instruction.

Why save the IP or EIP on the stack? The instruction pointer always points to the next instruction in the program. For the CALL instruction, the contents of IP/EIP are pushed onto the stack so program control passes to the instruction following the CALL after a procedure ends. Figure 5–6 shows the return address (IP) stored on the stack, and the call to the procedure for the 8086–80286.

Far CALL.   The far CALL instruction is like a far jump because it can CALL a procedure stored in any memory location in the system. The far CALL is a 5-byte instruction that contains an opcode followed by the next value for the IP and CS registers. Bytes 2 and 3 contain the new contents of the IP and bytes 4 and 5 contain the new contents for CS.

The far CALL instruction places the contents of both IP and CS on the stack before jumping to the address indicated by bytes 2–5 of the instruction. This allows the far CALL to call a procedure located anywhere in the memory and return from that procedure.

Figure 5–7 shows how the far CALL instruction calls a far procedure. Here the contents of IP and CS are pushed onto the stack. Next the program branches to the procedure.

CALLs with Register Operands.   Like jumps, CALLs also may contain a register operand. An example is the CALL BX instruction. This instruction pushes the contents of IP onto the stack. It then jumps to the offset address, located in register BX, in the current code

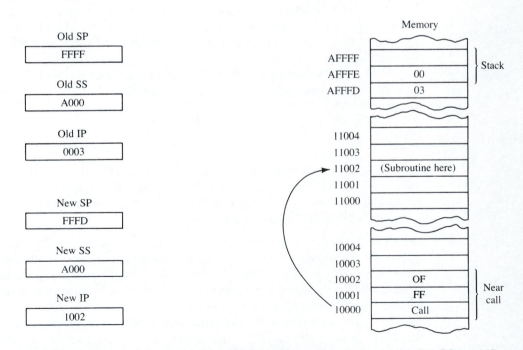

FIGURE 5–6 The effect of a near call instruction on the stack and the SP, SS, and IP registers. Notice how the old IP is stored on the stack.

FIGURE 5-7 The far CALL instruction.

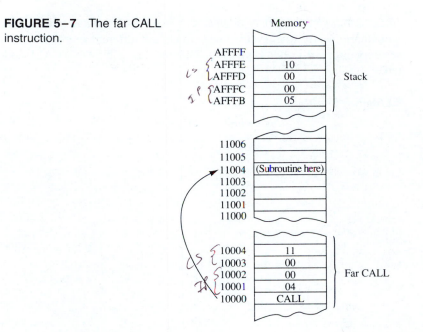

segment. This type of CALL always uses a 16-bit offset address stored in any 16-bit register except the segment registers.

EXAMPLE 5-9

```
                        ;calling sequence
                        ;
0000 BE 0005 R                    MOV   SI,OFFSET COMP
0003 FF D6                        CALL  SI


                        ;
                        ;procedure  COMP
                        ;
0005                    COMP       PROC NEAR


0005 52                           PUSH DX
0006 BA 03F8                      MOV  DX,03F8H
0009 EC                           IN   AL,DX
000A 42                           INC  DX
000B EE                           OUT  DX,AL
000C 5A                           POP  DX
000D C3                           RET

000E                    COMP       ENDP
```

Example 5-9 illustrates the use of the CALL register instruction to call a procedure that begins at offset address COMP. The OFFSET address COMP moves into the SI register and then the CALL SI instruction calls the procedure beginning at address COMP.

CALLs with Indirect Memory Addresses.   The CALL with an indirect memory address is particularly useful whenever we need to choose different subroutines in a program. This selection process is often keyed with a number that addresses a CALL address in a lookup table.

EXAMPLE 5–10

```
                            ;lookup table
                            ;
0000 0100 R                 TABLE      DW    ONE
0002 0200 R                            DW    TWO
0004 0300 R                            DW    THREE
                            ;
                            ;calling sequence
                            ;
0006 4B                                DEC   BX              ;scale BX
0007 03 DB                             ADD   BX,BX           ;double BX
0009 BF 0000 R                         MOV   DI,OFFSET TABLE ;address TABLE
000C 2E: FF 11                         CALL  CS:[BX+DI]
                            ;
                            ;procedures
                            ;
0100                        ONE        PROC  NEAR
                                        .          .
                                        .          .
0100                        ONE        ENDP

0200                        TWO        PROC  NEAR
                                        .          .
                                        .          .
0200                        TWO        ENDP

0300                        THREE      PROC  NEAR
                                        .          .
                                        .          .
0300                        THREE      ENDP
```

Example 5–10 shows three separate subroutines referenced by the numbers 1, 2, and 3 in AL. The calling sequence adjusts the value of AL and extends it to a 16-bit number before adding it to the location of the lookup table. This references one of the three subroutines using the CALL CS:[BX + DI] instruction. The CS: prefix appears before the CALL instruction's operand because the TABLE is in the code segment in this example.

The CALL instruction also can reference far pointers if the instruction appears as a CALL FAR PTR [SI]. This instruction retrieves a 32-bit address from the data segment memory location addressed by SI and uses it as the address of a far procedure.

RET

The return instruction (RET) removes either a 16-bit number (near return) from the stack and places it into IP or a 32-bit number (far return) and places it into IP and CS. The near and far return instructions are both defined in the procedure's PROC directive. This automatically selects the proper return instruction. In the 80386/80486 operated in the protected mode the far return removes 6 bytes from the stack; the first four contain the new value for EIP and the last two contain the new value for CS. The 80386/80486 protected mode near return removes 4 bytes from the stack and places them into EIP.

When IP/EIP or IP/EIP and CS are changed, the address of the next instruction is at a new memory location. This new location is the address of the instruction that immediately follows the most recent CALL to a procedure. Figure 5−8 shows how the CALL instruction links to a procedure and how the RET instruction returns in the 8086−80286 microprocessor.

There is one other form of the return instruction. This form adds a number to the contents of the stack pointer (SP) before the return. If the pushes must be deleted before a return, a 16-bit displacement adds to the SP before the return retrieves the return address from the stack. The effect of this is to delete stack data or skip stack data.

EXAMPLE 5−11

```
0000                        TESTS   PROC NEAR

0000 50                             PUSH AX
0001 53                             PUSH BX
                                      .     .
                                      .     .
                                      .     .
0030 C2 0004                        RET   4

0033                        TESTS   ENDP
```

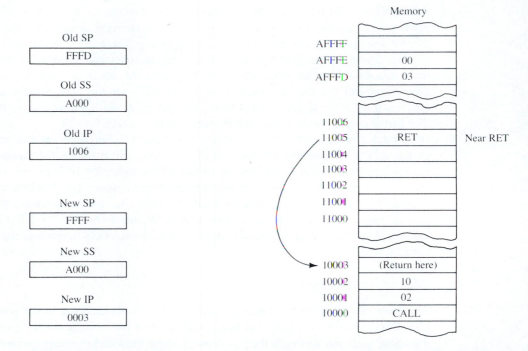

FIGURE 5−8 The effect of a near RET instruction on the stack and the SP, SS, and IP registers.

Example 5–11 shows how this type of return erases the data placed on the stack by a few pushes. The RET 4 adds a 4 to SP before removing the return address from the stack. Since the PUSH AX and PUSH BX together place 4 bytes of data on the stack, this return effectively deletes AX and BX from the stack. This type of return rarely appears in programs.

5–3   INTRODUCTION TO INTERRUPTS

An **interrupt** is either a hardware-generated CALL (externally derived from a hardware signal) or a software-generated CALL (internally derived from an instruction). Either will interrupt the program by calling an *interrupt service procedure* or *interrupt handler.*

This section explains software interrupts, which are special types of CALL instructions in the 8086–80486 microprocessor. We cover the three types of software interrupt instructions (INT, INTO, and INT 3), provide a map of the interrupt vectors, and explain the purpose of the special interrupt return instruction (IRET).

Interrupt Vectors

An **interrupt vector** is a 4-byte number stored in the first 1,024 bytes of the memory (000000H–0003FFH) when the microprocessor operates in the real mode. In the protected mode, the vector table is replaced by an interrupt descriptor table that uses 8-byte descriptors to describe each of the interrupts. There are 256 different interrupt vectors. Each vector contains the address of an interrupt service procedure—the procedure called by an interrupt. Table 5–3 lists the interrupt vectors with a brief description and the memory location of each vector for the real mode. Each vector contains a value for IP and CS that forms the address of the interrupt service procedure. The first 2 bytes contain the IP and the last 2 bytes contain the CS.

Intel reserves the first 32 interrupt vectors for the 8086–80486 and future products. The remaining interrupt vectors (32–255) are available for the user. Some reserved vectors are for errors that occur during the execution of software such as the divide error interrupt. Some vectors are reserved for the coprocessor. Still others occur for normal events in the system. In a personal computer, the reserved vectors are used for system functions as detailed later in this section. Vectors 1–6, 7, 9, 16, and 17 function in the real mode and protected mode; the remaining vectors only function in the protected mode.

Interrupt Instructions

The 8086–80486 has three different interrupt instructions available to the programmer: INT, INTO, and INT 3. In the real mode, each of these instructions fetches a vector from the vector table and then calls the procedure stored at the location addressed by the vector. In the protected mode, each of these instructions fetches an interrupt descriptor from the

TABLE 5-3 Interrupt vectors

Number	Address	Microprocessor	Function
0	0H–3H	8086–80486	Divide error
1	4H–7H	8086–80486	Single step
2	8H–BH	8086–80486	NMI (hardware interrupt)
3	CH–FH	8086–80486	Breakpoint
4	10H–13H	8086–80486	Interrupt on overflow
5	14H–17H	80286–80486	BOUND interrupt
6	18H–1BH	80286–80486	Invalid opcode
7	1CH–1FH	80286–80486	Coprocessor emulation interrupt
8	20H–23H	80386–80486	Double fault
9	24H–27H	80386	Coprocessor segment overrun
10	28H–2BH	80386–80486	Invalid task state segment
11	2CH–2FH	80386–80486	Segment not present
12	30H–33H	80386–80486	Stack fault
13	34H–37H	80386–80486	General protection fault
14	38H–3BH	80386–80486	Page fault
15	3CH–3FH		Reserved*
16	40H–43H	80286–80486	Floating-point error
17	44H–47H	80486SX	Alignment check interrupt
18–31	48H–7FH	8086–80486	Reserved*
32–255	80H–3FFH	8086–80486	User interrupts

* Some of these interrupts will appear on newer versions of the 8086–80486 when they become available.

interrupt descriptor table. The descriptor specifies the address of the interrupt service procedure. The interrupt call is similar to a far CALL instruction because it places the return address (IP/EIP and CS) on the stack.

INTs. There are 256 different software interrupt instructions (INT) available to the programmer. Each INT instruction has a numeric operand whose range is 0 to 255 (00H–FFH). For example, the INT 100 uses interrupt vector 100, which appears at memory address 190H–193H. We calculate the address of the interrupt vector by multiplying the interrupt type number times four. For example, the INT 10H instruction calls the interrupt service procedure whose address is stored beginning at memory location 40H (10H × 4) in the real mode. In protected mode, the interrupt descriptor is located by multiplying the type number by 8 instead of 4 because each descriptor is 8 bytes long.

Each INT instruction is 2 bytes in length. The first byte contains the opcode and the second byte contains the vector type number. The only exception to this is INT 3, a 1-byte special software interrupt used for breakpoints.

Whenever a software interrupt instruction executes, it (1) pushes the flags onto the stack, (2) clears the T and I flag bits, (3) pushes CS onto the stack, (4) fetches the new value for CS from the vector, (5) pushes IP/EIP onto the stack, (6) fetches the new value for IP/EIP from the vector, and (7) jumps to the new location addressed by CS and IP/EIP. The INT instruction performs as a far CALL except that it not only pushes CS and IP onto the stack, but it also pushes the flags onto the stack. The INT instruction is a combination PUSHF and far CALL instruction.

Notice that when the INT instruction executes, it clears the interrupt flag (I), which controls the external hardware interrupt input pin INTR (interrupt request). When I = 0, the microprocessor disables the INTR pin and when I = 1, the microprocessor enables the INTR pin.

Software interrupts are most commonly used to call system procedures. The system procedures are common to all system and application software. The interrupts often control printers, video displays, and disk drives. The INT instruction replaces a far CALL because the INT instruction is 2 bytes in length where the far CALL is 5 bytes. Each time that the INT instruction replaces a far CALL it saves 3 bytes of memory in a program. This can amount to a sizable savings if the INT instruction appears often in a program.

IRET/IRETD.   The interrupt return instruction (IRET) is used only with software or hardware interrupt service procedures. Unlike a simple return instruction (RET), the IRET instruction will (1) pop stack data back into the IP, (2) pop stack data back into CS, and (3) pop stack data back into the flag register. The IRET instruction accomplishes the same tasks as the POPF and RET instructions.

Whenever an IRET instruction executes, it restores the contents of I and T from the stack. This is important because it preserves the state of these flag bits. If interrupts were enabled before an interrupt service procedure, they are *automatically* re-enabled by the IRET instruction because it restores the flag register.

In the 80286–80486, the IRETD instruction is used to return from an interrupt service procedure that is called in the protected mode. It differs from the IRET because it pops a 32-bit instruction pointer (EIP) from the stack. The IRET is used in the real mode and the IRETD is used in the protected mode.

INT 3.   An INT 3 instruction is a special software interrupt designed to be used as a breakpoint. The difference between it and the other software interrupts is that INT 3 is a 1-byte instruction while the others are 2-byte instructions.

It is common to insert an INT 3 instruction in software to interrupt or break the flow of the software. This function is called a *breakpoint*. A breakpoint occurs for any software interrupt, but because INT 3 is 1 byte long, it is easier to use for this function. Breakpoints help to debug faulty software.

INTO.   Interrupt on overflow (INTO) is a conditional software interrupt that tests the overflow flag (O). If O = 0, the INTO instruction performs no operation, but if O = 1 and an INTO instruction executes, an interrupt occurs via vector type number 4.

The INTO instruction appears in software that adds or subtracts signed binary numbers. With these operations it is possible to have an overflow. Either the JO instruction or INTO instruction detects the overflow condition.

An Interrupt Service Procedure. Suppose that, in a particular system, we must add the contents of DI, SI, BP, and BX and save the sum in AX. Because this is a common task in this system, it is worthwhile to develop the task as a software interrupt. Example 5–12 shows this software interrupt. The main difference between this procedure and a normal far procedure is that it ends with the IRET instruction instead of the RET instruction.

EXAMPLE 5–12

```
0000                    INTS    PROC FAR

0000 03 C3                      ADD    AX,BX
0002 03 C5                      ADD    AX,BP
0004 03 C7                      ADD    AX,DI
0006 03 C6                      ADD    AX,SI
0008 CF                         IRET

0009                    INTS    ENDP
```

Interrupt Control

Although this section does not explain hardware interrupts, we introduce two instructions that control the INTR pin. The set interrupt flag instruction (STI) places a 1 into I, which enables the INTR pin. The clear interrupt flag instruction (CLI) places a 0 into I, which disables the INTR pin. The STI instruction enables INTR and the CLI instruction disables INTR. In a software interrupt service procedure we usually enable the hardware interrupts as one of the first steps. This is accomplished by the STI instruction.

Interrupts in the Personal Computer

The interrupts found in the personal computer differ somewhat from the ones presented in Table 5–3. The reason that they differ is that the original personal computers are 8086/8088-based systems. This meant that they only contained Intel specified interrupts 0–4. This design is carried forward so newer systems are compatible with the early personal computers.

Because the personal computer is operated in the real mode, the interrupt vector table is located at addresses 00000H–003FFH. The assignments used by computer systems are listed in Table 5–4. Notice that these differ somewhat from the assignments in Table 5–3. Some of the interrupts shown in this table are used in example programs in later chapters. An example is the clock tick, which is extremely useful for timing events because it occurs a constant 18.2 times a second in all personal computers.

Interrupts 00H–1FH and 70H–77H are present in the computer no matter what operating system is installed. If DOS is installed, interrupts 20H–2FH are also present.

TABLE 5–4 Interrupt assignments for the personal computer

Number	Function
0	Divide error
1	Single step (debug)
2	Nonmaskable interrupt pin
3	Breakpoint
4	Arithmetic overflow
5	Print screen key and BOUND instruction
6	Illegal instruction error
7	Coprocessor not present interrupt
8	Timer tick (hardware) (approximately 18.2 Hz)
9	Keyboard (hardware)
A	Hardware interrupt 2 (system bus) (cascade in AT)
B–F	Hardware interrupts 3–7 (system bus)
10	Video BIOS
11	Equipment environment
12	Conventional memory size
13	Direct disk service
14	Serial COM port service
15	Miscellaneous service
16	Keyboard service
17	Parallel port LPT service
18	ROM BASIC
19	Reboot
1A	Clock service
1B	Control-break handler
1C	User timer service
1D	Pointer for video parameter table
1E	Pointer for disk drive parameter table
1F	Pointer to graphics character pattern table
20	Terminate program
21	DOS services
22	Program termination handler
23	Control C handler
24	Critical error handler
25	Read disk
26	Write disk
27	Terminate and stay resident
28	DOS idle
2F	Multiplex handler
70–77	Hardware interrupts 8–15 (AT style computer)

5-4   MACHINE CONTROL AND MISCELLANEOUS INSTRUCTIONS

The last category of real mode instructions found in the 8086–80486 microprocessor includes the machine control and miscellaneous group. These instructions provide control of the carry bit, sample the $\overline{\text{BUSY/TEST}}$ pin, and perform various other functions. Because many of these instructions are used in hardware control, they need only be explained briefly at this point. We cover most of these instructions in more detail in later chapters that deal with the hardware and programs that control the hardware.

Controlling the Carry Flag Bit

The carry flag (C) propagates the carry or borrow in multiple-word/double-word addition and subtraction. It also indicates errors in procedures. There are three instructions that control the contents of the carry flag: STC (*set carry*), CLC (*clear carry*), and CMC (*complement carry*).

Because the carry flag is seldom used, except with multiple-word addition and subtraction, it is available for other uses. The most common task for the carry flag is to indicate error upon return from a procedure. Suppose that a procedure reads data from a disk memory file. This operation can be successful or an error can occur such as file-not-found. Upon return from this procedure, if C = 1, an error has occurred and if C = 0, no error occurred. Most of the DOS and BIOS procedures use the carry flag to indicate error conditions.

WAIT

The WAIT instruction monitors the hardware $\overline{\text{BUSY}}$ pin on the 80286–80386 and the $\overline{\text{TEST}}$ pin on the 8086/8088. The name of this pin was changed in the 80286 microprocessor from $\overline{\text{TEST}}$ to $\overline{\text{BUSY}}$. If the WAIT instruction executes while the $\overline{\text{BUSY}}$ pin = 0, nothing happens and the next instruction executes. If the $\overline{\text{BUSY}}$ pin = 1 when the WAIT instruction executes, the microprocessor waits for the $\overline{\text{BUSY}}$ pin to return to a logic 0.

The $\overline{\text{BUSY}}$ pin is usually connected to the $\overline{\text{BUSY}}$ pin of the 8087–80387 numeric coprocessor. This connection, with the WAIT instruction, allows the 8086–80386 to wait until the coprocessor finishes a task. Because the coprocessor is inside the 80486, the $\overline{\text{BUSY}}$ pin is not present.

HLT

The halt instruction (HLT) stops the execution of software. There are three ways to exit a halt: by an interrupt, by a hardware reset, or during a DMA operation. This instruction normally appears in a program to wait for an interrupt. It often synchronizes external hardware interrupts with the software system.

NOP

When the microprocessor encounters a no operation instruction (NOP), it takes a short time to execute. A NOP performs absolutely no operation and often pads software with space for future machine language instructions. If you are developing machine language programs, we recommend that you place NOPs into your program at 50-byte intervals. This is done in case you need to add instructions at some future point. A NOP also finds application in time delays that waste short periods of time.

LOCK Prefix

The LOCK prefix appends an instruction and causes the $\overline{\text{LOCK}}$ pin to become a logic 0. The $\overline{\text{LOCK}}$ pin often disables external bus masters or other system components. The LOCK prefix causes the lock pin to activate for the duration of a locked instruction. If we lock more than one sequential instruction, the $\overline{\text{LOCK}}$ pin remains a logic 0 for the duration of the sequence of locked instructions. The LOCK:MOV AL,[SI] instruction is an example of a locked instruction.

ESC

The escape (ESC) instruction passes information to the 8087–80387 numeric coprocessor. Whenever an ESC instruction executes, the microprocessor provides the memory address, if required, but otherwise performs a NOP. The 8087–80387 uses 6 bits of the ESC instruction to obtain its opcode and begin executing a coprocessor instruction.

The ESC opcode never appears in a program as ESC. In its place are a set of coprocessor instructions (FLD, FST, FMUL, etc.) that assemble as ESC instructions for the coprocessor. We provide more detail in the chapter that details the 8087–80387 coprocessor.

BOUND

The BOUND instruction is a compare instruction that can cause an interrupt (vector type number 5). This instruction compares the contents of any 16-bit or 32-bit register against the contents of two words or double words of memory: an upper and a lower boundary. If the value in the register compared with memory is *not* within the upper and lower boundary, a type 5 interrupt ensues. If it is within the boundary, the next instruction in the program executes.

For example, if the BOUND SI,DATA instruction executes, word-sized location DATA contains the lower boundary and word-sized location DATA + 2 bytes contains the upper boundary. If the number contained in SI is less than memory location DATA or greater than memory location DATA + 2 bytes, a type 5 interrupt occurs. Note that when this interrupt occurs the return address points to the BOUND instruction, not the instruction following BOUND. This differs from a normal interrupt where the return address points to the next instruction in the program.

ENTER and LEAVE

The ENTER and LEAVE instructions are used with stack frames. A stack frame is a mechanism used to pass parameters to a procedure through the stack memory. The stack frame also holds local memory variables for the procedure. Stack frames provide dynamic areas of memory for procedures in multi-user environments.

The ENTER instruction creates a stack frame by pushing BP onto the stack and then loading BP with the uppermost address of the stack frame. This allows stack frame variables to be accessed through the BP register. The ENTER instruction contains two operands: the first operand specifies the number of bytes to reserve for variables on the stack frame and the second specifies the level of the procedure.

Suppose that an ENTER 8,0 instruction executes. This instruction reserves 8 bytes of memory for the stack frame and the zero specifies level 0. Figure 5–9 shows the stack frame set up by this instruction. Note that this instruction stores BP onto the top of the stack. It then subtracts 8 from the stack pointer, leaving 8 bytes of memory space for temporary data storage. The uppermost location of this 8-byte temporary storage area is addressed by BP. The LEAVE instruction reverses this process by reloading both SP and BP with their prior values.

EXAMPLE 5–13

```
                         ;sequence used to call system software that
                         ;uses parameters stored in a stack frame
                         ;
0000 C8 0004 00             ENTER  4,0                    ;create 4 byte frame
0004 A1 00C8 R             MOV    AX,DATA1
0007 89 46FC              MOV    [BP-4],AX               ;save para 1
000A A1 00CA R             MOV    AX,DATA2
000D 89 46FE              MOV    [BP-2],AX               ;save para 2

0010 E8 0100 R             CALL   SYS                     ;call subroutine

0013 8B 46FC              MOV    AX,[BP-4]               ;get result 1
0016 A3 00C8 R             MOV    DATA1,AX                ;save result 1
0019 8B 46FE              MOV    AX,[BP-2]               ;get result 2
```

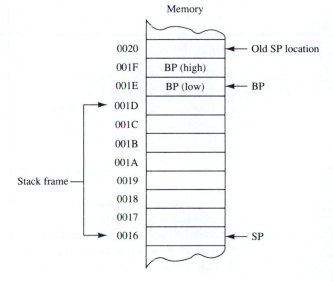

FIGURE 5–9 A stack frame generated by the ENTER 8,0 instruction. The BP register is stored beginning at the top of the stack frame. This is followed by an 8-byte area called a stack frame.

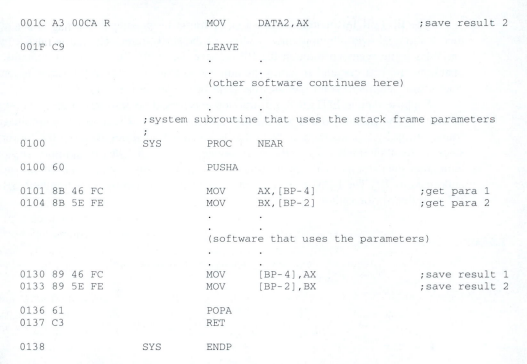

```
001C A3 00CA R              MOV    DATA2,AX                ;save result 2

001F C9                     LEAVE
                            .        .
                            .        .
                            (other software continues here)
                            .        .
                    ;system subroutine that uses the stack frame parameters
                    ;
0100                SYS     PROC   NEAR

0100 60                     PUSHA

0101 8B 46 FC               MOV    AX,[BP-4]               ;get para 1
0104 8B 5E FE               MOV    BX,[BP-2]               ;get para 2
                            .        .
                            .        .
                            (software that uses the parameters)
                            .        .
0130 89 46 FC               MOV    [BP-4],AX               ;save result 1
0133 89 5E FE               MOV    [BP-2],BX               ;save result 2

0136 61                     POPA
0137 C3                     RET

0138                SYS     ENDP
```

Example 5–13 shows how the ENTER instruction creates a stack frame so two 16-bit parameters are passed to a system level procedure. Notice how the ENTER and LEAVE instructions appear in this program, and how the parameters pass through the stack frame to and from the procedure. This procedure uses 2 parameters that pass to it and returns 2 results through the stack frame.

5–5   SUMMARY

1. There are three types of unconditional jump instructions: short, near, and far. The short jump allows a branch to within + 127 and −128 bytes. The near jump (using a displacement of ±32 K) allows a jump to anywhere in the current code segment (intrasegment). The far jump allows a jump to any location in the memory (intersegment). The near jump in an 80386/80486 microprocessor is within ±2G bytes.
2. Whenever a label appears with a JMP instruction, the label must be followed by a colon (LABEL:).
3. The displacement that follows a short or near jump is the distance from the next instruction to the jump location.
4. Indirect jumps are available in two forms: (1) jump to the location stored in a register, and (2) jump to the location stored in a memory word (near indirect) or double word (far indirect).

5. Conditional jumps are all short jumps that test one or more of the flag bits: C, Z, O, P, or S. If the condition is true, a jump occurs, and if the condition is false, the next sequential instruction executes.

6. A special conditional jump instruction (LOOP) decrements CX and jumps to the label when CX is not 0. Other forms of loop include: LOOPE, LOOPNE, LOOPZ, and LOOPNZ. The LOOPE instruction jumps if CX is not 0, and if an equal condition exists. In the 80386/80486 microprocessor the LOOP instruction can also use the ECX register as a counter.

7. In the 80386/80486 microprocessor a group of set according to condition instructions exist that either set a byte to 01H or clear it to 00H. If the condition under test is true, the operand byte is set to a 01H and if the condition under test is false, the operand byte is cleared to 00H.

8. Procedures are groups of instructions that perform one task and are used from any point in a program. The CALL instruction links to a procedure and the RET instruction returns from a procedure. In assembly language, the PROC directive defines the name and type of procedure. The ENDP directive declares the end of the procedure.

9. The CALL instruction is a combination of a PUSH and a JMP instruction. When CALL executes, it pushes the return address on the stack and then jumps to the procedure. A near CALL places the contents of IP on the stack and a far CALL places both IP and CS on the stack.

10. The RET instruction returns from a procedure by removing the return address from the stack and placing it into IP (near return) or IP and CS (far return).

11. Interrupts are either software instructions similar to CALL or hardware signals used to call procedures. This process interrupts the current program and calls a procedure. After the procedure, an IRET instruction returns control to the interrupted software.

12. Interrupt vectors are 4 bytes in length that contain the address (IP and CS) of the interrupt service procedure. The microprocessor contains 256 interrupt vectors in the first 1K byte of memory. The first 32 are defined by Intel, the remaining 224 are user interrupts.

13. Whenever an interrupt is accepted by the microprocessor, the flags, IP, and CS are pushed on the stack. Besides pushing the flags, the T and I flag bits are cleared to disable both the trace function and the INTR pin. The final event that occurs for the interrupt is that the interrupt vector is fetched from the vector table and a jump to the interrupt service procedure occurs.

14. Software interrupt instructions (INT) often replace system calls. Software interrupts save 3 bytes of memory each time they replace CALL instructions.

15. A special return instruction (IRET) must be used to return from an interrupt service procedure. The IRET instruction not only removes IP and CS from the stack, it also removes the flags from the stack.

16. Interrupt on an overflow (INTO) is a conditional interrupt that calls an interrupt service procedure if the overflow flag (O) = 1.

17. The interrupt enable flag (I) controls the INTR pin connection on the microprocessor. If the STI instruction executes, it sets I to enable the INTR pin. If the CLI instruction executes, it clears I to disable the INTR pin.

18. The carry flag bit (C) is clear, set, and complemented by the CLC, STC, and CMC instructions.

19. The WAIT instruction tests the condition of the $\overline{\text{BUSY}}$ pin on the microprocessor. If $\overline{\text{BUSY}}$ = 0, WAIT does not wait, but if $\overline{\text{BUSY}}$ = 1, WAIT continues testing the $\overline{\text{BUSY}}$ pin until it becomes a logic 0.

20. The LOCK prefix causes the $\overline{\text{LOCK}}$ pin to become a logic 0 for the duration of the locked instruction. The ESC instruction passes instruction to the 80287–80387 numeric coprocessor.

21. The BOUND instruction compares the contents of any 16-bit register against the contents of two words of memory: an upper and a lower boundary. If the value in the register compared with memory is *not* within the upper and lower boundary, a type 5 interrupt ensues.

22. The ENTER and LEAVE instructions are used with stack frames. A stack frame is a mechanism used to pass parameters to a procedure through the stack memory. The stack frame also holds local memory variables for the procedure. The ENTER instruction creates the stack frame, and the LEAVE instruction removes the stack frame from the stack. The BP register addresses stack frame data.

5–6   QUESTIONS AND PROBLEMS

1. What is a short JMP?
2. What type of JMP is used when jumping anywhere in a segment?
3. Which JMP instruction allows the program to continue execution at any memory location in the system?
4. What JMP instruction is 5 bytes long?
5. What is the range of a near jump in the 80386/80486 microprocessor?
6. What can be said about a label that is followed by a colon?
7. The near jump modifies the program address by changing which register or registers?
8. The far jump modifies the program address by changing which register or registers?
9. Explain what the JMP AX instruction accomplishes. Also identify it as a near or a far jump instruction.
10. Contrast the operation of a JMP DI with a JMP [DI].
11. Contrast the operation of a JMP [DI] with a JMP FAR PTR [DI].
12. List the five flag bits tested by the conditional jump instructions.
13. Describe how the JA instruction operates.
14. When will the JO instruction jump?
15. What conditional jump instructions follow the comparison of signed numbers?
16. What conditional jump instructions follow the comparison of unsigned numbers?
17. Which conditional jump instructions test both the Z and C flag bits?
18. When does the JCXZ instruction jump?
19. Which SET instruction is used to set AL if the flag bits indicate a zero condition?
20. The 8086 LOOP instruction decrements register _____ and tests it for a 0 to decide if a jump occurs.

21. The 80486 LOOP instruction decrements register _____ and tests it for a 0 to decide if a jump occurs.
22. Explain how the LOOPE instruction operates.
23. Develop a short sequence of instructions that stores a 00H into 150H bytes of memory beginning at extra segment memory location DATA. You must use the LOOP instruction to help perform this task.
24. Develop a sequence of instructions that searches through a block of 100H bytes of memory. This program must count all the unsigned numbers that are above 42H and all that are below 42H. Byte-sized memory location UP must contain the count of numbers above 42H and location DOWN must contain the count of numbers below 42H.
25. What is a procedure?
26. Explain how the near and far CALL instructions function.
27. How does the near RET instruction function?
28. The last executable instruction in a procedure must be a _____.
29. What directive identifies the start of a procedure?
30. How is a procedure identified as near or far?
31. Explain what the RET 6 instruction accomplishes.
32. Write a near procedure that cubes the contents of the CX register. This procedure may not affect any register except CX.
33. Write a procedure that multiplies DI by SI and then divides the result by 100H. Make sure that the result is left in AX upon returning from the procedure. This procedure may not change any register except AX.
34. Write a procedure that sums EAX, EBX, ECX, and EDX. If a carry occurs, place a logic 1 in EDI. If no carry occurs, place a 0 in EDI. The sum should be found in EAX after the execution of your procedure.
35. What is an interrupt?
36. What software instructions call an interrupt service procedure?
37. How many different interrupt types are available in the microprocessor?
38. What is the purpose of interrupt vector type number 0?
39. Illustrate the contents of an interrupt vector and explain the purpose of each part.
40. How does the IRET instruction differ from the RET instruction?
41. What is the IRETD instruction?
42. The INTO instruction only interrupts the program for what condition?
43. The interrupt vector for an INT 40H instruction is stored at what memory locations?
44. What instructions control the function of the INTR pin?
45. Which personal computer interrupt services the parallel LPT port?
46. Which personal computer interrupt services the keyboard?
47. What instruction tests the $\overline{\text{BUSY}}$ pin?
48. When will the BOUND instruction interrupt a program?
49. An ENTER 16,0 instruction creates a stack frame that contains _____ bytes.
50. What register moves to the stack when an ENTER instruction executes?
51. Which instruction passes opcodes to the numeric coprocessor?

CHAPTER 6

Programming
the Microprocessor

INTRODUCTION

This chapter develops programs and programming techniques using the MASM macro assembler program, the DOS function calls, and the BIOS function calls. Some of the DOS function calls and BIOS function calls are used in this chapter, but all are explained in complete detail in Appendix A. Please review the function calls as required as you read this chapter. The MASM assembler has already been explained and demonstrated in prior chapters, yet there are still more features to learn at this point.

Some programming techniques explained in this chapter include: macro sequences, keyboard and display manipulation, program modules, library files, interrupt hooks, and other important programming techniques. This chapter is meant as an introduction to programming, yet it includes valuable programming techniques that provide a wealth of background so that programs can be easily developed for the personal computer using either PCDOS[1] or MSDOS[2] as a springboard.

CHAPTER OBJECTIVES

Upon completion of this chapter, you will be able to:

1. Use the MASM assembler and linker program to create programs that contain more than one module.
2. Explain the use of EXTRN and PUBLIC as they apply to modular programming.
3. Set up a library file that contains commonly used subroutines.
4. Write and use MACRO and ENDM to develop macro sequences used with linear programming.

---

[1]PCDOS is a registered trademark of IBM Corporation.

[2]MSDOS is a register trademark of Microsoft Corporation.

5. Show how both sequential and random access files are developed for use in a system.
6. Develop programs using DOS function calls.
7. Differentiate a DOS function call from a BIOS function call.
8. Show how to hook into interrupts using DOS function calls.

6-1 MODULAR PROGRAMMING

Many programs are too large to be developed by one person. This means that programs are sometimes developed by teams of programmers. The linker program is provided with MSDOS or PCDOS so programming modules can be linked together into a complete program. This section of the text describes the linker, the linking task, library files, EXTRN, and PUBLIC as they apply to program modules and modular programming.

The Assembler and Linker

The *assembler program* converts a symbolic source module (file) into a hexadecimal object file. We have seen many examples of symbolic source files in prior chapters. Example 6–1 shows the assembler dialog that appears as a source module named FILE.ASM is assembled. Whenever you create a source file it must have an extension of ASM. Note that the extension (.ASM) is not typed into the assembler prompt when assembling a file. Source files are created using an editor that comes with the assembler or by almost any other word processor or editor that is capable of generating an ASCII file.

EXAMPLE 6–1

```
A>MASM

Microsoft (R) Macro Assembler Version 5.10
Copyright (C) Microsoft Corp 1981, 1989. All rights reserved.

Source filename [.ASM]: FILE
Object filename [FILE.OBJ]: FILE
Source listing [NULLST]: FILE
Cross reference [NUL.CRF]: FILE
```

The assembler program (MASM) asks for the source file name, the object file name, the list file name, and a cross-reference file name. In most cases the name for each of these will be the same as the source file. The object file (.OBJ) is not executable, but is designed as an input file to the linker. The source listing file (.LST) contains the assembled version of the source file and its hexadecimal machine language equivalent. The cross-reference file (.CRF) lists all labels and pertinent information required for cross-referencing.

The *linker program* reads the object files, created by the assembler program, and links them together into a single execution file. An *execution file* is created with the filename extension EXE. Execution files are executed by typing the file name at the DOS prompt (A>). An example execution file is FROG.EXE which is executed by typing FROG at the DOS command prompt.

If a file is short enough, less than 64K bytes in length, it can be converted from an execution file to a *command file* (.COM). The command file is slightly different from an execution file in that the program must be originated at location 100H before it can execute. The program EXE2BIN is used for converting an execution file into a command file. The main advantage of a command file is that it loads off the disk into the computer much more quickly than an execution file. It also requires less disk storage space than the equivalent execution file.

EXAMPLE 6–2

```
A>LINK

Microsoft (R) Overlay Linker Version 3.64
Copyright (C) Microsoft Corp 1983-1988. All rights reserved.

Object Modules [.OBJ]: FROG+WHAT+DONUT
Run File [FROG.EXE]: FROG
List File [NUL.MAP]: FROG
Libraries [.LIB]: LIBS
```

Example 6–2 shows the protocol involved with the linker program when it is used to link the files FROG, WHAT, and DONUT. The linker also links library files (LIBS) so procedures, located within LIBS, can be used with the linked execution file. To invoke the linker, type LINK at the DOS command prompt as illustrated in Example 6–2. Note that before files are linked, they must first be assembled and they must be *error free*.

In this example, after typing LINK, the linker program asks for the "Object Modules," which are created by the assembler. In this example, we have three object modules: FROG, WHAT, and DONUT. If more than one object file exists, the main program file (FROG in this example) is typed first followed by any other supporting modules. (We use a plus sign to separate module names.)

After the program module names are typed, the linker suggests that the execution (run-time) file name is FROG.EXE. This may be selected by typing the same name or if desired by typing the enter key. It may also be changed to any other name at this point.

The list file is where a map of the program segments appears as created by the linking. If enter is typed, no list file is created, but if a name is typed, the list file appears on the disk.

Library files are entered in the last line. In this example we entered library file name LIBS. This library contains procedures used by the other program modules.

PUBLIC and EXTRN

The PUBLIC and EXTRN directives are very important to modular programming. We use PUBLIC to declare that labels of code, data, or entire segments are available to other program modules. We use EXTRN (external) to declare that labels are external to a module. Without these statements, we could not link modules together to create a program using modular programming techniques.

EXAMPLE 6–3

```
                     DAT1    SEGMENT PUBLIC                ;declare entire segment public

                             PUBLIC DATA1                  ;declare DATA1, DATA2 public
                             PUBLIC DATA2
0000 0064[           DATA1   DB    100 DUP (?)             ;global
      ??
           ]
0064 0064[           DATA2   DB    100 DUP (?)             ;global
      ??
           ]
00C8                 DAT1    ENDS

0000                 CODES   SEGMENT

                             ASSUME CS:CODES,DS:DAT1

                             PUBLIC READ                   ;declare READ public

0000                 READ    PROC FAR

0000 B4 06                   MOV   AH,6                    ;read keyboard
0002 B2 FF                   MOV   DL,0FFH                 ;no echo
0004 CD 21                   INT   21H
0006 74 F8                   JE    READ
0008 CB                      RET

0009                 READ    ENDP

0009                 CODES   ENDS

                             END
```

The PUBLIC directive is normally placed in the opcode field of an assembly language statement to define a label as public so it can be used by other modules. This label can be a jump address, a data address, or an entire segment can be made public. Example 6–3 shows the PUBLIC statement used to define some labels public to other modules. When segments are made public they are combined with other public segments that contain data with the same segment name.

EXAMPLE 6–4

```
0000                 DAT1    SEGMENT PUBLIC                ;declare entire segment public

                             EXTRN DATA1:BYTE
                             EXTRN DATA2:BYTE
                             EXTRN DATA3:WORD
                             EXTRN DATA4:DWORD

0000                 DAT1    ENDS

0000                 CODES   SEGMENT

                             ASSUME CS:CODES,ES,DAT1

                             EXTRN READ:FAR
```

```
0000                          MAIN    PROC    FAR

0000  B8--R                           MOV     AX,DAT1
0003  8E C0                           MOV     ES,AX

0005  BF 0000 E                       MOV     DI,OFFSET DATA1
0008  B9 000A                         MOV     CX,10

000B                          MAIN1:

000B  9A 0000--E                      CALL    READ
0010  AA                              STOSB
0011  E2 F8                           LOOP    MAIN1
0013  CB                              RET

0014                          MAIN    ENDP

0014                          CODES   ENDS

                                      END     MAIN
```

The EXTRN statement appears in both data and code segments to define labels as external to the segment. If data are defined as external, their size must be represented as BYTE, WORD, or DWORD. If a jump or call address is external, it must be represented as NEAR or FAR. Example 6–4 shows how the external statement is used to indicate that several labels are external to the program listed. Notice in this example that any external address or data is defined with the letter E in the hexadecimal assembled listing.

Libraries

Library files are collections of procedures that can be used by many different programs. These procedures are assembled and compiled into a library file by the LIB program that accompanies the MASM assembler program. Libraries allow common procedures to be collected into one place so they can be used by many different applications. The library file (FILENAME.LIB) is invoked when a program is linked with the linker program.

Why bother with library files? A library file is a good place to store a collection of related procedures. When the library file is linked with a program, only the procedures required by the program are removed from the library file and added to the program. If any amount of assembly language programming is to be accomplished efficiently, a good set of library files is essential.

Creating a Library File.   A library file is created with the LIB command typed at the DOS prompt. A library file is a collection of assembled .OBJ files that each perform one procedure or task. Example 6–5 shows two separate files (READ_KEY and ECHO) that will be used to structure a library file. Please notice that the name of the procedure must be declared PUBLIC in a library file and does not necessarily need to match the file name, although it does in this example.

EXAMPLE 6–5

```
;The first library module is called READ_KEY.
;This procedure reads a key from the keyboard
```

```
                                    ;and returns with the ASCII character in AL.
                                    ;
0000                          LIB       SEGMENT

                                        ASSUME CS:LIB

                                        PUBLIC READ_KEY

0000                          READ_KEY      PROC    FAR

0000 52                                     PUSH    DX

0001                          READ_KEY1:
0001 B4 06                                  MOV     AH,6
0003 B2 0F                                  MOV     DL,0FH
0005 CD 21                                  INT     21H
0007 74 F8                                  JE      READ_KEY1
0009 5A                                     POP     DX
000A CB                                     RET
000B                          READ_KEY      ENDP

000B                          LIB       ENDS

                                        END
                                    ;
                                    ;This second library module is called ECHO
                                    ;This procedure displays the ASCII character
                                    ;in AL on the CRT screen.
                                    ;
0000                          LIB       SEGMENT

                                        ASSUME CS:LIB

                                        PUBLIC ECHO

0000                          ECHO          PROC    FAR
0000 52                                     PUSH    DX
0001 B4 06                                  MOV     AH,6
0003 8A D0                                  MOV     DL,AL
0005 CD 21                                  INT     21H
0007 5A                                     POP     DX
0008 CB                                     RET
0009                          ECHO          ENDP

0009                          LIB       ENDS

                                        END
```

After each file is assembled, the LIB program is used to combine them into a library file. The LIB program prompts for information as illustrated in Example 6-6 where these files are combined to form the library IO.

EXAMPLE 6-6

```
A>LIB

Microsoft (R) Library Manager Version 3.10
Copyright (C) Microsoft Corp 1983-1988. All rights reserved.
```

```
Library name:IO
Library file does not exist. Create? Y
Operations:READ_KEY+ECHO
List file:IO
```

The LIB program begins with the copyright message from Microsoft, followed by the prompt *Library name:*. The library name chosen is IO for the IO.LIB file. Because this is a new file, the library program asks if we wish to create the library file. The *Operations:* prompt is where the library module names are typed. In this case we created a library using two procedure files (READ_KEY and ECHO). The list file shows the contents of the library and is illustrated for this library in Example 6–7. The list file shows the size and names of the files used to create the library and also the public label (procedure name) that is used in the library file.

EXAMPLE 6–7

```
ECHO.......ECHO            READ_KEY......READ_KEY

READ_KEY    Offset: 00000010H Code and data size: BH
  READ_KEY

ECHO        Offset: 00000070H Code and data size: 9H
  ECHO
```

If you must add additional library modules at a later time, type the name of the library file after invoking LIB. At the *Operations:* type the new module name preceded with a *plus sign* to add a new procedure. If you must delete a library module, use a *minus sign* before the operation file name.

Once the library file is linked to your program file only the library procedures actually used by your program are placed in the execution file. Don't forget to use the label EXTRN when specifying library calls from your program module.

Macros

A macro is a group of instructions that perform one task just as a procedure performs one task. The difference is that a procedure is accessed via a CALL instruction, while a macro is inserted in the program as a new opcode containing a sequence of instructions. A *macro* is a new opcode that you create. Macro sequences execute faster than procedures because there is no CALL and RET instruction to execute. The instructions of the macro are placed in your program at the point they are invoked.

The MACRO and ENDM directives are used to delineate a macro sequence. The first statement of a macro is the MACRO statement that contains the name of the macro and any parameters associated with it. An example is MOVE MACRO A,B that defines the macro as MOVE. This new *opcode* uses two parameters A and B. The last statement of a macro is the ENDM instruction on a line by itself.

EXAMPLE 6–8

```
          MOVE    MACRO   A,B              ;;moves word from B to A

          PUSH    AX
```

```
                                        MOV       AX,B
                                        MOV       A,AX
                                        POP       AX

                                        ENDM

                                        MOVE      VAR1,VAR2          ;use macro MOVE

0000 50              1                   PUSH      AX
0001 A1 0002 R       1                   MOV       AX,VAR2
0004 A3 0000 R       1                   MOV       VAR1,AX
0007 58              1                   POP       AX

                                        MOVE      VAR3,VAR4          ;use macro MOVE

0008 50              1                   PUSH      AX
0009 A1 0006 R       1                   MOV       AX,VAR4
000C A3 0004 R       1                   MOV       VAR3,AX
000F 58              1                   POP       AX
```

Example 6-8 shows how a macro is created and used in a program. This macro moves the word-sized contents of memory location B into word-sized memory location A. After the macro is defined in the example, it is used twice. The macro is *expanded* in this example so that you can see how it assembles to generate the moves. A hexadecimal machine language statement followed by a number (a 1 in this example) is a macro expansion statement. The expansion statement was not typed in the source program. Notice that the comment in the macro is preceded with a ;; instead of ; as is customary.

Local Variable in a Macro.   Sometimes macros contain local variables. A *local variable* is one that appears in the macro, but is not available outside the macro. To define a local variable we use the LOCAL directive. Example 6-9 shows how a local variable, used as a jump address, appears in a macro definition. If this jump address is not defined as local, the assembler will flag it with errors on the second and subsequent attempts to use the macro.

EXAMPLE 6-9

```
                         READ     MACRO A              ;;reads keyboard
                                  LOCAL READ1          ;;define READ1 as local

                                  PUSH  DX

                         READ1:

                                  MOV   AH,6
                                  MOV   DL,0FFH
                                  INT   21H
                                  JE    READ1
                                  MOV   A,AL
                                  POP   DX

                                  ENDM

                                  READ  VAR5           ;read key

0000 52              1            MOV   DX
```

```
0001                    1       ??0000:
0001 B4 06              1               MOV     AH,6
0003 B2 FF              1               MOV     DL,0FFH
0005 CD 21              1               INT     21H
0007 74 F8              1               JE      ??0000
0009 A2 0008 R          1               MOV     VAR5,AL
000C 5A                 1               POP     DX

                                        READ    VAR6                    ;read key

000D 52                 1               PUSH    DX
000E                    1       ??0001:
000E B4 06              1               MOV     AH,6
0010 B2 FF              1               MOV     DL,0FFH
0012 CD 21              1               INT     21H
0014 74 F8              1               JE      ??0001
0016 A2 0009 R          1               MOV     VAR6,AL
0019 5A                 1               POP     DX
```

This example reads a character from the keyboard and stores it into the byte-sized memory location indicated as a parameter with the macro. Notice how the local label READ1 is treated in the expanded macros.

The LOCAL directive must always immediately follow the MACRO directive without any intervening spaces or comments. If a comment or space appears between MACRO and LOCAL, the assembler indicates an error and will not accept the variable as local.

Placing MACRO Definitions in their Own Module.   Macro definitions can be placed in the program file as shown, or can be placed in their own macro module. A file can be created that contains only macros that are to be included with other program files. We use the INCLUDE directive to indicate that a program file will include a module that contains external macro definitions. Although this is not a library file, it for all practical purposes functions as a library of macro sequences.

When macro sequences are placed in a file (often with the extension INC or MAC), they do not contain PUBLIC statements. If a file called MACRO.MAC contains macro sequences, the include statement is placed in the program file as INCLUDE C:\ASSM\MACRO.MAC. Notice that the macro file is on drive C, subdirectory ASSM in this example. The INCLUDE statement includes these macros just as if you had typed them into the file. No EXTRN statement is needed to access the macro statements that have been included.

The Modular Programming Approach

The modular programming approach often involves a team of people assigned different programming tasks. This allows the team manager to assign portions of the program to different team members. Often the team manager develops the system flowchart or shell and then divides it into modules for team members.

A team member might be assigned the task of developing a macro definition file. This file might contain macro definitions that handle the I/O operations for the system. Another team member might be assigned the task of developing the procedures used for the system. In most cases the procedures are organized as a library file that is linked to the program modules. Finally, several program files or modules might be used for the final system, each developed by different team members.

This approach requires considerable communications between team members and good documentation. Documentation is the key so that modules interface correctly. Also communication between members plays a key role in this approach.

6−2   USING THE KEYBOARD AND VIDEO DISPLAY

Today there are few programs that don't use the keyboard and video display. This section of the text explains how to use the keyboard and video display connected to the IBM PC or compatible computer running under either MSDOS or PCDOS.

Reading the Keyboard with DOS Functions

The keyboard of the personal computer is read via a DOS function call. A complete listing of the DOS function calls appears in Appendix A. This section uses INT 21H with various DOS function calls to read the keyboard. Data read from the keyboard is either in ASCII-coded form or in extended ASCII-coded form.

The ASCII-coded data appears as outlined in Table 1−7 in section 1−7. The extended character set of Table 1−8 applies to printed or displayed data only and not to keyboard data. Notice that the ASCII codes in Table 1−7 codes correspond to most of the keys on the keyboard. Also available through the keyboard are extended ASCII-coded keyboard data. Table 6−1 lists most of the extended ASCII codes obtained with various keys and key combinations. Notice that most keys on the keyboard have alternative key codes. The function keys have four sets of codes selected by the function keys, the shift function keys, alternate function keys, and the control function keys.

There are three ways to read the keyboard. The first method reads a key and echoes (or displays) the key on the video screen. A second way just tests to see if a key is pressed, and if it is, it reads the key; otherwise it returns without any key. The third way allows an entire character line to be read from the keyboard.

Reading a Key with an Echo.   Example 6−10 shows how a key is read from the keyboard and *echoed* (sent) back out to the video display. Although this is the easiest way to read a key, it is also the most limited because it always echoes the character to the screen even if it is an unwanted character. The DOS function number 01H also responds to the control C key and exits to DOS if it is typed.

EXAMPLE 6−10

```
0000                    KEY     PROC    FAR

0000 B4 01                      MOV     AH,1        ;function 01H
0002 CD 21                      INT     21H         ;read key
0004 0A C0                      OR      AL,AL       ;test for 00H
0006 75 03                      JNZ     KEY1
0008 CD 21                      INT     21H            ;get extended
```

```
000A F9                          STC                      ;indicate extended

000B                     KEY1:

000B CB                          RET

000C                     KEY     ENDP
```

To read and echo a character, the AH register is loaded with DOS function number 01H. This is followed by the INT 21H instruction. Upon return from the INT 21H, the AL register contains the ASCII character typed and the video display also shows the typed character. If AL = 0 after the return, the INT 21H instruction must again be executed to obtain the extended ASCII-coded character (see Table 6–1). The procedure of Example 6–10 returns with carry set (1) to indicate an extended ASCII character and carry cleared (0) to indicate a normal ASCII character.

Reading a Key with No Echo.   The best single character key reading function is function number 06H. This function reads a key without an echo to the screen. It also allows extended ASCII characters and *does not* respond to the control C key. This function uses AH for the function number (06H) and DL = 0FFH to indicate that the function call (INT 21H) will read the keyboard without an echo.

TABLE 6–1   Extended ASCII-coded keyboard data

First	0	1	2	3	4	5	6	7	8
Second									
0	—	aQ	aD	aB	—	down arrow	cF3	aF9	a9
1	aESC	aW	aF	aN	—	page down	cF4	aF10	a0
2	—	aE	aG	aM	—	insert	cF5	—	a-
3	c2	aR	aH	a,	—	delete	cF6	—	a=
4	—	aT	aJ	a.	—	sF1	cF7	—	—
5	—	aY	aK	a/	—	sF2	cF8	—	F11
6	—	aU	aL	—	—	sF3	cF9	—	F12
7	—	aI	a;	a*	home	sF4	cF10	—	sF11
8	—	aO	a'	—	up arrow	sF5	aF1	a1	sF12
9	—	aP	a'	—	page up	sF6	aF2	a2	cF11
A	—	a[	—	a-	—	sF7	aF3	a3	cF12
B	—	a]	a\	—	left arrow	sF8	aF4	a4	aF11
C	—	aENT	aZ	—	—	sF9	aF5	a5	aF12
D	—	—	aX	—	right arrow	sF10	aF6	a6	—
E	aBS	aA	aC	—	a+	cF1	aF7	a7	—
F	sTAB	aS	—	—	end key	cF2	aF8	a8	—

Notes: a = alternate key, c = control key, and s = shift key.

EXAMPLE 6–11

```
0000                    KEYS    PROC    FAR

0000 B4 06                      MOV     AH,6            ;function 01H
0002 B2 FF                      MOV     DL,0FFH
0004 CD 21                      INT     21H             ;read key
0006 74 F8                      JE      KEYS            ;if no key
0008 0A C0                      OR      AL,AL           ;test for 00H
000A 75 03                      JNE     KEYS1
000C CD 21                      INT     21H             ;get extended
000E F9                         STC                     ;indicate extended

000F                    KEYS1:

000F CB                         RET

0010                    KEYS    ENDP
```

Example 6–11 shows a procedure that uses function number 06H to read the keyboard. This performs as Example 6–10 except that no character is echoed to the video display.

If you examine the procedure, there is one other difference. Function call number 06H returns from the INT 21H even if no key is typed, while function call 01H waits for a key to be typed. This is an important difference that should be noted. This feature allows software to perform other tasks between checking the keyboard for a character.

Read an Entire Line with Echo.   Sometimes it is advantageous to read an entire line of data with one function call. Function call number 0AH reads an entire line of information—up to 255 characters—from the keyboard. It continues to acquire keyboard data until either the enter key (0DH) is typed, or the character count expires. This function requires that AH = 0AH and DS:DX addresses the keyboard buffer (a memory area where the ASCII data are stored). The first byte of the buffer area must contain the maximum number of keyboard characters read by this function. If the number typed exceeds this maximum number, the function returns just as if the enter key were typed. The second byte of the buffer contains the count of the actual number of characters typed and the remaining locations in the buffer contain the ASCII keyboard data.

EXAMPLE 6–12

```
0000                    COD     SEGMENT

                                ASSUME  CS:COD

0000 0101[                      BUF1    DB      257 DUP (?)
         ????
         ]
0102 0101[                      BUF2    DB      257 DUP (?)
         ????
         ]

0204                    MAIN    PROC    FAR

0204 8C C8                      MOV     AX,CS
0206 8E D8                      MOV     DS,AX
```

```
0208 BA 0000 R              MOV    DX,OFFSET BUF1      ;address buffer 1
020B C7 06 0000 R 00FF      MOV    BUF1,255           ;maximum count
0211 E8 0221 R              CALL   LINE               ;read first line

0214 BA 0102 R              MOV    DX,OFFSET BUF2      ;address buffer 2
0217 C7 06 0102 R 00FF      MOV    BUF2,255           ;maximum count
021D E8 0221 R              CALL   LINE               ;read second line

0220 CB                     RET

0221                 MAIN   ENDP

0221                 LINE   PROC   NEAR

0221 B4 0A                  MOV    AH,0AH             ;function 0AH
0223 CD 21                  INT    21H
0225 C3                     RET

0226                 LINE   ENDP

0226                 COD    ENDS

                            END    MAIN
```

Example 6–12 shows how this function reads 2 lines of information into 2 memory buffers (BUF1 and BUF2). Before the call to the DOS function through procedure LINE, the first byte of the buffer is loaded with a 255 so up to 255 characters can be typed. If you assemble and execute this program, the first line is accepted and so is the second. The only problem is that the second line appears on top of the first line. The next section of the text explains how to output characters to the video display to solve this problem.

Writing to the Video Display with DOS Functions

With almost any program written, data must be displayed on the video display. Video data are displayed in a number of different ways with DOS function calls. We use function 02H or 06H for displaying one character at a time or function 09H for displaying an entire string of characters. Because function 02H and 06H are identical, we tend to use function 06H because it is also used to read a key.

Displaying One ASCII Character. Both DOS functions 02H and 06H are explained together because they are identical for displaying ASCII data. Example 6–13 shows how this function is used to display a carriage return (0DH) and a line feed (0AH). Here a macro, called DISP (display), is used to display the carriage return and line feed. The combination of a carriage return and a line feed moves the cursor to the next line at the left margin of the video screen. This two-step process is used to correct the problem that occurred between the lines typed through the keyboard in Example 6–12.

EXAMPLE 6–13

```
        DISP    MACRO  A                    ;display A

                MOV    AH,06H
                MOV    DL,A
                INT    21H
```

```
                                ENDM

                                DISP    0DH                          ;carriage return

0000 B4 06          1           MOV     AH,06H
0002 B2 0D          1           MOV     DL,0DH
0004 CD 21          1           INT     21H

                                DISP    0AH                          ;line feed

0006 B4 06          1           MOV     AH,06H
0008 B2 0A          1           MOV     DL,0AH
000A CD 21          1           INT     21H
```

Display a Character String.   A character string is a series of ASCII-coded characters that end with a $ (24H) when used with DOS function call number 09H. Example 6–14 shows how a message is displayed at the current cursor position on the video display. Function call number 09H requires that DS:DX address the character string before executing the INT 21H.

EXAMPLE 6–14

```
0000                            COD     SEGMENT

                                        ASSUME  CS:COD,DS:COD

0000 0D 0A 0A 54 68 69  MES     DB      0DH,0AH,0AH,'This is a test line','$'
     73 20 69 73 20 61
     20 74 65 73 74 20
     6C 69 6E 65 24

0017                            MAIN    PROC    FAR

0017 8C C8                              MOV     AX,CS                ;load DS
0019 8E D8                              MOV     DS,AX

001B B4 09                              MOV     AH,09H               ;function 09H
001D BA 0000 R                          MOV     DX,OFFSET MES
0020 CD 21                              INT     21H

0022 B4 4C                              MOV     AH,4CH               ;function 4CH
0024 CD 21                              INT     21H

0026                            MAIN    ENDP


0026                            COD     ENDS

                                END     MAIN
```

This example program can be entered into the assembler, linked, and executed to produce *"This is a test line"* on the video display. Notice that an additional DOS function call is appended to the end of this program. Function call 4CH returns the system to the DOS prompt at the end of the program. We often use function number 4CH to end a program and return to DOS. (Note that with function 4CH, the AL register is cleared to 00H to indicate no error.)

Consolidated Read Key and Echo Library Procedures. Example 6–15 illustrates two procedures that could be assembled, linked, and added to a library file. The READ procedure reads a keyboard character and returns with either the ASCII or extended ASCII character in AL. If carry is set, AL contains the extended ASCII code and if carry is cleared, it contains the standard ASCII code. The ECHO procedure displays ASCII coded character located in AL at the current cursor position.

EXAMPLE 6–15

```
0000                 LIB     SEGMENT

                     ASSUME CS:LIB

                     PUBLIC READ

                     PUBLIC ECHO

                     ;
                     ;procedure that reads a key from the keyboard (no echo)
                     ;if CF = 0, AL = standard ASCII character
                     ;if CF = 1, AL = extended ASCII character
                     ;
0000                 READ    PROC    FAR

0000 52                      PUSH    DX              ;save DX
0001 B4 06                   MOV     AH,6            ;DOS function 06H
0003 B2 FF                   MOV     DL,0FFH

0005                 READ1:

0005 CD 21                   INT     21H
0007 74 FC                   JE      READ1           ;if no key
0009 0A C0                   OR      AL,AL           ;test for extended
000B 75 03                   JNZ     READ2           ;if standard ASCII

000D CD 21                   INT     21H             ;get extended
000F F9                      STC                     ;set carry

0010                 READ2:

0010 5A                      POP     DX
0011 CB                      RET

0012                 READ    ENDP
                     ;
                     ;procedure that displays the ASCII character in AL
                     ;
0012                 ECHO    PROC    FAR

0012 52                      PUSH    DX
0013 B4 06                   MOV     AH,6            ;DOS function 06H
0015 8A D0                   MOV     DL,AL           ;AL to DL
0017 CD 21                   INT     21H
0019 5A                      POP     DX
001A CB                      RET

001B                 ECHO    ENDP

001B                 LIB     ENDS

                     END
```

Using BIOS Video Function Calls

In addition to the DOS function call INT 21H, we also have BIOS (*basic I/O system*) function calls at INT 10H. The DOS function calls allow a key to be read and a character to be displayed with ease, but the cursor is difficult to position at the desired screen location. The BIOS function calls allow more control over the video display than do the DOS function calls. The BIOS function calls also require less time to execute than the DOS function calls.

Cursor Position.   Before any information is placed on the video screen, the position of the cursor should be known. This allows the screen to be cleared and started at any location that is desired. Function number 03H allows the cursor position to be read from the video interface. Function number 02H allows the cursor to be placed at any screen position. Table 6-2 shows the contents of various registers for both function 02H and 03H.

The page number, in register BH, should be 0 before setting the cursor position. Most software does not normally access the other pages (1–7) of the video display. The page number is often ignored after a cursor read. The 0 page is available in the CGA (*color graphics adaptor*), EGA (*enhanced graphics adapter*), and VGA (*variable graphics array*) text modes of operation.

The cursor position assumes that the lefthand page column is column 0 progressing across a line to column 79. The row number corresponds to the character line number on the screen. Row 0 is the uppermost line while row 23 is the last line on the screen. This assumes that the text mode selected for the video adapter is 80 characters per line by 24 lines. Other text modes are available such as 40×24 and 96×43.

EXAMPLE 6-16

```
0000                    CODE    SEGMENT

                                ASSUME CS:CODE

0000                    MAIN    PROC    FAR

                        HOME    MACRO

                                MOV     AH,2        ;;set cursor position
                                MOV     BH,0        ;;page 0
                                MOV     DX,0        ;;row 0, column 0
                                INT     10H

                                ENDM
```

TABLE 6-2 BIOS function INT 10H

AH	Description	Parameters
02H	Sets cursor position	DH = Row DL = Column BH = Page number
03H	Reads cursor position	BH = Page number DH = Row DL = Column

```
                              HOME
0000 B4 02      1            MOV    AH,2
0002 B7 00      1            MOV    BH,0
0004 BA 0000    1            MOV    DX,0
0007 CD 10      1            INT    10H

0009 B9 0780                 MOV    CX,1920
000C B4 06                   MOV    AH,6
000E B2 20                   MOV    DL,''                ;space

0010                 MAIN1:

0010 CD 21                   INT    21H                  ;display space
0012 E2 FC                   LOOP   MAIN1                ;repeat 1920 times

                              HOME
0014 B4 02      1            MOV    AH,2
0016 B7 00      1            MOV    BH,0
0018 BA 0000    1            MOV    DX,0
001B CD 10      1            INT    10H

001D B4 4C                   MOV    AH,4CH               ;exit to DOS
001F CD 21                   INT    21H

0021            MAIN  ENDP

0021            CODE  ENDS

                END   MAIN
```

Example 6–16 shows how the INT 10H, BIOS function call is used to clear the video screen. This is just one method of clearing the screen. Notice that the first function call positions the cursor to row 0 and column 0, which is called the *home* position. Next we use the DOS function call to write 1920 (80 characters per line × 24 character lines) blank spaces (20H) on the video display, then we again home the cursor.

If this example is assembled, linked, and executed, a problem surfaces. This program is far too slow to be useful in most cases. To correct this situation another BIOS function call is used. We can use the scroll function (06H) to clear the screen at a much higher speed.

EXAMPLE 6–17

```
0000            CODE  SEGMENT

                      ASSUME CS:CODE

0000            MAIN  PROC   FAR

                HOME  MACRO

                      MOV    AH,2                 ;;set cursor position
                      MOV    BH,0                 ;;page 0
                      MOV    DX,0                 ;;row 0, column 0
                      INT    10H

                      ENDM

0000 32 FF            XOR    BH,BH                ;page 0
```

```
0002 B4 08              MOV     AH,8              ;read attributes
0004 CD 10              INT     10H

0006 8A DF              MOV     BL,BH
0008 8A FC              MOV     BH,AH
000A 2B C9              SUB     CX,CX
000C BA 184F            MOV     DX,184FH
000F B8 0600            MOV     AX,0600H          ;clear page 0
0012 CD 10              INT     10H

                        HOME
0014 B4 02        1     MOV     AH,2
0016 B7 00        1     MOV     BH,0
0018 BA 0000      1     MOV     DX,0
001B CD 10        1     INT     10H

001D B4 4C              MOV     AH,4CH            ;exit to DOS
001F CD 21              INT     21H

0021            MAIN     ENDP

0021            CODE     ENDS

                        END     MAIN
```

Function 06H is used with a 00H in AL to blank the entire screen. This allows Example 6–16 to be rewritten so that the screen clears at a much higher speed. See Example 6–17 for a better clear and home cursor program. Here function call number 08H reads the character attributes for blanking the screen. Next, they are positioned in the correct registers and DX is loaded with the screen size, 4FH (79) and 18H (24). If this program is assembled, linked, executed, and compared with Example 6–16, there is a big difference in the speed at which the screen is cleared. Please refer to Appendix A for other BIOS INT 10H function calls that may prove useful in your applications. Also presented in Appendix A is a complete listing of all the INT functions available in most computers.

6-3   DATA CONVERSIONS

In computer systems, data are seldom in the correct form. One main task of the system is to convert data from one form to another. This section of the chapter describes conversions between binary and ASCII. Binary data are removed from a register or memory and converted to ASCII for the video display. In many cases, ASCII data are converted to binary as they are typed on the keyboard. We also explain converting between ASCII and hexadecimal data.

Converting from Binary to ASCII

Conversion from binary to ASCII is accomplished in two ways: (1) by the AAM instruction if the number is less than 100, or (2) by a series of decimal divisions (divide by 10). Both techniques are presented in this section.

The AAM instruction converts the value in AX into a two-digit unpacked BCD number in AX. If the number in AX is 0062H (98 decimal) before AAM executes, AX contains a 0908H after AAM executes. This is not ASCII code, but it is converted to ASCII code by adding a 3030H to AX. Example 6–18 illustrates a procedure that processes the binary value in AL (0–99) and displays it on the video screen as decimal. This procedure blanks a leading zero, which occurs for the numbers 0–9, with an ASCII space code.

EXAMPLE 6–18

```
0000                    DISP    PROC    FAR

0000 52                         PUSH    DX          ;save DX
0001 32 E4                      XOR     AH,AH       ;blank AH
0003 D4 0A                      AAM                 ;convert to BCD
0005 80 C4 20                   ADD     AH,20H      ;add 20H
0008 80 FC 20                   CMP     AH,20H      ;test for leading zero
000B 74 03                      JE      DISP1       ;if leading zero
000D 80 C4 10                   ADD     AH,10H      ;convert to ASCII

0010            DISP1:

0010 50                         PUSH    AX
0011 8A D4                      MOV     DL,AH       ;display first digit
0013 B4 06                      MOV     AH,6
0015 CD 21                      INT     21H
0017 58                         POP     AX
0018 04 30                      ADD     AL,30H      ;convert to ASCII
001A 8A D0                      MOV     DL,AL
001C B4 06                      MOV     AH,6        ;display second digit
001E CD 21                      INT     21H
0020 5A                         POP     DX          ;restore DX
0021 CB                         RET

0022                    DISP    ENDP
```

The reason that AAM converts any number between 0 and 99 to a two-digit unpacked BCD number is because it divides AX by 10. The result is left in AX so AH contains the quotient and AL the remainder. This same scheme of dividing by ten can be expanded to convert any whole number from binary to an ASCII coded character string that can be displayed on the video screen. The algorithm for converting from binary to ASCII is:

1. Divide by 10 and save the remainder on the stack as a significant BCD digit.
2. Repeat step 2 until the quotient is a 0.
3. Retrieve each remainder and add a 30H to convert to ASCII before displaying or printing.

Example 6–19 shows how the unsigned 16-bit contents of AX are converted to ASCII and displayed on the video screen. Here we divide AX by 10 and save the remainder on the stack after each division for later conversion to ASCII. After all the digits have been converted, the result is displayed on the video screen by removing the remainders from the stack and converting them to ASCII code. This procedure also blanks any leading zeros that occur.

EXAMPLE 6-19

```
0000                    DISPX   PROC    FAR

0000 52                         PUSH    DX              ;save BX, CX, and DX
0001 51                         PUSH    CX
0002 53                         PUSH    BX

0003 33 C9                      XOR     CX,CX           ;clear CX
0005 BB 000A                    MOV     BX,10           ;load 10

0008                    DISPX1:

0008 33 D2                      XOR     DX,DX           ;clear DX
000A F7 F3                      DIV     BX
000C 52                         PUSH    DX              ;save remainder
000D 41                         INC     CX              ;count remainder
000E 0B C0                      OR      AX,AX           ;test quotient
0010 75 F6                      JNZ     DISPX1          ;if not zero

0012                    DISPX2:

0012 5A                         POP     DX              ;display number
0013 B4 06                      MOV     AH,6
0015 80 C2 30                   ADD     DL,30H          ;convert to ASCII
0018 CD 21                      INT     21H
001A E2 F6                      LOOP    DISPX2          ;repeat

001C 5B                         POP     BX              ;restore BX, CX, and DX
001D 59                         POP     CX
001E 5A                         POP     DX
001F CB                         RET

0020                    DISPX   ENDP
```

Converting from ASCII to Binary

Conversions from ASCII to binary usually start with keyboard entry. If a single key is typed, the conversion occurs when a 30H is subtracted from the number. If more than one key is typed, conversion from ASCII to binary still requires that 30H is subtracted, but there is one additional step. After subtracting 30H, the number is added to the result after the prior result is first multiplied by a 10. The algorithm for converting from ASCII to binary is:

1. Begin with a binary result of 0.
2. Subtract 30H from the character typed on the keyboard to convert it to BCD.
3. Multiply the result by 10 and add the new BCD digit.
4. Repeat steps 2 and 3 until the character typed is not an ASCII-coded number.

EXAMPLE 6-20

```
0000                    READN   PROC    FAR

0000 53                         PUSH    BX              ;save BX and CX
0001 51                         PUSH    CX
0002 B9 000A                    MOV     CX,10           ;load 10
0005 33 DB                      XOR     BX,BX           ;clear result

0007                    READN1:
```

```
0007 B4 06                    MOV    AH,6              ;read key
0009 B2 FF                    MOV    DL,0FFH
000B CD 21                    INT    21H
000D 74 F8                    JE     READN1            ;wait for key

000F 3C 30                    CMP    AL,'0'            ;test against 0
0011 72 18                    JB     READN2            ;if below 0
0013 3C 39                    CMP    AL,'9'            ;test against 9
0015 77 14                    JA     READN2            ;if above 9

0017 8A D0                    MOV    DL,AL             ;echo key
0019 CD 21                    INT    21H

001B 2C 30                    SUB    AL,'0'            ;convert to BCD

001D 50                       PUSH   AX
001E 8B C3                    MOV    AX,BX             ;multiply by 10
0020 F7 E1                    MUL    CX
0022 8B D8                    MOV    BX,AX             ;save product
0024 58                       POP    AX
0025 32 E4                    XOR    AH,AH
0027 03 D8                    ADD    BX,AX             ;add BCD to product
0029 EB DC                    JMP    READN1            ;repeat

002B              READN2:

002B 8B C3                    MOV    AX,BX             ;move binary to AX
002D 59                       POP    CX                ;restore BX and CX
002E 5B                       POP    BX
002F CB                       RET

0030              READN    ENDP
```

Example 6–20 illustrates a procedure that implements this algorithm. Here the binary number returns in the AX register as a 16-bit result. If a larger result is required, the procedure must be reworked for 32-bit addition. Each time this procedure is called, it reads a number from the keyboard until any key other than 0 through 9 is typed.

Displaying and Reading Hexadecimal Data

Hexadecimal data is easier to read from the keyboard and display than decimal data. This type of date is not used at the applications level, but at the system level. System level data is often hexadecimal and must be either displayed in hexadecimal form or read from the keyboard as hexadecimal data.

Reading Hexadecimal Data.   Hexadecimal data appears as 0 to 9 and A to F. The ASCII codes obtained from the keyboard for hexadecimal data are 30H to 39H for the numbers 0 through 9 and 41H to 46H (A–F) or 61H to 66H (a–f) for the letters. To be useful, a procedure that reads hexadecimal data must be able to accept both lowercase and uppercase letters.

EXAMPLE 6–21

```
0000                         CONV   PROC   NEAR

0000 3C 39                          CMP    AL,'9'
0002 76 08                          JBE    CONV2             ;if a number
```

```
0004 3C 61                          CMP     AL,'a'
0006 72 02                          JB      CONV1              ;if uppercase
0008 2C 20                          SUB     AL,20H

000A                 CONV1:

000A 2C 07                          SUB     AL,7

000C                 CONV2:

000C 2C 30                          SUB     AL,'0'
000E C3                             RET

000F                 CONV    ENDP

000F                 READH   PROC    FAR

000F 51                             PUSH    CX                 ;save BX and CX
0010 53                             PUSH    BX
0011 B9 0004                        MOV     CX,4               ;load shift count
0014 8B F1                          MOV     SI,CX              ;load count
0016 33 DB                          XOR     BX,BX              ;clear result

0018                 READH1:

0018 B4 06                          MOV     AH,6               ;read key
001A B2 FF                          MOV     DL,0FFH
001C CD 21                          INT     21H
001E 74 F8                          JE      READH1             ;wait for key
0020 8A D0                          MOV     DL,AL              ;echo
0022 CD 21                          INT     21H
0024 E8 0000 R                      CALL    CONV               ;convert to hexadecimal
0027 D3 E3                          SHL     BX,CL              ;shift result
0029 02 D8                          ADD     BL,AL              ;add AL to result
002B 4E                             DEC     SI
002C 75 EA                          JNZ     READH1             ;repeat 4 times
002E 5B                             POP     BX                 ;restore BX and CX
002F 59                             POP     CX
0030 CB                             RET

0031                 READH   ENDP
```

Example 6–21 shows two procedures: one converts the contents of the data in AL from ASCII code to a single hexadecimal digit, while the other reads a 4-digit hexadecimal number from the keyboard and returns with it in register AX. This procedure can be modified to read any size hexadecimal number from the keyboard.

Displaying Hexadecimal Data. To display hexadecimal data, a number must be divided into 4-bit segments that are converted into hexadecimal digits. Conversion is accomplished by adding a 30H to the numbers 0 to 9 and a 37H to the letters A to F.

EXAMPLE 6–22

```
0000                 DISPH   PROC    FAR

0000 51                             PUSH    CX                 ;save CX and DX
0001 52                             PUSH    DX
0002 B1 04                          MOV     CL,4               ;load rotate count
```

```
0004 B5 04                    MOV     CH,4              ;load digit count

0006              DISPH1:

0006 D3 C0                    ROL     AX,CL             ;position number
0008 50                       PUSH    AX                ;save it
0009 24 0F                    AND     AL,0FH            ;get hex digit
000B 04 30                    ADD     AL,30H            ;adjust it
000D 3C 39                    CMP     AL,'9'            ;test against 9
000F 76 02                    JBE     DISPH2            ;if 0 - 9
0011 04 07                    ADD     AL,7              ;adjust it

0013              DISPH2:

0013 B4 06                    MOV     AH,6
0015 8A D0                    MOV     DL,AL
0017 CD 21                    INT     21H               ;display digit
0019 58                       POP     AX                ;restore AX
001A FE CD                    DEC     CH
001C 75 E8                    JNZ     DISPH1            ;repeat

001E 5A                       POP     DX                ;restore CX and DX
001F 59                       POP     CX
0020 CB                       RET

0021              DISPH   ENDP
```

A procedure that displays the contents of the AX register on the video display appears in Example 6–22. Here the number is rotated left so the leftmost digit is displayed first. Because AX contains a 4-digit hexadecimal number, the procedure displays 4 hexadecimal digits.

Using Lookup Tables for Data Conversions

Lookup tables are often used to convert from one data form to another. A lookup table is formed in the memory as a list of data that is referenced by a procedure to perform conversions. In the case of many lookup tables, the XLAT instruction can often be used to lookup data in a table provided the table contains 8-bit wide data and its length is less than or equal to 256 bytes.

Converting from BCD to 7-Segment Code.   One simple application that uses a lookup table is BCD to 7-segment code conversion. Example 6–23 illustrates a lookup table that contains the 7-segment codes for the numbers 0 to 9. These codes are used with the 7-segment display pictured in Figure 6–1. This 7-segment display uses active high (logic 1) inputs to light a segment. The code is arranged so that the *a* segment is in bit position 0 and the *g* segment is in bit position 6. Bit position seven is zero in this example, but can be used for displaying a decimal point.

EXAMPLE 6–23

```
0000              SEG7    PROC    FAR

0000 53                   PUSH    BX
0001 BB 0008 R            MOV     BX,OFFSET TABLE
0004 2E: D7               XLAT    CS:TABLE          ;see text
```

FIGURE 6-1 The 7-segment display.

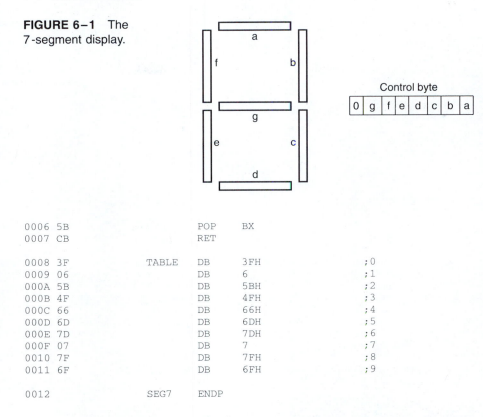

Control byte

0	g	f	e	d	c	b	a

```
0006  5B                   POP     BX
0007  CB                   RET

0008  3F          TABLE    DB      3FH            ;0
0009  06                   DB      6              ;1
000A  5B                   DB      5BH            ;2
000B  4F                   DB      4FH            ;3
000C  66                   DB      66H            ;4
000D  6D                   DB      6DH            ;5
000E  7D                   DB      7DH            ;6
000F  07                   DB      7              ;7
0010  7F                   DB      7FH            ;8
0011  6F                   DB      6FH            ;9

0012              SEG7     ENDP
```

The procedure that performs the conversion contains only two instructions and assumes that AL contains the BCD digit to be converted to 7-segment code. One of the instructions addresses the lookup table by loading its address into BX and the other performs the conversion and returns the 7-segment code in AL.

Because the lookup table is located in the code segment, and the XLAT instruction accesses the data segment by default, the XLAT instruction includes a segment override. Notice that a dummy operand (TABLE) is added to the XLAT instruction so the (CS:) code segment override prefix can be added to the instruction. Normally XLAT does not contain an operand unless its default segment must be overridden. The LODS and MOVS instructions are also overridden in the same manner as XLAT by using a dummy operand.

Using a Lookup Table to Access ASCII Data. Some programming techniques require that numeric codes are converted to ASCII character strings. For example, suppose that you need to display the days of the week for a calendar program. Because the number of ASCII characters in each day is different, some type of lookup table must be used to reference the ASCII coded days of the week.

EXAMPLE 6-24

```
0000              DAYS     PROC    FAR

0000  52                   PUSH    DX             ;save DX and SI
0001  56                   PUSH    SI
```

```
0002 BE 001B R              MOV    SI,OFFSET DTAB      ;address DTAB
0005 32 E4                  XOR    AH,AH               ;clear AH
0007 03 C0                  ADD    AX,AX               ;double AX
0009 03 F0                  ADD    SI,AX               ;modify table address
000B 2E: 8B 14              MOV    DX,CS:[SI]          ;get string address
000E 8C C8                  MOV    AX,CS               ;change data segment
0010 1E                     PUSH   DS
0011 8E D8                  MOV    DS,AX
0013 B4 09                  MOV    AH,9
0015 CD 21                  INT    21H                 ;display string
0017 1F                     POP    DS
0018 5E                     POP    SI                  ;restore DX and SI
0019 5A                     POP    DX
001A CB                     RET

001B 0029 R 0031 R    DTAB  DW     SUN,MON,TUE,WED,THU,FRI,SAT
     0039 R 0042 R
     004D R 0057 R
     005F R

0029 53 75 6E 64 61   SUN   DB     'Sunday $'
     79 20 24

0031 4D 6F 6E 64 61   MON   DB     'Monday $'
     79 20 24

0039 54 75 65 73 64   TUE   DB     'Tuesday $'
     61 79 20 24

0042 57 65 64 6E 65   WED   DB     'Wednesday $'
     73 64 61 79 20 24

004D 54 68 75 72 73   THU   DB     'Thursday $'
     64 61 79 20 24

0057 46 72 69 64 61   FRI   DB     'Friday $'
     79 20 24

005F 53 61 74 75 72   SAT   DB     'Saturday $'
     64 61 79 20 24

0069                  DAYS  ENDP
```

Example 6–24 shows a table that references ASCII coded character strings located in the code segment. Each character string contains an ASCII coded day of the week. The table references each day of the week. The procedure that accesses the day of the week uses the AL register and the numbers 0 to 6 to refer to Sunday through Saturday. If AL contains a 2 when this procedure is called, the word *"Tuesday"* is displayed on the video screen.

This procedure first addresses the table by loading its address into the SI register. Next the number in AL is converted into a 16-bit number and doubled because the table contains 2 bytes for each entry. This index is then added to SI to address the correct entry in the lookup table. The address of the ASCII character string is now loaded into DX by the MOV DX,CS:[SI] instruction.

Before the INT 21H DOS function is called, the DS register is placed on the stack and loaded with the segment address of CS. This allows DOS function number 09H (display a string) to be used to display the day of the week. This procedure converts the numbers 0 to 6 to the days of the week.

An Example Program Using Data Conversions

A program example is required to combine some of the data conversion DOS functions. Suppose that you must display the time and date on the video screen. This example program (see Example 6–25) displays the time as 10:45 P.M. and the date as Tuesday, May 14, 1991. The program is short because it calls a procedure that displays the time and a second that displays the date.

EXAMPLE 6–25 (page 1 of 4)

```
0000                         STAC    SEGMENT STACK

0000 0100[                   DW      256 DUP (?)              ;set up stack
               ????
            ]

0200                         STAC    ENDS

0000                         DAT     SEGMENT

0000 0026 R 002F R 0038 R    DAY     DW      SUN,MON,TUE,WED,THU,FRI,SAT
     0042 R 004E R 0059 R
     0062 R
000E 006D R 0076 R 0080 R    MONT    DW      JAN,FEB,MAR,APR,MAY,JUN,JUL,AUG,SEP,OCT,NOV,DC
     0087 R 008E R 0093 R
     0099 R 009F R 00A7 R
     00B2 R 00BB R 00C5 R

0026 53 75 6E 64 61 79       SUN     DB      'Sunday, $'
     2C 20 24
002F 4D 6F 6E 64 61 79       MON     DB      'Monday, $'
     2C 20 24
0038 54 75 65 73 64 61       TUE     DB      'Tuesday, $'
     79 2C 20 24
0042 57 65 64 6E 65 73       WE      DB      'Wednesday, $'
     64 61 79 2C 20 24
004E 54 68 75 72 73 64       THU     DB      'Thursday, $'
     61 79 2C 20 24
0059 46 72 69 64 61 79       FRI     DB      'Friday, $'
     2C 20 24
0062 53 61 74 75 72 64       SAT     DB      'Saturday, $'
     61 79 2C 20 24

006D 4A 61 6E 75 61 72       JAN     DB      'January $'
     79 20 24
0076 46 65 62 72 75 61       FEB     DB      'February $'
     72 79 20 24
0080 4D 61 72 63 68 20       MAR     DB      'March $'
     24
0087 41 70 72 69 6C 20       APR     DB      'April $'
     24
008E 4D 61 79 20 24          MAY     DB      'May $'
0093 4A 75 6E 65 20 24       JUN     DB      'June $'
0099 4A 75 6C 79 20 24       JUL     DB      'July $'
009F 41 75 67 75 73 74       AUG     DB      'August $'
```

EXAMPLE 6-25 (page 2 of 4)

```
        20 24
00A7 53 65 70 74 65 6D      SEP     DB      'September $'
     62 65 72 20 24
00B2 4F 63 74 6F 62 65      OCT     DB      'October $'
     72 20 24
00BB 4E 6F 76 65 6D 62      NOV     DB      'November $'
     65 72 20 24
00C5 44 65 63 65 6D 62      DC      DB      'December $'
     65 72 20 24

00CF 0D 0A 24               CRLF    DB      13,10,'$'
00D2 2E 4D 2E 20 20 24      MES1    DB      '.M. $'
00D8 2C 20 31 39 24         MES2    DB      ',19$'
00DD 2C 20 32 30 24         MES3    DB      ',20$'

00E2                DAT     ENDS

0000                COD     SEGMENT

                            ASSUME  CS:COD,DS:DAT,SS:STAC

0000                MAIN    PROC    FAR             ;main program

0000 B8 -- R                MOV     AX,DAT          ;load DS
0003 8E D8                  MOV     DS,AX

0005 BA 00CF R              MOV     DX,OFFSET CRLF  ;get new line
0008 B4 09                  MOV     AH,9
000A CD 21                  INT     21H

000C E8 001D R              CALL    TIMES           ;display time
000F E8 007E R              CALL    DATES           ;display date

0012 BA 00CF R              MOV     DX,OFFSET CRLF  ;get new line
0015 B4 09                  MOV     AH,9
0017 CD 21                  INT     21H

0019 B4 4C                  MOV     AH,4CH          ;exit to DOS
001B CD 21                  INT     21H

001D                MAIN    ENDP

001D                TIMES   PROC    NEAR            ;display time XX:XX A.M.

001D B4 2C                  MOV     AH,2CH          ;get time
001F CD 21                  INT     21H

0021 B7 41                  MOV     BH,'A'          ;set AM

0023 80 FD 0C               CMP     CH,12           ;test against 12
0026 72 05                  JB      TIMES1          ;if AM

0028 B7 50                  MOV     BH,'P'          ;set PM
002A 80 ED 0C               SUB     CH,12           ;adjust time
002D                TIMES1:

002D 0A ED                  OR      CH,CH           ;test for 0 hours
002F 75 02                  JNE     TIMES2          ;if not 0 hours
0031 B5 0C                  MOV     CH,12           ;replace with 12 hours
```

EXAMPLE 6-25 (page 3 of 4)

```
0033                    TIMES2:

0033 8A C5                      MOV     AL,CH           ;get hours
0035 32 E4                      XOR     AH,AH           ;clear AH
0037 D4 0A                      AAM                     ;convert to BCD
0039 0A E4                      OR      AH,AH           ;test tens of hours
003B 74 09                      JZ      TIMES3          ;if no tens of hours
003D 50                         PUSH    AX
003E 8A C4                      MOV     AL,AH
0040 04 30                      ADD     AL,'0'          ;convert to ASCII
0042 E8 0075 R                  CALL    DISP            ;display tens of hours
0045 58                         POP     AX

0046                    TIMES3:

0046 04 30                      ADD     AL,'0'          ;convert to ASCII
0048 E8 0075 R                  CALL    DISP            ;display units of hours
004B B0 3A                      MOV     AL,':'          ;display colon
004D E8 0075 R                  CALL    DISP

0050 8A C1                      MOV     AL,CL           ;get minutes
0052 32 E4                      XOR     AH,AH           ;clear AH
0054 D4 0A                      AAM                     ;convert to BCD

0056 05 3030                    ADD     AX,3030H        ;convert to ASCII
0059 50                         PUSH    AX
005A 8A C4                      MOV     AL,AH
005C E8 0075 R                  CALL    DISP            ;display tens of minutes
005F 58                         POP     AX
0060 E8 0075 R                  CALL    DISP            ;display units of minutes

0063 B0 20                      MOV     AL,''           ;display space
0065 E8 0075 R                  CALL    DISP

0068 8A C7                      MOV     AL,BH           ;display A or P
006A E8 0075 R                  CALL    DISP

006D BA 00D2 R                  MOV     DX,OFFSET MES1  ;display .M.
0070 B4 09                      MOV     AH,9
0072 CD 21                      INT     21H
0074 C3                         RET

0075                    TIMES   ENDP
0075                    DISP    PROC    NEAR            ;display ASCII

0075 50                         PUSH    AX
0076 B4 06                      MOV     AH,6
0078 8A D0                      MOV     DL,AL
007A CD 21                      INT     21H
007C 58                         POP     AX
007D C3                         RET

007E                    DISP    ENDP

007E                    DATES   PROC    NEAR            ;display date

007E B4 2A                      MOV     AH,2AH          ;get date
0080 CD 21                      INT     21H
0082 52                         PUSH    DX              ;save month and day
```

EXAMPLE 6–25 (page 4 of 4)

```
0083 32 E4                    XOR    AH,AH              ;clear AH
0085 03 C0                    ADD    AX,AX              ;double AX
0087 BE 0000 R                MOV    SI,OFFSET DAY      ;address day table
008A 03 F0                    ADD    SI,AX
008C 8B 14                    MOV    DX,[SI]            ;get string address
008E B4 09                    MOV    AH,9
0090 CD 21                    INT    21H                ;display day

0092 5A                       POP    DX
0093 52                       PUSH   DX
0094 8A C6                    MOV    AL,DH              ;get month
0096 FE C8                    DEC    AL
0098 32 E4                    XOR    AH,AH
009A 03 C0                    ADD    AX,AX
009C BE 000E R                MOV    SI,OFFSET MONT     ;address month table
009F 03 F0                    ADD    SI,AX
00A1 8B 14                    MOV    DX,[SI]            ;get string address
00A3 B4 09                    MOV    AH,9
00A5 CD 21                    INT    21H                ;display month

00A7 5A                       POP    DX                 ;get day
00A8 8A C2                    MOV    AL,DL
00AA 32 E4                    XOR    AH,AH              ;clear AH
00AC D4 0A                    AAM                       ;convert to BCD
00AE 0A E4                    OR     AH,AH              ;test tens of day
00B0 74 09                    JZ     DATES1             ;if zero
00B2 50                       PUSH   AX
00B3 8A C4                    MOV    AL,AH
00B5 04 30                    ADD    AL,'O'             ;convert to ASCII
00B7 E8 0075 R                CALL   DISP               ;display tens of day
00BA 58                       POP    AX

00BB             DATES1:
00BB 04 30                    ADD    AL,'0'             ;convert to ASCII
00BD E8 0075 R                CALL   DISP               ;display units of day
00C0 BA 00D8 R                MOV    DX,OFFSET MES2
00C3 81 F9 07D0               CMP    CX,2000            ;test for year 2000
00C7 72 06                    JB     DATES2             ;if year 19XX
00C9 83 E9 64                 SUB    CX,100
00CC BA 00DD R                MOV    DX,OFFSET MES3

00CF             DATES2:

00CF B4 09                    MOV    AH,9               ;display 19 or 20
00D1 CD 21                    INT    21H
00D3 81 E9 076C               SUB    CX,1900            ;adjust year
00D7 8B C1                    MOV    AX,CX
00D9 D4 0A                    AAM                       ;convert to BCD
00DB 05 3030                  ADD    AX,3030H           ;convert to ASCII
00DE 50                       PUSH   AX
00DF 8A C4                    MOV    AL,AH
00E1 E8 0075 R                CALL   DISP               ;display tens of year
00E4 58                       POP    AX
00E5 E8 0075 R                CALL   DISP               ;display units of year
00E8 C3                       RET

00E9             DATES   ENDP

00E9             COD     ENDS

                         END    MAIN
```

The time is available from DOS using and INT 21H function call number 2CH. This returns with the hours in CH and minutes in CL. Also available are seconds in DH and hundredths of seconds in DL. The date is available using INT 21H function call number 2AH. This leaves the day of the week in AL, the year in CX, the day of the month in DH, and the month in DL.

This procedure uses two ASCII lookup tables that convert the day and month to ASCII character strings. It also uses the AAM instruction to convert from binary to BCD for the time and date. The displaying of data is handled in two ways: by character string (function 09H) and by single character (function 06H).

The memory consists of three segments: stack (STAC), data (DAT), and code (COD). The data segment contains the characters strings used with the procedures that display time and date. The code segment contains MAIN, TIMES, DATES, and DISP procedures. The MAIN procedure is a FAR procedure because it is the program or main module. The other procedures are NEAR or local procedures used by MAIN.

6-4   DISK FILES

Data are found stored on the disk in the form of files. The disk itself is organized in four main parts: the boot sector, the file allocation table (FAT), the root directory, and the data storage areas. The first sector on the disk is the boot sector. The boot sector is used to load the disk operating system (DOS) from the disk into the memory when power is applied to the computer. The FAT is where the names of files/subdirectories and their locations on the disk are stored by DOS. All references to any disk file are handled through the FAT. The root directory is where all other subdirectories and files are referenced through. The disk files are all considered sequential access files meaning that they are accessed a byte at a time from the beginning of the file toward the end.

Disk Organization

Figure 6-2 illustrates the organization of sectors and tracks on the surface of the disk. This organization applies to both floppy and hard disk memory systems. The outer track is always track 0 and the inner track is 39 (double-density) or 79 (high-density) on floppy disks. The inner track on a hard disk is determined by the disk size and could be 10000 or higher for very large hard disks.

Figure 6-3 shows the organization of data on a disk. The length of the FAT is determined by the size of the disk. Likewise, the length of the root directory is determined by the number of files and subdirectories located within it. The boot sector is always a single *512-byte* long sector located in the outer track at sector 0, the first sector.

The boot sector contains a *bootstrap loader* program that is read into RAM when the system is powered. The bootstrap loader then executes and loads the IO.SYS[3] and MSDOS.SYS[4] programs into RAM. Next the bootstrap loader passes control to the

---

[3]IO.SYS is an I/O control program provided by Microsoft Corporation with Microsoft DOS.
[4]MSDOS.SYS is the Microsoft Disk Operating System.

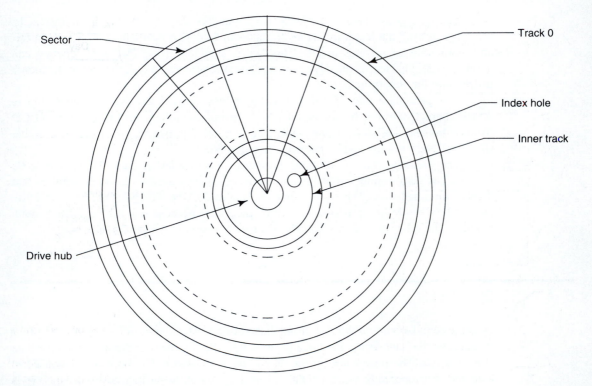

FIGURE 6–2   The format of a 5¼" floppy disk.

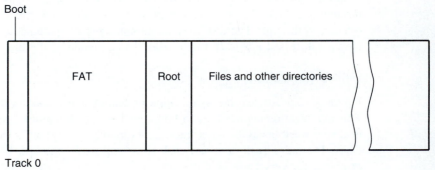

FIGURE 6–3   The main data storage areas on a disk.

MSDOS control program and the computer is now under the control of the DOS command processor.

The FAT indicates which sectors are free, which are corrupted (unusable), and which contain data. The FAT table is referenced each time that DOS writes data to the disk so that it can find a free sector. Each free cluster is indicated by a 0000H in the FAT and each occupied sector is indicated by the cluster number. A *cluster* can be anything from one sector to any number of sectors in length. Many hard disk memory

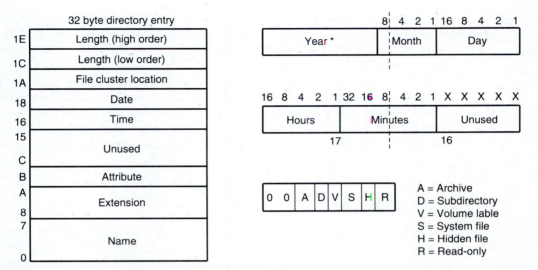

FIGURE 6-4 The format for any directory or subdirectory entry.

systems use 4 sectors per cluster, which means the smallest file is 512 × 4 or 2048 bytes in length.

Figure 6-4 shows the format of each directory entry in the root or any other directory or subdirectory. Each entry contains the name, extension, attribute, time, date, location, and length. The length of the file is stored as a 32-bit number. This means that a file can have a maximum length of 4G bytes. The location is the starting cluster number.

EXAMPLE 6-26

```
0000 49 4F 20 20 20 20 20 20 53 59 53 07 00 00 00 00  IO      SYS
0010 00 00 00 00 00 00 00 00 93 11 02 00 39 82 00 00

0020 4D 53 44 4F 53 20 20 20 53 59 53 07 00 00 00 00  MSDOS   SYS
0030 00 00 00 00 00 00 C0 44 93 12 13 00 92 00 00 00

0040 43 4F 4D 4D 41 4E 44 20 43 4F 4D 00 00 00 00 00  COMMAND COM
0050 00 00 00 00 00 00 00 00 93 11 26 00 B5 92 00 00

0060 42 41 52 52 59 20 42 52 45 59 20 28 00 00 00 00  BARRY BREY
0070 00 00 00 00 00 00 E0 AD 6A 13 00 00 00 00 00 00

0080 50 43 54 4F 4F 4C 53 20 20 20 20 10 00 00 00 00  PCTOOLS
0090 00 00 00 00 00 00 80 AE 6A 13 5C 00 00 00 00 00

00A0 44 4F 53 20 20 20 20 20 20 20 20 10 00 00 00 00  DOS
00B0 00 00 00 00 00 00 E0 B0 6A 13 4E 00 00 00 00 00

00C0 52 55 4E 5F 46 57 20 20 42 41 54 00 00 00 00 00  FUN_FW  BAT
00D0 00 00 00 00 00 00 40 BD 6A 13 97 0F 4A 00 00 00

00E0 46 4F 4E 54 57 41 52 45 20 20 20 10 00 00 00 00  FONTWARE
00F0 00 00 00 00 00 00 60 BD 6A 13 6E 00 00 00 00 00
```

Example 6–26 shows how part of the root directory appears in a hexadecimal dump. Try to identify the date, time, location, and length of each entry. Also identify the attribute for each entry. The listing shows hexadecimal data and also ASCII data as is customary for most computer dumps.

Files are usually accessed through DOS INT 21H function calls. There are two ways to access a file using INT 21H. One way uses a file control block and the other uses a file handle. Today, all software accesses files via a file handle, so this text also uses file handles for file access. File control blocks are a carryover from an earlier operating system called CPM (control program micro) that was used with 8-bit computer systems based on the Z80 or 8080 microprocessor.

Sequential File Access

All DOS files are sequential files. A sequential file is stored and accessed from the beginning of the file toward the end—the first byte and all bytes between it and the last must be accessed to read the last byte. Fortunately, files are read and written with the DOS INT 21H function calls (refer to Appendix A), which makes their access and manipulation easy. This section of the text describes how to create, read, write, delete, and rename a sequential access file.

File Creation.   Before a file can be used, it must exist on the disk. A file is *created* by the INT 21H function call number 3CH. The file name must be stored at a location addressed by DS:DX before calling the function and CX must contain the attribute of the file (or subdirectory) created.

EXAMPLE 6–27

```
0000                    DAT     SEGMENT

0000 44 4F 47 2E 54 58      FILE1   DB      'DOG.TXT',0             ;file name DOG.TXT
     54 00
0008 43 3A 44 41 54 41      FILE2   DB      'C:DATA.DOC',0         ;file C:DATA.DOC
     2E 44 4F 43 00
0013 43 3A 5C 44 52 45      FILE3   DB      'C:\DREAD\ERROR.FIL',0 ;file C:\DREAD\ERROR.FIL
     41 44 5C 45 52 52
     4F 52 2E 46 49 4C
     00

0026                    DAT     ENDS
```

A *file name* is always stored as an ASCII-Z string and may contain the drive and directory path(s) if needed. Example 6–27 shows several ASCII-Z string file names stored in a data segment for access by the file utilities. An *ASCII-Z string* is a character string that ends with a 00H or null character.

Suppose that you have filled a 256 memory buffer area with data that must be stored in a new file called DATA.NEW on the default disk drive. Before data can be written to this new file, it must first be created. Example 6–28 lists a short procedure that creates this new file on the disk.

EXAMPLE 6-28

```
0000                        DAT     SEGMENT

0000 44 41 54 41 2E 4E      FILE1   DB      'DATA.NEW',0    ;file name DATA.NEW
     45 57 00
0009 0100[                  BUFFER  DB      256 DUP (?)     ;data buffer
              ??
           ]

0109                        DAT     ENDS

0000                        COD     SEGMENT
                                    ASSUME  CS:COD,DS:DAT

0000 B8 ---- R              MOV     AX,DAT
0003 8E D8                  MOV     DX,AX                   ;load DS

0005 B4 3C                  MOV     AH,3CH                  ;load create function
0007 33 C9                  XOR     CX,CX                   ;00H = attribute
0009 BA 0000 R              MOV     DX,OFFSET FILE1         ;address ASCII-Z name
000C CD 21                  INT     21H                     ;create DATA.NEW

000E 72 20                  JC      ERROR                   ;on creation error
                                .       .
                                .       .
                                .       .
0030                        COD     ENDS

                                    END
```

Whenever a file is created, the CX register must contain the attributes or characteristics of the file. Table 6-3 lists the attribute bit positions and defines them. A logic one in a bit selects the attribute, while a logic zero does not.

After returning from the INT 21H, the carry flag indicates whether an error occurred (CF = 1) during the creation of the file. Some errors that can occur, which are obtained if needed by INT 21H function call number 59H, are: path not found, no file handles available, or media error. If carry is cleared, no error has occurred and the AX

TABLE 6-3 File attribute definitions

Bit Position	Attribute	Function
0	Read-only	A read-only file or subdirectory
1	Hidden	Prevents the file or subdirectory name from appearing in the directory when a DIR is used from the DOS command line
2	System	Specifies a file as a system file
3	Volume	Specifies the disk volume label
4	Subdirectory	Specifies a subdirectory name
5	Archive	Indicates that a file has been changed and that it should be archived

register contains a file handle. The **file handle** is a number that is used to refer to the file after it is created or opened. The file handle allows a file to be accessed without using the ASCII-Z string name of the file speeding the operation.

Writing to a File.   Now that we have created a new file, called FILE.NEW, data can be written to it. Before writing to a file it must have been created or opened. When a file is created or opened, the file handle returns in the AX register. The file handle is used to refer to the file whenever data are written.

Function number 40H is used to write data to an opened or newly created file. In addition to loading a 40H into AH, we must load BX = the file handle, CX = the number of bytes to be written, and DS:DX = the address of the area to be written to the disk.

EXAMPLE 6–29

```
                                    .        .
                                    .        .
                                    .        .
0010 8B D8              MOV     BX,AX                ;move handle to BX
0012 B4 40              MOV     AH,40H               ;load write function
0014 B9 0100            MOV     CX,256               ;load count
0017 BA 0009 R          MOV     DX,OFFSET BUFFER     ;address BUFFER
001A CD 21              INT     21H                  ;write 256 bytes from BUFFER

001C 72 32              JC      ERROR1               ;on write error
```

Suppose that we must write all 256 bytes of BUFFER to the file. This is accomplished as illustrated in Example 6–29 using function 40H. If an error occurs during a write operation, the carry flag is set. If no error occurs, the carry flag is cleared and the number of bytes written to the file is returned in the AX register. Errors that occur for writes usually indicate that the disk is full or that there is some type of media error.

Opening, Reading, and Closing a File.   To read a file, it must be opened first. When a file is opened, DOS checks the directory to determine if the file exists and returns the DOS file handle in register AX. The DOS file handle must be used for reading, writing, and closing a file.

EXAMPLE 6–30

```
0000                   READ    PROC    NEAR

0000 B4 3D             MOV     AH,3DH               ;load open function
0002 B0 00             MOV     AL,0                 ;select read
0004 BA 0000 R         MOV     DX,OFFSET FILE1      ;address file name
0007 CD 21             INT     21H                  ;open file

0009 72 15             JC      ERROR                ;on error

000B 8B D8             MOV     BX,AX                ;move file handle to BX

000D B4 3F             MOV     AH,3FH               ;load read function
000F B9 0100           MOV     CX,256               ;number of bytes
0012 BA 0009 R         MOV     DX,OFFSET BUFFER     ;address BUFFER
0015 CD 21             INT     21H                  ;read 256 bytes

0017 72 07             JC      ERROR                ;on error
```

```
0019 B4 3E                    MOV     AH,3EH            ;load close function
001B CD 21                    INT     21H               ;close file

001D 72 01                    JC      ERROR             ;on error

001F C3                       RET

0020             READ         ENDP
```

Example 6–30 shows a sequence of instructions that open a file, read 256 bytes from the file into memory area BUFFER, and then close the file. When a file is opened (AH = 3DH), the AL register specifies the type of operation allowed for the opened file. If AL = 00H, the file is opened for a read; if AL = 01H, the file is opened for a write; and if AL = 02H, the file is opened for a read or a write.

Function number 3FH causes a file to be read. As with the write function, BX contains the file handle, CX, the number of bytes to be read, and DS:DX contains the location of a memory area where the data are stored. As with all disk functions, the carry flag indicates an error when a logic one. If a logic zero, the AX register indicates the number of bytes read from the file.

Closing a file is very important. If a file is left open, some serious problems can occur that can actually destroy the disk and all its data. If a file is written and not closed, the FAT can become corrupted, making it difficult or impossible to retrieve data from the disk. Always be certain to close a file after it is read or written.

The File Pointer. When a file is opened, written, or read, the file pointer addresses the current location in the sequential file. When a file is opened, the file pointer always addresses the first byte of the file. If a file is 1,024 bytes in length, and a read function reads 1,023 bytes, the file pointer addresses the last byte of the file, but not the end of the file.

The **file pointer** is a 32-bit number that addresses any byte in a file. Once a file is opened, the file pointer can be changed with the move file pointer function number 42H. A file pointer can be moved from the start of the file (AL = 00H), from the current location (AL = 01H), or from the end of the file (AL = 02H). In practice all three directions of the move are used to access different parts of the file. The distance moved by the file pointer is specified by registers CX and DX. The DX register holds the least significant part and CX the most significant part of the distance. Register BX must contain the file handle before using function 42H to move the file pointer.

Suppose that a file exists on the disk and that you must append the file with 256 bytes of new information. When the file is opened, the file pointer addresses the first byte of the file. If you attempt to write without moving the file pointer to the end of the file, the new data will overwrite the first 256 bytes of the file. Example 6–31 shows a procedure that opens a file, moves the file pointer to the end of the file, writes 256 bytes of data, and then closes the file. This *appends* the file with 256 new bytes of data.

EXAMPLE 6–31

```
0000             APPEND       PROC    NEAR

0000 B4 3D                    MOV     AH,3DH            ;load open function
0002 B0 01                    MOV     AL,1              ;select write
0004 BA 0000 R                MOV     DX,OFFSET FILE1   ;address file name
```

```
0007 CD 21                    INT     21H              ;open file

0009 72 21                    JC      ERROR            ;on error

000B 8B D8                    MOV     BX,AX            ;move file handle to BX

000D B4 42                    MOV     AH,42H           ;load move file pointer function
000F B0 02                    MOV     AL,02H           ;move from end
0011 33 C9                    XOR     CX,CX            ;move 0 bytes from end
0013 33 D2                    XOR     DX,DX
0015 CD 21                    INT     21H              ;move pointer to end

0017 72 13                    JC      ERROR            ;on error

0019 B4 40                    MOV     AH,40H           ;load write function
001B B9 0100                  MOV     CX,256           ;number of bytes
001E BA 0009 R                MOV     DX,OFFSET BUFFER ;address BUFFER
0021 CD 21                    INT     21H              ;write 256 bytes

0023 72 07                    JC      ERROR            ;on error

0025 B4 3E                    MOV     AH,3EH           ;load close function
0027 CD 21                    INT     21H              ;close file

0029 72 01                    JC      ERROR            ;on error

002B C3                       RET

002C              APPEND      ENDP
```

One of the more difficult file maneuvers is inserting new data in the middle of the file. Figure 6–5 shows how this is accomplished by creating a second file. Notice that the part of the file before the insertion point is copied into the new file. This is followed by the new information before the remainder of the file is appended after the insertion in the new file. Once the new file is complete, the old file is deleted and the new file is renamed to the old file name.

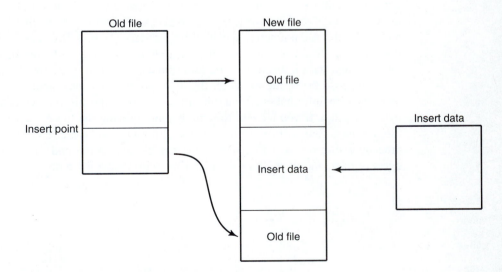

FIGURE 6–5   Inserting new data within an old file.

Example 6–32 shows a procedure that inserts new data, up to 64K bytes in length, into an old file. This procedure required some input parameters to make it a general-purpose procedure. The first parameter is the old file name that is passed to the procedure through the DS:DX register. The second parameter (register CX) is the number of new bytes of information to write to the new file. The third parameter is the location (ES:SI) of the new data to be inserted in the file. The final parameter is the insertion point located in registers BP and DI, where BP contains the most significant insert point and DI the least.

EXAMPLE 6–32 (page 1 of 3)

```
0000                    DATA    SEGMENT PUBLIC

0000 0100[              BUFFER  DB    256 DUP (?)    ;buffer
           ??
         ]
0100 0000              TEMP     DW    ?              ;temporary data
0102 0000              TEMP1    DW    ?              ;temporary data
0104 0000              OLD_HAN  DW    ?              ;old handle
0106 0000              NEW_HAN  DW    ?              ;temp handle
0108 54 45 4D 50 2E 24 TEMPS    DB    'TEMP.$$$',0   ;temp file
     24 24 00

0111                    DATA    ENDS

0000                    CODE    SEGMENT

                        ASUMME CS:CODE,DS:DATA

0000                    INSERT  PROC    FAR

0000 89 16 0100 R               MOV     TEMP,DX       ;save old file address
0004 89 0E 0102 R               MOV     TEMP1,CX      ;save count

0008 B8 3D02                    MOV     AX,3D02H      ;open old file
000B CD 21                      INT     21H
000D A3 0104 R                  MOV     OLD_HAN,AX    ;save old file handle
0010 73 05                      JNC     INSERT1       ;if no error

0012 E8 009F R                  CALL    C_OLD         ;close old file
0015 F9                         STC                   ;indicate error
0016 CB                         RET

0017                    INSERT1:

0017 B4 3C                      MOV     AH,3CH        ;create temp file
0019 33 C9                      XOR     CX,CX
001B BA 0108 R                  MOV     DX,OFFSET TEMPS
001E CD 21                      INT     21H
0020 A3 0106 R                  MOV     NEW_HAN,AX    ;save temp file handle
0023 73 08                      JNC     INSERT2

0025                    EXIT:

0025 E8 00A8 R                  CALL    C_TEMP        ;close temp file
0028 E8 009F R                  CALL    C_OLD         ;close old file
002B F9                         STC                   ;indicate error
002C CB                         RET
002D                    INSERT2:
```

EXAMPLE 6–32 (page 2 of 3)

```
002D 81 FF 0100          CMP    DI,256        ;test insert point
0031 77 07               JA     INSERT3       ;if greater than 256
0033 0B ED               OR     BP,BP
0035 75 03               JNE    INSERT3       ;if greater than 256
0037 EB 17 90            JMP    INSERT4       ;if less than 256

003A              INSERT3:

003A B9 0100             MOV    CX,256
003D E8 00B1 R           CALL   R_OLD         ;read old file
0040 72 E3               JC     EXIT          ;on error
0042 E8 00BD R           CALL   W_TEMP        ;write temp file
0045 72 DE               JC     EXIT          ;on error

0047 81 EF 0100          SUB    DI,256        ;decrement BP-DI by 256
004B 83 DD 00            SBB    BP,0
004E EB DD               JMP    INSERT2

0050              INSERT4:

0050 8B CF               MOV    CX,DI         ;get count
0052 E8 00B1 R           CALL   R_OLD         ;read old file
0055 72 CE               JC     EXIT          ;on error
0057 E8 00BD R           CALL   W_TEMP        ;write temp file
005A 72 C9               JC     EXIT          ;on error

005C 8B 0E 0102 R        MOV    CX,TEMP1      ;get insert count
0060 1E                  PUSH   DS            ;save data segment
0061 8C C0               MOV    AX,ES
0063 8E D8               MOV    DS,AX         ;load DS with ES

0065 8B D6               MOV    DX,SI         ;get address
0067 B4 40               MOV    AH,40H        ;write insert data
0069 CD 21               INT    21H
006B 1F                  POP    DS            ;restore DS
006C 72 B7               JC     EXIT          ;on error

006E              INSERT5:

006E B9 0100             MOV    CX,256        ;write remainder of file
0071 E8 00B1 R           CALL   R_OLD         ;read old file
0074 72 AF               JC     EXIT          ;on error
0076 0B C0               OR     AX,AX         ;test for end of file
0078 74 05               JE     INSERT6       ;if end file
007A E8 00BD R           CALL   W_TEMP        ;write temp file
007D EB EF               JMP    INSERT5       ;repeat until end

007F              INSERT6:

007F E8 009F R           CALL   C_OLD         ;close old file
0082 E8 00A8 R           CALL   C_TEMP        ;close temp file
0085 8B 16 0100 R        MOV    DX,TEMP       ;delete old file
0089 B4 41               MOV    AH,41H
008B CD 21               INT    21H

008D 06                  PUSH   ES            ;save ES
008E 8C D8               MOV    AX,DS
0090 8E C0               MOV    ES,AX         ;load ES with DS

0092 8B 3E 0100 R        MOV    DI,TEMP       ;get old file name
```

EXAMPLE 6–32 (page 3 of 3)

```
0096 BA 0108 R              MOV     DX,OFFSET TEMPS
0099 B4 56                  MOV     AH,56H                ;rename file
009B CD 21                  INT     21H
009D 07                     POP     ES
009E CB                     RET

009F             INSERT     ENDP

009F             C_OLD      PROC    NEAR

009F 8B 1E 0104 R           MOV     BX,OLD_HAN            ;close old file
00A3 B4 3E                  MOV     AH,3EH
00A5 CD 21                  INT     21H
00A7 C3                     RET

00A8             C_OLD      ENDP

00A8             C_TEMP     PROC    NEAR                  ;close temp file

00A8 8B 1E 0106 R           MOV     BX,NEW_HAN
00AC B4 3E                  MOV     AH,3EH
00AE CD 21                  INT     21H
00B0 C3                     RET

00B1             C_TEMP     ENDP

00B1             R_OLD      PROC    NEAR

00B1 8B 1E 0104 R           MOV     BX,OLD_HAN
00B5 BA 0000 R              MOV     DX,OFFSET BUFFER
00B8 B4 3F                  MOV     AH,3FH
00BA CD 21                  INT     21H
00BC C3                     RET

00BD             R_OLD      ENDP
00BD             W_TEMP     PROC    NEAR

00BD 8B C8                  MOV     CX,AX
00BF 8B 1E 0106 R           MOV     BX,NEW_HAN
00C3 BA 0000 R              MOV     DX,OFFSET BUFFER
00C6 B4 40                  MOV     AH,40H
00C8 CD 21                  INT     21H
00CA C3                     RET

00CB             W_TEMP     ENDP

00CB             CODE       ENDS

                            END
```

This procedure uses two new INT 21H function calls. The delete and rename function calls are used to delete the old file before the temporary file is renamed to the old file name.

Random Access Files

Random access files are developed through software using sequential access files. A random access file is addressed by a record number rather than by going through the file searching for data. The move pointer function call becomes very important when random access files are created. Random access files are much easier to use for large volumes of data.

Creating a Random Access File.   Planning ahead is paramount to creating a random access file system. Suppose that a random access file is required for storing the names of customers. Each customer record requires 16 bytes for the last name, 16 bytes for the first name, and 1 byte for the middle initial. Each customer record contains two street address lines of 32 bytes each, a city line of 16 bytes, 2 bytes for the state code, and 9 bytes for the zip code. Just the basic customer information requires 105 bytes. Additional information expands the record to 256 bytes in length. Because the business is growing, provisions are made for 5,000 customers. This means that the total random access file is 1,280,000 bytes in length.

EXAMPLE 6–33

```
0000                    DATA     SEGMENT

0000 0100[              BUFFER   DB   256 DUP (0)      ;buffer of 00H
           00
         ]
0100 41 3A 43 55 53 54  FILE     DB   'A:CUST.FIL',0  ;file name
     2E 46 49 4C 00

010B                    DATA     ENDS

0000                    CODE     SEGMENT

                        ASSUME CS:CODE,DS:DATA

0000            MAKE    PROC     FAR

0000 B8 ---- R          MOV      AX,DATA              ;load DS
0003 8E D8              MOV      DS,AX

0005 B4 3C             MOV      AH,3CH               ;create CUST.FIL
0007 33 C9             XOR      CX,CX
0009 BA 0100 R         MOV      DX,OFFSET FILE
000C CD 21             INT      21H

000E 8B D8             MOV      BX,AX                ;handle to BX

0010 BF 1388           MOV      DI,5000          .   ;load record count

0013              MAKE1:

0013 B4 40             MOV      AH,40H               ;write a record of 00H
0015 B9 0100           MOV      CX,256
0018 BA 0000 R         MOV      DX,OFFSET BUFFER
001B CD 21             INT      21H
001D 4F               DEC      DI
001E 75 F3            JNZ      MAKE1                ;repeat 5000 times

0020 B4 3E             MOV      AH,3EH               ;close file
0022 CD 21             INT      21H

0024 B4 4C             MOV      AH,4CH               ;exit to DOS
```

```
0026 CD 21                              INT     21H

0028                            MAKE    ENDP

0028                            CODE    ENDS

                                        END     MAKE
```

Example 6–33 illustrates a short program that created a file called CUST.FIL and inserts 5,000 blank records of 256 bytes each. A blank record contains 00H in each byte. This appears to be a large file, but it fits on a single high-density 5-¼″ or 3-½″ floppy disk drive; in fact this program assumes that the disk is in drive A.

Reading and Writing a Record.   Whenever a record must be read, the record number is loaded into the BP register and the procedure listed in Example 6–34 is called. This procedure assumes that FIL contains the handle number and that the CUST.FIL remains open at all times.

EXAMPLE 6–34

```
0000                            READ    PROC    FAR

0000 8B 1E 0100 R                       MOV     BX,FIL              ;get handle
0004 B8 0100                            MOV     AX,256              ;multiply by 256
0007 F7 E5                              MUL     BP
0009 8B CA                              MOV     CX,DX
000B 8B D0                              MOV     DX,AX
000D B8 4200                            MOV     AX,4200H            ;move pointer
0010 CD 21                              INT     21H

0012 B4 3F                              MOV     AH,3FH              ;read record
0014 B9 0100                            MOV     CX,256
0017 BA 0000 R                          MOV     DX,OFFSET BUFFER
001A CD 21                              INT     21H
001C CB                                 RET

001D                            READ    ENDP
```

Notice how the record number is multiplied by 256 to obtain a count for the move pointer function. In each case the file pointer is moved from the start of the file to the desired record before it is read into memory area BUFFER. Although not shown, writing a record is performed in the same manner as reading.

6–5   EXAMPLE PROGRAMS

Now that the basic programming building blocks have been discussed, we present some example application programs. Although these example programs may seem trivial, they present some additional programming techniques and illustrate programming styles for the 80286 microprocessor.

Calculator Program

This program demonstrates how data conversion plays an important part in many application programs. Example 6–35 illustrates a program that accepts two numbers and adds, subtracts, multiplies, or divides them. To limit the complexity of the program, the numbers are limited to 2-digit numbers. For example, if you type a 12 + 24 =, the program will calculate the result and display a 36 as an answer. To further simplify the program, the numbers 0–9 must be entered as 2-digit numbers 00–09.

EXAMPLE 6–35 (page 1 of 4)

```
0000                    STAC    SEGMENT STACK

0000 0400[              DW      1024 DUP (?)        ;set stack
           ????
            ]

0800                    STAC    ENDS

0000                    DATA    SEGMENT

0000 0D 0A 24           MES1    DB      13,10,'$'

0003                    DATA    ENDS

0000                    CODE    SEGMENT

                        ASSUME CS:CODE,DS:DATA,SS:STAC

0000                    MAIN    PROC    FAR
0000 B8 ---- R                  MOV     AX,DATA     ;load DS
0003 8E D8                      MOV     DS,AX

0005                    MAIN1:

0005 E8 0069 R                  CALL    NEW         ;get new line

0008 E8 0071 R                  CALL    READ        ;get first number

000B                    MAIN2:

000B E8 0097 R                  CALL    KEY         ;get operation
000E 3C 2D                      CMP     AL,'-'
0010 74 0C                      JE      MAIN3       ;op ok
0012 3C 2B                      CMP     AL,'+'
0014 74 08                      JE      MAIN3       ;op ok
0016 3C 2F                      CMP     AL,'/'
0018 74 04                      JE      MAIN3       ;op ok
001A 3C 2A                      CMP     AL,'*'
001C 75 ED                      JNE     MAIN2       ;invalid op

001E                    MAIN3:

001E 8A D0                      MOV     DL,AL       ;echo op
0020 CD 21                      INT     21H

0022 8A D8                      MOV     BL,AL       ;save operation
```

EXAMPLE 6-35 (page 2 of 4)

```
0024 8B F5                      MOV    SI,BP            ;save first number
0026 E8 00A0 R                  CALL   SPACE
0029 E8 0071 R                  CALL   READ             ;get second number

002C               MAIN4:

002C E8 0097 R                  CALL   KEY              ;get equal
002F 3C 3D                      CMP    AL,'='
0031 75 F9                      JNE    MAIN4            ;if not equal

0033 8A D0                      MOV    DL,AL            ;echo equal
0035 CD 21                      INT    21H
0037 E8 00A0 R                  CALL   SPACE

003A 80 FB 2B                   CMP    BL,'+'           ;test for +
003D 74 11                      JE     PLUS
003F 80 FB 2D                   CMP    BL,'-'           ;test for -
0042 74 13                      JE     MIN
0044 80 FB 2F                   CMP    BL,'/'           ;test for /
0047 74 15                      JE     DIVS

0049 8B C5                      MOV    AX,BP            ;multiply
004B F7 E6                      MUL    SI
004D EB 15 90                   JMP    MAIN5            ;display product

0050               PLUS:

0050 8B C5                      MOV    AX,BP            ;add
0052 03 C6                      ADD    AX,SI
0054 EB 0E 90                   JMP    MAIN5            ;display sum

0057               MIN:

0057 8B C6                      MOV    AX,SI            ;subtract
0059 2B C5                      SUB    AX,BP
005B EB 07 90                   JMP    MAIN5            ;display difference

005E               DIVS:

005E 33 D2                      XOR    DX,DX            ;divide
0060 8B C6                      MOV    AX,SI
0062 F7 F5                      DIV    BP               ;display quotient

0064               MAIN5:

0064 E8 00A7 R                  CALL   DISP             ;display result
0067 EB 9C                      JMP    MAIN1            ;repeat forever

0069           MAIN    ENDP
0069           NEW     PROC   NEAR

0069 B4 09                      MOV    AH,9             ;display new line
006B BA 0000 R                  MOV    DX,OFFSET MES1
006E CD 21                      INT    21H
0070 C3                         RET

0071           NEW     ENDP

0071           READ    PROC   NEAR
```

EXAMPLE 6–35 (page 3 of 4)

```
0071 33 ED                   XOR    BP,BP           ;clear number
0073 B9 0002                 MOV    CX,2            ;load count
0076 B7 0A                   MOV    BH,10           ;load 10

0078              READ1:

0078 E8 0097 R               CALL   KEY             ;read key
007B 3C 30                   CMP    AL,'0'          ;test for number
007D 72 F9                   JB     READ1           ;if not a number
007F 3C 39                   CMP    AL,'9'
0081 77 F5                   JA     READ1           ;if not a number

0083 8A D0                   MOV    DL,AL           ;echo to video
0085 CD 21                   INT    21H

0087 32 E4                   XOR    AH,AH
0089 2C 30                   SUB    AL,'0'

008B 95                      XCHG   BP,AX           ;form number
008C F6 E7                   MUL    BH
008E 95                      XCHG   BP,AX
008F 03 E8                   ADD    BP,AX

0091 E2 E5                   LOOP   READ1           ;repeat twice

0093 E8 00A0 R               CALL   SPACE           ;display space
0096 C3                      RET

0097             READ   ENDP

0097             KEY    PROC   NEAR

0097 B4 06                   MOV    AH,6            ;read key
0099 B2 FF                   MOV    DL,0FFH
009B CD 21                   INT    21H
009D 74 F8                   JE     KEY
009F C3                      RET

00A0            KEY    ENDP
00A0            SPACE  PROC   NEAR

00A0 B4 06                   MOV    AH,6            ;display space
00A2 B2 20                   MOV    DL,' '
00A4 CD 21                   INT    21H
00A6 C3                      RET

00A7            SPACE  ENDP

00A7            DISP   PROC   NEAR

00A7 33 C9                   XOR    CX,CX           ;clear count
00A9 BB 000A                 MOV    BX,10           ;load 10
00AC 3D 8000                 CMP    AX,8000H        ;test for negative
00AF 72 0A                   JB     DISP1           ;if positive
00B1 F7 D8                   NEG    AX              ;make positive
00B3 50                      PUSH   AX
00B4 B2 2D                   MOV    DL,'-'          ;display -
00B6 B4 06                   MOV    AH,6
```

EXAMPLE 6–35 (page 4 of 4)

```
00B8 CD 21                      INT     21H
OOBA 58                         POP     AX

00BB                    DISP1:

00BB 33 D2                      XOR     DX,DX
00BD F7 F3                      DIV     BX              ;divide by 10
00BF 52                         PUSH    DX              ;save remainder
00C0 41                         INC     CX              ;count digit
00C1 0B C0                      OR      AX,AX           ;test quotient
00C3 75 F6                      JNE     DISP1           ;repeat until 0

00C5 B4 06                      MOV     AH,6

00C7                    DISP2:

00C7 5A                         POP     DX              ;display digit
00C8 80 C2 30                   ADD     DL,'O'
00CB CD 21                      INT     21H
00CD E2 F8                      LOOP    DISP2           ;repeat
00CF C3                         RET

00D0            DISP    ENDP

00D0            CODE    ENDS

                END     MAIN
```

Note that this program is an infinite loop. When you have tested it and found that it functions, the control and alternate keys are held down, then the delete key is pressed to reboot the computer and DOS. If you wish you can place an exit function in the software. This program does not support a backspace to correct an erroneous entry. No attempt has been made to recover from any errors.

Numeric Sort Program

At times numbers must be sorted into numeric order. This is often accomplished with a bubble sort. Figure 6–6 shows 5 numbers that are sorted with a bubble sort. Notice that the set of 5 numbers is tested 4 times with 4 passes. For each pass 2 consecutive numbers are compared and sometimes exchanged. Also notice that during the first pass, there are 4 comparisons, during the second 3, etc.

Example 6–36 illustrates a program that accepts 10 numbers from the keyboard (0–65535). After these 16-bit numbers are accepted and stored in memory section ARRAY, they are sorted using the bubble sorting technique. This bubble sort uses a flag to determine if any numbers were exchanged in a pass. If no numbers are exchanged, the numbers are in order and the sort terminates.

EXAMPLE 6–36 (page 1 of 5)

```
0000                    STAC    SEGMENT STACK

0000 0400[                      DW      1024 DUP (?)            ;set stack
```

FIGURE 6-6 A bubble sort showing data as they are sorted. Note: Sorting five numbers may require four passes.

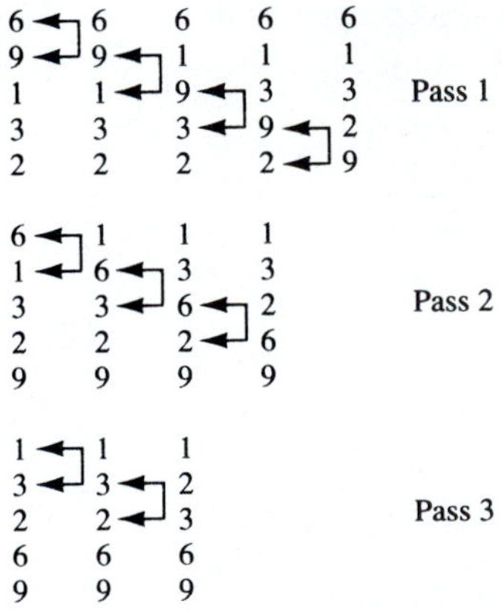

```
                ????
                        ]

0800                        STAC    ENDS

0000                        DATA    SEGMENT

0000 000A[                  ARRAY   DW      10 DUP (?)           ;space for numbers
          ????
                  ]
0014 0D 0A 24               MES1    DB      13,10,'$'
0017 0D 0A 45 6E 74 65      MES2    DB      13,10,'Enter 10 numbers:'13,100,'$'
     72 20 31 30 20 6E
     75 6D 62 65 72 73
     3A 0D 0A 24
002D 0D 0A 53 6F 72 74      MES3    DB      13,10,'Sorted Data:',13,10,'$'
     65 64 20 44 61 74
     61 3A 0D 0A 24

003E                        DATA    ENDS

0000                        CODE    SEGMENT

                            ASSUME CS:CODE,DS:DATA,SS:STAC

0000                        MAIN    PROC    FAR

0000 B8 -- R                        MOV     AX,DATA              ;load DS
0003 8E D8                          MOV     DS,AX
0005 8E C0                          MOV     ES,AX                ;load ES

0007 B4 09                          MOV     AH,9                 ;display MES2
0009 BA 0017 R                      MOV     DX,OFFSET MES2
000C CD 21                          INT     21H

000E FC                             CLD                          ;select auto-increment
000F BF 0000 R                      MOV     DI,OFFSET ARRAY      ;address ARRAY
0012 B9 000A                        MOV     CX,10                ;load count
```

EXAMPLE 6-36 (page 2 of 5)

EXAMPLE 6-36 (page 3 of 5)

```
0015                          MAIN1:

0015 E8 0039 R                      CALL    READ              ;read number
0018 E2 FB                          LOOP    MAIN1             ;repeat 10 times

001A BF 0000 R                      MOV     DI,OFFSET ARRAY   ;address ARRAY
001D B9 000A                        MOV     CX,10             ;load count
0020 E8 007A R                      CALL    SORT              ;sort numbers
0023 B4 09                          MOV     AH,9              ;display MES3
0025 BA 002D R                      MOV     DX,OFFSET MES3
0028 CD 21                          INT     21H

002A B9 000A                        MOV     CX,10             ;load count
002D BE 0000 R                      MOV     SI,OFFSET ARRAY   ;address ARRAY

0030                          MAIN2:

0030 E8 009A R                      CALL    DISP              ;display number
0033 E2 FB                          LOOP    MAIN2

0035 B4 4C                          MOV     AH,4CH            ;return to DOS
0037 CD 21                          INT     21H

0039                          MAIN    ENDP

0039                          READ    PROC    NEAR

0039 33 ED                          XOR     BP,BP             ;clear result
003B BB 000A                        MOV     BX,10             ;load 10

003E                          READ1:

003E B4 06                          MOV     AH,6              ;read key
0040 B2 FF                          MOV     DL,OFFH
0042 CD 21                          INT     21H
0044 74 F8                          JE      READ1             ;if no key
0046 3C 0D                          CMP     AL,13
0048 74 25                          JE      READ2             ;if enter key
004A 3C 30                          CMP     AL,'0'
004C 72 F0                          JB      READ1             ;if not a number
004E 3C 39                          CMP     AL,'9'
0050 77 EC                          JA      READ1             ;if not a number

0052 50                             PUSH    AX
0053 8B C5                          MOV     AX,BP             ;multiply by 10
0055 F7 E3                          MUL     BX
0057 0B D2                          OR      DX,DX             ;test for too big
0059 5A                             POP     DX
005A 75 E2                          JNZ     READ1             ;too big
005C 52                             PUSH    DX
005D 32 F6                          XOR     DH,DH
005F 80 EA 30                       SUB     DL,'0'            ;make BCD
0062 03 C2                          ADD     AX,DX             ;form number
0064 5A                             POP     DX
0065 72 D7                          JC      READ1             ;if too big
0067 8B E8                          MOV     BP,AX             ;save number
0069 B4 06                          MQV     AH,6              ;echo
006B CD 21                          INT     21H
006D EB CF                          JMP     READ1
```

EXAMPLE 6–36 (page 4 of 5)

```
006F                         READ2:

006F 8B C5                          MOV     AX,BP
0071 AB                             STOSW
0072 B4 09                          MOV     AH,9            ;get new line
0074 BA 0014 R                      MOV     DX,OFFSET MES1
0077 CD 21                          INT     21H
0079 C3                             RET

007A                         READ    ENDP

007A                         SORT    PROC    NEAR

007A 49                             DEC     CX              ;adjust count

007B                         SORT1:

007B 8B F7                          MOV     SI,DI           ;duplicate address
007D 8B D9                          MOV     BX,CX           ;duplicate count
007F 33 ED                          XOR     BP,BP           ;clear swap flag

0081                         SORT2:

0081 AD                             LODSW                   ;get data
0082 3B 04                          CMP     AX,[SI]
0084 72 0A                          JB      SORT3           ;no swap
0086 8B 14                          MOV     DX,[SI]         ;swap
0088 89 04                          MOV     [SI],AX
008A 89 54 FE                       MOV     [SI-2],DX
008D BD 0001                        MOV     BP,1            ;indicate swap

0090                         SORT3:

0090 4B                             DEC     BX
0091 75 EE                          JNE     SORT2           ;repeat
0093 0B ED                          OR      BP,BP
0095 74 02                          JE      SORT4           ;done
0097 E2 E2                          LOOP    SORT1           ;repeat

0099                         SORT4:

0099 C3                             RET

009A                         SORT    ENDP
009A                         DISP    PROC    NEAR

009A 51                             PUSH    CX              ;save external count
009B 33 C9                          XOR     CX,CX           ;clear count
009D BB 000A                        MOV     BX,10           ;load 10
00A0 AD                             LODSW                   ;get number

00A1                         DISP1:

00A1 33 D2                          XOR     DX,DX           ;clear DX
00A3 F7 F3                          DIV     BX              ;divide by 10
00A5 52                             PUSH    DX              ;save remainder
00A6 41                             INC     CX
00A7 0B C0                          OR      AX,AX           ;test quotient
00A9 75 F6                          JNZ     DISP1           ;repeat
```

EXAMPLE 6–36 (page 5 of 5)

```
00AB B4 06                     MOV      AH,6

00AD                  DISP2:

00AD 5A                        POP      DX              ;get digit
00AE 80 C2 30                  ADD      DL,'0'          ;make ASCII
00B1 CD 21                     INT      21H             ;display it
00B3 E2 F8                     LOOP     DISP2           ;repeat

00B5 B4 09                     MOV      AH,9            ;get new line
00B7 BA 0014 R                 MOV      DX,OFFSET MES1
00BA CD 21                     INT      21H

00BC 59                        POP      CX              ;restore CX
00BD C3                        RET

00BE            DISP           ENDP

00BE            CODE           ENDS

               END      MAIN
```

Once the numbers are sorted, they are displayed on the video screen in ascending numeric order. No provision is made for errors as each number is typed. The program terminates after sorting one set of 10 numbers and must be invoked again to sort 10 new numbers.

Hexadecimal File Dump

An example program that displays a file in hexadecimal format allows us to practice disk memory access. It also gives us the opportunity to read a parameter (the file name) from the DOS command line.

Whenever a command (program name) is typed at the DOS command line, any parameters that follow are placed in a *program segment prefix*. The program segment prefix (PSP) is listed in Appendix A, Figure A–6. Notice that the length of the command line and the command line parameters appear in the PSP along with other information. Upon execution of a program, the DS segment register addresses the PSP so an offset address of 80H is used to access the length (byte-sized) of the command line. After obtaining the length, the command line and its parameters can be accessed.

EXAMPLE 6–37 (page 1 of 5)

```
0000                 STAC    SEGMENT STACK

0000 0400[                    DW       1024 DUP (?)        ;set stack
         ????
             ]
0800                 STAC    ENDS

0000                 DATA    SEGMENT

0000 0100[                    BUFFER  DB    256 DUP (?)
         ??
```

EXAMPLE 6–37 (page 2 of 5)

```
                    ]
0100 0040[                        FILE    DB    64 DUP (?)
            ??
                    ]

0140 0D 0A 2A 2A 2A 20            MES1    DB    13,10,'***You enter file name    ***',13,10,'$'
     59 6F 75 20 65 6E
     74 65 72 20 66 69
     6C 65 20 6E 61 6D
     65 20 2A 2A 2A 0D
     0A 24
0160 0D 0A 2A 2A 2A 20            MES2    DB    13,10,'***File not found***',13,10,'$'
     46 69 6C 65 20 6E
     6F 74 20 66 6F 75
     6E 64 20 2A 2A 2A
     0D 0A 24
017B 0D 0A 2A 2A 2A 20            MES3    DB    13,10,'***File corrupt***',13,10,'$'
     46 69 6C 65 20 63
     6F 72 72 75 70 74
     20 2A 2A 2A 0D 0A
     24
0194 0D 0A 53 65 63 74            MES4    DB    13,10,'Section: $'
     69 6F 6E 3A 20 24
01A0 0D 0A 24                     MES5    DB    13,10,'$'
01A3 00                          SECT    DB    ?

01A4                     DATA    ENDS

0000                     CODE    SEGMENT

                         ASSUME CS:CODE,DS:DATA,SS:STAC

0000                     MAIN    PROC    FAR

0000 B8 -- R             MOV     AX,DATA          ;load ES
0003 8E C0               MOV     ES,AX
0005 BE 0082             MOV     SI,82H           ;address length
0008 80 7C FE 00         CMP     BYTE PTR [SI-2],0
000C 75 0D               JNE     MAIN2            ;if file name

000E 8E D8               MOV     DS,AX            ;load DS
0010 BA 0140 R           MOV     DX,OFFSET MES1   ;display error

0013                     MAIN1:

0013 B4 09               MOV     AH,9
0015 CD 21               INT     21H

0017 B4 4C               MOV     AH,4CH           ;return to DOS
0019 CD 21               INT     21H

001B                     MAIN2:

001B 8A 4C FE            MOV     CL,[SI-2]        ;get length
001E 32 ED               XOR     CH,CH            ;make 16 bits
0020 49                  DEC     CX               ;adjust count
0021 BF 0100 R           MOV     DI,OFFSET FILE   ;address file name
0024 F3/ A4              REP MOVSB                 ;save file name
0026 C6 05 00            MOV     BYTE PTR [DI],0  ;make ASCII-Z string
```

EXAMPLE 6-37 (page 3 of 5)

```
0029 8C C0                    MOV     AX,ES              ;load DS
002B 8E D8                    MOV     DS,AX

002D B8 3D02                  MOV     AX,3D02H           ;open file
0030 BA 0100 R                MOV     DX,OFFSET FILE
0033 CD 21                    INT     21H
0035 73 05                    JNC     MAIN3              ;if file found
0037 BA 0160 R                MOV     DX,OFFSET MES2     ;display file not found
003A EB D7                    JMP     MAIN1

003C               MAIN3:

003C 8B D8                    MOV     BX,AX              ;get file handle
003E C6 06 01A3 R FF          MOV     SECT,-1            ;set first section

0043               MAIN4:

0043 FE 06 01A3 R             INC     SECT
0047 B4 3F                    MOV     AH,3FH             ;read 256 bytes
0049 B9 0100                  MOV     CX,256
004C BA 0000 R                MOV     DX,OFFSET BUFFER
004F CD 21                    INT     21H
0051 73 05                    JNC     MAIN5              ;if read good
0053 BA 017B R                MOV     DX,OFFSET MES3     ;display file corrupt
0056 EB BB                    JMP     MAIN1
0058               MAIN5:

0058 3D 0000                  CMP     AX,0               ;test for end of file
005B 75 0B                    JNE     MAIN6              ;not end

005D B4 3E                    MOV     AH,3EH             ;close file
005F CD 21                    INT     21H

0061 E8 00BF R                CALL    NEW

0064 B4 4C                    MOV     AH,4CH             ;exit to DOS
0066 CD 21                    INT     21H

0068               MAIN6:

0068 E8 006D R                CALL    DUMP               ;display 256-byte section
006B EB D6                    JMP     MAIN4              ;repeat

006D               MAIN    ENDP

006D               DUMP    PROC    NEAR                  ;display 256-byte section

006D 8B C8                    MOV     CX,AX              ;save count
006F B4 09                    MOV     AH,9               ;display header
0071 BA 0194 R                MOV     DX,OFFSET MES4
0074 CD 21                    INT     21H

0076 A0 01A3 R                MOV     AL,SECT            ;display number
0079 E8 009C R                CALL    DISP

007C BE 0000 R                MOV     SI,OFFSET BUFFER

007F               DUMP1:
```

EXAMPLE 6–37 (page 4 of 5)

```
007F E8 00C7 R              CALL    DISPA               ;display address

0082                        DUMP1A:

0082 E8 00FA R                      CALL    DISPN       ;display number
0085 49                             DEC     CX
0086 74 08                          JE      DUMP2
0088 8B C6                          MOV     AX,SI
008A 24 0F                          AND     AL,0FH      ;test address
008C 74 F1                          JZ      DUMP1
008E EB F2                          JMP     DUMP1A
0090                        DUMP2:

0090 B4 06                          MOV     AH,6        ;get a key
0092 B2 FF                          MOV     DL,0FFH
0094 CD 21                          INT     21H
0096 74 F8                          JE      DUMP2
0098 E8 00BF R                      CALL    NEW
009B C3                             RET

009C                        DUMP    ENDP

009C                        DISP    PROC    NEAR        ;display decimal

009C 51                             PUSH    CX          ;save CX
009D 53                             PUSH    BX          ;save BX
009E 32 E4                          XOR     AH,AH
00A0 BB 000A                        MOV     BX,10       ;load 10
00A3 33 C9                          XOR     CX,CX       ;clear count

00A5                        DISP1:

00A5 33 D2                          XOR     DX,DX
00A7 F7 F3                          DIV     BX          ;divide by 10
00A9 52                             PUSH    DX          ;save remainder
00AA 41                             INC     CX          ;count remainder
00AB 0B C0                          OR      AX,AX       ;test quotient
00AD 75 F6                          JNE     DISP1       ;repeat
00AF B4 06                          MOV     AH,6

00B1                        DISP2:

00B1 5A                             POP     DX          ;get digit
00B2 80 C2 30                       ADD     DL,'0'      ;convert to ASCII
00B5 CD 21                          INT     21H
00B7 E2 F8                          LOOP    DISP2       ;repeat
00B9 E8 00BF R                      CALL    NEW         ;get new line
00BC 5B                             POP     BX
00BD 59                             POP     CX
00BE C3                             RET

00BF                        DISP    ENDP

00BF                        NEW     PROC    NEAR        ;display new line

00BF B4 09                          MOV     AH,9
00C1 BA 01A0 R                      MOV     DX,OFFSET MES5
00C4 CD 21                          INT     21H
00C6 C3                             RET
```

EXAMPLE 6-37 (page 5 of 5)

```
00C7                    NEW     ENDP
00C7                    DISPA   PROC    NEAR                    ;display address

00C7 E8 00BF R                  CALL    NEW                     ;get new line
00CA 8B C6                      MOV     AX,SI                   ;get address
00CC E8 00DF R                  CALL    DIG                     ;display digit
00CF E8 00DF R                  CALL    DIG
00D2 E8 00DF R                  CALL    DIG
00D5 E8 00DF R                  CALL    DIG

00D8 B4 06                      MOV     AH,6                    :display space
00DA B2 20                      MOV     DL,''
00DC CD 21                      INT     21H

00DE C3                         RET

00DF                    DISPA   ENDP

00DF                    DIG     PROC    NEAR                    ;display hex digit

00DF D1 C0                      ROL     AX,1                    ;position digit
00E1 D1 C0                      ROL     AX,1
00E3 D1 C0                      ROL     AX,1
00E5 D1 C0                      ROL     AX,1
00E7 50                         PUSH    AX
00E8 24 0F                      AND     AL,0FH                  ;mask
00EA 04 30                      ADD     AL,'0'                  ;convert to ASCII
00EC 3C 39                      CMP     AL'9'
00EE 76 02                      JBE     DIG1
00F0 04 07                      ADD     AL,7

00F2                    DIG1:

00F2 8A D0                      MOV     DL,AL                   ;display digit
00F4 B4 06                      MOV     AH,6
00F6 CD 21                      INT     21H
00F8 58                         POP     AX
00F9 C3                         RET

00FA                    DIG     ENDP

00FA                    DISPN   PROC    NEAR                    ;display number

00FA AC                         LODSB                           ;get number

00FB 8A E0                      MOV     AH,AL
00FD E8 00DF R                  CALL    DIG                     ;display digit
0100 E8 00DF R                  CALL    DIG

0103 B4 06                      MOV     AH,6
0105 B2 20                      MOV     DL,''                   ;display space
0107 CD 21                      INT     21H
0109 C3                         RET

010A                    DISPN   ENDP

010A                    CODE    ENDS

                                END     MAIN
```

Example 6–37 lists a program that obtains a file name from the command line and then displays the file in a hexadecimal listing. This program is useful for debugging faulty programs and also as practice with disk file access and conversions. The parameter following the command always starts with a space (20H) at offset address 81H and always ends with a carriage return (0DH). The length of the parameter is always one greater. For example, if DUMPS FROG is typed at the command line and DUMPS is the name of the program, the parameter FROG is stored beginning with a 20H at offset 81H and the length is 5.

6–6   HOOKS

Hooks are used to tap into the interrupt structure of the microprocessor. For example, we might hook into the keyboard interrupt so we can detect a special keystroke called a hot key. Whenever the hot key is typed, we can access a terminate and stay resident (TSR) program that performs a special task. Some examples of hot key software are pop-up calculators, pop-up clocks, and so forth.

Taping into an Interrupt

In order to tap into an interrupt, we must use a DOS function call that reads the current address from the interrupt vector. The DOS function call number 35H is used to read the current interrupt vector and DOS function call number 25H is used to change the address of the current vector. In both DOS function calls, AL indicates the vector type number (00H–FFH) and AH indicates the DOS function call number.

When the vector is read using function 35H, the offset address is returned in register BX and the segment address is in register ES. These two registers are saved so they can be restored when the interrupt hook is removed from memory. When the vector is set, it is set to the address stored at the memory location addressed by DS:DX.

EXAMPLE 6–38

```
                        ORG     100H                    ;origin for a COM program
0100                    START:

0100 EB 04                      JMP     MAIN

0102 00000000           ADRESSS DD      ?               ;old interrupt vector

0106                    MAIN:

0106 8C C8                      MOV     AX,CS           ;address CS with DS
0108 8E D8                      MOV     DS,AX

            ;get vector 0 address

010A B8 3500                    MOV             AX,3500H
010D CD 21                      INT             21H
```

```
                            ;save vector address

010F 2E: 89 1E 0102 R       MOV     WORD PTR ADDRESS,BX
0114 2E: 8C 06 0104 R       MOV     WORD PTR ADDRESS+2,ES

                            ;install new interrupt vector 0 address

0119 B8 2500                MOV     AX,2500H
011C BA 0300 R              MOV     DX,OFFSET NEW
011F CD 21                  INT     21H
```

The process of installing an interrupt handler through a hook is illustrated in Example 6–38. This procedure reads the current interrupt vector address and stores it into a double-word memory location for access by the new interrupt service procedure. Next, the address of the new interrupt service procedure stored in DS:DX is placed into the vector using DOS function call number 25H.

Example TSR Alarm Clock

A fairly simple example showing an interrupt hook and TSR causes a beep on the speaker after a set amount of time elapses. The amount of time is specified in 10-second intervals as defined by an equate statement found in this software. For example, if the amount of the time interval specified is 60, then a beep will occur after 10 minutes once this program is installed. The timing interval of the beep can be adjusted by changing the number stored with the equate statement.

EXAMPLE 6–39 (page 1 of 3)

```
0000                        CODES   SEGMENT  'CODE'

                            ASSUME  CS:CODES

                            ORG     5DH

005D 0000                   COUNTS  DW      ?               ;timer interval

                            ORG     100H            ;origin for a COM program

0100                        START:

0100 E9 0091                        JMP     MAIN

0103 00000000               ADDR1   DD      ?               ;old interrupt vector
0107 B6                     SEC10   DB      182             ;10 second counter
0108 00                     ACTIVE  DB      0               ;timer flag

=  000A                     ALARM   EQU     10              ;alarm times 10 seconds
=  0320                     TONE    EQU     800             ;frequency in Hertz
=  0006                     LENG    EQU     6               ;duration = leng/18.2

0109                        BEEP    PROC    NEAR

0109 50                             PUSH    AX              ;save registers
010A 53                             PUSH    BX
010B 51                             PUSH    CX
010C 52                             PUSH    DX
```

EXAMPLE 6-39 (page 2 of 3)

```
010D 06                     PUSH    ES
010E B0 B6                  MOV     AL,0B6H         ;initialize timer 2
0110 E6 43                  OUT     43H,AL

0112 BA 0012                MOV     DX,12H          ;calculate count
0115 B8 34DC                MOV     AX,34DCH
0118 BB 0320                MOV     BX,TONE
011B F7 F3                  DIV     BX

011D E6 42                  OUT     42H,AL          ;program timer 2
011F 8A C4                  MOV     AL,AH
0121 E6 42                  OUT     42H,AL

0123 E4 61                  IN      AL,61H          ;speaker on
0125 0C 03                  OR      AL,3
0127 E6 61                  OUT     61H,AL

0129 BA 0006                MOV     DX,LENG
012C 2B C9                  SUB     CX,CX
012E 8E C1                  MOV     ES,CX
0130 26: 03 16 046C         ADD     DX,ES:[46CH]
0135 26: 13 0E 046E         ADC     CX,ES:[46EH]
013A                BEEPS:

013A 26: 8B 1E 046C         MOV     BX,ES:[46CH]    ;wait leng clock ticks
013F 26: A1 046E            MOV     AX,ES:[46EH]
0143 2B DA                  SUB     BX,DX
0145 1B C1                  SBB     AX,CX
0147 72 F1                  JC      BEEPS
0149 E4 61                  IN      AL,61H          ;speaker off
014B 34 03                  XOR     AL,3
014D E6 61                  OUT     61H,AL

014F 07                     POP     ES              ;restore registers
0150 5A                     POP     DX
0151 59                     POP     CX
0152 5B                     POP     BX
0153 58                     POP     AX
0154 C3                     RET

0155                BEEP    ENDP

0155                TIMES   PROC    FAR             ;new interrupt

0155 2E: 80 3E 0108 R       CMP     ACTIVE,0        ;test active
     00
015B 74 05                  JZ      TIMES1          ;if armed
015D 2E: FF 2E 0103 R       JMP     ADDR1           ;do original interrupt

0162                TIMES1:
0162 2E: FE 06 0108 R       INC     ACTIVE          ;set active
0167 9C                     PUSHF                   ;simulate interrupt
0168 2E: FF 1E 0103 R       CALL    ADDR1           ;do interrupt
016D FB                     STI                     ;enable INTR
016E 1E                     PUSH    DS              ;save registers
016F 0E                     PUSH    CS
0170 1F                     POP     DS              ;get current code segment
0171 2E: FE 0E 0107 R       DEC     SEC10           ;decrement counter
0176 75 15                  JNZ     TIMES2          ;if not 10 seconds
0178 2E: C6 06 0107 R       MOV     SEC10,182       ;reload SEC10
```

EXAMPLE 6–39 (page 2 of 3)

```
        B6
017E 2E: FF 0E 005D R         DEC     COUNTS          ;decrement counter
0183 75 08                     JNZ     TIMES2          ;if no alarm
0185 E8 FF81                   CALL    BEEP            ;sound alarm
0188 2E: FE 06 0108 R          INC     ACTIVE

018D                 TIMES2:
018D 2E: FE 0E 0108 R          DEC     ACTIVE          ;decrement active
0192 1F                        POP     DS
0193 CF                        IRET

0194                 TIMES     ENDP
0194                 MAIN:
0194 8C C8                     MOV     AX,CS
0196 8E D8                     MOV     DS,AX

0198 B8 000A                   MOV     AX,ALARM
019B 2E: A3 005D R             MOV     COUNTS,AX       ;save alarm interval
019F B8 3508                   MOV     AX,3508H        ;get vector 8
01A2 CD 21                     INT     21H
01A4 2E: 89 1E 0103 R          MOV     WORD PTR ADDR1,BX  ;save address
01A9 2E: 8C 06 0105 R          MOV     WORD PTR ADDR1+2,ES
01AE B8 2508                   MOV     AX,2508H        ;install new interrupt
01B1 BA 0155 R                 MOV     DX,OFFSET TIMES
01B4 CD 21                     INT     21H
01B6 BA 0194 R                 MOV     DX,OFFSET MAIN  ;set length
01B9 B1 04                     MOV     CL,4
01BB D3 EA                     SHR     DX,CL
01BD 42                        INC     DX
01BE B8 3100                   MOV     AX,3100H        ;TSR
01C1 CD 21                     INT     21H

01C3                 CODES     ENDS

                     END       START
```

The beep is caused by using timer 2 of the timer found inside the PC so it generates an audio tone at the speaker. (Refer to section 9–5 for a discussion of the timer and see Figure 6–7 for its connection in the computer.) Programming timer 2 with a particular beep frequency or tone is accomplished by programming timer 2 with 1,193,180 divided by the desired tone. For example, if we divide 1,193,180 by 800, the speaker generates an 800 Hz audio tone. Refer to the BEEP procedure (see Example 6–39) for programming the timer and turning the speaker on and off after a short wait determined by the number of clock ticks. This procedure uses 6 clock ticks that produce about a $\frac{1}{3}$ second beep. Note that each clock tick occurs about 18.2 times a second (the actual time is 18.2064819336). This is accomplished by using the user wait timer locations in the first segment of the memory. The user wait timer is updated 18.2 times per second by the computer so it can be used to time events.

The MAIN program initializes the alarm counter with a 10 causing a 100-second delay before the speaker beeps. After initializing the alarm delay, the address of the original timer interrupt vector (type 8) is obtained using DOS function call number 35H and stored in memory location ADDR1. After obtaining the original interrupt vector, DOS function call 25H is used to store the address of TIMES (the new interrupt service procedure) into vector number 8. The very last few instructions of MAIN are used to

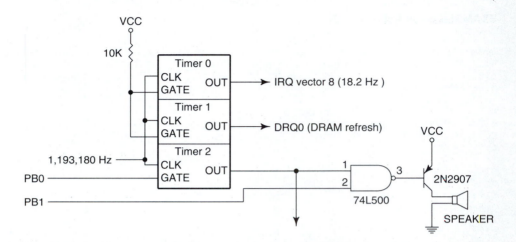

FIGURE 6–7   The speaker circuit connected to the timer inside the personal computer. (The 8255 is at I/O ports 60H–63H and the 8253 is at I/O ports 40H–43H.)

make the interrupt service procedure and BEEP memory resident. This is accomplished by first calculating the length of these procedures. Note that the length is given as the number of 16-byte paragraphs. When DOS function call 31H is executed, the new interrupt service procedure and BEEP become memory resident. There is no provision for removing this memory resident software from the system once it is installed. All that happens after the alarm goes off is that the interrupt service procedure deactivates itself.

The program is assembled and linked as any other program, but in this example it is converted from an .EXE file into a .COM file. Conversion is accomplished by using the EXE2BIN program. All .COM files must begin executing software at location 100H and may not exceed 64K bytes in length. A .COM file is used in place of an .EXE file because it requires less memory to store. This is important for memory resident software, but not an absolute requirement.

This example remains resident even after the alarm has sounded. If it is desirable to remove the program, it must terminate with DOS function call 4CH just as we terminate most other software instead of an interrupt return. This DOS function call removes the program from the memory and returns to DOS when activated. If you wish to terminate with DOS function 4CH, make sure that you replace the original interrupt vector into vector 8 before executing the DOS function 4CH call.

Example Hot Key Program

Hot keys are keystrokes that invoke programs that are terminate and stay resident. For example, an ALT C key could be defined as a hot key that calls a program that displays the time. Note that the hot key is detected inside most applications, but not at the DOS command line, where if used may lock up the system. To detect a hot key we usually hook into interrupt vector 9, which is the keyboard interrupt that occurs if any key is typed. This allows us to test the keyboard and detect a hot key before the normal interrupt processes the keystroke.

EXAMPLE 6-40

```
0108 00000000          OLD9    DD    ?           ;original vector address
010C 00                CODE    DB    ?           ;scan code of hot key
010D 00                MASKS   DB    ?           ;shift/alternate mask
010E 00                HOT     DB    ?           ;correct hot shift/alternate
010F 00                FLAG    DB    0           ;TSR flag


0200 FB                VEC9:   STI               ;interrupt on
0201 50                        PUSH  AX
0202 E4 60                     IN    AL,60H      ;get scan code
0204 2E: 3A 06 010C R          CMP   AL,CODE     ;check for hot key scan code
0209 75 2E                     JNE   VEC91       ;if not hot key
020B 06                        PUSH  ES
020C 2B C0                     SUB   AX,AX
020E 8E C0                     MOV   ES,AX
0210 26: A0 0417               MOV   AL,ES:[417H] ;get shift/alternate status
0214 2E: 22 06 010D R          AND   AL,MASKS    ;isolate bit(s)
0219 2E: 3A 06 010E R          CMP   AL,HOT      ;test for shift/alternate
021E 07                        POP   ES
021F 75 18                     JNE   VEC91       ;if not hot key


                ;HOT KEY pressed


0221FA                         CLI               ;interrupt off
0222 E4 61                     IN    AL,61H      ;throw away keystroke
0224 0C 80                     OR    AL,80H      ;clear keyboard
0226 E6 61                     OUT   61H,AL
0228 24 7F                     AND   AL,7FH      ;signal break
022A E6 61                     OUT   61H,AL
022C B0 20                     MOV   AL,20H      ;reset interrupt controller
022E E6 20                     OUT   20H,AL
0230 FB                        STI               ;interrupts on
0231 58                        POP   AX
0232 2E: C6 06 010F R          MOV   FLAG,1      ;indicate hot key
     01
0238 CF                        IRET              ;exit handler


                ;HOT KEY NOT pressed


0239                   VEC91:


0239 58                        POP   AX
023A FA                        CLI               ;interrupts off
023B 9C                        PUSHF             ;simulate interrupt
023C 2E: FF 1E 0108 R          CALL  OLD9        ;call original keyboard interrupt
0241 CF                        IRET
```

Example 6–40 shows a short replacement interrupt service procedure that tests for a hot key and sets a flag if it is detected. This example does not illustrate the software to install this replacement procedure. The CODE variable is the scan code (see Figure 6–8) of the hot key to be detected, the MASKS are the mask bits to extract the shift key or alternate key from the memory at location 0000:0471 (see Appendix A for details), and the HOT code is the desired combination of shift/alternate keys for the hot key. The procedure detects a hot key and if it is active, the procedure places a 01H into the FLAG byte. The FLAG byte is usually detected by a replacement clock tick interrupt at vector 8.

Example 6–41 shows a program that hooks into interrupt vectors 9 and 8. Interrupt vector 9 is captured to access a hot key and interrupt vector 8 is captured to execute a

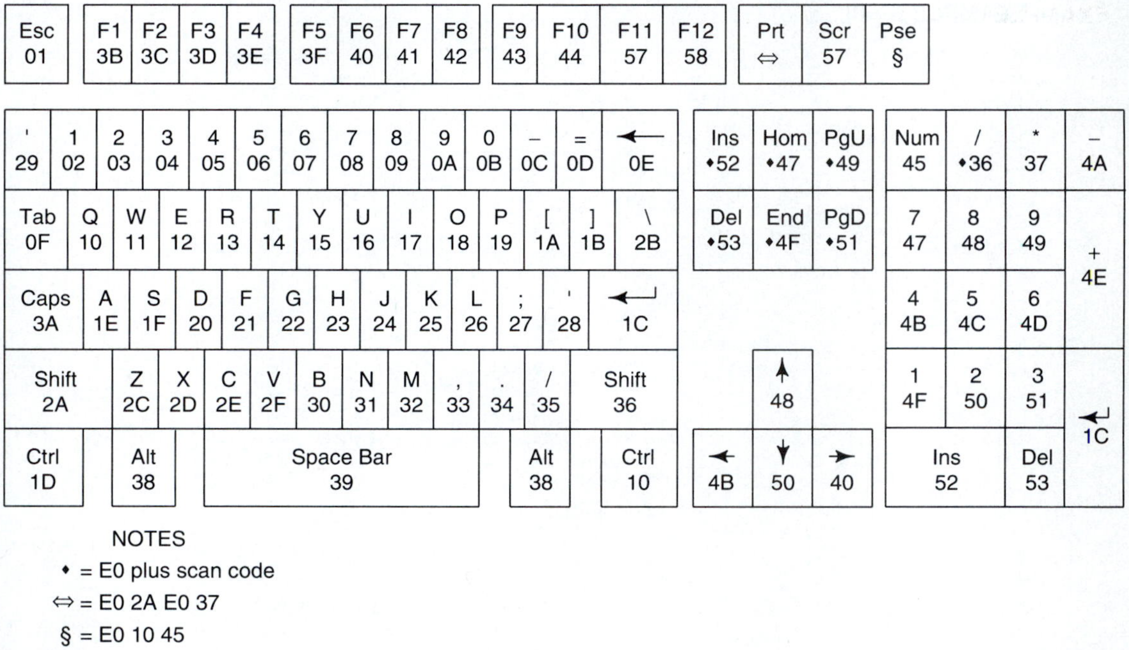

| Esc 01 | F1 3B | F2 3C | F3 3D | F4 3E | | F5 3F | F6 40 | F7 41 | F8 42 | | F9 43 | F10 44 | F11 57 | F12 58 | | Prt ⇔ | Scr 57 | Pse § |

' 29	1 02	2 03	3 04	4 05	5 06	6 07	7 08	8 09	9 0A	0 0B	– 0C	= 0D	← 0E		Ins ♦52	Hom ♦47	PgU ♦49		Num 45	/ ♦36	* 37	– 4A
Tab 0F	Q 10	W 11	E 12	R 13	T 14	Y 15	U 16	I 17	O 18	P 19	[1A	] 1B	\ 2B		Del ♦53	End ♦4F	PgD ♦51		7 47	8 48	9 49	+ 4E
Caps 3A	A 1E	S 1F	D 20	F 21	G 22	H 23	J 24	K 25	L 26	; 27	' 28	←┘ 1C					4 4B	5 4C	6 4D	
Shift 2A	Z 2C	X 2D	C 2E	V 2F	B 30	N 31	M 32	, 33	. 34	/ 35	Shift 36		↑ 48		1 4F	2 50	3 51	←┘ 1C
Ctrl 1D	Alt 38	Space Bar 39	Alt 38	Ctrl 10	← 4B	↓ 50	→ 40	Ins 52	Del 53

NOTES

♦ = E0 plus scan code
⇔ = E0 2A E0 37
§ = E0 10 45

FIGURE 6–8 The keyboard scan codes.

TSR program that is activated by the hot key. In this example, we use the hot key A that accesses a TSR program to display the time of day on the video screen. The time is displayed until the escape key is typed on the keyboard. When escape is typed, the original data is redisplayed over the time. This program only functions if the display adapter is in text mode.

EXAMPLE 6–41 (page 1 of 6)

```
                        .286
                        ;
                        ;This program displays the time when hot key ALT T is typed.
                        ;This program is set up as a .COM file with ORG 100H
                        ;
0000                    CODE    SEGMENT

                                ASSUME  CS:CODE

                                ORG     100H

0100 E9 0962            BEGIN:  JMP     START

0103 00000000           VEC8    DD      ?           ;original vector 8 address
0107 00000000           VEC9    DD      ?           ;original vector 9 address
010B 00000000           STPT    DD      ?           ;original stack pointer
010F 00                 H_FLAG  DB      0           ;hot key flag
0110 14                 H_CODE  DB      14H         ;scan code of hot key ''T''
0111 08                 MASKS   DB      8           ;alternate mask
0112 08                 HOT     DB      8           ;correct hot shift/alternate
```

EXAMPLE 6-41 (page 2 of 6)

```
0113 00                     COL     DB      0                   ;display column
0114 00                     ROW     DB      0                   ;display row
0115 00                     T_ROW   DB      ?                   ;temp row
0116 00                     T_COL   DB      ?                   ;temp column
0117 0005 [                 BUF     DB      5 DUP (?)           ;old display data
        00
           ]
011C 24                             DB      '$'
011D 0005 [                 BUF1    DB      5 DUP (?)           ;time buffer
        00
           ]
0122 24                             DB      '$'
0123 0000                   TEMP    DW      ?
0125 0400 [                         DW      400H DUP (?)
        0000
           ]
0925 = 0925                 STAC    EQU     THIS WORD


                            ;keyboard hot key intercept

0925                        KEY     PROC    FAR

0925 FB                             STI                         ;interrupts on
0926 50                             PUSH    AX
0927 E4 60                          IN      AL,60H              ;get scan code
0929 2E: 3A 06 0110 R               CMP     AL,H_CODE           ;test for hot scan code
092E 75 2E                          JNE     KEY1                ;if not hot key
0930 06                             PUSH    ES
0931 2B C0                          SUB     AX,AX
0933 8E C0                          MOV     ES,AX
0935 26: A0 0417                    MOV     AL,ES:[417H]        ;get shift/alternate status
0939 2E: 22 06 0111 R               AND     AL,MASKS            ;isolate alternate
093E 2E: 3A 06 0112 R               CMP     AL,HOT              ;test for alternate
0943 07                             POP     ES
0944 75 18                          JNE     KEY1                ;if not hot key


                            ;if HOT KEY detected

0946 FA                             CLI                         ;interrupts off
0947 E4 61                          IN      AL,61H              ;throw away keystroke
0949 0C 80                          OR      AL,80H              ;clear keyboard
094B E6 61                          OUT     61H,AL
094D 24 7F                          AND     AL,7FH              ;signal break
094F E6 61                          OUT     61H,AL
0951 B0 20                          MOV     AL,20H              ;reset interrupt controller
0953 E6 20                          OUT     20H,AL
0955 FB                             STI                         ;interrupts on
0956 58                             POP     AX
0957 2E: C6 06 010F R               MOV     H_FLAG,0FFH         ;indicate hot key
     FF
095D CF                             IRET


                            ;if HOT KEY not detected

095E                        KEY1:

095E 58                             POP     AX
095F FA                             CLI                         ;interrupts off
```

EXAMPLE 6–41 (page 3 of 6)

```
0960 9C                          PUSHF                        ;simulate interrupt
0961 2E: FF 1E 0107 R            CALL    CS:VEC9
0966 CF                          IRET

0967                     KEY     ENDP

                        ;clock tick interrupt TICK

0967                     TICK    PROC    FAR

0967 2E: 80 3E 010F R            CMP     H_FLAG,0             ;test for HOT KEY
     00
096D 75 05                       JNZ     TICK1               ;if HOT KEY active
096F 2E: FF 2E 0103 R            JMP     CS:VEC8             ;do normal interrupt

                        ;if HOT KEY ACTIVE

0974                     TICK1:

0974 2E: C6 06 010F R            MOV     H_FLAG,0             ;clear HOT KEY request
     00
097A 9C                          PUSHF                        ;do clock tick interrupt
097B 2E: FF 1E 0103 R CALL       CS:VEC8

0980 FA                          CLI
0981 2E: A3 0123 R               MOV     TEMP,AX              ;save old stack area
0985 8C D0                       MOV     AX,SS
0987 2E: A3 010D R               MOV     WORD PTR STPT+2,AX
098B 2E: 89 26 010B R            MOV     WORK PTR STPT,SP

0990 BC 0925 R                   MOV     SP,OFFSET STAC       ;get new stack area
0993 8C C8                       MOV     AX,CS
0995 8E D0                       MOV     SS,AX
0997 FB                          STI

0998 E8 0012                     CALL    CLOCK                ;display time until any key

099B FA                          CLI
099C 2E: A1 010D R               MOV     AX,WORD PTR STPT+2   ;adress old stack area
09A0 8E D0                       MOV     SS,AX
09A2 2E: 8B 26 010B R            MOV     SP,WORD PTR STPT
09A7 2E: A1 0123 R               MOV     AX,TEMP
09AB FB                          STI

09AC CF                          IRET

09AD                     TICK    ENDP

                        ;CLOCK procedure to display the time at COL, ROW

09AD                     CLOCK   PROC    NEAR


09AD 50                          PUSH    AX                   ;save registers
09AE 53                          PUSH    BX
09AF 51                          PUSH    CX
09B0 52                          PUSH    DX
09B1 57                          PUSH    DI
09B2 1E                          PUSH    DS
```

EXAMPLE 6-41 (page 4 of 6)

```
09B3 8C C8              MOV    AX,CS
09B5 8E D8              MOV    DS,AX

09B7 B4 03              MOV    AH,3              ;get current cursor position
09B9 B7 00              MOV    BH,0
09BB CD 10              INT    10H
09BD 2E: 88 36 0115 R   MOV    T_ROW,DH          ;save row and column
09C2 2E: 88 16 0116 R   MOV    T_COL,DL
09C7 B4 02              MOV    AH,2              ;move cursor
09C9 2E: 8A 36 0114 R   MOV    DH,ROW
09CE 2E: 8A 16 0113 R   MOV    DL,COL
09D3 B7 00              MOV    BH,0
09D5 CD 10              INT    10H

09D7 BF 0117 R          MOV    DI,OFFSET BUF     ;save current screen
09DA B9 0005            MOV    CX,5


09DD            CLOCK1:

09DD B4 08              MOV    AH,8              ;read character
09DF B7 00              MOV    BH,0
09E1 CD 10              INT    10H
09E3 88 05              MOV    [DI],AL
09E5 47                 INC    DI
09E6 FE C2              INC    DL                ;next column
09E8 B4 02              MOV    AH,2
09EA CD 10              INT    10H
09EC E2 EF              LOOP   CLOCK1

09EE B4 02              MOV    AH,2              ;reposition cursor
09F0 80 EA 05           SUB    DL,5
09F3 CD 10              INT    10H

09F5 BF 011D R          MOV    DI,OFFSET BUF1

09F8 B4 2C              MOV    AH,2CH            ;get time
09FA CD 21              INT    21H
09FC 8A C5              MOV    AL,CH
09FE 32 E4              XOR    AH,AH
0A00 D4 0A              AAM                      ;convert tens of hours
0A02 80 C4 20           ADD    AH,20H
0A05 80 FC 20           CMP    AH,20H
0A08 74 03              JE     CLOCK2
0A0A 80 C4 10           ADD    AH,10H


0A0D            CLOCK2:

0A0D 88 25              MOV    [DI],AH
0A0F 04 30              ADD    AL,30H
0A11 88 45 01           MOV    [DI+1],AL
0A14 2E:C6 45 02 3A     MOV    BYTE PTR CS:[DI+2],':'
0A19 8A C1              MOV    AL,CL
0A1B 32 E4              XOR    AH,AH             ;convert units of hours
0A1D D4 0A              AAM
0A1F 05 3030            ADD    AX,3030H
0A22 88 65 03           MOV    [DI+3],AH
0A25 88 45 04           MOV    [DI+4],AL
0A28 BA 011D R          MOV    DX,OFFSET BUF1
0A2B B4 09              MOV    AH,9              ;display time
```

EXAMPLE 6-41 (page 5 of 6)

```
0A2D CD 21                          INT     21H
0A2F                        CLOCK3:

0A2F B4 06                          MOV     AH,6              ;test any key
0A31 B2 FF                          MOV     DL,0FFH
0A33 CD 21                          INT     21H
0A35 74 F8                          JZ      CLOCK3

0A37 B4 02                          MOV     AH,2
0A39 2E: 8A 36 0114 R               MOV     DH,ROW
0A3E 2E: 8A 16 0113 R               MOV     DL,COL
0A43 B7 00                          MOV     BH,0
0A45 CD 10                          INT     10H

0A47 B4 09                          MOV     AH,9
0A49 BA 0017 R                      MOV     DX,OFFSET BUF
0A4C CD 21                          INT     21H

0A4E B4 02                          MOV     AH,2
0A50 2E: 8A 36 0115 R               MOV     DH,T_ROW
0A55 2E: 8A 16 0116 R               MOV     DL,T_COL
0A5A B7 00                          MOV     BH,0
0A5C CD 10                          INT     10H

0A5E 1F                             POP     DS
0A5F 5F                             POP     DI
0A60 5A                             POP     DX
0A61 59                             POP     CX
0A62 5B                             POP     BX
0A63 58                             POP     AX
0A64 C3                             RET

0A65                        CLOCK   ENDP

                            ;install interrupt procedure 8 and 9

0A65                        START:

0A65 8C C8                          MOV     AX,CS
0A67 8E D8                          MOV     DS,AX

0A69 B8 3508                        MOV     AX,3508H           ;get vector 8
0A6C CD 21                          INT     21H
0A6E 2E: 89 1E 0103 R               MOV     WORD PTR VEC8,BX
0A73 2E: 8C 06 0105 R               MOV     WORD PTR VEC8+2,ES

0A78 B8 3509                        MOV     AX,3509H           ;get vector 9
0A7B CD 21                          INT     21H
0A7D 2E: 89 1E 0107 R               MOV     WORD PTR VEC9,BX
0A82 2E: 8C 06 0109 R               MOV     WORD PTR VEC9+2,ES
0A87 B8 2508                        MOV     AX,2508H           ;install TICK as 8
0A8A BA 0967 R                      MOV     DX,OFFSET TICK
0A8D CD 21                          INT     21H

0A8F B8 2509                        MOV     AX,2509H
0A92 BA 0925 R                      MOV     DX,OFFSET KEY      ;install KEY as 9
0A95 CD 21                          INT     21H

0A97 BA 0A65 R                      MOV     DX,OFFSET START    ;make resident
```

EXAMPLE 6–41 (page 6 of 6)

```
0A9A C1 EA 04                    SHR      DX,4
0A9D 42                          INC      DX
0A9E B8 3100                     MOV      AX,3100H
0AA1 CD 21                       INT      21H

0AA3                    CODE     ENDS

                                 END      BEGIN
```

6–7   SUMMARY

1. The assembler program assembles modules that contain PUBLIC variables and segments plus EXTRN (external) variables. The linker program links modules and library files to create a run-time program executed from the DOS command line. The run-time program usually has the extension EXE.

2. The MACRO and ENDM directives create a new opcode for use in programs. These macros are similar to procedures except there is no call or return. In place of them, the assembler inserts the code of the macro sequence into a program each time it is invoked. Macros can include variables that pass information and data to the macro sequence.

3. The DOS INT 21H function call provides a method of using the keyboard and video display. Function number 06H, placed into register AH, provides an interface to the keyboard and display. If DL = 0FFH, this function tests the keyboard for a keystroke. If no keystroke is detected, it returns equal. If a keystroke is detected, the standard ASCII character returns in AL. If an extended ASCII character is typed, it returns with AL = 00H, where the function must again be called to return with the extended ASCII character in AL. To display a character, DL is loaded with the character and AH with 06H before the INT 21H is used in a program.

4. Character strings are displayed using function number 09H. The DS:DX register combination addresses the character string, which must end with a $.

5. The INT 10H instruction accesses BIOS (basic I/O system) procedures that control the video display and keyboard. The BIOS functions are independent of DOS and function with any operating system.

6. Data conversion from binary to BCD is accomplished with the AAM instruction for numbers that are less than 100 or by repeated division by 10 for larger numbers. Once converted to BCD, a 30H is added to convert each digit to ASCII code for the video display.

7. When converting from an ASCII number to BCD, a 30H is subtracted from each digit. To obtain the binary equivalent, we multiply by 10.

8. Lookup tables are used for code conversion with the XLAT instruction if the code is an 8-bit code. If the code is wider than 8 bits, then a short procedure that accesses a lookup table provides the conversion. Lookup tables are also used to hold addresses so that different parts of a program or different procedures can be selected.

9. The disk memory system contains tracks that hold information stored in sectors. Many disk systems store 512 bytes of information per sector. Data on the disk is

organized in a boot sector, file allocation table, root directory, and a data storage area. The boot sector loads the DOS system from the disk into the computer memory system. The FAT indicates which sectors are present and whether they contain data. The root directory contains file names and subdirectories, through which all disk files are accessed. The data storage area contains all subdirectories and data files.

10. Files are manipulated with the DOS INT 21H function call. To read a disk file, the file must be opened, read, and then closed. To write to a disk file, it must be opened, written, and then closed. When a file is opened, the file pointer addresses the first byte of the file. To access data at other locations, the file pointer is moved before data are read or written.

11. A sequential access file is a file that is accessed sequentially from the beginning to the end. A random access file is a file that is accessed at any point. Although all disk files are sequential, they can be treated as random access files by using software procedures.

12. The program segment prefix (PSP) contains information about a program. One important part of the PSP is the command line parameters.

13. Interrupt hooks allow application software to gain access to or intercept an interrupt. We often hook into the timer click interrupt (vector 8) or the keyboard interrupt (vector 9).

14. A terminate and stay resident (TSR) program is a program that remains in the memory that is often accessed through a hooked interrupt using either the timer click or a hot key.

15. A hot key is a key that activates a terminate and stay resident program through the keyboard interrupt hook.

6–8   QUESTIONS AND PROBLEMS

1. The assembler converts a source file to an _____ file.

2. What files are generated from the source file TEST.ASM as it is processed by MASM?

3. The linker program links object files and _____ files to create an execution file.

4. What does the PUBLIC directive indicate when placed in a program module?

5. What does the EXTRN directive indicate when placed in a program module?

6. What directives appear with labels defined external?

7. Describe how a library file works when it is linked to other object files by the linker program.

8. What assembler language directives delineate a macro sequence?

9. What is a macro sequence?

10. How are parameters transferred to a macro sequence?

11. Develop a macro called ADD32 that adds the 32-bit contents of DX—CX to the 32-bit contents of BX—AX.

12. How is the LOCAL directive used within a macro sequence?

13. Develop a macro called ADDLIST PARA1,PARA2 that adds the contents of PARA1 to PARA2. Each of these parameters represents an area of memory. The number of bytes added are indicated by register CX before the macro is invoked.

14. Develop a macro that sums a list of byte-sized data invoked by the macro ADDM LIST,LENGTH. The label LIST is the starting address of the data block and length is the number of data added. The result must be a 16-bit sum found in AX at the end of the macro sequence.

15. What is the purpose of the INCLUDE directive?

16. Develop a procedure called RANDOM. This procedure must return an 8-bit random number in register CL at the end of the subroutine. (One way to generate a random number is to increment CL each time the DOS function 06H tests the keyboard and finds *no* keystroke. In this way a random number is generated.)

17. Develop a procedure that displays a character string that ends with a 00H. Your procedure must use the DS:DX register to address the start of the character string.

18. Develop a procedure that reads a key and displays the hexadecimal value of an extended ASCII coded keyboard character if it is typed. If a normal character is typed, ignore it.

19. Use BIOS INT 10H to develop a procedure that positions the cursor at line 3, column 6.

20. When a number is converted from binary to BCD, the _____ instruction accomplishes the conversion provided the number is less than 100 decimal.

21. How is a large number (over 100 decimal) converted from binary to BCD?

22. A BCD digit is converted to ASCII code by adding a _____ .

23. An ASCII coded number is converted to BCD by subtracting _____ .

24. Develop a procedure that reads an ASCII number from the keyboard and stores it as a BCD number into memory array DATA. The number ends when anything other than a number is typed.

25. Explain how a 3-digit ASCII coded number is converted to binary.

26. Develop a procedure that converts all lowercase ASCII coded letters into uppercase ASCII coded letters. Your procedure may not change any other character except the letter a-z.

27. Develop a lookup table that converts hexadecimal data 00H-0FH into the ASCII coded characters that represent the hexadecimal digits. Make sure to show the lookup table and any software required for the conversion.

28. Develop a program sequence that jumps to memory location ONE if AL = 6, TWO if AL = 7, and THREE if AL = 8.

29. Show how to use the XLAT instruction to access a lookup table called LOOK that is located in the stack segment.

30. Explain the purpose of a boot sector, FAT, and root directory.

31. The surface of a disk is divided into tracks that are further subdivided into _____ .

32. What is a bootstrap loader and where is it found?

33. What is a cluster?

34. A directory entry contains an attribute byte. This byte indicates what information about the entry?

35. A directory entry contains the length of the disk file or subdirectory stored in _____ bytes of memory.

36. What is the maximum length of a file?
37. Develop a procedure that opens a file called TEST.LST, reads 512 bytes from the file into data segment memory area ARRAY, and closes the file.
38. Develop a procedure that renames file TEST.LST to TEST.LIS.
39. Write a program that reads any decimal number between 0 and 65,535 and displays the 16-bit binary version on the video display.
40. Write a program that displays the binary powers of two (in decimal) on the video screen for the powers 0 through 7. Your display shows 2^n = value for each power of 2.
41. Using the technique learned in question 15, develop a program that displays random numbers between 1 and 47 (or whatever) for your state's lottery.
42. Develop a program that displays the hexadecimal contents of a block of 256 bytes of memory. Your software must be able to accept the starting address as a hexadecimal number between 00000H and FFF00H.
43. Develop a program that hooks into interrupt vector 0 to display the following message on a divide error: "Oops, you have attempted to divide by 0."

CHAPTER 7

8086/8088 Hardware Specifications

INTRODUCTION

In this chapter, we describe the pin functions of both the 8086 and 8088 microprocessors and provide details on the following hardware topics: clock generation, bus buffering, bus latching, timing, wait states, and minimum mode operation versus maximum mode operation.

Before it is possible to connect or interface anything to the microprocessor, it is necessary to understand the pin functions and timing. Thus, the information in this chapter is essential to a complete understanding of memory and I/O interfacing, which we cover in the later chapters of the text.

CHAPTER OBJECTIVES

Upon completion of this chapter, you will be able to:

1. Describe the function of each 8086 and 8088 pin.
2. Understand the microprocessor's DC characteristics and indicate its fanout to common logic families.
3. Use the clock generator chip (8284A) to provide the clock for the microprocessor.
4. Connect buffers and latches to the buses.
5. Interpret the timing diagrams.
6. Describe wait states and connect the circuitry required to cause various numbers waits.
7. Explain the difference between minimum and maximum mode operation.

7–1   PINOUTS AND THE PIN FUNCTIONS

In this section we explain the function, and in some cases the multiple functions, of each of the microprocessor's pins. In addition, we discuss the DC characteristics to provide a basis for understanding the later sections on buffering and latching.

The Pinout

Figure 7–1 illustrates the pinouts of the 8086 and 8088 microprocessors. As a close comparison reveals, there is virtually no difference between these two microprocessors—both are packaged in 40-pin dual in-line packages (DIPs).

As we mentioned in Chapter 1, the 8086 is a 16-bit microprocessor with a 16-bit data bus, and the 8088 is a 16-bit microprocessor with an 8-bit data bus. (As the pinouts show, the 8086 has pin connections AD_0–AD_{15}, and the 8088 has pin connections AD_0–AD_7). Data bus width is therefore the only major difference between these microprocessors.

There is, however, a minor difference in one of the control signals. The 8086 has an $M/\overline{IO}$ pin, and the 8088 has an $IO/\overline{M}$ pin. The only other hardware difference appears on Pin 34 of both chips: on the 8088, it is an $\overline{SSO}$ pin, while on the 8086, it is a $\overline{BHE}/S_7$ pin.

Power Supply Requirements

Both the 8086 and 8088 microprocessors require +5.0 V with a supply voltage tolerance of ±10 percent. The 8086 draws a maximum supply current of 360 mA, and the 8088 draws a maximum of 340 mA. Both microprocessors operate in ambient temperatures of between 32°F and about 180°F. This range is not wide enough to be used outdoors in the

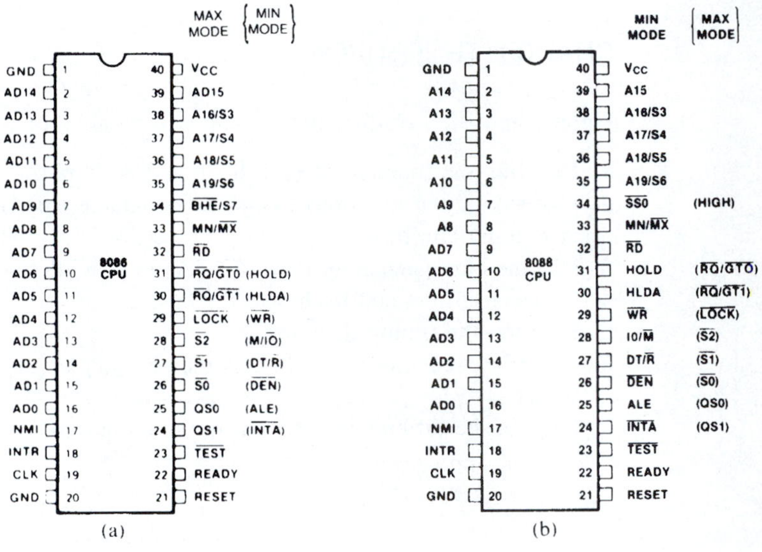

FIGURE 7–1   (a) The pinout of the 8086 microprocessor; (b) the pinout of the 8088 microprocessor.

winter or even in the summer, but extended temperature range versions of the 8086 and 8088 microprocessors are available. There is also a CMOS version, which requires a very low supply current and also has an extended temperature range. The 80C88 and 80C86 are CMOS versions that require only 10 mA of power supply current and function in temperature extremes of −40°F through +225°F.

DC Characteristics

It is impossible to connect anything to the pins of the microprocessor without knowing the input current requirement for an input pin and the output current drive capability for an output pin. This knowledge allows the hardware designer to select the proper interface components for use with the microprocessor without the fear of damaging anything.

Input Characteristics.   The input characteristics of these microprocessors are compatible with all the standard logic components available today. Table 7–1 depicts the input voltage levels and also the input current requirements for any input pin on either microprocessor. The input current levels are very small because the inputs are the gate connections of MOSFETs and represent only leakage currents.

Input Characteristics.   Table 7–2 illustrates the output characteristics of all the output pins of these microprocessors. The logic 1 voltage level of the 8086/8088 is compatible with that of most standard logic families, but the logic 0 level is not. Standard logic circuits have a maximum logic 0 voltage of 0.4 V, and the 8086/8088 has a maximum of 0.45 V. Thus there is a difference of 0.05 V.

This difference reduces the noise immunity from a standard level of 400 mV (0.8 V − 0.45 V) to 350 mV. (The noise immunity is the difference between the logic 0 output voltage and the logic 0 input voltage levels.) This reduced noise immunity may result in problems with long wire connections or too many loads. It is therefore recommended that no more than 10 loads of any type or combination be connected to an output pin without buffers. If this loading is exceeded, noise will begin to take its toll in timing problems.

Table 7–3 lists some of the more common logic families and the recommended fanout from the 8086/8088. The best choice of component types for the connection to an 8086/8088 output pin is a LS, 74ALS, or 74HC logic component.

TABLE 7–1 Input characteristics of the 8086 and 8088 microprocessors

Logic Level	Voltage	Current
0	0.8 V maximum	10 μA maximum
1	2.0 V minimum	10 μA maximum

TABLE 7–2 Output characteristics of the 8086 and 8088 microprocessors

Logic Level	Voltage	Current
0	0.45 V maximum	2.0 mA maximum
1	2.4 V minimum	−400 μA maximum

TABLE 7–3 Recommended fanout from any 8086/8088 pin connection

Family	Fanout	Sink Current	Source Current
TTL (74XX)	1	−1.6 mA	40 μA
TTL (74LSXX)	5	−0.4 mA	20 μA
TTL (74SXX)	1	−2.0 mA	50 μA
TTL (74ALSXX)	10	−0.2 mA	20 μA
CMOS (74HCXX)	10	−1.0 μA	1.0 μA
CMOS (CD4XXX)	10	−1.0 μA	1.0 μA
NMOS	10	−10 μA	10 μA

Pin Connections

1. AD_7–AD_0 (8088)—*Address/Data Bus*: compose the multiplexed address data bus of the 8088 and contain the rightmost 8 bits of the memory address or I/O port number whenever ALE is active (logic 1) or data whenever ALE is inactive (logic 0). These pins are at their high-impedance state during a hold acknowledge.

2. A_{15}–A_8 (8088)—*Address Bus*: provide the upper-half memory address bits that are present throughout a bus cycle. These address connections go to their high-impedance state during a hold acknowledge.

3. AD_{15}–AD_7 (8086)—*Address/Data Bus*: lines compose the upper multiplexed address/data bus on the 8086. These lines contain address bits A_{15}–A_8 whenever ALE is a logic 1 and data bus connections D_{15}–D_8. These pins enter a high-impedance state whenever a hold acknowledge occurs.

4. A_{19}/S_6, A_{18}/S_5, A_{17}/S_4, and A_{16}/S_3—*Address/Status Bus*: are multiplexed to provide address signals A_{19}–A_{16} and also status bits S_6–S_3. These pins also attain a high-impedance state during the hold acknowledge.

   Status bit S_6 always remains a logic 0, bit S_5 indicates the condition of the IF flag bits, and S_4 and S_3 show which segment is accessed during the current bus cycle. Refer to Table 7–4 for the truth table of S_4 and S_3. These two status bits could be used to address four separate 1M byte memory banks.

5. $\overline{RD}$—*Read*: signals (when a logic 0) that the data bus is receptive to data from the memory or I/O devices connected to the system. This pin floats to its high-impedance state during a hold acknowledge.

TABLE 7–4 Function of S_4 and S_3

S_4	S_3	Function
0	0	Extra segment
0	1	Stack segment
1	0	Code or no segment
1	1	Data segment

6. READY—*Ready*: is an input that when controlled can be used to insert wait states into the timing of the microprocessor. If the READY pin is placed at a logic 0 level, the microprocessor enters into wait states and remains idle. If the READY pin is placed at a logic 1 level, it has no effect on the operation of the microprocessor.

7. INTR—*Interrupt Request*: is used to request a hardware interrupt. If INTR is held high when IF = 1, the 8086/8088 enters an interrupt acknowledge cycle ($\overline{INTA}$ becomes active) after the current instruction has completed execution.

8. $\overline{TEST}$—*Test*: is an input pin that is tested by the WAIT instruction. If $\overline{TEST}$ is a logic 0, the WAIT instruction functions as a NOP. If $\overline{TEST}$ is a logic 1, then the WAIT instruction waits for $\overline{TEST}$ to become a logic 0. This pin is most often connected to the 8087 numeric coprocessor.

9. NMI—*Nonmaskable Interrupt*: is similar to INTR except the NMI interrupt does not check to see if the IF flag bit is a logic 1. If NMI is activated, this interrupt input uses interrupt vector 2.

10. RESET—*Reset*: causes the microprocessor to reset itself if this pin is held high for a minimum of 4 clocking periods. Whenever the 8086/8088 is reset, it begins executing instructions at memory location FFFF0H and disables future interrupts by clearing the IF flag bit.

11. CLK—*Clock*: provides the basic timing signal to the microprocessor. The clock signal must have a duty cycle of 33% (high one third of the clocking period and low for two thirds) to provide proper internal timing for the 8086/8088.

12. V_{cc}—*Power supply*: input V_{cc} provides a +5.0 V, ±10% signal to the microprocessor.

13. GND—*Ground*: is the return connection for the power supply. Note that the 8086/8088 has two pins labeled GND—both must be connected to ground for proper operation.

14. MN/$\overline{MX}$—*Minimum/Maximum Mode*: selects either minimum mode or maximum mode operation for the microprocessor. If minimum mode is selected, the MN/$\overline{MX}$ pin must be connected directly to +5.0 V.

15. $\overline{BHE}$/S_7—*Bus High Enable*: is used in the 8086 to enable the most significant data bus bits (D_{15}–D_8) during a read or a write operation. The state of S_7 is always a logic 1.

Minimum Mode Pins. Minimum mode operation of the 8086/8088 is obtained by connecting the MN/$\overline{MX}$ pin directly to +5.0 V. Do not connect this pin to +5.0 V through a pullup resistor, or it will not function correctly.

1. IO/$\overline{M}$ (8088), M/$\overline{IO}$ (8086)—*Memory or Input/Output*: is a pin that indicates to the memory and I/O that the microprocessor address bus contains either a memory address or an I/O port address. This pin is at its high-impedance state during a hold acknowledge.

2. $\overline{WR}$—*Write*: is a strobe that indicates that the 8086/8088 is outputting data to a memory or I/O device. During the time that the $\overline{WR}$ is a logic 0, the data bus contains valid data for memory or I/O. This pin floats to a high-impedance during a hold acknowledge.

3. $\overline{INTA}$—*Interrupt Acknowledge*: is a response to the INTR input pin. The $\overline{INTA}$ pin is normally used to gate the interrupt vector number onto the data bus in response to an interrupt request.

4. ALE—*Address Latch Enable*: shows that the 8086/8088 address/data bus contains address information. This address can be a memory address or an I/O port number. Note that the ALE signal does not float during a hold acknowledge.

5. DT/$\overline{R}$—*Data Transmit/Receive*: shows that the microprocessor data bus is transmitting (DT/$\overline{R}$ = 1) or receiving (DT/$\overline{R}$ = 0) data. This signal is used to enable external data bus buffers.

6. $\overline{DEN}$—*Data Bus Enable*: is used to enable external data bus buffers.

7. HOLD—*Hold*: requests a direct memory access (DMA). If the HOLD signal is a logic 1, the microprocessor stops executing software and places its address, data, and control bus at the high-impedance state. If the HOLD pin is a logic 0, the microprocessor executes software normally.

8. HLDA—*Hold Acknowledge*: indicates that the 8086/8088 has entered the hold state.

9. $\overline{SS0}$ (8088)—*Status Line 0*: is equivalent to the $\overline{S0}$ pin in maximum mode operation of the microprocessor. This signal is combined with IO/$\overline{M}$ and DT/$\overline{R}$ to decode the function of the current bus cycle (refer to Table 7–5).

Maximum Mode Pins.   In order to achieve maximum mode for use with external coprocessors, connect the MN/$\overline{MX}$ pin to ground.

1. $\overline{S2}$, $\overline{S1}$, and $\overline{S0}$—*Status Bits*: indicate the function of the current bus cycle. These signals are normally decoded by the 8288 bus controller described later in this chapter. Table 7–6 shows the function of these three status bits in the maximum mode.

2. $\overline{RQ/GT0}$ and $\overline{RQ/GT1}$—*Request/Grant*: pins that request direct memory accesses (DMA) during maximum mode operation. Each of these lines is bidirectional and used to both request and grant a DMA operation.

3. $\overline{LOCK}$—*Lock*: is an output that can be used to lock peripherals off the system. This pin is activated by using the LOCK prefix on any instruction.

4. QS1 and QS0—*Queue Status*: show the status of the internal instruction queue. These pins are provided for access by the numeric coprocessor (8087). Refer to Table 7–7 for the operation of the queue status bits.

TABLE 7–5 Bus cycle status (8088) using $\overline{SS0}$

IO/$\overline{M}$	DT/$\overline{R}$	$\overline{SS0}$	Function
0	0	0	Interrupt acknowledge
0	0	1	Memory read
0	1	0	Memory write
0	1	1	Halt
1	0	0	Code access
1	0	1	I/O read
1	1	0	I/O write
1	1	1	Passive

TABLE 7–6 Bus control functions generated by the bus controller (8288) using $\overline{S2}$, $\overline{S1}$, and $\overline{S0}$

$\overline{S2}$	$\overline{S1}$	$\overline{S0}$	Function
0	0	0	Interrupt acknowledge
0	0	1	I/O read
0	1	0	I/O write
0	1	1	Halt
1	0	0	Code access
1	0	1	Memory read
1	1	0	Memory write
1	1	1	Passive

TABLE 7–7 Queue status bits

QS1	QS0	Function
0	0	No operation (queue is idle)
0	1	First byte of an opcode
1	0	Queue is empty
1	1	Subsequent byte of an opcode

7–2   CLOCK GENERATOR (8284A)

This section describes the clock generator (8284A), the RESET signal, and introduces the READY signal for the 8086/8088 microprocessor. The READY signal and its associated circuitry are treated in detail in section 7–5.

The 8284A Clock Generator

The 8284A is an ancillary component to the 8086/8088 microprocessor. Without the clock generator, many additional circuits are required to generate the clock (CLK) in an 8086/8088-based system. The 8284A provides the following basic functions or signals: clock generation, RESET synchronization, READY synchronization, and a TTL level peripheral clock signal. Figure 7–2 illustrates the pinout of the 8284A clock generator.

FIGURE 7–2 The pinout of the 8284A clock generator.

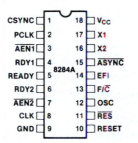

Pin Functions.   The 8284A is an 18-pin integrated circuit designed specifically for use with the 8086/8088 microprocessor. The following is a list of each pin and its function:

1. $\overline{\text{AEN1}}$ and $\overline{\text{AEN2}}$—*Address Enable*: pins are provided to qualify the bus ready signals, RDY1 and RDY2, respectively. Section 7–5 illustrates the use of these two pins, which are used to cause wait states, along with the RDY1 and RDY2 inputs. Wait states are generated by the READY pin of the 8086/8088 microprocessor, which is controlled by these two inputs.

2. RDY1 and RDY2—*Bus Ready*: inputs are provided in conjunction with the $\overline{\text{AEN1}}$ and $\overline{\text{AEN2}}$ pins to cause wait states in an 8086/8088-based system.

3. $\overline{\text{ASYNC}}$—*Ready Synchronization Select*: an input used to select either one or two stages of synchronization for the RDY1 and RDY2 inputs.

4. READY—*Ready*: this output pin connects to the 8086/8088 READY input. This signal is synchronized with the RDY1 and RDY2 inputs.

5. X1 and X2—*Crystal Inputs*: pins connect to an external crystal used as the timing source for the clock generator and all its functions.

6. $\text{F}/\overline{\text{C}}$—*Frequency/Crystal*: selects the clocking source for the 8284A. If this pin is held high, an external clock is provided to the EFI input pin, and if it is held low, the internal crystal oscillator provides the timing signal.

7. EFI—*External Frequency Input*: an input used when the $\text{F}/\overline{\text{C}}$ pin is pulled high. EFI supplies the timing whenever the $\text{F}/\overline{\text{C}}$ pin is high.

8. CLK—*Clock*: an output pin that provides the CLK input signal to the 8086/8088 microprocessor and other components in the system. The CLK pin has an output signal that is one third of the crystal or EFI input frequency and has a 33 percent duty cycle, which is required by the 8086/8088.

9. PCLK—*Peripheral Clock*: a signal that is one sixth the crystal or EFI input frequency and has a 50 percent duty cycle. The PCLK output provides a clock signal to the peripheral equipment in the system.

10. OSC—*Oscillator Output*: a TTL level signal that is at the same frequency as the crystal or EFI input. The OSC output provides an EFI input to other 8284A clock generators in some multiple-processor systems.

11. $\overline{\text{RES}}$—*Reset Input*: the active-low reset input to the 8284A. The $\overline{\text{RES}}$ pin is often connected to an RC network that provides power-on resetting.

12. RESET—*Reset Output*: the signal connected to the 8086/8088 RESET input pin.

13. CSYNC—*Clock Synchronization*: a pin used whenever the EFI input provides synchronization in systems with multiple processors. If the internal crystal oscillator is used, this pin must be grounded.

14. GND—*Ground*: a pin connected to ground.

15. V_{cc}—*Power Supply Input*: a pin connected to +5.0 V with a tolerance of ±10 percent.

Operation of the 8284A

The 8284A is a relatively easy component to understand. Figure 7–3 illustrates the internal logic diagram of the 8284A clock generator.

Operation of the Clock Section.   The top half of the logic diagram represents the clock and reset synchronization section of the 8284A clock generator. As the diagram shows, the crystal oscillator has two inputs: X1 and X2. If a crystal is attached to X1 and X2, the

D = AND
⟩ = OR

Schmitt trigger

flip-flop

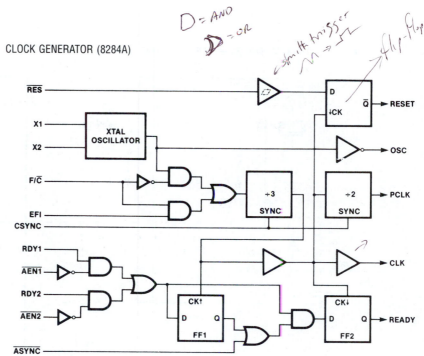

FIGURE 7–3   The internal block diagram of the 8284A clock generator.

oscillator generates a square-wave signal at the same frequency as the crystal. The square-wave signal is fed to an AND gate and also an inverting buffer that provides the OSC output signal. The OSC signal is sometimes used as an EFI input to other 8284As.

A close inspection of the AND gate reveals that when F/$\overline{C}$ is a logic 0, the oscillator output is steered through to the divide-by-3 counter. If F/$\overline{C}$ is a logic 1, then EFI is steered through to the counter.

The output of the divide-by-3 counter generates the timing for ready synchronization, a signal for another counter (divide-by-2), and the CLK signal to the 8086/8088 microprocessor. The CLK signal is also buffered before it leaves the clock generator. Notice that the output of the first counter feeds the second. These two cascaded counters provide the divide-by-6 output at PCLK, the peripheral clock output.

Figure 7–4 shows how an 8284A is connected to the 8086/8088. Notice (1) that F/$\overline{C}$ and CSYNC are grounded to select the crystal oscillator, and (2) that a 15 MHz crystal provides the normal 5 MHz clock signal to the 8086/8088 as well as a 2.5 MH⁻ peripheral clock signal.

Operation of the Reset Section.   The reset section of the 8284A is very simple. It consists of a Schmitt trigger buffer and a single D-type flip-flop circuit. The D-type flip-flop ensures that the timing requirements of the 8086/8088 RESET input are met. This circuit applies the RESET signal to the microprocessor on the negative edge (1-to-0 transition) of each clock. The 8086/8088 samples RESET at the positive edge (0-to-1 transition) of the clocks; therefore, this circuit meets the timing requirements of the 8086/8088.

Refer again to Figure 7–4. Notice that an RC circuit provides a logic 0 to the $\overline{RES}$ input pin when power is first applied to the system. After a short time, the $\overline{RES}$ input becomes a logic 1 because the capacitor charges toward +5.0 V through the resistor. A pushbutton switch allows the microprocessor to be reset by the operator. Correct reset timing requires the

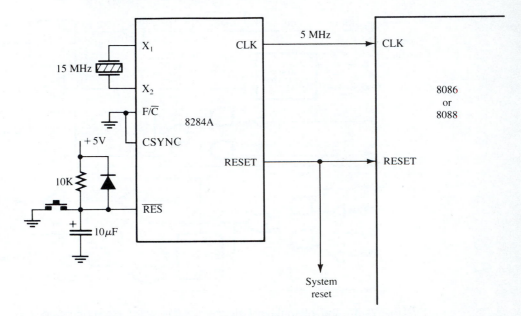

FIGURE 7–4   The clock generator (8284A) and the 8086 or 8088 microprocessor illustrating the connection for the clock and reset signals. A 15-MHz crystal provides the 5-MHz clock for the microprocessor.

RESET input to become a logic 1 no later than four clocks after system power is applied and to be held high for at least 50 μs. The flip-flop makes certain that RESET goes high in four clocks and the RC time constant ensures that it stays high for at least 50 μs.

7–3   BUS BUFFERING AND LATCHING

Before the 8086/8088 can be used with memory or I/O interfaces, its multiplexed buses must be demultiplexed. This section provides the detail required to demultiplex the buses and illustrates how the buses are buffered for very large systems. (Because the maximum fanout is 10, the system must be buffered if it contains more than 10 other components.)

Demultiplexing the Buses

The address/data bus on the 8086/8088 is multiplexed (shared) to reduce the number of pins required for the 8086/8088 microprocessor integrated circuit. Unfortunately, this burdens the hardware designer with the task of extracting or demultiplexing information from these multiplexed pins.

Why not leave the buses multiplexed? Memory and I/O require that the address remains valid and stable throughout a read or write cycle. If the buses are multiplexed, the address changes at the memory and I/O, which causes them to read or write data in the wrong locations.

All computer systems have three buses: (1) an address bus that provides the memory and I/O with the memory address or the I/O port number, (2) a data bus that transfers data between the microprocessor and the memory and I/O in the system, and (3) a control bus that provides control signals to the memory and I/O. These buses must be present in order to interface to memory and I/O.

Demultiplexing the 8088. Figure 7–5 illustrates the 8088 microprocessor and the components required to demultiplex its buses. In this case, two 74LS373 transparent latches are used to demultiplex the address/data bus connections AD_7–AD_0 and the multiplexed address/status connections A_{19}/S_6–A_{16}/S_3.

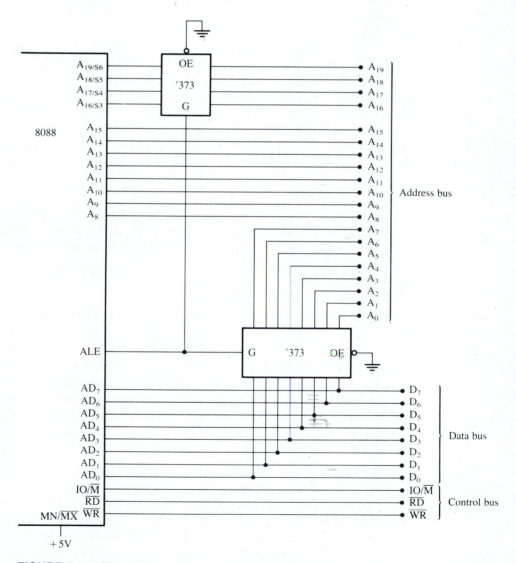

FIGURE 7–5 The 8088 microprocessor shown with a demultiplexed address bus. This is the model used to build many 8088-based systems.

These transparent latches, which are like wires whenever the address latch enable pin (ALE) becomes a logic 1, pass the inputs to the outputs. After a short time, ALE returns to its logic 0 condition, which causes the latches to remember the inputs at the time of the change to a logic 0. In this case, A_7–A_0 are remembered in the bottom latch and A_{19}–A_{16} in the top latch. This yields a separate address bus with connections A_{19}–A_0. These address connections allow the 8088 to address IM bytes of memory space. The fact that the data bus is separate allows it to be connected to any 8-bit peripheral device or memory component.

Demultiplexing the 8086.   Like the 8088, the 8086 system requires separate address, data, and control buses. It differs primarily in the number of multiplexed pins. In the 8088, only AD_7–AD_0 and A_{19}/S_6–A_{16}/S_3 are multiplexed. In the 8086 the multiplexed pins include AD_{15}–AD_0, A_{19}/S_6–A_{16}/S_3, and $\overline{BHE}/S_7$. All of these signals must be demultiplexed.

Figure 7–6 illustrates a demultiplexed 8086 with all three buses: address (A_{19}–A_0 and $\overline{BHE}$, data (D_{15}–D_0), and control (M/$\overline{IO}$, $\overline{RD}$, and $\overline{WR}$).

This circuit is almost identical to the one pictured in Figure 7–5, except that an additional 74LS373 latch has been added to demultiplex the address/data bus pins AD_{15}–AD_8 and a $\overline{BHE}/S_7$ input has been added to the top 74LS373 to select the high-order memory bank in the 16-bit memory system of the 8086. Here the memory and I/O system see the 8086 as a device with a 20-bit address bus (A_{19}–A_0), a 16-bit data bus (D_{15}–D_0), and a 3-line control bus (M/$\overline{IO}$, $\overline{RD}$, and $\overline{WR}$).

The Buffered System

If more than 10 unit loads are attached to any bus pin, the entire 8086 or 8088 system must be buffered. The demultiplexed pins are already buffered by the 74LS373 latches, which have been designed to drive the high-capacitance buses encountered in microcomputer systems. The buffer's output currents have been increased so more TTL unit loads may be driven: a logic 0 output provides up to 32 mA of sink current, and a logic 1 output provides up to 5.2 mA of source current.

A fully buffered signal will introduce a timing delay to the system. This causes no difficulty unless memory or I/O devices are used which function at near the maximum speed of the bus. Section 7–4 treats this problem and the time delays involved in more detail.

The Fully Buffered 8088.   Figure 7–7 depicts a fully buffered 8088 microprocessor. Notice that the remaining eight address pins, A_{15}–A_8, use a 74LS244 octal buffer; the eight data bus pins, D_7–D_0, use a 74LS245 octal bidirectional bus buffer; and the control bus signals, IO/$\overline{M}$, $\overline{RD}$, and $\overline{WR}$, use a 74LS244 buffer. A fully buffered 8088 system requires two 74LS244s, one 74LS245, and two 74LS373s. The direction of the 74LS245 is controlled by the DT/$\overline{R}$ signal and is enabled and disabled by the $\overline{DEN}$ signal.

The Fully Buffered 8086.   Figure 7–8 illustrates a fully buffered 8086 microprocessor. Its address pins are already buffered by the 74LS373 address latches; its data bus employs two 74LS245 octal bidirectional bus buffers; and the control bus signals, M/$\overline{IO}$, $\overline{RD}$, and $\overline{WR}$, use a 74LS244 buffer. A fully buffered 8086 system requires one 74LS244, two 74LS245s, and three 74LS373s. The 8086 requires one more buffer than the 8088 because of the extra eight data bus connections D_{15}–D_8. It also has a $\overline{BHE}$ signal that is buffered for memory-bank selection.

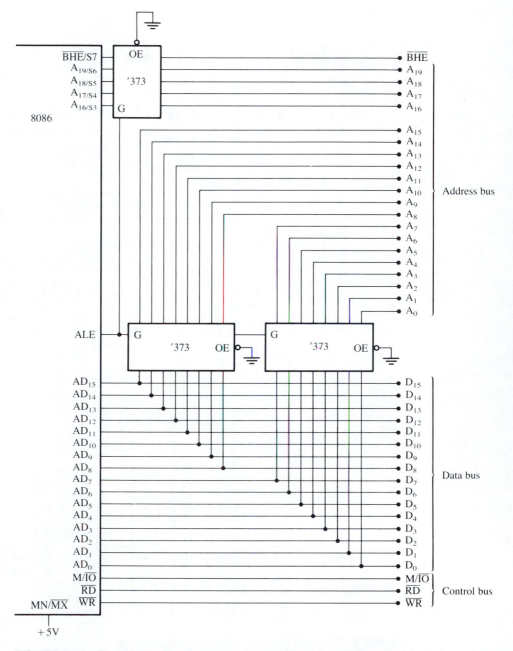

FIGURE 7-6 The 8086 microprocessor shown with a demultiplexed address bus. This is the model used to build many 8086-based systems.

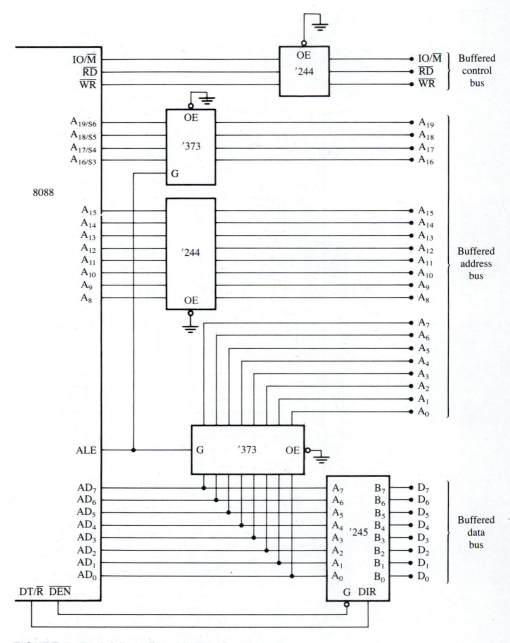

FIGURE 7–7   A fully buffered 8088 microprocessor.

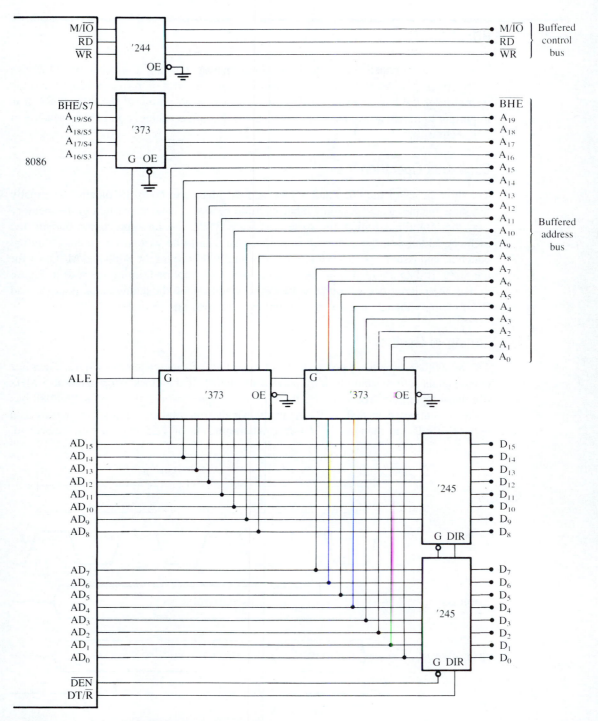

FIGURE 7-8 A fully buffered 8086 microprocessor.

7–4   BUS TIMING

It is essential to understand system bus timing before choosing a memory or I/O device for interfacing to the 8086 or 8088 microprocessor. This section provides insight into the operation of the bus signals and the basic read and write timing of the 8086/8088. It is important to note that we discuss only the times that affect memory and I/O interfacing in this section.

Basic Bus Operation

The three buses of the 8086 and 8088—address, data, and control—function in exactly the same manner as those of any other microprocessor. If data are written to the memory (see the simplified timing for write in Figure 7–9), the microprocessor outputs the memory address on the address bus, outputs the data to be written into memory on the data bus, and issues a write ($\overline{WR}$) to memory and IO/$\overline{M}$ = 0 for the 8088 and M/$\overline{IO}$ = 1 for the 8086. If data are read from the memory (see the simplified timing for read in Figure 7–10), the microprocessor outputs the memory address on the address bus, issues a read ($\overline{RD}$) memory signal, and accepts the data via the data bus.

Timing in General

The 8086/8088 uses the memory and I/O in periods of time called *bus cycles*. Each bus cycle equals four system-clocking periods (T states). If the clock is operated at 5 MHz (the basic operating frequency for these two microprocessors), then one 8086/8088 bus cycle is completed in 800 ns. This means that the microprocessor reads or writes data between itself and memory or I/O at a maximum rate of 1.25 million times a second.

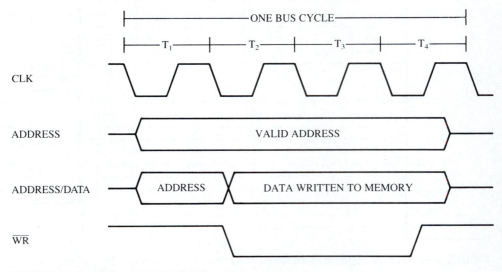

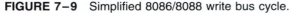

FIGURE 7–9   Simplified 8086/8088 write bus cycle.

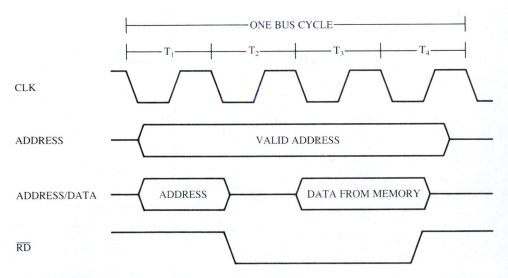

FIGURE 7-10 Simplified 8086/8088 read bus cycle.

(Because of the internal queue, the 8086/8088 can execute 2.5 million instructions per second (MIPS) in bursts.) Other available versions of these microprocessors operate at much higher transfer rates due to higher clock frequencies.

T1. During the first clocking period in a bus cycle, which is called T1, many things happen. The address of the memory or I/O location is sent out via the address bus and the address/data bus connections. (The address/data bus is multiplexed and at times contains memory-addressing information and at other times data.) Also output during T1 are the control signals ALE, DT/$\overline{R}$, and IO/$\overline{M}$ (8088) or M/$\overline{IO}$ (8086). The $\overline{IO}$/M or M/$\overline{IO}$ signal indicates whether the address bus contains a memory address or an I/O device (port) number.

T2. During T2, the 8086/8088 issues the $\overline{RD}$ or $\overline{WR}$ signal, $\overline{DEN}$, and, in the case of a write, the data to be written appear on the data bus. These events cause the memory or I/O device to begin to perform a read or a write. The $\overline{DEN}$ signal turns on the data bus buffers, if they are present in the system, so the memory or I/O can receive data to be written or so the microprocessor can accept the data read from the memory or I/O for a read operation. If this happens to be a write bus cycle, then the data are sent out to the memory or I/O through the data bus.

READY is sampled at the end of T2, as illustrated in Figure 7-11. If READY is low at this time, T3 becomes a wait state (Tw). More detail is provided in section 7-5.

T3. This clocking period is provided to allow the memory time to access data. If the bus cycle happens to be a read bus cycle, the data bus is sampled at the end of T3.

T4. In T4, all bus signals are deactivated in preparation for the next bus cycle. This is also the time when the 8086/8088 samples the data bus connections for data that are read from memory or I/O. In addition, at this point, the trailing edge of the $\overline{WR}$ signal transfers data to the memory or I/O, which activate and write when the $\overline{WR}$ signal returns to a logic 1 level.

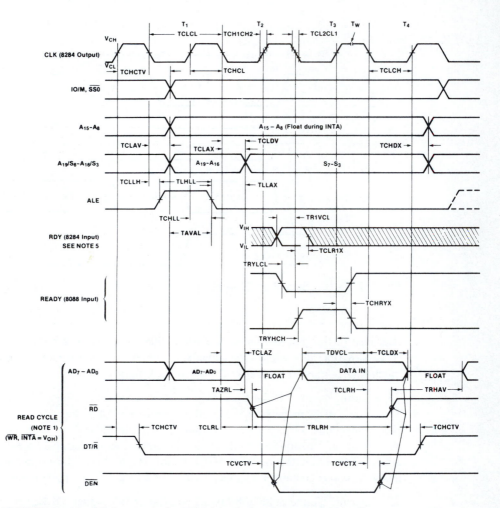

FIGURE 7–11   Minimum mode 8088 bus timing for a read operation.

Read Timing

Figure 7–11 also depicts the read timing for the 8088 microprocessor. The 8086 read timing is identical except that the 8086 has 16 rather than 8 data bus bits. A close look at this timing diagram should allow you to identify all the main events described for each T state.

The most important item contained in the read timing diagram is the amount of time allowed the memory or I/O to read the data. Memory is chosen by its access time, which is the fixed amount of time the microprocessor allows it to access data for the read operation. It is therefore extremely important that the memory you choose comply with the limitations of the system.

The microprocessor timing diagram does not, however, provide a straightforward memory access time. Instead it is necessary to combine several times to arrive at the access time. To find memory access time in this diagram, we must first locate the point in T3 when data are sampled. If you examine the timing diagram closely, you will notice a line that extends from the end of T3 down to the data bus. The end of T3 is where the microprocessor samples the data bus.

Memory access time starts when the address appears on the memory address bus and continues until the microprocessor samples the memory data at T3. Approximately three T states elapse between these times but not exactly. (Refer to Figure 7–12 for the following times.) The address does not appear until T_{CLAV} time (110 ns if the clock is 5 MHz) after the start of T1. This means that T_{CLAV} time must be subtracted from the three clocking states (600 ns) that separate the appearance of the address (T1) and the sampling of the data (T3). One other time must also be subtracted: the data setup time (T_{DVCL}), which occurs before T3. Memory access time is thus three clocking states minus the sum of T_{CLAV} and T_{DVCL}. Because T_{DVCL} is 30 ns with a 5 MHz clock, the allowed memory access time is only 460 ns (access time = 600 ns – 110 ns – 30 ns).

Actually, the memory devices chosen for connection to the 8086/8088 operated at 5 MHz must be able to access data in *less* than 460 ns, because of the time delay introduced by the address decoders and buffers in the system. At least a 30 or 40 ns margin should exist for the operation of these circuits. Therefore, the memory speed should be no slower than about 420 ns to operate correctly with the 8086/8088 microprocessor.

The only other timing factor that may affect memory operation is the width of the $\overline{RD}$ strobe. On the timing diagram, the read strobe width is given as T_{RLRH}. The time for this strobe is 325 ns (5 MHz clock rate), which is wide enough for almost all memory devices manufactured with an access time of 400 ns or less.

Write Timing

Figure 7–13 illustrates the write timing diagram for the 8088 microprocessor. Again, the 8086 is so nearly identical that it need not be presented here in a separate timing diagram.

The main differences between read and write timing are minimal. The $\overline{RD}$ strobe is replaced by the $\overline{WR}$ strobe, the data bus contains information for the memory rather than information from the memory, and $DT/\overline{R}$ remains a logic 1 instead of a logic 0 throughout the bus cycle.

When interfacing some memory devices, timing may be especially critical between the point at which $\overline{WR}$ becomes a logic 1 and the time when the data are removed from the data bus. This is the case because, as you will recall, memory data are written at the trailing edge of the $\overline{WR}$ strobe. According to the timing diagram, this critical period is T_{WHDX} or 88 ns when the 8088 is operated with a 5 MHz clock. Hold time is often much less than this, and is in fact often 0 ns for memory devices. The width of the $\overline{WR}$ strobe is T_{WLWH} or 340 ns at a 5 MHz clock rate. This rate, too, is compatible with most memory devices that have an access time of 400 ns or less.

FIGURE 7–12   8088 AC characteristics.

A.C. CHARACTERISTICS (8088: T$_A$ = 0°C to 70°C, V$_{CC}$ = 5V ±10%)*
(8088-2: T$_A$ = 0°C to 70°C, V$_{CC}$ = 5V ±5%)

MINIMUM COMPLEXITY SYSTEM TIMING REQUIREMENTS

Symbol	Parameter	8088		8088-2		Units	Test Conditions
		Min.	Max.	Min.	Max.		
TCLCL	CLK Cycle Period	200	500	125	500	ns	
TCLCH	CLK Low Time	118		68		ns	
TCHCL	CLK High Time	69		44		ns	
TCH1CH2	CLK Rise Time		10		10	ns	From 1.0V to 3.5V
TCL2CL1	CLK Fall Time		10		10	ns	From 3.5V to 1.0V
TDVCL	Data in Setup Time	30		20		ns	
TCLDX	Data in Hold Time	10		10		ns	
TR1VCL	RDY Setup Time into 8284 (See Notes 1, 2)	35		35		ns	
TCLR1X	RDY Hold Time into 8284 (See Notes 1, 2)	0		0		ns	
TRYHCH	READY Setup Time into 8088	118		68		ns	
TCHRYX	READY Hold Time into 8088	30		20		ns	
TRYLCL	READY Inactive to CLK (See Note 3)	−8		−8		ns	
THVCH	HOLD Setup Time	35		20		ns	
TINVCH	INTR, NMI, TEST Setup Time (See Note 2)	30		15		ns	
TILIH	Input Rise Time (Except CLK)		20		20	ns	From 0.8V to 2.0V
TIHIL	Input Fall Time (Except CLK)		12		12	ns	From 2.0V to 0.8V

A.C. CHARACTERISTICS (Continued)

TIMING RESPONSES

Symbol	Parameter	8088		8088-2		Units	Test Conditions
		Min.	Max.	Min.	Max.		
TCLAV	Address Valid Delay	10	110	10	60	ns	
TCLAX	Address Hold Time	10		10		ns	
TCLAZ	Address Float Delay	TCLAX	80	TCLAX	50	ns	
TLHLL	ALE Width	TCLCH−20		TCLCH−10		ns	
TCLLH	ALE Active Delay		80		50	ns	
TCHLL	ALE Inactive Delay		85		55	ns	
TLLAX	Address Hold Time to ALE Inactive	TCHCL−10		TCHCL−10		ns	
TCLDV	Data Valid Delay	10	110	10	60	ns	C$_L$ = 20-100 pF for all 8088 Outputs in addition to internal loads
TCHDX	Data Hold Time	10		10		ns	
TWHDX	Data Hold Time After WR	TCLCH−30		TCLCH−30		ns	
TCVCTV	Control Active Delay 1	10	110	10	70	ns	
TCHCTV	Control Active Delay 2	10	110	10	60	ns	
TCVCTX	Control Inactive Delay	10	110	10	70	ns	
TAZRL	Address Float to READ Active	0		0		ns	
TCLRL	RD Active Delay	10	165	10	100	ns	
TCLRH	RD Inactive Delay	10	150	10	80	ns	
TRHAV	RD Inactive to Next Address Active	TCLCL−45		TCLCL−40		ns	
TCLHAV	HLDA Valid Delay	10	160	10	100	ns	
TRLRH	RD Width	2TCLCL−75		2TCLCL−50		ns	
TWLWH	WR Width	2TCLCL−60		2TCLCL−40		ns	
TAVAL	Address Valid to ALE Low	TCLCH−60		TCLCH−40		ns	
TOLOH	Output Rise Time		20		20	ns	From 0.8V to 2.0V
TOHOL	Output Fall Time		12		12	ns	From 2.0V to 0.8V

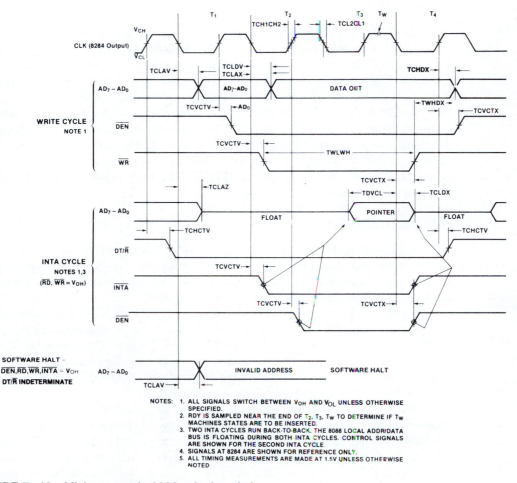

FIGURE 7-13   Minimum mode 8088 write bus timing.

7-5   READY AND THE WAIT STATE

As we mentioned earlier in this chapter, the READY input causes wait states for slower memory and I/O components. A *wait state* (Tw) is an extra clocking period inserted between T2 and T3, to lengthen the bus cycle. If one wait state is inserted, then the memory access time, normally 460 ns with a 5 MHz clock, is lengthened by one clocking period (200 ns) to 660 ns.

In this section, we discuss the READY synchronization circuitry inside the 8284A clock generator, show how to insert one or more wait states selectively into the bus cycle, and examine the READY input and the synchronization times it requires.

The READY Input

The READY input is sampled at the end of T2 and again, if applicable, in the middle of Tw. If READY is a logic 0 at the end of T2, then T3 is delayed and Tw is inserted between T2 and T3. READY is next sampled at the middle of Tw to determine if the next state is Tw or T3. It is tested for a logic 0 on the 1-to-0 transition of the clock at the end of T2 and for a 1 on the 0-to-1 transition of the clock in the middle of Tw.

The READY input to the 8086/8088 has some stringent timing requirements. The timing diagram in Figure 7–14 shows READY causing one wait state (Tw) along with the required setup and hold times from the system clock. The timing requirement for this operation is met by the internal READY synchronization circuitry of the 8284A clock generator. When the 8284A is used for READY, the RDY (ready input to the 8284A) input occurs at the end of each T state.

RDY and the 8284A

RDY is the synchronized ready input to the 8284A clock generator. The timing diagram for this input is provided in Figure 7–15. Although it differs from the timing for the READY input to the 8086/8088, the internal 8284A circuitry guarantees the accuracy of the READY synchronization provided to the 8086/8088.

Figure 7–16 again depicts the internal structure of the 8284A. The bottom half of this diagram is the READY synchronization circuitry. At the leftmost side, the RDY1 and $\overline{\text{AEN1}}$ inputs are ANDed, as are the RDY2 and $\overline{\text{AEN2}}$ inputs. The outputs of the AND gates are then ORed to generate the input to the one or two stages of synchronization. In order to obtain a logic 1 at the inputs to the flip-flops, RDY1 ANDed with $\overline{\text{AEN1}}$ must be active or RDY2 ANDed with $\overline{\text{AEN2}}$ must be active.

The $\overline{\text{ASYNC}}$ input selects one stage of synchronization when it is a logic 1 and two stages when a logic 0. If one stage is selected, then the RDY signal is kept from reaching the 8086/8088 READY pin until the next negative edge of the clock. If two stages are selected, the first positive edge of the clock captures RDY in the first flip-flop. The output of this flip-flop is fed to the second flip-flop so on the next negative edge of the clock, the second flip-flop captures RDY.

Figure 7–17 illustrates a circuit used to introduce almost any number of wait states for the 8086/8088 microprocessor. Here an 8-bit serial shift register (74LS164) shifts a logic 0 for one or more clock periods from one of its Q outputs through to the RDY1 input of the 8284A. With appropriate strapping, this circuit can provide various numbers of wait states. Notice also how the shift register is cleared back to its starting

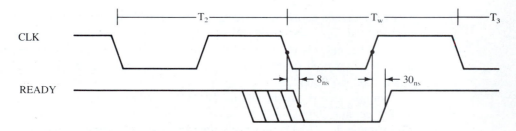

FIGURE 7–14   8086/8088 READY input timing.

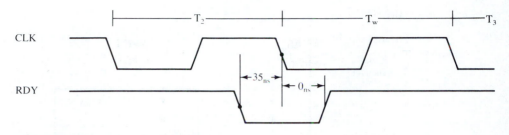

FIGURE 7–15 8284A RDY input timing.

point. The output of the register is forced high when the $\overline{RD}$, $\overline{WR}$obx, and $\overline{INTA}$ pins are all logic 1's. These three signals are high until state T2, so the shift register shifts for the first time when the positive edge of the T2 arrives. If one wait is desired, then output Q_B is connected to the OR gate. If two waits are desired, output Q_C is connected, and so forth.

Also notice in Figure 7–17 that this circuit does not always generate wait states. It is enabled from the memory only for memory devices that require the insertion of waits. If the selection signal from a memory device is a logic 0, the device is selected; then this circuit will generate a wait state.

Figure 7–18 illustrates the timing diagram for this shift register wait state generator when it is wired to insert one wait state. The timing diagram also illustrates the internal contents of the shift register's flip-flops to present a more detailed view of its operation. In this example, one wait state is generated.

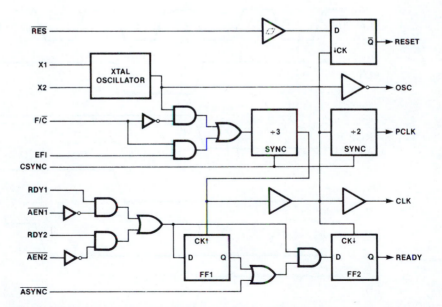

FIGURE 7–16 The internal block diagram of the 8284A clock generator. (Courtesy of Intel Corporation)

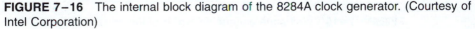

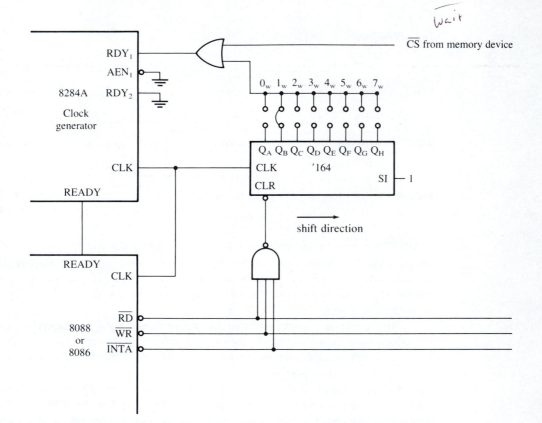

FIGURE 7–17 A circuit that will cause between 0 and 7 wait states.

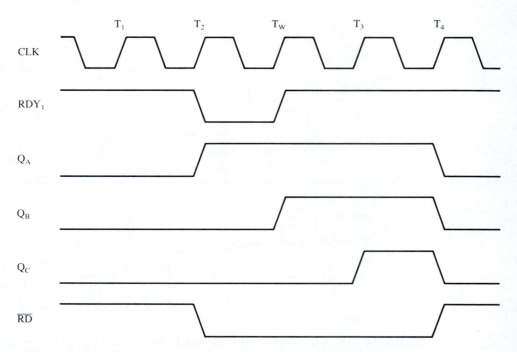

FIGURE 7–18 Wait state generation timing of the circuit of Figure 7–17.

7-6   MINIMUM MODE VERSUS MAXIMUM MODE

There are two available modes of operation for the 8086/8088 microprocessor: minimum mode and maximum mode. Minimum mode operation is obtained by connecting the mode selection pin MN/$\overline{\text{MX}}$ to +5.0 V, and maximum mode is selected by grounding this pin. Both modes enable different control structures for the 8086/8088 microprocessor. The mode of operation provided by minimum mode is similar to that of the 8085A, the most recent Intel 8-bit microprocessor, whereas maximum mode is new and unique and designed to be used whenever a coprocessor exists in a system.

Minimum Mode Operation

Minimum mode operation is the least expensive way to operate the 8086/8088 microprocessor (see Figure 7-19 for the minimum mode 8088 system). It costs less because all the control signals for the memory and I/O are generated inside the microprocessor. Its control signals are identical to those of the Intel 8085A, an earlier 8-bit microprocessor. This configuration allows 8085A peripherals to be used with the 8086/8088 without any special considerations.

Maximum Mode Operation

Maximum mode operation differs from minimum mode in that some of the control signals must be externally generated. This requires the addition of an external bus

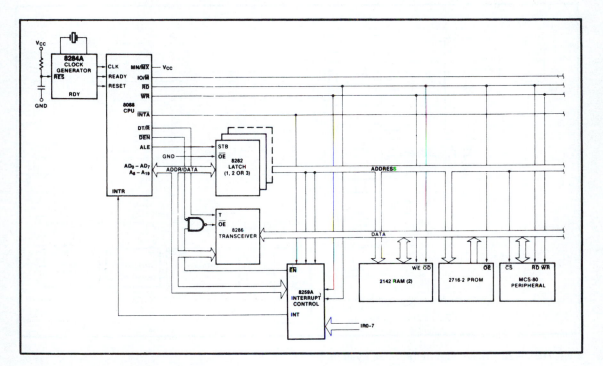

FIGURE 7-19   Minimum mode 8088 system.

controller—the 8288 bus controller (see Figure 7–20 for the maximum mode 8088 system). There are not enough pins on the 8086/8088 for bus control during maximum mode because new pins and new features have replaced some of them. Maximum mode is used only when the system contains external coprocessors such as the 8087 arithmetic coprocessor.

The 8288 Bus Controller

An 8086/8088 system that is operated in maximum mode must have an 8288 bus controller to provide the signals that are eliminated from the 8086/8088 by the maximum mode operation. Figure 7–21 illustrates the block diagram and pinout of the 8288 bus controller circuit.

Notice that the control bus developed by the 8288 bus controller contains separate signals for I/O ($\overline{IORC}$ and $\overline{IOWC}$) and memory ($\overline{MRDC}$ and $\overline{MWTC}$). It also contains advanced memory ($\overline{AMWC}$) and I/O ($\overline{AIOWC}$) write strobes and the $\overline{INTA}$ signal. These signals replace ALE, $\overline{WR}$, IO/$\overline{M}$, DT/$\overline{R}$, $\overline{DEN}$, and $\overline{INTA}$, which are lost when the 8086/8088 is switched to maximum mode from the minimum mode.

Pin functions.   The following list provides a description of each pin of the 8288 bus controller.

1. $\overline{S2}$, $\overline{S1}$, and $\overline{S0}$—*Status Inputs*: are connected to the status output pins on the 8086/8088 microprocessor. These three signals are decoded to generate the timing signals for the system.

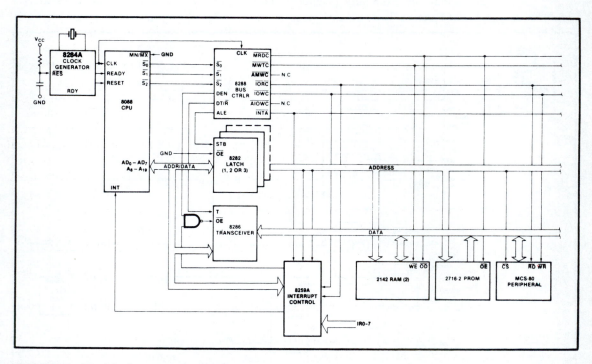

FIGURE 7–20   Maximum mode 8088 system.

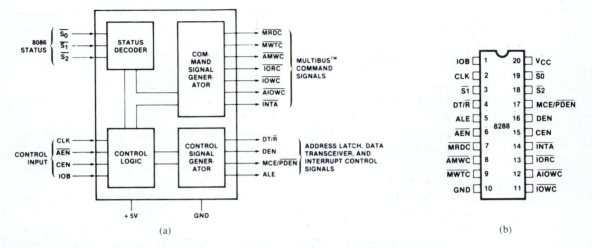

FIGURE 7-21 The 8288 bus controller. (a) Block diagram. (b) pinout.

2. CLK—*Clock*: is an input that provides internal timing and must be connected to the CLK output pin of the 8284A clock generator.

3. ALE—*Address Latch Enable*: an output that is used to demultiplex the address/data bus.

4. DEN—*Data Bus Enable*: a pin that controls the bidirectional data bus buffers in the system. Note that this is an active high-output pin that is the opposite polarity from the $\overline{DEN}$ signal found on the microprocessor when operated in the minimum mode.

5. DT/$\overline{R}$—*Data Transmit/Receive*: a signal output by the 8288 to control the direction of the bidirectional data bus buffers.

6. $\overline{AEN}$—*Address Enable*: an input to the 8288 that enables the memory control signals.

7. CEN—*Control Enable*: an input that enables the command output pins on the 8288.

8. IOB—*I/O Bus Mode*: selects either the I/O bus mode or system bus mode operation.

9. $\overline{AIOWC}$—*Advanced I/O Write*: a command output used to provide I/O with an advanced I/O write control signal.

10. $\overline{IOWC}$—*I/O Write*: a command output used to provide I/O with its main write signal.

11. $\overline{IORC}$—*I/O Read*: a command output used to provide I/O with its read control signal.

12. $\overline{AMWC}$—*Advanced Memory Write*: a command used to provide memory with an early or advanced write signal.

13. $\overline{MWTC}$—*Memory Write*: a command used to provide memory with its normal write control signal.

14. $\overline{MRDC}$—*Memory Read*: a command that provides memory with a read control signal.

15. $\overline{INTA}$—*Interrupt Acknowledge*: an output that acknowledges an interrupt request input applied to the INTR pin.

16. MCE/$\overline{PDEN}$—*Master Cascade/Peripheral Data*: an output that selects cascade operation for an interrupt controller if IOB is grounded and enables the I/O bus transceivers if IOB is tied high.

7-7   SUMMARY

1. The main difference between the 8086 and 8088 are (a) an 8-bit data bus on the 8088 and a 16-bit data bus on the 8086, (b) an $\overline{SS0}$ pin on the 8088 in place of $\overline{BHE}/S_7$ on the 8086, and (c) an IO/$\overline{M}$ pin on the 8088 instead of an M/$\overline{IO}$ on the 8086.

2. Both the 8086 and 8088 require a single +5.0 V power supply with a tolerance of ±10 percent.

3. The 8086/8088 is TTL compatible if the noise immunity figure is derated to 350 mV from the customary 400 mV.

4. The 8086/8088 can drive one 74XX, five 74LSXX, one 74SXX, ten 74ALSXX, and ten 74HCXX unit loads.

5. The 8284A clock generator provides the system clock (CLK), READY synchronization, and RESET synchronization.

6. The standard 5 MHz 8086/8088 operating frequency is obtained by attaching a 15 MHz crystal to the 8284A clock generator. The PCLK output contains a TTL compatible signal at one half the CLK frequency.

7. Whenever the 8086/8088 is reset, it begins executing software at memory location FFFF0H (FFFF:0000) with the interrupt request pin disabled.

8. Because the 8086/8088 buses are multiplexed and most memory and I/O devices aren't, the system must be demultiplexed before interfacing with memory or I/O. Demultiplexing is accomplished by an 8-bit latch whose clock pulse is obtained from the ALE signal.

9. In a large system, the buses must be buffered because the 8086/8088 is capable of driving only ten unit loads and large systems often have many more.

10. Bus timing is very important to the remaining chapters in the text. A bus cycle that consists of four clocking periods acts as the basic system timing. Each bus cycle is able to read or write data between the microprocessor and the memory or I/O system.

11. A bus cycle is broken into four states or T periods. T1 is used by the microprocessor to send the address to the memory or I/O and the ALE signal to the demultiplexers; T2 is used to send data to memory for a write and to test the READY pin and activate control signals $\overline{RD}$ or $\overline{WR}$; T3 allows the memory time to access data and allows data to be transferred between the microprocessor and the memory or I/O; T4 is where data are written.

12. The 8086/8088 allows the memory and I/0 460 ns to access data when they are operated with a 5 MHz clock.

13. Wait states (Tw) stretch the bus cycle by one or more clocking periods to allow the memory and I/0 additional access time. Wait states are inserted by controlling the READY input to the 8086/8088. READY is sampled at the end of T2 and during Tw.

14. Minimum mode operation is similar to that of the Intel 8085A microprocessor, while maximum mode operation is new and specifically designed for the operation of the 8087 arithmetic coprocessor.

15. The 8288 bus controller must be used in the maximum mode to provide the control bus signals to the memory and I/O. This is because the maximum mode operation of the 8086/8088 removes some of the system's control signal lines in favor of control signals for the coprocessors. The 8288 reconstructs these removed control signals.

7-8 QUESTIONS AND PROBLEMS

1. List the differences between the 8086 and the 8088 microprocessors.
2. Is the 8086/8088 TTL compatible? Explain your answer.
3. What is the fanout from the 8086/8088 to the following devices:
   a. 74XXX TTL
   b. 74ALSXXX TTL
   c. 74HCXXX CMOS
   d. NMOS
4. What information appears on the address/data bus of the 8088 while ALE is active?
5. What is the purpose of status bits S3 and S4?
6. What condition does a logic 0 on the 8086/8088 $\overline{RD}$ pin indicate?
7. Explain the operation of the TEST pin and the WAIT instruction.
8. Describe the signal that is applied to the CLK input pin of the 8086/8088 microprocessor.
9. What mode of operation is selected when MN/$\overline{MX}$ is grounded?
10. What does the $\overline{WR}$ strobe signal from the 8086/8088 indicate about the operation of the 8086/8088?
11. When does ALE float to its high-impedance state?
12. When DT/$\overline{R}$ is a logic 1, what condition does it indicate about the operation of the 8086/8088?
13. What happens when the HOLD input to the 8086/8088 is placed at its logic 1 level?
14. What three minimum mode 8086/8088 pins are decoded to discover if the processor is halted?
15. Explain the operation of the $\overline{LOCK}$ pin.
16. What conditions do the QS_1 and QS_0 pins indicate about the 8086/8088?
17. What three housekeeping chores are provided by the 8284A clock generator?
18. By what factor does the 8284A clock generator divide the crystal oscillator's output frequency?
19. If the F/$\overline{C}$ pin is placed at a logic 1 level, the crystal oscillator is disabled. Where is the timing input signal attached to the 8284A under this condition?
20. The PCLK output of the 8284A is _____ MHz if the crystal oscillator is operating at 14 MHz.
21. The $\overline{RES}$ input to the 8284A is placed at a logic _____ level in order to reset the 8086/8088.
22. Which bus connections on the 8086 microprocessor are typically demultiplexed?
23. Which bus connections on the 8088 microprocessor are typically demultiplexed?
24. What TTL integrated circuit is often used to demultiplex the buses on the 8086/8088?
25. What is the purpose of the demultiplexed $\overline{BHE}$ signal on the 8086 microprocessor?
26. Why are buffers often required in an 8086/8088-based system?
27. What 8086/8088 signal is used to select the direction of the data flows through the 74LS245 bidirectional bus buffer?
28. A bus cycle is equal to clocking ____ periods.
29. If the CLK input to the 8086/8088 is 4 MHz, how long is one bus cycle?
30. What two 8086/8088 operations occur during a bus cycle?

31. How many MIPS is the 8086/8088 capable of obtaining when operated with a 10 MHz clock?
32. Briefly describe the purpose of each T state listed:
    a. T1
    b. T2
    c. T3
    d. T4
33. How much time is allowed for memory access when the 8086/8088 is operated with a 5 MHz clock?
34. How wide is $\overline{\text{DEN}}$ if the 8088 is operated with a 5 MHz clock?
35. If the READY pin is grounded, it will introduce _____ states into the bus cycle of the 8086/8088.
36. What does the $\overline{\text{ASYNC}}$ input to the 8284A accomplish?
37. What logic levels must be applied to $\overline{\text{AEN1}}$ and RDY1 to obtain a logic 1 at the READY pin? (Assume that $\overline{\text{AEN2}}$ is at a logic 1 level.)
38. Contrast minimum and maximum mode 8086/8088 operation.
39. What main function is provided by the 8288 bus controller when used with 8086/8088 maximum mode operation?

CHAPTER 8

Memory Interface

INTRODUCTION

Whether simple or complex, every microprocessor-based system has a memory system. The Intel family of microprocessors is no different from any other in this respect.

Almost all systems contain two main types of memory, *read-only memory* (ROM) and *random access memory* (RAM) or read/write memory. Read-only memory contains system software and permanent system data, while RAM contains temporary data and application software. This chapter explains how to interface both memory types to the Intel family of microprocessors. We demonstrate memory interface to an 8-, 16-, and 32-bit data bus using various memory address sizes. This allows virtually any microprocessor to be interfaced to any memory system.

CHAPTER OBJECTIVES

Upon completion of this chapter, you will be able to:

1. Decode the memory address and use the outputs of the decoder to select various memory components.
2. Use programmable logic devices (PLDs) to decode memory addresses.
3. Explain how to interface both RAM and ROM to a microprocessor.
4. Explain how parity can detect memory errors.
5. Interface memory to an 8-, 16-, and 32-bit data bus.
6. Explain the operation of a dynamic RAM controller.
7. Interface dynamic RAM to the microprocessor.

8–1   MEMORY DEVICES

Before attempting to interface memory to the microprocessor, it is essential to completely understand the operation of memory components. In this section, we explain the function of the three common types of memory: *read-only memory* (ROM), *static random access memory* (SRAM), and *dynamic random access memory* (DRAM).

Memory Pin Connections

Pin connections common to all memory devices are the address inputs, data outputs or input/outputs, some type of selection input, and at least one control input used to select a read or write operation. See Figure 8–1 for ROM and RAM generic-memory devices.

Address Connections.   All memory devices have address inputs that select a memory location within the memory device. The number of address pins found on a memory device is determined by the number of memory locations found within it.

Today, the more common memory devices have between 1K (1,024) and 4M (4,194,304) memory locations, with 16M and 256M memory location devices on the horizon. A 1K memory device has 10 address pins (A_0–A_9); therefore, 10 address inputs are required to select any of its 1,024 memory locations. It takes a 10-bit binary number (1,024 different combinations) to select any single location on a 1,024-location device. If a memory device has 11 address connections (A_0–A_{10}), it has 2,048 (2K) internal memory locations. The number of memory locations can thus be extrapolated from the number of address pins. For example, a 4K memory device has 12 address connections, an 8K device has 13, and so forth. A device that contains 1M locations requires a 20-bit address (A_0–A_{19}).

A 400H represents a 1K byte section of the memory system. If a memory device is decoded to begin at memory address 10000H and it is a 1K device, its last location is at address 103FFH—one location less than 400H. Another important hexadecimal number to remember is a 1000H, because 1000H is 4K. A memory device that contains a starting address of 14000H that is 4K bytes in size ends at location 14FFFH—one location less

FIGURE 8–1   A pseudo-memory component illustrating the address, data, and control connections.

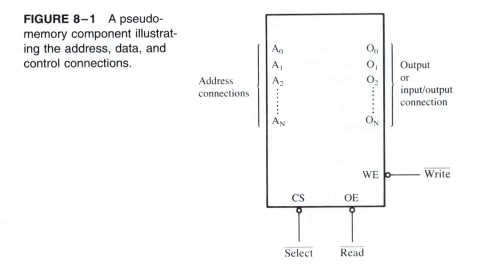

than 1000H. A third number is 64K or 10000H. A memory that starts at location 30000H and ends at location 3FFFFH is a 64K byte memory.

Data Connections. All memory devices have a set of data outputs or input/outputs. The device illustrated in Figure 8–1 has a common set of input/output (I/O) connections. Today many memory devices have bidirectional common I/O pins.

The data connections are the points at which data are entered for storage or extracted for reading. In this sample memory device, there are eight I/O connections, which means that the memory device stores 8 bits of data in each of its memory locations. An 8-bit-wide memory device is often called a *bytewide* memory. Although most devices are currently 8 bits wide, not all memory devices are 8 bits wide. Some devices are 16 bits, 4 bits, or just 1 bit wide.

Catalog listings of memory devices often refer to memory locations times bits per location. For example, a memory device with 1K memory locations and 8 bits in each location is often listed as a 1K × 8 by the manufacturer. A 16K × 1 is a memory device that contains 16K 1-bit memory locations. Memory devices are also often classified according to total bit capacity. For example, a 1K × 8-bit memory device is sometimes listed as an 8K memory device, or a 64K × 4 memory device is listed as a 256K device. These variations occur from one manufacturer to another.

Selection Connections. Each memory device has an input—sometimes more than one—that selects or enables the memory device. This kind of input is most often called a *chip select* ($\overline{CS}$), *chip enable* ($\overline{CE}$), or *select* ($\overline{S}$) input. RAM memory generally has at least one $\overline{CS}$ or $\overline{S}$ input, and ROM at least one $\overline{CE}$. If the $\overline{CE}$, $\overline{CS}$, or $\overline{S}$ input is active (a logic 0 in this case because of the overbar), the memory device performs a read or a write; if it is inactive (a logic 1 in this case), the memory device cannot do a read or a write because it is turned off or disabled. If more than one $\overline{CS}$ connection is present, all must be activated to read or write data.

Control Connections. All memory devices have some form of control input. A ROM usually has only one control input, while a RAM often has one or two control inputs.

The control input most often found on a ROM is the *output enable* ($\overline{OE}$) or *gate* ($\overline{G}$) connection, which allows data to flow out of the output data pins of the ROM. If $\overline{OE}$ and the selection input are both active, then the output is enabled; if $\overline{OE}$ is inactive, the output is disabled at its high-impedance state. The $\overline{OE}$ connection enables and disables a set of three-state buffers located within the memory device and must be active to read data.

A RAM memory device has either one or two control inputs. If there is one control input, it is often called R/$\overline{W}$. This pin selects a read operation or a write operation only if the device is selected by the selection input ($\overline{CS}$). If the RAM has two control inputs, they are usually labeled $\overline{WE}$ (or $\overline{W}$) and $\overline{OE}$ (or $\overline{G}$). Here $\overline{WE}$ (*write enable*) must be active to perform a memory write, and $\overline{OE}$ must be active to perform a memory read operation. When these two controls ($\overline{WE}$ and $\overline{OE}$) are present, they must never both be active at the same time. If both control inputs are inactive (logic 1's), then data are neither written nor read and the data connections are at their high-impedance state.

ROM Memory

The read-only memory (ROM) permanently stores programs and data that are resident to the system and must not change when power is disconnected. The ROM is permanently programmed so data are always present, even when power is disconnected.

The ROM is available in many forms today. A device we call a ROM is purchased in mass quantities from a manufacturer and programmed during its fabrication at the factory. The EPROM (*erasable programmable read-only memory*), a type of ROM, is more commonly used when software must be changed often or when too limited a number are in demand to make the ROM economical. For a ROM to be practical we usually must purchase at least 10,000 devices. An EPROM is programmed in the field on a device called an EPROM programmer. The EPROM is also erasable if exposed to high-intensity ultraviolet light for about 20 minutes or less, depending on the type of EPROM.

PROM memory devices are also available, but they are not as common today. The PROM (*programmable read-only memory*) is also programmed in the field by burning open tiny Nichrome or silicon oxide fuses, but once programmed it cannot be erased.

Still another, newer type of *read-mostly* memory is called the flash memory.[1] The flash memory is also often called an EEPROM (electrically erasable programmable ROM), EAROM (electrically alterable ROM), or a NOVRAM (nonvolatile ROM). These memory devices are electrically erasable in the system, but require more time to erase than a normal RAM. The flash memory device is used to store setup information for systems such as the video card in the computer. It may also soon replace the EPROM in the computer for the BIOS memory. Some systems contain a password stored in the flash memory device.

Figure 8–2 illustrates the 2716 EPROM. This device contains 11 address inputs and 8 data outputs. The 2716 is a 2K × 8 memory device. The 27XXX series of the EPROMs contains the following part numbers: 2704 (512 × 8), 2708 (1K × 8), 2716 (2K × 8), 2732 (4K × 8), 2764 (8K × 8), 27128 (16K × 8), 27256 (32K × 8), 27512 (64K × 8), and 271024

MODE SELECTION

MODE \ PINS	PD/PGM (18)	$\overline{CS}$ (20)	V_{PP} (21)	V_{CC} (24)	OUTPUTS (9-11, 13-17)
Read	V_{IL}	V_{IL}	+5	+5	D_{OUT}
Deselect	Don't Care	V_{IH}	+5	+5	High Z
Power Down	V_{IH}	Don't Care	+5	+5	High Z
Program	Pulsed V_{IL} to V_{IH}	V_{IH}	+25	+5	D_{IN}
Program Verify	V_{IL}	V_{IL}	+25	+5	D_{OUT}
Program Inhibit	V_{IL}	V_{IH}	+25	+5	High Z

PIN CONFIGURATION

```
A7  [ 1      24 ] VCC
A6  [ 2      23 ] A8
A5  [ 3      22 ] A9
A4  [ 4      21 ] VPP
A3  [ 5      20 ] CS
A2  [ 6      19 ] A10
A1  [ 7      18 ] PD/PGM
A0  [ 8      17 ] O7
O0  [ 9      16 ] O6
O1  [ 10     15 ] O5
O2  [ 11     14 ] O4
GND [ 12     13 ] O3
```

PIN NAMES

A_0–A_{10}	ADDRESSES
PD/PGM	POWER DOWN/PROGRAM
$\overline{CS}$	CHIP SELECT
O_0–O_7	OUTPUTS

BLOCK DIAGRAM

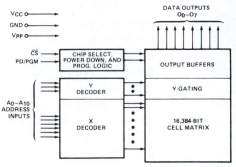

FIGURE 8–2   The pinout of the 2716, 2K × 8 EPROM. (Courtesy of Intel Corporation)

---

[1]Flash memory is a registered trademark of Intel Corporation.

(128K × 8). Each of these parts contains address pins, 8 data connections, one chip selection input ($\overline{CE}$), and an output enable pin ($\overline{OE}$).

Figure 8–3 illustrates the timing diagram for the 2716 EPROM. Data only appear on the output connections after a logic 0 is placed on both the $\overline{CE}$ and $\overline{OE}$ pin connections. If $\overline{CE}$ and $\overline{OE}$ are not both logic 0's, the data output connections remain at their high-impedance or off states. Note that the Vpp pin must be placed at a logic 1 for data to be read from the EPROM. In some cases, the Vpp pin is in the same position as the $\overline{WE}$ pin on the SRAM. This can allow a single socket to hold either an EPROM or an SRAM. An example is the 2716 EPROM and the 6116 SRAM, both 2K × 8 devices that have the same pinout except for Vpp on the EPROM and $\overline{WE}$ on the SRAM.

A.C. Characteristics

$T_A = 0°C$ to $70°C$, V_{CC}[1] = +5V ±5%, V_{PP}[2] = V_{CC} ±0.6V [3]

Symbol	Parameter	Limits			Unit	Test Conditions
		Min.	Typ.[4]	Max.		
t_{ACC1}	Address to Output Delay		250	450	ns	PD/PGM = $\overline{CS}$ = V_{IL}
t_{ACC2}	PD/PGM to Output Delay		280	450	ns	$\overline{CS}$ = V_{IL}
t_{CO}	Chip Select to Output Delay			120	ns	PD/PGM = V_{IL}
t_{PF}	PD/PGM to Output Float	0		100	ns	$\overline{CS}$ = V_{IL}
t_{DF}	Chip Deselect to Output Float	0		100	ns	PD/PGM = V_{IL}
t_{OH}	Address to Output Hold	0			ns	PD/PGM = $\overline{CS}$ = V_{IL}

Capacitance [5] $T_A = 25°C$, f = 1 MHz

Symbol	Parameter	Typ.	Max.	Unit	Conditions
C_{IN}	Input Capacitance	4	6	pF	$V_{IN} = 0V$
C_{OUT}	Output Capacitance	8	12	pF	$V_{OUT} = 0V$

A.C. Test Conditions:

Output Load: 1 TTL gate and C_L = 100 pF
Input Rise and Fall Times: ≤20 ns
Input Pulse Levels: 0.8V to 2.2V
Timing Measurement Reference Level:
    Inputs   1V and 2V
    Outputs 0.8V and 2V

WAVEFORMS

A. Read Mode
PD/PGM = V_{IL}

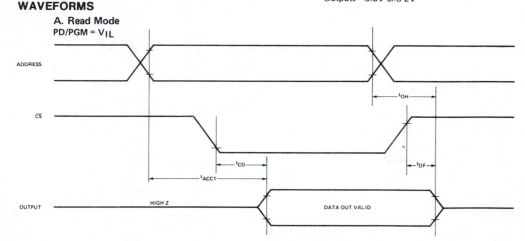

FIGURE 8–3 The timing diagram and AC characteristics of the 2716 EPROM. (Courtesy of Intel Corporation)

One important piece of information provided by the timing diagram and data sheet is the memory access time—the time that it takes the memory to read information. As Figure 8–3 illustrates, memory access time (T_{acc}) is measured from the appearance of the address at the address inputs until the appearance of the data at the output connections. This is based on the assumption that the $\overline{CE}$ input goes low at the same time that the address inputs become stable. Also, $\overline{OE}$ must be a logic 0 for the output connections to become active. The basic speed of this EPROM is 450 ns (recall that the 8086/8088 operated with a 5 MHz clock allowed memory 460 ns to access data). This type of memory component requires wait states to operate properly with the 8086/8088 microprocessor because of its rather long access time. If wait states are not desired, higher speed versions of the EPROM are available at an additional cost. Today EPROM memory is available with access times of as little as 100 ns.

Static RAM (SRAM) Devices

Static RAM memory devices retain data for as long as DC power is applied. Because no special action (except power) is required to retain stored data, this device is called a *static memory*. The main difference between a ROM and a RAM is that a RAM is written under normal operation and a ROM is programmed outside the computer and is only normally read. The SRAM stores temporary data and is used when the size of the read/write memory is relatively small. Today, a small memory is one that is less than 1M bytes.

Figure 8–4 illustrates the 4016 SRAM, which is a 2K × 8 read/write memory. This device has 11 address inputs and 8 data input/output connections.

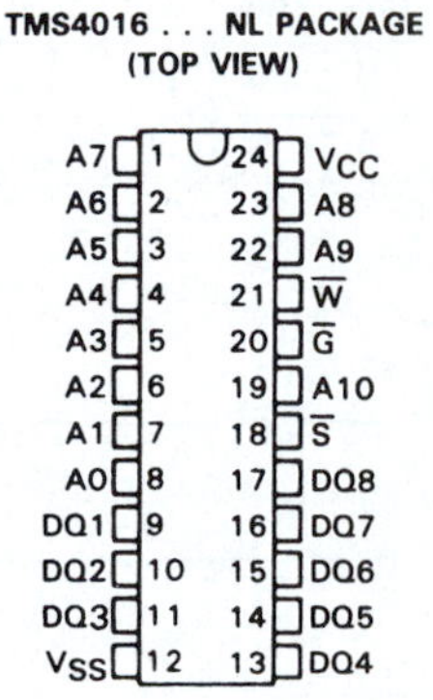

FIGURE 8–4   The pinout of the TMS4016. 2K × 8 static RAM (SRAM). (Courtesy of Texas Instruments Incorporated)

TMS4016 . . . NL PACKAGE
(TOP VIEW)

```
        A7  [ 1  ᴗ 24 ]  Vcc
        A6  [ 2    23 ]  A8
        A5  [ 3    22 ]  A9
        A4  [ 4    21 ]  W̅
        A3  [ 5    20 ]  G̅
        A2  [ 6    19 ]  A10
        A1  [ 7    18 ]  S̅
        A0  [ 8    17 ]  DQ8
       DQ1  [ 9    16 ]  DQ7
       DQ2  [10    15 ]  DQ6
       DQ3  [11    14 ]  DQ5
       Vss  [12    13 ]  DQ4
```

PIN NOMENCLATURE	
A0 – A10	Addresses
DQ1 – DQ8	Data In/Data Out
G̅	Output Enable
S̅	Chip Select
Vcc	+ 5-V Supply
Vss	Ground
W̅	Write Enable

The control inputs of this RAM are slightly different from those presented earlier. The $\overline{OE}$ pin is labeled $\overline{G}$, the $\overline{CS}$ pin $\overline{S}$, and the $\overline{WE}$ pin $\overline{W}$. Despite the altered designations, the control pins function exactly the same as those outlined previously. Other manufacturers make this popular SRAM under the part numbers 2016 and 6116.

Figure 8–5 depicts the timing diagram for the 4016 SRAM. As the read cycle timing reveals, the access time is $t_a(A)$. On the slowest version of the 4016, this time is 250 ns, which is fast enough to connect to an 8088 or an 8086 operated at 5 MHz without wait states. Again, it is important to remember that the access time must be checked to determine the compatibility of memory components with the microprocessor.

Figure 8–6 illustrates the pinout of the 62256, 32K × 8 static RAM. This device is packaged in a 28-pin integrated circuit, and is available with access times of 120 ns or 150 ns. Other common SRAM devices are available in 8K × 8 and 128K × 8 sizes.

Dynamic RAM (DRAM) Memory

About the largest static RAM available today is a 128K × 8. Dynamic RAMs, on the other hand, are available in much larger sizes: up to 16M × 1. In all other respects, DRAM is essentially the same as SRAM except it retains data for only 2 or 4 ms on an integrated capacitor. After 2 or 4 ms, the contents of the DRAM must be completely rewritten (*refreshed*) because the capacitors, which store a logic 1 or logic 0, lose their charges.

Instead of requiring the almost impossible task of reading the contents of each memory location with a program and then rewriting them, the manufacturer has internally constructed the DRAM so, in the 64K × 1 version, the entire contents of the memory is refreshed with 256 reads in a 4 ms interval. Refreshing also occurs during a write, a read, or during a special refresh cycle. Much more information on refreshing DRAMs is provided in section 8–6.

Another disadvantage of DRAM memory is that it requires so many address pins that the manufacturers have multiplexed the address inputs. Figure 8–7 illustrates a 64K × 4 DRAM, the TMS4464. Notice that it contains only 8 address inputs where it should contain 16—the number required to address 64K memory locations. The only way that 16 address bits can be crammed into 8 address pins is in two 8-bit increments. This operation requires two special pins called *column address strobe* ($\overline{CAS}$) and *row address strobe* ($\overline{RAS}$). First, A_0–A_7 are placed on the address pins and strobed into an internal row latch by $\overline{RAS}$ as the row address. Next, the address bits A_8–A_{15} are placed on the same eight address inputs and strobed into an internal column latch by $\overline{CAS}$ as the column address (see Figure 8–8 for this timing). The 16-bit address held in these internal latches addresses the contents of one of the 4-bit memory locations.

Figure 8–9 illustrates a set of multiplexers used to strobe the column and row addresses into the eight address inputs of a pair of TMS4464 DRAMs. Here the $\overline{RAS}$ not only strobes the row address into the DRAMs, but it also changes the address applied to the address inputs. This is possible due to the long propagation delay time of

electrical characteristics over recommended operating free-air temperature range (unless otherwise noted)

	PARAMETER	TEST CONDITIONS		MIN	TYP†	MAX	UNIT
V_{OH}	High level voltage	$I_{OH} = -1$ mA,	$V_{CC} = 4.5$ V	2.4			V
V_{OL}	Low level voltage	$I_{OL} = 2.1$ mA,	$V_{CC} = 4.5$ V			0.4	V
I_I	Input current	$V_I = 0$ V to 5.5 V				10	μA
I_{OZ}	Off-state output current	$\overline{S}$ or $\overline{G}$ at 2 V or $\overline{W}$ at 0.8 V, $V_O = 0$ V to 5.5 V				10	μA
I_{CC}	Supply current from V_{CC}	$I_O = 0$ mA, $T_A = 0°C$ (worst case)	$V_{CC} = 5.5$ V,		40	70	mA
C_i	Input capacitance	$V_I = 0$ V,	$f = 1$ MHz			8	pF
C_O	Output capacitance	$V_O = 0$ V,	$f = 1$ MHz			12	pF

†All typical values are at $V_{CC} = 5$ V, $T_A = 25°C$.

timing requirements over recommended supply voltage range and operating free-air temperature range

	PARAMETER	TMS4016-12		TMS4016-15		TMS4016-20		TMS4016-25		UNIT
		MIN	MAX	MIN	MAX	MIN	MAX	MIN	MAX	
$t_{c(rd)}$	Read cycle time	120		150		200		250		ns
$t_{c(wr)}$	Write cycle time	120		150		200		250		ns
$t_{w(W)}$	Write pulse width	60		80		100		120		ns
$t_{su(A)}$	Address setup time	20		20		20		20		ns
$t_{su(S)}$	Chip select setup time	60		80		100		120		ns
$t_{su(D)}$	Data setup time	50		60		80		100		ns
$t_{h(A)}$	Address hold time	0		0		0		0		ns
$t_{h(D)}$	Data hold time	5		10		10		10		ns

switching characteristics over recommended voltage range, $T_A = 0°C$ to $70°C$

	PARAMETER	TMS4016-12		TMS4016-15		TMS4016-20		TMS4016-25		UNIT
		MIN	MAX	MIN	MAX	MIN	MAX	MIN	MAX	
$t_{a(A)}$	Access time from address		120		150		200		250	ns
$t_{a(S)}$	Access time from chip select low		60		75		100		120	ns
$t_{a(G)}$	Access time from output enable low		50		60		80		100	ns
$t_{v(A)}$	Output data valid after address change	10		15		15		15		ns
$t_{dis(S)}$	Output disable time after chip select high		40		50		60		80	ns
$t_{dis(G)}$	Output disable time after output enable high		40		50		60		80	ns
$t_{dis(W)}$	Output disable time after write enable high		50		60		60		80	ns
$t_{en(S)}$	Output enable time after chip select low	5		5		10		10		ns
$t_{en(G)}$	Output enable time after output enable low	5		5		10		10		ns
$t_{en(W)}$	Output enable time after write enable high	5		5		10		10		ns

NOTES: 3. C_L = 100pF for all measurements except $t_{dis(W)}$ and $t_{en(W)}$.
C_L = 5 pF for $t_{dis(W)}$ and $t_{en(W)}$.
4. t_{dis} and t_{en} parameters are sampled and not 100% tested.

FIGURE 8-5 (a) The AC characteristics of the TMS4016 SRAM. (b) The timing diagrams of the TMS4016 SRAM. (Courtesy of Texas Instruments Incorporated)

timing waveform of read cycle (see note 5)

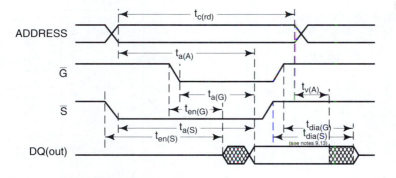

timing waveform of write cycle no. 1 (see note 6)

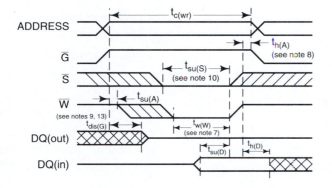

timing waveform of write cycle no. 2 (see notes 6 and 11)

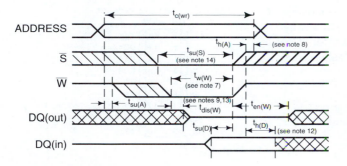

NOTES: 5. $\overline{W}$ is high Read Cycle.
6. $\overline{W}$ must be high during all address transitions.
7. A write occurs during the overlap of a low $\overline{S}$ and a low $\overline{W}$.
8. $t_{h(A)}$ is measured from the earlier of $\overline{S}$ or $\overline{W}$ going high to the end of the write cycle.
9. During this period, I/O pins are in the output state so that the input signals of opposite phase to the outputs must not be applied.
10. If the Slow transition occurs simultaneously with the $\overline{W}$ low transitions or after the $\overline{W}$ transition, output remains in a high impedance state.
11. G is continuously low ($G = V_{IL}$).
12. If $\overline{S}$ is low during this period, I/O pins are in the output state. Data input signals of opposite phase to the outputs must not be applied.
13. Transition is measured ± 200 mV from steady-state voltage.
14. If the $\overline{S}$ low transition occurs before the W low transition, then the data input signals of opposite phase to the outputs must not be applied for the duration of $t_{dis(W)}$ after the $\overline{W}$ low transition.

FIGURE 8-5 *continued*

FIGURE 8-6 Pin diagram of the 62256, 32K × 8 static RAM.

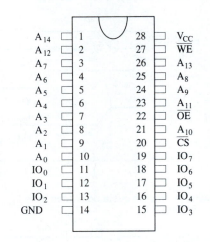

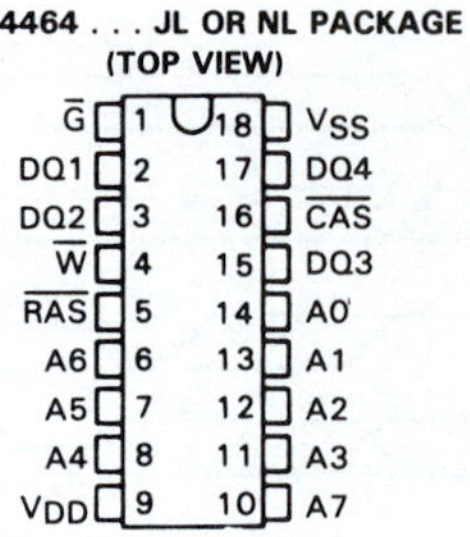

A_{14}	1	28	V_{CC}
A_{12}	2	27	$\overline{WE}$
A_7	3	26	A_{13}
A_6	4	25	A_8
A_5	5	24	A_9
A_4	6	23	A_{11}
A_3	7	22	$\overline{OE}$
A_2	8	21	A_{10}
A_1	9	20	$\overline{CS}$
A_0	10	19	IO_7
IO_0	11	18	IO_6
IO_1	12	17	IO_5
IO_2	13	16	IO_4
GND	14	15	IO_3

PIN FUNCTION

A_0 - A_{14}	Addresses
IO_0 - IO_7	Data connections
$\overline{CS}$	Chip select
$\overline{OE}$	Output enable
$\overline{WE}$	Write enable
V_{CC}	+5V Supply
GND	Ground

FIGURE 8-7 The pinout of the TMS4464, 64K × 4 dynamic RAM (DRAM). (Courtesy of Texas Instruments Incorporated)

TMS4464 . . . JL OR NL PACKAGE
(TOP VIEW)

$\overline{G}$	1	18	V_{SS}
DQ1	2	17	DQ4
DQ2	3	16	$\overline{CAS}$
$\overline{W}$	4	15	DQ3
$\overline{RAS}$	5	14	A0
A6	6	13	A1
A5	7	12	A2
A4	8	11	A3
V_{DD}	9	10	A7

(a)

PIN NOMENCLATURE	
A0-A7	Address Inputs
$\overline{CAS}$	Column Address Strobe
DQ1-DQ4	Data-In/Data-Out
$\overline{G}$	Output Enable
$\overline{RAS}$	Row Address Strobe
V_{DD}	+ 5-V Supply
V_{SS}	Ground
$\overline{W}$	Write Enable

(b)

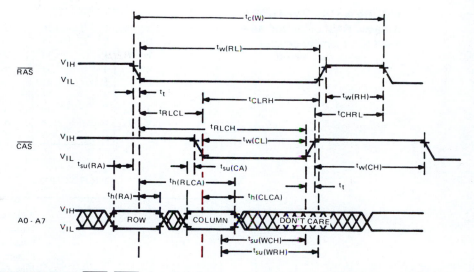

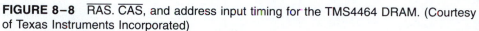

FIGURE 8-8 $\overline{\text{RAS}}$. $\overline{\text{CAS}}$, and address input timing for the TMS4464 DRAM. (Courtesy of Texas Instruments Incorporated)

FIGURE 8-9 Address multiplexer for the TMS4464 DRAM.

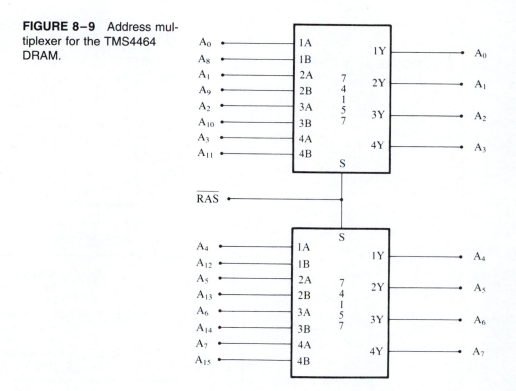

FIGURE 8–10 The 41256 dynamic RAM organized as a 256K × 1 memory device.

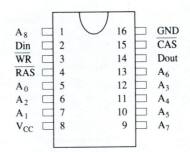

PIN FUNCTIONS

A_0 - A_8	Addresses
Din	Data in
$\overline{Dout}$	Data out
$\overline{CAS}$	Column Address Strobe
$\overline{RAS}$	Row Address Strobe
$\overline{WR}$	Write enable
V_{CC}	+5V Supply
GND	Ground

FIGURE 8–11 The 1M × 1 DRAM.

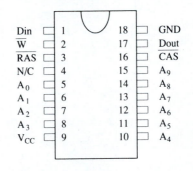

PIN FUNCTIONS

A_0 - A_9	Addresses
Din	Data in
Dout	Data out
$\overline{CAS}$	Column Address Strobe
$\overline{RAS}$	Row Address Strobe
$\overline{W}$	Write enable
V_{CC}	+5V Supply
GND	Ground

the multiplexers. When $\overline{RAS}$ is a logic 1, the B inputs are connected to the Y outputs of the multiplexers, and when the $\overline{RAS}$ input goes to a logic 0, the A inputs connect to the Y outputs. Because the internal row address latch is edge-triggered, it captures the row address before the address at the inputs changes to the column address. More detail on DRAM and DRAM interfacing is provided in section 8–6.

As with the SRAM, the $\overline{W}$ pin writes data to the DRAM and the $\overline{G}$ pin enables the output connections for a read operation. ($\overline{W}$ replaces $\overline{WE}$, and $\overline{G}$ replaces $\overline{OE}$.) Figure 8–10 shows the pinout of the 41256 dynamic RAM. This device is organized as a 256K × 1 memory requiring as little as 70 ns to access data.

More recently, a larger DRAM has become available that is organized as a 1M × 1 memory. On the horizon is the 16M × 1 and a 256M × 1 memory is in the planning stages. Figure 8–11 lists the pinout of a 1M × 1 memory, the TMX4C1024 by Texas Instruments. This device is also often numbered a 511000P.

8–2   ADDRESS DECODING

In order to attach a memory device to the microprocessor, it is necessary to decode the address from the microprocessor to make the memory function at a unique section or partition of the memory map. Without an address decoder, only one memory device can be connected to a microprocessor, which would make it virtually useless. In this section, we describe a few of the more common address-decoding techniques as well as the decoders that are found in many systems.

Why Decode Memory?

When the 8088 microprocessor is compared to the 2716 EPROM, a difference in the number of address connections surfaces—the EPROM has 11 address connections and the microprocessor has 20. This means that the microprocessor sends out a 20-bit memory address whenever it reads or writes data. Since the EPROM has only 11 address inputs, there is a mismatch that must somehow be corrected. If only 11 of the 8088's address pins are connected to the memory, then the 8088 will see only 2K bytes of memory instead of the 1M bytes that it "expects" the memory to contain. The decoder is used to match the microprocessor with the memory component.

Simple NAND Gate Decoder

Address connections A_{10}–A_0 of the 8088 are connected to address inputs A_{10}–A_0 of the EPROM, and the remaining nine address pins (A_{19}–A_{11}) are connected to the inputs of a NAND gate decoder (see Figure 8–12). The decoder selects the EPROM from one of the many 2K byte sections of the entire 1M byte address range of the 8088 microprocessor.

In this circuit, a single NAND gate decodes the memory address. The output of the NAND gate is a logic 0 whenever the 8088 address pins attached to its inputs (A_{19}–A_{11}) are all logic 1's. The active low, logic 0 output of the NAND gate decoder is connected

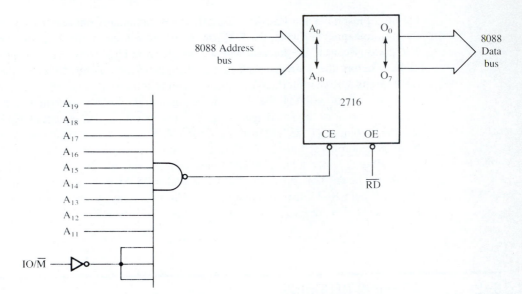

FIGURE 8–12   A simple NAND gate decoder used to select a 2716 EPROM memory component for memory locations FF800H–FFFFFH.

to the $\overline{CE}$ input, which selects (*enables*) the EPROM. Recall that whenever $\overline{CE}$ is a logic 0, data will be read from the EPROM only if $\overline{OE}$ is also a logic 0. The $\overline{OE}$ pin is activated by the 8088 $\overline{RD}$ signal or the $\overline{MRDC}$ (memory read control) signal of other family members.

If the 20-bit binary address, decoded by the NAND gate, is written so the leftmost 9 bits are 1's and the rightmost 11 bits are don't cares (X), the actual address range of the EPROM can be determined. (A don't care is a logic 1 or a logic 0, whichever is appropriate.)

EXAMPLE 8–1

```
1111 1111 1XXX XXXX XXXX

        or

1111 1111 1000 0000 0000 = FF800H

        to

1111 1111 1111 1111 1111 = FFFFFH
```

Example 8–1 illustrates how the address range for this EPROM is determined by writing down the externally decoded address bits (A_{19}–A_{11}) and the address bits decided by the EPROM (A_{10}–A_0) as don't cares. As the example illustrates, the don't cares are first written as 0's to locate the lowest address and then as 1's to find the highest address. Example 8–1 also shows these binary boundaries as hexadecimal addresses. Here the 2K EPROM is decoded at memory address locations FF800H–FFFFFH. Notice that this is a

2K byte section of the memory and is also located at the reset location for the 8086/8088, the most likely place for an EPROM.

Although this example serves to illustrate decoding, NAND gates are rarely used to decode memory because each memory device requires its own NAND gate decoder. Because of the excessive cost of the NAND gate decoder, this option requires that an alternate be found.

The 3-to-8 Line Decoder (74LS138)

One of the more common, although not only, integrated circuit decoders found in many microprocessor-based systems is the 74LS138 3-to-8 line decoder. Figure 8–13 illustrates this decoder and its truth table.

The truth table shows that only one of the eight outputs ever goes low at any time. For any of the decoder's outputs to go low, the three enable inputs ($\overline{G2A}$, $\overline{G2B}$, and $\overline{G1}$) must all be active. To be active, the $\overline{G2A}$ and $\overline{G2B}$ inputs must both be low (logic 0), and G1 must be high (logic 1).

Once the 74LS138 is enabled, the address inputs (C, B, and A) select which output pin goes low. Imagine eight EPROM $\overline{CE}$ inputs connected to the eight outputs of the

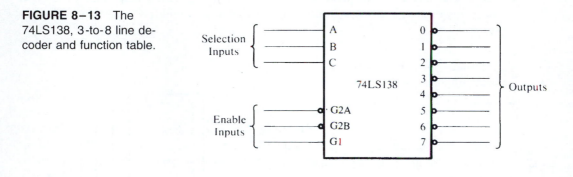

FIGURE 8–13 The 74LS138, 3-to-8 line decoder and function table.

Inputs						Outputs							
Enable			Select										
G2A	G2B	G1	C	B	A	$\overline{0}$	$\overline{1}$	$\overline{2}$	$\overline{3}$	$\overline{4}$	$\overline{5}$	$\overline{6}$	$\overline{7}$
1	X	X	X	X	X	1	1	1	1	1	1	1	1
X	1	X	X	X	X	1	1	1	1	1	1	1	1
X	X	0	X	X	X	1	1	1	1	1	1	1	1
0	0	1	0	0	0	0	1	1	1	1	1	1	1
0	0	1	0	0	1	1	0	1	1	1	1	1	1
0	0	1	0	1	0	1	1	0	1	1	1	1	1
0	0	1	0	1	1	1	1	1	0	1	1	1	1
0	0	1	1	0	0	1	1	1	1	0	1	1	1
0	0	1	1	0	1	1	1	1	1	1	0	1	1
0	0	1	1	1	0	1	1	1	1	1	1	0	1
0	0	1	1	1	1	1	1	1	1	1	1	1	0

decoder! This is a very powerful device because it selects eight different memory devices at the same time.

Sample Decoder Circuit.   Notice that the outputs of the decoder illustrated in Figure 8–14 are connected to eight different 2764 EPROM memory devices. Here the decoder selects eight, 8K byte blocks of memory for a total of 64K bytes of memory. This figure also illustrates the address range of each memory device and the common connections to the memory devices. Notice that all the address connections from the 8088 are connected to this circuit. Also notice that the decoder's outputs are connected to the $\overline{CE}$ inputs of the EPROMs, and the $\overline{RD}$ signal from the 8088 is connected to the $\overline{OE}$ inputs of the EPROMs. This allows only the selected EPROM to be enabled and to send its data to the microprocessor through the data bus whenever $\overline{RD}$ becomes a logic 0.

In this circuit, a 3-input NAND gate is connected to address bits A_{19}–A_{17}. When all three address inputs are high, the output of this NAND gate goes low and enables input $\overline{G2B}$ of the 74LS138. Input G1 is connected directly to A_{16}. In other words, in order to enable this decoder, the first four address connections (A_{19}–A_{16}) must all be high.

The address inputs C, B, and A connect to microprocessor address pins A_{15}–A_{13}. These three address inputs determine which output pin goes low and which EPROM is selected whenever the 8088 outputs a memory address within this range to the memory system.

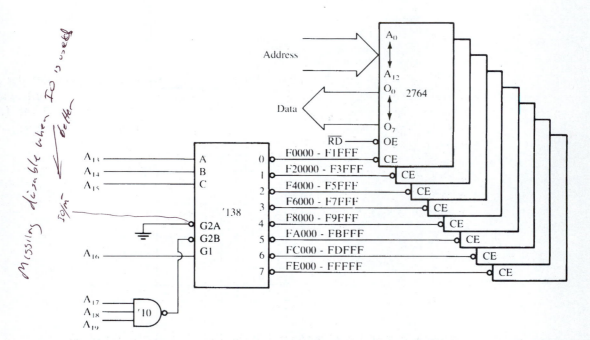

FIGURE 8–14 A circuit that uses eight 2764 EPROMs for a 64K × 8 section of memory in an 8088 microprocessor-based system. The addresses selected in this circuit are F0000H–FFFFFH.

EXAMPLE 8–2

```
1111 XXXX XXXX XXXX XXXX

        or

1111 0000 0000 0000 0000 = F0000H

        to

1111 1111 1111 1111 1111 = FFFFFH
```

Example 8–2 shows how the address range of the entire decoder is determined. Notice that the range is location F0000H–FFFFFH. This is a 64K-byte span of the memory.

How is it possible to determine the address range of each memory device attached to the decoder's outputs? Again, the binary bit pattern is written down, and this time the C, B, and A address inputs are not don't cares. Example 8–3 shows how output 0 of the decoder is made to go low to select the EPROM attached to that pin. Here C, B, and A are shown as logic 0's.

EXAMPLE 8–3

```
     CBA
1111 0000 XXXX XXXX XXXX

        or

1111 0000 0000 0000 0000 = F0000H

        to

1111 0001 1111 1111 1111 = F1FFFH
```

If the address range of the EPROM connected to output 1 of the decoder is required, it is determined in exactly the same way as that of output 0. The only difference is that now the C, B, and A inputs contain a 001 instead of a 000 (see Example 8–4). The remaining output address ranges are determined in the same manner by substituting the binary address of the output pin into C, B, and A.

EXAMPLE 8–4

```
     CBA
1111 001X XXXX XXXX XXXX

        or

1111 0010 0000 0000 0000 = F2000H

        to

1111 0011 1111 1111 1111 = F3FFFH
```

The Dual 2-to-4 Line Decoder (74LS139)

Another decoder that finds some application is the 74LS139 dual 2-to-4 line decoder. Figure 8–15 illustrates both the pinout and the truth table for this decoder. The 74LS139

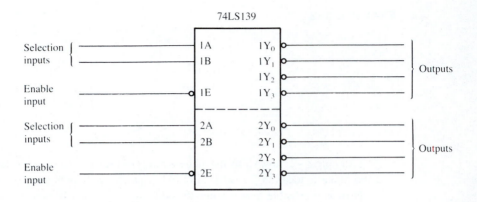

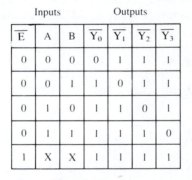

Inputs			Outputs			
$\overline{E}$	A	B	$\overline{Y_0}$	$\overline{Y_1}$	$\overline{Y_2}$	$\overline{Y_3}$
0	0	0	0	1	1	1
0	0	1	1	0	1	1
0	1	0	1	1	0	1
0	1	1	1	1	1	0
1	X	X	1	1	1	1

FIGURE 8–15   The pinout and truth table of the 74LS139, dual 2-to-4 line decoder.

contains two separate 2-to-4 line decoders—each with its own address, enable, and output connections.

PROM Address Decoder

Another common address decoder is the bipolar PROM, used because of its larger number of input connections, which reduces the number of other circuits required in a system memory address decoder. The 74LS138 decoder has six inputs used for address connections. The PROM decoder may have many more inputs for address decoding.

For example, a 82S147 (512 × 8) PROM used as an address decoder has 10 input connections and 8 output connections. It can replace the circuit illustrated in Figure 8–14 without the extra 3-input NAND gate. This saves space on the printed circuit board and reduces the cost of a system.

Figure 8–16 illustrates this address decoder with the PROM in place. The PROM is a memory device that must be programmed with the correct binary bit pattern to select the eight EPROM memory devices. The PROM itself has 9 address inputs that select one of the 512 internal 8-bit memory locations. The remaining input ($\overline{CE}$) must be grounded

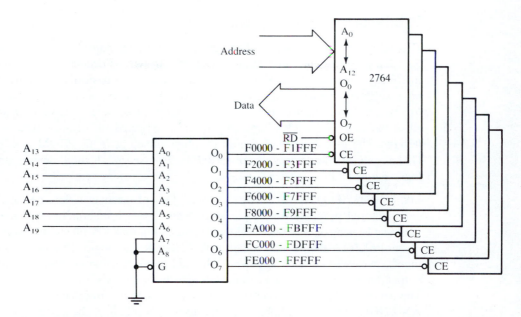

FIGURE 8-16 A memory system using the TPB28L42, 512 × 8 PROM as an address.

because if this PROM's outputs float to their high-impedance state, then one or more of the EPROMs might be selected by noise impulses in the system.

Table 8-1 illustrates the binary bit pattern programmed into each PROM location in order to select the eight different EPROMs. The main advantage to using a PROM is that the address map is easily changed in the field. Because the PROM comes with all the locations programmed as logic 1's, only 8 of the 512 locations must be programmed. This saves valuable time for the manufacturer.

TABLE 8-1 The 82S147 PROM programming pattern for the circuit of Figure 8-16

				Inputs									Outputs				
$\overline{OE}$	A8	A7	A6	A5	A4	A3	A2	A1	A0	O0	O1	O2	O3	O4	O5	O6	O7
0	0	0	1	1	1	1	0	0	0	0	1	1	1	1	1	1	1
0	0	0	1	1	1	1	0	0	1	1	0	1	1	1	1	1	1
0	0	0	1	1	1	1	0	1	0	1	1	0	1	1	1	1	1
0	0	0	1	1	1	1	0	1	1	1	1	1	0	1	1	1	1
0	0	0	1	1	1	1	1	0	0	1	1	1	1	0	1	1	1
0	0	0	1	1	1	1	1	0	1	1	1	1	1	1	0	1	1
0	0	0	1	1	1	1	1	1	0	1	1	1	1	1	1	0	1
0	0	0	1	1	1	1	1	1	1	1	1	1	1	1	1	1	0
all other address combinations										1	1	1	1	1	1	1	1

PLD Programmable Decoders

This section of the text explains the use of the programmable logic device or PLD as a decoder. Recently, the PAL[2] has replaced PROM address decoders in the latest memory interfaces. There are three PLD devices that function in basically the same manner, but have different names: PLA (*programmable logic array*), PAL (*programmable array logic*), and GAL[3] (*gated array logic*). Although these devices have been in existence since the mid-1970s, they have only recently appeared in memory system and digital designs. The PAL and the PLA are fuse programmed as is the PROM, and some of the GALs are erasable devices as are EPROMs. In essence, all three devices are arrays of logic elements that are programmable.

Combinatorial Programmable Logic Arrays.   One of the two basic types of PALs is the combinatorial programmable logic array. This device is internally structured as a programmable array of combinational logic circuits. Figure 8–17 illustrates internal structure of the PAL16L8 that is constructed with AND/OR gate logic. This device has 10 fixed inputs, two fixed outputs, and 6 pins that are programmable as inputs or outputs. Each output pin is generated from a 7-input OR gate that has an AND gate attached to each input. The outputs of the OR gates pass through a three state inverter that defines each out as an AND/NOR function. Initially all of the fuses connect all of the vertical/horizontal connections illustrated in this figure. Programming is accomplished by blowing fuses to connect various inputs to the OR gate array. The wired-AND function is performed at each input connection that allows a product term of up to 16 inputs. A logic expression using the PAL16L8 can have 7 product terms with 16 inputs NORed together to generate the output expression. This device is ideal as a memory address decoder because of its structure. It is also ideal because the outputs are active low.

Fortunately we don't have to choose the fuses by number for programming. We program the PAL using a software package called PALASM[4] (the PAL assembler). The PALASM program and its syntax are an industry standard for programming PAL devices. Example 8–5 shows a program that decodes the same areas of memory as decoded in Figure 8–16. Note that this program was developed using a text editor such as EDIT available with Microsoft DOS version 5.0; it can also be developed using an editor that comes with the PALASM package. Various editors attempt to ease the task of defining the pins, but we believe it is easier to use EDIT and the listing as shown.

EXAMPLE 8–5

```
TITLE      Address Decoder
PATTERN    Test 1
REVISION   A
AUTHOR     Barry B. Brey
COMPANY    Symbiotic Systems
DATE       6/23/93
CHIP       Decoder1 PAL16L8
```

---

[2]PAL is a registered trademark of Monolithic Memories, Inc.

[3]GAL is a registered trademark of LATTICE Semiconductors, Inc.

[4]PALASM is a register trademark of Monolithic Memories, Inc.

Logic Diagram   16L8

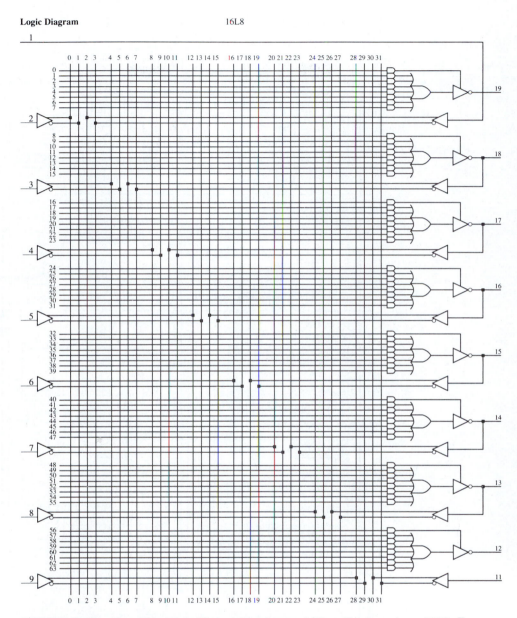

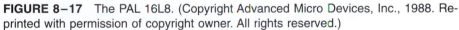

FIGURE 8-17 The PAL 16L8. (Copyright Advanced Micro Devices, Inc., 1988. Reprinted with permission of copyright owner. All rights reserved.)

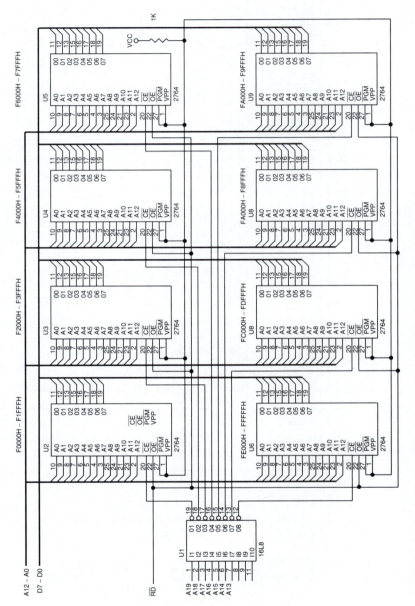

FIGURE 8–18 A PAL16L8 that decodes 8 2764 (8K × 8) memory devices.

```
;pins 1    2    3    4    5    6   7   8   9   10
      A19  A18  A17  A16  A13  NC  NC  NC  NC  GND

;pins 11   12   13   14   15   16   17   18   19   20
      NC   O8   O7   O6   O5   O4   O3   O2   O1   VCC

EQUATIONS

/O1 = A19 * A18 * A17 * A16 * /A15 * /A14 * /A13
/O2 = A19 * A18 * A17 * A16 * /A15 * /A14 * A13
/O3 = A19 * A18 * A17 * A16 * /A15 * A14 * /A13
/O4 = A19 * A18 * A17 * A16 * /A15 * A14 * A13
/O5 = A19 * A18 * A17 * A16 * A15 * /A14 * /A13
/O6 = A19 * A18 * A17 * A16 * A15 * /A14 * A13
/O7 = A19 * A18 * A17 * A16 * A15 * A14 * /A13
/O8 = A19 * A18 * A17 * A16 * A15 * A14 * A13
```

The first 8 lines of the program illustrated in Example 8–5 identify the program title, pattern, revision, author, company, date, and chip type with the program name. Here the chip type is a PAL16L8 and the program is called decoder1. After the program is identified, a comment statement (;pins) identifies the pin numbers. Below this comment appear the pins as defined for this application. Once all the pins are defined, we use the EQUATIONS statement to indicate that the equations for this application follow. In this example, the equations define the 8 chip enable outputs for the 8 EPROM memory devices. Refer to Figure 8–18 for the complete schematic diagram of this PAL decoder.

8-3   8088 MEMORY INTERFACE

This text contains separate sections on memory interfacing for the 8088 with its 8-bit data bus; the 8086, 80286, and 80386SX with their 16-bit data buses; and for the 80386DX and 80486 with their 32-bit data buses. Separate sections are provided because the methods used to address the memory are slightly different in these microprocessors. Hardware engineers or technicians who wish to broaden their expertise in interfacing 16-bit and 32-bit microprocessors should cover all sections. This section is much more complete than the section on the 16- and 32-bit memory interface, which covers only material not covered in the 8088 section.

In this section, we examine the memory interface to both RAM and ROM and explain parity checking, which is commonplace in many microprocessor-based computer systems. We also briefly mention error correction schemes currently available to memory system designers.

Basic 8088 Memory Interface

The 8088 microprocessor has an 8-bit data bus, which makes it ideal to connect to the common 8-bit memory devices available today. It also makes it ideal as a simple controller. For the 8088 to function correctly with the memory, however, the memory system must decode the address to select a memory component, and it must use the $\overline{RD}$, $\overline{WR}$, and IO/$\overline{M}$ control signals provided by the 8088 to control the memory system.

The minimum mode configuration for the 8088 is used in this section and is essentially the same as the maximum mode system for memory interface. The main difference is that, in maximum mode IO/$\overline{M}$ is combined with $\overline{RD}$ to generate an $\overline{MRDC}$ signal, and IO/$\overline{M}$ is combined with $\overline{WR}$ to generate an $\overline{MWTC}$ signal. These maximum mode control signals are developed inside the 8288 bus controller. In the minimum mode, the memory sees the 8088 as a device with 20 address connections (A_{19}–A_0), 8 data bus connections (AD_7–AD_0), and the control signals IO/$\overline{M}$, $\overline{RD}$, and $\overline{WR}$.

Interfacing EPROM to the 8088.   You will find this section very similar to section 8–2 on decoders. The only difference is that, in this section, we discuss wait states and the use of the IO/$\overline{M}$ signal to enable the decoder.

Figure 8–19 illustrates an 8088 microprocessor connected to eight 2732 EPROMs, 4K × 8 memory devices that are in very common use today. The 2732 has one more address input (A_{11}) than the 2716 and twice the memory. The device in this illustration decodes eight 4K × 8 blocks of memory, for a total of 32K × 8 bits of the physical address space for the 8088.

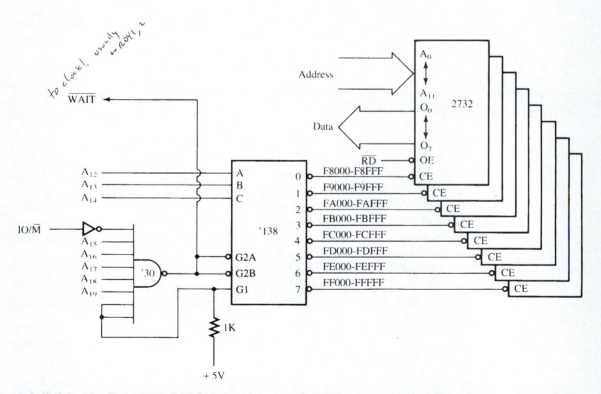

FIGURE 8–19 Eight 2732 EPROMs interfaced to the 8088 microprocessor. Note that the output of the NAND gate is used to cause a wait state whenever this section of the memory is selected.

The decoder (74LS138) is connected a little differently than might be expected because the slower version of this type of EPROM has a memory access time of 450 ns. Recall from Chapter 7 that when the 8088 is operated with a 5 MHz clock, it allows 460 ns for the memory to access data. Because of the decoder's added time delay (12 ns), it is impossible for this memory to function within 460 ns. In order to correct this problem, we must add a NAND gate to generate a signal to enable the decoder and a signal for the wait state generator, covered in Chapter 7. With a wait state inserted every time this section of the memory is accessed, the 8088 will allow 660 ns for the EPROM to access data. Recall that an extra wait state adds 200 ns (1 clock) to the access time. The 660 ns is ample time for a 450 ns memory component to access data, even with the delays introduced by the decoder and any buffers added to the data bus.

Notice that the decoder is selected for a memory address range that begins at location F8000H and continues through location FFFFFH—the upper 64K bytes of memory. This section of memory is an EPROM because FFFF0H is where the 8088 starts to execute instructions after a hardware reset. We often call location FFFF0H the *cold-start* location. The software stored in this section of memory contains a JMP instruction at location FFFF0H that jumps to location F8000H so the remainder of the program can execute.

Interfacing RAM to the 8088.   RAM is a little easier to interface than EPROM because most RAM memory components do not require wait states. An ideal section of the memory for the RAM is the very bottom, which contains vectors for interrupts. Interrupt vectors (discussed in more detail in Chapter 10) are often modified by software packages, so it is rather important to encode this section of the memory with RAM.

In Figure 8–20, sixteen 62256 32K × 8 static RAMS are interfaced to the 8088, beginning at memory location 00000H. This circuit board uses two decoders to select the sixteen different RAM memory components and a third to select the other decoders for the appropriate memory sections. Sixteen 32K RAMs fill memory from location 00000H through location 7FFFFH, for 512K bytes of memory.

The first decoder (U4) in this circuit selects the other two decoders. An address beginning with 00 selects decoder U3 and 01 selects decoder U9. Notice that extra pins remain at the output of decoder U4 for future expansion. These allow more 256K × 8 blocks of RAM, for a total of 1M × 8, simply by adding the RAM and the additional secondary decoders.

Also notice from the circuit in Figure 8–20 that all the address inputs to this section of memory are buffered, as are the data bus connections and control signals $\overline{RD}$ and $\overline{WR}$. Buffering is important when many devices appear on a single board or in a single system. Suppose that three other boards like this are plugged into a system. Without the buffers on each board, the load on the system address, data, and control buses would be enough to prevent proper operation. (Excessive loading causes the logic 0 output to rise above the 0.8V maximum allowed in a system.) Buffers are normally used if the memory will contain additions at some future date. If the memory will never grow, then buffers may not be needed.

Parity for Memory Error Detection

Because such large memories are available in today's systems, and because circuit costs are minimal, many memory board manufacturers have added parity checking to their

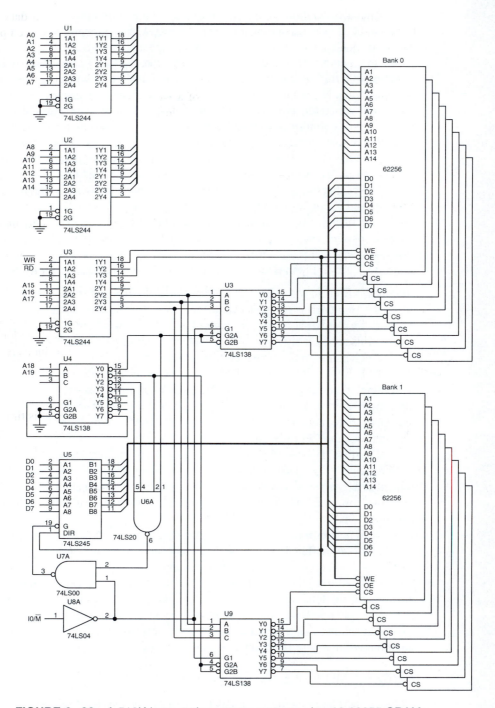

FIGURE 8-20   A 512K byte static memory system using 16 62255 SRAMs.

RAM memory boards. Parity checking counts the number of 1's in data and indicates whether there is an even or odd number. If all data are stored as with even parity (with an even number of 1 bits), a 1-bit error can be detected.

Figure 8–21 illustrates the 74AS280 parity generator/detector integrated circuit. This circuit has nine inputs and generates even or odd parity for the 9-bit number placed on its inputs. It also checks the parity of a 9-bit number connected to its inputs.

Figure 8–22 illustrates a 16K × 8 static RAM system that has parity generation and detection. Notice that a 74AS280 (A) generates a parity bit stored in one of four different TMS4044 4K × 1 RAM memories. Here the eight data bus connections are attached to the parity generator's inputs A–H. Input I is grounded so if an even number of 1's appear on the data bus, a 1 (at the even output) is stored in the parity RAM. If an odd number of 1's appears, a 0 is stored in the parity RAM. Here odd parity is stored for each byte of data, including the parity bit written to the memory.

When data are read from the memory, each datum is connected to another 74AS280 (B) to check its parity. In this case, all the inputs to the checker are connected. Inputs A–H are connected to the data RAM's outputs, and input I is connected to the parity RAM. If parity is odd, as it is if everything is correct, the even parity output of the 74AS280 is a logic 0. If a bit of the information read from the memory changes for any reason, then the even output pin of the 74AS280 will become a logic 1.

This pin is connected to a special input of the 8088 called the nonmaskable interrupt (NMI) input. The NMI input can never be turned off. If it is placed at its logic 1 level, the program being executed is interrupted, and a special subroutine indicates that a parity error has been detected by the memory system. (More detail on interrupts is provided in Chapter 10.)

The application of the parity error is timed so the data read from the memory are settled to their final state before an NMI input occurs. The operation is timed by a D-type flip-flop that latches the output of the parity checker at the end of an $\overline{RD}$ cycle from this section of the memory. In this way, the memory has enough time to read the information

FIGURE 8–21 The pinout and function table of the 74AS280 9-bit parity generator/detector. (Courtesy of Texas Instruments Incorporated)

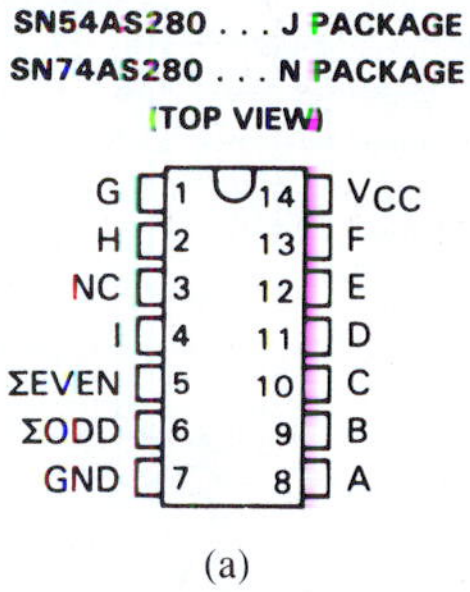

SN54AS280 . . . J PACKAGE
SN74AS280 . . . N PACKAGE
(TOP VIEW)

(a)

FUNCTION TABLE

NUMBER OF INPUTS A	OUTPUTS	
THRU I THAT ARE HIGH	Σ EVEN	Σ ODD
0,2,4,6,8	H	L
1,3,5,7,9	L	H

(b)

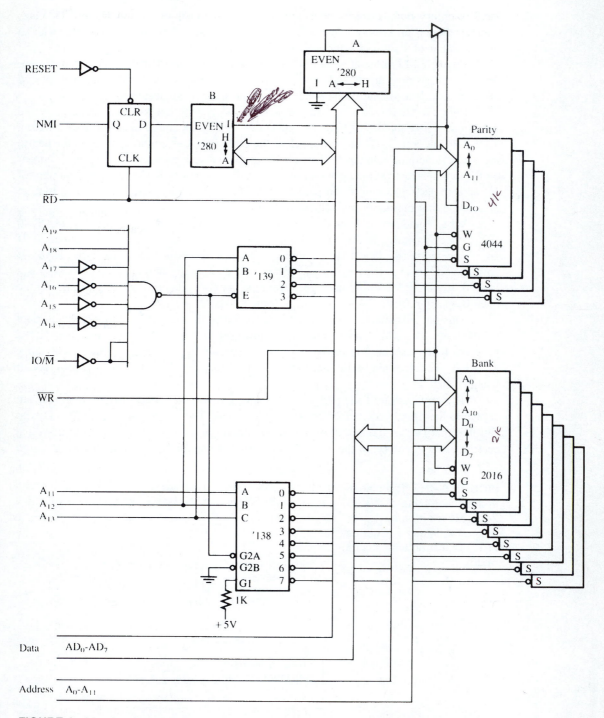

FIGURE 8–22 A 16K × 8 memory system that contains a parity error detection circuit.

and pass it through the generator before the output of the generator is sampled by the NMI input.

Error Correction

Error correction schemes have been around for a long time, but integrated circuit manufacturers have only recently started to produce error correcting circuits. One such circuit is the 74LS636, an 8-bit error correction and detection circuit that corrects any single-bit memory read error and flags any 2-bit error.

This device corrects errors by storing 5 parity bits with each byte of memory data. This does increase the amount of memory required, but it also provides automatic error correction for single-bit errors. If more than two bits are in error, this circuit may not detect it. Fortunately, this is rare, and the extra effort required to correct more than a single-bit error is very expensive and not worth the effort. Whenever a memory component fails completely, its bits are all high or all low. In this case, the circuit flags the processor with a multiple-bit error indication.

Figure 8–23 depicts the pinout of the 74LS636. Notice that it has eight data I/O pins, five check bit I/O pins, two control inputs (S_0 and S_1), and two error outputs: single-error flag (SEF) and double-error flag (DEF). The control inputs select the type of operation to be performed and are listed in the truth table of Table 8–2.

When a single error is detected, the 74LS636 goes through an error correction cycle: it places a 01 on S_0 and S_1 by causing a wait and then a read following error correction.

Figure 8–24 illustrates a circuit used to correct single-bit errors with the 74LS636 and to interrupt the processor through the NMI pin for double-bit errors. To simplify the illustration, we depict only one 2K × 8 RAM and a second 2K × 8 RAM to store the 5-bit check code.

The connection of this memory component is different from that of the previous example. Notice that the $\overline{S}$ or $\overline{CS}$ pin is grounded, and data bus buffers control the flow to the system bus. This is necessary if the data are to be accessed from the memory before the $\overline{RD}$ strobe goes low.

On the next negative edge of the clock after an $\overline{RD}$, the 74LS636 checks the single-error flag (SEF) to determine whether an error has occurred. If so, then a correction cycle causes the single-error defect to be corrected. If a double error occurs, then an interrupt request is generated by the double-error flag (DEF) output, which is connected to the NMI pin of the microprocessor.

TABLE 8–2   Control bits S_0 and S_1

			Error Flags	
S_0	S_1	Function	SEF	DEF
0	0	Write check word	0	0
0	1	Correct data word	*	*
1	0	Read data	0	0
1	1	Latch data	*	*

Note: These levels are determined by the type of error.

pin assignments

	J, N PACKAGES		
1	DEF	11	CB4
2	DB0	12	nc
3	DB1	13	CB3
4	DB2	14	CB2
5	DB3	15	CB1
6	DB4	16	CB0
7	DB5	17	S0
8	DB6	18	S1
9	DB7	19	SEF
10	GND	20	V_{CC}

(a)

functional block diagram

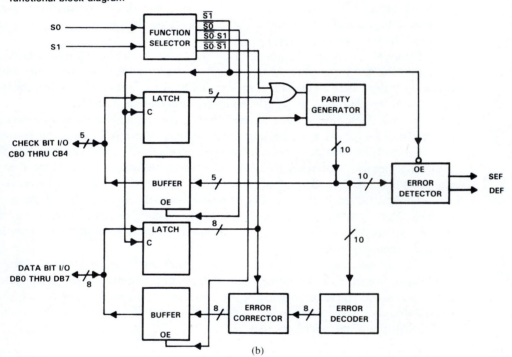

(b)

FIGURE 8–23   (a) The pin connections of the 74LS636. (b) The block diagram of the 74LS636. (Courtesy of Texas Instruments Incorporated)

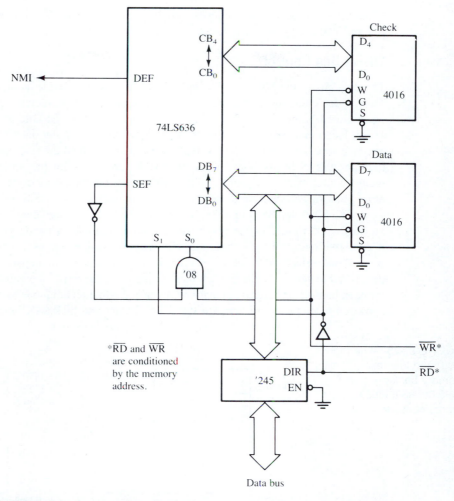

*RD and WR
are conditioned
by the memory
address.

FIGURE 8-24   An error detection and correction circuit using the 74LS636.

8-4   8086, 80286, AND 80386SX MEMORY INTERFACE

The 8086, 80286, and 80386SX microprocessors differ from the 8088 in three ways: (1) the data bus is 16 bits wide instead of 8 bits wide as on the 8088, (2) the IO/$\overline{M}$ pin of the 8088 is an M/$\overline{IO}$ pin on the 8086, and (3) there is a new control signal called bus high enable ($\overline{BHE}$). The address bit A_0 is also used differently. Because this section is based on information provided in section 8-3, it is extremely important that you read the previous section first. A few other differences exist between the 8086 and the 80286/80386SX. The 80286/80386SX contains a 24-bit address bus ($A_{23}-A_0$) instead of the 20-bit address bus ($A_{19}-A_0$) of the 8086. The 8086 contains an M/$\overline{IO}$ signal while the 80286 system and

80386SX microprocessor contain control signals $\overline{\text{MRDC}}$ and $\overline{\text{MWTC}}$ instead of $\overline{\text{RD}}$ and $\overline{\text{WR}}$.

16-Bit Bus Control

The data bus of the 8086, 80286, and 80386SX is twice as wide as the bus for the 8088. This wider data bus presents us with a unique set of problems that have not been encountered before. The 8086, 80286, and 80386SX must be able to write data to any 16-bit location *or* any 8-bit location. This means that the 16-bit data bus must be divided into two separate sections (*banks*) that are 8 bits in width so the microprocessor can write to either half (8-bit) or both halves (16-bit). Figure 8–25 illustrates the two banks of the memory. One bank (*low bank*) holds all the even-numbered memory locations, and the other bank (*high bank*) holds all the odd-numbered memory locations.

The 8086, 80286, and 80386SX use the $\overline{\text{BHE}}$ signal (high bank) and the A_0 address bit (low bank) to select one or both banks of memory used for the data transfer. Table 8–3 depicts the logic levels on these two pins and the bank or banks selected.

Bank selection is accomplished in two ways: (1) a separate write signal is developed to select a write to each bank of the memory, or (2) separate decoders are used for each bank. As a careful comparison reveals, the first technique is by far the least costly approach to memory interface for the 8086, 80286, and 80386SX microprocessors.

FIGURE 8–25 The high (odd) and low (even) 8-bit memory banks of the 8086/80286/83865X microprocessor.

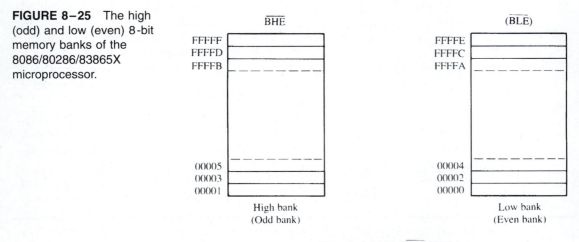

Note: A_0 is labeled $\overline{\text{BLE}}$ (BUS Low enable) on the 80386SX.

TABLE 8–3 Memory bank selection using $\overline{\text{BHE}}$ and A_0

$\overline{BHE}$	A_0	Function
0	0	Both banks active (16-bit transfer through D_{15}–D_0)
0	1	High bank active (8-bit transfer through D_{15}–D_8)
1	0	Low bank active (8-bit transfer through D_7–D_0)
1	1	No banks active

Separate Bank Decoders.   The use of separate bank decoders is often the least effective way to decode memory addresses for the 8086, 80286, and 80386SX. This method is sometimes used, but it is difficult to understand why in most cases.

Figure 8–26 illustrates two 74LS138 decoders used to select 64K RAM memory components for the 8086 microprocessor (20-bit address). Here decoder A has the A_0 pin attached to $\overline{G2A}$, and decoder B has the $\overline{BHE}$ signal attached to its $\overline{G2A}$ input. Because the decoder will not activate until all its enable inputs are active, decoder A only activates for a 16-bit operation or an 8-bit operation from the low bank, and decoder B activates for a 16-bit operation or an 8-bit operation to the high bank. These two decoders and the sixteen 64K-byte RAMs they control represent the entire 1M range of the 8086 memory system. Yes, two decoders are used for the entire memory.

Notice from this figure that the A_0 address pin does not connect to the memory; instead it connects to the decoder. Also notice that address bus bit position A_1 is connected to memory address input A_0, A_2 is connected to A_1, and so forth. The reason is that A_0 from the 8086 (or 80286/80386SX) is already connected to decoder A and does not need to be connected again to the memory. If A_0 is attached to the A_0 address pin of memory, every other memory location in each bank of memory would be used. This means that half of the memory is wasted if A_0 is connected to A_0.

Separate Bank Write Strobes.   The most effective way to handle bank selection is to develop a separate write strobe for each memory bank. This technique requires only one decoder to select a 16-bit-wide memory. This often saves money and reduces the number of components in a system.

Why not also generate separate read strobes for each memory bank? This is usually unnecessary, because the 8086, 80286, and 80386SX reads only the byte of data that it needs at any given time from half of the data bus. If 16-bit sections of data are always presented to the data bus during a read, the microprocessor ignores the 8-bit section it doesn't need without any conflicts or special problems.

Figure 8–27 depicts the generation of separate 8086 write strobes for the memory. Here a 74LS32 OR gate combines A_0 with $\overline{WR}$ for the low bank selection signal ($\overline{LWR}$) and $\overline{BHE}$ with $\overline{WR}$ for the high bank selection signal ($\overline{HWR}$). Write strobes for the 80286/80386SX are generated using the $\overline{MWTC}$ signal instead of $\overline{WR}$.

A memory system that uses separate write strobes is constructed differently from either the 8-bit system (8088) or the system using separate memory banks. Memory in a system that uses separate write strobes is decoded as 16-bit-wide memory. For example, suppose that a memory system will contain 64K bytes of SRAM memory. This memory requires two 32K byte memory devices (62256) so a 16-bit-wide memory can be constructed. Because the memory is 16 bits wide, and another circuit generated the bank write signals, address bit A0 becomes a don't care.

EXAMPLE 8–6

```
0000 0110 0000 0000 0000 0000 = 060000H

         to

0000 0110 1111 1111 1111 1111 = 06FFFFH


0000 0110 XXXX XXXX XXXX XXXX = 06XXXXH
```

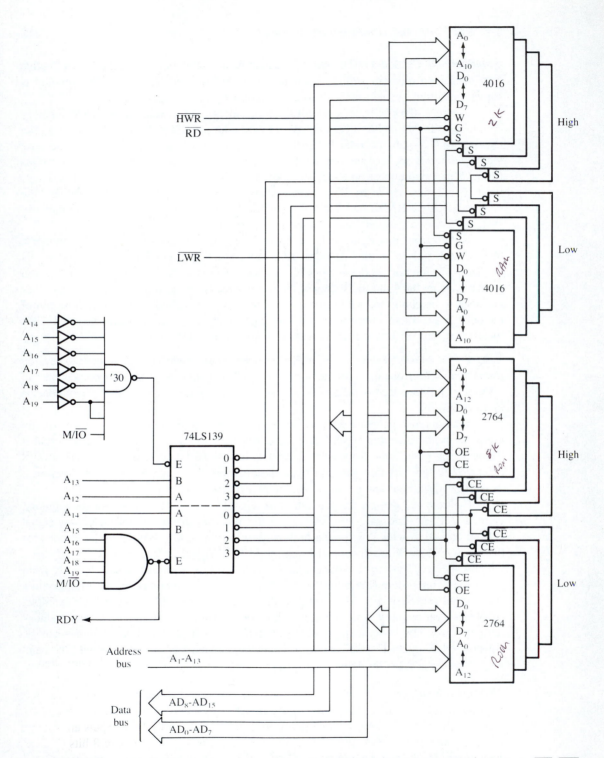

FIGURE 8–26 An 8086 1M byte memory interface. Note that no attempt is made to illustrate $\overline{RD}$, $\overline{WR}$, and the DRAM selection inputs $\overline{CAS}$ and $\overline{RAS}$.

(handwritten annotation: Only have to gate (block) one Read!! write Both bytes are on bus for read, but processor selects.)

FIGURE 8–27   The memory bank write selection inputs signals: $\overline{HWR}$ (high bank write) and $\overline{LWR}$ (low bank write).

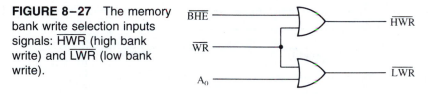

Example 8–6 shows how a 16-bit-wide memory stored at locations 060000H–06FFFFH is decoded for the 80286 or 80386 microprocessor. Memory in this example is decoded so bit A0 is a don't care for the decoder bits A1–A15 are connected to address pins A0–A14 of both memory components and the decoder (PAL16L8) enables both memory devices. Figure 8–28 illustrates this simple circuit using a PAL16L8 to both decode memory and generate the separate write strobe. The program for the PAL16L8 decoder is illustrated in Example 8–7.

EXAMPLE 8–7

```
TITLE       Address Decoder
PATTERN     Test 1R
REVISION    A
AUTHOR      Barry B. Brey
COMPANY     Symbiotic Systems
DATE        6/24/93
CHIP        Decoder1R PAL16L8

;pins 1    2    3    4    5    6    7    8    9    10
          A23  A22  A21  A20  A19  A18  A17  A16  A0  GND

;pins 11   12   13   14   15   16   17    18  19   20
          BHE  SEL  LWR  HWR  NC   NC   MWTC  NC  NC  VCC

EQUATIONS

/SEL = /A23 * /A22 * /A21 * /A20 * /A19 * A18 * A17 * /A16
/LWR = /MWTC * /A0
/HWR = /MWTC * /BHE
```

Figure 8–29 depicts a small memory system for the 8086 microprocessor that contains an EPROM section and a RAM section. Here there are four 27128 EPROMs (16K × 8) that compose a 32K × 16-bit memory at location F0000H–FFFFFH and four 62256 (32K × 8) RAMs that compose a 64K × 16-bit memory at location 00000H–1FFFFH. (Remember that even though the memory is 16 bits wide, it is still numbered in bytes.)

This circuit uses a 74LS139 dual 2-to-4 line decoder that selects EPROM with one half and RAM with the other half. It decodes memory that is 16 bits wide and not 8 bits as before. Notice that the $\overline{RD}$ strobe is connected to all the EPROM $\overline{OE}$ inputs and all the RAM $\overline{G}$ input pins. This is done because even if the 8086 is only reading 8 bits of data, the application of the remaining 8 bits to the data bus has no effect on the operation of the 8086.

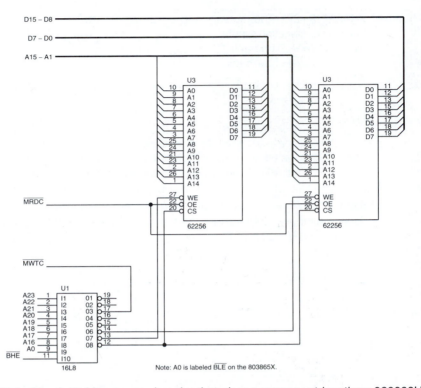

FIGURE 8–28 A 16-bit memory decoder that places memory at locations 060000H–06FFFFH.

The $\overline{\text{LWR}}$ and $\overline{\text{HWR}}$ strobes are connected to different banks of the RAM memory. Here it does matter if the microprocessor is doing a 16-bit or an 8-bit write. If the 8086 writes a 16-bit number to memory, both $\overline{\text{LWR}}$ and $\overline{\text{HWR}}$ go low and enable the $\overline{\text{W}}$ pins of both memory banks. But, if the 8086 does an 8-bit write, then only one of the write strobes goes low, writing to only one memory bank. Again the only time that the banks make a difference is for a memory write operation.

Notice that an EPROM decoder signal is sent to the 8086 wait state generator because EPROM memory usually requires a wait state. The signal comes from the NAND gate used to select the EPROM decoder section so that if EPROM is selected, a wait state is requested.

Figure 8–30 illustrates a memory system connected to the 80386SX microprocessor using a PAL16L8 as a decoder. This interface contains 256K bytes of EPROM in the form of four 27512 (64K × 8) EPROMs and 128K bytes of SRAM memory found in four 62256 (32K × 8)SRAMs.

Notice from Figure 8–30 that the PAL also generates the memory bank write signals $\overline{\text{LWR}}$ and $\overline{\text{HWR}}$. As can be gleaned from this circuit, the number of components required to interface memory has been reduced to just one in most cases (the PAL). The program listing for the PAL is located in Example 8–8. The PAL decodes the 16-bit-wide memory addresses at locations 000000H–01FFFFH for the SRAM and locations FC0000H–FFFFFFH for the EPROM.

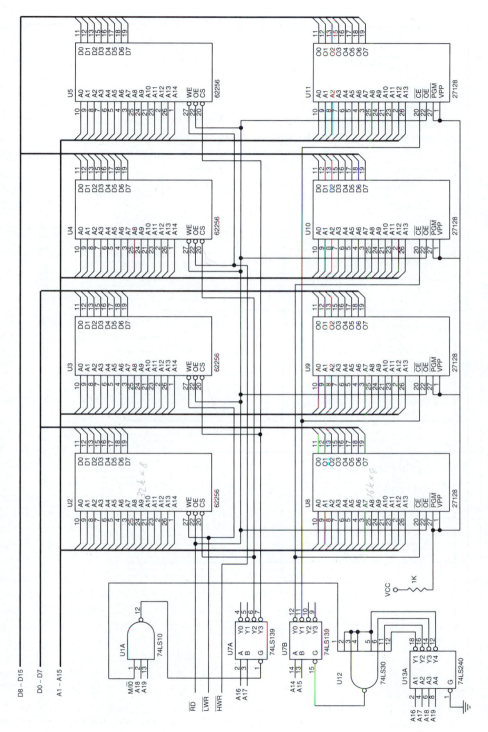

FIGURE 8–29 A memory system for the 8086 that contains a 64K byte EPROM and a 128K byte SRAM.

317

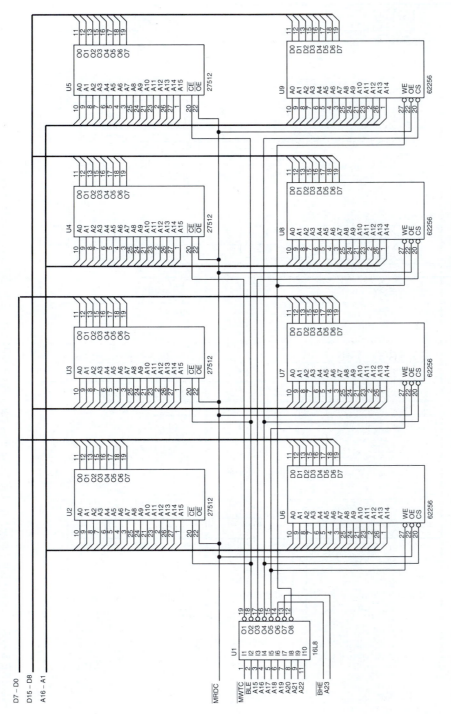

FIGURE 8–30 An 80386SX memory system containing 256K of EPROM and 128K of SRAM.

EXAMPLE 8–8

```
TITLE       Address Decoder
PATTERN     Test 1Z
REVISION    A
AUTHOR      Barry B. Brey
COMPANY     Symbiotic Systems
DATE        6/25/93
CHIP        Decoder1Z PAL16L8

;pins 1    2    3    4    5    6    7    8    9    10
       MWTC A0   A15  A16  A17  A18  A19  A20  A21  GND

;pins 11   12   13   14   15   16   17   18   19   20
       A22  HWR  A23  BHE  LWR  RB0  RB1  EB0  EB1  VCC

EQUATIONS

/LWR = /MWTC * /A0
/HWR = /MWTC * /BHE
/RB0 = /A23 * /A22 * /A21 * /A20 * /A19 * /A18 * /A17 * /A16
/RB1 = /A23 * /A22 * /A21 * /A20 * /A19 * /A18 * /A17 * A16
/EB0 = A23 * A22 * A21 * A20 * A19 * A18 * /A17
/EB1 = A23 * A22 * A21 * A20 * A19 * A18 * A17
```

8–5   80386DX AND 80486 MEMORY INTERFACE

As with 8- and 16-bit memory systems, the microprocessor interfaces to memory through its data bus and control signals that select separate memory banks. The only difference with a 32-bit memory system is that the microprocessor has a 32-bit data bus and four banks of memory instead of one or two. Another difference is that both the 80386DX and 80486 (both SX and DX) contain a 32-bit address bus that usually requires PLD decoders instead of integrated decoders, because of the sizable number of address bits.

Memory Banks

The memory banks for both the 80386DX and 80486 microprocessor are illustrated in Figure 8–31. Notice that these large memory systems contain four 8-bit-wide banks that each contain up to 1G bytes of memory. Bank selection is accomplished by the bank selection signals $\overline{BE3}$, $\overline{BE2}$, $\overline{BE1}$, and $\overline{BE0}$. If a 32-bit number is transferred, all four banks are selected; if a 16-bit number is transferred, two banks (usually $\overline{BE3}$ and $\overline{BE2}$ or $\overline{BE1}$ and $\overline{BE0}$) are selected; and if 8 bits are transferred, a single bank is selected.

As with the 8086/80286/80386SX, the 80386DX and 80486 require separate write strobe signals for each memory bank. These separate write strobes are developed as illustrated in Figure 8–32 using a simple OR gate or other logic component.

A 32-Bit Memory Interface

As can be gathered from the prior discussion, a memory interface for the 80386DX or 80486 requires that we generate four bank write strobes and also decode a 32-bit address.

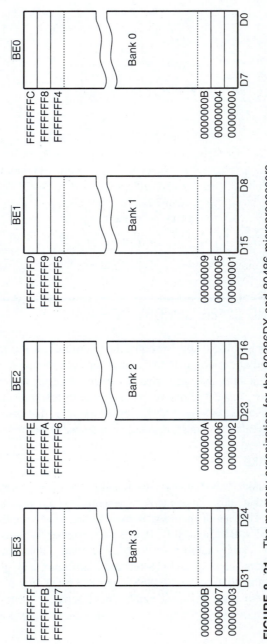

FIGURE 8–31 The memory organization for the 80386DX and 80486 microprocessors.

FIGURE 8–32 Bank write signals for the 80386DX and 80486 microprocessors.

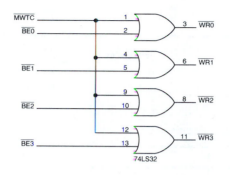

There are no integrated decoders, such as the 74LS138, that can easily accommodate a memory interface for the 80386DX or 80486 microprocessors. Note that address bits A0 and A1 are don't cares when 32-bit-wide memory is decoded. These address bits are used within the microprocessor to generate the bank enable signals. Also notice that address bus connected A2 connects to memory address pin A0.

Figure 8–33 shows a 256K × 8 memory system for the 80486 microprocessor. This interface uses eight 32K × 8 SRAM memory devices and two PAL16L8 devices. Two devices are required because of the number of address connections found on the microprocessor. This system places the SRAM memory at locations 02000000H–0203FFFFH. The programs for the PAL devices are found in Example 8–9.

EXAMPLE 8–9

```
TITLE       Address Decoder
PATTERN     Test 1U1 (PAL U1)
REVISION    A
AUTHOR      Barry B. Brey
COMPANY     Symbiotic Systems
DATE        6/26/93
CHIP        Decoder1U1 PAL16L8

;pins 1     2    3    4    5    6    7    8    9    10
      MWTC  BE0  BE1  BE2  BE3  A17  A28  A29  A30  GND

;pins 11    12   13   14   15   16   17   18   19   20
      A31   RB1  U2   NC   WR0  WR1  WR2  WR3  RB0  VCC


EQUATIONS

/WR0 = /MWTC * /BE0
/WR1 = /MWTC * /BE1
/WR2 = /MWTC * /BE2
/WR3 = /MWTC * /BE3
/RB0 = /A31 * /A32 * /A30 * /A29 * /A28 * /A17 * /U2
/RB1 = /A31 * /A32 * /A30 * /A29 * /A28 * A17 * /U2



TITLE       Address Decoder
PATTERN     Test 1U2 (PAL U2)
REVISION    A
AUTHOR      Barry B. Brey
COMPANY     Symbiotic Systems
DATE        6/26/93
```

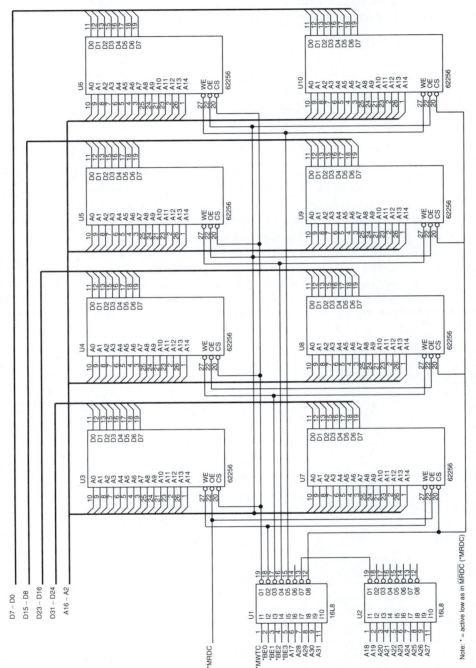

FIGURE 8–33 A small 256K SRAM memory system interfaced to the 80486 microprocessor.

Note: * = active low as in MRDC (*MRDC)

```
CHIP        Decoder1U2 PAL16L8

;pins 1    2    3    4    5    6    7    8    9    10
      A18  A19  A20  A21  A22  A23  A24  A25  A26  GND

;pins  11   12 13 14 15 16 17 18 19 20
       A27  U2 NC NC NC NC NC NC NC VCC

EQUATIONS

/U2 = /A27 * /A26 * A25 * /A24 * /A23 * /A22 * /A21 * /A20 * /A19 * /A18
```

Although not mentioned in this section of the text, the 80386DX and 80486 microprocessors operate with very high clock rates that usually require wait states for memory access. Access time calculations for these microprocessors are discussed in Chapters 13 and 14. The interface provides a signal used with the wait state generator that is not illustrated in this section of the text. Other devices found with these higher speed microprocessors are *cache memory* and *interleaved memory systems*. These also are presented in Chapters 13 and 14 with the 80386DX and 80486 microprocessors.

8-6   DYNAMIC RAM

Because RAM memory is often very large, it requires many SRAM devices at a great cost or just a few DRAMs (dynamic RAMs) at a much reduced cost. The DRAM memory, as briefly discussed in section 8-1, is fairly complex because it requires address multiplexing and refreshing. Luckily, the integrated circuit manufacturers have provided a dynamic RAM controller that includes the address multiplexers and all the timing circuitry necessary for refreshing.

This section of the text covers the DRAM memory device in much more detail than section 8-1 and provides information on the use of a dynamic controller in a memory system.

DRAM Revisited

As mentioned in section 8-1, a DRAM retains data for only 2-4 ms and requires the multiplexing of address inputs. We have already covered address multiplexers in section 8-1, but we will examine the operation of the DRAM during refresh in detail here.

As we mentioned previously, a DRAM must be refreshed periodically because it stores data internally on capacitors that lose their charge in a short period of time. In order to refresh a DRAM, the contents of a section of the memory must periodically be read or written. Any read or write automatically refreshes an entire section of the DRAM. The number of bits refreshed depends on the size of the memory component and its internal organization.

Refresh cycles are accomplished by doing a read, a write, or a special refresh cycle that doesn't read or write data. The refresh cycle is totally internal to the DRAM and is accomplished while other memory components in the system operate. This type of refresh is called either hidden refresh, transparent refresh, or sometimes cycle stealing.

In order to accomplish a hidden refresh while other memory components are functioning, a $\overline{RAS}$-only cycle strobes a row address into the DRAM to select a row of bits to be refreshed. $\overline{RAS}$ also causes the selected row to be read out internally and rewritten into the selected bits. This recharges the internal capacitors that store the data. This type of refresh is hidden from the system because it occurs while the microprocessor is reading or writing to other sections of the memory.

The DRAM's internal organization contains a series of rows and columns. A 256K × 1 DRAM has 256 columns, each containing 256 bits, or rows organized into four sections of 64K bits each. Whenever a memory location is addressed, the column address selects a column (or internal memory word) of 1,024 bit (one per section of the DRAM). Refer to Figure 8–34 for the internal structure of a 256K × 1 DRAM.

Figure 8–35 illustrates the timing for a $\overline{RAS}$-only refresh cycle. The main difference between the $\overline{RAS}$ and a read or write is that it applies only a refresh address, which is usually obtained from a 7- or 8-bit binary counter. The size of the counter is determined by the type of DRAM being refreshed. The refresh counter is incremented at the end of each refresh cycle so all the rows are refreshed in 2 or 4 ms, depending on the type of DRAM.

If there are 256 rows to be refreshed within 4 ms, as in a 256K × 1 DRAM, then the refresh cycle must be activated at least once every 15.6 μs in order to meet the refresh specification. For example, it takes the 8086/8088, running at a 5 MHz clock rate, 800 ns to do a read or a write. Because the DRAM must have a refresh cycle every 15.6 μs, this means that for every 19 memory reads or writes, the memory system must run a refresh cycle or memory data will be lost. This represents a loss of 5 percent of the computer's time, a small price to pay for the savings represented by using the dynamic RAM.

DRAM Controllers

Of the many DRAM controllers available, this text focuses on the TMS4500A (see Figure 8–36 for a block diagram). Like all DRAM controllers, the TMS4500A contains address multiplexers and some mechanism for requesting a refresh, but, unlike the others, it does not need a special high-frequency clock signal for proper operation during a refresh. Notice that the TMS4500A has the internal multiplexer, the refresh counter, and all the timing necessary to accomplish a refresh.

Pin Description.   A complete understanding of the operation of the TMS4500A depends on a familiarity with the function of the pins described here:

1. RA_7–RA_0 (*Row Address Inputs*): the pins connected to the microprocessor's address bus. They are often connected to address bus bits A_7–A_0.
2. CA_7–CA_0 (*Column Address Inputs*): pins that are also connected to the address bus. If the row address inputs are connected to A_7–A_0, then these inputs are connected to A_{15}–A_8. The order of these connections doesn't affect the operation of the system.
3. MA_7–MA_0 (*Memory Address Outputs*): these pins connect directly to DRAM address pins A_7–A_0.

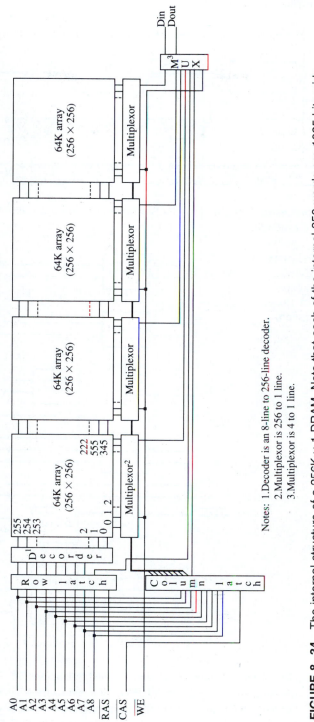
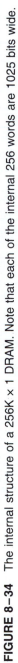

Notes: 1. Decoder is an 8-line to 256-line decoder.
2. Multiplexor is 256 to 1 line.
3. Multiplexor is 4 to 1 line.

FIGURE 8–34 The internal structure of a 256K × 1 DRAM. Note that each of the internal 256 words are 1025 bits wide.

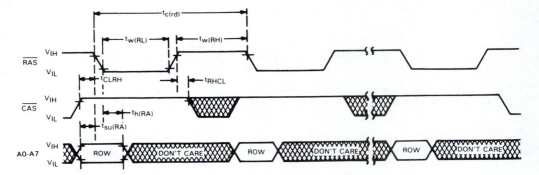

FIGURE 8–35   The timing diagram of the $\overline{\text{RAS}}$ refresh cycle for the TMS4464 DRAM. (Courtesy of Texas Instruments Corporation)

FIGURE 8–36   The block diagram of the TMS4500A dynamic RAM controller. DRAM. (Courtesy of Texas Instruments Corporation)

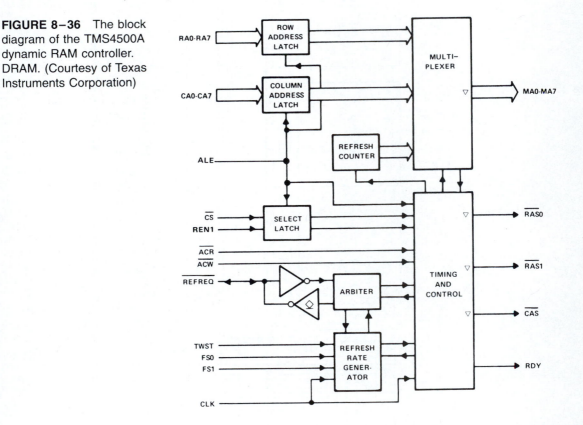

4. ALE (*Address Latch Enable Input*): used to latch the 16 address inputs applied to RA_7–RA_0 and CA_7–CA_0, $\overline{\text{CS}}$, and REN1. Notice how these latches replace the address latches discussed in Chapter 7 if DRAM is the only memory in a system. Because this input must be active to cause a cycle, it must be connected to ALE from the microprocessor.

5. $\overline{\text{CS}}$ (*Chip Select Input*): starts a memory read or write for the DRAMs connected to the DRAM controller whenever it is a logic 0 at ALE's 1-to-0 transition.

6. REN1 (*Enable Input*): selects one of two banks of DRAMs connected to the DRAM controller. (Notice that there are two $\overline{RAS}$ outputs.) When REN1 is high, $\overline{RAS1}$ is selected, and when it is low $\overline{RAS2}$ is selected.

7. $\overline{ACR}$ (*Access Control Read Input*): ends a memory read cycle on the 0-to-1 transition. This pin is connected to the 8086/8088 minimum mode $\overline{RD}$ control signal or the $\overline{MRDC}$ signal for maximum mode operation.

8. $\overline{ACW}$ (*Access Control Write Input*): ends a memory write cycle on the 0-to-1 transition. It is connected to $\overline{WR}$ or $\overline{MWTC}$.

9. CLK (*Clock Input*): connects to the system clock of the microprocessor.

10. REFREQ (*Refresh Request*): starts a refresh cycle or when used as an output, indicates that an internal refresh cycle is in progress.

11. $\overline{RAS1}$, $\overline{RAS0}$ (*Row Address Strobes*): connect to the DRAM $\overline{RAS}$ inputs. Both signals are low for a refresh operation, but only one goes low during a normal read or a write cycle. REN1 selects which $\overline{RAS}$ pin goes low during a memory operation.

12. $\overline{CAS}$ (*Column Address Strobe*): connects to the $\overline{CAS}$ inputs of all of the DRAM memories in both memory banks.

13. RDY (*Ready Output*): connects to the RDY input of the 8284A clock generator in an 8086/8088 system. RDY becomes active when the DRAM controller performs an internal refresh cycle.

14. TWST (*Timing/Wait Strap Input*): select waits and/or certain timing constraints when used with the FS1 and FS0 inputs. A logic 1 on this pin inserts one wait state for every memory access.

15. FS0, FS1 (*Frequency Select Inputs*): select various mode and frequency options (refer to Table 8–4).

TMS4500A Operation

Figure 8–37 illustrates the basic connection of the DRAM controller to the buses of the 8088 microprocessor in the minimum mode configuration. Here the $\overline{RD}$ and $\overline{WR}$ pins are connected to the $\overline{ACR}$ and $\overline{ACW}$ pins, respectively. The $\overline{CS}$ input is connected to a 4-input NAND gate that decodes the three most significant address bits. REN1 connects to address

TABLE 8–4 Mode selection for the TMS4500 DRAM controller

TWST	FS1	FS0	Wait States	Refresh Rate	Minimum Clock (MHz)	Refresh Freq. (KHz)	Clocks per Refresh
0	0	0	0	External	—	REFREQ	4
0	0	1	0	CLK÷31	1.984	64–95	3
0	1	0	0	CLK÷46	2.944	64–85	3
0	1	1	0	CLK÷61	3.904	64–82	4
1	0	0	1	CLK÷46	2.944	64–85	3
1	0	1	1	CLK÷61	3.904	64–80	4
1	1	0	1	CLK÷76	4.864	64–77	4
1	1	1	1	CLK÷91	5.824	64–88	4

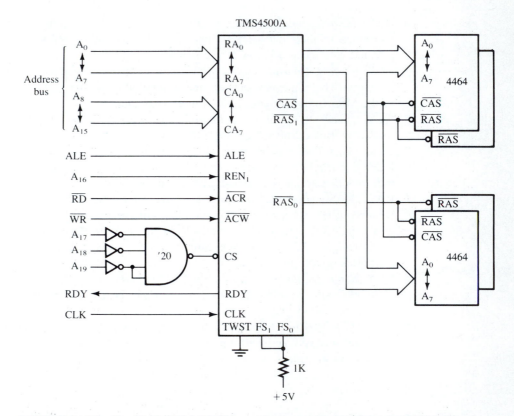

FIGURE 8–37 The TMS4500A DRAM controller used to interface to 128K bytes of DRAM. Here four TMS4464 DRAMs provide the memory located at locations 00000H–1FFFFH.

bus connection A_{16} so it selects one bank of memory or the other. If A_{16} is high, the bank attached to $\overline{RAS1}$ is selected, and if low, the bank that connects to $\overline{RAS0}$ is selected. In this example, two banks of 64K × 8 DRAMs are selected for a total of 128K × 8 of memory. The address range begins at location 00000H and extends through location 1FFFFH.

The programming pins TWST, FS1, and FS0 are selected (0, 1, and 1) so there are no waits, the refresh occurs every 61 clocks, and there are 4 clocks for every refresh. This ensures that a refresh occurs once every 12.2 µs, which is well within the tolerance of the 15.6 µs calculated earlier.

When an internal clocking signal is generated every 61 clock periods, an internal refresh request occurs. The request is delayed until current bus cycle is completed, which adds another four clocks to the time. When the request is honored, the RDY pin goes to a logic 0. This causes wait states to be inserted while the DRAM controller refreshes the memory. After the refresh is completed, the bus is free to do a read or a write until the next refresh request.

Figure 8–38 shows the timing diagram for the TMS4500A during the request for and completion of a refresh. Notice that the RDY line goes low to request wait states during the refresh operation.

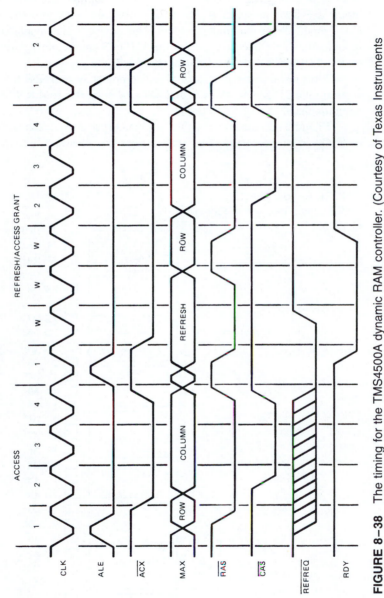

FIGURE 8-38 The timing for the TMS4500A dynamic RAM controller. (Courtesy of Texas Instruments Corporation)

DRAM Interface

Figure 8–39 illustrates a 1M × 9 SIMM (*single in-line memory module*) that contains 10 address pins that are provided with a 20-bit multiplexed address. The $\overline{CAS}$ and $\overline{RAS}$ inputs are used to select ($\overline{CAS}$) and strobe addresses into the memory module. The $\overline{CAS}_9$ input selects the ninth parity bit. This device is also available as a 1M × 8 memory module, the 421000C8. The pins of the 42100C9 for the ninth parity bit are not connected on the 421000C8 and only 8 memory devices are present.

Most newer microprocessor-based computer systems use SIMM memory. Common sizes are the 256K × 9, 1M × 9, and 4M × 9. Soon the 16M × 9 SIMM will also become commonplace.

Figure 8–40 illustrates an 8M × 8 memory system designed for either the 80386DX or 80486 microprocessor. This system does not illustrate the circuit that generates the

FIGURE 8–39 The 1M × 9 SIMM (single in-line memory module).

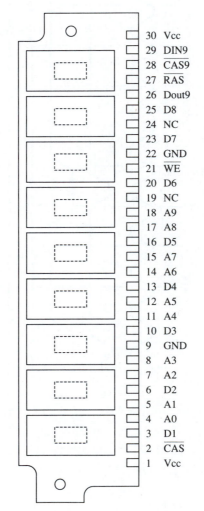

Pin	Signal
30	Vcc
29	DIN9
28	$\overline{CAS9}$
27	$\overline{RAS}$
26	Dout9
25	D8
24	NC
23	D7
22	GND
21	$\overline{WE}$
20	D6
19	NC
18	A9
17	A8
16	D5
15	A7
14	A6
13	D4
12	A5
11	A4
10	D3
9	GND
8	A3
7	A2
6	D2
5	A1
4	A0
3	D1
2	$\overline{CAS}$
1	Vcc

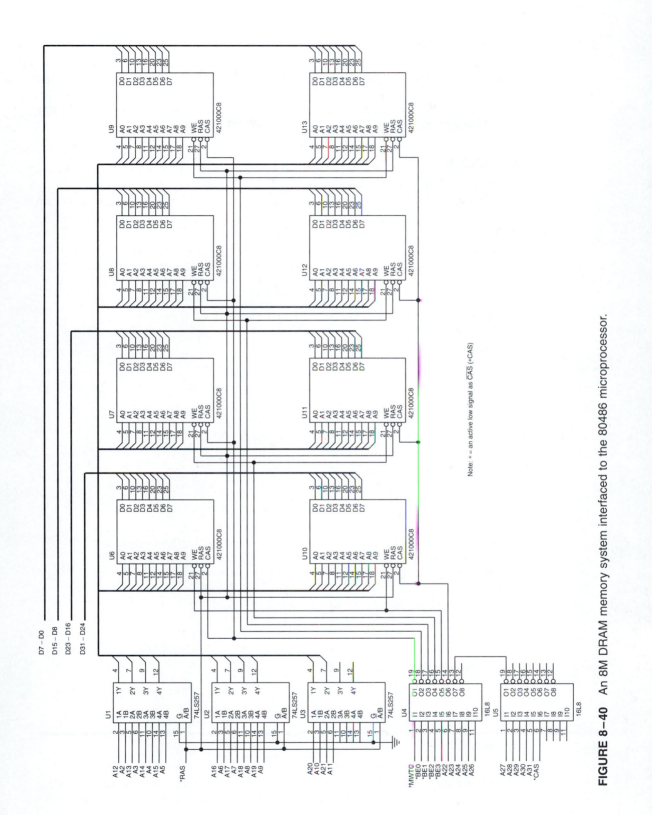

Note: * = an active low signal as $\overline{CAS}$ (*CAS)

FIGURE 8–40 An 8M DRAM memory system interfaced to the 80486 microprocessor.

331

$\overline{\text{CAS}}$ and $\overline{\text{RAS}}$ signals, but does show the address multiplexer. Notice again that the PAL16L8s are used (see Example 8–10) to develop the bank write strobe signals and also to decode the memory address. Here the memory system is decoded to provide an 8M byte memory from location 00000000H through 007FFFFFH.

EXAMPLE 8–10

```
TITLE      Address Decoder
PATTERN    Test 1U4 (PAL U4)
REVISION   A
AUTHOR     Barry B. Brey
COMPANY    Symbiotic Systems
DATE       6/27/93
CHIP       Decoder1U4 PAL16L8

;pins 1    2    3    4    5    6    7    8    9    10
           MWTC BE0  BE1  BE2  BE3  A22  A23  A24  A25  GND

;pins 11   12 13 14   15   16   17   18   19   20
           A26  NC U2 MB1  WR0  WR1  WR2  WR3  MB0  VCC

EQUATIONS

/WR0 = /MWTC * /BE0
/WR1 = /MWTC * /BE1
/WR2 = /MWTC * /BE2
/WR3 = /MWTC * /BE3
/MB0 = /A26 * /A25 * /A24 * /A23 * /A22 * /U2
/MB1 = /A26 * /A25 * /A24 * /A23 * A22 * /U2


TITLE      Address Decoder
PATTERN    Test 1U5 (PAL U5)
REVISION   A
AUTHOR     Barry B. Brey
COMPANY    Symbiotic Systems
DATE       6/27/93
CHIP       Decoder1U5 PAL16L8

;pins 1    2    3    4    5    6    7  8  9    10
           A27  A28  A29  A30  A31  CAS NC NC NC  GND

;pins 11 12 13 14 15 16 17 18 19 20
           NC NC NC NC NC NC NC NC U2 VCC

EQUATIONS

/U2 = /A31 * /A30 * /A29 * /A28 * /A27 * /CAS
```

8–7   SUMMARY

1. All memory devices have address inputs; data inputs and outputs, or just outputs; a pin for selection; and one or more pins that control the operation of the memory.

2. Address connections on a memory component are used to select one of the memory locations within the device. Ten address pins have 1,024 combinations and therefore are able to address 1,024 different memory locations.

3. Data connections on a memory are used to enter information to be stored in a memory location and also to retrieve information read from a memory location. Manufacturers list their memory as, for example, 4K × 4, which means that the device has 4K memory locations (4,096) and 4 bits are stored in each location.

4. Memory selection is accomplished via a chip selection pin ($\overline{CS}$) on many RAMs or a chip enable pin ($\overline{CE}$) on many EPROM or ROM memories.

5. Memory function is selected by an output enable pin ($\overline{OE}$) for reading data and a write enable pin ($\overline{WE}$) for writing data.

6. An EPROM memory is programmed by an EPROM programmer and can be erased if exposed to ultraviolet light. Today EPROMs are available in sizes from 1K × 8 all the way up to 128K × 8 and larger.

7. Static (SRAM) retains data for as long as the system power supply is attached. These memory types are available in sizes up to 128K × 8.

8. Dynamic RAM (DRAM) retains data for only a short period, usually 2–4 ms. This creates problems for the memory system designer because the DRAM must be refreshed periodically. DRAMs also have multiplexed address inputs that require an external multiplexer to provide each half of the address at the appropriate time.

9. Memory address decoders select an EPROM or RAM at a particular area of the memory. Commonly found address decoders include the 74LS138 3-to-8 line decoder, the 74LS139 2-to-4 line decoder, and programmed selection logic in the form of a PROM or PLD.

10. The PROM and PLD address decoders for microprocessors like the 8088 through the 80486 reduce the number of integrated circuits required to complete a functioning memory system.

11. The 8088 minimum mode memory interface contains 20 address lines, 8 data lines, and 3 control lines: $\overline{RD}$, $\overline{WR}$, and IO/$\overline{M}$. The 8088 memory functions correctly only when all these lines are used for memory interface.

12. The access speed of the EPROM must be compatible with the microprocessor to which it is interfaced. Many EPROMs available today have an access time of 450 ns, which is too slow for the 5 MHz 8088. In order to circumvent this problem, a wait state is inserted to increase memory access time to 660 ns.

13. Parity checkers are becoming commonplace today in many microprocessor-based microcomputer systems. An extra bit is stored with each byte of memory, making the memory 9 bits wide instead of 8.

14. Error correction features are also available for memory systems, but these require the storage of many more bits. If an 8-bit number is stored with an error correction circuit, it actually takes 13 bits of memory: 5 for an error checking code and 8 for the data. Most error correction integrated circuits are able to correct only a single-bit error.

15. The 8086/80286/80386SX memory interface has a 16-bit data bus and contains an M/$\overline{IO}$ control pin, whereas the 8088 has an 8-bit data bus and contains an IO/$\overline{M}$ pin. In addition to these changes, there is an extra control signal, bus high enable ($\overline{BHE}$).

16. The 8086/80386/80386SX memory is organized in two 8-bit banks: high bank and low bank. The high bank of memory is enabled by the $\overline{\text{BHE}}$ control signal and the low bank by the A_0 address signal.

17. Two common schemes for selecting the banks in an 8086/80286/80386SX-based system include (1) a separate decoder for each bank and (2) separate $\overline{\text{WR}}$ control signals for each bank with a common decoder.

18. Memory interfaced to the 80386DX and 80486 is 32 bits wide as selected by a 32-bit address bus. Because of the width of this memory, it is organized in four memory banks that are each 8 bits in width. Bank selection signals are provided by the microprocessor as $\overline{\text{BE0}}$, $\overline{\text{BE1}}$, $\overline{\text{BE2}}$, and $\overline{\text{BE3}}$.

19. Dynamic RAM controllers are designed to control DRAM memory components. Many DRAM controllers today contain address multiplexers, refresh counters, and the circuitry required to do a periodic DRAM memory refresh.

8-8   QUESTIONS AND PROBLEMS

1. What types of connections are common to all memory devices?
2. List the number of words found in each memory device for the following numbers of address connections:
   a. 8
   b. 11
   c. 12
   d. 13
3. List the number of data items stored in each of the following memory devices and the number of bits in each datum:
   a. 2K × 4
   b. 1K × 1
   c. 4K × 8
   d. 16K × 1
   e. 64K × 4
4. What is the purpose of the $\overline{\text{CS}}$ or $\overline{\text{CE}}$ pin on a memory component?
5. What is the purpose of the $\overline{\text{OE}}$ pin on a memory device?
6. What is the purpose of the $\overline{\text{WE}}$ pin on a RAM?
7. How many words of storage do the following EPROM memory devices contain?
   a. 2708
   b. 2716
   c. 2732
   d. 2764
   e. 27128
8. Why won't a 450 ns EPROM work directly with a 5 MHz 8088?
9. SRAM is an acronym for what type of device?
10. The 4016 memory has a $\overline{\text{G}}$ pin, an $\overline{\text{S}}$ pin, and a $\overline{\text{W}}$ pin. What are these pins used for in this RAM?
11. How much memory access time is required by the slowest 4016?
12. DRAM is an acronym for what type of device?

13. The TMS4464 has eight address inputs, yet it is a 64K DRAM. Explain how a 16-bit memory address is forced into eight address inputs.
14. What are the purposes of the $\overline{CAS}$ and $\overline{RAS}$ inputs of a DRAM?
15. How much time is required to refresh the typical DRAM?
16. Why are memory address decoders important?
17. Modify the NAND gate decoder of Figure 8–12 so it selects the memory for address range DF800H–DFFFFH.
18. Modify the NAND gate decoder in Figure 8–12 so it selects the memory for address range 40000H–407FFH.
19. When the $\overline{G1}$ input is high and $\overline{G2A}$ and $\overline{G2B}$ are both low, what happens to the outputs of the 74LS138 3-to-8 line decoder?
20. Modify the circuit of Figure 8–18 so it addresses memory range 70000H–7FFFFH.
21. Modify the circuit of Figure 8–18 so it addresses memory range 40000H–4FFFFH.
22. Describe the 74LS139 decoder.
23. Why is a PROM address decoder often found in a memory system?
24. Reprogram the PROM in Table 8–1 so it decodes memory address range 80000H–8FFFFH.
25. Reprogram the PROM in Table 8–1 so it decodes memory address range 30000H–3FFFFH.
26. The $\overline{RD}$ and $\overline{WR}$ minimum mode control signals are replaced by what two control signals in the 8086 maximum mode?
27. Modify the circuit of Figure 8–18 so it selects memory at location 68000H–6BFFFH.
28. Modify the circuit of Figure 8–18 so it selects eight 2764 8K × 8 EPROMs at memory location 10000H–1FFFFH.
29. Add another decoder to the circuit of Figure 8–20 so an additional eight 4016 2K × 8 SRAMs are added at location 10000H–13FFFH.
30. Redesign the main decoder in Figure 8–20 so memory addressing begins at location 80000H.
31. Explain how odd parity is stored in a memory system and how it is checked.
32. The 74LS636 error correction and detection circuit stores a check code with each byte of data. How many bits are stored for the check code?
33. What is the purpose of the SEF pin on the 74LS636?
34. The 74LS636 will correct _____ bits that are in error.
35. Outline the major difference between the buses of the 8086 and 8088 microprocessors.
36. What is the purpose of the $\overline{BHE}$ and A_0 pins on the 8086 microprocessor?
37. What two methods are used to select the memory in the 8086 microprocessor?
38. If $\overline{BHE}$ is a logic 0, then the _____ memory bank is selected.
39. If A_0 is a logic 0, then the _____ memory bank is selected.
40. Why don't separate bank read ($\overline{RD}$) strobes need to be developed when interfacing memory to the 8086?
41. Modify the circuit of Figure 8–29 so the EPROM is located at memory range C0000H–CFFFFH and the RAM is located at memory range 30000H–33FFFH.
42. Develop a 16-bit-wide memory interface that contains SRAM memory at locations 200000H–21FFFFH for the 80386SX microprocessor.
43. Develop a 32-bit-wide memory interface that contains EPROM memory at locations FFFF0000H–FFFFFFFFH.

44. What is a $\overline{\text{RAS}}$-only cycle?
45. When DRAM is refreshed, can it be done while other sections of the memory operate?
46. If a 16K × 1 DRAM requires 2 ms for a refresh and has 128 rows to be refreshed, no more than _____ of time must pass before another row is refreshed.
47. Where is the memory address applied to the TMS4500A DRAM controller?
48. What is the purpose of the REN1 pin on the TMS4500A?
49. What is normally connected to the $\overline{\text{ACW}}$ pin of the TMS4500A?
50. What operating condition on the TMS4500A is TWST used to select?
51. Modify the circuit of Figure 8–37 so it selects memory range 40000H–5FFFFH.
52. Modify the PAL program in Example 8–10 so memory is decoded at addresses 80000000H–87FFFFFFH.

CHAPTER 9

Basic I/O Interface

INTRODUCTION

A microprocessor is great at solving problems, but if it can't communicate with the outside world, it is of little worth. This chapter outlines some of the basic methods of communications, both serial and parallel, between humans or machines and the microprocessor.

In this chapter, we first introduce the basic I/O interface and discuss decoding for I/O devices. Then we provide detail on parallel and serial interfacing, both of which have a wide variety of applications. As applications, we connect analog-to-digital and digital-to-analog converters as well as both DC and stepper motors to the microprocessor.

CHAPTER OBJECTIVES

Upon completion of this chapter, you will be able to:

1. Explain the operation of the basic input and output interfaces.
2. Decode an 8-bit and a 16-bit I/O device so it can be used at any I/O port address.
3. Define handshaking and explain how to use it with I/O devices.
4. Interface and program the 8255 programmable parallel interface.
5. Interface and program the 8279 programmable keyboard/display controller.
6. Interface and program the 8251A serial communications interface adapter.
7. Interface and program the 8254 programmable interval timer.
8. Interface an analog-to-digital converter and a digital-to-analog converter to the microprocessor.
9. Interface both DC and stepper motors to the microprocessor.

9–1   INTRODUCTION TO I/O INTERFACE

In this section of the text, we explain the operation of the I/O instructions (IN, INS, OUT, and OUTS). We also explain the concept of isolated (sometimes called direct or I/O mapped I/O) and memory-mapped I/O, the basic input and output interfaces, and handshaking. A working knowledge of these topics will make it easier to understand the connection and operation of the programmable interface components and I/O techniques presented in the remainder of this chapter and text.

I/O Instructions

The instruction set contains one type of instruction that transfers information to an I/O device (OUT) and another to read information from an I/O device (IN). Instructions (INS and OUTS found on all versions except the 8086/8088) are also provided to transfer strings of data between the memory and an I/O device. Table 9–1 lists all versions of each instruction found in the microprocessor's instruction set.

Both the IN and OUT instructions transfer data between an I/O device and the microprocessor's accumulator (AL, AX, or EAX). The I/O address is stored in register DX as a 16-bit I/O address or in the byte (p8) immediately following the opcode as an 8-bit I/O address. Intel calls the 8-bit form (p8) a *fixed address* because it is stored with the instruction, usually in a ROM. The 16-bit I/O address in DX is called a *variable address* because it is stored in a register, which can be varied. Both the INS and OUTS instructions use a variable I/O address contained in the DX register.

Whenever data are transferred using the IN or OUT instruction, the I/O address, often called a *port number,* appears on the address bus. The external I/O interface decodes it in the same manner that it decodes a memory address. The 8-bit fixed port number (p8) appears on address bus connections A7–A0 with bits A15–A8 = 0000 0000. The address connections above A15 are undefined for an I/O instruction. The 16-bit variable port number (DX) appears on address connection A15–A0. This means that the first 256 I/O port addresses (00H–FFH) are accessed by both the fixed and variable I/O instructions, but any I/O address from 0100H–FFFFH is only accessed by the variable I/O address. In many dedicated task systems, only the rightmost 8 bits of the address are decoded, thus reducing the amount of circuitry required for decoding. In a PC computer, all 16 address bus bits are decoded with location 00XXH–03XXH being used for most I/O inside the PC.

The INS and OUTS instructions address the I/O device using the DX register, but do not transfer data between the accumulator and the I/O device as IN and OUT. Instead, these instructions transfer data between memory and the I/O device. The memory address is located by ES:DI for the INS instruction and DS:SI for the OUTS instruction. As with other string instructions, the contents of the pointers are incremented or decremented as dictated by the state of the direction flag (DF). Both INS and OUTS can also be prefixed with the REP prefix allowing more than one byte or word to be transferred between I/O and memory.

Isolated and Memory-Mapped I/O

There are two completely different methods of interfacing I/O to the microprocessor: *isolated I/O* and *memory-mapped I/O.* In isolated I/O the IN, INS, OUT, and OUTS

TABLE 9–1 Input/output instructions

Instruction	Data Width	Comment
IN AL,p8	8	Read a byte from I/O address p8 into AL
IN AL,DX	8	Read a byte from the I/O address indexed by DX into AL
IN AX,p8	16	Read a word from I/O address p8 into AX
IN AX,DX	16	Read a word from the I/O address indexed by DX into AX
IN EAX,p8	32	Read a double word from I/O address p8 into EAX
IN EAX,DX	32	Read a double word from the I/O address indexed by DX into EAX
INSB	8	Read a byte from the I/O address indexed by DX and store it in the location indexed by ES:DI, then increment/decrement DI by 1
INSW	16	Read a word from the I/O address indexed by DX and store it in the location indexed by ES:DI, then increment/decrement DI by 2
INSD	32	Read a double word from the I/O address indexed by DX and store it in the location indexed by ES:DI, then increment/decrement DI by 4
OUT p8,AL	8	Write a byte from AL into I/O address p8
OUT DX,AL	8	Write a byte from AL into the I/O address indexed by DX
OUT p8,AX	16	Write a word from AX into I/O address p8
OUT DX,AX	16	Write a word from AX into the I/O address indexed by DX
OUT p8,EAX	32	Write a double word from EAX into I/O address p8
OUT p8,EAX	32	Write a double word from EAX into the I/O address indexed by DX
OUTSB	8	Write a byte from the memory location indexed by DS:SI into the I/O address indexed by DX, then increment/decrement SI by 1
OUTSW	16	Write a word from the memory location indexed by DS:SI into the I/O address indexed by DX, then increment/decrement SI by 2
OUTSD	32	Write a double word from the memory location indexed by DS:SI into the I/O address indexed by DX, then increment/decrement SI by 4

instructions transfer data between the microprocessor accumulator or memory and the I/O device. In memory-mapped I/O, any instruction that references memory can accomplish the transfer. Both isolated and memory-mapped I/O are in use, so both are discussed in this text.

Isolated I/O. The most common I/O transfer technique used in the Intel microprocessor-based system is isolated I/O. The term isolated describes how the I/O locations are isolated from the memory system in a separate I/O address space. (Figure 9–1 illustrates both the isolated and memory-mapped address spaces for an 8088 microprocessor.) The addresses for isolated I/O devices, called *ports,* are separate from the memory. As a result, the user can expand the memory to its full size without using any of this space for I/O devices. A disadvantage of isolated I/O is that the data transferred between I/O and the microprocessor must be accessed by the IN, INS, OUT, and OUTS instructions. Separate control signals for the I/O space are developed that indicate an I/O read ($\overline{IORC}$) or an I/O write ($\overline{IOWC}$) operation. These signals indicate that an I/O port address appears on the

FIGURE 9–1 The memory and I/O maps for the 8086/8088 microprocessor. (a) Isolated I/O. (b) Memory-mapped I/O.

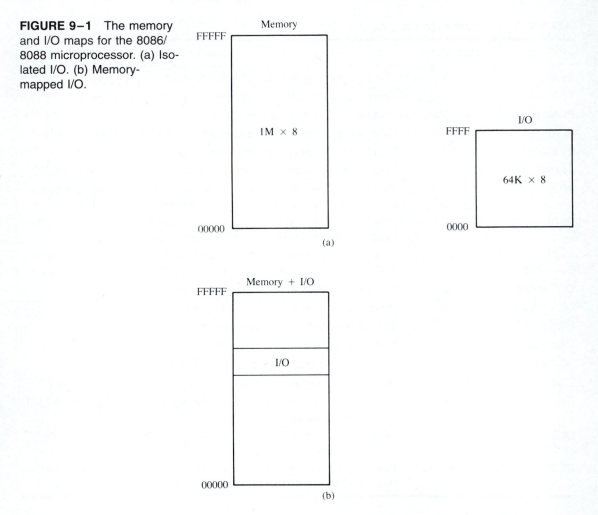

address bus that is used to select the I/O device. In the personal computer, isolated I/O ports are used for controlling peripheral devices. As a rule, an 8-bit port address is used to access devices located on the system board such as the timer and keyboard interface and a 16-bit port is used to access serial and parallel ports as well as video and disk drive systems.

Memory-Mapped I/O. Unlike isolated I/O, memory-mapped I/O does not use the IN, INS, OUT, or OUTS instructions. Instead, it uses any instruction that transfers data between the microprocessor and memory. A memory-mapped I/O device is treated as a memory location in the memory map. The main advantage of memory-mapped I/O is that any memory transfer instruction can be used to access the I/O device. The main disadvantage is that a portion of the memory system is used as the I/O map. This reduces the amount of memory available to applications. [Another advantage is that the $\overline{\text{IORC}}$ and $\overline{\text{IOWC}}$ signals have no function in a memory-mapped I/O system which reduces the amount of circuitry required for decoding.]

Personal Computer I/O Map

The personal computer uses part of the I/O map for dedicated funtions. Figure 9–2 shows the I/O map for the PC. Note that I/O space between ports 0000H and 3FFH is normally reserved for the computer system. The I/O ports located at 0400H–FFFFH are generally available for user applications. Note that the 80287 arithmetic coprocessor uses I/O address 00F8–00FD for communications. The I/O ports located between 0000H and 00FFH are accessed via the fixed port I/O instructions and the ports located above 00FFH are accessed via the variable I/O port instructions.

FIGURE 9–2 The I/O map of a personal computer illustrating many of the fixed I/O areas.

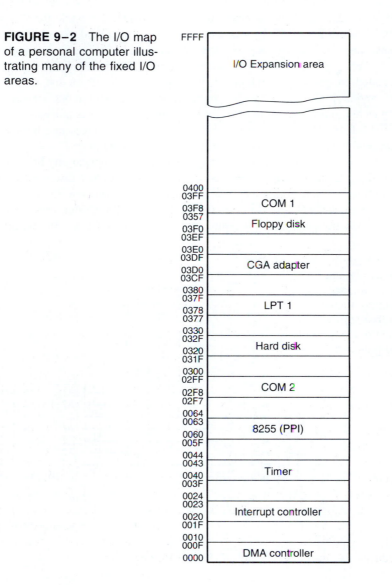

Basic Input and Output Interfaces

The basic input device is a set of three-state buffers. The basic output device is a set of data latches. The term IN refers to moving data from the I/O device into the microprocessor and the term OUT refers to moving data out of the microprocessor to the I/O device.

The Basic Input Interface.   Three-state buffers are used to construct the 8-bit input port depicted in Figure 9–3. Notice that the external TTL data (simple toggle switches in this example) are connected to the inputs of the buffers. The outputs of the buffers connect to the data bus. The exact data bus connections depend on the version of the microprocessor. For example, the 8088 has data bus connections D7–D0, while the 80486 has D31–D0. The circuit of Figure 9–3 allows the microprocessor to read the contents of the 8 switches that connect to the data bus when the select signal $\overline{SEL}$ becomes a logic 0.

When the microprocessor executes an IN instruction, the I/O port address is decoded to generate the logic 0 on $\overline{SEL}$. A 0 placed on the output control inputs ($\overline{1G}$ and $\overline{2G}$) of the 74ALS244 buffer causes the data input connections (A) to be connected to the data output (Y) connections. If a logic 1 is placed on the output control inputs of the 74ALS244 buffer, the device enters the three-state high-impedance mode that effectively disconnects the switches from the data bus.

This basic input circuit is not optional and must appear any time that input data are interfaced to the microprocessor. Sometimes it appears as a discrete part of the circuit as in Figure 9–3 and sometimes it is built into a programmable I/O device.

Sixteen- or 32-bit data can also be interfaced to various versions of the microprocessor, but not nearly as commonly as 8-bit data. To interface 16 bits of data, the circuit

FIGURE 9–3 The basic input interface illustrating the connection of eight switches. Note that the 74ALS244 is a three-state buffer that controls the application of the switch data to the data bus.

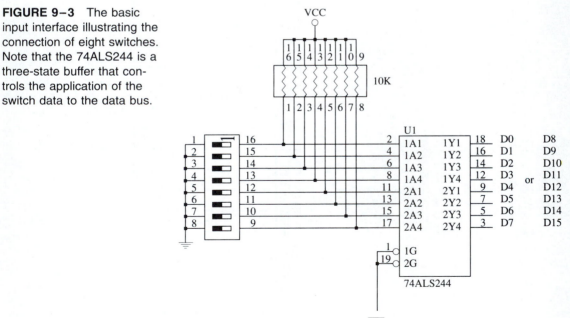

in Figure 9–3 is doubled to include two 74ALS244 buffers that connect 16 bits of input data to the 16-bit data bus. To interface 32 bits of data, the circuit is expanded by a factor of 4.

The Basic Output Interface. The basic output interface receives data from the microprocessor and must usually hold it for some external device. Its latches, like the buffers found in the input device, are often built into the I/O device.

Figure 9–4 shows how 8 simple light-emitting diodes (LEDs) connect to the microprocessor through a set of 8 data latches. The latch stores the number output by the microprocessor from the data bus so the LEDs can be lit with any 8-bit binary number. Latches are needed to hold the data because when the microprocessor executes an OUT instruction, the data are only present on the data bus for less than 1.0 μs. Without a latch, the viewer would never see the LEDs illuminate.

When the OUT instruction executes, the data from AL, AX, or EAX are transferred to the latch via the data bus. Here the D inputs of a 74ALS374 octal latch are connected to the data bus to capture the output data, and the Q outputs of the latch are attached to the LEDs. When a Q output becomes a logic 0, the LED lights. Each time that the OUT instruction executes, the $\overline{\text{SEL}}$ signal to the latch activates, capturing the data output to the latch from the data bus. The data are held until the next OUT instruction executes.

Handshaking

Many I/O devices accept or release information at a much slower rate than the microprocessor. Another method of I/O control, called *handshaking* or *polling*, synchro-

FIGURE 9–4 The basic output interface connected to a set of LED displays.

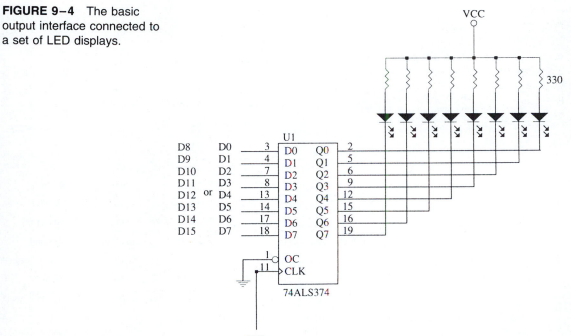

nizes the I/O device with the microprocessor. An example device that requires handshaking is a parallel printer that prints 100 characters per second (CPS). It is obvious that the microprocessor can definitely send more than 100 CPS to the printer, so a way to slow the microprocessor down to match speeds with the printer must be developed.

Figure 9–5 illustrates the typical input and output connections found on a printer. Here data are transferred through a series of data connections (D7–D0), BUSY indicates that the printer is busy, and $\overline{\text{STB}}$ is a clock pulse used to send data into the printer for printing.

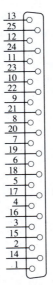

Connector DB25

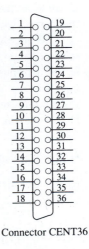

Connector CENT36

DB25 Pin number	CENT36 Pin number	Function	DB25 Pin number	CENT36 Pin number	Function
1	1	$\overline{\text{Data Strobe}}$	12	12	Paper empty
2	2	Data 0 (D0)	13	13	Select
3	3	Data 1 (D1)	14	14	Afd
4	4	Data 2 (D2)	15	32	$\overline{\text{Error}}$
5	5	Data 3 (D3)	16	—	$\overline{\text{RESET}}$
6	6	Data 4 (D4)	17	31	Select in
7	7	Data 5 (D5)	18—25	19—30	Ground
8	8	Data 6 (D6)	—	17	Frame ground
9	9	Data 7 (D7)	—	16	Ground
10	10	$\overline{\text{Ack}}$	—	33	Ground
11	11	Busy			

FIGURE 9–5 The DB25 connector found on computers and the Centronics 36-pin connector found on printers for the Centronics parallel printer interface.

The ASCII data to be printed by the printer are placed on D7–D0 and a pulse is applied to the $\overline{\text{STB}}$ connection. The strobe signal sends the data into the printer so it can be printed. As soon as the printer receives the data, it places a logic 1 on the BUSY pin indicating that it is busy printing data. The microprocessor polls or tests the BUSY pin to decide if the printer is busy. If the printer is busy, the microprocessor waits; if it is not busy, the microprocessor sends another ASCII character to the printer. The process of *interrogating* the printer is called handshaking or polling. Example 9–1 illustrates a simple procedure that tests the printer BUSY flag and sends data to the printer if it is not busy. The PRINT procedure prints the ASCII-coded contents of BL only if the BUSY flag is a logic 0 indicating the printer is not busy.

EXAMPLE 9–1

```
                        ;procedure that prints the contents of BL
                        ;
0000                    PRINT  PROC     FAR

0000 E4  4B                    IN       AL,BUSY          ;get BUSY flag
0002 A8  04                    TEST     AL,BUSY_BIT      ;test BUSY
0004 75  FA                    JNE      PRINT            ;if busy = 1
0006 8A  C3                    MOV      AL,BL            ;print character
0008 E6  4A                    OUT      PRINTER,AL
000A CB                        RET

000B                    PRINT  ENDP
```

9–2   I/O PORT ADDRESS DECODING

I/O port address decoding is very similar to memory address decoding, especially for memory-mapped I/O devices. In fact, we do not discuss memory-mapped I/O decoding because it is treated exactly the same as memory, except that the $\overline{\text{IORC}}$ and $\overline{\text{IOWC}}$ are not used, since there is no IN or OUT instruction. The decision to use memory-mapped I/O is often determined by the size of the memory system and the placement of the I/O devices in the system.

The main difference between memory decoding and isolated I/O decoding is the number of address pins connected to the decoder. We decode A32–A0, A23–A0, or A19–A0 for memory and A15–A0 for isolated I/O. Sometimes, if the I/O devices use only fixed I/O addressing, we decode only A7–A0. Another difference is that we use the $\overline{\text{IORC}}$ and $\overline{\text{IOWC}}$ to activate I/O devices for a read or a write operation. On earlier versions of the microprocessor, IO/$\overline{\text{M}}$ = 1 and $\overline{\text{RD}}$ or $\overline{\text{WR}}$ are used to activate I/O devices.

Decoding 8-Bit I/O Addresses

As mentioned, the fixed I/O instruction uses an 8-bit I/O port address that appears on A15–A0 as 0000H–00FFH. If a system contains less than 256 I/O devices, we often decode only address connections A7–A0 for an 8-bit I/O port address. Please note that the DX register can also address I/O ports 00H–FFH. Also note that if the address is decoded as an 8-bit address, then we can never include I/O devices that use a 16-bit I/O address.

FIGURE 9–6 A port decoder that decodes 8-bit I/O ports. This decoder generates active low outputs for ports F0H–F7H.

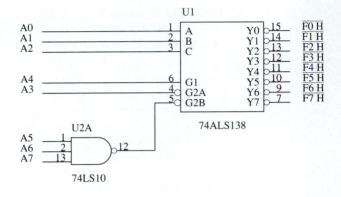

Figure 9–6 illustrates a 74ALS138 decoder that decodes 8-bit I/O ports F0H through F7H. (We assume that the system will only use I/O ports 00H–FFH for this decoder.) This decoder is identical to a memory address decoder except we only connect address bits A7–A0 to the inputs of the decoder. Figure 9–7 shows the PAL version of this decoder. Notice that this is a better decoder circuit because the number of integrated circuits has been reduced to one device, the PAL. The program for the PAL appears in Example 9–2.

EXAMPLE 9–2

```
TITLE       Address Decoder
PATTERN     Test 2
REVISION    A
AUTHOR      Barry B. Brey
COMPANY     Symbiotic Systems
DATE        6/28/93
CHIP        Decoder2 PAL16L8

;pins 1  2  3  4  5  6  7  8  9   10
      A0 A1 A2 A3 A4 A5 A6 A7 NC  GND

;pins 11 12 13 14 15 16 17 18 19 20
      NC F7 F6 F5 F4 F3 F2 F1 F0 VCC

EQUATIONS

/F0 = A7 * A6 * A5 * A4 * A3 * /A2 * /A1 * /A0
/F1 = A7 * A6 * A5 * A4 * A3 * /A2 * /A1 * A0
/F2 = A7 * A6 * A5 * A4 * A3 * /A2 * A1 * /A0
/F3 = A7 * A6 * A5 * A4 * A3 * /A2 * A1 * A0
/F4 = A7 * A6 * A5 * A4 * A3 * A2 * /A1 * /A0
/F5 = A7 * A6 * A5 * A4 * A3 * A2 * /A1 * A0
/F6 = A7 * A6 * A5 * A4 * A3 * A2 * A1 * /A0
/F7 = A7 * A6 * A5 * A4 * A3 * A2 * A1 * A0
```

Decoding 16-Bit I/O Addresses

We also decode 16-bit I/O addresses, especially in a personal computer system. The main difference between decoding an 8-bit I/O address and a 16-bit I/O address is that 8 additional address lines (A15–A8) must be decoded. Figure 9–8 illustrates a circuit that contains 2 PAL16L8s used to decode I/O ports 3F8H–3FFH. These are common I/O port assignments in a PC used for the serial communications port.

FIGURE 9-7 A PAL16L8 decoder that generates I/O port signals for ports F0H–F7H.

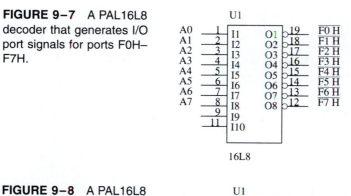

FIGURE 9-8 A PAL16L8 circuit that decodes 16-bit I/O ports 3F8H–3FFH.

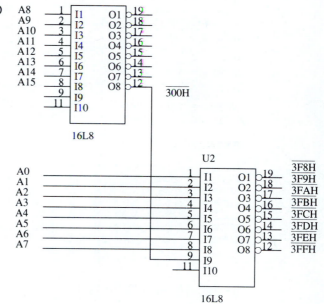

The first PAL16L8 (U1) decodes the first 8 bits of the I/O port address (A15–A8) so it generates a signal to enable the second PAL16L8 (U2) for any I/O address between 0300H and 03FFH. The second PAL16L8 further decodes the I/O address to produce 8 active low-output strobes 3F8H–3FFH. The programs for both PAL16L8 devices, U1 and U2, appear in Examples 9-3 and 9-4.

EXAMPLE 9-3

```
TITLE      Address Decoder
PATTERN    Test 3
REVISION   A
AUTHOR     Barry B. Brey
COMPANY    Symbiotic Systems
DATE       6/29/93
CHIP       Decoder3 PAL16L8
```

```
;pins 1   2   3    4    5    6    7    8    9   10
      A8  A9  A10  A11  A12  A13  A14  A15  NC  GND

;pins 11  12    13  14  15  16  17  18  19  20
      NC  300H  NC  NC  NC  NC  NC  NC  NC  VCC

EQUATIONS

/300H = /A15 * /A14 * /A13 * /A12 * /A11 * /A10 * A9 * A8
```

EXAMPLE 9–4

```
TITLE      Address Decoder
PATTERN    Test 4
REVISION   A
AUTHOR     Barry B. Brey
COMPANY    Symbiotic Systems
DATE       6/30/93
CHIP       Decoder4 PAL16L8

;pins 1   2   3   4   5   6   7   8   9     10
      A0  A1  A2  A3  A4  A5  A6  A7  300H  GND

;pins 11  12    13    14    15    16    17    18    19    20
      NC  3FFH  3FEH  3FDH  3FCH  3FBH  3FAH  3F9H  3F8H  VCC

EQUATIONS

/3F8H = /300H * A7 * A6 * A5 * A4 * A3 * /A2 * /A1 * /A0
/3F9H = /300H * A7 * A6 * A5 * A4 * A3 * /A2 * /A1 * A0
/3FAH = /300H * A7 * A6 * A5 * A4 * A3 * /A2 * A1 * /A0
/3FBH = /300H * A7 * A6 * A5 * A4 * A3 * /A2 * A1 * A0
/3FCH = /300H * A7 * A6 * A5 * A4 * A3 * A2 * /A1 * /A0
/3FDH = /300H * A7 * A6 * A5 * A4 * A3 * A2 * /A1 */A0
/3FEH = /300H * A7 * A6 * A5 * A4 * A3 * A2 * A1 * /A0
/3FFH = /300H * A7 * A6 * A5 * A4 * A3 * A2 * A1 * A0
```

8- and 16-Bit I/O Ports

Now that we understand that decoding the I/O port address is probably simpler than decoding a memory address (because of the number of bits), we explain how data are transferred between the microprocessor and 8- or 16-bit I/O devices. Data transferred to an 8-bit I/O device exists in one of the I/O banks of the 8086, 80286, or 80386SX. The I/O system contains two 8-bit memory banks just as memory does. This is illustrated in Figure 9–9, which shows the separate I/O banks for a 16-bit system such as the 80286 or 80386SX.

Because two I/O banks exist, any 8-bit I/O write requires a separate write strobe to function correctly. I/O reads do not requires separate read strobes because, as with memory, the microprocessor only reads the byte it expects and ignores the other byte. The only time that a read can cause problems is when the I/O device responds incorrectly to a read operation. In the case of an I/O device that responds to a read from the wrong bank, we may need to include separate read signals. This is discussed if the case arises later in this chapter.

Figure 9–10 illustrates a system that contains two different 8-bit output devices located at 8-bit I/O address 40H and 41H. Because these are 8-bit devices and because

FIGURE 9–9 The I/O banks found in the 80286 microprocessor-based system.

FIGURE 9–10 An I/O port decoder that selects ports 40H and 41H for output data.

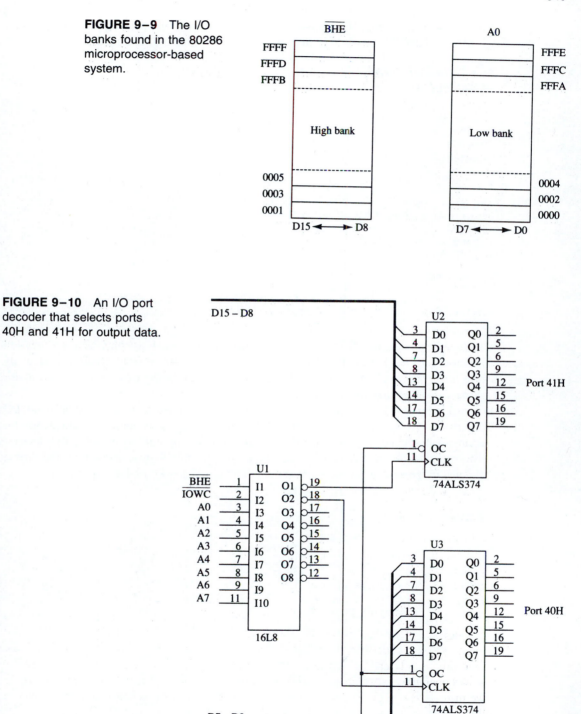

they appear in different I/O banks, we generate separate I/O write signals. The program for the PAL16L8 decoder used in Figure 9–9 is illustrated in Example 9–5.

EXAMPLE 9–5

```
TITLE      Address Decoder
PATTERN    Test 5
REVISION   A
AUTHOR     Barry B. Brey
COMPANY    Symbiotic Systems
DATE       7/1/93
CHIP       Decoder5 PAL16L8

;pins 1    2    3  4  5  6  7  8  9  10
      BHE IOWC A0 A1 A2 A3 A4 A5 A6 GND

;pins 11 12 13 14 15 16 17 18  19  20
      A7 NC NC NC NC NC NC 040 041 VCC

EQUATIONS

O40 = /A0 * /IOWC * /A7 * A6 * /A5 * /A4 * /A3 * /A2 * /A1
O41 = /BHE * /IOWC * /A7 * A6 * /A5 * /A4 * /A3 * /A2 * /A1
```

When selecting 16-bit-wide I/O devices, the A0 and $\overline{BHE}$ pins have no function because both I/O banks are selected together. Although 16-bit I/O devices are relatively rare, a few do exist for analog-to-digital and digital-to-analog converters as well as for some video and disk memory interfaces.

Figure 9–11 illustrates a 16-bit input device connected to function at 8-bit I/O addresses 64H and 65H. Notice that the PAL16L8 decoder does not have a connection for address bit A0 and $\overline{BHE}$ because these signals do not apply to 16-bit-wide I/O devices. The program for the PAL16L8 is illustrated in Example 9–6 to show how the enable signals are generated for the three-state buffers (74ALS244) used as input devices.

EXAMPLE 9–6

```
TITLE      Address Decoder
PATTERN    Test 6
REVISION   A
AUTHOR     Barry B. Brey
COMPANY    Symbiotic Systems
DATE       7/2/93
CHIP       Decoder6 PAL16L8

;pins 1    2   3  4  5  6  7  8  9  10
      IORC A1 A2 A3 A4 A5 A6 A7 NC GND

;pins 11 12 13 14 15 16 17 18 19  20
      NC NC NC NC NC NC NC NC O6X VCC

EQUATIONS

/O6X = /IORC * /A7 * A6 * A5 * /A4 * /A3 * /A2 * /A1
```

FIGURE 9–11 A 16-bit I/O port decoded at I/O addresses 64H and 65H.

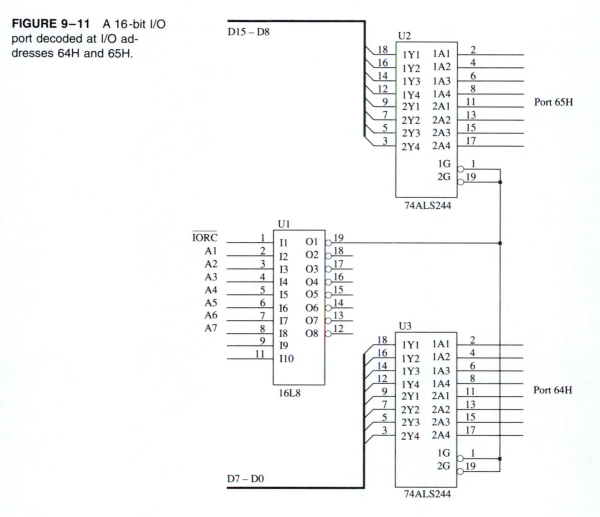

32-Bit-Wide I/O Ports

Although 32-bit-wide I/O ports are not common, they may eventually become commonplace because of new buses found in computer systems. The EISA system bus supports 32-bit I/O, but it is only found on some computer systems.

The circuit of Figure 9–12 illustrates a 32-bit input port for the 80386DX or 80486 microprocessor. As with prior interfaces, this circuit uses a single PAL to decode the I/O ports and four 74LS244 buffers to connect the I/O data to the data bus. The I/O ports decoded by this interface are 8-bit ports 70H–73H as illustrated by the PAL program in Example 9–7.

EXAMPLE 9–7

```
TITLE     Address Decoder
PATTERN   Test 7
```

FIGURE 9–12 A 32-bit input port decoded at bytes
70H–73H.

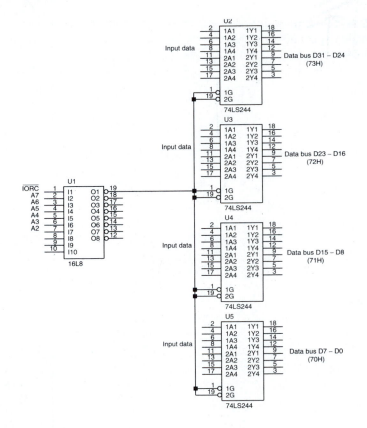

```
REVISION    A
AUTHOR      Barry B. Brey
COMPANY     Symbiotic Systems
DATE        7/3/93
CHIP        Decoder7 PAL16L8

;pins 1    2   3   4   5   6   7   8   9   10
      IORC A7  A6  A5  A4  A3  A2  NC  NC  GND

;pins 11 12 13 14 15 16 17 18 19   20
      NC NC NC NC NC NC NC NC SEL  VCC

EQUATIONS

/SEL = /IORC * /A7 * A6 * A5 * A4 * /A3 * /A2
```

9–3   THE PROGRAMMABLE PERIPHERAL INTERFACE

The 8255 *programmable peripheral interface* (PPI) is a very popular low-cost interfacing
component found in many applications. The PPI has 24 pins for I/O, programmable in
groups of 12 pins, that are used in three separate modes of operation. The 8255 can

interface any TTL-compatible I/O device to the microprocessor. The 82C55A (CMOS version) requires the insertion wait states if operated with a microprocessor using higher than an 8 MHz clock. Because I/O devices are inherently slow, wait states used during I/O transfers do not impact significantly upon the speed of the system. The 8255 still finds application (compatible for programming, although it may not appear in the system as a discrete 8255) even in the latest 80486-based computer system. The 8255 is used for interface to the keyboard and the parallel printer port in these personal computers.

Basic Description of the 8255

Figure 9–13 illustrates the pinout diagram of the 8255. Its three I/O ports (labeled A, B, and C) are programmed in groups of 12 pins. Group A connections consist of port A (PA7–PA0) and the upper half of port C (PC7–PC4) and group B consists of port B (PB7–PB0) and the lower half of port C (PC3–PC0). The 8255 is selected by its $\overline{CS}$ pin for programming and for reading or writing to a port. Register selection is accomplished through the A1 and A0 pins that select an internal register for programming or operation. Table 9–2 shows the I/O port assignments used for programming and access to the I/O ports. In the personal computer an 8255 or its equivalent is decoded at I/O ports 60H–63H.

The 8255 is a fairly simple device to interface to the microprocessor and program. For the 8255 to be read or written, the $\overline{CS}$ input must be a logic 0 and the correct I/O address must be applied to the A1 and A0 pins. The remaining port address pins are don't cares and are externally decoded to select the 8255.

Figure 9–14 shows an 8255 connected to the 8086 so it functions at 8-bit I/O port addresses C0H (port A), C2H (port B), C4H (port C), and C6H (command register). This

FIGURE 9–13 The pinout of the 8255A peripheral interface adapter (PPI).

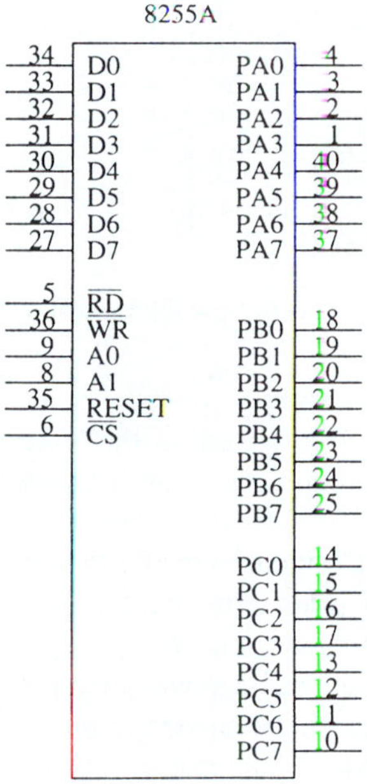

TABLE 9-2 I/O port assignments for the 8255

A1	A0	Function
0	0	Port A
0	1	Port B
1	0	Port C
1	1	Command Register

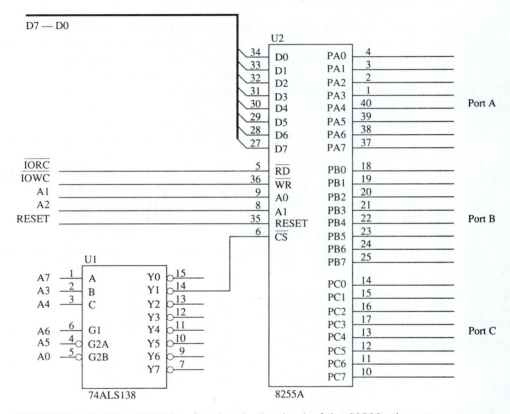

FIGURE 9-14 The 8255A interfaced to the low bank of the 80286 microprocessor.

interface uses the low bank of the 8086 I/O map. Notice from this interface that all the 8255 pins are direct connections to the 8086 except for the $\overline{CS}$ pin. The $\overline{CS}$ pin is decoded and selected by a 74ALS138 decoder.

The RESET input to the 8255 initializes the device whenever the microprocessor is reset. A RESET input to the 8255 causes all ports to be set up as simple input ports using mode 0 operation. Because the port pins are internally programmed as input pins on a reset, this prevents damage when the power is first applied to the system. After a RESET, no other commands are needed to program the 8255 as long as it used as an input device at all three ports. Note that an 8255 is interfaced to the personal computer at port addresses 60H–63H for keyboard control and also for controlling the speaker, timer, and other internal devices such as memory expansion.

Programming the 8255

The 8255 is easy to program because it only contains two internal command registers as illustrated in Figure 9–15. Notice that bit position 7 selects either command byte A or command byte B. Command byte A programs the function of group A and B, while command byte B sets (1) or resets (0) bits of port C only if the 8255 is programmed in mode 1 or 2.

Group B pins (port B and the lower part of port C) are programmed as either input or output pins. Group B can operate in either mode 0 or mode 1. Mode 0 is the basic input/output mode that allows the pins of group B to be programmed as simple input and

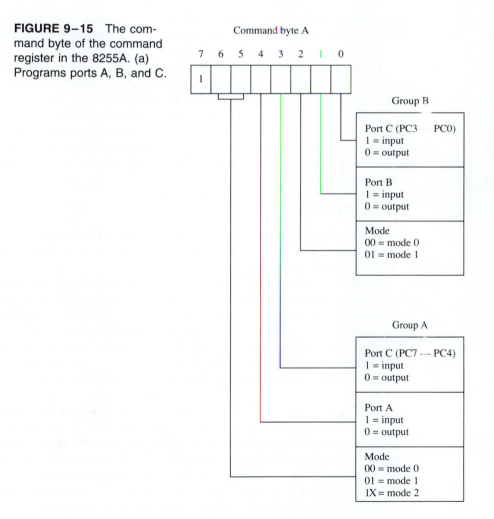

FIGURE 9–15 The command byte of the command register in the 8255A. (a) Programs ports A, B, and C.

(a)

FIGURE 9–15 (*continued*)
(b) Sets or resets the bit indicated in the select a bit field.

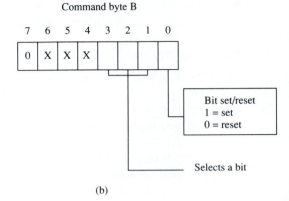

(b)

latched output connections. Mode 1 operation is the strobed operation for group B connections where data are transferred through port B and port C provides handshaking signals.

Group A pins (port A and the upper part of port C) are also programmed as either input or output pins. The difference is that group A can operate in modes 0, 1, and 2. Mode 2 operation is a bidirectional mode of operation for port A.

If a 0 is placed in bit position 7 of the command byte, command byte B is selected. This command allows any bit of port C to be set (1) or reset (0) if the 8255 is operated in either mode 1 or 2. Otherwise this command byte is not used for programming. We often use the bit set/reset function in control systems to set or clear a control bit at port C.

Mode 0 Operation

Mode 0 operation allows the 8255 to function either as a buffered input device or as a latched output device. These are the same as the basic input and output circuits discussed in the first section of this chapter.

Figure 9–16 shows the 8255 connected to a set of 8 seven-segment LED displays. In this circuit, both ports A and B are programmed as (mode 0) simple latched output ports. Port A provides the segment data inputs to the display and port B provides a means of selecting a display position at a time for multiplexing the displays. The 8255 is interfaced to an 8088 through a PAL16L8 so it functions at I/O port numbers 0700H–0703H. The program for the PAL16L8 is listed in Example 9–8. The PAL decodes the I/O address and also develops the lower write strobe for the $\overline{WR}$ pin of the 8255.

The resistor values are chosen in Figure 9–16 so the segment current is 80 mA. This current is required to produce an average current of 10 mA per segment as the displays are multiplexed. In this type of display system, only one of the eight display positions is on at any given instant. The peak anode current is 560 mA, but the average anode current is 70 mA. Whenever displays are multiplexed, we increase the segment current from 10 mA to a value equal to the number of display positions times 10 mA. This means that a 4-digit display uses 40 mA per segment, a 5-digit display uses 50 mA, and etc.

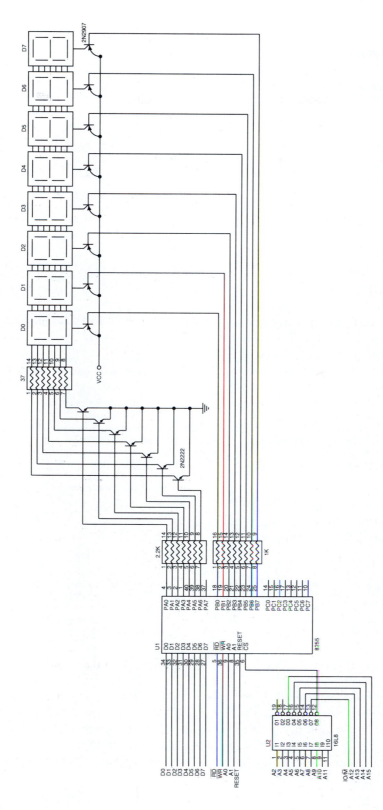

FIGURE 9–16 An 8-digit LED display interfaced to the 8088 microprocessor through an 8255A PIA.

EXAMPLE 9–8

```
TITLE      Address Decoder
PATTERN    Test 8
REVISION   A
AUTHOR     Barry B. Brey
COMPANY    Symbiotic Systems
DATE       7/5/93
CHIP       Decoder8 PAL16L8


;pins 1  2  3  4  5  6  7  8  9   10
      A2 A3 A4 A5 A6 A7 A8 A9 A10 GND

;pins 11  12 13  14  15  16  17  18 19 20
      A11 CS IOM A12 A13 A14 A15 NC NC VCC

EQUATIONS

/CS = /A15*/A14*/A13*/A12*/A11*A10*A9*A8*/A7*/A6*/A5*/A4*/A3*A2*IOM
```

EXAMPLE 9–9

```
                          ;software to program the 8255A
                          ;
0000 B0 80                MOV    AL,10000000B          ;set up command
0002 BA 0703              MOV    DX,COMMAND            ;address command register
0005 EE                   OUT    DX,AL                 ;program the 8255A
```

EXAMPLE 9–10

```
                          ;Procedure to scan the 8 digits of the multiplexed LED display.
                          ;This procedure must be called continuously from a program to
                          ;display the 7-segment coded information in area MEMORY.
0006                      ;DISP   PROC   NEAR

0006 9C                          PUSHF                       ;save registers
0007 50                          PUSH   AX
0008 53                          PUSH   BX
0009 52                          PUSH   DX
000A 56                          PUSH   SI

                          ;set up register for display

000B BB 0008              MOV    BX,8                  ;load count
000E B4 7F                MOV    AH,7FH                ;load select pattern
0010 BE FFFF R            MOV    SI,OFFSET MEMORY-1    ;address display RAM
0013 BA 0701              MOV    DX,PORTB              ;address port B

                          ;display eight digits

0016                      DISP1:

0016 8A C4                MOV    AL,AH                 ;select digit
0018 EE                   OUT    DX,AL
0019 4A                   DEC    DX                    ;address port A
001A 8A 00                MOV    AL,[BX+SI]            ;get data
001C EE                   OUT    DX,AL                 ;display data

001D E8 029A R            CALL   DELAY                 ;wait 1 ms
```

```
0020 D0 CC              ROR     AH,1            ;adjust selection code
0022 42                 INC     DX              ;address port B
0023 4B                 DEC     BX              ;adjust count
0024 75 F0              JNZ     DISP1           ;repeat 8 times

0026 5E                 POP     SI              ;restore registers
0027 5A                 POP     DX
0028 5B                 POP     BX
0029 58                 POP     AX
002A 9D                 POPF
002B C3                 RET

002C           DISP     ENDP
```

Before software to operate the display is examined, we must first program the 8255. This is accomplished with the short sequence of instructions listed in Example 9–9. Here ports A and B are both programmed as outputs.

The procedure to drive these displays is listed in Example 9–10. For this display system to function correctly, we must call this procedure often. Notice that the procedure calls another procedure (DELAY) that causes a 1 ms time delay. This time delay is not illustrated in this example, but is used to allow time for each display position to turn on. It is recommended by the manufacturers of LED displays that the display flash is between 100 Hz and 1,500 Hz. Using a 1 ms time delay we light each digit for 1 ms, for a total display flash rate of 1000 Hz / 8 display or a flash rate of 125.

The display procedure addresses an area of memory where the data, in 7-segment code, is stored for the 8 display digits. The AH register is loaded with a code (7FH) that initially addresses the most significant display position. Once this position is selected, the contents of memory location MEMORY + 7 is addressed and sent to the most significant digit. The selection code is then adjusted to select the next display digit as is the address. This process repeats 8 times to display the contents of location MEMORY through MEMORY + 7 on the 8 display digits.

A Stepper Motor Interfaced to the 8255.   Another device often interfaced to a computer system is the stepper motor. A stepper motor is a digital motor because it is moved in discrete steps as it traverses through 360°. A common stepper motor is geared to move perhaps 15° per step in an inexpensive stepper motor to 1° per step on a more costly high-precision stepper motor. In all cases, these steps are gained through many magnetic poles an/or gearing. Notice that two coils are energized in this illustration. If less power is required, one coil may be energized at a time causing the motor to step at 0°, 90°, 180°, and 270°.

Figure 9–17 shows a four-coil stepper motor that uses an armature with a single pole. Notice in this illustration, the stepper motor is shown four times with the armature (permanent magnetic) rotated to four discrete places. This is accomplished by energizing the coils as shown. This is an illustration of full stepping. The stepper motor is driven using NPN darlington pairs to provide a large current to each coil.

A circuit that can drive this stepper motor is illustrated in Figure 9–18 with the four coils shown in place. This circuit uses the 8255 to provide it with the drive signals used to rotate the armature of the motor in either the right-hand or left-hand direction.

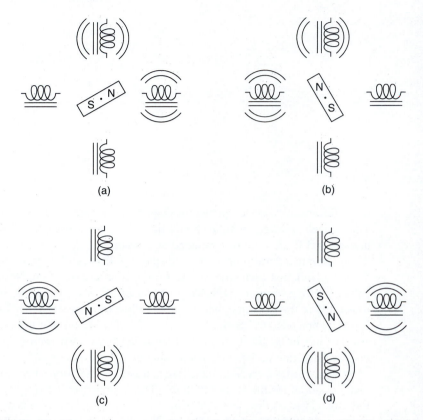

(a)

(b)

(c)

(d)

FIGURE 9–17   The stepper motor showing full-step operation. (a) 45° (b) 135° (c) 225° (d) 317°.

FIGURE 9–18   A stepper motor interfaced to the 8255. This illustration does not show the decoder.

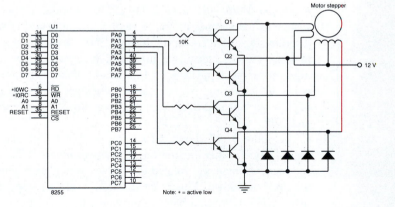

EXAMPLE 9-11

```
0000                    DATA      SEGMENT

0000 33                 POS            DB      33H                         ;position

0001                    DATA      ENDS

0000                    CODE      SEGMENT 'CODE'
                                  ASSUME CS:CODE,DS:DATA

= 0040                  PORTA     EQU   40H                               ;port number

                        ;Procedure to control a stepper motor.

0000                    STEP      PROC FAR

0000 A0 0000 R                    MOV   AL,POS                            ;get position
0003 81 F9 8000                   CMP   CX,8000H
0007 77 10                        JA    RH                                ;if right-hand direction
0009 83 F9 00                     CMP   CX,0
000C 74 14                        JE    STEP_OUT                          ;if no steps
000E                    STEP1:
000E D0 C0                         ROL   AL,1                             ;step left
0010 E6 40                         OUT   PORTA,AL
0012 E8 0011                       CALL  DELAY
0015 E2 F7                         LOOP  STEP1
0017 EB 09                         JMP   STEP_OUT
0019                    RH:
0019 81 E1 7FFF                    AND   CX,7FFFH                         ;clear bit 15
001D                    RH1:
001D D0 C8                         ROR   AL,1                             ;step right
001F E6 40                         OUT   PORTA,AL
0021 E8 0006                       CALL  DELAY
0024 E2 F7                         LOOP  RH1
0026                    STEP_OUT:
0026 A2 0000                       MOV   POS,AL                           ;save position
0029 C9                            RET

002A                    STEP      ENDP
002A                    CODE      ENDS
                                  END   STEP
```

A simple procedure that drives the motor (assuming port A is programmed in Mode 0 as an output device) is listed in Example 9-11. This subroutine is called with CX holding the number of steps and direction of the rotation. If CX > 8000H the motor spins in the right-hand direction, and if CX < 8000H it spins in the left-hand direction. The leftmost bit of CX is removed and the remaining 15 bits contain the number of steps. Notice that the procedure uses a time delay (not illustrated) that causes a 1 ms time delay. This time delay allows the stepper motor armature time to move to its next position.

The current position is stored in memory location POS, which must be initialized with 33H, 66H, 99H, or CCH. This allows a simple ROR (step right) or ROL (step left) instruction to rotate the binary bit pattern for the next step.

Mode 1 Strobed Input

Mode 1 operation causes port A and/or port B to function as latching input devices. This allows external data to be stored into the port until the microprocessor is ready to retrieve it. Port C is also used in mode 1 operation, not for data, but for control or handshaking signals that help operate either or both port A and port B as strobed input ports. Figure 9–19 shows how both ports are structured for mode 1 strobed input operation and also the timing diagram.

The strobed input port captures data from the port pins when the strobe ($\overline{STB}$) is activated. Note that strobe captures the port data on the 0-to-1 transition. The $\overline{STB}$ signal causes data to be captured in the port and it also activates the IBF (input buffer full) and

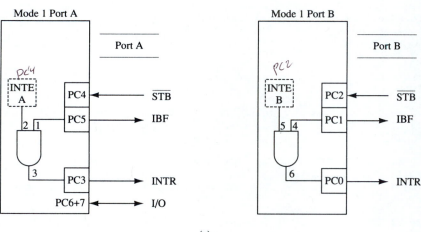

(a)

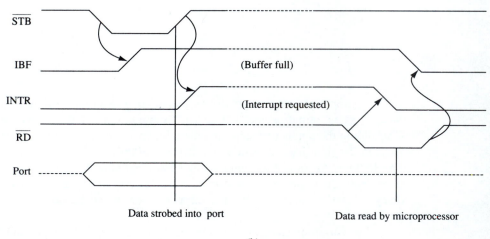

(b)

FIGURE 9–19 Strobed input operation (mode 1) of the 8255A. (a) Internal structure. (b) Timing diagram.

INTR (interrupt request) signals. Once the microprocessor, through software (IBF) or hardware (INTR), notices that data are strobed into the port, it executes an IN instruction to read the port ($\overline{RD}$). The act of reading the port restores both IBF and INTR to their inactive states until the next datum is strobed into the port.

Signal Definitions for Mode 1 Strobed Input

1. $\overline{STB}$—Strobe: an input used to load data into the port latch, which holds the information until it is input to the microprocessor via the IN instruction.
2. IBF—Input Buffer Full: an output that indicates the input latch contains information.
3. INTR—Interrupt Request: an output that requests an interrupt. The INTR pin becomes a logic 1 when the $\overline{STB}$ input returns to a logic 1 and is cleared when the data are input from the port by the microprocessor.
4. INTE—Interrupt Enable: neither an input nor an output, but an internal bit programmed via the port PC4 (port A) or PC2 (port B) bit position.
5. PC7, PC6—Port Pins 7 and 6: general-purpose I/O pins that are available for any purpose.

Strobe Input Example. An excellent example of a strobed input device is a keyboard. The keyboard encoder debounces the keyswitches and provides a strobe signal whenever a key is depressed and the data output contain the ASCII-coded keycode. Figure 9–20 illustrates a keyboard connected to strobed input port A. Here $\overline{DAV}$ (data available) is activated for 1 μs each time that a key is typed on the keyboard. This causes data to be strobed into port A because $\overline{DAV}$ is connected to the $\overline{STB}$ input of port A. So each time a key is typed, it is stored into port A of the 8255. The $\overline{STB}$ input also activates the IBF signal indicating that date is in port A.

Example 9–12 shows a procedure that reads data from the keyboard each time a key is typed. This procedure read the key from port A and returns with the ASCII code in AL. To detect a key, port C is read and the IBF bit (bit position PC5) is tested to see if the buffer is full. If the buffer is empty (IBF = 0) then the procedure keeps testing this bit waiting for a character to be typed on the keyboard.

FIGURE 9–20 Using the 8255A for strobed input operation of a keyboard.

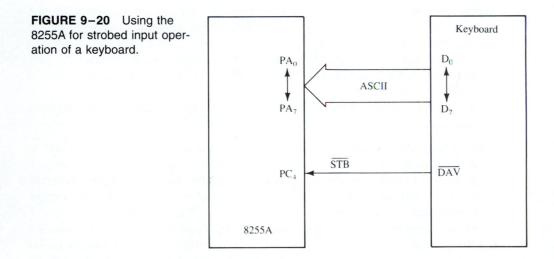

EXAMPLE 9–12

```
                            ;procedure that reads the keyboard encoder and returns
                            ;with the ASCII character in AL
= 0020                      BIT5    EQU     20H

0000                        READ    PROC    NEAR

0000 E4 22                          IN      AL,PORTC        ;read port C
0002 A8 20                          TEST    AL,BIT5         ;test IBF
0004 74 FA                          JZ      READ            ;if IBF = 0

0006 E4 20                          IN      AL,PORTA        ;read ASCII code
0008 C3                             RET

0009                        READ    ENDP
```

Mode 1 Strobed Output

Figure 9–21 illustrates the internal configuration and timing diagram of the 8255 when it is operated as a strobed output device under mode 1. Strobed output operation is similar to mode 0 output except that control signals are included to provide handshaking.

Whenever data are written to a port programmed as a strobed output port, the $\overline{\text{OBF}}$ (output buffer full) signal becomes a logic 0 to indicate that data are present in the port latch. This signal indicates that data are available to an external I/O device that removes the data by strobing the $\overline{\text{ACK}}$ (acknowledge) input to the port. The $\overline{\text{ACK}}$ signal returns the $\overline{\text{OBF}}$ signal to a logic 1 indicating that the buffer is not full.

Signal Definitions for Mode 1 Strobed Output

1. $\overline{\text{OBF}}$—Output Buffer Full: an output that goes low whenever data are output (OUT) to the port A or port B latch. This signal is set to a logic 1 whenever the $\overline{\text{ACK}}$ pulse returns from the external device.
2. $\overline{\text{ACK}}$—Acknowledge: a signal that causes the $\overline{\text{OBF}}$ pin to return to a logic 1 level. The $\overline{\text{ACK}}$ is a response from an external device that indicates it has received the data from the 8255 port.
3. INTR—Interrupt Request: a signal that interrupts the microprocessor when the external device receives the data via the $\overline{\text{ACK}}$ signal. This pin is qualified by the internal INTE (interrupt enable) bit.
4. INTE—Interrupt Enable: neither an input nor an output, but an internal bit programmed to enable or disable the INTR pin. The INTE A bit is programmed as PC6 and INTE B is PC2.
5. PC5, PC4—Port C bits 5 and 4 are general-purpose I/O pins. The bit set and reset command may be used to set or reset these two pins.

Strobed Output Example.
The printer interface discussed in section 9–1 is used here to demonstrate how to achieve strobed output synchronization between the printer and the 8255. Figure 9–22 illustrates port B connected to a parallel printer with eight data inputs for receiving ASCII-coded data, a $\overline{\text{DS}}$ (data strobe) input to strobe data into the printer, and an $\overline{\text{ACK}}$ output to acknowledge the receipt of the ASCII character.

In this circuit, there is no signal to generate the $\overline{\text{DS}}$ signal to the printer, so PC4 is used with software that generates the $\overline{\text{DS}}$ signal. The $\overline{\text{ACK}}$ signal that is returned from the printer acknowledges the receipt of the data and is connected to the $\overline{\text{ACK}}$ input of the 8255.

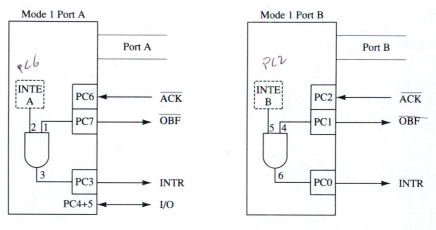

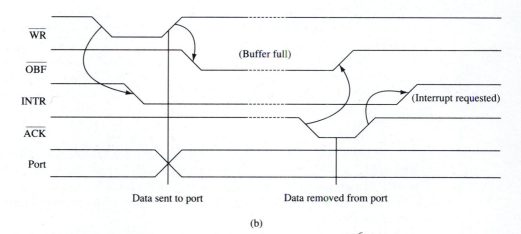

(b)

FIGURE 9–21 Strobed output operation (mode 1) of the 8266A. (a) Internal structure. (b) Timing diagram.

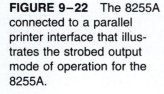

FIGURE 9–22 The 8255A connected to a parallel printer interface that illustrates the strobed output mode of operation for the 8255A.

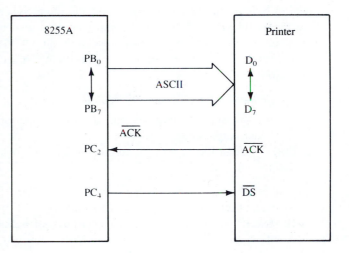

EXAMPLE 9-13

```
                 ;Procedure that transfers the ASCII-coded character from AH
                 ;to the printer via port B
                 ;
= 0002           BIT1    EQU     2H

0000             PRINT   PROC    NEAR

                 ;check for printer ready

0000 E4 62               IN      AL,PORTC            ;get OBF
0002 A8 02               TEST    AL,BIT1             ;test OBF
0004 74 FA               JZ      PRINT               ;if OBF = 0

                 ;send character to printer via port B

0006 8A C4               MOV     AL,AH               ;get character
0008 E6 61               OUT     PORTB,AL            ;send it

                 ;send DS to printer

000A B0 08               MOV     AL,8                ;clear DS
000C E6 63               OUT     COMMAND,AL
000E B0 09               MOV     AL,9                ;set DS
0010 E6 63               OUT     COMMAND,AL
0012 C3                  RET

0013             PRINT   ENDP
```

Example 9-13 lists the software that sends the ASCII-coded character in AH to the printer. The procedure first tests $\overline{\text{OBF}}$ to decide if the printer has removed the data from port B. If not, the procedure waits for the $\overline{\text{ACK}}$ signal to return from the printer. If $\overline{\text{OBF}} = 1$, then the procedure sends the contents of AH to the printer through port B and also sends the $\overline{\text{DS}}$ signal.

Mode 2 Bidirectional Operation

In mode 2, which is allowed only for group A, port A becomes bidirectional, allowing data to be transmitted and received over the same eight wires. Bidirectional bused data are useful when interfacing two computers. It is also used for the IEEE-488 parallel high-speed (general-purpose instrumentation bus—GPIB[1]) interface standard. Figure 9-23 shows the internal structure and timing diagram for mode 2 bidirectional operation.

Signal Definitions for Bidirectional Mode 2

1. INTR—Interrupt Request: an output used to interrupt the microprocessor for both input and output conditions.
2. $\overline{\text{OBF}}$—Output Buffer Full: an output that indicates that the output buffer contains data for the bidirectional bus.

---

[1]GPIB (general-purpose instrumentation bus) is a registered trademark of Hewlett-Packard Corporation.

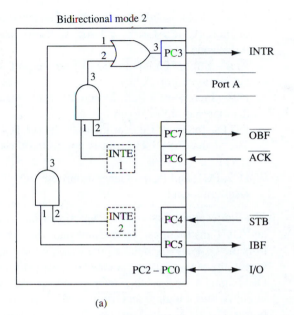

(a)

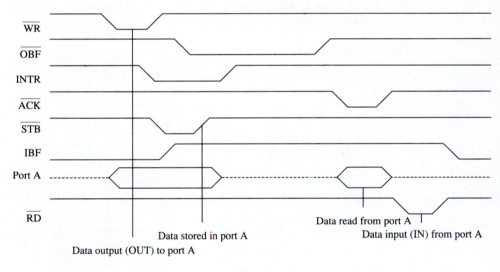

(b)

FIGURE 9–23   Mode 2 operation of the 8255A. (a) Internal structure. (b) Timing diagram.

3. $\overline{ACK}$—Acknowledge: an input that enables the three-state buffers so data can appear on port A. If $\overline{ACK}$ is a logic 1, the output buffers of port A are at their high-impedance state.

4. $\overline{STB}$—Strobe: an input used to load the port A input latch with external data from the bidirectional port A bus.

5. IBF—Input Buffer Full: an output used to signal that the input buffer contains data for the external bidirectional bus.

6. INTE—Interrupt Enable: internal bits (INTE1 and INTE2) that enable the INTR pin. The state of the INTR pin is controlled through port C bits PC6 (INTE1) and PC4 (INTE2).

7. PC2, PC1, and PC0—General-purpose I/O pins in mode 2 controlled by the bit set and reset command.

The Bidirectional Bus.   The bidirectional bus is used by referencing port A with the IN and OUT instructions. To transmit data through the bidirectional bus, the program first tests the $\overline{OBF}$ signal to determine whether the output buffer is empty. If it is, then data are sent to the output buffer via the OUT instruction. The external circuitry also monitors the $\overline{OBF}$ signal to decide if the microprocessor has sent data to the bus. As soon as the output circuitry sees a logic 0 on $\overline{OBF}$ it sends back the $\overline{ACK}$ signal to remove it from the output buffer. The $\overline{ACK}$ signal sets the $\overline{OBF}$ bit and also enables the three-state output buffers so data may be read. Example 9–14 lists a procedure that transmits the contents of the AH register through bidirectional port A.

EXAMPLE 9–14

```
                        ;Procedure that transmits AH through the bidirectional
                        ;bus of port A
                        ;
= 0080                  BIT7    EQU     80H

0000                    TRANS   PROC    NEAR

                        ;test OBF

0000 E4 62                      IN      AL,PORTC        ;get OBF
0002 A8 80                      TEST    AL,BIT7         ;test OBF
0004 74 FA                      JZ      TRANS           ;if OBF = 0

                        ;send data

0006 8A C4                      MOV     AL,AH           ;get data
0008 E6 60                      OUT     PORTA,AL
000A C3                         RET

000B         —          TRANS   ENDP
```

To receive data through the bidirectional port A bus, the IBF bit is tested with software to decide if data have been strobed into the port. If IBF = 1, then data are input using the IN instruction. The external interface sends data into the port using the $\overline{STB}$ signal. When $\overline{STB}$ is activated, the IBF signal becomes a logic 1 and the data at port A are held inside the port in a latch. When the IN instruction executes, the IBF bit is cleared and the data in the port are moved into AL. Example 9–15 lists a procedure that reads data from the port.

FIGURE 9-24 A summary of the port connections for the 8255A PIA.

		Mode 0		Mode 1		Mode 2
Port A		IN	OUT	IN	OUT	I/O
Port B		IN	OUT	IN	OUT	Not used
Port C	0	IN	OUT	$INTR_B$	$INTR_B$	I/O
	1			IBF_B	$\overline{OBF_B}$	I/O
	2			$\overline{STB_B}$	$\overline{ACK_B}$	I/O
	3			$INTR_A$	$INTR_A$	INTR
	4			$\overline{STB_A}$	I/O	$\overline{STB}$
	5			IBF_A	I/O	IBF
	6			I/O	$\overline{ACK_A}$	$\overline{ACK}$
	7			I/O	$\overline{OBF_A}$	$\overline{OBF}$

EXAMPLE 9-15

```
                        ;Procedure that inputs data from the bidirectional
                        ;bus and returns with it in AL
                        ;
= 0020                  BIT5    EQU     20H

0000                    READ    PROC    NEAR

                        ;test IBF

0000 E4 62                      IN      AL,PORTC        ;get IBF
0002 A8 20                      TEST    AL,BIT5         ;test IBF
0004 74 FA                      JZ      READ            ;if IBF = 0

                        ;read data

0006 E4 60                      IN      AL,PORTA
0008 C3                         RET

0009                    READ    ENDP
```

The INTR (interrupt request) pin can be activated from both directions of data flow through the bus. If INTR is enabled by both INTE bits, then the output and input buffers both cause interrupt requests. This occurs when data are strobed into the buffer using $\overline{STB}$ or when data are written using OUT.

8255 Mode Summary

Figure 9-24 shows a graphical summary of the three modes of operation for the 8255. Mode 0 provides simple I/O, mode 1 provides strobed I/O, and mode 2 provides bidirectional I/O. As mentioned, these modes are selected through the command register of the 8255.

9-4   THE 8279 PROGRAMMABLE KEYBOARD/DISPLAY INTERFACE

The 8279 is a programmable keyboard and display interfacing component that scans and encodes up to a 64-key keyboard and controls up to a 16-digit numerical display. The keyboard interface has a built-in first-in, first-out (FIFO) buffer that allows it to store up to eight keystrokes before the microprocessor must retrieve a character. The display section controls up to 16 numeric displays from an internal 16 x 8 RAM that stores the coded display information.

Basic Description of the 8279

As we shall see, the 8279 is designed for ease of interfacing with any microprocessor. Figure 9–25 illustrates the pinout of this device, and the definition of each pin connection follows.

Pin Definition for the 8279

1. A0—Address Input: a pin that selects data or control for reads and writes between the microprocessor and the 8279. A logic 0 selects data and a logic 1 selects control or status register.
2. $\overline{BD}$—Blank: an output used to blank the displays.
3. CLK—Clock: an input that generates the internal timing for the 8279. The maximum allowable frequency on the CLK pin is 3.125 MHz. Other timings require wait states in microprocessors executing at above 5 MHz.
4. CN/ST—Control/Strobe: an input normally connected to the control key on a keyboard.
5. $\overline{CS}$—Chip Select: an input used to enable the 8279 for programming, reading the keyboard and status information, and writing control and display data.

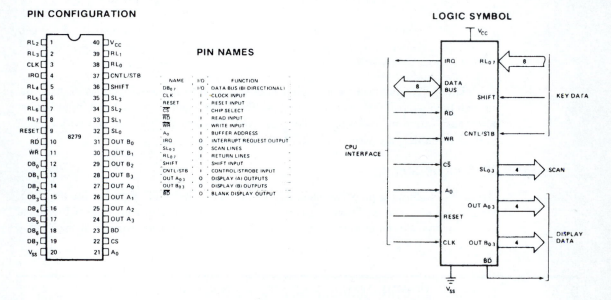

FIGURE 9–25 The pinout and logic symbol of the 8279 programmable keyboard/display interface. (Courtesy of Intel Corporation)

6. DB7–DB0—Data Bus: bidirectional pins that connect to the data bus on the microprocessor.

7. IRQ—Interrupt Request: an output that becomes a logic 1 whenever a key is pressed on the keyboard. This signal indicates that keyboard data are available for the microprocessor.

8. OUTA3–OUTA0—Outputs: used to send data to the displays (most significant).

9. OUTB3–OUTB0—Outputs: used to send data to the displays (least significant).

10. $\overline{\text{RD}}$—Read: an input directly connected to the $\overline{\text{IORC}}$ or $\overline{\text{RD}}$ signal from the system. The $\overline{\text{RD}}$ input causes, when $\overline{\text{CS}}$ is a logic 0, a read from the data registers or status register.

11. RESET—Reset: an input that connects to the system RESET signal.

12. RL7–RL0—Return Lines: inputs used to sense any key depression in the keyboard matrix.

13. SHIFT—Shift: an input normally connected to the shift key on a keyboard.

14. SL3–SL0—Scan Lines: outputs that scan both the keyboard and the displays.

15. $\overline{\text{WR}}$—Write: an input that connects to the write strobe signal that is developed with external logic. The $\overline{\text{WR}}$ input causes data to be written to either the data registers or control registers within the 8279.

16. Vcc—Supply: a pin connected to the system + 5.0 V bus.

17. Vss—Ground: a pin connected to the system ground.

Interfacing the 8279 to the Microprocessor

In Figure 9–26, the 8279 is connected to the 8088 microprocessor. The 8279 is decoded to function at 8-bit I/O address 10H and 11H where port 10H is the data port and 11H is the control port. This circuit uses a PAL16L8 (see Example 9–16) to decode the I/O address as well as to generate the low bank I/O write signal for the 8279. Address bus bit A0 selects either the data or control port. Notice that the $\overline{\text{CS}}$ signal selects the 8279 and also provides a signal called $\overline{\text{WAIT2}}$ that is used to cause 2 wait states so that this device functions with an 8MHz 8088.

FIGURE 9–26 The 8279 interfaced to the 8088 microprocessor to function at 8-bit I/O ports 10H and 11H.

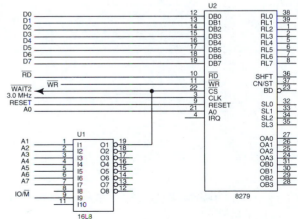

EXAMPLE 9–16

```
TITLE       Address Decoder
PATTERN     Test 9
REVISION    A
AUTHOR      Barry B. Brey
COMPANY     Symbiotic Systems
DATE        7/5/93
CHIP        Decoder9 PAL16L8

;pins 1   2   3   4   5   6   7   8   9    10
      A1  A2  A3  A4  A5  A6  A7  NC  IOM  GND

;pins 11 12 13 14 15 16 17 18 19  20
      NC NC NC NC NC NC NC CS NC  VCC

EQUATIONS

/CS = IOM * /A7 * /A6 * /A5 * A4 * /A3 * /A2 * /A1
```

The only signal not connected to the microprocessor is the IRQ output. This is an interrupt request pin and is beyond the scope of this section of the text. The next chapter explains interrupts, where their operation and function in a system are explained.

Keyboard Interface

Suppose that a 64-key keyboard (with no numeric displays) is connected through the 8279 to the 8088 microprocessor. Figure 9–27 shows this connection as well as the keyboard. With the 8279, the keyboard matrix is any size between 2 × 2 (4 keys) and an 8 × 8 (64 keys). (Note that each crossover point in the matrix contains a normally open pushbutton switch that connects one vertical column with one horizontal row when a key is pressed.)

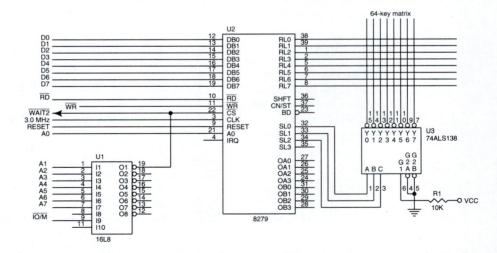

FIGURE 9–27   A 64-key keyboard interfaced to the 8088 microprocessor through the 8279.

The I/O port number decoded is the same as that decoded for Figure 9–26. The I/O port number is 10H for the data port and 11H for the control port in this circuit.

The 74ALS138 decoder generates eight active low column strobe signals for the keyboard. The selection pins SL2–SL0 sequentially scan each column of the keyboard, and the internal circuitry of the 8279 scans the RL pins searching for a keyswitch closure. Pullup resisters, normally found on input lines of a keyboard, are not required because the 8279 contains its own internal pullups on the RL inputs.

Programming the Keyboard Interface. Before any keystroke is detected, the 8279 must be programmed—a more involved procedure than with the 8255. The 8279 has 8 control words to consider before it is programmed. The first 3 bits of the number sent to the control port (11H in this example) select one of the 8 different control words. Table 9–3 lists all 8 control words and briefly describes them.

Control Word Descriptions. Following is a list of the control words that program the 8279. Note that the first three bits are the control register number, which are followed by other binary bits of information as they apply to each control.

1. 000DDKKK—Mode Set: a command with an opcode of 000 and two fields programmed to select the mode of operation for the 8279. The DD field selects the mode of operation for the displays (see Table 9–4) and the KKK field selects the mode of operation (see Table 9–5) for the keyboard.

    The DD field selects either an 8- or 16-digit display and determines whether new data are entered to the rightmost or leftmost display position. The KKK field is quite a bit more complex. It provides encoded, decoded, or strobed keyboard operation.

    In encoded mode, the SL outputs are active-high and follow the binary bit pattern 0 through 7 or 0 through 15 depending on whether 8- or 16-digit displays are

TABLE 9–3 The 8279 control word summary

D7	D6	D5	Function	Purpose
0	0	0	Mode set	Selects the number of display positions, left or right entry, and type of keyboard scan
0	0	1	Clock	Programs the internal clock and sets the scan and debounce times
0	1	0	Read FIFO	Selects the type of FIFO read and the address to be read
0	1	1	Read display	Selects the type of display read and the address of the display position
1	0	0	Write display	Selects the type of display write and the address of the display position
1	0	1	Display write inhibit	Allows half-byte to be blanked or inhibited
1	1	0	Clear	Allows the display or FIFO to be cleared
1	1	1	End interrupt	Clears the IRQ pin at the end of an interrupt service procedure

TABLE 9–4 Binary bit assignment for DD of the mode set control word

D	D	Function
0	0	8-character display with left entry
0	1	16-character display with left entry
1	0	8-character display with right entry
1	1	16-character display with right entry

TABLE 9–5 Binary bit assignment for KKK of the mode set control word

K	K	K	Function
0	0	0	Encoded keyboard with 2-key lockout
0	0	1	Decoded keyboard with 2-key lockout
0	1	0	Encoded keyboard with N-key rollover
0	1	1	Decoded keyboard with N-key rollover
1	0	0	Encoded sensor matrix
1	0	1	Decoded sensor matrix
1	1	0	Strobed keyboard, encoded display scan
1	1	1	Strobed keyboard, decoded display scan

selected. In decoded mode, the SL outputs are active-low, and only one of the four outputs is low at any given instant. The decoded outputs repeat the pattern: 1110, 1101, 1011, and 0111. In strobed mode, an active-high pulse on the CN/ST input pin strobes data from the RL pins into an internal FIFO where they are held for the microprocessor.

It is also possible to select either 2-key lockout or N-key rollover. Two-key lockout prevents two keys from being recognized if pressed simultaneously. N-key rollover will accept all keys pressed simultaneously, from first to last.

2. 001PPPPP—Clock: a command word that programs the internal clock divider. The code PPPPP is a prescaler that divides the clock input pin (CLK) to achieve the desired operating frequency or approximately 100 KHz. An input clock of 1 MHz thus requires a prescaler of 01010_2 for PPPPP.

3. 010Z0AAA—Read FIFO: a control word that selects the address of a keystroke from the internal FIFO buffer. Bit positions AAA select the desired FIFO location from 000 to 111, and Z selects auto-increment for the address. Under normal operation, this control word is used only with the sensor matrix operation of the 8279.

4. 011ZAAAA—Display Read: a control word that selects the read address of one of the display RAM positions for reading through the data port. AAAA is the address of the position to be read and Z selects auto-increment mode. This command is used if the information stored in the display RAM must be read.

5. 100ZAAAA—Write Display: a control word that selects the write address of one of the displays. AAAA addresses the position to be written to through the data port and Z selects auto-increment so subsequent writes through the data port are to subsequent display positions.

6. 1010WWBB—Display Write Inhibit: a control word that inhibits writing to either half of each display RAM location. The leftmost W inhibits writing to the leftmost 4 bits of the display RAM location, and the rightmost W inhibits the rightmost 4 bits. The BB field functions in a like manner, except they blank (turn off) either half of the output pins.

7. 1100CCFA—Clear: a control word that clears the display, the FIFO, or both the display and FIFO. Bit F clears the FIFO, the display RAM status, and sets the address pointer to 000. If the CC bits are 00 or 01, then all display RAM locations become 0000000, if CC = 10, all locations become 00100000, and if CC = 11, all locations become 11111111.

8. 111E000—End Interrupt: a control word that is issued to clear the IRQ pin to zero in the sensor matrix mode.

The large number of control words make programming the keyboard interface appear complex. Before anything is programmed, the clock divider rate must be determined. In the circuit illustrated in Figure 9–26, we use a 3.0 MHz clock input signal. To program the presCaler to generate a 100 KHz internal rate, we program PPPPP of the clock control word with a 30 or 11110_2.

The next step involves programming the keyboard type. In the example keyboard of Figure 9–27, we have an encoded keyboard. Notice the circuit includes an external decoder that converts the encoded data from the SL pins into decoded column selection signals. We are free in this example to choose either 2-key lockout or N-key rollover, but most applications use 2-key lockout.

Finally, we program the operation of the FIFO. Once the FIFO is programmed, it never needs to be reprogrammed unless we need to read prior keyboard codes. Each time a key is typed, the data are stored in the FIFO; if it is read from the FIFO before the FIFO is full (8 characters), then the data from the FIFO follow the same order as the typed data. Example 9–17 provides the software required to initialize the 8279 to control the keyboard illustrated in Figure 9–27.

EXAMPLE 9–17

```
                        ;Initialization dialog for the keyboard interface
                        ;
                        ;program clock

0000 B0 3E                      MOV   AL,00111110B
0002 E6 11                      OUT   CNTR,AL

                        ;program mode set

0004 B0 00                      MOV   AL,0
0006 E6 11                      OUT   CNTR,AL

                        ;program to read FIFO and keyboard

0008 B0 50                      MOV   AL,01010000B
000A E6 11                      OUT   CNTR,AL
```

Once the 8279 is initialized, a procedure is required to read data from the keyboard. We determine if a character is typed in the keyboard by looking at the FIFO status register. Whenever the control port is addressed by the IN instruction, the contents of the FIFO status word is copied into the AL register. Figure 9–28 shows the contents of the FIFO status register and defines the purpose of each status bit.

The procedure listed in Example 9–18 first tests the FIFO status register to see if it contains any data. If NNN = 000, the FIFO is empty. Upon determining that the FIFO is not empty, the procedure inputs data to AL and returns with the keyboard code in AL.

EXAMPLE 9–18

```
                       ;Procedure that reads data from the FIFO and returns
                       ;with it in AL
                       ;
= 0007                 MASKS    EQU      7

0000                   READ     PROC     FAR

                       ;test FIFO status

0000 E4 11                      IN    AL,STATUS          ;get status
0002 A8 07                      TEST  AL,MASKS           ;test NNN
0004 74 FA                      JZ    READ               ;if NNN = 000

                       ;read FIFO

0006 E4 10                      IN    AL,DATA            ;get data
0008 CB                         RET

0009                   READ     ENDP
```

The data found in AL upon returning from the subroutine contain raw data from the keyboard. Figure 9–29 shows the format of this data for both the scanned and strobed modes of operation. The scanned code is returned from our keyboard interface and is converted to ASCII code by using the XLAT instruction with an ASCII code lookup table. The scanned code is returned with the row and column number occupying the rightmost 6 bits. The SH shows the state of the shift pin and the CT bit shows the state of the control pin. In the strobed mode, the contents of the eight RL inputs appear as they are sampled by placing a logic one on the strobe input pin to the 8279.

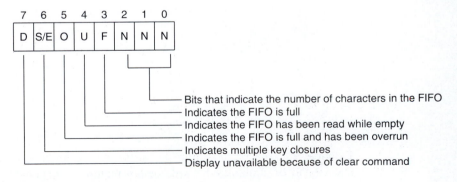

FIGURE 9–28   The 8279-5 FIFO status register.

FIGURE 9–29 The (a) scanned keyboard code and (b) strobed keyboard code for the 8279–5 FIFO.

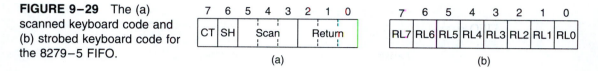

(a)

(b)

Six-Digit Display Interface

Figure 9–30 depicts the 8279 connected to the 8088 microprocessor and a 6-digit numeric display. This interface uses a PAL16L8 (program not shown) to decode the 8279 at I/O ports 20H (data) and 21H (control/status). The segment data are supplied to the displays through the OUTA and OUTB pins of the 8279. These bits are buffered by a segment driver (ULN2003A) to drive the segment inputs to the display.

A 74ALS138 3-to-8 line decoder enables the anode switches of each display position. The SL2–SL0 pins supply the decoder with the encoded display position from the 8279. Notice that the left-hand display is at position 0101 and the right-hand display is at position 0000. These are the addresses of the display positions as indicated in control words for the 8279.

It is necessary to choose resistor values that allow 60 mA of current flow per segment. In this circuit we use 47 Ω resistors. If we allow 60 mA of segment current, then the average segment current is 10 mA, or one sixth of 60 mA because current only flows for one sixth of the time through a segment. The anode switches must supply the current for all seven segments plus the decimal point. Here the total anode current is 8 × 60 mA or 480 mA.

Example 9–19 lists the initialization dialog for programming the 8279 to function with this 6-digit display. This software programs the display and clears the display RAM.

EXAMPLE 9–19

```
                        ;Initialization dialog for the 6-digit display
                        ;
                        ;program the clock

0000 B0 3E                      MOV   AL,00111110B
0002 E6 21                      OUT   CNTR,AL

                        ;program mode set

0004 B0 00                      MOV   AL,0
0006 E6 21                      OUT   CNTR,AL

                        ;clear display

0008 B0 C1                      MOV   AL,11000001B
000A E6 21                      OUT   CNTR,AL
```

Example 9–20 lists a procedure for displaying information on the displays. Data are transferred to the procedure through the AX register. AH contains the seven-segment display code and AL contains the address of the displayed digit.

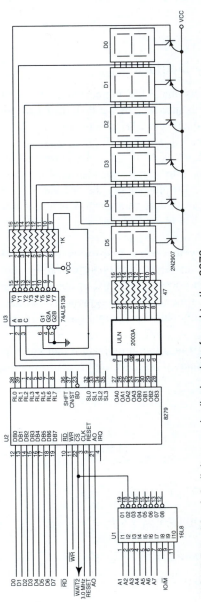

FIGURE 9–30 A 6-digit numeric display interfaced to the 8279.

EXAMPLE 9–20

```
                              ;Procedure to display AH on the display position
                              ;addressed by AL
                              ;
= 0080                        MASKS    EQU     80H

000C                          DISP     PROC    NEAR

000C 50                                PUSH AX                    ;save data
000D 0C 80                             OR    AL,MASKS             ;select display
000F E6 21                             OUT   CNTR,AL

                              ;display data

0011 8A C4                             MOV   AL,AH
0013 E6 20                             OUT   DATA,AL
0015 58                                POP   AX
0016 C3                                RET

0017                          DISP     ENDP
```

9–5   8254 PROGRAMMABLE INTERVAL TIMER

The 8254 programmable interval timer consists of three independent 16-bit programmable counters (timers). Each counter is capable of counting in binary or binary-coded decimal (BCD). The maximum allowable input frequency to any counter is 10 MHz. This device is useful wherever the microprocessor must control real-time events. Some examples of usage include: real-time clock, events counter, and motor speed and direction control.

This timer also appears in the personal computer decoded at ports 40H–43H to (1) generate a basic timer interrupt that occurs at approximately 18.2 Hz, (2) cause the DRAM memory system to be refreshed, and (3) provide a timing source to the internal speaker and other devices. The timer in the personal computer is an 8253 instead of an 8254.

8254 Functional Description

Figure 9–31 shows the pinout of the 8254, which is a higher-speed version of the 8253, and a diagram of one of the three counters. Each timer contains a CLK input, a gate input, and an output (OUT) connection. The CLK input provides the basic operating frequency to the timer, the gate pin controls the timer in some modes, and the OUT pin is where we obtain the output of the timer.

The signals that connect to the microprocessor are the data bus pins (D7–D0), $\overline{RD}$, $\overline{WR}$, $\overline{CS}$, and address inputs A1 and A0. The address inputs are present to select any of the four internal registers used for programming, reading, or writing to a counter. The personal computer contains an 8253 timer or its equivalent decoded at I/O ports 40H–43H. Timer zero is programmed to generate an 18.2 Hz signal that interrupts the microprocessor at interrupt vector 8 for a clock tick. The tick is often used to time

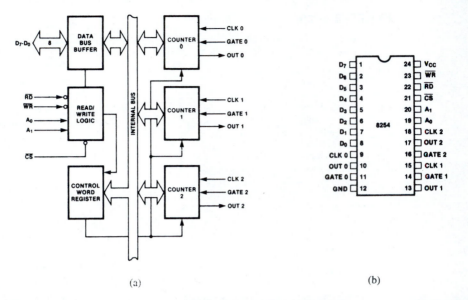

FIGURE 9–31   The 8254 programmable interval timer. (a) Internal structure. (b) Pinout. (Courtesy of Intel Corporation)

programs and events. Timer 1 is programmed for a 15 μs output that is used on the PC/XT personal computer to request a DMA action used to refresh the dynamic RAM. Timer 2 is programmed to generate tone on the personal computer speaker.

Pin Definitions

1. A1, A0—Address Inputs: select one of four internal registers within the 8254. See Table 9–6 for the function of the A1 and A0 address bits.
2. CLK—Clock Input: used as a timing source for each of the internal counters. This input is often connected to the PCLK signal from the microprocessor system bus controller.
3. $\overline{\text{CS}}$—Chip Select: enables the 8254 for programming and reading or writing a counter.
4. G—Gate Input: controls the operation of the counter in some modes of operation.
5. GND—Ground: connected to the system ground bus.
6. OUT—Counter Output: the output is where the waveform generated by the timer is available.

TABLE 9–6   Address selection inputs to the 8254

A1	A0	Function
0	0	Counter 0
0	1	Counter 1
1	0	Counter 2
1	1	Control word

7. $\overline{RD}$—Read: reads data from the 8254 with the $\overline{IORC}$ signal.
8. Vcc—Power: connected to the + 5.0 V power supply.
9. $\overline{WR}$—Write: writes data to the 8254 with the write strobe ($\overline{IOWC}$).

Programming the 8254

Each counter is individually programmed by writing a control word followed by the initial count. Figure 9–32 lists the program control word structure of the 8254. The control word allows the programmer to select the counter, mode of operation, and type of operation (read/write). The control word also selects either a binary or BCD count. Each counter may be programmed with a count of 1 to FFFFH. A count of 0 is equal to FFFFH+1 (65,536) or 10,000 in BCD. The minimum count of 1 applies to all modes of operation except modes 2 and 3, which have a minimum count of 2. Timer 0 is used in the personal computer with a divide by count of 64K (FFFFH) to generate the 18.2 Hz (18.19638 Hz) interrupt clock tick. Timer 0 has a clock input frequency of 4.77 MHz ÷ 4 or 1.1925 Mhz.

The control word uses the BCD bit to select a BCD count (BCD = 1) or a binary count (BCD = 0). The M2, M1, and M0 bits select one of the 6 different modes of operation (000–101) for the counter. The RW1 and RW0 bits determine how the data are read from or written to the counter. The SC1 and SC0 bits select a counter or the special read-back mode of operation discussed later in this section.

Each counter has a program control word used to select the way the counter operates. If 2 bytes are programmed into a counter, then the first byte (LSB) will stop the count, and the second byte (MSB) will start the counter with the new count. The order of programming is important for each counter, but programming of different counters may be interleaved for better control. For example, the control word may be sent to each counter before the counts for individual programming. Example 9–21 shows a few ways

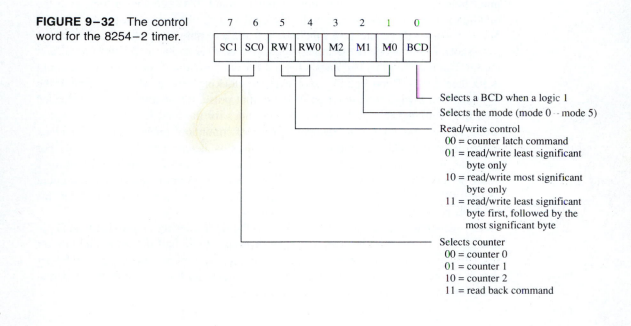

FIGURE 9–32 The control word for the 8254–2 timer.

to program counters 1 and 2. The first method programs both control words, then the LSB of the count for each counter, which stops them from counting. Finally, the MSB portion of the count is programmed starting both counters with the new count. The second example shows one counter programmed before the other.

EXAMPLE 9–21

```
PROGRAM CONTROL WORD 1          ;set up counter 1
PROGRAM CONTROL WORD 2          ;set up counter 2
PROGRAM LSB 1                   ;stop counter 1 and program LSB
PROGRAM LSB 2                   ;stop counter 2 and program LSB
PROGRAM MSB 1                   ;program MSB and start counter 1
PROGRAM MSB 2                   ;program MSB and start counter 2

    or

PROGRAM CONTROL WORD 1          ;set up counter 1
PROGRAM LSB 1                   ;stop counter 1 and program LSB
PROGRAM MSB 1                   ;program MSB and start counter 1
PROGRAM CONTROL WORD 2          ;set up counter 2
PROGRAM LSB 2                   ;stop counter 2 and program LSB
PROGRAM MSB 2                   ;program MSB and start counter 2
```

Modes of Operation.   Six modes (mode 0–mode 5) of operation are available to each of the 8254 counters. Figure 9–33 shows how each of these modes functions with the CLK input, the gate (G) control signal, and OUT signal. A description of each mode follows:

1. *Mode 0* allows the 8254 counter to be used as an events counter. In this mode, the output becomes a logic 0 when the control word is written and remains there until N plus the number of programmed counts. For example, if a count of 5 is programmed the output will remain a logic 0 for 6 counts beginning with N. Note that the gate (G) input must be a logic 1 to allow the counter to count. If G becomes a logic 0 in the middle of the count, the counter will stop until G again becomes a logic 1.

2. *Mode 1* causes the counter to function as a retriggerable monostable multivibrator (one-shot). In this mode the G input triggers the counter so that it develops a pulse at the OUT connection that becomes a logic 0 for the duration of the count. If the count is 10, then the OUT connection goes low for 10 clocking periods when triggered. If the G input occurs within the duration of the output pulse, the counter is again reloaded with the count and the OUT connection continues for the total length of the count.

3. *Mode 2* allows the counter to generate a series of continuous pulses that are one clock pulse in width. The separation between pulses is determined by the count. For example, for a count of 10, the output is a logic 1 for 9 clock periods and low for 1 clock period. This cycle is repeated until the counter is programmed with a new count or until the G pin is placed at a logic 0 level. The G input must be a logic 1 for this mode to generate a continuous series of pulses.

4. *Mode 3* generates a continuous square wave at the OUT connection provided the G pin is a logic 1. If the count is even, the output is high for one half the count and low for one half the count. If the count is odd, the output is high for one clocking period longer than it is low. For example, if the counter is programmed for a count of 5, the output is high for 3 clocks and low for 2.

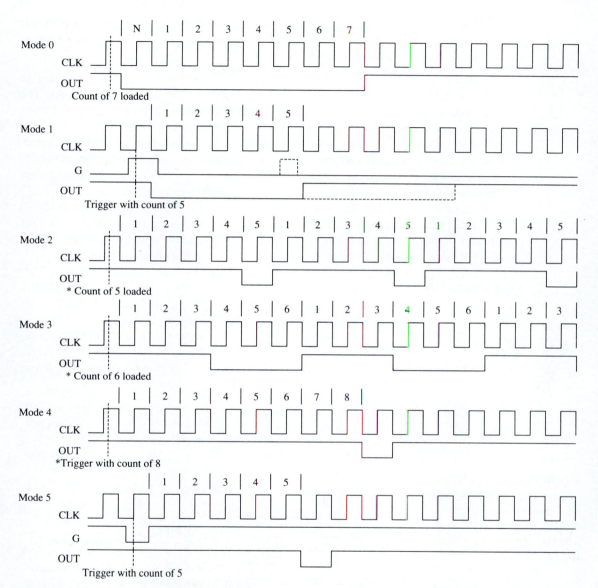

FIGURE 9-33 The six modes of operation for the 8254-2 programmable interval timer. *The G input stops the count when 0 in modes 2, 3, and 4.

5. *Mode 4* allows the counter to produce a single pulse at the output. If the count is programmed as a 10, the output is high for 10 clocking periods and then low for one clocking period. The cycle does not begin until the counter is loaded with its complete count. This mode operates as a software triggered one-shot. As with modes 2 and 3, this mode also uses the G input to enable the counter. The G input must be a logic 1 for the counter to operate for these three modes.

6. *Mode 5* is a hardware triggered one-shot that functions as mode 4 except it is started by a trigger pulse on the G pin instead of by software. This mode is also similar to mode 1 because it is retriggerable.

Generating a Waveform with the 8254.   Figure 9–34 shows an 8254 connected to function at I/O ports 0700H, 0702H, 0704H, and 0706H of an 8086 microprocessor. The addresses are decoded using a PAL16L8 that also generates a write strobe signal for the 8254, which is connected to the low order data bus connections. The PAL also generates a wait signal for the microprocessor that causes 2 waits states when the 8254 is accessed. The wait state generator connected to the microprocessor actually controls the number of wait states inserted into the timing. The program for the PAL is not illustrated here because it is basically the same as many of the other prior examples.

Example 9–22 lists the program that generates a 100 KHz square wave at OUT0 and a 200 KHz continuous pulse at OUT1. We use mode 3 for counter 0 and mode 2 for counter 1. The count programmed into counter 0 is 80 and the count for counter 1 is 40. These counts generate the desired output frequencies with an 8 MHz input clock.

EXAMPLE 9–22

```
                         ;Procedure that programs the 8254 timer to
                         ;function as indicated in Figure 9-34
                         ;
0000                     TIME     PROC     NEAR

0000 50                          PUSH AX                  ;save registers
0001 52                          PUSH DX

0002 BA 0706                     MOV   DX,706H            ;address control word
0005 B0 36                       MOV   AL,00110110B       ;mode 3
0007 EE                          OUT   DX,AL              ;program control for 0
0008 B0 74                       MOV   AL,01110100B       ;mode 2
```

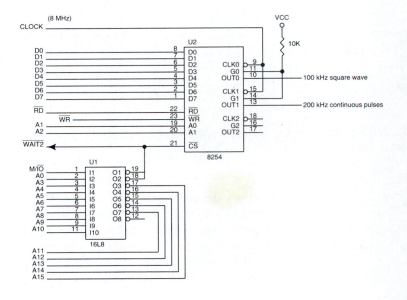

FIGURE 9–34   The 8254 interfaced to an 8 MHz 8086 so it generates a 100 KHz square wave at OUT0 and a 200KHz continous pulse at OUT1.

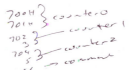

```
000A EE                        OUT    DX,AL                ;program control for 1

000B BA 0700                   MOV    DX,700H              ;address counter 0
000E B0 50                     MOV    AL,80                ;load count of 80
0010 EE                        OUT    DX,AL
0011 32 C0                     XOR    AL,AL
0013 EE                        OUT    DX,AL

0014 BA 0702                   MOV    DX,702H              ;address counter 1
0017 B0 28                     MOV    AL,40                ;load count of 40
0019 EE                        OUT    DX,AL
001A 32 C0                     XOR    AL,AL
001C EE                        OUT    DX,AL

001D 5A                        POP    DX                   ;restore registers
001E 58                        POP    AX
001F C3                        RET

0020             TIME    ENDP
```

Reading a Counter.   Each counter has an internal latch that is read with the read counter port operation. These latches will normally follow the count. If the contents of the counter are needed at a particular time, then the latch can remember the count by programming the counter latch control word (see Figure 9–35), which causes the contents of the counter to be held in a latch until it is read. Whenever a read from the latch or the counter is programmed, the latch tracks the contents of the counter.

When it is necessary for the contents of more than one counter to be read at the same time, we use the read-back control word illustrated in Figure 9–36. With the

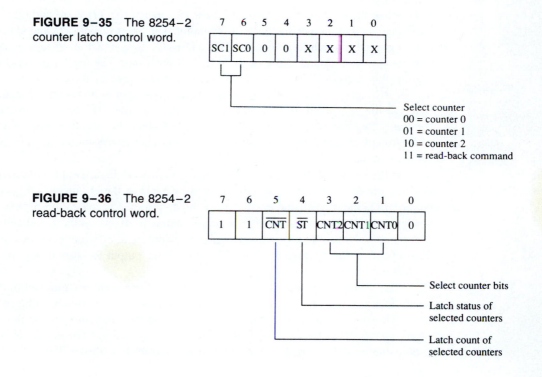

FIGURE 9–35 The 8254–2 counter latch control word.

FIGURE 9–36 The 8254–2 read-back control word.

FIGURE 9–37 The 8254–2 status register.

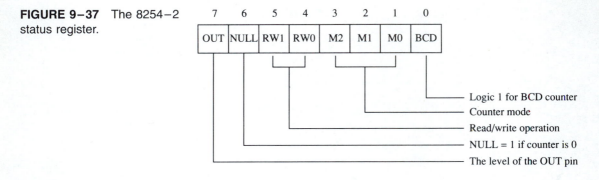

read-back control word, the $\overline{\text{CNT}}$ bit is a logic 0 to cause the counters selected by CNT0, CNT1, and CNT2 to be latched. If the status register is to be latched, then the $\overline{\text{ST}}$ bit is placed at a logic 0. Figure 9–37 shows the status register, which shows the state of the output pin, whether the counter is at its null state (0), and how the counter is programmed.

DC Motor Speed and Direction Control

One application of the 8254 timer is as a motor speed controller for a DC motor. Figure 9–38 shows the schematic diagram of the motor and its associated driver circuitry. It also illustrates the interconnection of the 8254, a flip-flop, and the motor and its driver.

The operation of the motor driver circuitry is fairly straightforward. If the Q output of the 74ALS112 is a logic 1, the base Q2 is pulled up to +12 V through the base pullup resistor and the base of Q2 is open circuited. This means that Q1 is off and Q2 is on, with ground applied to the positive lead of the motor. The bases of both Q3 and Q4 are pulled low to ground through the inverters. This causes Q3 to conduction or turn on and Q4 to turn off applying ground to the negative lead of the motor. The logic 1 at the Q output of the flip-flop therefore connects +12 V to the positive lead of the motor and ground to the negative lead. This connection causes the motor to spin in its forward direction. If the state of the Q output of the flip-flop becomes a logic 0, then the conditions of the transistors are reversed and +12 V is attached to the negative lead of the motor with ground attached to the positive lead. This causes the motor to spin in the reverse direction.

If the output of the flip-flop is alternated between a logic 1 and 0, the motor spins in either direction at various speeds. If the duty cycle of the Q output is 50 percent, the motor will not spin at all and exhibits some holding torque because current flows through it. Figure 9–39 shows some timing diagrams and their effects on the speed and direction of the motor. Notice how each counter generates pulses at different positions to vary the duty cycle at the Q output of the flip-flop. This output is also called pulse-width modulation.

To generate these waveforms, counters 0 and 1 are both programmed to divide the input clock (PCLK) by 30,720. We change the duty cycle of Q by changing the point at which counter 1 is started in relationship to counter 0. This changes the direction and speed of the motor. But why divide the 8MHz clock by 30,720? The divide rate of 30,720 is divisible by 256 so we can develop a short program that allows 256 different speeds.

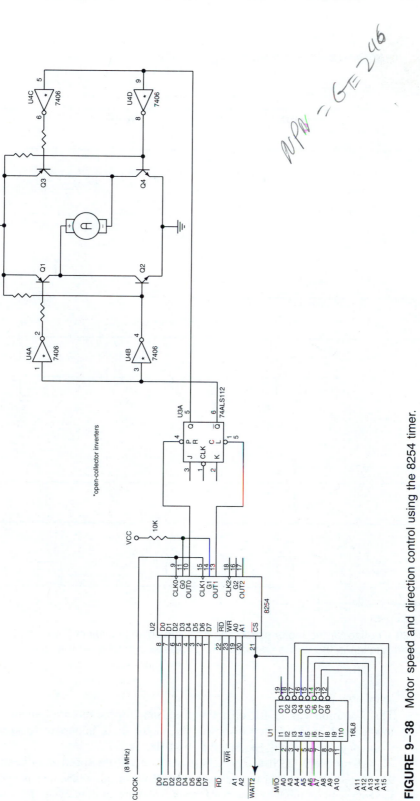

FIGURE 9–38 Motor speed and direction control using the 8254 timer.

387

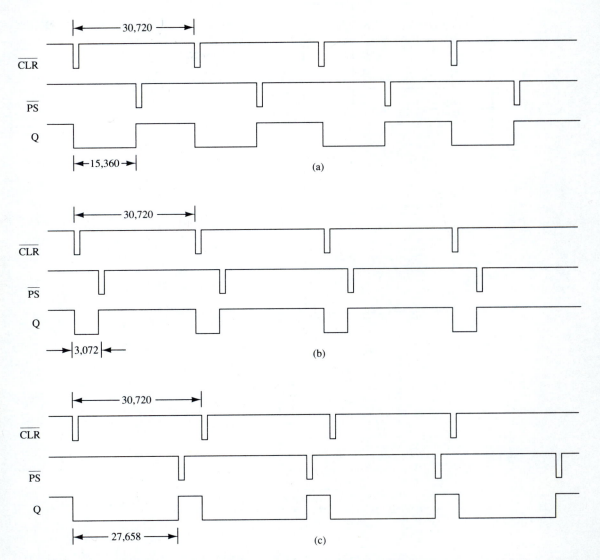

FIGURE 9–39 Timing for the motor speed and direction control circuit of Figure 9–38. (a) No rotation. (b) High-speed rotation in the reverse direction. (c) High-speed rotation in the forward direction.

This also produces a basic operating frequency for the motor of about 260 Hz, which is low enough in frequency to power the motor. It is important to keep this operating frequency below 1,000 Hz, but above 60 Hz.

Example 9–23 lists a procedure that controls the speed and direction of the motor. The speed is controlled by the value of AH when this procedure is called. Because we have an 8-bit number to represent speed, a 50 percent duty cycle, for a stopped motor, is a count of 128. By changing the value in AH, when the procedure is called, we can adjust the motor speed. The speed of the motor will increase in either direction by changing the number in AH when this procedure is called. As the value in AH approaches 00H, the motor begins to increase its speed in the reverse direction. As the value of AH approaches FFH, the motor increases its speed in the forward direction.

EXAMPLE 9–23

```
                        ;Procedure that controls the duty cycle of Q and
                        ;therefore the speed and direction of the motor.
                        ;
                        ;AH contains a number between 00H and FFH that
                        ;selects both direction and speed of the motor.
                        ;
= 0706                  CNTR    EQU    706H            ;control port
= 0700                  CNT0    EQU    700H            ;counter 0 port
= 0702                  CNT1    EQU    702H            ;counter 1 port
= 7800                  COUNT   EQU    30720           ;count of 30,720

0000                    SPEED   PROC   NEAR

0000 50                         PUSH AX                ;save registers
0001 51                         PUSH DX
000253                          PUSH BX

                        ;calculate count

0003 8A DC                      MOV   BL,AH
0005 B8 0078                    MOV   AX,120
0008 F6 E3                      MUL   BL
000A 8B D8                      MOV   BX,AX
000C B8 7800                    MOV   AX,COUNT
000F 2B C3                      SUB   AX,BX
0011 8B D8                      MOV   BX,AX

                        ;program counter control words

0013 BA 0706                    MOV   DX,CNTR          ;load port address of control
0016 B0 34                      MOV   AL,00110100B     ;control for CNT0
0018 EE                         OUT   DX,AL
0019 B0 74                      MOV   AL,01110100B     ;control for CNT1
001B EE                         OUT   DX,AL

                        ;start counter 1 to generate clear

001C BA 0702                    MOV   DX,CNT1          ;address counter 1
001F B8 7800                    MOV   AX,COUNT         ;get count
0022 EE                         OUT   DX,AL            ;stop counter 1
0023 8A C4                      MOV   AL,AH
0025 EE                         OUT   DX,AL            ;start counter 1

                        ;wait for counter 1 to reach calculated count

0026                    SPE:

0026 EC                         IN    AL,DX            ;get count
0027 86 C4                      XCHG AL,AH
0029 EC                         IN    AL,DX
002A 86 C4                      XCHG AL,AH
002C 3B C3                      CMP   AX,BX            ;test count
002E 72 F6                      JB    SPE              ;if CNT1 below count

                        ;start counter 0 to generate set
```

```
0030 BA 0700              MOV   DX,CNT0      ;address counter 0
0033 B8 7800              MOV   AX,COUNT     ;get count
0036 EE                   OUT   DX,AL        ;stop counter 0
0037 8A C4                MOV   AL,AH
0039 EE         .         OUT   DX,AL        ;start counter 1

003A 5B                   POP   BX           ;restore registers
003B 5A                   POP   DX
003C 58                   POP   AX
003D C3                   RET

003E            SPEED     ENDP
```

The procedure adjusts the waveform at Q by first calculating the count that counter 0 is to start in relationship to counter 1. This is accomplished by multiplying AH by 120 and then subtracting it from 30,720. This is required because the counters are down-counters that count from the programmed count to 0, before restarting. Next counter 1 is programmed with a count of 30,720 and started to generate the clear waveform for the flip-flop. After counter 1 is started, it is read and compared with the calculated count. Once it reaches this count, counter 0 is started with a count of 30,720. From this point forward, both counters continue generating the clear and set waveforms until the procedure is again called to adjust the speed and direction of the motor.

9-6   8251A PROGRAMMABLE COMMUNICATIONS INTERFACE

The 8251A is a programmable communications interface designed to connect to virtually any type of serial interface. The 8251A is a *universal synchronous/ asynchronous receiver/transmitter* (USART) that is fully compatible with the Intel microprocessors provided that 2 wait states are inserted if operated at 8 MHz. For connection to higher speed microprocessors, additional wait states must be inserted. The 8251A is capable of operating at 0–64 KBaud (Bd—bits per second) in the synchronous mode and 0–19.2 KBd in the asynchronous mode. *Baud rate* is the number of bits transferred per second, including start, stop, data, and parity. The programmer of the 8251A selects the number of data bits, number of stop bits, type of parity (even or odd), and the clock rate in the asynchronous mode. In the synchronous mode, the programmer selects the number of data bits, parity, and the number of synchronization characters (one or two).

Asynchronous Serial Data

Asynchronous serial data is information that is transmitted and received without a clock or timing signal. Figure 9–40 illustrates two frames of asynchronous serial data. Each frame contains a start bit, seven data bits, parity, and one stop bit. In this figure, a frame, which contains one ASCII character, has 10 bits. Most communications systems use 10 bits for asynchronous serial data with even parity.

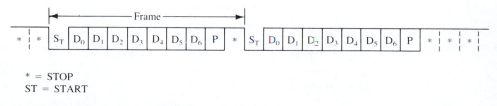

* = STOP
ST = START

FIGURE 9–40 Asynchronous serial data.

Synchronous Serial Data

Figure 9–41 shows the format of synchronous serial data. Notice that this information contains no start or stop bits, only data and parity. Also notice that the data are referenced or synchronized to a clock or timing element. Instead of using the start and stop bits for synchronizing each character, synchronous data use a sync character or characters to synchronize blocks of data. A sync character or characters are sent followed by a block of data in a synchronous system. If we use 2 sync characters, the system is called *bi-sync*, and is the most common. The advantage of the synchronous system is that more bits of information are transferred per second, but the disadvantage is that the clock signal must also be transmitted with the data.

8251A Functional Description

Figure 9–42 illustrates the pinout of the 8251A USART. Two completely separate sections are responsible for data communications: the receiver and the transmitter. Because each of these sections is independent of each other, the 8251A is able to function in *simplex, half-duplex,* or *full-duplex* modes.

An example simplex system is where the transmitter or receiver is used by itself such as in an FM (frequency modulation) radio station. An example half-duplex system is a CB (citizens band) radio where we transmit and receive, but not both at the same time. The full-duplex system allows transmission and reception in both directions simultaneously. An example full-duplex system is the telephone.

The 8251A can control a *modem* (modulator/demodulator), which is a device that converts TTL levels of serial data into audio tones that can pass through the telephone system. Four pins on the 8251A are devoted to modem control: $\overline{\text{DSR}}$ (data set ready), $\overline{\text{DTR}}$ (data terminal ready), $\overline{\text{CTS}}$ (clear-to-send), and $\overline{\text{RTS}}$ (request-to-send). The modem is referred to as the *data set* and the 8251A is referred to as the *data terminal*.

Pin Functions

1. $C/\overline{D}$—Command/Data Input: selects either the command/status register or data for the transmitter or from the receiver. This pin is a logic 1 to access the command/status register and a logic 0 to access data.

FIGURE 9–41 Synchronous serial data.

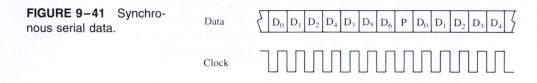

Data

Clock

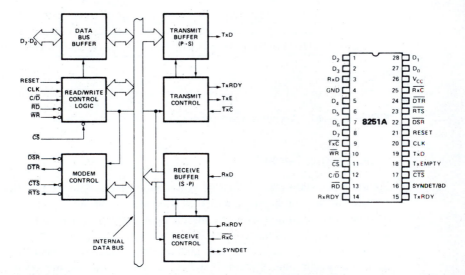

FIGURE 9–42   The pinout and block diagram of the 8251A programmable communications interface. (Courtesy of Intel Corporation)

2. CLK—Clock Input: provides the 8251A with its timing source. The frequency of the clock signal must be 3.125 MHz or less. This input does not determine the transmission rate of the digital data, but it must be at least 16 times higher than the transmit or receive clocks.

3. $\overline{CS}$—Chip Select: enables the 8251A when a logic 0.

4. $\overline{CTS}$—Clear-to-Send: is a return signal from the modem that indicates it is ready to begin sending information. Note that this pin must be grounded in order to transmit data.

5. D7–D0—Data Bus: pins that connect to the data bus.

6. $\overline{DSR}$—Data Set Ready: an inverting input used to test the $\overline{DSR}$ signal from the modem (data set). The $\overline{DSR}$ input indicates that the data set is ready to begin transferring information.

7. $\overline{DTR}$—Data Terminal Ready: an inverting output that signals the data set that the data terminal (8251A) is ready to transfer information.

8. RESET—Reset Input: clears the internal circuitry of the 8251A selecting the synchronous mode of operation. This input is connected to the RESET signal on the system bus.

9. $\overline{RD}$—Read Input: used to read data from the receiver or to read the status register.

10. $\overline{RTS}$—Request-to-Send: an inverting output that signals the data set that the 8251A is requesting that the line be turned around for transmission. This signal is used in the half-duplex mode of operation.

11. $\overline{RxC}$—Receiver Clock: provides a timing signal for the receiver.

12. RxD—Receiver Data: accepts serial data for the receiver.

13. RxRDY—Receiver Ready: shows that the receiver has received a serial datum that is ready for transfer, in parallel, for the microprocessor from the 8251A.

14. SY/BD—Sync Detect/Break Detect: an output that indicates either synchronization in the synchronous mode or the receipt of a break character in the asynchronous mode. A break character is two complete frames of start pulses and is often used to break communications.
15. $\overline{T \times C}$—Transmitter Clock: provides the 8251A transmitter with its Baud rate determining clock frequency. This input can be scaled by factors of 1, 16, or 64 in the asynchronous mode, and represents the actual Baud rate for synchronous operation.
16. T×D—Transmit Data: serial data output connection.
17. T×EMPTY—Transmitter Empty: indicates that the transmitter, within the 8251A, has finished transmitting all data.
18. T×RDY—Transmitter Ready: a signal that indicates the transmitter, within the 8251A, is ready to receive another character for transmission.
19. $\overline{WR}$—Write Input: strobes data into the transmitter or the internal command register for programming.

Programming the 8251A

Programming the 8251A is simple when compared to some of the other programmable interfaces described in this chapter. Programming is a two-part process that includes initialization dialog and operational dialog.

Initialization dialog, which occurs after a hardware or software reset, consists of two parts: reset and mode. Because of an apparent design flaw, the 8251A does not reset properly from the RESET input pin. Instead, it must be reset by a series of instructions that send the command register three 00H's followed by a 40H (the software reset command).

Once the 8251A is reset, it may be programmed with the mode word, which directs the 8251A to function as either an asynchronous or synchronous device. Figure 9–43 shows both the synchronous and asynchronous mode command words. Both words specify the number of data bits and parity. In the asynchronous mode, the number of stop bits and clock divider are programmed and in the synchronous mode, the number of sync characters and the function of SY are programmed. The SY pin is programmed as either an input, which indicates synchronization, or as an output, which indicates the sync characters have been received.

In the asynchronous mode, once the mode instruction is programmed, the initialization programming is complete. In the synchronous mode, the one or two sync characters are programmed following the mode command to complete initialization programming.

Suppose that an asynchronous system requires seven data bits, odd parity, a clock divider of 64, and one stop bit. Example 9–24 lists a procedure that initializes the 8251A to function in this manner. Figure 9–44 shows the interface to the 8086 microprocessor using a PAL16L8 to decode the 8-bit port addresses FDH and FFH. Here port FDH accesses the data register and FFH the command register. Notice that the Baud clock input is 76,800 Hz and the transmitted and received serial data are at 1200 Baud. The reason is that the Baud rate multiplier is programmed to divide the input clock by a factor of 64 in this example.

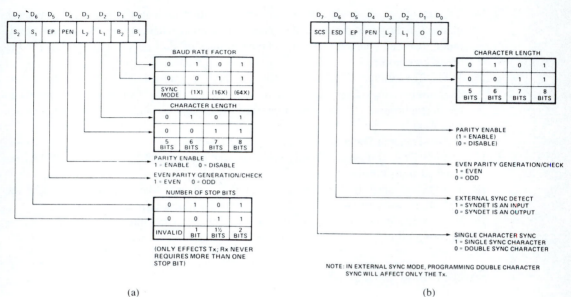

FIGURE 9–43 8251A mode instruction words. (a) Asynchronous. (b) Synchronous. (Courtesy of Intel Corporation)

FIGURE 9–44 The 8251A interfaced to the upper data bus of the 8086 at I/O ports FDH and FFH.

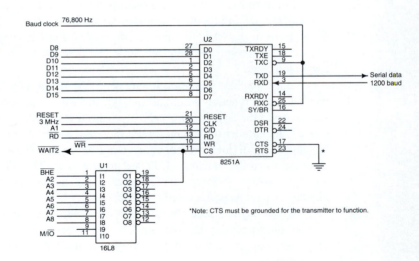

*Note: CTS must be grounded for the transmitter to function.

EXAMPLE 9–24

```
              ;Initialization procedure for the 8251A used in
              ;asynchronous operation.
              ;
= 00FF        CNTR    EQU     0FFH            ;command port
= 0040        RESET   EQU     40H             ;reset code

0000          PROG    PROC    NEAR

0000 50               PUSH AX                 ;save AX
```

```
                                ;reset the 8251A

0001 32 C0                              XOR    AL,AL
0003 E6 FF                              OUT    CNTR,AL
0005 E6 FF                              OUT    CNTR,AL
0007 E6 FF                              OUT    CNTR,AL
0009 B0 40                              MOV    AL,RESET
000B E6 FF                              OUT    CNTR,AL


                                ;program mode

000D B0 5B                              MOV    AL,01011011B
000F E6 FF                              OUT    CNTR,AL


                                ;enable receiver and transmitter

0011 B0 15                              MOV    AL,00010101B
0013 E6 FF                              OUT    CNTR,AL

0015 58                                 POP    AX                      ;restore AX
0016 C3                                 RET

0017                      PROG          ENDP
```

If the 8251A is operated in synchronous mode, the programming sequence is very similar except that one or two sync characters are also programmed. Example 9–25 lists a procedure that programs the 8251A for synchronous operation using seven data bits, even parity, SY as an output, and two sync characters.

EXAMPLE 9–25

```
                                ;Initialization procedure for the 8251A used in
                                ;synchronous operation.
                                ;
= 00FF                  CNTR    EQU    0FFH                    ;command port
= 0040                  RESET   EQU    40H                     ;reset code
= 007F                  SYNC1   EQU    7FH                     ;sync code 1
= 007E                  SYNC2   EQU    7EH                     ;sync code 2


0000                    PROGS   PROC   NEAR

0000 50                                 PUSH AX                ;save AX


                                ;reset the 8251A

0001 32 C0                              XOR    AL,AL
0003 E6 FF                              OUT    CNTR,AL
0005 E6 FF                              OUT    CNTR,AL
0007 E6 FF                              OUT    CNTR,AL
0009 B0 40                              MOV    AL,RESET
000B E6 FF                              OUT    CNTR,AL


                                ;program mode

000D B0 B8                              MOV    AL,10111000B
000F E6 FF                              OUT    CNTR,AL


                                ;program sync characters
```

```
0011 B0 7F                     MOV   AL,SYNC1
0013 E6 FF                     OUT   CNTR,AL
0015 B0 7E                     MOV   AL,SYNC2
0017 E6 FF                     OUT   CNTR,AL

                      ;enable receiver and transmitter

0019 B0 15                     MOV   AL,00010101B
001B E6 FF                     OUT   CNTR,AL

001D 58                        POP   AX                        ;restore AX
001E C3                        RET

001F          PROGS            ENDP
```

After the mode instruction is programmed into the 8251A, it is still not ready to function. After programming the mode, in asynchronous operation, and after programming the mode and sync characters, in synchronous operation, we still must program the command register. Figure 9–45 illustrates the command word for the 8251A. The command word enables the transmitter and receiver, controls DTR and RTS, sends a break character in asynchronous mode, resets errors, resets the 8251A, and enters the hunt mode for synchronous operation. Refer to example command words as programmed in Examples 9–24 and 9–25.

FIGURE 9–45 The 8251A command word. (Courtesy of Intel Corporation)

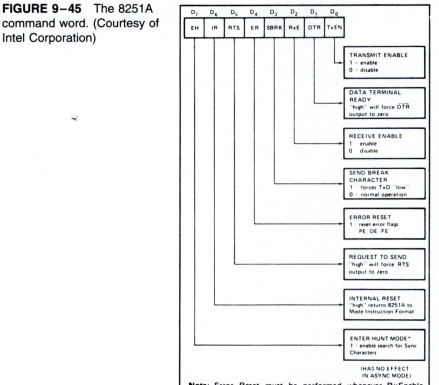

Before it is possible to write software to send or receive serial data through the 8251A, we need to know the function of the status register (see Figure 9–46). The status word contains information about error conditions, the states of DSR, SY/BD, TxEMPTY, RxRDY, and TxRDY.

Suppose that a procedure (see Example 9–26) is written to transmit the contents of AH to the 8251A and out through its serial data pin (TxD). The TxRDY bit is polled by software to determine if the transmitter is ready to receive data. This procedure uses the circuit of Figure 9–44.

EXAMPLE 9–26

```
                    ;Procedure that transmits the contents of AH
                    ;
= 00FF              CNTR    EQU    0FFH                    ;command port
= 00FD              DATA    EQU    0FDH                    ;data port

0000                SEND    PROC   NEAR

0000 50                     PUSH AX                        ;save AX
```

FIGURE 9–46 The 8251A status word. (Courtesy of Intel Corporation)

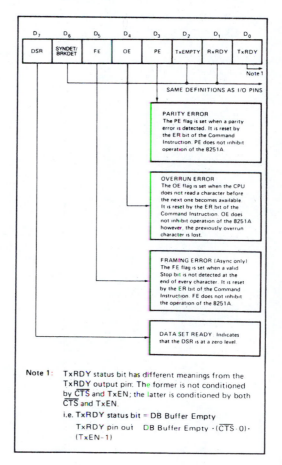

```
                              ;test TxRDY

0001                    SEND1:

0001 E4 FF                       IN    AL,CNTR          ;read status
0003 D0 C8                       ROR   AL,1             ;rotate TxRDY to CF
0005 73 FA                       JNC   SEND1            ;if not ready

                              ;transmit data

0007 8A C4                       MOV   AL,AH
0009 E6 FD                       OUT   DATA,AL

000B 58                          POP   AX               ;restore AX
000C C3                          RET

000D                    SEND    ENDP
```

To read received information from the 8251A we test the RxRDY bit of the status register. Example 9–27 lists a procedure that tests the RxRDY bit to decide if the 8251A has received data. Upon reception of data, the procedure tests for errors. If an error is detected, the procedure returns with AL = ?. If no error has occurred, then the procedure returns with AL equal to the received character.

EXAMPLE 9–27

```
                         ;Procedure that receives data from the 8251A
                         ;
= 00FF                   CNTR    EQU    0FFH           ;command port
= 00FD                   DATA    EQU    0FDH           ;data port
= 0004                   MASKS   EQU    4              ;RxRDY mask
= 0038                   ERROR   EQU    38H            ;error mask
= 0015                   E_Res   EQU    15H            ;error reset
= 003F                   QUES    EQU    '?'            ;question mark

0000                     RECV    PROC   NEAR

                         ;test RxRDY

0000                     RECV1:

0000 E4 FF                       IN    AL,CNTR          ;read status
0002 A8 04                       TEST  AL,MASKS         ;test RxRDY
0004 74 FA                       JZ    RECV1            ;if not ready

                         ;test for errors

0006 A8 38                       TEST  AL,ERROR
0008 75 03                       JNZ   ERR              ;if an error

                         ;read data

000A E4 FD                       IN    AL,DATA
000C C3                          RET

                         ;error

000D                     ERR:

000D B0 15                       MOV   AL,E_RES         ;reset error
```

```
000F E6 FF                 OUT   CNTR,AL
0011 B0 3F                 MOV   AL,QUES              ;get ?
0013 C3                    RET

0014            RECV        ENDP
```

The types of errors detected by the 8251A are: parity error, framing error, and overrun error. A parity error indicates that the received data contain the wrong parity. A framing error indicates that the start and stop bits are not in their proper places. An overrun error indicates that data have overrun the internal receiver buffer. These errors should not occur during normal operation. If a parity error occurs, it indicates that noise was encountered during reception. A framing error occurs if the receiver is receiving data at an incorrect Baud rate. An overrun error only occurs if the software fails to read the data from the USART.

9–7   ANALOG-TO-DIGITAL (ADC) AND DIGITAL-TO-ANALOG CONVERTERS (DAC)

Analog-to digital (ADC) and digital-to-analog (DAC) converters are used to interface the microprocessor to the analog world. Many events that are monitored and controlled by the microprocessor are analog events. These often include monitoring all forms of events, even speech, to controlling motors and like devices. In order to interface the microprocessor to these events, we must have an understanding of the interface and control of the ADC and DAC, which convert between analog and digital data.

The DAC0830 Digital-to-Analog Converter

A fairly common and low-cost digital-to-analog converter is the DAC0830.[2] This device is an 8-bit converter that transforms an 8-bit binary number into an analog voltage. Other converters are available that convert from 10, 12, or 16 bits into analog voltages. The number of voltage steps generated by the converter is equal to the number of binary input combinations. Therefore, an 8-bit converter generates 256 different voltage levels, a 10-bit converter generates 1,024 levels, and so forth. The DAC0830 is a medium speed converter that transforms a digital input to an analog output in approximately 1.0 μs.

Figure 9–47 illustrates the pinout of the DAC0830. This device has a set of eight data bus connections for the application of the digital input code and a pair of analog outputs labeled Iout1 and Iout2 that are designed as inputs to an external operational amplifier. Because this is an 8-bit converter, its output step voltage is defined as −Vref (reference voltage) divided by 255. For example, if the reference voltage is −5.0 V, its output step voltage is +.0196078431373 V. Note that the output voltage is the opposite polarity of the reference voltage. If an input of 1001 0010 is applied to the device, the output voltage will be the step voltage times 1001 0010, or in this case +2.86274509804 V.

---

[2]The DAC0830 is a product of National Semiconductor Corporation.

FIGURE 9-47 The pinout of the DAC0830 digital-to-analog converter.

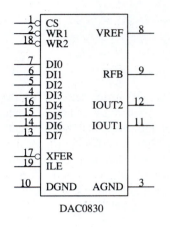

DAC0830

By changing the reference voltage to −5.1 V, the step voltage becomes +.02 V. The step voltage is also often called the resolution of the converter.

Internal Structure of the DAC0830.   Figure 9–48 illustrates the internal structure of the DAC0830. Notice that this device contains two internal registers. The first is a holding register while the second connects to the R-2R internal ladder converter. The two latches allow one byte to be held while another is converted. In many cases we disable the first latch and only use the second for entering data into the converter. This is accomplished by connecting a logic 1 to ILE and a logic zero to $\overline{CS}$ (chip select).

Both latches within the DAC0830 are transparent latches. When the G input to the latch is a logic 1, data pass through the latch, but when the G input becomes a logic 0, data are latched or held. The converter has a reference input pin (Vref) that establishes the full scale output voltage. If −10 V is placed on Vref, the full scale (1111 1111) output

FIGURE 9-48 The internal structure of the DAC0830.

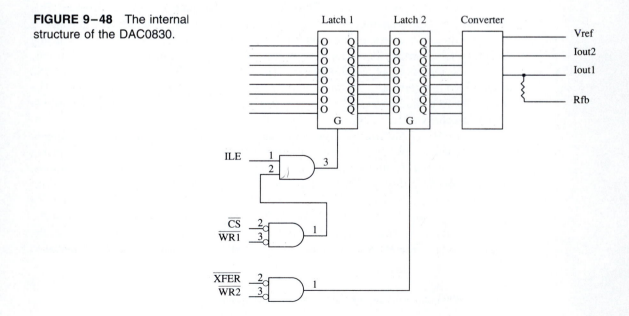

voltage is +10 V. The output of the R-2R ladder within the converter appears at Iout1 and Iout2. These outputs are designed to be applied to an operational amplifier such as a 741 or similar device.

Connecting the DAC0830 to the Microprocessor. The DAC0830 is connected to the microprocessor as illustrated in Figure 9–49. Here a PAL16L8 is used to decode the DAC0830 at 8-bit I/O port address 20H. Whenever an OUT 20H,AL instruction is executed, the contents of data bus connection AD0–AD7 are passed to the converter within the DAC0830. The 741 operational amplifier along with the −12V zener reference voltage causes the full-scale output voltage to equal +12 V. The output of the operational amplifier feeds a driver that powers a 12 V DC motor. This driver is a darlington amplifier for large motors. This example shows the converter driving a motor, but other devices could be used as an output.

The ADC080X Analog-to-Digital Converter

A common low-cost ADC is the ADC0804, which belongs to a family of converters that are all identical except for accuracy. This device is compatible with a wide range of microprocessors such as the 8086. There are faster ADCs available and some with more resolution than 8 bits, but this device is ideal for many applications that do not require a high degree of accuracy. The ADC0804 requires up to 100 μs to convert an analog input voltage into a digital output code.

Figure 9–50 shows the pinout of the ADC0804[3] converter. To operate the converter, the $\overline{WR}$ pin is pulsed with $\overline{CS}$ grounded to start the conversion process. Because this converter requires a considerable amount of time for the conversion, a pin

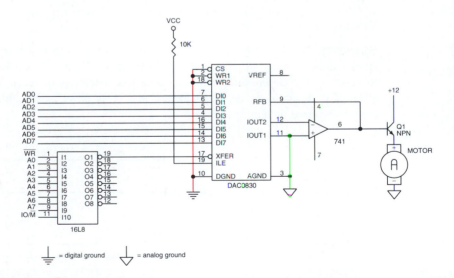

FIGURE 9–49 A DAC0830 interfaced to the 8086 microprocessor at 8-bit I/O location 20H.

---

[3]The ADC0804 is a product of National Semiconductor Corporation.

FIGURE 9–50   The pinout of the ADC0804 analog-to-digital converter.

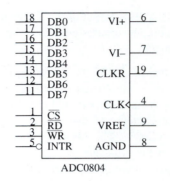

ADC0804

labeled INTR signals the end of the conversion. Refer to Figure 9–51 for a timing diagram that shows the interaction of the control signals. As can be seen, we start the converter with the $\overline{WR}$ pulse, we wait for INTR to return to a logic 0 level, and then we read the data from the converter. If a time delay is used that allows at least 100 μs of time, then we don't need to test the INTR pin. Another option is to connect the INTR pin to an interrupt input so when the conversion is complete, an interrupt occurs.

The Analog Input Signal.   Before the ADC0804 can be connected to the microprocessor, its analog inputs must be understood. There are two analog inputs to the ADC0804: Vin (+) and Vin (–). These inputs are connected to an internal operational amplifier and are differential inputs as shown in Figure 9–52. The differential inputs are summed by the operational amplifier to produce a signal for the internal analog-to-digital converter. Figure 9–52 shows a few ways to use these differential inputs. The first way (Figure 9–52a) uses a single input that can vary between 0 V and + 5.0 V. The second (Figure 9–52b) shows a variable voltage applied to the Vin (–) pin so the zero reference for VIN (+) can be adjusted.

Generating the Clock Signal.   The ADC0804 requires a clock source for operation. The clock can be an external clock applied to the CLK IN pin or it can be generated with an RC circuit. The permissible range of clock frequencies is between 100 KHz and 1460 KHz. It is desirable to use a frequency that is as close as possible to 1460 KHz so conversion time is kept to a minimum.

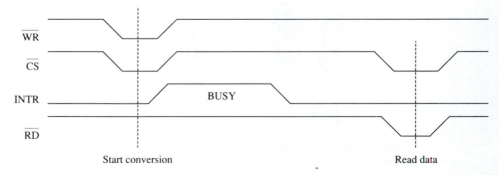

FIGURE 9–51   The timing for the ADC0804 analog-to-digital converter.

FIGURE 9–52 The analog inputs to the ADC0804 converter. (a) To sense a 0- to +5.0–V input. (b) To sense an input offset from ground.

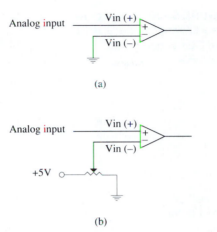

If the clock is generated with an RC circuit, we use the CLK IN and CLK R pins connected to an RC circuit as illustrated in Figure 9–53. When this connection is in use, the clock frequency is calculated by the following equation:

$$\text{Fclk} = \frac{1}{1.1\ RC}$$

Connecting the ADC0804 to the Microprocessor. The ADC0804 is interfaced to the 8088 microprocessor as illustrated in Figure 9–54. Note the Vref signal is not attached to anything and this is normal. Suppose that the ADC0804 is decoded at 8-bit I/O port address 40H for the data and port address 42H for the INTR signal and a procedure is required to start and read the data from the ADC. This procedure is listed in Example 9–28. Notice that the INTR bit is polled and if it becomes a logic 0, the procedure ends with AL containing the converted digital code.

EXAMPLE 9–28

```
                      ;Procedure that reads data from the ADC and returns
                      ;with it in AL
                      ;
0000                  ADCX    PROC    NEAR

0000 E6 40                    OUT    40H,AL               ;start conversion

0002                  ADCX1:

0002 E4 42                    IN     AL,42H               ;read INTR
0004 A8 80                    TEST   AL,80H               ;test INTR
0006 75 FA                    JNZ    ADCX1                ;repeat until INTR = 0

0008 E4 40                    IN     AL,40H               ;get data from ADC
000A C3                       RET

000B                  ADCX    ENDP
```

FIGURE 9–53 Connecting the RC circuit to the CLK IN and CLK R pins on the ADC0804.

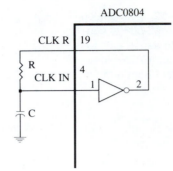

FIGURE 9–54 The ADC0804 interfaced to the microprocessor.

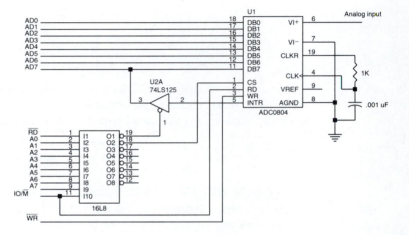

Using the ADC0804 and the DAC0830

This section of the text illustrates an example using both the ADC0804 and the DAC0830 to capture and replay audio signals or speech. In the past we often used a speech synthesizer to generate speech, but the quality of the speech was poor. For human quality speech we can use the ADC0804 to capture an audio signal and store it in memory for later playback through the DAC0830.

Figure 9–55 illustrates the circuitry required to connect the ADC0804 at 16-bit I/O ports 0700H and 0702H. The DAC0830 is interfaced at I/O port 704H. The software used to run these converters appears in Example 9–29. This software reads a 1 second burst of speech and then plays it back 10 times. This process repeats until the system is turned off.

EXAMPLE 9–29 (page 1 of 4)

```
                ;Software that records a 1 second passage of speech and
                ;plays it back 10 times before recording the next 1 second
                ;of speech.
                ;
                ;Assumes that the clock is 8 MHz
                ;
0000            STAC    SEGMENT STACK

0000 0800 [             DW     2048 DUP (?)          ;stack space
```

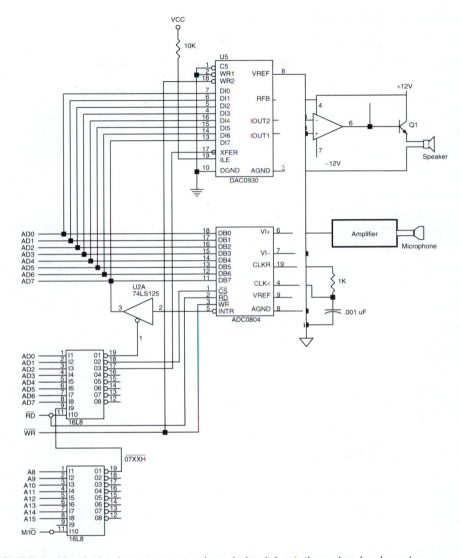

FIGURE 9-55 A circuit to store speech and play it back through a loudspeaker.

EXAMPLE 9-29 (page 2 of 4)

```
            0000
                    ]

1000                    STAC    ENDS

0000                    DATA1   SEGMENT 'DATA'

0000 03E8 [             WORDS   DB  1000 DUP (?)          ;space for 1 second of speech
        00
            ]
```

EXAMPLE 9–29 (page 3 of 4)

```
03E8                    DATA1   ENDS

0000                    CODE1   SEGMENT 'CODE'

                        ASSUME    CS:CODE1,DS:DATA1,SS:STAC

0000                    START   PROC    FAR

0000 B8 ---- R          MOV  AX,DATA1            ;load DS
0003 8E D8              MOV  DS,AX
0005 33 C0              XOR  AX,AX               ;load ES
0007 8E C0              MOV  ES,AX

0009 E8 000A            CALL  READ               ;read speech

000C B9 000A            MOV  CX,10

000F            START1:

000F E8 0023            CALL WRITE               ;talk
0012 E2 FB              LOOP START1              ;repeat 10 times

0014 EB EA              JMP  START               ;redo all

0016            START   ENDP

0016       READ         PROC    NEAR

0016 BF 0000 R          MOV  DI,OFFSET WORDS     ;address data
0019 B9 03E8            MOV  CX,1000             ;load count
001C BA 0700            MOV  DX,0700H            ;address port

001F            READ1:

001F EE                 OUT  DX,AL               ;start converter
0020 83 C2 02           ADD  DX,2

0023            READ2:

0023 EC                 IN   AL,DX               ;get INTR
0024 A8 80              TEST AL,80H              ;test INTR
0026 75 FB              JNZ  READ2               ;wait for INTR = 0

0028 83 EA 02           SUB  DX,2
002B EC                 IN   AL,DX               ;get data
002C 88 05              MOV  [DI],AL             ;save data
002E 47                 INC  DI

002F E8 0018            CALL DELAY               ;wait 1/1000 second

0032 E2 EB              LOOP READ1               ;repeat 1024 times
0034 C3                 RET

0035            READ    ENDP

0035            WRITE   PROC    NEAR

0035 51                 PUSH CX
0036 BF 0000 R          MOV  DI,OFFSET WORDS     ;address data
```

EXAMPLE 9-29 (page 4 of 4)

```
0039 B9 03E8                    MOV  CX,1000             ;load count
003C BA 0704                    MOV  DX,0704H            ;address port
003F                  WRITE1:

003F 8A 05                      MOV  AL,[DI]             ;get data
0041 EE                         OUT  DX,AL               ;output data
0042 47                         INC  DI

0043 E8 0004                    CALL DELAY               ;wait 1/1000 second

0046 E2 F7                      LOOP WRITE1
0048 59                         POP  CX
0049 C3                         RET

004A                  WRITE     ENDP

004A                  DELAY     PROC    NEAR

                  ;wait 1/1000 second

004A 51                         PUSH CX
004B B9 03E8                    MOV  CX,1000

004E                  DELAY1:

004E E2 FE                      LOOP DELAY1
0050 59                         POP  CX
0051 C3                         RET

0052                  DELAY     ENDP

0052                  CODE1     ENDS

                                END     START
```

9-8   SUMMARY

1. The 8086 has two basic types of I/O instructions: IN and OUT. The IN instruction inputs data from an external I/O device into either the AL (8-bit) or AX (16-bit) register. The IN instruction is available as a fixed port instruction, a variable port instruction, or as a string instruction (80286–80486) INSB or INSW. The OUT instruction outputs data from AL or AX to an external I/O device and is also available as a fixed, variable, or string instruction OUTSB or OUTSW. The fixed port instruction uses an 8-bit I/O port address, while the variable and string I/O instructions use a 16-bit port number found in the DX register.

2. Isolated I/O, sometimes called direct I/O, uses a separate map for the I/O space, freeing the entire memory for use by the program. Isolated I/O uses the IN and OUT instructions to transfer data between the I/O device and the microprocessor. The control structure of the I/O map uses $\overline{\text{IORC}}$ (I/O read control) and $\overline{\text{IOWC}}$ (I/O write control) plus the bank selection signals $\overline{\text{BHE}}$ and A0 to effect the I/O transfer. The early 8086/8088 uses the M/$\overline{\text{IO}}$ (IO/$\overline{\text{M}}$) signal with RD and WR to generate the I/O control signals.

3. Memory-mapped I/O uses a portion of the memory space for I/O transfers. This reduces the amount of memory available, but it negates the need to use the $\overline{IORC}$ and $\overline{IOWC}$ signals for I/O transfers. In addition, any instruction that addresses a memory location using any addressing mode can be used to transfer data between the microprocessor and the I/O device using memory-mapped I/O.

4. All input devices are buffered so the I/O data are only connected to the data bus during the execution of the IN instruction. The buffer is either built into a programmable peripheral or located separately.

5. All output devices use a latch to capture output data during the execution of the OUT instruction. This is necessary because data appear on the data bus for less than 100 ns for an OUT instruction and most output devices require the data for a longer time. In many cases, the latch is built into the peripheral.

6. Handshaking or polling is the act of two independent devices synchronizing with a few control lines. For example, the computer asks a printer if it is busy by inputting the BUSY signal from the printer. If it isn't busy, the computer outputs data to the printer and informs the printer that data are available with a data strobe ($\overline{DS}$) signal. This communication between the computer and the printer is called a handshake or a poll.

7. The I/O port number appears on address bus connections A7–A0 for a fixed port I/O instruction and on A15–A0 for a variable port I/O instruction. In both cases, address bits above A15 are zero. The 8-bit I/O address found on A7–A0 also contains logic 0's on address connections A15–A8.

8. Because the 8086/80286/80386SX contain a 16-bit data bus and the I/O addresses reference byte-sized I/O locations, the I/O space is also organized in banks as is the memory system. In order to interface an 8-bit I/O device to the 16-bit data bus, we often require separate write strobes, an upper and a lower, for I/O write operations.

9. The I/O port decoder is much like the memory address decoder except instead of decoding the entire address, the I/O port decoder decodes only a 16-bit address for variable port instructions and often an 8-bit port number for fixed I/O instructions.

10. The 8255 is a programmable peripheral interface (PIA) that has 24 I/O pins that are programmable in two groups of 12 pins each (group A and group B). The 8255 operates in three modes: simple I/O (mode 0), strobed I/O (mode 1), and bidirectional I/O (mode 2). When the 8255 is interfaced to the 8086 operating at 8 MHz, we insert two wait states because the speed of the microprocessor is faster than the 8255 can handle.

11. The 8279 is a programmable keyboard/display controller that can control a 64-key keyboard and a 16-digit numeric display.

12. The 8254 is a programmable interval timer that contains three 16-bit counters that count in binary or binary-coded decimal (BCD). Each counter is independent of each other, and operates in six different modes. The six modes of the counter are (1) events counter, (2) retriggerable monostable multivibrator, (3) pulse generator, (4) square-wave generator, (5) software-triggered pulse generator, and (6) hardware-triggered pulse generator.

13. The 8251A is a programmable communications interface capable of receiving and transmitting either asynchronous or synchronous serial data.

14. The DAC0830 is an 8-bit digital-to-analog converter that converts a digital signal to an analog voltage within 1 μs.
15. The ADC0804 is an 8-bit analog-to-digital converter that converts an analog signal into a digital signal within 100 μs.

9-9 QUESTIONS AND PROBLEMS

1. Explain which way the data flow for an IN and an OUT instruction.
2. Where is the I/O port number stored for a fixed I/O instruction?
3. Where is the I/O port number stored for a variable I/O instruction?
4. Where is the I/O port number stored for a string I/O instruction?
5. To which register are data input to by the 16-bit IN instruction?
6. Describe the operation of the OUTSB instruction.
7. Describe the operation of the INSW instruction.
8. Contrast a memory-mapped I/O system with an isolated I/O system.
9. What is the basic input interface?
10. What is the basic output interface?
11. Explain the term *handshaking* as it applies to computer I/O systems.
12. An even-number I/O port address is found in the _____ I/O bank in the 8086 microprocessor.
13. Show the circuitry required to generate the upper and lower I/O write strobes.
14. Develop an I/O port decoder, using a 74ALS138, that generates low bank I/O strobes for the 8-bit I/O port addresses: 10H, 12H, 14H, 16H, 18H, 1AH, 1CH, and 1EH.
15. Develop an I/O port decoder, using a 74ALS138, that generates high bank I/O strobes for the 8-bit I/O port addresses: 11H, 13H, 15H, 17H, 19H, 1BH, 1DH, and 1FH.
16. Develop an I/O port decoder, using a PAL16L8, that generates 16-bit I/O strobes for the 16-bit I/O port addresses: 1000H–1001H, 1002H–1003H, 1004H–1005H, 1006H–1007H, 1008H–1009H, 100AH–100BH, 100CH–100DH, and 100EH–100FH.
17. Develop an I/O port decoder, using the PAL16L8, that generates the following low bank I/O strobes: 00A8H, 00B6H, and 00EEH.
18. Develop an I/O port decoder, using the PAL16L8, that generates the following high bank I/O strobes: 300DH, 300BH, 1005H, and 1007H.
19. Why are both $\overline{BHE}$ and A0 ignored in a 16-bit port address decoder?
20. An 8-bit I/O device, located at I/O port address 0010H, is connected to which data bus connections?
21. An 8-bit I/O device located at I/O port address 100DH is connected to which data bus connections?
22. The 8255 has how many programmable I/O pin connections?
23. List the pins that belong to group A and to group B in the 8255.
24. What two 8255 pins accomplish internal I/O port address selection?
25. The $\overline{RD}$ connection on the 8255 is attached to which 8086 system control bus connection?

26. Using a PAL16L8, interface an 8255 to the 8086 microprocessor so it functions at I/O locations 0380H, 0382H, 0384H and 0386H.
27. When the 8255 is reset, its I/O ports are all initialized as _____ .
28. What three modes of operation are available to the 8255?
29. What is the purpose of the $\overline{STB}$ signal in strobed input operation of the 8255?
30. Explain the operation of a simple four-coil stepper motor.
31. What sets the IBF pin in strobed input operation of the 8255?
32. Write the software required to place a logic 1 on the PC7 pin of the 8255 during strobed input operation.
33. How is the interrupt request pin (INTR) enabled in the strobed input mode of operation of the 8255?
34. In strobed output operation of the 8255, what is the purpose of the $\overline{ACK}$ signal?
35. What clears the $\overline{OBF}$ signal in strobed output operation of the 8255?
36. Write the software required to decide if PC4 is a logic 1 when the 8255 is operated in the strobed output mode.
37. Which group of pins is used during bidirectional operation of the 8255?
38. What pins are general-purpose I/O pins during mode 2 operation of the 8255?
39. What is normally connected to the CLK pin of the 8279?
40. How many wait states are required to interface the 8279 to the 8086 microprocessor operating with an 8 MHz clock?
41. If the 8279 CLK pin is connected to a 3.0 MHz clock, program the internal clock.
42. What is an overrun error in the 8279?
43. What is the difference between encoded and decoded as defined for the 8279?
44. Interface the 8279 so it functions at 8-bit I/O ports 40H–7FH. Use the 74ALS138 as a decoder and use either the upper or lower data bus.
45. Interface a 16-key keyboard and an 8-digit numeric display to the 8279.
46. The 8254 interval timer functions from DC to _____ Hz.
47. Each counter in the 8254 functions in how many different modes?
48. Interface an 8254 to function at I/O port addresses XX10H, XX12H, XX14H, and XX16H. Write the software required to cause counter 2 to generate an 80 KHz square wave if the CLK input to counter 2 is 8 MHz.
49. What number is programmed in an 8254 counter to count 300 events?
50. If a 16-bit count is programmed into the 8254, which byte of the count is programmed first?
51. Explain how the read-back control word functions in the 8254.
52. Program counter 1 of the 8254 so it generates a continuous series of pulses that have a high time of 100 μs and low time of 1 μs. Make sure to indicate the CLK frequency required to accomplish this task.
53. Why does a 50 percent duty cycle cause the motor to stand still in the motor speed and direction control circuit presented in this chapter?
54. What is asynchronous serial data?
55. What is synchronous serial data?
56. What is Baud rate?
57. Program the 8251A for asynchronous operation using 6 data bits, even parity, one stop bit, and a Baud rate divider of 1. (Assume that the I/O ports are numbered 20H and 22H.)

58. If the 8251A is to generate an asynchronous serial signal at a Baud rate of 2400 Baud, and the divider is programmed for 16, what is the frequency of the signal attached to the T×C pin?

59. Describe the following terms: simplex, half-duplex, and full-duplex.

60. How is the 8251A reset?

61. The DAC0830 converts an 8-bit digital input to an analog output in approximately _____ .

62. What is the step voltage at the output of the DAC0830 if the reference voltage is −2.55 V?

63. Interface a DAC0830 to the 8086 so it operates at I/O port 400H.

64. Program the interface of question 62 so the DAC0830 generates a triangular voltage waveform. The frequency of this waveform must be approximately 100 Hz.

65. The ADC080X requires approximately _____ to convert an analog voltage into a digital code.

66. What is the purpose of the INTR pin on the ADC080X?

67. The $\overline{WR}$ pin on the ADC080X is used for what purpose?

68. Interface an ADC080X at I/O port 0260H for data and 0270H to test the INTR pin.

69. Develop a program for the ADC080X in question 68 so it reads an input voltage once per 100 ms and stores the results in a memory array that is 100H bytes in length.

CHAPTER 10

Interrupts

INTRODUCTION

In this chapter, we expand our coverage of basic I/O and programmable peripheral interfaces by examining a technique called interrupt-processed I/O. An interrupt is a hardware-initialed procedure that interrupts whatever program is currently executing.

This chapter provides examples and a detailed explanation of the interrupt structure of the entire Intel family of microprocessors.

CHAPTER OBJECTIVES

Upon completion of this chapter, you will be able to:

1. Explain the interrupt structure of the Intel family of microprocessors.
2. Explain the operation of software interrupt instructions: INT, INTO, INT 3, and BOUND.
3. Explain how the interrupt enable flag bit (IF) modifies the interrupt structure.
4. Describe the function of the trap interrupt flag bit (TF) and the operation of trap-generated tracing.
5. Develop interrupt service procedures that control lower speed external peripheral devices.
6. Expand the interrupt structure of the microprocessor using the 8259A programmable interrupt controller and other techniques.
7. Explain the purpose and operation of a real-time clock.

10–1   BASIC INTERRUPT PROCESSING

In this section, we discuss the function of an interrupt in a microprocessor-based system and the structure and features of interrupts available to the Intel family of microprocessors.

The Purpose of Interrupts

Interrupts are particularly useful when interfacing I/O devices that provide or require data at relatively low data transfer rates. In Chapter 9, for instance, we saw a keyboard example using strobed input operation of the 8255. In that example, software polled the 8255 and its IBF bit to decide if data were available from the keyboard. If the person using the keyboard typed one character per second, the software for the 8255 waited an entire second between each keystroke for the person to type another key. This process is such a tremendous waste of time that designers have developed another process called interrupt processing to handle this situation.

Unlike the polling technique, interrupt processing allows the microprocessor to execute other software while the keyboard operator is thinking about what key to type next. As soon as a key is pressed, the keyboard encoder debounces the switch and puts out one pulse that interrupts the microprocessor. In this way, the microprocessor executes other software until the key is actually pressed when it reads a key and returns to the program that was interrupted. As a result, the microprocessor can print reports or complete any other task while the operator is typing a document and thinking about what to type next.

Figure 10–1 shows a time line that indicates a typist typing data on a keyboard, a printer removing data from the memory, and a program executing. The program is the main program that is interrupted for each keystroke and each character that is to print on the printer. Note that the keyboard interrupt service procedure, called by the keyboard interrupt, and the printer interrupt service procedure each take little time to execute.

Interrupts

The interrupts of the entire Intel family of microprocessors include two hardware pins that request interrupts (INTR and NMI) and one hardware pin ($\overline{\text{INTA}}$) that acknowledges the interrupt requested through INTR. In addition to the pins, the microprocessor also has software interrupts INT, INTO, INT 3, and BOUND. Two flag bits, IF (interrupt flag) and TF (trap flag), are also used with the interrupt structure and a special return instruction IRET (or IRETD in the 80386 or 80486).

Interrupt Vectors. The interrupt vectors and vector table are crucial to an understanding of hardware and software interrupts. The *interrupt vector table* is located in the first 1,024 bytes of memory at addresses 000000H–0003FFH. It contains 256 different four-byte

FIGURE 10–1 A time line that indicates interrupt usage in a typical system.

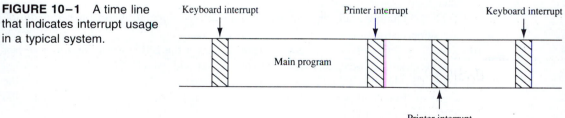

interrupt vectors. An *interrupt vector* contains the address (segment and offset) of the interrupt service procedure.

Figure 10–2 illustrates the interrupt vector table for the microprocessor. The first five interrupt vectors are identical in all Intel microprocessor family members from the 8086 to the 80486. Other interrupt vectors exist for the 80286 that are upward compatible to the 80386 and 80486, but not downward compatible to the 8086 or 8088. Intel reserves the first 32 interrupt vectors for their use in various microprocessor family members. The last 224 vectors are available as user interrupt vectors. Each vector is 4 bytes in length and contains the *starting address* of the interrupt service procedure. The first two bytes of the vector contain the offset address and the last two bytes contain the segment address.

The following list describes the function of each dedicated interrupt in the microprocessor:

1. Type 0—Divide Error: occurs whenever the result of a division overflows or whenever an attempt is made to divide by zero.
2. Type 1—Single-Step or Trap: occurs after the execution of each instruction if the trap (TF) flag bit is set. Upon accepting this interrupt, the TF bit is cleared so the interrupt service procedure executes at full speed. More detail is provided about this interrupt later in this section of the chapter.
3. Type 2—Nonmaskable Hardware Interrupt: a result of placing a logic 1 on the NMI input pin to the microprocessor. This input is nonmaskable which means that it cannot be disabled.
4. Type 3—One-Byte Interrupt: is a special one-byte instruction (INT 3) that uses this vector to access its interrupt service procedure. The INT 3 instruction is often used to store a breakpoint in a program for debugging.
5. Type 4—Overflow: is a special vector used with the INTO instruction. The INTO instruction interrupts the program if an overflow condition exists as reflected by the overflow flag (OF).
6. Type 5—BOUND: is an instruction that compares a register with boundaries stored in the memory. If the contents of the register is greater than or equal to the first word in memory and less than or equal to the second word, no interrupt occurs because the contents of the register is within bounds. If the contents of the register is out of bounds, a type 5 interrupt ensues.
7. Type 6—Invalid Opcode: occurs whenever an undefined opcode is encountered in a program.
8. Type 7—Coprocessor Not Available: occurs when a coprocessor is not found in the system as dictated by the machine status word (MSW) coprocessor control bits. If an ESC or WAIT instruction executes and the coprocessor is not found, a type 7 exception or interrupt occurs.
9. Type 8—Double Fault: is activated whenever two separate interrupts occur during the same instruction.
10. Type 9—Coprocessor Segment Overrun: occurs if the ESC instruction (coprocessor opcode) memory operand extends beyond offset address FFFFH.
11. Type 10—Invalid Task State Segment: occurs if the TSS is invalid because the segment limit field is not 002BH or higher. In most cases this is caused because the TSS is not initialized.

FIGURE 10–2 (a) The interrupt vector table for the microprocessor. (b) The contents of an interrupt vector.

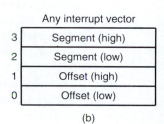

080H	Type 32 — 255 User interrupt vectors
	Type 14 — 31 Reserved
040H	Type 16 Coprocessor error
03CH	Type 15 Unassigned
038H	Type 14 Page fault
034H	Type 13 General protection
030H	Type 12 Stack segment overrun
02CH	Type 11 Segment not present
028H	Type 10 Invalid task state segment
024H	Type 9 Coprocessor segment overrun
020H	Type 8 Double fault
01CH	Type 7 Coprocessor not available
018H	Type 6 Undefined opcode
014H	Type 5 BOUND
010H	Type 4 Overflow (INTO)
00CH	Type 3 1-byte breakpoint
008H	Type 2 NMI pin
004H	Type 1 Single-step
000H	Type 0 Divide error

(a)

Any interrupt vector

3	Segment (high)
2	Segment (low)
1	Offset (high)
0	Offset (low)

(b)

12. Type 11—Segment not Present: interrupts occur when the P bit (P = 0) in a descriptor indicates that the segment is not present or not valid.

13. Type 12—Stack Segment Overrun: occurs if the stack segment is not present (P = 0) or if the limit of the stack segment is exceeded.

14. Type 13—General Protection: occurs for most protection violation in the 80286/80386/80486 protected mode system. A list of these protection violations follows:
   a. descriptor table limit exceeded
   b. privilege rules violated
   c. invalid descriptor segment type loaded
   d. write to code segment that is protected
   e. read from execute-only code segment
   f. write to read-only data segment
   g. segment limit exceeded
   h. CPL ≠ 0 when executing CTS, HLT, LGDT, LIDT, LLDT, LMSW, or LTR
   i. CPL > IOPL when executing CLI, IN, INS, LOCK, OUT, OUTS, and STI

15. Type 14—Page Fault: occurs for any page fault memory or code access in the 80386 and 80486 microprocessors.

16. Type 16—Coprocessor Error: takes effect whenever a coprocessor error ($\overline{ERROR}$ = 0) occurs for the ESCape or WAIT instructions for the 80386 microprocessor only.

Interrupt Instructions: BOUND, INTO, INT, INT 3, and IRET

Of the five software interrupt instructions available to the microprocessor, INT and INT 3 are very similar, BOUND and INTO are conditional, and IRET is a special interrupt return instruction.

The BOUND instruction, which has two operands, compares a register with two words of memory data. For example, if the instruction BOUND AX,DATA is executed, AX is compared with the contents of DATA and DATA+1 and also with DATA+2 and DATA+3. If AX is less than the contents of DATA and DATA+1, a type 5 interrupt occurs. If AX is greater than DATA+2 and DATA+3, a type 5 interrupt occurs. If AX is within the bounds of these two memory words, no interrupt occurs.

The INTO instruction checks the overflow flag (OF). If OF = 1, the INTO instruction calls the procedure whose address is stored in interrupt vector type number 4. If OF = 0, then the INTO instruction performs a NOP and the next sequential instruction in the program executes.

The INT n instruction calls the interrupt service procedure that begins at the address represented in vector number n. For example, an INT 80H or INT 128 calls the interrupt service procedure whose address is stored in vector type number 80H (000200H–000203H). To determine the vector address, just multiply the vector type number (n) by 4. This gives the beginning address of the four-byte long interrupt vector. For example, an INT 5 = 4 × 5 or 20 (14H). The vector for INT 5 begins at address 000014H and continues to 000017H. Each INT instruction is stored in two bytes of memory with the first byte containing the opcode and the second the interrupt type number. The only exception to this is the INT 3 instruction, a one-byte instruction. The INT 3 instruction is often used as a breakpoint interrupt because it is easy to insert a 1-byte instruction into a program. Breakpoints are often used to debug faulty software.

The IRET instruction is a special return instruction used to return for both software and hardware interrupts. The IRET instruction is much like a normal far RET, because it retrieves the return address from the stack. It is unlike the normal return because it also retrieves a copy of the flag register from the stack. An IRET instruction removes 6 bytes from the stack, 2 for the IP, 2 for the CS, and 2 for the flags.

In the 80386 and 80486 microprocessors, there is also an IRETD instruction because these microprocessors can push the EFLAG register (32 bits) on the stack as well as the 32-bit EIP in the protected mode. If operated in the real mode, we use the IRET instruction with the 80386/80486 microprocessor.

The Operation of an Interrupt

When the microprocessor completes executing the current instruction, it determines whether an interrupt is active by checking (1) instruction executions, (2) single-step, (3) NMI, (4) coprocessor segment overrun, (5) INTR, and (6) INT instruction in the order presented. If one or more of these interrupt conditions are present, the following sequence of events occurs:

1. The contents of the flag register are pushed onto the stack.
2. Both the interrupt (IF) and trap (TF) flags are cleared. This disables the INTR pin and also the trap or single-step feature.
3. The contents of the code segment register (CS) are pushed onto the stack.
4. The contents of the instruction pointer (IP) are pushed onto the stack.
5. The interrupt vector contents are fetched and placed into both IP and CS so the next instruction executes at the interrupt service procedure addressed by the vector.

Whenever an interrupt is accepted, the microprocessor stacks the contents of the flag register, CS and IP; clears both IF and TF; and jumps to the procedure addressed by the interrupt vector. After the flags are pushed onto the stack, IF and TF are cleared. These flags are returned to the state prior to the interrupt when the IRET instruction is encountered at the end of the interrupt service procedure. Therefore, if interrupts were enabled prior to the interrupt service procedure, they are automatically reenabled by the IRET instruction at the end of the procedure.

The return address (in CS and IP) is pushed onto the stack during the interrupt. Sometimes the return address points to the next instruction in the program and sometimes it points to the instruction or point in the program where the interrupt occurred. Interrupt type numbers 0, 5, 6, 7, 8, 10, 11, 12, and 13 push a return address that points to the offending instruction, instead of the next instruction in the program. This allows the interrupt service procedure to possibly retry the instruction in certain error cases.

Some of the protected mode interrupts (types 8, 10, 11, 12, and 13) place an error code on the stack following the return address. The error code identifies the selector that caused the interrupt. In cases where no selector is involved, the error code is a 0.

Interrupt Flag Bits

The interrupt flag (IF) and the trap flag (TF) are both cleared after the contents of the flag register are stacked during an interrupt. Figure 10–3 illustrates the contents of the flag register and the location of IF and TF. When the IF bit is set, it allows the INTR pin to

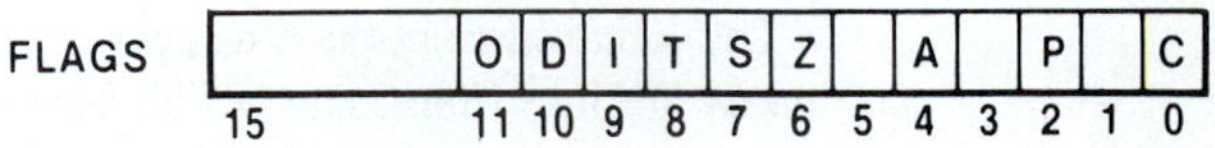

FIGURE 10–3 The 80286 flag register. (Courtesy of Intel Corporcation)

FLAGS

	O	D	I	T	S	Z		A		P		C
15	11	10	9	8	7	6	5	4	3	2	1	0

cause an interrupt; when the IF bit is cleared, it prevents the INTR pin from causing an interrupt. When TF = 1, it causes a trap interrupt (type number 1) to occur after each instruction executes. This is why we often call trap a single-step. When TF = 0, normal program execution occurs. This flag bit allows debugging in the 80386/80486 as explained in Chapter 14.

The interrupt flag is set and cleared by the STI and CLI instructions respectively. There are no special instructions that set or clear the trap flag. Example 10–1 shows an interrupt service procedure that turns tracing on by setting the trap flag bit on the stack from inside the procedure. Example 10–2 shows an interrupt service procedure that turns tracing off by clearing the trap flag on the stack from within the procedure.

EXAMPLE 10–1

```
                    ;Procedure that sets TF to enable trap
                    ;
0000                TRON     PROC    FAR

0000 50                      PUSH AX                    ;save registers
0001 55                      PUSH BP

0002 8B EC                   MOV   BP,SP                ;get SP
0004 8B 46 08                MOV   AX,[BP+8]            ;get flags
0007 80 CC 01                OR    AH,1                 ;set TF
000A 89 46 08                MOV   [BP+8],AX            ;save flags

000D 5D                      POP   BP                   ;restore registers
000E 58                      POP   AX
000F CF                      IRET

0010                TRON     ENDP
```

EXAMPLE 10–2

```
                    ;Procedure that clears TF to disable trap
                    ;
0010                TROFF    PROC    FAR

0010 50                      PUSH AX                    ;save registers
0011 55                      PUSH BP

0012 8B EC                   MOV   BP,SP                ;get SP
0014 8B 46 08                MOV   AX,[BP+8]            ;get flags
0017 80 E4 FE                AND   AH,0FEH              ;clear TF
001A 89 46 08                MOV   [BP+8],AX            ;save flags

001D 5D                      POP   BP                   ;restore registers
001E 58                      POP   AX
001F CF                      IRET

0020                TROFF    ENDP
```

In both examples, the flag register is retrieved from the stack by using the BP register, which by default addresses the stack segment. After the flags are retrieved, the TF bit is either set (TRON) or clears (TROFF) before returning from the interrupt service procedure. The IRET instruction restores the flag register with the new state of the trap flag.

Trace Procedure. Assuming that TRON is accessed by an INT 40H instruction and TROFF is accessed by an INT 41H instruction, Example 10–3 traces through a program immediately following the INT 40H instruction. The interrupt service procedure illustrated in Example 10–3 responds to interrupt type number 1 or a trap interrupt. Each time that this occurs—after each instruction executes following INT 40H—the TRACE procedure displays the contents of all the 16-bit microprocessor registers on the CRT screen. This provides a register trace of all the instructions between the INT 40H (TRON) and INT 41H (TROFF).

EXAMPLE 10–3 (page 1 of 3)

```
                         ;Procedure that displays all the registers and their contents
                         ;on the video screen in response to a trap interrupt.
                         ;
0000                     TRACE    PROC    FAR

0000 50                           PUSH AX                    ;save registers
0001 55                           PUSH BP
0002 53                           PUSH BX

0003 BB 0054 R                    MOV  BX,OFFSET NAMES       ;address register names

                         ;display registers

0006 E8 009A R                    CALL CRLF                  ;get new display line
0009 E8 00A9 R                    CALL DISP                  ;display AX
000C 8B C3                        MOV  AX,BX
000E E8 00A9 R                    CALL DISP                  ;display BX
0011 8B C1                        MOV  AX,CX
0013 E8 00A9 R                    CALL DISP                  ;display CX
0016 8B C2                        MOV  AX,DX
0018 E8 00A9 R                    CALL DISP                  ;display DX
001B 8B C4                        MOV  AX,SP
001D 05 000C                      ADD  AX,12
0020 E8 00A9 R                    CALL DISP                  ;display SP
0023 8B C5                        MOV  AX,BP
0025 E8 00A9 R                    CALL DISP                  ;display BP
0028 8B C6                        MOV  AX,SI
002A E8 00A9 R                    CALL DISP                  ;display SI
002D 8B EC                        MOV  BP,SP                 ;address stack with BP
002F 8B 46 06                     MOV  AX,[BP+6]
0032 E8 00A9 R                    CALL DISP                  ;display IP
0035 8B 46 0A                     MOV  AX,[BP+10]
0038 E8 00A9 R                    CALL DISP                  ;display flags
003B 8B 46 08                     MOV  AX,[BP+8]
003E E8 00A9 R                    CALL DISP                  ;display CS
0041 8C D8                        MOV  AX,DS
0043 E8 00A9 R                    CALL DISP                  ;display DS
0046 8C C0                        MOV  AX,ES
0048 E8 00A9 R                    CALL DISP                  ;display ES
004B 8C D0                        MOV  AX,SS
004D E8 00A9 R                    CALL DISP                  ;display SS
```

EXAMPLE 10–3 (page 2 of 3)

```
0050 5B                    POP   BX              ;restore registers
0051 5D                    POP   BP
0052 58                    POP   AX
0053 CF                    IRET

0054               TRACE   ENDP

0054 41 58 20 3D 20  NAMES DB    'AX = '
0059 42 58 20 3D 20        DB    'BX = '
005E 43 58 20 3D 20        DB    'CX = '
0063 44 58 20 3D 20        DB    'DX = '
0068 53 50 20 3D 20        DB    'SP = '
006D 42 50 20 3D 20        DB    'BP = '
0072 53 49 20 3D 20        DB    'SI = '
0077 44 49 20 3D 20        DB    'DI = '
007C 49 50 20 3D 20        DB    'IP = '
0081 46 4C 20 3D 20        DB    'FL = '
0086 43 53 20 3D 20        DB    'CS = '
008B 44 53 20 3D 20        DB    'DS = '
0090 45 53 20 3D 20        DB    'ES = '
0095 53 53 20 3D 20        DB    'SS = '

009A               CRLF    PROC       NEAR

009A 50                    PUSH  AX              ;save registers
009B 52                    PUSH  DX

009C B4 06                 MOV   AH,6
009E B2 0D                 MOV   DL,13
00A0 CD 21                 INT   21H             ;display CR
00A2 B2 0A                 MOV   DL,10
00A4 CD 21                 INT   21H             ;display LF

00A6 5A                    POP   DX              ;restore registers
00A7 58                    POP   AX
00A8 C3                    RET

00A9               CRLF    ENDP

00A9               DISP    PROC       NEAR

00A9 52                    PUSH  DX              ;save registers
00AA 57                    PUSH  DI
00AB 51                    PUSH  CX
00AC 50                    PUSH  AX

00AD B4 06                 MOV   AH,6
00AF B9 0005               MOV   CX,5

00B2               DISP1:

00B2 2E: 8A 17             MOV   DL,CS:[BX]      ;display name
00B5 CD 21                 INT   21H
00B7 43                    INC   BX
00B8 E2 F8                 LOOP  DISP1
00BA 5F                    POP   DI              ;get numeric value
00BB 57                    PUSH  DI
00BC B6 04                 MOV   DH,4            ;set count
```

EXAMPLE 10-3 (page 3 of 3)

```
00BE                      DISP2:

00BE B9 0004                  MOV   CX,4
00C1 D3 C7                    ROL   DI,CL
00C3 8B C7                    MOV   AX,DI
00C5 B4 06                    MOV   AH,6
00C7 8A D0                    MOV   DL,AL
00C9 80 E2 0F                 AND   DL,15
00CC 80 C2 30                 ADD   DL,30H          ;convert to ASCII
00CF 80 FA 39                 CMP   DL,39H
00D2 76 03                    JBE   DISP3
00D4 80 C2 07                 ADD   DL,7

00D7                      DISP3:

00D7 CD 21                    INT   21H
00D9 FE CE                    DEC   DH
00DB 75 E1                    JNZ   DISP2           ;repeat for 4 digits

00DD B4 06                    MOV   AH,6
00DF B2 20                    MOV   DL,' '          ;display space
00E1 CD 21                    INT   21H

00E3 58                       POP   AX              ;restore registers
00E4 59                       POP   CX
00E5 5F                       POP   DI
00E6 5A                       POP   DX
00E7 C3                       RET

00E8                  DISP    ENDP
```

Storing an Interrupt Vector in the Vector Table

In order to install an interrupt vector—sometimes called a *hook*—the assembler must address absolute memory. Example 10–4 shows how a new vector is added to the interrupt vector table by using the assembler and a DOS function call. Here INT 21H function call number 25H initializes the interrupt vector. Notice that the first thing done in this procedure is to save the old interrupt vector number using DOS INT 21H function call number 35H to read the current vector. Refer to Appendix A for more detail on DOS function calls.

EXAMPLE 10–4

```
                          ;Procedure that installs a new interrupt vector at interrupt
                          ;type number 40H
                          ;
0000 0000             OLDOFF   DW    ?
0002 0000             OLDSEG   DW    ?
= 0004                NEWOFF   EQU   THIS WORD
= 0006                NEWSEG   EQU   THIS WORD+2
0004 0200 ---- R      NEW      DD    FAR PTR TRON

0008                  IN_40H   PROC    NEAR

0008 06                        PUSH  ES              ;save registers
0009 1E                        PUSH  DS
```

```
000A 50                         PUSH AX
000B 53                         PUSH BX
000C 52                         PUSH DX

000D B4 35                      MOV  AH,35H               ;get current vector
000F B0 40                      MOV  AL,40H               ;type number
0011 CD 21                      INT  21H

0013 2E: 89 1E 0000 R           MOV  CS:OLDOFF,BX         ;save old offset
0018 8C C0                      MOV  AX,ES
001A 2E: A3 0002 R              MOV  CS:OLDSEG,AX         ;save old segment

001E 2E: 8B 16 0004 R           MOV  DX,NEWOFF            ;get new offset
0023 2E: A1 0006 R              MOV  AX,NEWSEG            ;get new segment
0027 8E D8                      MOV  DS,AX

0029 B4 25                      MOV  AH,25H               ;install new vector
002B B0 40                      MOV  AL,40H               ;type number
002D CD 21                      INT  21H

002F 5A                         POP  DX                   ;restore registers
0030 5B                         POP  BX
0031 58                         POP  AX
0032 1F                         POP  DS
0033 07                         POP  ES
0034 C3                         RET

0035              MIN_40H  ENDP
```

10-2   HARDWARE INTERRUPTS

The microprocessor has two hardware interrupt inputs: nonmaskable interrupt (NMI) and interrupt request (INTR). Whenever the NMI input is activated, a type 2 interrupt occurs because NMI is internally decoded. The INTR input must be externally decoded to select a vector. Any interrupt vector can be chosen for the INTR pin, but we usually use an interrupt type number between 20H and FFH. The INTA signal is also an interrupt pin on the microprocessor, but it is an output that is used in response to the INTR input to apply a vector type number to the data bus connections D7–D0. Figure 10–4 shows the three interrupt connections on the microprocessor.

NMI

The nonmaskable interrupt (NMI) is an edge-triggered input that requests an interrupt on the positive edge (0-to-1 transition). After a positive edge, the NMI pin must remain a logic 1 until it is recognized by the microprocessor. Note that before the positive edge is recognized, the NMI pin must be a logic 0 for at least 2 clocking periods.

The NMI input is often used for parity errors and other major system faults such as power failures. Power failures are easily detected by monitoring the AC power line and causing an NMI interrupt whenever AC power drops out. In response to this type of interrupt, the microprocessor stores all the internal registers in a battery-backed-up

FIGURE 10-4 The 80286 interrupt pins.

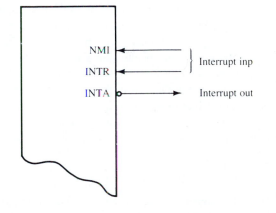

memory or an EEPROM. Figure 10-5 shows a power failure detection circuit that provides a logic 1 to the NMI input whenever AC power is interrupted.

In this circuit, an optical isolator provides isolation from the AC power line. The output of the isolator is shaped by a Schmitt-trigger inverter that provides a 60 Hz pulse to the trigger input of the 74LS122 retriggerable monostable multivibrator. The values of R and C are chosen so the 74LS122 has an active pulse width of 33 ms or 2 AC input periods. Because the 74LS122 is retriggerable, as long as AC power is applied, the Q output remains triggered at a logic 1 and $\overline{Q}$ remains a logic 0.

If the AC power fails, the 74LS122 no longer receives trigger pulses from the 74ALS14, which means that Q returns to a logic 0 and $\overline{Q}$ returns to a logic 1 interrupting the microprocessor through the NMI pin. The interrupt service procedure, not shown here, stores the contents of all internal registers and other data into a battery-backed-up memory. This system assumes that the system power supply has a large enough filter capacitor to provide energy for at least 75 ms after the AC power ceases.

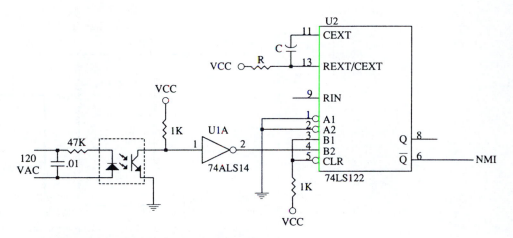

FIGURE 10-5 A power failure detection circuit.

Figure 10–6 shows a circuit that supplies power to a memory after the DC power fails. Here diodes are used to switch supply voltages from the DC power supply to the battery. The diodes used are standard silicon diodes because the power supply to this memory circuit is elevated above +5.0 V to +5.7 V. Also notice that the resistor is used to trickle-charge the battery which is either NiCad, lithium, or a gel cell.

When DC power fails, the battery provides a reduced voltage to the Vcc connection on the memory device. Most memory devices will retain data with Vcc voltages as low as 1.5 V so the battery voltage does not need to be +5.0 V. The $\overline{WR}$ pin is pulled to Vcc during a power outage so no data will be written to the memory.

INTR and INTA

The interrupt request input (INTR) is level-sensitive, which means that it must be held at a logic 1 level until it is recognized. The INTR pin is set by an external event and cleared inside the interrupt service procedure. This input is automatically disabled once it is accepted by the microprocessor and reenabled by the IRET instruction at the end of the interrupt service procedure. The 80386 and 80486 use the IRETD instruction in the protected mode of operation.

The microprocessor responds to the INTR input by pulsing the $\overline{INTA}$ output in anticipation of receiving an interrupt vector type number on data bus connection D7–D0. Figure 10–7 shows the timing diagram for the INTR and $\overline{INTA}$ pins of the microprocessor. There are two $\overline{INTA}$ pulses generated by the system that are used to insert the vector type number on the data bus.

Figure 10–8 illustrates a simple circuit that applies interrupt vector type number FFH to the data bus in response to an INTR. Notice that the $\overline{INTA}$ pin is not connected in this circuit. Because resistors are used to pull the data bus connections (D0–D7) high, the microprocessor automatically sees vector type number FFH in response to the INTR input. This is possibly the least expensive way to implement the INTR pin on the microprocessor.

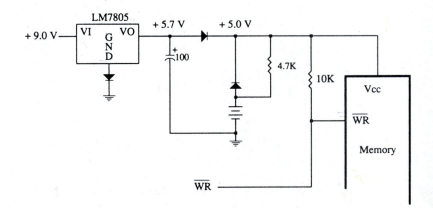

FIGURE 10–6   A battery-backed-up memory system using a NiCad, lithium, or gel cell.

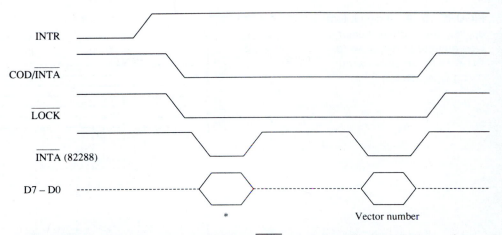

FIGURE 10–7 The timing for the INTR and $\overline{\text{INTA}}$ pulses from the 82288 system bus controller. *Note: This portion of the data bus is ignored and usually contains the vector type number.

FIGURE 10–8 A simple method for generating interrupt vector type number FFH in response to INTR.

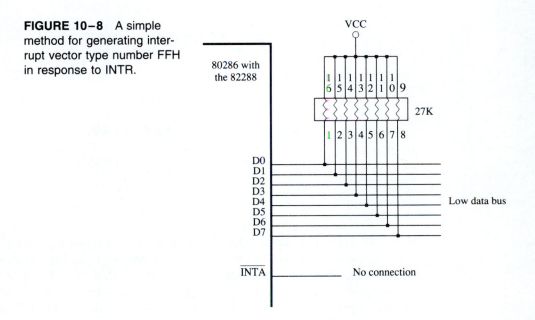

Using a Three-State Buffer for INTA. Figure 10–9 shows how interrupt vector type number 80H is applied to the data bus (D0–D7) in response to an INTR. In response to the INTR, the microprocessor outputs the $\overline{\text{INTA}}$ that is used to enable a 74ALS244 three-state octal buffer. The octal buffer applies the interrupt vector type number to the data bus in response to the $\overline{\text{INTA}}$ pulse. The vector type number is easily changed with the DIP switches that are shown in this illustration.

FIGURE 10–9 A circuit that applies any interrupt vector type number in response to INTA. Here the circuit is applying type number 80H.

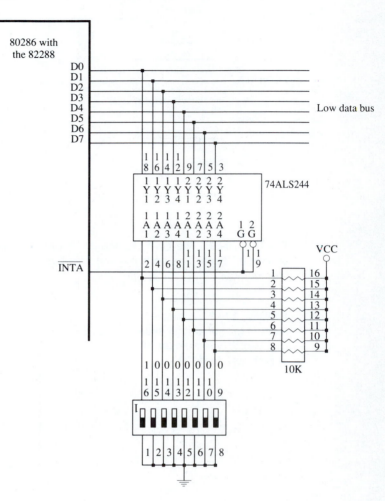

Making the INTR Input Edge-Triggered. Often we need an edge-triggered input instead of a level-sensitive input. The INTR input can be converted to an edge-triggered input by using a D-type flip-flop as illustrated in Figure 10–10. Here the clock input becomes an edge-triggered interrupt request input and the clear input is used to clear the request when the INTA signal is output by the microprocessor. Also note that the RESET signal initially clears the flip-flop so no interrupt is requested when the system is first powered.

The 8255 Keyboard Interrupt

The keyboard example presented in the last chapter provides a simple example of the operation of the INTR input and an interrupt. Figure 10–11 illustrates the interconnection of the 8255 with the microprocessor and the keyboard. It also shows how a 74ALS244 octal buffer is used to provide the microprocessor with interrupt vector type number 40H in response to the keyboard interrupt during the INTA pulse.

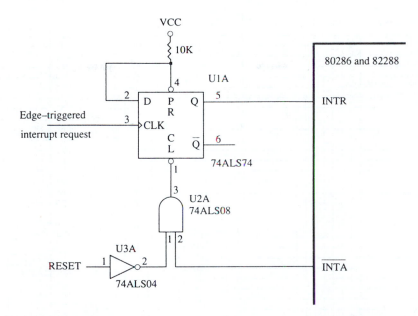

FIGURE 10–10 Converting INTR into an edge-triggered interrupt request input.

The 8255 is decoded at 8086 I/O port address 0500H, 0502H, 0504H, and 0506H by a PAL16L8 (the program is not illustrated). The 8255 is operated in mode 1 (strobed input mode) so whenever a key is typed, the INTR output (PC3) becomes a logic 1, requesting an interrupt through the INTR pin on the microprocessor. The INTR pin remains high until the ASCII data are read from port A. In other words, every time a key is typed, the 8255 requests a type 40H interrupt through the INTR pin. The $\overline{DAV}$ signal from the keyboard causes data to be latched into port A and also causes INTR to become a logic 1.

Example 10–5 illustrates the interrupt service procedure for the keyboard. It is very important that all registers affected by an interrupt are saved before they are used. In the software required to initialize the 8255 (not shown here), the FIFO is initialized so both pointers are equal, the INTR request pin is enabled through the INTE bit inside the 8255, and the mode of operation is programmed.

EXAMPLE 10–5 (page 1 of 3)

```
                       ;Interrupt service procedure that reads a key
                       ;from the keyboard.
= 0500                 PORTA   EQU   500H                  ;port A
= 0506                 CNTR    EQU   506H                  ;control register
0000 0100[             FIFO    DB    256 DUP (?)           ;FIFO buffer
        ??
     ]
0100 0000              INP     DW    ?                     ;input pointer
0102 0000              OUTP    DW    ?                     ;output pointer

0104                   KEY     PROC  FAR
```

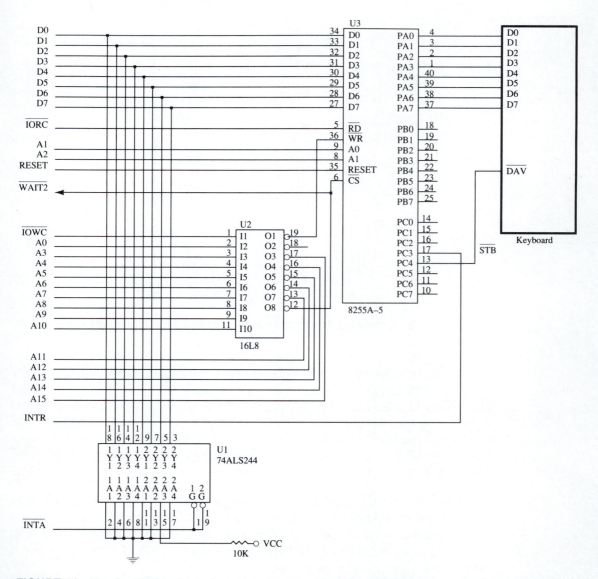

FIGURE 10–11   An 8255A–5 interfaced to a keyboard from the 80286 system using interrupt vector 40H.

EXAMPLE 10–5 (page 2 of 3)

```
0104 50                         PUSH  AX                    ;save registers
0105 53                         PUSH  BX
0106 57                         PUSH  DI
0107 52                         PUSH  DX

0108 2E: 8B 1E 0100 R           MOV   BX,INP                ;address FIFO
010D 2E: 8B 3E 0102 R           MOV   DI,OUTP
```

EXAMPLE 10–5 (page 3 of 3)

```
0112 FE C3                    INC   BL                        ;test for full
0114 3B DF                    CMP   BX,DI
0116 74 11                    JE    FULL                      ;if full

0118 FE CB                    DEC   BL
011A BA 0500                  MOV   DX,PORTA
011D EC                       IN    AL,DX                     ;get data
011E 2E: 88 07                MOV   CS:[BX],AL                ;save data
0121 2E: FE 06 0100 R         INC   BYTE PTR INP
0126 EB 07 90                 JMP   DONE

0129              FULL:

0129 B0 08                    MOV   AL,8                      ;disable interrupts
012B BA 0506                  MOV   DX,CNTR
012E EE                       OUT   DX,AL

012F              DONE:

012F 5A                       POP   DX                        ;restore registers
0130 5F                       POP   DI
0131 5B                       POP   BX
0132 58                       POP   AX
0133 CF                       IRET

0134              KEY   ENDP
```

The procedure is fairly short because the 8086 already knows that keyboard data are available when the procedure is called. Data are input from the keyboard and then stored in the FIFO (first-in, first-out) buffer. Most keyboard interfaces contain a FIFO that is at least 16 bytes in depth. The FIFO in this example is 256 bytes, which is more than adequate for a keyboard interface.

This procedure first checks to see if the FIFO is full. A full condition is indicated when the input point (INP) is one byte below the output pointer (OUTP). If the FIFO is full, the interrupt is disabled with a bit set/reset command to the 8255, and a return from the interrupt occurs. If the FIFO is not full, the data are input from port A, and the input pointer is incremented before a return occurs.

Example 10–6 shows the procedure that removes data from the FIFO. This procedure first determines whether the FIFO is empty by comparing the two pointers. If the pointers are equal, the FIFO is empty, and the software waits at the EMPTY loop where it continuously tests the pointers. The EMPTY loop is interrupted by the keyboard interrupt, which stores data into the FIFO so it is no longer empty. This procedure returns with the character in register AH.

EXAMPLE 10–6

```
                 ;Procedure that reads a key from the FIFO and
                 ;returns with it in AH
                 ;
0104             READ   PROC   FAR

0104 53                 PUSH BX                               ;save registers
0105 57                 PUSH DI
0106 52                 PUSH DX
```

```
0107                       EMPTY:

0107 2E: 8B 1E 0100 R          MOV  BX,INP                ;address FIFO
010C 2E: 8B 3E 0102 R          MOV  DI,OUTP
0111 3B DF                     CMP  BX,DI                 ;test for empty
0113 74 F2                     JE   EMPTY                 ;if empty

0115 2E: 8A 25                 MOV  AH,CS:[DI]            ;get data

0118 B0 09                     MOV  AL,9                  ;enable 8255A interrupt
011A BA 0506                   MOV  DX,CNTR
011D EE                        OUT  DX,AL

011E 2E: FE 06 0102 R          INC  BYTE PTR OUTP         ;increment pointer

0123 5A                        POP  DX                    ;restore registers
0124 5F                        POP  DI
0125 5B                        POP  BX
0126 CB                        RET

0127                   READ    ENDP
```

10-3   EXPANDING THE INTERRUPT STRUCTURE

This text covers three of the more common methods of expanding the interrupt structure of the microprocessor. In this section we explain how, with software and some hardware modification of the circuit of Figure 10–9, it is possible to expand the INTR input so it accepts 7 interrupt inputs. We also explain how to "daisy-chain" interrupts by software polling. In the next section, we describe a third technique in which up to 63 interrupting inputs can be added by means of the 8259A programmable interrupt controller.

Using the 74ALS244 to Expand Interrupts

The modification shown in Figure 10–12 allows the circuit of Figure 10–9 to accommodate up to seven additional interrupt inputs. The only hardware change is the addition of an 8-input NAND gate, which provides the INTR signal to the microprocessor when any of the $\overline{IR}$ inputs becomes active.

Operation.   If any of the $\overline{IR}$ inputs become a logic 0, then the output of the NAND gate goes to a logic 1 and requests an interrupt through the INTR input. Which interrupt vector is fetched during the $\overline{INTA}$ pulse depends on which interrupt request line becomes active. Table 10–1 shows the interrupt vectors used by a single interrupt request input.

If two or more interrupt request inputs are simultaneously active, a new interrupt vector is generated. For example, if $\overline{IR1}$ and $\overline{IR0}$ are both active, the interrupt vector generated is FCH (252). Priority is resolved at this location. If the $\overline{IR0}$ input is to have the higher priority, the vector address for $\overline{IR0}$ is stored at vector location FCH. The entire top half of the vector table and its 128 interrupt vectors must be used to accommodate all possible conditions of these seven interrupt request inputs. This seems wasteful, but in many dedicated applications it is a cost-effective approach to interrupt expansion.

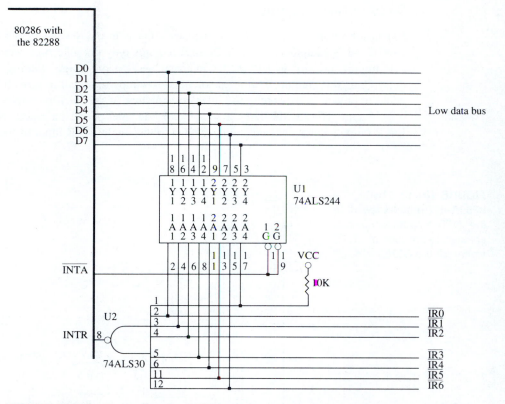

FIGURE 10-12 Expanding the INTR input from one to seven interrupt request lines.

TABLE 10-1 Single interrupt request for Figure 10-12

AD7	$\overline{IR6}$	$\overline{IR5}$	$\overline{IR4}$	$\overline{IR3}$	$\overline{IR2}$	$\overline{IR1}$	$\overline{IR0}$	Vector
1	1	1	1	1	1	1	0	FEH (254)
1	1	1	1	1	1	0	1	FDH (253)
1	1	1	1	1	0	1	1	FBH (251)
1	1	1	1	0	1	1	1	F7H (247)
1	1	1	0	1	1	1	1	EFH (239)
1	1	0	1	1	1	1	1	DFH (223)
1	0	1	1	1	1	1	1	BFH (191)

Daisy-Chained Interrupt

Expansion by means of a daisy-chained interrupt is in many ways better than using the 74ALS244 interrupt expansion because it requires only one interrupt vector. The task of determining priority is left to the interrupt service procedure. Setting priority for a daisy-chain does require additional software execution time, but in general this is a much better approach to expanding the interrupt structure of the microprocessor.

Figure 10–13 illustrates a set of two 8255 peripheral interfaces with their four INTR outputs daisy-chained and connected to the single INTR input of the microproces-

FIGURE 10–13 Two 8255A–5 PIAs connected to the INTR outputs are daisy-chained to produce an INTR signal for the 80286.

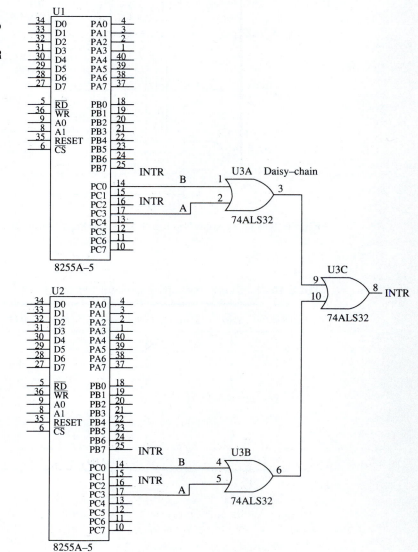

sor. If any interrupt output becomes a logic 1, so does the INTR input to the micro-processor causing an interrupt.

When a daisy-chain is used to request an interrupt it is better to pull the data bus connections (D0–D7) high using pullup resisters so interrupt vector FFH is used for the chain. Actually any interrupt vector can be used to respond to a daisy-chain. In the circuit, any of the four INTR outputs from the two 8255s will cause the INTR pin on the microprocessor to go high requesting an interrupt.

When the INTR pin does go high with a daisy-chain, the hardware gives no direct indication as to which 8255 or which INTR output caused the interrupt. The task of locating which INTR output became active is up to the interrupt service procedure, which must poll the 8255s to determine who caused the interrupt.

Example 10–7 illustrates the interrupt service procedure that responds to the daisy-chain interrupt request. This procedure polls each 8255 and each INTR output to decide which interrupt service procedure to utilize.

EXAMPLE 10–7

```
                        ;Procedure that services the daisy-chain interrupt
                        ;
= 0504                  C1      EQU   504H              ;first 8255A
= 0604                  C2      EQU   604H              ;second 8255A
= 0001                  MASK1   EQU   1                 ;INTRB
= 0008                  MASK2   EQU   8                 ;INTRA

0000                    POLL    PROC  FAR

0000 50                         PUSH  AX                ;save registers
0001 52                         PUSH  DX

0002 BA 0504                    MOV   DX,C1             ;address port C
0005 EC                         IN    AL,DX
0006 A8 01                      TEST  AL,MASK1
0008 75 0F                      JNZ   LEVEL_0           ;if INTRB of first 8255A

000A A8 08                      TEST  AL,MASK2
000C 75 13                      JNZ   LEVEL_1           ;if INTRA of first 8255A

000E BA 0604                    MOV   DX,C2             ;address port C
0011 EC                         IN    AL,DX
0012 A8 01                      TEST  AL,MASK1
0014 75 1B                      JNZ   LEVEL_2           ;if INTRB of second 8255A
0016 EB 29 9                    JMP   LEVEL_3           ;if INTRA of second 8255A

0019                    POLL    ENDP
```

10–4   8259A PROGRAMMABLE INTERRUPT CONTROLLER

The 8259A programmable interrupt controller (PIC) adds eight vectored priority encoded interrupts to the microprocessor. This controller can be expanded without additional hardware to accept up to 64 interrupt request inputs. This expansion requires a master 8259A and eight 8259A slaves.

General Description of the 8259A

Figure 10–14 shows the pinout of the 8259A. The 8259A is easy to connect to the microprocessor because all of its pins are direct connections except the $\overline{CS}$ pin, which must be decoded, and the $\overline{WR}$ pin, which must have an I/O bank write pulse. Following is a description of each pin on the 8259A:

1. D7–D0—Bidirectional Data Connections: pins normally connected to either the upper or lower data bus on the 8086 microprocessor or the data bus on the 8088.
2. IR7–IR0—Interrupt Request Inputs: used to request an interrupt and to connect to a slave in a system with multiple 8259As.
3. $\overline{WR}$—Write: an input connected to either the lower or upper write strobe signal.
4. $\overline{RD}$—Read: an input connected to the $\overline{IORC}$ signal.
5. INT—Interrupt: an output connected to the INTR pin on the microprocessor from the master, and connected to a master IR pin on a slave.
6. $\overline{INTA}$—Interrupt Acknowledge: an input connected to the $\overline{INTA}$ signal on the system. In a system with a master and slaves, only the master $\overline{INTA}$ signal is connected.
7. A0—Address: an input that selects different command words within the 8259A.
8. $\overline{CS}$—Chip Select: used to enable the 8259A for program and control.
9. SP/EN—Slave Program/Enable Buffer: A dual-function pin. When the 8259A is in buffered mode, this is an output that controls the data bus transceivers. When the 8259A is not in the buffered mode, this pin programs the device as a master (1) or a slave (0).
10. CAS2–CAS0—Cascade Lines: used as outputs from the master to the slaves for cascading multiple 8259As in a system.

Connecting a Single 8259A

Figure 10–15 shows a single 8259A connected to the 8086 microprocessor. Here the $\overline{SP/EN}$ pin is pulled high to indicate that it is a master. Also note that the 8259A is decoded at I/O ports 0400H and 0402H by the PAL16L8 (no program shown). Like other peripherals discussed in the prior chapter, the 8259A requires two wait states for it to function properly with an 8MHz 8086.

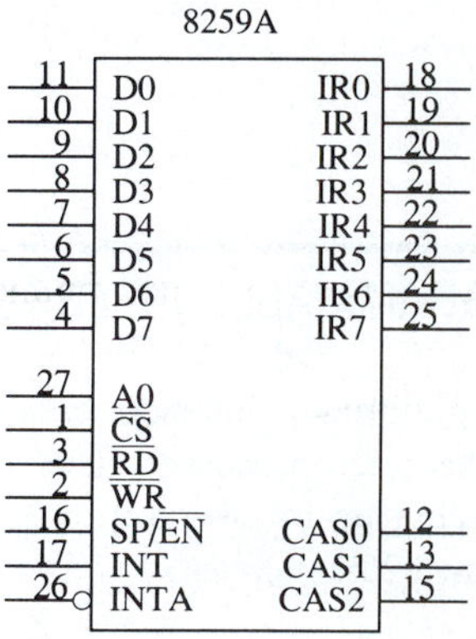

FIGURE 10–14 The pinout of the 8259A programmable interrupt controller (PIC).

FIGURE 10-15 An 8259A interfaced to the 8086 microprocessor.

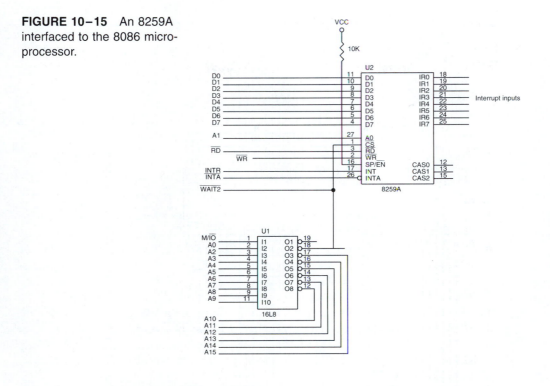

Cascading Multiple 8259As

Figure 10-16 shows two 8259As connected to the 8086 microprocessor in a way that is often found in the AT-style computer, which has 2 8259As for interrupts. The XT- or PC-style computer uses one 8259A at interrupt vectors 08H through 0FH. The AT-style computer uses interrupt vector 0AH as a cascade input from a second 8259A located at vectors 70H through 77H. Appendix A contains a table that lists the functions of all the interrupt vectors used in the PC-, XT-, and AT-style computers.

This circuit uses vectors 08H–0FH and I/O ports 0300H and 0302H for U1, the master, and vectors 70H–77H and I/O ports 0304H and 0306H for U2, the slave. Notice that we also include data bus buffers to illustrate the use of the $\overline{SP/EN}$ pin on the 8259A. These buffers are only used in various large systems that have many devices connected to their data bus connections. In practice, we seldom find these buffers.

Programming the 8259A

The 8259A is programmed by initialization and operation command words. *Initialization command words* (ICWs) are programmed before the 8259A is able to function in the system and dictate the basic operation of the 8259A. *Operation command words* (OCWs) are programmed during the normal course of operation and allow the 8259A to function properly.

Initialization Command Words.   There are four initialization command words (ICWs) for the 8259A that are selected when the A0 pin is a logic 1. When the 8259A is first powered up, it must be sent ICW1, ICW2, and ICW4. If the 8259A is programmed in cascade

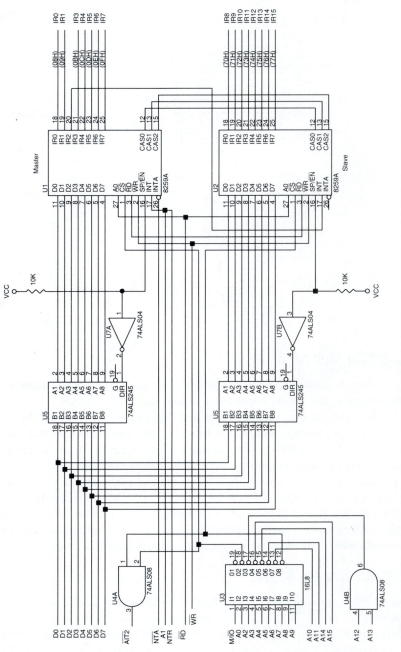

FIGURE 10–16 Two 8259As interfaced to the 8259A at I/O ports 0300H and 0302H for the master and 0304H and 0306H for the slave.

mode by ICW1, then we also must program ICW3. So if a single 8259A is used in a system, ICW1, ICW2, and ICW4 must be programmed. If cascade mode is used in a system, then all four ICWs must be programmed. Refer to Figure 10–17 for the format of all four ICWs. The following is a description of each ICW:

1. ICW1—programs the basic operation of the 8259A. To program this ICW for 8086–80486 operation, we place a logic 1 in bit IC4. Bits ADI, A7, A6, and A5 are don't cares for microprocessor operation and only apply to the 8259A when used with an 8-bit 8085 microprocessor. This ICW selects single or cascade operation by programming the SNGL bit. If cascade operation is selected, we must also program ICW3. The LTIM bit determines whether the interrupt request inputs are positive edge-triggered or level-triggered.

2. ICW2—selects the vector number used with the interrupt request inputs. For example, if we decide to program the 8259A so it functions at vector locations 08H–0FH, we place a 08H into this command word. Likewise, if we decide to program the 8259A for vectors 70H–77H, we place a 70H in this ICW.

3. ICW3—is only used when ICW1 indicates that the system is operated in cascade mode. This ICW indicates where the slave is connected to the master. For example, in Figure 10–16 we connected a slave to IR2. To program ICW3 for this connection, in both master and slave, we place a 04H in ICW3. Suppose we have two slaves connected to a master using IR0 and IR1. The master is programmed with an ICW3 of 03H and one slave is programmed with an ICW3 of 01H and the other with an ICW3 of 02H.

4. ICW4—is programmed for use with the 8086–80486 microprocessor. This ICW is not programmed in a system that functions with the 8085 microprocessor. The rightmost bit must be a logic 1 to select operation with the 8086–80486 microprocessor, and the remaining bits are programmed as follows:
   a. SFNM—selects the special fully nested mode of operation for the 8259A if a logic 1 is placed in this bit. This allows the highest priority interrupt request from a slave to be recognized by the master while it is processing another interrupt from a slave. Normally only one interrupt request is processed at a time and others are ignored until the process is complete.
   b. BUF and M/S—buffer and master slave are used together to select buffered operation or nonbuffered operation for the 8259A as a master or a slave
   c. AEOI—selects automatic or normal end of interrupt (discussed more fully under operation command words). The EOI commands of OCW2 are only used if the AEOI mode is not selected by ICW4. If AEOI is selected, the interrupt automatically resets the interrupt request bit and does not modify priority. This is the preferred mode of operation for the 8259A and reduces the length of the interrupt service procedure.

Operation Command Words.   The operation command words (OCWs) are used to direct the operation of the 8259A once it is programmed with the ICWs. The OCWs are selected when the A0 pin is at a logic 0 level, except for OCW1, which is selected when A0 is a logic 1. Figure 10–18 lists the binary bit patterns for all three operation command words of the 8259A. Following is a list describing the function of each OCW:

FIGURE 10–17 The 8259A initialization command words (ICWS). (Courtesy of Intel Corporation)

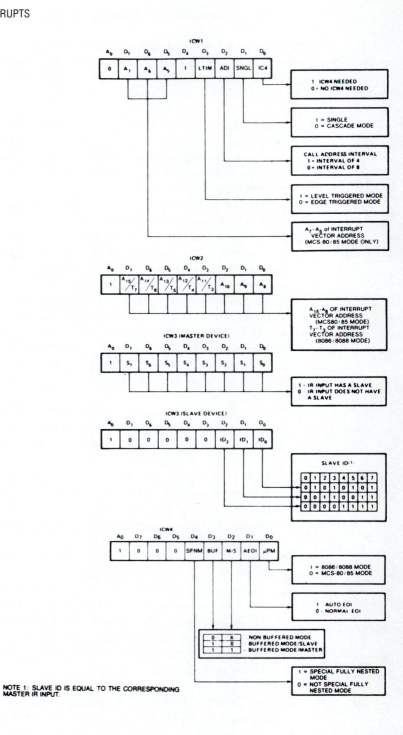

FIGURE 10–18 The 8259A operational command words (OCWs). (Courtesy of Intel Corporation)

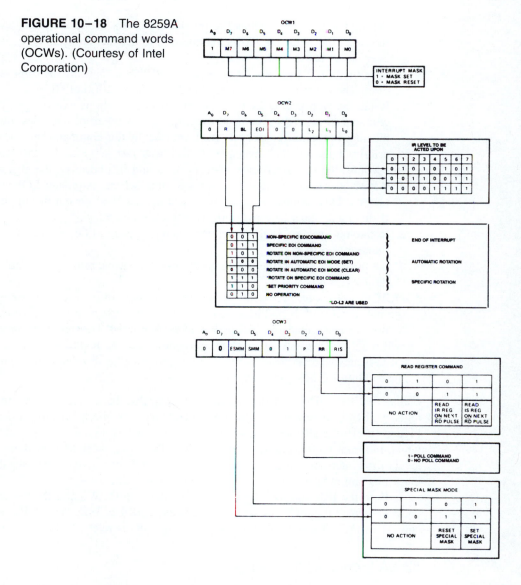

1. OCW1—is used to set and read the interrupt mask register. When a mask bit is set, it will *turn off* (mask) the corresponding interrupt input. The mask register is read when OCW1 is read. Because the state of the mask bits is unknown when the 8259A is first initialized, OCW1 must be programmed after programming the ICWs upon initialization.

2. OCW2—is programmed only when the AEOI mode is not selected for the 8259A. In this case, this OCW selects how the 8259A responds to an interrupt. The modes are listed as follows:

   a. Nonspecific End-of-Interrupt—a command sent by the interrupt service procedure to signal the end of the interrupt. The 8259A automatically determines which interrupt level was active and resets the correct bit of the interrupt status register. Resetting the status bit allows the interrupt to take action again or a lower priority interrupt to take effect.

    b. Specific End-of-Interrupt—a command that allows a specific interrupt request to be reset. The exact position is determined with bits L2–L0 of OCW2.

    c. Rotate-on-Nonspecific EOI—A command that functions exactly like the nonspecific end-of-interrupt command except it rotates interrupt priorities after resetting the interrupt status register bit. The level reset by this command becomes the lowest priority interrupt. For example, if IR4 was just serviced by this command, it becomes the lowest priority interrupt input and IR5 becomes the highest priority.

    d. Rotate-on-Automatic EOI—a command that selects automatic EOI with rotating priority. This command must only be sent to the 8259A once if this mode is desired. If this mode must be turned off, use the clear command.

    e. Rotate-on-Specific EOI—functions as the specific EOI, except that it selects rotating priority.

    f. Set priority—allows the programmer to set the lowest priority interrupt input using the L2–L0 bits.

3. OCW3—selects the register to be read, the operation of the special mask register, and the poll command. If polling is selected, the P-bit must be set and then output to the 8259A. The next read operation will read the poll word. The rightmost three bits of the poll word indicate the active interrupt request with the highest priority. The leftmost bit indicates whether there is an interrupt, and must be checked to determine whether the rightmost 3 bits contain valid information.

Status Register.   Three status registers are readable in the 8259A: interrupt request register (IRR), in-service register (ISR), and interrupt mask register (IMR) (refer to Figure 10–19 for all three status registers). The IRR is an 8-bit register that indicates which interrupt request inputs are active. The ISR is an 8-bit register that contains the level of the interrupt being serviced. The IMR is an 8-bit register that holds the interrupt mask bits and indicates which interrupts are masked off.

    Both the IRR and ISR are read by programming OCW3 and IMR is read through OCW1. To read the IMR, A0 = 1 and to read either IRR or ISR, A0 = 0. Bit positions D0 and D1 of OCW3 select which register (IRR or ISR) is read when A0 = 0.

8259A Programming Example

Figure 10–20 illustrates the 8259A programmable interrupt controller connected to an 8251A programmable communications controller. In this circuit, three interrupt output

FIGURE 10–19   The 8259A in-service register (ISR). (a) Before IR$_4$ is accepted, and (b) after IR$_4$ is accepted. (Courtesy of Intel Corporation)

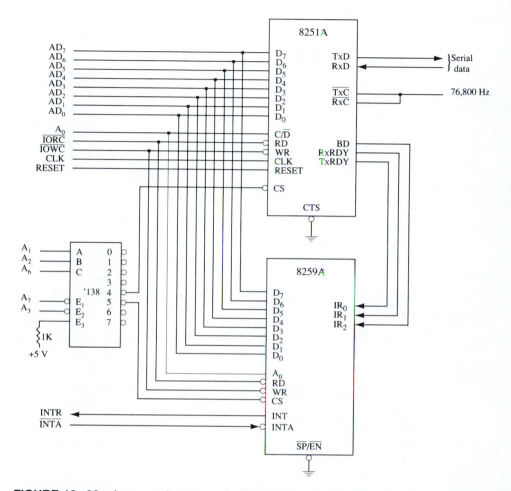

FIGURE 10–20   An example communications circuit using the 8251A and the 8259A.

pins from the 8251A (TxRDY, RxRDY, and SY/BR) are connected to the PICs interrupt request inputs IR0, IR1, and IR2. An IR0 occurs whenever the transmitter is ready to send another character. When the receiver has received a character for the 8086, IR1 is active because of RxRDY. The IR2 input is used for break detection. Notice that the 8251A is decoded at 8-bit I/O ports 40H and 42H, and the 8259A is decoded at 8-bit I/O ports 44H and 46H. Because A5 is not connected to the decoder (partially decoded ports), the 8251A also functions at ports 60H and 62H and the 8259A functions at ports 64H and 66H. Both devices are interfaced to the lower data bus.

Initialization Software.   The first portion of the software for this system must program both the 8251A and the 8259A and then enable the INTR pin on the 8086 so interrupts can take effect. Example 10–8 lists the software required to program both devices and enable INTR.

EXAMPLE 10–8

```
                          ;Initialization dialog for the 8251A and the 8259A
                          ;
= 0042              PCC_C    EQU   42H              ;8251A control register
= 0044              PIC_C1   EQU   44H              ;8259A control A0 = 0
= 0046              PIC_C2   EQU   46H              ;8259A control A0 = 1
= 0040              FORTY    EQU   40H              ;reset command for 8251A
= 007B              INST1    EQU   7BH              ;8251A mode word
= 0015              INST2    EQU   15H              ;8251A command word
= 001B              ICW1     EQU   1BH              ;8259A ICW1
= 0080              ICW2     EQU   80H              ;8259A ICW2
= 0003              ICW4     EQU   03H              ;8259A ICW4
= 00F9              OCW1     EQU   0F9H             ;8259A OCW1


0000                START    PROC  FAR

                          ;set up the 8251A for 7 data bits, even parity, one stop bit,
                          ;and a clock divider of 64.
                          ;
                          ;program 8251A
                          ;
0000 32 C0                         XOR   AL,AL               ;reset 8251A
0002 E6 42                         OUT   PCC_C,AL
0004 E6 42                         OUT   PCC_C,AL
0006 E6 42                         OUT   PCC_C,AL
0008 B0 40                         MOV   AL,FORTY
000A E6 42                         OUT   PCC_C,AL

000C B0 7B                         MOV   AL,INST1            ;program 8251A mode
000E E6 42                         OUT   PCC_C,AL
0010 B0 15                         MOV   AL,INST2            ;program 8251A command
0012 E6 42                         OUT   PCC_C,AL


                          ;program 8259A

0014 B0 1B                         MOV   AL,ICW1             ;program ICW1
0016 E6 44                         OUT   PIC_C1,AL
0018 B0 80                         MOV   AL,ICW2             ;program ICW2
001A E6 46                         OUT   PIC_C2,AL
001C B0 03                         MOV   AL,ICW4             ;program ICW4
001E E6 46                         OUT   PIC_C2,AL

0020 B0 F9                         MOV   AL,OCW1             ;program OCW1
0022 E6 46                         OUT   PIC_C2,AL

0024 FB                            STI                       ;enable INTR
0025 CB                            RET

0026                START    ENDP
```

The first portion of the procedure (START) resets the 8251A and programs the mode and command words. The mode selects 7 data bits, even parity, one stop bit, and a clock divider of 64 that causes the transmitter and receiver to transfer serial data at 1200 Baud. The command enables both the transmitter and receiver.

The second part of the procedure programs the 8259A with its three ICWs and its one OCW. The 8259A is set up so it functions at interrupt vectors 80H–87H and operates with automatic EOI. The ICW enables the break detection interrupt and the receiver interrupt, but not the transmitter interrupt. The transmitter interrupt is only enabled when there is data to transmit. The transmitter is periodically enabled and disabled during normal operation by reading OCW1, modifying the mask bits, and then rewriting OCW1.

The last thing that the START procedure does is enable the INTR pin so a receiver or break detection interrupt can take effect immediately.

Receiving Data from the 8251A. The data received by the 8251A are stored in a FIFO memory until the software in the main program can use them. The FIFO memory used for received data is 16K bytes in length, so many characters can easily be stored and received before any intervention from the 8086 is required to empty the receiver FIFO. The receiver FIFO is stored in the extra segment so string instructions, using the DI register, can be used to access it.

Receiving data from the 8251A requires two procedures: one reads the data register of the 8251A each time that the RxRDY pin requests an interrupt and stores it into the FIFO, and the other reads data from the FIFO from the main program.

Example 10-9 lists the procedure used to read data from the FIFO from the main program. This procedure assumes that the pointers (IIN and IOUT) are initialized in the initialization dialog for the system (not shown). The READ procedure returns with AL containing a character read from the FIFO. If the FIFO is empty, the procedure returns with the character FEH in AL. This means that FEH is not allowed as a character at the receiver.

EXAMPLE 10-9

```
                      ;Main procedure to read a character from the FIFO
                      ;AL is the character upon return or FEH if FIFO is empty.
                      ;
= 0046                OCW1    EQU   46H                       ;address of OCW1
= 00FD                MASK1   EQU   0FDH

0000                  READ    PROC  FAR

0000 53                       PUSH  BX                        ;save registers
0001 57                       PUSH  DI

                      ;test for empty FIFO

0002 26: 8B 3E 4002 R         MOV   DI,IOUT                   ;get output pointer
0007 26: 8B 1E 4000 R         MOV   BX,IIN                    ;get input pointer

000C 3B DF                    CMP   BX,DI                     ;test for empty
000E B0 FE                    MOV   AL,0FEH                   ;indicate empty
0010 74 16                    JE    DONE                      ;if empty

                      ;get character from FIFO

0012 26: 8A 06                MOV   AL,ES:[DI]                ;get data

                      ;modify and save output pointer

0015 47                       INC   DI                        ;adjust pointer
0016 81 FF 4000 R             CMP   DI,OFFSET FIFO+16*1024
001A 26: 89 3E 4002 R         MOV   IOUT,DI
001F 76 07                    JBE   DONE                      ;if within bounds
```

```
0021 26: C7 06 4002 R 0000 R MOV  IOUT,OFFSET FIFO          ;point to FIFO start

                        ;enable RxRDY interrupt

0028                    DONE:

0028 50                        PUSH AX
0029 E4 46                     IN   AL,OCW1
002B 24 FD                     AND  AL,MASK1
002D E6 46                     OUT  OCW1,AL

002F 58                        POP  AX                        ;restore registers
0030 5F                        POP  DI
0031 5B                        POP  BX
0032 CB                        RET

0033                    READ   ENDP
```

Example 10–10 lists the RxRDY interrupt service procedure that is called each time the 8251A receives a character for the 8086. In this example, this interrupt uses vector type number 81H, which must contain the address of the RxRDY interrupt service procedure. Each time this interrupt occurs the RxRDY procedure reads a character from the 8251A and stores it into the FIFO. If the FIFO is full, the IR1 input to the 8259A is disabled. This may result in lost data, but at least it will not cause the interrupt to overrun valid data already stored in the FIFO. Any error conditions detected by the 8251A store a ? (3FH) in the FIFO.

EXAMPLE 10–10

```
                        ;Interrupt service procedure for RxRDY (IR1)
                        ;
= 0040                  DATA   EQU   40H              ;8251A data port
= 0046                  OCW1   EQU   46H              ;8259A OCW1 port
= 0002                  MASK2  EQU   02H              ;turn off IR1 mask
= 0042                  PCC_C  EQU   42H              ;8251A command port
= 0038                  MASK3  EQU   38H               ;8251A error mask

0000                    RXRDY  PROC   FAR

0000 50                        PUSH AX                ;save registers
0001 53                        PUSH BX
0002 57                        PUSH DI
0003 56                        PUSH SI
0004 26: 8B 1E 4002 R          MOV  BX,IOUT           ;load output pointer
0009 26: 8B 36 4000 R          MOV  SI,IIN            ;load input pointer

                        ;is FIFO full?

000E 8B FE                     MOV  DI,SI
0010 46                        INC  SI
0011 81 FE 4000 R              CMP  SI,OFFSET FIFO+16*1024
0015 76 03                     JBE  NEXT
0017 BE 0000 R                 MOV  SI,OFFSET FIFO

001A                    NEXT:

001A 3B DE                     CMP  BX,SI
001C 74 20                     JE   FULL
```

```
                        ;test for 8251A errors

001E E4 42                          IN    AL,PCC_C                 ;get 8251A status register
0020 24 38                          AND   AL,MASK3
0022 74 0F                          JZ    NEXT1                    ;if no errors
0024 B0 10                          MOV   AL,10H                   ;reset errors
0026 E6 42                          OUT   PCC_C,AL
0028 B0 3F                          MOV   AL,'?'
002A AA                             STOSB
002B 26: 89 36 4000 R               MOV   IIN,SI
0030 EB 12 90                       JMP   DONE                     ;if an error

                        ;read character

0033                    NEXT1:

0033 E4 40                          IN    AL,DATA                  ;get 8251A data
0035 AA                             STOSB
0036 26: 89 36 4000 R               MOV   IIN,SI
003B EB 07 90                       JMP   DONE

                        ;if full

003E                    FULL:

003E E4 46                          IN    AL,OCW1                  ;disable IR1
0040 0C 02                          OR    AL,MASK2
0042 E6 46                          OUT   OCW1,AL

0044                    DONE:

0044 5E                             POP   SI                       ;restore registers
0045 5F                             POP   DI
0046 5B                             POP   BX
0047 58                             POP   AX
0048 CF                             IRET

0049                    RXRDY   ENDP
```

Transmitting Data to the 8251A.   Data are transmitted to the 8251A in much the same manner as they are received, except the interrupt service procedure removes transmitted data from a second 16K byte FIFO.

Example 10–11 lists the procedure that fills the output FIFO. It is similar to the procedure listed in Example 10–9, except it determines whether the FIFO is full instead of empty.

EXAMPLE 10–11

```
                        ;Procedure that places data into the output FIFO for
                        ;transmission by the transmitter interrupt service procedure.
                        ;AL = character to be transmitted.
                        ;
= 0046                  OCW1    EQU   46H                          ;8259A OCW1 port
= 00FE                  MASK4   EQU   0FEH                         ;turn IR0 on

0000                    TRANS   PROC   FAR
```

```
0000 53                              PUSH  BX                          ;save registers
0001 57                              PUSH  DI
0002 56                              PUSH  SI

                     ;check if FIFO is full

0003 26: 8B 36 8004 R               MOV   SI,OIN                       ;get input pointer
0008 26: 8B 1E 8006 R               MOV   BX,OOUT                      ;get output pointer
000D 8B FE                          MOV   DI,SI
000F 46                             INC   SI
0010 81 FE 8004 R                   CMP   SI,OFFSET OFIFO+16*1024
0014 76 03                          JBE   NEXT
0016 BE 4004 R                      MOV   SI,OFFSET OFIFO

0019                 NEXT:

0019 3B DE                          CMP   BX,SI
001B 74 06                          JE    DONE                         ;if full
001D AA                             STOSB
001E 26: 89 36 8004 R               MOV   OIN,SI

                    DONE:

0023 E4 46                          IN    AL,OCW1                      ;enable transmitter interrupt
0025 24 FE                          AND   AL,MASK4
0027 E6 46                          OUT   OCW1,AL

0029 5E                             POP   SI                           ;restore registers
002A 5F                             POP   DI
002B 5B                             POP   BX
002C CB                             RET

002D                TRANS ENDP
```

Example 10–12 lists the interrupt service subroutine for the 8251A transmitter, T×RDY, using interrupt vector number 80H. This procedure is similar to the RXRDY procedure of Example 10–10, except it determines whether the FIFO is empty rather than full. Note that we do not include an interrupt service procedure for the break interrupt.

EXAMPLE 10–12

```
                    ;Interrupt service procedure for the 8251A transmitter
                    ;
= 0040              DATA  EQU   40H                      ;8251A data port
= 0001              MASK5 EQU   01H                      ;turn IR0 off

002D                TXRDY PROC  FAR

002D 50                             PUSH  AX                           ;save registers
002E 53                             PUSH  BX
002F 57                             PUSH  DI
0030 26: 8B 1E 8004 R               MOV   BX,OIN                       ;load input pointer
0035 26: 8B 3E 8006 R               MOV   DI,OOUT  ;load output pointer

                    ;is FIFO empty?

003A 3B DF                          CMP   BX,DI
003C 74 17                          JE    EMPTY                        ;if empty
```

```
                        ;write character

003E 26: 8A 05                 MOV   AL,ES:[DI]
0041 E6 40                     OUT   DATA,AL
0043 47                        INC   DI
0044 81 FF 8004 R              CMP   DI,OFFSET OFIFO+16*1024
0048 76 03                     JBE   NEXT1
004A BF 4004 R                 MOV   DI,OFFSET OFIFO

004D                  NEXT1:

004D 26: 89 3E 8006 R          MOV   OOUT,DI
0052 EB 07 90                  JMP   DONES

0055                  EMPTY:

0055 E4 46                     IN    AL,OCW1
0057 0C 01                     OR    AL,MASK5
0059 E6 46                     OUT   OCW1,AL

005B                  DONES:

005B 5F                        POP   DI                      ;restore registers
005C 5B                        POP   BX
005D 58                        POP   AX
005E CF                        IRET

005F                  TXRDY     ENDP
```

10-5   REAL-TIME CLOCK

This section of the text presents a real-time clock as an example use of an interrupt. A real-time clock keeps time in real time, that is in hours and minutes. The example illustrated here keeps time in hours, minutes, seconds, and 1/60 seconds using four memory locations to hold the BCD time of day.

Figure 10-21 illustrates a simple circuit that uses the 60 Hz AC power line to generate a periodic interrupt request signal for the NMI interrupt input pin. Although we are using a signal from the AC power line, which varies slightly in frequency from time to time, it is accurate over a period of time. The circuit uses a signal from the 120 VAC power line that is conditioned by a Schmitt trigger inverter before it is applied to the NMI interrupt input. Note that you must make certain that the power line ground is connected

FIGURE 10-21 Converting the AC power line to a 60-Hz TTL signal for the NMI input.

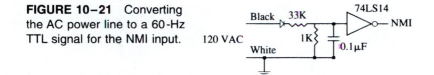

to the system ground in this schematic. The power line ground (neutral) connection is the large flat pin on the power line. The narrow flat pin is the hot side or 120 VAC side of the line.

The software for the real-time clock contains an interrupt service procedure that is called 60 times per second and a procedure that updates the count located in four memory locations. Example 10–13 lists both procedures along with the four bytes of memory used to hold the BCD time of day.

EXAMPLE 10–13

```
0000 00                TIME     DB    ?          ;1/60 seconds counter
0001 00                         DB    ?          ;seconds counter
0002 00                         DB    ?          ;minutes counter
0003 00                         DB    ?          ;hours counter (24 hour clock)

                       ;Interrupt service procedure for NMI

0004                   TIMES    PROC    FAR

0004 50                         PUSH AX           ;save registers
0005 56                         PUSH SI

0006 B4 60                      MOV  AH,60H       ;load modulus of counter
0008 BE 0000 R                  MOV  SI,OFFSET TIME   ;address time
000B E8 0022 R                  CALL UP           ;adjust 1/60 counter
000E 75 0F                      JNZ  DONE
0010 E8 0022 R                  CALL UP           ;adjust seconds counter
0013 75 0A                      JZ   DONE
0015 E8 0022 R                  CALL UP           ;adjust minutes
0018 75 05                      JZ   DONE
001A B4 24                      MOV  AH,24H       ;modulus 24
001C E8 0022 R                  CALL UP

001F                   DONE:

001F 5E                         POP  SI           ;restore registers
0020 58                         POP  AX
0021 CF                         IRET

0022                   TIMES    ENDP

0022                   UP       PROC    NEAR

0022 2E: 8A 04                  MOV  AL,CS:[SI]
0025 46                         INC  SI
0026 04 01                      ADD  AL,1         ;increment counter
0028 27                         DAA
0029 2E: 88 44 FF               MOV  CS:[SI-1],AL
002D 2A C4                      SUB  AL,AH
002F 75 04                      JNZ  UP1
0031 2E: 88 44 FF               MOV  CS:[SI-1],AL

0035                   UP1:

0035 C3                         RET

0036                   UP       ENDP
```

10–6   SUMMARY

1. An interrupt is a hardware- or software-initiated call that interrupts the currently executing program at any point and calls a procedure. The procedure called by the interrupt is an interrupt service procedure.
2. Interrupts are useful when an I/O device needs to be serviced only occasionally at low data transfer rates.
3. The microprocessor has five instructions that apply to interrupts: BOUND, INT, INT 3, INTO, and IRET. The INT and INT 3 instructions call procedures with addresses stored in interrupt vector whose type is indicated by the instruction. The BOUND instruction is a conditional interrupt that uses interrupt vector type number 5. The INTO instruction is a conditional interrupt that only interrupts a program if the overflow flag is set. Finally, the IRET instruction is used to return from interrupt service procedures.
4. The microprocessor has three pins that apply to its hardware interrupt structure: INTR, NMI, and $\overline{\text{INTA}}$. The interrupt inputs are INTR and NMI that are used to request interrupts and $\overline{\text{INTA}}$ is an output used to acknowledge the INTR interrupt request.
5. Interrupts are referenced through a vector table that occupies memory locations 00000H–003FFH. Each interrupt vector is four bytes in length and contains the offset and segment addresses of the interrupt service procedure.
6. Two flag bits are used with the interrupt structure of the microprocessor: trap (TF) and interrupt enable (IF). The IF flag bit enables the INTR interrupt input, and the TF flag bit causes interrupts to occur after the execution of each instruction as long as TF is active.
7. The first 32 interrupt vector locations are reserved for Intel use with many predefined in the microprocessor. The last 224 interrupt vectors are for user use and can perform any function desired.
8. Whenever an interrupt is detected, the following events occur: (1) the flags are pushed onto the stack, (2) the IF and TF flag bits are both cleared, (3) the IP and CS registers are both pushed onto the stack, and (4) the interrupt vector is fetched from the interrupt vector table and the interrupt service subroutine is accessed through the vector address.
9. Tracing or single-stepping is accomplished by setting the TF flag bit. This causes an interrupt to occur after the execution of each instruction for debugging.
10. The nonmaskable interrupt input (NMI) calls the procedure whose address is stored at interrupt vector type number 2. This input is positive-edge triggered.
11. The INTR pin is not internally decoded as is the NMI pin. Instead, $\overline{\text{INTA}}$ is used to apply the interrupt vector type number to data bus connections D0–D7 during the $\overline{\text{INTA}}$ pulse.
12. Methods of applying the interrupt vector type number to the data bus during $\overline{\text{INTA}}$ vary widely. One method uses resistors to apply interrupt type number FFH to the data bus, while another uses a three-state buffer to apply any vector type number.
13. The 8259A programmable interrupt controller (PIC) adds at least eight interrupt inputs to the microprocessor. If more interrupts are needed, this device can be cascaded to provide up to 64 interrupt inputs.

14. Programming the 8259A is a two-step process. First a series of initialization command words (ICWs) are sent to the 8259A, then a series of operation command words (OCWs) are sent.
15. The 8259A contains three status registers: IMR (interrupt mask register), ISR (in-service register), and IRR (interrupt request register).
16. A real-time clock is used to keep time in real time. In most cases time is stored in either binary or BCD form in several memory locations.

10–7   QUESTIONS AND PROBLEMS

1. What is interrupted by an interrupt?
2. Define the term *interrupt*.
3. What is called by an interrupt?
4. Why do interrupts free up time for the microprocessor?
5. List the interrupt pins found on the microprocessor.
6. List the five interrupt instructions for the microprocessor.
7. What is an interrupt vector?
8. Where are the interrupt vectors located in the microprocessor's memory?
9. How many different interrupt vectors are found in the interrupt vector table?
10. Which interrupt vectors are reserved by Intel?
11. Explain how a type 0 interrupt occurs.
12. Describe the operation of the BOUND instruction.
13. Describe the operation of the INTO instruction.
14. What memory locations contain the vector for an INT 44H instruction?
15. Explain the operation of the IRET instruction.
16. What is the purpose of interrupt vector type number 7?
17. List the events that occur when an interrupt becomes active.
18. Explain the purpose of the interrupt flag (IF).
19. Explain the purpose of the trap flag (TF).
20. How is IF cleared and set?
21. How is TF cleared and set?
22. The NMI interrupt input automatically vectors through which vector type number?
23. Does the $\overline{\text{INTA}}$ signal activate for the NMI pin?
24. The INTR input is _____-sensitive.
25. The NMI input is _____-sensitive.
26. When the $\overline{\text{INTA}}$ signal becomes a logic 0, it indicates that the microprocessor is waiting for an interrupt _____ number to be placed on the data bus (D0–D7).
27. What is a FIFO?
28. Develop a circuit that places interrupt type number 86H on the data bus in response to the INTR input.
29. Develop a circuit that places interrupt type number CCH on the data bus in response to the INTR input.

30. Explain why pullup resistors on D0–D7 cause the microprocessor to respond with interrupt vector type number FFH for the $\overline{\text{INTA}}$ pulse.
31. What is a daisy-chain?
32. Why must interrupting devices be polled in a daisy-chained interrupt system?
33. What is the 8259A?
34. How many 8259As are required to have 64 interrupt inputs?
35. What is the purpose of the IR0–IR7 pins on the 8259A?
36. When are the CAS2–CAS0 pins used on the 8259A?
37. Where is a slave INT pin connected on the master 8259A in a cascaded system?
38. What is an ICW?
39. What is an OCW?
40. How many ICWs are needed to program the 8259A when operated as a single master in a system?
41. Where is the vector type number stored in the 8259A?
42. Where is the sensitivity of the IR pins programmed in the 8259A?
43. What is the purpose of ICW1?
44. What is a nonspecific EOI?
45. Explain priority rotation in the 8259A.
46. What is the purpose of IRR in the 8259A?

CHAPTER 11

Direct Memory Access and DMA-Controlled I/O

INTRODUCTION

In previous chapters, we discussed basic and interrupt-processed I/O. Now we turn to the final form of I/O called *direct memory access* (DMA). The DMA I/O technique provides direct access to the memory while the microprocessor is temporarily disabled. This allows data to be transferred between memory and the I/O device at a rate that is limited only by the speed of the memory components in the system or the DMA controller. The DMA transfer speed can approach 10–12 M-byte transfer rates with today's high-speed RAM memory components.

DMA transfers are used for many purposes, but more common are DRAM refresh, video displays for refreshing the screen, and disk memory system reads and writes. The DMA transfer is also used to do high-speed memory-to-memory transfers.

This chapter also explains the operation of disk memory systems and video systems that are often DMA processed. Disk memory includes: floppy, fixed, and optical disk storage. Video systems include: digital and analog monitors.

CHAPTER OBJECTIVES

Upon completion of this chapter, you will be able to:

1. Describe a DMA transfer.
2. Explain the operation of the HOLD and HLDA direct memory access control signals.
3. Explain the function of the 8237 DMA controller when used for DMA transfers.
4. Program the 8237 to accomplish DMA transfers.
5. Describe the disk standards found in personal computer systems.
6. Describe the various video interface standards that are found in the personal computer.

11-1   BASIC DMA OPERATION

Two control signals are used to request and acknowledge a direct memory access (DMA) transfer in the microprocessor-based system. The HOLD pin is an input used to request a DMA action and the HLDA pin is an output that acknowledges the DMA action. Figure 11–1 shows the timing that is typically found on these two DMA control pins.

Whenever the HOLD input is placed at a logic 1 level, a DMA action (hold) is requested. The microprocessor responds, within a few clocks, by suspending the execution of the program and by placing its address, data, and control bus at their high-impedance states. The high-impedance state causes the microprocessor to appear as if it has been removed from its socket. This state allows external I/O devices or other microprocessors to gain access to the system buses so memory can be accessed directly.

As the timing diagram indicates, HOLD is sampled in the middle of any clocking cycle. Thus, the hold can take effect at any time during the operation of any instruction in the microprocessor. As soon as the microprocessor recognizes the hold, it stops executing software and enters hold cycles. Note that the HOLD input has a higher priority than the INTR or NMI interrupt inputs. Interrupts take effect at the end of an instruction, while a HOLD takes effect in the middle of an instruction. The only microprocessor pin that has a higher priority than a HOLD is the RESET pin. Note that the HOLD input may not be active during a RESET or the reset is not guaranteed.

The HLDA signal becomes active to indicate that the microprocessor has indeed placed its buses at their high-impedance state as can be seen in the timing diagram. Note that there are a few clock cycles between the time that HOLD changes until the time that HLDA changes. The HLDA output is a signal to the external requesting device that the microprocessor has relinquished control of its memory and I/O space. You could call the HOLD input a DMA request input and the HLDA output a DMA grant signal.

Basic DMA Definitions

Direct memory accesses normally occur between an I/O device and memory without the use of the microprocessor. A *DMA read* transfers data from the memory to the I/O device. A *DMA write* transfers data from an I/O device to memory. In both operations, the memory and I/O are controlled simultaneously and that is why the system contains

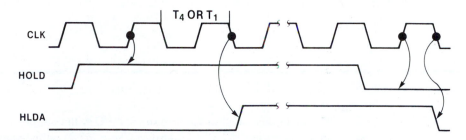

FIGURE 11–1   HOLD and HLDA timing for the 8086/8088 microprocessor.

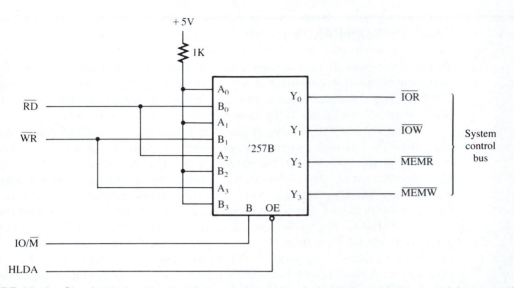

FIGURE 11-2 Circuit used to develop the control bus signals in a system that uses minimum mode DMA for the 8088 microprocessor.

separate memory and I/O control signals. This special control bus structure of the microprocessor allows DMA transfers. A DMA read causes the $\overline{MRDC}$ ($\overline{MEMR}$) and $\overline{IOWC}$ ($\overline{IOW}$) signals to both activate transferring data from the memory to the I/O device. A DMA write causes the $\overline{MWTC}$ ($\overline{MEMW}$) and $\overline{IORC}$ ($\overline{IOR}$) signals to both activate. These control bus signals are available to all microprocessors in the Intel family except the 8086/8088 system. The 8086/8088 require their generation with either a system controller or a circuit such as the one illustrated in Figure 11-2. The DMA controller provides the memory with its address and a signal from the controller ($\overline{DACK}$) selects the I/O device during the DMA transfer.

The data transfer speed is determined by the speed of the memory device or a DMA controller that often controls DMA transfers. If the memory speed is 100 ns, DMA transfers occur at rates of up to 1/100 ns or 10 M-bytes per second. If the DMA controller in a system functions at a maximum rate of 5 MHz and we still use 100 ns memory, the maximum transfer rate is 5 MHz because the DMA controller is slower than the memory. In many cases the DMA controller slows the speed of the system when DMA transfers occur.

11-2   THE 8237 DMA CONTROLLER

The 8237 DMA controller supplies the memory and I/O with control signals and memory address information during the DMA transfer. The 8237 is actually a special-purpose microprocessor whose job is high-speed data transfer between memory and the I/O.

Figure 11–3 shows the pinout and block diagram of the 8237 programmable DMA controller. Although this device may not appear as a discrete component in modern microprocessor-based systems, it does appear within system controller chip sets found in most newer systems. Although not described because of its complexity, the chip set (82357 ISP or integrated peripheral controller) and its integral set of two DMA controllers are programmed exactly as the 8237. The ISP also provides a pair of 8259A programmable interrupt controllers for the system.

The 8237 is a four-channel device that is compatible to the 8086/8088 microprocessor. The 8237 can be expanded to include any number of DMA channel inputs, although four channels seem to be adequate for many small systems. The 8237 is capable of DMA transfers at rates of up to 1.6M bytes per second. Each channel is capable of addressing a full 64K byte section of memory and can transfer up to 64K bytes with a single programming.

Pin Definitions

1. CLK (clock) is connected to the system clock signal as long as that signal is 5 MHz or less. In the 8086/8088 system, the clock must be inverted for the proper operation of the 8237.
2. $\overline{CS}$ (chip select) selects the 8237 during programming. The CS pin is normally connected to the output of a decoder. The decoder does not use the 8086/8088 control signal IO/$\overline{M}$ (M/$\overline{IO}$) because it contains the new memory and I/O control signals ($\overline{MEMR}$, $\overline{MEMW}$, $\overline{IOR}$, and $\overline{IOW}$).
3. RESET (reset) clears the command, status, request, and temporary registers. It also clears the first/last flip-flop and sets the mask register. This input primes the 8237 so it is disabled until programmed otherwise.

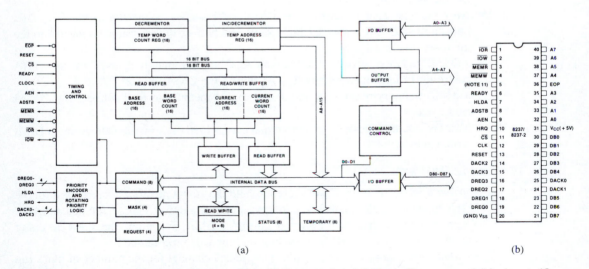

(a)   (b)

FIGURE 11–3   The 8237A–5 programmable DMA controller. (a) Block diagram, and (b) pinout. (Courtesy of Intel Corporation)

4. READY (ready) causes the 8237 to enter wait states for slower memory and/or I/O components.

5. HLDA (hold acknowledge) signals the 8237 that the microprocessor has relinquished control of the address, data, and control buses.

6. $DREQ_3$–$DREQ_0$ (DMA request) inputs are used to request a DMA transfer for each of the four DMA channels. Because the polarity of these inputs is programmable, they are either active-high or active-low inputs.

7. DB_7–DB_0 (data bus) pins are connected to the microprocessor data bus connections and are used during the programming of the DMA controller.

8. $\overline{IOR}$ (I/O read) is a bidirectional pin used during programming and during a DMA write cycle.

9. $\overline{IOW}$ (I/O write) is a bidirectional pin used during programming and during a DMA read cycle.

10. $\overline{EOP}$ (end-of-process) is a bidirectional signal that is used as an input to terminate a DMA process or as an output to signal the end of the DMA transfer. This input is often used to interrupt a DMA transfer at the end of a DMA cycle.

11. A_3–A_0 (address) are pins that are used to select an internal register during programming and also provide part of the DMA transfer address during a DMA action.

12. A_7–A_4 (address) are outputs that provide part of the DMA transfer address during a DMA action.

13. HRQ (hold request) is an output that connects to the HOLD input of the microprocessor in order to request a DMA transfer.

14. $DACK_3$–$DACK_0$ (DMA channel acknowledge) are outputs that acknowledge a channel DMA request. These outputs are programmable as either active-high or active-low signals. The DACK outputs are often used to select the DMA controlled I/O device during the DMA transfer.

15. AEN (address enable) enables the DMA address latch connected to the DB_7–DB_0 pins on the 8237. It is also used to disable any buffers in the system connected to the microprocessor.

16. ADSTB (address strobe) functions as ALE, except that it is used by the DMA controller to latch address bits A_{15}–A_8 during the DMA transfer.

17. $\overline{MEMR}$ (memory read) is an output that causes memory to read data during a DMA read cycle.

18. $\overline{MEMW}$ (memory write) is an output that causes memory to write data during a DMA write cycle.

Internal Registers

1. *Current address register (CAR)* is used to hold the 16-bit memory address used for the DMA transfer. Each channel has its own current address register for this purpose. When a byte of data is transferred during a DMA operation, the CAR is either incremented or decremented, depending on how it is programmed.

2. *Current word count register (CWCR)* programs a channel for the number of bytes (up to 64K) transferred during a DMA action. The number loaded into this register is one less than the number of bytes transferred. For example, if a 10 is loaded into the CWCR, then 11 bytes are transferred during the DMA action.

3. *Base address (BA) and base word count (BWC) registers* are used when autoinitial-ization is selected for a channel. In the autoinitialization mode, these registers are used to reload both the CAR and CWCR after the DMA action is completed. This allows the same count and address to be used to transfer data from the same memory area.

4. *Command register (CR)* programs the operation of the 8237 DMA controller. Figure 11-4 depicts the function of the command register.

   The command register uses bit position 0 to select the memory-to-memory DMA transfer mode. Memory-to-memory DMA transfers use DMA channel 0 to hold the source address and DMA channel 1 to hold the destination address. (This is similar to the operation of a MOVSB instruction.) A byte is read from the address accessed by channel 0 and saved within the 8237 in a temporary holding register. Next the 8237 initiates a memory write cycle where the contents of the temporary holding register are written into the address selected by DMA channel 1. The number of bytes transferred is determined by the channel 1 count register.

   The channel 0 address hold enable bit (bit position 1) programs channel 0 for memory-to-memory transfers. For example, suppose that you must fill an area of memory with data; channel 0 can be held at the same address while channel 1 changes for memory-to-memory transfer. This copies the contents of the address accessed by channel 0 into a block of memory accessed by channel 1.

   The controller enable/disable bit (bit position 2) turns the entire controller on and off. The normal and compressed bit (bit position 3) determines whether a DMA cycle contains 2 (compressed) or 4 (normal) clocking periods. Bit position 5 is used in normal timing to extend the write pulse so it appears one clock earlier in the timing for I/I devices that require a wider write pulse.

   Bit position 4 selects priority for the 4 DMA channel DREQ inputs. In the fixed priority scheme, channel 0 has the highest priority and channel 3 has the lowest. In the

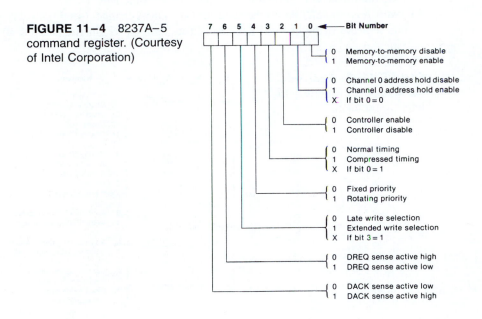

FIGURE 11-4 8237A-5 command register. (Courtesy of Intel Corporation)

rotating priority scheme, the most recently serviced channel assumes the lowest priority. For example, if channel 2 just had access to a DMA transfer, it assumes the lowest priority and channel 3 assumes the highest priority position. Rotating priority is an attempt to give all channels equal priority.

The remaining two bits (bit positions 6 and 7) program the polarities of the DREQ inputs and the DACK outputs.

5. *Mode register (MR)* programs the mode of operation for a channel. Note that each channel has its own mode register (see Figure 11−5) as selected by bit positions 1 and 0. The remaining bits of the mode register select the operation, autoinitialization, increment/decrement, and mode for the channel. Verification operations generate the DMA addresses without generating the DMA memory and I/O control signals.

The modes of operation include demand mode, single mode, block mode, and cascade mode. Demand mode transfers data until an external $\overline{EOP}$ is input or until the DREQ input becomes inactive. Single mode releases the HOLD after each byte of data is transferred. If the DREQ pin is held active, the 8237 again requests a DMA transfer through the DREQ line to the microprocessor's HOLD input. Block mode automatically transfers the number of bytes indicated by the count register for the channel. DREQ need not be held active through the block mode transfer. Cascade mode is used when more than one 8237 is present in a system.

6. *Request register (RR)* is used to request a DMA transfer via software (see Figure 11−6). This is very useful in memory-to-memory transfers where an external signal is not available to begin the DMA transfer.

7. *Mask register set/reset (MRSR)* sets or clears the channel mask as illustrated in Figure 11−7. If the mask is set, the channel is disabled. Recall that the RESET signal sets all channel masks to disable them.

8. *Mask register (MSR)* (see Figure 11−8) clears or sets all of the masks with one command instead of individual channels as with the MRSR.

9. *Status register (SR)* shows the status of each DMA channel (see Figure 11−9). The TC bits indicate if the channel has reached its terminal count (transferred all its bytes).

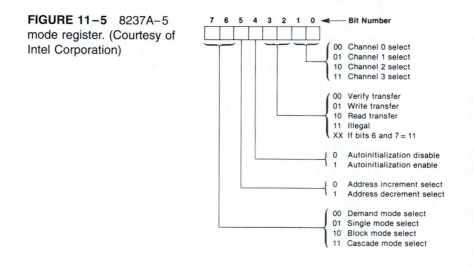

FIGURE 11−5 8237A−5 mode register. (Courtesy of Intel Corporation)

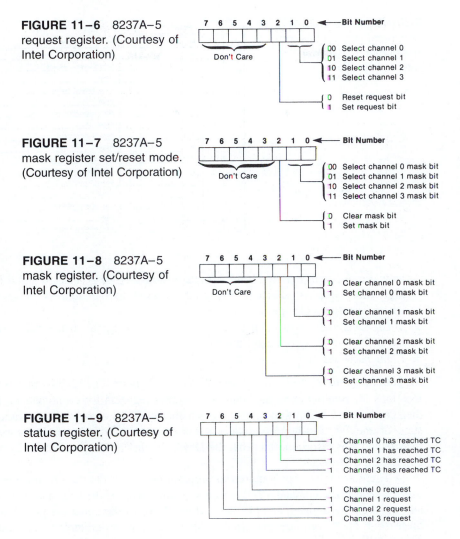

FIGURE 11-6 8237A-5 request register. (Courtesy of Intel Corporation)

FIGURE 11-7 8237A-5 mask register set/reset mode. (Courtesy of Intel Corporation)

FIGURE 11-8 8237A-5 mask register. (Courtesy of Intel Corporation)

FIGURE 11-9 8237A-5 status register. (Courtesy of Intel Corporation)

Whenever the terminal count is reached, the DMA transfer is terminated for most modes of operation. The request bits indicate if the DREQ input for a given channel is active.

Software Command. Three software commands are used to control the operation of the 8237. These commands do not have a binary bit pattern as do the various control registers within the 8237. A simple output to the correct port number enables the software command. Figure 11-10 shows the I/O port assignments that access all registers and the software commands.

The functions of the software commands are explained in the following list:

1. *Clear the first/last flip-flop* clears the first/last (F/L) flip-flop within the 8237. The F/L flip-flop selects which byte (low or high order) is read/written in the current address

FIGURE 11–10 8237A–5 command and control port assignments. (Courtesy of Intel Corporation)

Signals						Operation
A3	A2	A1	A0	IOR	IOW	
1	0	0	0	0	1	Read Status Register
1	0	0	0	1	0	Write Command Register
1	0	0	1	0	1	Illegal
1	0	0	1	1	0	Write Request Register
1	0	1	0	0	1	Illegal
1	0	1	0	1	0	Write Single Mask Register Bit
1	0	1	1	0	1	Illegal
1	0	1	1	1	0	Write Mode Register
1	1	0	0	0	1	Illegal
1	1	0	0	1	0	Clear Byte Pointer Flip/Flop
1	1	0	1	0	1	Read Temporary Register
1	1	0	1	1	0	Master Clear
1	1	1	0	0	1	Illegal
1	1	1	0	1	0	Clear Mask Register
1	1	1	1	0	1	Illegal
1	1	1	1	1	0	Write All Mask Register Bits

and current count registers. If F/L = 0, the low order byte is selected and if F/L = 1, the high order byte is selected. Any read or write to the address or count register automatically toggles the F/L flip-flop.

2. *Master clear* acts exactly the same as the RESET signal to the 8237. As with the RESET signal this command disables all channels.

3. *Clear mask register* enables all four DMA channels.

Programming the Address and Count Registers. Figure 11–11 illustrates the I/O port locations for programming the count and address registers for each channel. Notice that the state of the F/L flip-flop determines whether the LSB or MSB is programmed. If the state of the F/L flip-flop is unknown, the count and address could be programmed incorrectly. It is also important that the DMA channel is disabled before its address and count are programmed.

There are four steps required to program the 8237: (1) the F/L flip-flop is cleared using a clear F/L command, (2) the channel is disabled, (3) the LSB and then MSB of the address are programmed, and (4) the LSB and MSB of the count are programmed. Once these four operations are performed, the channel is programmed and ready to use. Additional programming is required to select the mode of operation before the channel is enabled and started.

The 8237 Connected to the 8088 Microprocessor

Figure 11–12 shows an 8088-based system that contains the 8237 DMA controller.

The address enable (AEN) output of the 8237 controls the output pins of the latches and the outputs of the 74LS257 (E). During normal 8088 operation (AEN = 0), latches A and C and the multiplexer (E) provide address bus bits A_{19}–A_{16} and A_7–A_0. The multiplexer provides the system control signals as long as the 8088 is in control of the system. During a DMA action (AEN = 1), latches A and C are disabled along with the multiplexer (E). Latches D and B now provide address bits A_{19}–A_{16} and A_{15}–A_8. Address bus bits A_7–A_0 are provided directly by the 8237 and contain a part of the DMA transfer address. The control signals $\overline{MEMR}$, $\overline{MEMW}$, $\overline{IOR}$, and $\overline{IOW}$ are also provided by the DMA controller.

Channel	Register	Operation	Signals $\overline{CS}$	$\overline{IOR}$	$\overline{IOW}$	A3	A2	A1	A0	Internal Flip-Flop	Data Bus DB0–DB7
0	Base and Current Address	Write	0	1	0	0	0	0	0	0	A0–A7
			0	1	0	0	0	0	0	1	A8–A15
	Current Address	Read	0	0	1	0	0	0	0	0	A0–A7
			0	0	1	0	0	0	0	1	A8–A15
	Base and Current Word Count	Write	0	1	0	0	0	0	1	0	W0–W7
			0	1	0	0	0	0	1	1	W8–W15
	Current Word Count	Read	0	0	1	0	0	0	1	0	W)0–W7
			0	0	1	0	0	0	1	1	W8–W15
1	Base and Current Address	Write	0	1	0	0	0	1	0	0	A0–A7
			0	1	0	0	0	1	0	1	A8–A15
	Current Address	Read	0	0	1	0	0	1	0	0	A0–A7
			0	0	1	0	0	1	0	1	A8–A15
	Base and Current Word Count	Write	0	1	0	0	0	1	1	0	W0–W7
			0	1	0	0	0	1	1	1	W8–W15
	Current Word Count	Read	0	0	1	0	0	1	1	0	W)0–W7
			0	0	1	0	0	1	1	1	W8–W15
2	Base and Current Address	Write	0	1	0	0	1	0	0	0	A0–A7
			0	1	0	0	1	0	0	1	A8–A15
	Current Address	Read	0	0	1	0	1	0	0	0	A0–A7
			0	0	1	0	1	0	0	1	A8–A15
	Base and Current Word Count	Write	0	1	0	0	1	0	1	0	W0–W7
			0	1	0	0	1	0	1	1	W8–W15
	Current Word Count	Read	0	0	1	0	1	0	1	0	W)0–W7
			0	0	1	0	1	0	1	1	W8–W15
3	Base and Current Address	Write	0	1	0	0	1	1	0	0	A0–A7
			0	1	0	0	1	1	0	1	A8–A15
	Current Address	Read	0	0	1	0	1	1	0	0	A0–A7
			0	0	1	0	1	1	0	1	A8–A15
	Base and Current Word Count	Write	0	1	0	0	1	1	1	0	W0–W7
			0	1	0	0	1	1	1	1	W8–W15
	Current Word Count	Read	0	0	1	0	1	1	1	0	W)0–W7
			0	0	1	0	1	1	1	1	W8–W15

FIGURE 11–11   8237A–5 DMA channel I/O port addresses. (Courtesy of Intel Corporation)

The address strobe output (ADSTB) of the 8237 clocks the address (A_{15}–A_8) into latch D during the DMA action so the entire DMA transfer address becomes available on the address bus. Address bus bits A_{19}–A_{16} are provided by latch B, which must be programmed with these four address bits before the controller is enabled for the DMA transfer. The DMA operation of the 8237 is limited to a transfer of not more than 64K bytes within the same 64K byte section of the memory.

The decoder (F) selects the 8237 for programming and also the 4-bit latch (B) for the uppermost four address bits. The decoder in this system enables the 8237 for I/O port addresses XX70H–XX7FH and the I/O latch (B) for ports XX10H–XX1FH. Notice that the decoder output is combined with the $\overline{IOW}$ signal to generate an active-high clock for the latch (B).

During normal 8088 operation, the DMA controller and integrated circuits B and D are disabled. During a DMA action, integrated circuits A, C, and E are disabled so the 8237 can take control of the system through the address, data, and control buses.

In the personal computer, the two DMA controllers are programmed at I/O ports 0000H–000FH for DMA channels 0–3 and ports 00C0H–00DFH for DMA channels

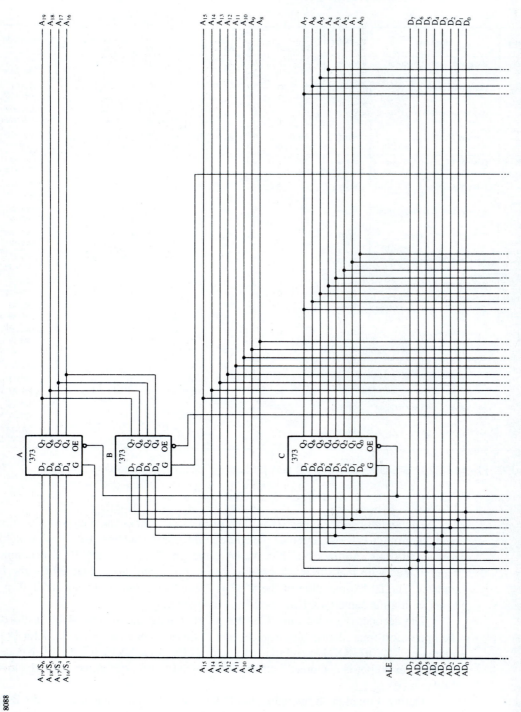

FIGURE 11–12 Complete 8088 minimum mode DMA system.

462

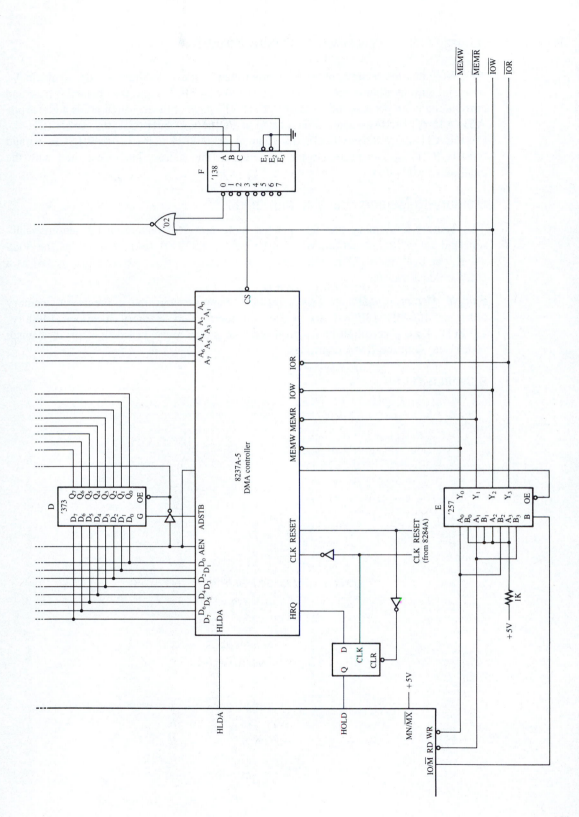

4–7. Note that the second controller is programmed at even addresses only, so channel 4 base and current address are programmed at I/O port 00C0H and the channel 4 base and current count are programmed at port 00C2H. The page register, which holds address bits A23–A16 of the DMA address, is located at I/O ports 0087H (CH–0), 0083H (CH–1), 0081H (CH–2), 0082H (CH–3), (no channel 4), 008BH (CH–5), 0089H (CH–6) and 008AH (CH–7). The page register functions as the address latch described with the examples in this text.

Memory-to-Memory Transfer with the 8237

The memory-to-memory transfer is much more powerful than even the automatically repeated MOVSB instruction. While the repeated MOVSB instruction tables the 8088 4.2 μs per byte, the 8237 requires only 2.0 μs per byte. This is over twice as fast as a software data transfer.

Sample Memory-to-Memory DMA Transfer. Suppose that the contents of memory locations 10000H–13FFFH are to be transferred into memory locations 14000H–17FFFH. This is accomplished with a repeated string move instruction, or, at a much faster rate, with the DMA controller.

EXAMPLE 11–1

```
        ;Procedure that will transfer a block of data using the 8237A-5
        ;DMA controller. This transfer is a memory-memory transfer.
        ;
        ;Source address is assumed to be in SI
        ;Destination address is assumed to be in DI
        ;Count is assumed to be in CX
        ;
        ;All data are assumed to be in the ES which contains the location
        ;of the 64K byte block.
        ;
= 0010              LATCHB    EQU  10H        ;latch (B)
= 007C              CLEAR_FL  EQU  7CH        ;F/L flip-flop
= 0070              CH0_ADD   EQU  70H        ;CH0 address
= 0072              CH1_ADD   EQU  72H        ;CH1 address
= 0073              CH1_CNT   EQU  73H        ;CH1 count
= 007B              MODE      EQU  7BH        ;mode
= 0078              CMMD      EQU  78H        ;command
= 007F              MASKS     EQU  7FH        ;mask
= 0079              REQ       EQU  79H        ;request register
= 0078              STATUS    EQU  78H        ;status register

0000                TRANSFER  PROC FAR

0000 50                       PUSH AX

0001 8C C0                    MOV  AX,ES      ;program latch (B)
0003 8A C4                    MOV  AL,AH
0005 D0 E8                    SHR  AL,1
0007 D0 E8                    SHR  AL,1
0009 D0 E8                    SHR  AL,1
000B D0 E8                    SHR  AL,1
000D E6 10                    OUT  LATCHB,AL

000F E6 7C                    OUT  CLEAR_FL,AL    ;clear F/L
```

```
0011 8B C6                              MOV    AX,SI              ;program source
0013 E6 70                              OUT    CH0_ADD,AL
0015 8A C4                              MOV    AL,AH
0017 E6 70                              OUT    CH0_ADD,AL

0019 8B C7                              MOV    AX,DI              ;program destination
001B E6 72                              OUT    CH1_ADD,AL
001D 8A C4                              MOV    AL,AH
001F E6 72                              OUT    CH1_ADD,AL

0021 8B C1                              MOV    AX,CX              ;program count
0023 48                                 DEC    AX                 ;adjust count
0024 E6 73                              OUT    CH1_CNT,AL
0026 8A C4                              MOV    AL,AH
0028 E6 73                              OUT    CH1_CNT,AL
002A B0 88                              MOV    AL,88H             ;program mode
002C E6 7B                              OUT    MODE,AL
002E B0 85                              MOV    AL,85H
0030 E6 7B                              OUT    MODE,AL

0032 B0 01                              MOV    AL,1               ;enable block move
0034 E6 78                              OUT    CMMD,AL

0036 B0 0E                              MOV    AL,0EH             ;unmask channel 0
0038 E6 7F                              OUT    MASKS,AL

003A B0 04                              MOV    AL,4               ;request DMA
003C E6 79                              OUT    REQ,AL

003E                                    AGAIN:

003E E4 78                              IN     AL,STATUS          ;wait till DMA complete
0040 A8 01                              TEST   AL,1
0042 74 FA                              JZ     AGAIN

0044 58                                 POP    AX
0045 CB                                 RET

0046                       TRANSFER     ENDP
```

Example 11–1 illustrates the software required to initialize the 8237 and program latch B in Figure 11–12 for this DMA transfer.

Programming the DMA controller requires a few steps as illustrated in the example. The leftmost digit of the 5-digit address is sent to latch B. Next, the channels are programmed after the F/L flip-flop is cleared. Note that we use channel 0 as the source and channel 1 as the destination for a memory-to-memory transfer. The count is next programmed with a value that is one less than the number of bytes to be transferred. Next the mode register of each channel is programmed, the command register selects a block move, channel 0 is enabled, and a software DMA request is initiated. Before return is made from the procedure, the status register is tested for a terminal count. Recall that the terminal count flag indicates that the DMA transfer is completed. The TC also disables the channel, preventing additional transfers.

Sample Memory Fill Using the 8237.   In order to fill an area of memory with the same data, the channel 0 source register is programmed to point to the same address throughout the transfer. This is accomplished with the channel 0 hold mode. The controller copies the contents of this single memory location to an entire block of memory addressed by channel 1. This has many useful applications.

For example, suppose that a video display must be cleared. This operation can be performed using the DMA controller with the channel 0 hold mode and a memory-to-memory transfer. If the video display contains 80 columns and 24 lines, it has 1,920 display positions that must be set to 20H (an ASCII space) to clear the screen.

EXAMPLE 11-2

```
                            ;Procedure that will clear the screen.
                            ;
= 0002          ADDRESS   EQU   02H              ;screen address
= 0010          LATCHB    EQU   10H              ;latch (B)
= 007C          CLEAR_FL  EQU   7CH              ;F/L flip-flop
= 0070          CH0_ADD   EQU   70H              ;CH0 address
= 0072          CH1_ADD   EQU   72H              ;CH1 address
= 0073          CH1_CNT   EQU   73H              ;CH1 count
= 007B          MODE      EQU   7BH              ;mode
= 0078          CMMD      EQU   78H              ;command
= 007F          MASKS     EQU   7FH              ;mask
= 0079          REQ       EQU   79H              ;request register
= 0078          STATUS    EQU   78H              ;status register
= 0020          SPACE     EQU   ' '              ;ASCII space

0000            CLEAR_SCREEN  PROC  FAR

0000 50                       PUSH  AX
0001 06                       PUSH  ES
0002 53                       PUSH  BX

0003 B0 02                    MOV   AL,ADDRESS
0005 E6 10                    OUT   LATCHB,AL
0007 D0 E0                    SHL   AL,1
0009 D0 E0                    SHL   AL,1
000B D0 E0                    SHL   AL,1
000D D0 E0                    SHL   AL,1
000F 8A E0                    MOV   AH,AL
0011 32 C0                    XOR   AL,AL
0013 8E C0                    MOV   ES,AX       ;address segment

0015 E6 7C                    OUT   CLEAR_FL,AL    ;clear F/L

0017 B8 0014 R                MOV   AX,OFFSET SCREEN
001A 8B D8                    MOV   BX,AX
001C 26: C6 07 20             MOV   BYTE PTR ES:[BX],SPACE

0020 E6 70                    OUT   CH0_ADD,AL
0022 8A C4                    MOV   AL,AH
0024 E6 70                    OUT   CH0_ADD,AL

0026 8B C3                    MOV   AX,BX
0028 40                       INC   AX
0029 E6 72                    OUT   CH1_ADD,AL
002B 8A C4                    MOV   AL,AH
002D E6 72                    OUT   CH1_ADD,AL
002F B8 077E                  MOV   AX,1918    ;program count
0032 E6 73                    OUT   CH1_CNT,AL
0034 8A C4                    MOV   AL,AH
0036 E6 73                    OUT   CH1_CNT,AL

0038 B0 88                    MOV   AL,88H     ;program mode CH0
003A E6 7B                    OUT   MODE,AL
```

```
003C  B0 85                        MOV    AL,85H     ;program mode CH1
003E  E6 7B                        OUT    MODE,AL

0040  B0 03                        MOV    AL,3       ;program copy
0042  E6 78                        OUT    CMMD,AL

0044  B0 0E                        MOV    AL,0EH     ;unmask CH0
0046  E6 7F                        OUT    MASKS,AL

0048  B0 04                        MOV    AL,4       ;request DMA
004A  E6 79                        OUT    REQ,AL

004C                       AGAIN:

004C  E4 78                        IN     AL,STATUS  ;wait until complete
004E  A8 01                        TEST   AL,1
0050  74 FA                        JZ     AGAIN

0052  5B                           POP    BX
0053  07                           POP    ES
0054  58                           POP    AX
0055  CB                           RET

0056             CLEAR_SCREEN      ENDP
```

Example 11-2 shows a procedure that clears the video display. Here the screen address is known, as are the number of bytes on the screen. Notice that this procedure is nearly identical to Example 11-1, except the command register is programmed so the channel 0 address is held.

DMA Processed Printer Interface

Figure 11-13 illustrates the hardware added to Figure 11-12 for a DMA controlled printer interface. Little additional circuitry is added for this interface to a Centronics-type parallel printer. The latch is used to capture the data as it is sent to the printer during the DMA transfer. The write pulse passed through to the latch during the DMA action also generates the data strobe ($\overline{DS}$) signal to the printer through the single-shot. The $\overline{ACK}$ signal returns from the printer each time it is ready for additional data. In this circuit $\overline{ACK}$ is used to request a DMA action through a flip-flop.

Notice that the I/O device is not selected by decoding the address on the address bus. During the DMA transfer, the address bus contains the memory address and cannot contain the I/O port address. In place of the I/O port address, the $\overline{DACK_3}$ output from the 8237 selects the latch by gating the write pulse through an OR gate.

Software that controls this interface is simple because only the address of the data and the number of characters to be printed are programmed. Once programmed, the channel is enabled, and the DMA action transfers a byte at a time to the printer interface each time that the interface receives the $\overline{ACK}$ signal from the printer.

EXAMPLE 11-3 (page 1 of 3)

```
;Procedure that prints data beginning at the location
;addressed by DS:BX. The number of characters printed is
;in CX when this procedure is called.
;
```

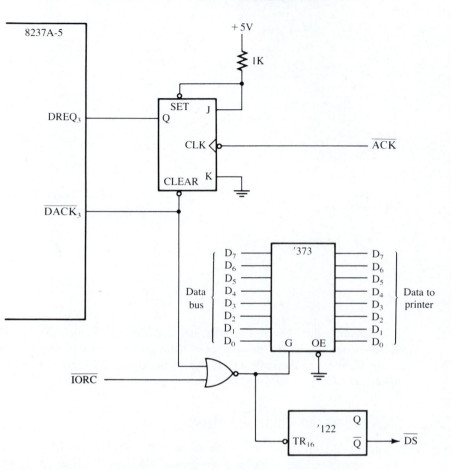

FIGURE 11–13   DMA process printer interface.

EXAMPLE 11–3 (page 2 of 3)

```
= 0010                 LATCHB    EQU   10H              ;latch (B)
= 007C                 CLEAR_FL  EQU   7CH              ;F/L flip-flop
= 0076                 CH3_ADD   EQU   76H              ;CH3 address
= 0077                 CH3_CNT   EQU   77H              ;CH3 count
= 007B                 MODE            EQU   7BH        ;mode
= 0078                 CMMD            EQU   78H        ;command
= 007F                 MASKS     EQU   7FH              ;mask
= 0079                 REQ             EQU   79H        ;request register

0000                   PRINT     PROC  FAR

0000 50                          PUSH    AX
0001 51                          PUSH    CX
0002 53                          PUSH    BX

0003 8C D8                       MOV     AX,DS          ;program A19--A16
0005 B1 04                       MOV     CL,4
0007 D3 EB                       SHR     BX,CL
```

```
0009 03 C3                              ADD     AX,BX
000B B1 0C                              MOV     CL,12
000D 50                                 PUSH    AX
000E D3 E8                              SHR     AX,CL
0010 E6 10                              OUT     LATCHB,AL
0012 58                                 POP     AX
0013 5B                                 POP     BX
0014 B1 04                              MOV     CL,4
0016 D3 E0                              SHL     AX,CL
0018 83 E3 0F                           AND     BX,15
001B 03 C3                              ADD     AX,BX

001D E6 7C                              OUT     CLEAR_FL,AL      ;clear F/L

001F E6 76                              OUT     CH3_ADD,AL       ;program
address
0021 8A C4                              MOV     AL,AH
0023 E6 76                              OUT     CH3_ADD,AL

0025 58                                 POP     AX                        ;program count
0026 50                                 PUSH    AX
0027 53                                 PUSH    BX
0028 48                                 DEC     AX

0029 E6 77                              OUT     CH3_CNT,AL
002B 8A C4                              MOV     AL,AH
002D E6 77                              OUT     CH3_CNT,AL
002F B0 00                              MOV     AL,0          ;enable controller
0031 E6 78                              OUT     CMMD,AL

0033 B0 07                              MOV     AL,7          ;unmask CH3
0035 E6 7F                              OUT     MASKS,AL

0037 5B                                 POP     BX
0038 59                                 POP     CX
0039 58                                 POP     AX
003A CB                                 RET

003B                        PRINT       ENDP
```

The procedure that prints data from the current data segment is illustrated in Example 11–3. This procedure programs the 8237, but doesn't actually print anything. Printing is accomplished by the DMA controller and the printer interface.

EXAMPLE 11–4

```
                            ;Procedure to test for a completed DMA action.
                            ;
= 0078                      STATUS      EQU   78H              ;status

0000                        TEST_P      PROC  NEAR

0000 E4 78                              IN    AL,STATUS        ;test CH3
0002 A8 08                              TEST  AL,8
0004 74 FA                              JZ    TEST_P
0006 C3                                 RET

0007                        TEST_P      ENDP
```

A secondary procedure is needed to determine if the DMA action has been completed. Example 11–4 lists the secondary procedure that tests the DMA controller to see if the DMA transfer is complete. The TEST_P procedure is called before programming the DMA controller to see if the prior transfer is complete.

Printed data can be double-buffered by first loading buffer 1 with data to be printed. Next, the PRINT procedure is called to begin printing buffer 1. Because it takes very little time to program the DMA controller, a second buffer (buffer 2) can be filled with new printer data while the first buffer (buffer 1) is printed by the printer interface and DMA controller. This process is repeated until all data are printed.

11–3   SHARED-BUS OPERATION

Complex present-day computer systems have so many tasks to perform that some systems are using more than one microprocessor to accomplish the work. This is called a *multiprocessing* system. We also sometimes call this a *distributed* system. A system that performs more than one task is called a *multitasking* system. In systems that contain more than one microprocessor, some method of control must be developed and employed. In a distributed, multiprocessing, multitasking environment, each microprocessor accesses two buses: (1) the *local bus* and (2) the *remote* or *shared bus.*

This section of the text describes shared-bus operation for the 8086 and 8088 microprocessor using the 8289 bus arbiter. The 80286 uses the 82289 bus arbiter and the 80386/80486 uses the 82389. These systems are much more complex and difficult to illustrate at this point in the text, but their terminology and opertation are essentially the same as for the 8086/8088.

The local bus is connected to memory and I/O devices that are directly accessed by a single microprocessor without any special protocol or access rules. The remote (shared) bus contains memory and I/O that are accessed by any microprocessor in the system. Figure 11–14 illustrates this idea with a few microprocessors.

Types of Buses Defined

The local bus is the bus that is resident to the microprocessor. The local bus contains the resident or local memory and I/O. All microprocessors studied thus far in this text are considered local bus systems. The local memory and local I/O are accessed by the microprocessor that is directly connected to them.

A shared bus is one that is connected to all microprocessors in the system. The shared bus is used to exchange data between microprocessors in the system. A shared bus may contain memory and I/O devices that are accessed by all microprocessors in the system. Access to the shared bus is controlled by some form or arbiter that allows only a single microprocessor to access the system's shared bus space.

Figure 11–15 shows an 8088 microprocessor that is connected as a remote bus master. The term *bus master* applies to any device (microprocessor or otherwise) that can control a bus containing memory and I/O. The 8237 DMA controller presented earlier in the chapter is an example of a remote bus master. The DMA controller gained access to

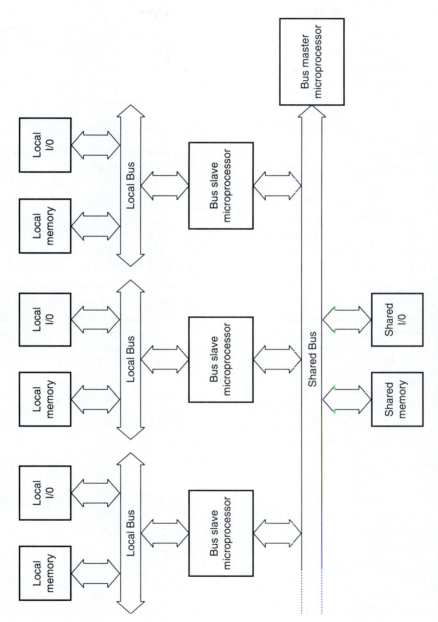

FIGURE 11–14 A block diagram illustrating the shared and local buses.

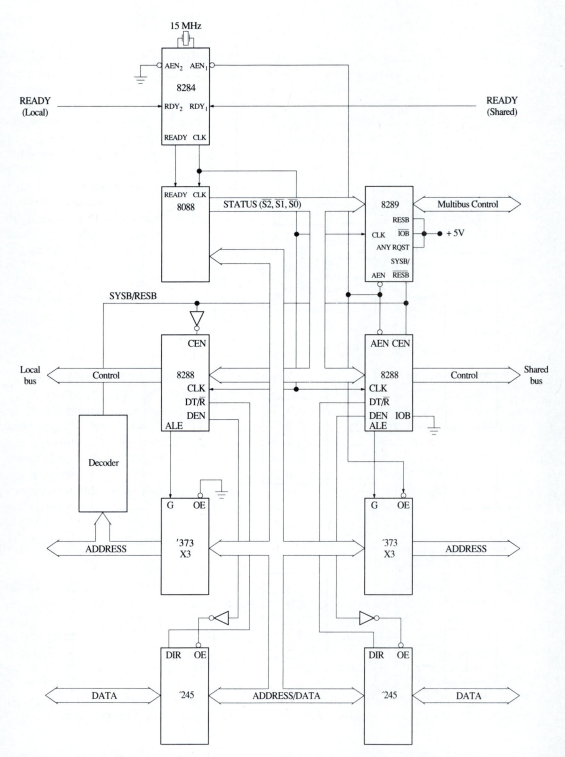

FIGURE 11–15 The 8088 operated in the remote mode illustrating the local and shared bus connections.

the system memory and I/O space to cause a data transfer. Likewise, a remote bus master gains access to the shared bus for the same purpose. The difference is that the remote bus master microprocessor can execute variable software, where the DMA controller can only transfer data.

Access to the shared bus is accomplished using the HOLD pin on the microprocessor for the DMA controller. Access to the shared bus for the remote bus master is accomplished via a bus arbiter. The *bus arbiter* functions to resolve priority between bus masters and allows only one device at a time to access the shared bus.

Notice in Figure 11–15 that the 8088 microprocessor has an interface to both a local, resident bus and the shared bus. This configuration allows the 8088 to access local memory and I/O or, through the bus arbiter and buffers, the shared bus. The task assigned to the microprocessor might be data communications and it may, after collecting a block of data from the communications interface, pass those data on to the shared bus and shared memory so other microprocessors attached to the system can access the data. This allows many microprocessors to share common data. In the same manner, multiple microprocessors can be assigned various tasks in the system, drastically improving throughput.

The Bus Arbiter

Before Figure 11–17 can be fully understood, the operation of the bus arbiter must be grasped. The 8289 bus arbiter controls the interface of a bus master to a shared bus. Although the 8289 is not the only bus arbiter, it is designed to function with the 8086/8088 microprocessor so it is presented here. Each bus master or microprocessor requires an arbiter for the interface to the shared bus, which Intel calls the Multibus[1] and IBM calls the Micro Channel.[2] The shared bus is used only to pass information from one microprocessor to another; otherwise, the bus masters function in their own local bus modes using their own local programs, memory, and I/O space. Microprocessors connected in a system such as this are often called *parallel* or *distributed* processors because they can execute software and perform tasks in parallel.

8289 Architecture

Figure 11–16 illustrates the pinout and block diagram of the 8289 bus arbiter. The left side of the block diagram depicts the connections to the microprocessor. The right side denotes the 8289 connection to the shared (remote) bus or Multibus.

The 8289 controls the shared bus by causing the READY input to the microprocessor to become a logic 0 (not ready) if access to the shared bus is denied. The *blocking* occurs whenever another microprocessor is accessing the shared bus. As a result, the microprocessor requesting access is blocked by the logic 0 applied to its READY input. When the READY pin is a logic 0, the microprocessor and its software wait until access to the shared bus is granted by the arbiter. In this manner, one microprocessor at a time

---

[1]Multibus is a trademark of Intel Corporation.

[2]Micro Channel is a trademark of International Business Machines.

FIGURE 11–16 The 8289 pinout and block diagram. (Courtesy of Intel Corporation)

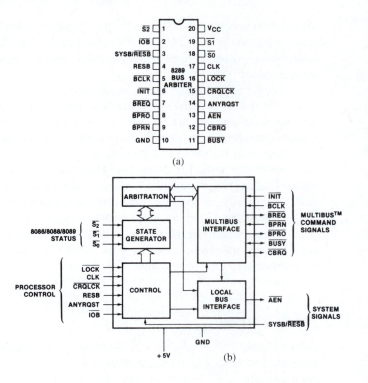

gains access to the shared bus. No special instructions are required for bus arbitration with the 8289 bus arbiter since arbitration is accomplished strictly by the hardware.

Pin Definitions

1. $\overline{\text{AEN}}$ (address enable output) causes the bus drivers in a system to switch to their three-state, high-impedance state.

2. ANYRQST (any request input) is a strapping option that prevents a lower priority microprocessor from gaining access to the shared bus. If tied to a logic 0, normal arbitration occurs, and a lower priority microprocessor can gain access to the shared bus if $\overline{\text{CBRQ}}$ is also a logic 0.

3. $\overline{\text{BCLK}}$ (bus clock input) synchronizes all shared-bus masters.

4. $\overline{\text{BPRN}}$ (bus priority input) allows the 8289 to acquire the shared bus on the next falling edge of the $\overline{\text{BCLK}}$ signal.

5. $\overline{\text{BPRO}}$ (bus priority output) is a signal that is used to resolve priority in a system that contains multiple bus masters.

6. $\overline{\text{BREQ}}$ (bus request output) is used to request access to the shared bus.

7. $\overline{\text{BUSY}}$ (busy input/output) indicates, as an output, that an 8289 has acquired the shared bus. As an input, $\overline{\text{BUSY}}$ is used to detect that another 8289 has acquired the shared bus.

8. $\overline{\text{CBRQ}}$ (common bus request input/output) is used when a lower priority microprocessor is asking for the use of the shared bus. As an output, $\overline{\text{CBRQ}}$ becomes a logic 0 whenever the 8289 requests the shared bus, and remains low until the 8289 obtains access to the shared bus.

9. CLK (clock input) is generated by the 8284A clock generator and provides the internal timing source to the 8289.

10. $\overline{\text{CRQLCK}}$ (common request lock input) prevents the 8289 from surrendering the shared bus to any of the 8289s in the system. This signal functions in conjunction with the $\overline{\text{CBRQ}}$ pin.

11. $\overline{\text{INIT}}$ (initialization input) resets the 8289 and is normally connected to the system RESET signal.

12. $\overline{\text{IOB}}$ (I/O bus input) selects whether the 8289 operates in a shared-bus system (if selected by RESB) with I/O ($\overline{\text{IOB}} = 0$) or with memory and I/O ($\overline{\text{IOB}} = 1$).

13. $\overline{\text{LOCK}}$ (lock input) prevents the 8289 from allowing any other microprocessor from gaining access to the shared bus. An 8086/8088 instruction that contains a LOCK prefix will prevent other microprocessors from accessing the shared bus.

14. RESB (resident-bus input) is a strapping connection that allows the 8289 to operate in systems that have either a shared-bus or resident-bus system. If RESB is a logic 1, the 8289 is configured as a shared-bus master. If RESB is a logic 0, the 8289 is configured as a local-bus master. When configured as a shared-bus master, access is requested through the SYSB/$\overline{\text{RESB}}$ input pin.

15. $\overline{\text{S2}}$, $\overline{\text{S1}}$, and $\overline{\text{S0}}$ (status inputs) initiate shared-bus requests and surrenders. These pins connect to the 8288 system bus controller status pins.

16. SYSB/$\overline{\text{RESB}}$ (system bus/resident bus input) selects the shared-bus system when placed at a logic 1 or the resident local bus when placed at a logic 0.

General 8289 Operation. As the pin descriptions demonstrate, the 8289 can be operated in three basic modes: (1) I/O peripheral bus mode, (2) resident-bus mode, and (3) single-bus mode. Refer to Table 11–1 for the connections required to operate the 8289 in these modes. In the *I/O peripheral bus mode,* all devices on the local bus are treated as I/O, including memory, and are accessed by I/I instructions. All memory references access the shared bus and all I/O access the resident local bus. The *resident bus mode* allows memory and I/O accesses on both the local and shared buses. Finally, *the single-bus mode* interfaces a microprocessor to a shared bus, but the microprocessor has no local memory or local I/O. In many systems, one microprocessor is set up as the shared-bus master (single-bus mode) to control the shared bus and become the shared-bus master. The *shared-bus master* controls the system through shared memory and I/O. Additional microprocessors are connected to the shared bus as resident or I/O peripheral bus masters. These additional bus masters usually perform independent tasks that are reported to the shared-bus master through the shared bus.

System Illustrating Single-Bus and Resident-Bus Connections. Single-bus operation interfaces a microprocessor to a shared bus that contains both I/O and memory resources

TABLE 11–1 8289 modes of operation.

Mode	Pin Connections
Single bus	$\overline{\text{IOB}} = 1$ and RESB = 0
Resident bus	$\overline{\text{IOB}} = 1$ and RESB = 1
I/O bus	$\overline{\text{IOB}} = 0$ and RESB = 0
I/O bus and resident bus	$\overline{\text{IOB}} = 0$ and RESB = 1

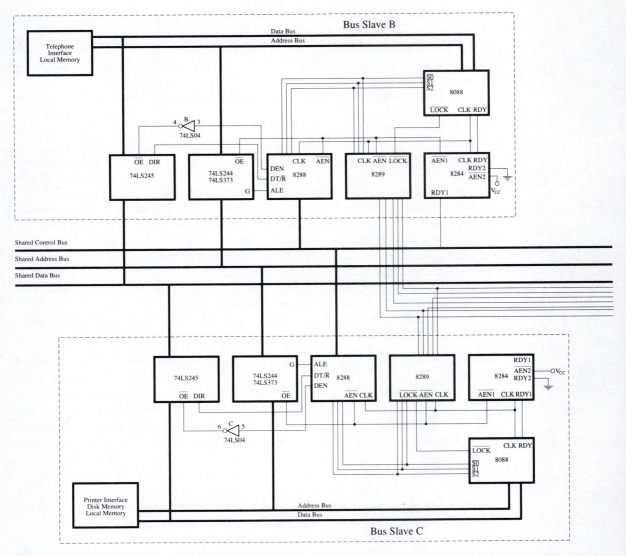

FIGURE 11–17 Three 8088 microprocessors that share a common bus system. Microprocessor A is the bus master in control of the shared memory and CRT terminal. Microprocessor B is a bus slave controlling its local telephone interface and memory. Microprocessor C is also a slave that controls a printer, disk memory system, and local memory.

that are shared by other microprocessors. Figure 11–17 illustrates three 8088 microprocessors, each connected to a shared bus. Two of the three microprocessors operate in the
resident-bus mode, while the third operates in the single-bus mode. Microprocessor A, in
Figure 11–17, operates in the single-bus mode and has no local bus. This microprocessor
only accesses the shared memory and I/O space. Microprocessor A is often referred to as
the *system bus master* because it is responsible for coordinating the main memory and I/O

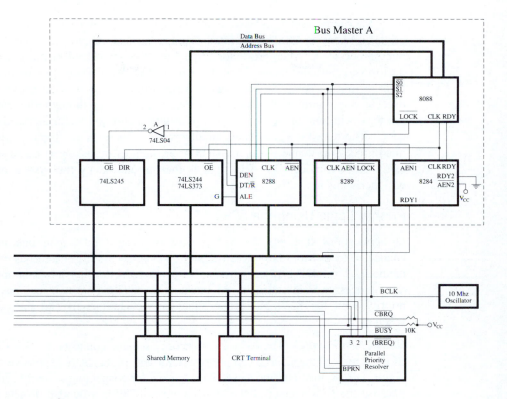

tasks. The remaining two microprocessors (B and C) are connected in the resident-bus mode, which allows them access to both the shared bus and their own local buses. These resident-bus microprocessors are used to perform tasks that are independent from the system bus master. In fact, the only time that the system bus master is interrupted from performing its tasks is when one of the two resident-bus microprocessors needs to transfer data between itself and the shared bus. This connection allows all three microprocessors to perform tasks simultaneously, yet data can be shared between microprocessors when needed.

In Figure 11–17, the bus master (A) allows the user to operate with a video terminal that allows the execution of programs and generally controls the system. Microprocessor B handles all telephone communications and passes this information to the shared memory in blocks. This means that microprocessor B waits for each character to be transmitted or received and controls the protocol used for the transfers. For example, suppose that a 1K byte block of data is transmitted across the telephone interface and this occurs at the rate of 100 characters per second. This means that the transfer requires 10 seconds. Rather than tie up the bus master for 10 seconds, microprocessor B patiently performs the data transfer from its own local memory and the local communications interface. This frees the bus master for other tasks. The only time that microprocessor B interrupts the bus master is to transfer data between the shared memory and its local memory system. This requires only a few hundred microseconds from the bus master and the main system.

Microprocessor C is used as a print spooler. Its only task is to print data on the printer. Whenever the bus master requires printed output, it transfers the task to microprocessor C. Microprocessor C then accesses the shared memory and captures the data to be printed and stores it in its own local memory. Data are then printed from the local memory, freeing the bus master to perform other tasks. This allows the system to execute a program with the bus master, transfer data through the communications interface with microprocessor B, and print information on the printer with microprocessor C. These tasks all execute simultaneously. There is no limit to the number of microprocessors connected to a system or the number of tasks performed simultaneously using this technique. The only limit is that introduced by the system design and the designer's ingenuity.

Priority Logic Using the 8289

In applications that use the 8289, there is always more than one microprocessor connected to a shared bus. Because only one can access the shared bus at a time, some method of resolving priority must be employed. Priority prevents more than one microprocessor from accessing the bus at a time. There are two methods for resolving priority with the 8289 bus arbiter: the daisy-chain (serial) and the parallel-priority schemes.

Daisy-Chain Priority. The daisy-chain priority scheme connects the $\overline{\text{BPRO}}$ output to the $\overline{\text{BPRN}}$ input of the next-lower priority 8289 and is the least expensive to implement. Figure 11–18 illustrates the daisy-chain scheme for connecting several 8289s in a system. Because the $\overline{\text{BPRN}}$ input of the higher priority 8289 is grounded, it gets an immediate acknowledgement whenever its microprocessor requests access to the shared bus. The $\overline{\text{BPRO}}$ output is a logic 0 if the 8289 and its microprocessor are inactive and a logic 1 if the 8289 and its microprocessor are actively using the shared bus. If no requests are active, all $\overline{\text{BPRN}}$ inputs will see a logic 0. As soon as the highest priority 8289 receives a bus acknowledgement, its $\overline{\text{BPRO}}$ output goes high, blocking all lower priority 8289 from accessing the shared bus. If more than one 8289 receives an acknowledgement, more than one 8289 will function at the same time. This scheme is seldom used because two microprocessors can access the shared bus at a time. For this reason, Intel

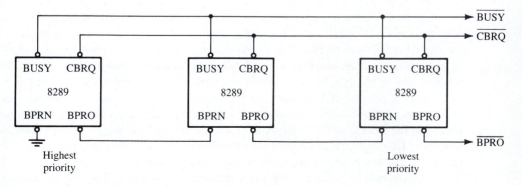

FIGURE 11–18   Daisy-chain 8289 priority resolver.

recommends that this scheme is limited to no more than three 8289s in a system that uses a bus clock of 10 MHz or less. With this frequency bus clock, no conflict occurs and only one microprocessor accesses the shared bus at a time. If more arbiters are connected, Intel suggests that the priority is resolved using the parallel scheme.

Parallel Priority

Figure 11–19 illustrates a parallel-priority scheme where four 8289 bus arbiters are connected with a parallel circuit. Here a 74LS148, eight-input priority encoder is used to resolve priority conflicts in parallel. In this example only four of the inputs are used to resolve priority for the four 8289s. The four unused encoder inputs are pulled up to a

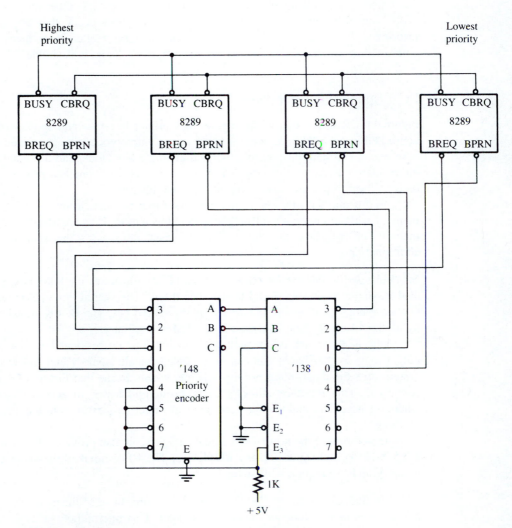

FIGURE 11–19   Parallel-priority resolver for the 8289.

logic 1 to disable these unneeded inputs to the encoder. Note that this circuit can be expanded to provide priority for up to eight 8289s with their microprocessors.

The circuit in Figure 11–19 functions as follows. If all 8289 arbiters are idle (no requests for the shared bus through the SYSB/$\overline{\text{RESB}}$ input), all $\overline{\text{BREQ}}$ outputs are high and the outputs of the 74LS148 are logic 1s ($\overline{\text{A}}$ and $\overline{\text{B}}$ are both 1). This means that the highest priority 8289 will gain access to the shared bus if it is requested by its microprocessor. On the other hand, if a lower priority request is made, the $\overline{\text{BREQ}}$ output becomes a logic 0. This causes the priority encoder to place a logic 0 on the corresponding $\overline{\text{BPRN}}$ input pin of the 8289 allowing access to the shared bus. For example, if the rightmost 8289 places a logic 0 on its $\overline{\text{BREQ}}$ output pin, the priority encoder will have a zero on input $\overline{3}$. This causes the 74LS148 to generate a 00 on its output pins. The 00 causes the 74LS138 to activate the $\overline{\text{BPRN}}$ input of the rightmost 8289, giving it access to the shared bus. This also locks out any other request because the $\overline{\text{BUSY}}$ signal becomes a logic 0. If simultaneous requests occur, they are automatically prioritized by the 74LS148, preventing conflicts no matter how many 8289s are connected in a system. For this reason, this priority scheme is desirable.

Print Spooler and Interface

Figure 11–20 shows the block diagram of a printer interface and spooler (print queue) controlled by an 8088 microprocessor. Here two microprocessors are placed in a system with one, the system bus master, operated in single-bus mode, and a second operated in the resident-bus mode. Because two microprocessors exist, one can print data while the other is used to process new information in the interim.

In this interface, the slave microprocessor transfers data to the printer from its local memory without intervention from the system bus master. Data are transferred to the local memory of the slave microprocessor whenever it accesses the shared memory for additional data.

Single-Mode-Bus-Master Interface. Figure 11–21 illustrates the 8088 bus master, operated in single mode, interfaced to the shared bus. The shared bus master has access to every memory location and I/O device on the shared bus. The $\overline{\text{BCLK}}$ signal is generated by an 8284A clock generator used as a 10 MHz oscillator.

The 8289 arbiter is operated with no I/O bus, no resident bus, and ANYRQST pulled high so the shared bus can be accessed for all memory and I/O transfers. This system uses the daisy-chain priority scheme, which means that the $\overline{\text{BREQ}}$ signal is not connected. This interface allows the slave microprocessor to access shared memory whenever necessary and thus prevents the slave microprocessor from locking the bus for too long.

In addition to the normal bus signals, this circuit also provides the shared bus with a 2.5 MHz PCLK signal for any I/O device. The RDY input is shown in case system memory and I/O require wait states.

Resident-Bus Operation of the Slave 8088. Figure 11–22 illustrates the slave 8088 microprocessor that functions as a print spooler. This microprocessor is connected as a

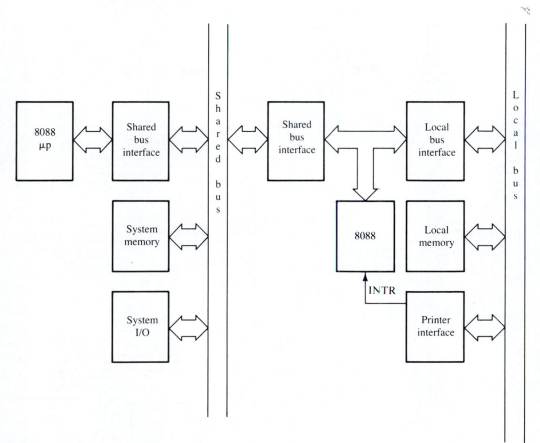

FIGURE 11–20 Block diagram of two 8088s used to control a printer interface and print spooler.

resident-bus master. This illustration depicts the resident-local-bus interface as well as the shared-bus interface.

Whenever the slave 8088 microprocessor accesses memory above location 7FFFFH, it places a logic 1 on the SYS/$\overline{\text{RESB}}$ input to the 8289 and the CEN pin of the shared-bus master's 8288. This requests access to the shared bus through the 8289 bus arbiter. If the address is below 80000H, the SYS/$\overline{\text{RESB}}$ pin on the 8289 is grounded and a logic 1 is placed on the CEN pin of the local bus 8288. This requests access to the resident-local bus for control of the printer and resident-local bus memory. Notice that no attempt is made to access the shared-bus I/O because the purpose of the slave 8088 is to access the printer interface on its local bus as local I/O.

Figure 11–23 shows the memory maps of both the slave 8088 local memory and the shared memory and the local memory of the 8088 bus master. The bus master has access to all of the shared memory, while the slave can only access locations 80000H–FFFFFH. Transfers to the print spooler are made through the upper half of the shared memory.

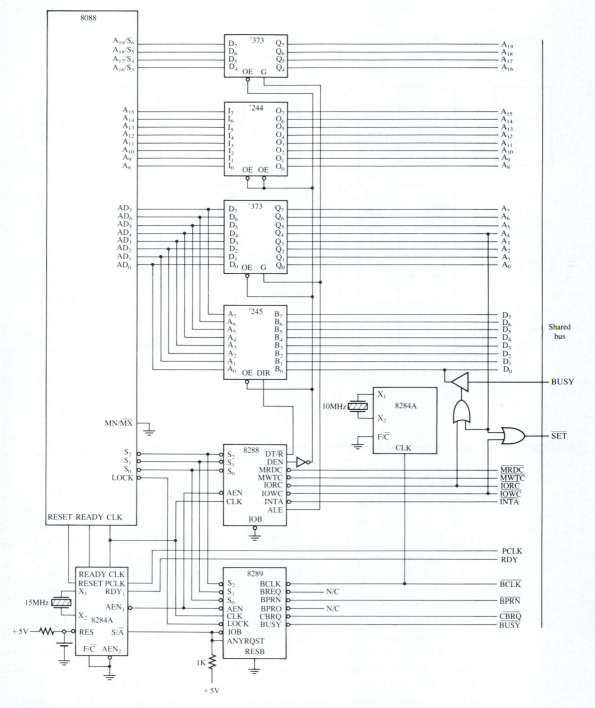

FIGURE 11–21   An 8088 connected for the single-bus mode of operation.

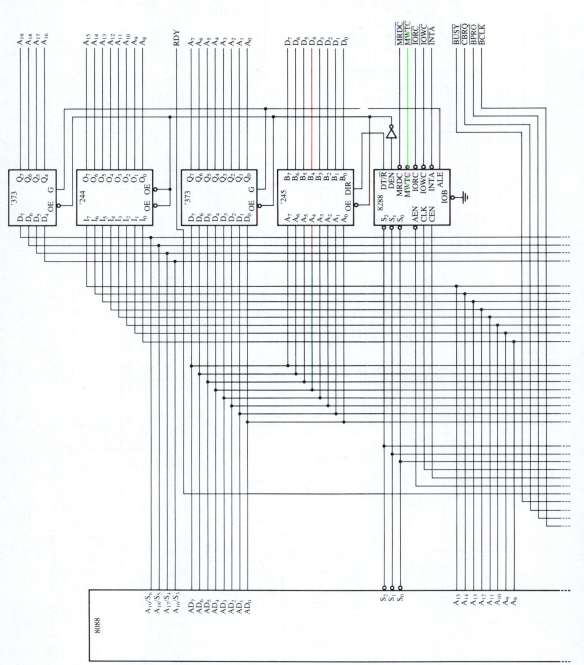

FIGURE 11-22 The 8088 shown with both a shared and a local bus.

483

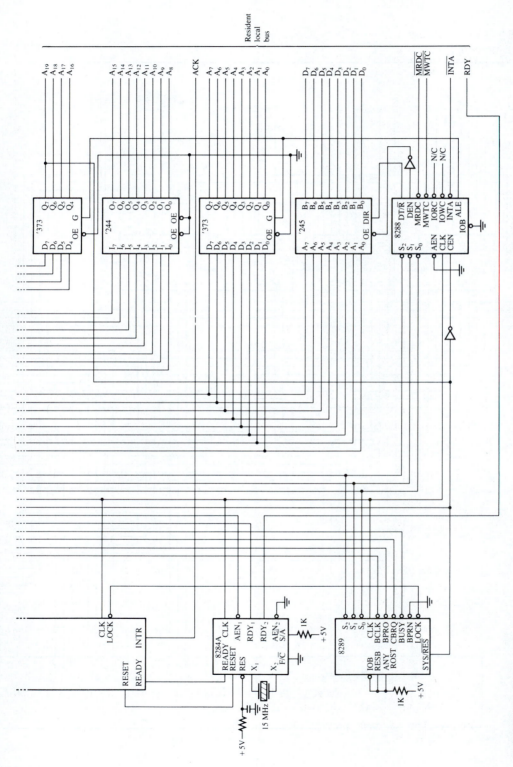

FIGURE 11–22 *(continued)*

FIGURE 11–23 Memory maps for the print spooler. (a) Shared-bus master. (b) Bus-slave memory map.

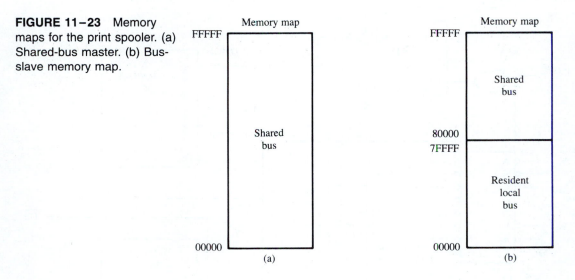

The resident-local bus in this system contains EPROM, DRAM, and a printer interface. The EPROM contains the program that controls the slave 8088, the DRAM contains the data for the printer, and printer interface controls the printer. Figure 11–24 illustrates these three devices on the resident-local bus of the slave 8088 microprocessor.

The decoder in this illustration selects EPROM for locations 00000H–0FFFFH, the printer for locations 10000H–1FFFFH, and the DRAM for locations 20000H–7FFFFH. This allows the spooler to hold up to 384K bytes of data (see Figure 11–25). If the printer can produce 1,000 lines per minute (high-speed printer), then this represents about three minutes of printing and about 50–75 printed pages of data. If the system is expanded with a fixed memory system, the capacity of the spooler can become almost boundless because of the huge capacity of a modern fixed-disk memory system. For simplicity's sake, this is not added to this example.

The printer is interfaced to the slave microprocessor through a 74LS244 that is operated as a strobed output interrupting device. Whenever the printer completes printing a character, as signaled by the $\overline{\text{ACK}}$ signal, an interrupt is generated, causing the slave microprocessor to retrieve data from the print queue for the printer. This process continues until the queue is empty, at which time the slave microprocessor disables interrupt requests until new information is placed in the queue for printing.

Print Spooler Software. The software for the print spooler is fairly straightforward. The entire software listing is provided in sections, so a study can be made of initialization, data transfer, and interrupt-controlled printer service procedures. The only software not illustrated is that which is required to program and initialize the system. When the system is initialized, the input and output pointers of the queue are both set up with address 20000H. This condition (equal pointers) indicates that the queue is empty. The segment portion of the pointers contains 2000H and the offset portion contains 0000H.

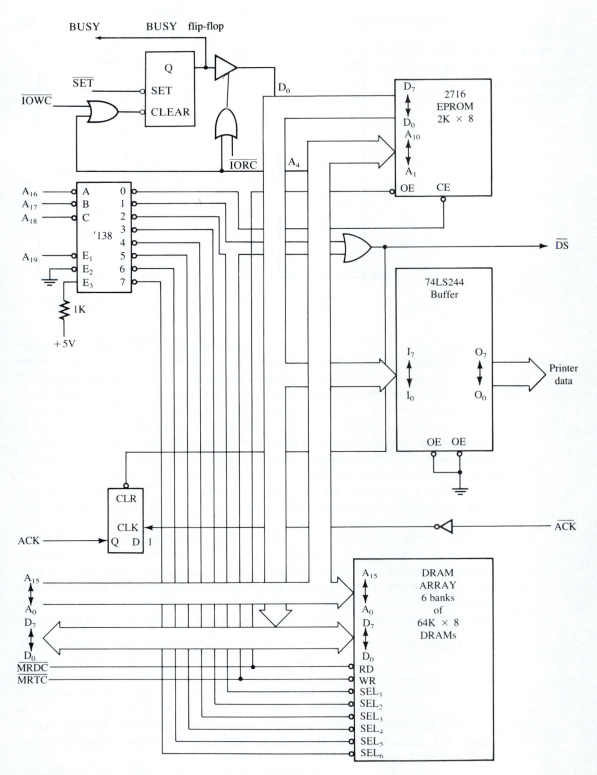

FIGURE 11–24 Resident local bus for the print spooler.

FIGURE 11-25 8088 resident local bus memory map.

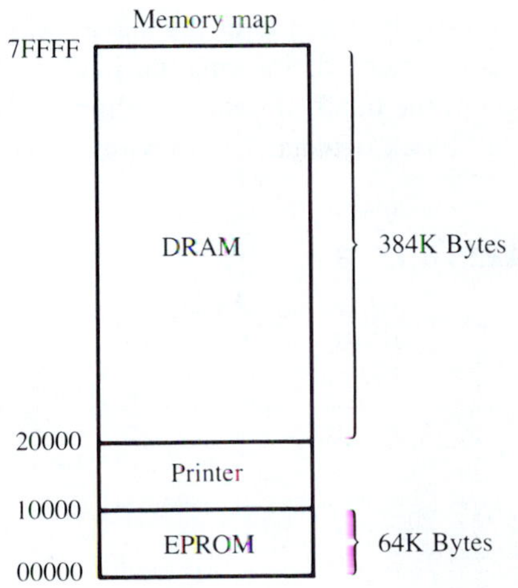

EXAMPLE 11-5

```
;Procedure found in the master microprocessor that tests the
;FLAG to determine if the slave is busy. If the slave is not busy
;data are transferred into the print buffer and the flag is set
;to indicate that data are available for the slave to print.
;
;The contents of CX = the number of characters to be loaded

;The contents of DS:SI = the location of the data to be sent to
;the slave for printing
;
0000                    LOAD    PROC    FAR

0000 E4 00                      IN      AL,00H
0002 A8 01                      TEST    AL,1
0004 75 FA                      JNZ     LOAD        ;wait for slave to finish

0006 06                         PUSH    ES
0007 BF 0002 R                  MOV     DI,OFFSET BUFFER
000A B8 8000                    MOV     AX,8000H
000D 8E C0                      MOV     ES,AX
000F 26: 89 0E 0000 R           MOV     ES:LENGTH,CX

0014 F3/ A4                     REP     MOVSB

0016 07                         POP     ES
0017 B0 FF                      MOV     AL,0FFH
0019 E6 00                      OUT     00H,AL      ;set data available flag

001B CB                         RET

001C                    LOAD    ENDP
```

Example 11-5 lists the software that transfers data into the print spooler from the shared bus. In this software, the bus master loads a block of shared memory with printer data, called a print buffer (BUFFER beginning at location 80002H), and then signals the slave 8088 that data are available through a flip-flop, which acts as an indicator to the slave. This flag flip-flop is set by the master whenever printer data are available and cleared by the slave after the slave has removed the data from the shared memory. One additional piece of information is also placed in the shared memory for the slave—the length of the block of data. Location 80000H holds a word that indicates the length of the printed block of data. The maximum size of the buffer is 64K bytes.

EXAMPLE 11–6

```
                        ;Procedure found in the slave microprocessor that tests the
                        ;FLAG to determine if data are available for printing. If
                        ;data are available, this procedure transfers it into the
                        ;local memory of the slave processor for printing.
                        ;
0000                            TRANSFER    PROC    FAR

0000 E4 00                      IN      AL,00H
0002 A8 01                      TEST    AL,1
0004 74 FA                      JZ      TRANSFER            ;if no data

0006 B8 8000                    MOV     AX,8000H            ;load segments
0009 8E D8                      MOV     DS,AX
000B BE 0000                    MOV     SI,0                ;load source
000E 8B 0C                      MOV     CX,[SI]             ;get count
0010 83 C6 02                   ADD     SI,2                ;adjust pointer

0013 E8 0023 R                  CALL    FILL_QUEUE          ;fill queue

0016 FB                         STI                         ;enable interrupt

0017 E6 00                      OUT     00H,AL              ;clear flip-flop
0019 EB E5                      JMP     TRANSFER

001B                            TRANSFER    ENDP

001B 0000              IN_POINT_SEG    DW      ?           ;input pointer
001D 0000              IN_POINT_OFF    DW      ?
001F 0000              OUT_POINT_SEG   DW      ?           ;output pointer
0021 0000              OUT_POINT_OFF   DW      ?

                        ;Procedure that will transfer data from the master BUFFER to
                        ;the slave queue. DS:SI address the source data in the
                        ;shared memory and CX contains the count.
                        ;
0023                      FILL_QUEUE PROC    NEAR

0023 FC                         CLD
0024 2E: A1 001B R              MOV     AX,CS:IN_POINT_SEG
0028 8E C0                      MOV     ES,AX
002A 2E: 8B 3E 001D R           MOV     DI,CS:IN_POINT_OFF

002F                            FULL:

002F E8 0046 R                  CALL    TEST_FULL           ;test for full
0032 74 FB                      JZ FULL                     ;if full

0034 A4                         MOVSB
0035 E8 005C R                  CALL    INC_IN_POINT        ;increment
                                                            ;in_pointer
0038 8C C0                      MOV     AX,ES
003A 2E: A3 001B R              MOV     CS:IN_POINT_SEG,AX
003E 2E: 89 3E 001D R           MOV     CS:IN_POINT_OFF,DI
```

```
0043 E2 EA                     LOOP     FULL            ;repeat for all data
0045 C3                        RET

0046                   FILL_QUEUE     ENDP

       ;Procedure to test for a full queue
       ;
0046               TEST_FULL  PROC   NEAR

0046 1E                        PUSH     DS
0047 57                        PUSH     DI
0048 E8 005C R                 CALL     INC_IN_POINT
004B 8C D8                     MOV      AX,DS
004D 2E: 3B 06 001F R          CMP      AX,CS:OUT_POINT_SEG
0052 75 05                     JNE      TEST_FULL_END
0054 2E: 3B 3E 0021 R          CMP      DI,OUT_POINT_OFF

0059                   TEST_FULL_END:

0059 5F                        POP      DI
005A 1F                        POP      DS
005B C3                        RET

005C               TEST_FULL       ENDP

       ;Procedure to increment the in_pointer.
       ;
005C           INC_IN_POINT PROC      NEAR

005C 47                        INC      DI
005D 0B FF                     OR DI,DI
005F 75 0F                     JNE      INC_IN_POINT_END
0061 8C C0                     MOV      AX,ES
0063 05 1000                   ADD      AX,1000H
0066 3D 8000                   CMP      AX,8000H
0069 75 03                     JNE      INC_IN_POINT1
006B B8 2000                   MOV      AX,2000H

006E                   INC_IN_POINT1:

006E 8E C0                     MOV      ES,AX

0070                   INC_IN_POINT_END:

0070 C3                        RET

0071          INC_IN_POINT     ENDP
```

Once the slave notices a logic 1 in the flag flip-flop, it begins transferring data from the shared memory into its own local memory. The data are stored in the local memory organized as a FIFO (first-in, first out) or queue. In this example, the size of the queue is 384K bytes. Example 11–6 lists the software used by the slave to load the queue from the shared memory buffer. In this software the slave tests the flag flip-flop to see if the master has filled the buffer in the shared memory. If the buffer is filled, the slave microprocessor transfers its contents form the shared memory into its queue. Once the transfer is complete, the slave clears the flag flip-flop so the master may begin filling the buffer with additional printer data.

EXAMPLE 11–7

```
                ;Interrupt service procedure that prints data from the queue.
                ;If all data are printed, interrupts are disabled by this
                ;procedure.
                ;
0071                    PRINT   PROC    FAR

0071 50                         PUSH    AX          ;save registers
0072 55                         PUSH    BP
0073 1E                         PUSH    DS
0074 57                         PUSH    DI
0075 06                         PUSH    ES

0076 E8 009D R                  CALL    TEST_EMPTY
0079 75 0E                      JNE     PRINT1      ;if not empty

007B 8B EC                      MOV     BP,SP
007D 8B 46 0C                   MOV     AX,[BP+12]
0080 80 E4 FD                   AND     AH,0FDH     ;interrupt off
0083 89 46 0C                   MOV     [BP+12],AX
0086 EB 0F 90                   JMP     PRINT_END

0089                    PRINT1:

0089 B8 1000                    MOV     AX,1000H
008C 8E C0                      MOV     ES,AX
008E 8A 05                      MOV     AL,[DI]
0090 26: A2 0000 R              MOV     ES:DATA,AL  ;print character

0094 E8 00B5 R                  CALL    INC_OUT

0097                    PRINT_END:

0097 07                         POP     ES          ;restore registers
0098 5F                         POP     DI
0099 1F                         POP     DS
009A 5D                         POP     BP
009B 58                         POP     AX
009C CF                         IRET

009D                    PRINT   ENDP

009D                    TEST_EMPTY   PROC    NEAR

009D 2E: A1 001F R              MOV     AX,CS:OUT_POINT_SEG
00A1 8E D8                      MOV     DS,AX
00A3 2E: 8B 3E 0021 R           MOV     DI,CS:OUT_POINT_OFF
00A8 2E: 3B 06 001B R           CMP     AX,CS:IN_POINT_SEG
00AD 75 05                      JNE     TEST_EMPTY_END
00AF 2E: 3B 3E 001D R           CMP     DI,CS:IN_POINT_OFF
00B4                    TEST_EMPTY_END:

00B4 C3                         RET

00B5                    TEST_EMPTY   ENDP

00B5                    INC_OUT PROC    NEAR

00B5 47                         INC     DI
00B6 0B FF                      OR      DI,DI
```

```
00B8  75 0D                    JNE        INC_OUT_END
00BA  8C C0                    MOV        AX,DS
00BC  05 1000                  ADD        AX,1000H
00BF  3D 8000                  CMP        AX,8000H
00C2  75 03                    JNE        INC_OUT_END
00C4  B8 2000                  MOV        AX,2000H

00C7                           INC_OUT_END:

00C7  2E: A3 001F R            MOV        CS:OUT_POINT_SEG,AX
00CB  2E: 89 3E 0021 R         MOV        CS:OUT_POINT_OFF,DI
00D0  C3                       RET

00D1                    INC_OUT ENDP
```

Example 11-7 lists the software that prints data from the queue. This software is interrupt driven, and therefore runs as a background program virtually hidden from the software listed in Example 11-6 except for the interrupt enable instruction. Whenever the printer interface, through a flip-flop, indicates that it is ready to accept additional data, an interrupt occurs calling this interrupt service procedure. The procedure extracts data from the queue and sends them to the printer.

11-4   DISK MEMORY SYSTEMS

Disk memory is used to store long-term data. Many types of disk storage systems are available today. All disk memory systems use magnetic media except the optical disk memory that stores data on a plastic disk. Optical disk memory is either a *CDROM* (compact disk/read only memory) that is read, but never written, or a *WORM* (write once/read mostly) that is read most of the time, but can be written once by a laser beam. Also becoming available is optical disk memory that can be read and written many times, but there is still a limitation on the number of write operations allowed. This section of the chapter provides an introduction to disk memory systems so that they may be used with computer systems. It also provides detail of their operation.

Floppy Disk Memory

The most common and the most basic form of disk memory is the floppy or flexible disk. This magnetic recording media is available in three sizes: the 8″ *standard,* 5¼″ *minifloppy,* and the 3½″ *microfloppy.* Today the 8″ standard version has but disappeared, giving way to the mini- and microfloppy disks. The 8″ disk is too large and unwielding to handle and stockpile. To solve this problem, industry developed the 5¼″ minifloppy disk. Today, the microfloppy disk is quickly replacing the minifloppy in newer systems because of its reduced size, ease of storage, and its durability. Even so, many systems are still marketed with both the mini- and microfloppy disk drives. In fact, one vendor markets a single disk drive that accepts both the 5¼″ and 3½″ floppy disks.

All disks have several things in common. They are all organized so data are stored in tracks. A **track** is a concentric ring of data that is stored on a surface of a disk. Figure

11–26 illustrates the surface of a 5¼″ minifloppy disk showing a track that is divided into sectors. A **sector** is a common subdivision of a track that is designed to hold a reasonable amount of data. In many systems a sector holds either 512 or 1,024 bytes of data. The size of a sector can vary from 128 bytes to the length of one entire track.

Notice from the illustration that there is a hole through the disk that is labeled an index hole. The *index hole* is designed so the electronic system that reads the disk is able to find the beginning of a track and its first sector (00). Tracks are numbered from track 00, the outermost track, in increasing value toward the center or innermost track. Sectors are often numbered from sector 00 on the outermost track, to whatever value is required to reach the innermost track and its last sector.

The 5¼″ Minifloppy Disk.   Today, the 5¼″ floppy is probably the most popular disk size used with older microcomputer systems. Figure 11–27 illustrates this minifloppy disk. The floppy disk is rotated at 300 RPMs inside its semirigid plastic jacket. The head mechanism in a floppy disk drive makes physical contact with the surface of the disk, which eventually causes wear and damage to the disk. This could present a potential problem, but disks usually last many years before data are lost due to wear.

Today most minifloppy disks are double-sided. This means that data are written on both the top and bottom surfaces of the disk. A set of tracks is called a *cylinder* and consists of one top and one bottom track. Cylinder 00, for example, consists of the outermost top and bottom tracks.

Floppy disk data are stored in the double-density format which uses a recording technique called *MFM* (modified frequency modulation) to store the information.

FIGURE 11–26 The format of a 5¼″ floppy disk.

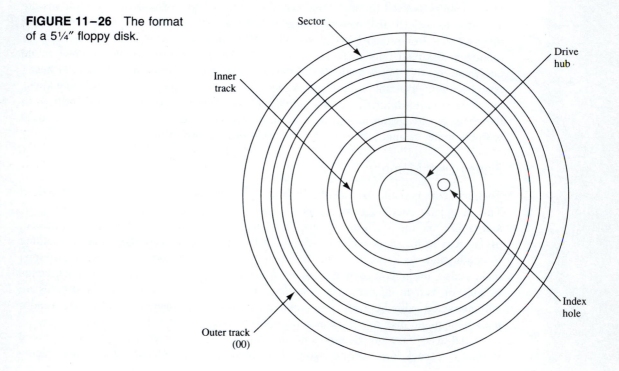

Sector

Drive hub

Inner track

Index hole

Outer track (00)

FIGURE 11–27 The 5¼″ minifloppy disk.

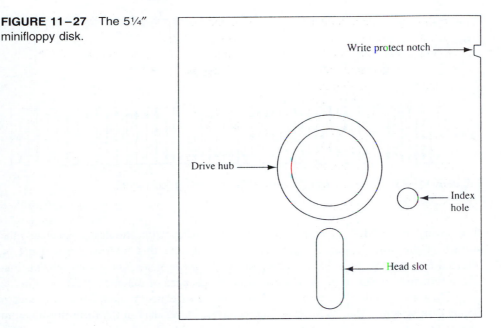

Double-density, double-sided (*DSDD*) disks are normally organized with 40 tracks of data on each side of the disk. A double-density disk track is typically divided into 9 sectors with each sector containing 512 bytes of information. This means that the total capacity of a double-density, double-sided disk is 40 tracks per side × 2 sides × 9 sectors per track × 512 bytes per sector or 368,640 (360 K) bytes of information.

Earlier disk memory systems used single-density and *FM* (frequency modulation) to store information in 40 tracks on one or two sides of the disk. Each of the 8 or 9 sectors on the single-density disk stored 256 bytes of data. This meant that a single-density disk stored 90K bytes of data per side. A single-density, double-sided disk stored 180K bytes of data.

Also common today are *high-density (HD)* minifloppy disks. A high-density minifloppy disk contains 80 tracks of information per side with 8 sectors per track. Each sector contains 1,024 bytes of information. This gives the 5¼″ high-density minifloppy disk a total capacity of 80 tracks per side × 2 sides × 8 sectors per track × 1,024 bytes per sector or 1,310,720 (1.2M) bytes of information.

The magnetic recording technique used to store data on the surface of the disk is called *nonreturn to zero* (NRZ) recording. With NRZ recording, magnetic flux placed on the surface of the disk never returns to zero. Figure 11–28 illustrates the information stored in a portion of a track. It also shows how the magnetic field encodes the data. Note that arrows are used in this illustration to show polarity of the magnetic field stored on the surface of the disk.

The main reason that this form of magnetic encoding was chosen is that it automatically erases old information when new information is recorded. If another technique were used, a separate erase head is required. The mechanical alignment of a separate erase head and a separate read/write head is virtually impossible. The magnetic

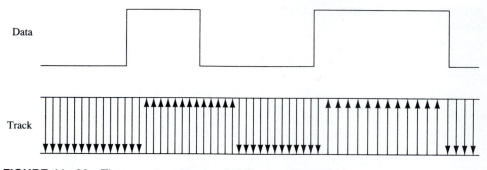

FIGURE 11–28   The nonreturn to zero (NRZ) recording technique.

flux density of the NRZ signal is so intense that it completely saturates (magnetizes) the surface of the disk, erasing all prior data. It also insures that information will not be affected by noise because the amplitude of the magnetic field contains no information. The information is stored in the placement of the changes of magnetic field.

Data are stored in the form of MFM (modified frequency modulation) in modern floppy disk systems. The MFM recording technique stores data in the form illustrated in Figure 11–29. Notice that each bit time is 2 μs in width on a double-density disk. This means that data are recorded at the rate of 500,000 bits per second. Each 2 μs bit time is divided into two parts. One part is designated to hold a clock pulse and the other holds a data pulse. If a clock pulse is present, it is 1 μs in width as is a data pulse. Clock and data pulses are never present at the same time in one bit period. (Note that high-density disk drives halve these times so that a bit time is 1 μs and a clock or data pulse is 0.5 μs in width. This also doubles the transfer rate to 1 million bits per second.)

If a data pulse is present, the bit time represents a logic one. If no data or no clock is present, the bit time represents a logic zero. If a clock pulse is present with no data pulse, the bit time also represents a logic zero. The rules followed when data are stored using MFM are:

1. A data pulse is always stored for a logic one.
2. No data and no clock are stored for the first logic zero in a string of logic zeros.
3. The second and subsequent logic zeros in a row contain a clock pulse, but no data pulse.

The reason that a clock is inserted as the second and subsequent zero in a row is to maintain synchronization as data are read from the disk. The electronics used to recapture

FIGURE 11–29   Modified frequency modulation (MFM) used with disk memory.

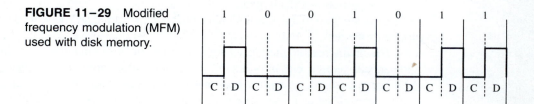

the data from the disk drive use a phase-locked loop to generate a clock and a data window. The phase-locked loop needs a clock or data to maintain synchronized operation.

The 3½" Microfloppy Disk.   Another very popular disk size is the 3½" microfloppy disk. Recently this size floppy disk has begun to sell very well and in the future promises to be the dominant size floppy disk. The microfloppy disk is a much improved version of the minifloppy disk described earlier. Figure 11–30 illustrates the 3½" microfloppy disk.

Disk designers noticed several shortcomings of the minifloppy, a scaled down version of the 8" standard floppy, soon after it was released. Probably one of the biggest problems with the minifloppy is that it is packaged in a semirigid plastic cover that bends easily. The microfloppy is packaged in a rigid plastic jacket that will not bend easily. This provides a much greater degree of protection to the disk inside the jacket.

Another problem with the minifloppy is the head slot that continually exposes the surface of the disk to contaminants. This problem is also corrected on the microfloppy because it is constructed with a spring-loaded sliding head door. The head door remains closed until the disk is inserted into the drive. Once inside the drive, the drive mechanism slides open the door, exposing the surface of the disk to the read/write heads. This provides a great deal of protection to the surface of the microfloppy disk.

Yet another improvement is the sliding plastic write protection mechanism on the microfloppy disk. On the minifloppy disk, a piece of tape was placed over a notch on the side of the jacket to prevent writing. This plastic tape easily became dislodged inside disk drives, causing problems. On the microfloppy, an integrated plastic slide has replaced the tape write protection mechanism. To write protect (prevent writing) the microfloppy disk, the plastic slide is moved to *open* the hole though the disk jacket. This allows light to strike a sensor which inhibits writing.

Still another improvement is the replacement of the index hole with a different drive mechanism. The drive mechanism on the minifloppy allowed the disk drive to grab

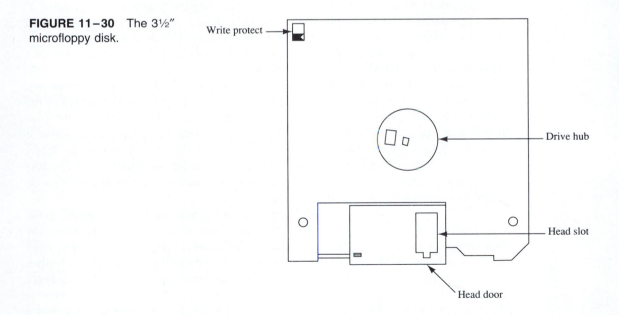

FIGURE 11–30   The 3½" microfloppy disk.

Write protect

Drive hub

Head slot

Head door

the disk at any point. This required the index hole so that the electronics could find the beginning of a track. The index hole was another trouble spot because it collected dirt and dust. The microfloppy has a drive mechanism that is keyed so that it only fits one way inside the disk drive. The index hole is no longer required because of this keyed drive mechanism. Because of the sliding head mechanism and the fact that no index hole exists, the microfloppy disk has no place to catch dust or dirt.

Two types of microfloppy disks are widely available: the double-sided, double-density *(DSDD)* and the high-density *(HD)*. The double-sided, double-density micro-floppy disk has 80 tracks per side with each track containing 9 sectors. Each sector contains 512 bytes of information. This allows 80 tracks per side × 2 sides × 9 sectors × 512 bytes per sector or 737,280 (720K) bytes of data to be stored on a double-density, double-sided floppy disk.

The high-density, double-sided microfloppy disk stores even more information. The high-density version has 80 tracks per side, but the number of sectors is doubled to 18 per track. This format still uses 512 bytes per sector, as did the double-density format. The total number of bytes on a high-density, double-sided microfloppy disk is 80 tracks per side × 2 sides × 18 sectors per track × 512 bytes per sector or 1,474,560 (1.44M) bytes of information.

Recently a new size 3½″ floppy disk has been introduced, the EHD (extended high-density) floppy disk. This new format stores 2.88M bytes of data on a single floppy disk. At this time this format is expensive and will take time to become common. Also available is the floptical disk that stores data magnetically using an optical tracking system. The floptical disk stores 21M bytes of data.

Hard Disk Memory

Larger disk memory is available in the form of the hard disk drive. The hard disk drive is often called a *fixed disk* because it is not removable like the floppy disk. A hard disk is also often called a *rigid disk*. The term *Winchester drive* is also used to describe a hard disk drive. Hard disk memory has a much larger capacity than the floppy disk memory. Hard disk memory is available in sizes approaching 1G byte of data. Common, low-cost sizes are presently 170M bytes or 213M bytes.

There are several differences between the floppy disk and the hard disk memory. The hard disk memory uses a flying head to store and read data from the surface of the disk. A flying head, which is very small and light, does not touch the surface of the disk. It flies above the surface on a film of air that is carried with the surface of the disk as it spins. The hard disk typically spins at 3000 RPM, which is 10 times faster than the floppy disk. This higher rotational speed allows the head to fly (just as an airplane flies) just over the top of the surface of the disk. This is an important feature because there is no wear on the surface as there is with the floppy disk.

Problems can arise because of flying heads. One problem is a head crash. If the power is abruptly interrupted or the hard disk drive is jarred, the head can crash onto the disk surface. This can damage the disk surface or the head. To help prevent crashes, some drive manufacturers have included a system that automatically parks the head when power is interrupted. This type of disk drive has auto-parking heads. When the heads are parked they are moved to a safe landing zone (unused track) when the power is disconnected. Some drives are not auto-parking. This type of drive usually requires a program that parks the heads on the innermost track before power is disconnected. The innermost track is a safe landing area because it is the very last track filled by the disk drive. Parking is the responsibility of the operator in this type of disk drive.

Another difference between a floppy disk drive and a hard disk drive are the number of heads and disk surfaces. A floppy disk drive has two heads, one for the upper surface and one for the lower surface. The hard disk drive may have up to eight disk surfaces (four platters) with up to two heads per surface. Each time that a new cylinder is obtained by moving the head assembly, 16 new tracks are available under the heads. Refer to Figure 11–31, which illustrates a hard disk system.

Heads are moved from track to track using either a stepper motor or a voice coil. The stepper motor is slow and noisy while the voice coil mechanism is quiet and quick. Moving the head assembly requires one step per cylinder in a system that uses a stepper motor to position the heads. In a system that uses a voice coil, the heads can be moved many cylinders with one sweeping motion. This makes the disk drive faster when seeking new cylinders.

Another advantage of the voice coil system is that a servo mechanism can monitor the amplitude of the signal as it comes from the read head and make slight adjustments in the position of the heads. This is not possible with a stepper motor which relies strictly on mechanics to position the head. Stepper motor type head positioning mechanisms can often become misaligned with use, while the voice coil mechanism corrects for any misalignment.

Hard disk drives often store information in sectors that are 1,024 bytes in length. Data are addressed in *clusters* of four sectors which contain 4,096 bytes on most hard disk drives. Hard disk drives use either MFM or RLL to store information. MFM is described with floppy disk drives. *Run-length limited* (RLL) is described here.

A typical MFM hard disk drive uses 18 sectors per track so that 18K bytes of data are stored per track. If a hard disk drive has a capacity of 40M bytes, it contains approximately 2,280 tracks. If the disk drive has two heads, this means that it contains 1,140 cylinders. If it contains four heads, then it has 570 cylinders. These specifications vary from disk drive to disk drive.

FIGURE 11–31 A hard disk drive that uses four heads per platter.

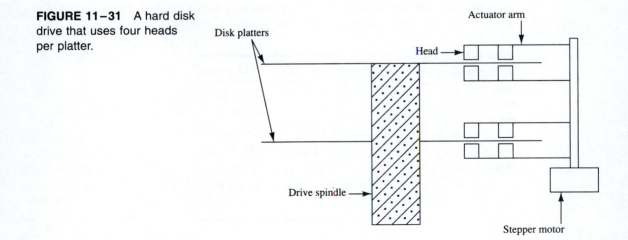

RLL Storage.   Run-length limited (RLL) disk drives use a different method for encoding the data than MFM. The term *RLL* means that the run of zeros (zeros in a row) is limited. A common RLL encoding scheme in use today is *RLL 2,7.* This means that the run of zeros is always between two and seven. Table 11–2 illustrates the coding used with standard RLL.

Data are first encoded using Table 11–2 before being sent to the drive electronics for storage on the disk surface. Because of this encoding technique, it is possible to achieve a 50 percent increase in data storage on a disk drive when compared to MFM. The main difference is that the RLL drive often contains 27 tracks instead of the 18 found on the MFM drive. (Some RLL drives also use 35 sectors per track.)

It is interesting to note that RLL encoding requires no change to the drive electronics or surface of the disk in most cases. The only difference is a slight decrease in the pulse width using RLL which may require slightly finer oxide particles on the surface of the disk. Disk manufacturers test the surface of the disk and grade the disk drive as either an MFM certified or an RLL certified drive. Other than grading, there is no difference in the construction of the disk drive or the magnetic material which coats the surface of the disks.

Figure 11–32 shows a comparison of MFM data and RLL data. Notice that the amount of time (space) required to store RLL data is reduced when compared to MFM. Here a 101001011 is coded in both MFM and RLL so that these two standards can be compared. Notice that the width of the RLL signal has been reduced so that 3 pulses fit in the same space as a clock and a data pulse for MFM. A 40M byte MFM disk can hold 60M bytes of RLL encoded data. Besides holding more information, the RLL drive can be written and read at a higher rate.

All hard disk drives use either MFM or RLL encoding. There are a number of disk drive interfaces in use today. The oldest is the ST-506 interface, which uses either MFM or RLL data. A disk system using this interface is also called either MFM or RLL disk system. Newer standards are also found in use today. These include ESDI, SCSI, and IDE. All of these newer standards use RLL even though they normally do not call attention to it. The main difference is the interface between the computer and the disk drive. The IDE system is becoming the standard hard disk memory interface.

The *enhanced small disk interface* (ESDI) system is capable of transferring data between itself and the computer at rates approaching 10M bytes per second. An ST-506 interface can approach a transfer rate of 860K bytes per second.

TABLE 11–2   Standard RLL 2,7 coding

Input Data	RLL output
000	000100
10	0100
010	100100
0010	00100100
11	1000
011	001000
0011	00001000

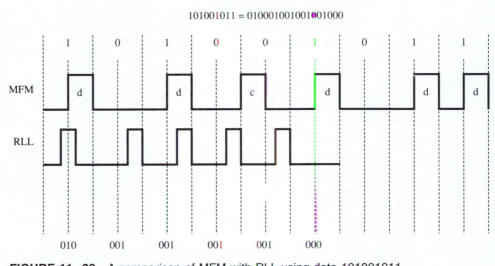

FIGURE 11–32 A comparison of MFM with RLL using data 101001011.

The *small computer system interface* (SCSI) system is also in use because it allows up to seven different disks or other interfaces to be connected to the computer through the same interface controller. SCSI is found in some PC type computers and also in the Apple Macintosh system. An improved version, SCSI-II, has started to appear in some systems.

The newest system is *integrated drive electronics* (IDE), which incorporates the disk controller in the disk drive and attaches the disk drive to the host system through a small interface cable. This allows many disk drives to be connected to a system without worrying about bus conflicts or controller conflicts. IDE drives are found in newer IBM PS-2 systems and many clones. The IDE interface is also capable of driving other I/O devices besides the hard disk. This interface also usually contains at least a 32K byte cache memory for disk data. The cache speeds disk transfers. Common access times for an IDE drive are often less than 12 ms, where the access time for a floppy disk is about 200 ms.

Optical Disk Memory

Optical disk memory (see Figure 11–33) is commonly available in two forms: the *CDROM* (compact disk/read only memory) and the *WORM* (write once/read mostly). The CDROM is the lowest cost optical disk, but it suffers from lack of speed. Access times for a CDROM are typically 300 ms or longer, about the same as a floppy disk. (Note that slower CDROM devices are on the market and should be avoided.) Hard disk magnetic memory can have access times as little as 16 ms. The CDROM also suffers from lack of software applications at this time. The CDROM is available with large volume data storage such as the Bible, encyclopedia, clip art, magazine articles, etc. None of these applications have wide appeal at the current prices. At some future date if access times decrease and more applications are introduced, the CDROM may become very popular. A

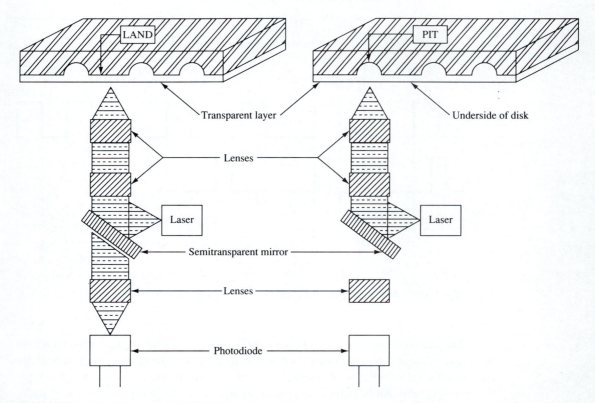

FIGURE 11–33   The optical CDROM memory system.

CDROM stores 660M bytes of data or a combination of data and musical passages. As systems develop and become more visually active, the use of the CDROM drive will become more common.

The WORM drive sees far more commercial application than the CDROM. The problem is that its application is very specialized due to the nature of the WORM. Because data may only be written once, the main application is in the banking industry, insurance industry, and other massive data storing organizations. The WORM is normally used to form an audit trail of transactions that are spooled onto the WORM and retrieved only during an audit. You might call the WORM an archiving device.

Many WORM and read/write optical disk memory systems are interfaced to the microprocessor using the SCSI or ESDI interface standards used with hard disk memory. The difference is that the current optical disk drives are no faster than most floppy drives. Some CDROM drives are interfaced to the microprocessor through proprietary interfaces that are not compatible with other disk drives.

The main advantage of the optical disk is its durability. Because a solid-state laser beam is used to read the data from the disk, and the focus point is below a protective plastic coating, the surface of the disk may contain small scratches and dirt particles and still be read correctly. This feature allows less care of the optical disk than a comparable floppy disk. About the only way to destroy data on an optical disk is to break it or deeply scar it.

11-5   VIDEO DISPLAYS

Modern video displays are *OEM* (original equipment manufacturer) devices that are usually purchased and incorporated into a system. Today there are many different types of video displays available. Of the types available, either color or monochrome versions are found.

Monochrome versions usually display information using amber, green, or paper-white displays. The paper-white display is becoming extremely popular for many applications. The most common of these applications are desk-top publishing and computer aided drafting (CAD).

The color displays are more diverse. Color display systems are available that accept information as a composite video signal much as your home television, as TTL voltage level signals (0 or 5 V), and as analog signals (0–0.7 V). Composite video displays are disappearing because the resolution available is too low. Today many applications require high resolution graphics which cannot be displayed on a composite display such as a home television receiver. Early composite video displays were found with Commodore 64, Apple 2, and similar computer systems.

Video Signals

Figure 11–34 illustrates the signal sent to a composite video display. This signal is composed of several parts that are required for this type of display. The signals illustrated represent the signals sent to a color composite video monitor. Notice that these signals include not only video, but sync pulses, sync pedestals, and a color burst. Also notice that no audio signal is illustrated because one often does not exist. Rather than include audio with the composite video signal, audio is developed in the computer and output from a

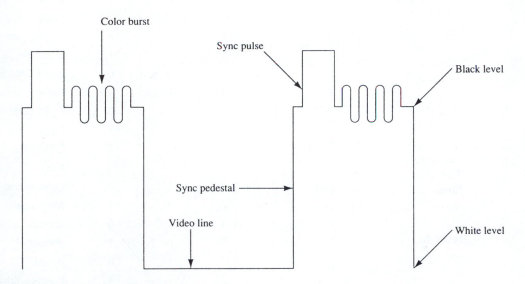

FIGURE 11–34 The composite video signal.

speaker inside the computer cabinet. The major disadvantage of the composite video display is the resolution and color limitations. Composite video signals were designed to emulate television video signals so a home television receiver could function as a video monitor.

Most modern video systems use direct video signals that are generated with separate sync signals. In a direct video system, video information is passed to the monitor through a cable that uses separate lines for video and also synchronization pulses. Recall that these signals were combined in a composite video signal.

A monochrome (one color) monitor uses one wire for video, one for horizontal sync, and one for vertical sync. Often these are the only signal wires found. A color video monitor uses three video signals. One signal represents red, another green, and the third blue. These monitors are often called RGB monitors for the video primary colors of light: red (R), green (G), and blue (B).

The TTL RGB Monitor

The RGB monitor is available as either an analog or TTL monitor. The RGB monitor uses TTL level signals (0 or 5 V) as video inputs and a fourth line called intensity to allow a change in intensity. The RGB video TTL display can display a total of 16 different colors. The TTL RGB monitor is used in the *CGA* (color graphics adaptor) system found in older computer systems.

Table 11–3 lists these 16 colors and also the TTL signals present to generate them. Eight of the 16 colors are generated at high intensity and the other eight at low intensity.

TABLE 11–3 The 16 colors available on a TTL color (CGA) RGB display

Red	Green	Blue	Intensity	Color
0	0	0	0	Black
0	0	0	1	Gray
0	0	1	0	Light Blue
0	0	1	1	Blue
0	1	0	0	Light Green
0	1	0	1	Green
0	1	1	0	Light Cyan
0	1	1	1	Cyan
1	0	0	0	Light Red
1	0	0	1	Red
1	0	1	0	Light Magenta
1	0	1	1	Magenta
1	1	0	0	Brown
1	1	0	1	Yellow
1	1	1	0	White
1	1	1	1	Intense White

The three video colors are red, green, and blue. These are primary colors of light. The secondary colors are cyan, magenta, and yellow. Cyan is a combination of blue and green video signals and is blue-green in color. Magenta is a combination of blue and red video signals and is a purple color. Yellow (high-intensity) and brown (low-intensity) are both a combination of red and green video signals. If additional colors are desired, TTL video is not normally used. A scheme was developed using low and medium color TTL video signals, which provided 32 colors, but it proved of little application and never found widespread use in the field.

Figure 11–35 illustrates the connector most often found on the TTL RGB monitor or a TTL monochrome monitor. The connector illustrated is a 9-pin connector. Two of the connections are used for ground, three for video, two for synchronization or retrace signals, and one for intensity. Notice that pin 7 is labeled normal video. This is the pin used on a monochrome monitor for the luminance or brightness signal. Monochrome TTL monitors use the same 9-pin connector as RGB TTL monitors.

The Analog RGB Monitor

In order to display more than 16 colors, an analog video display is required. These are often called analog RGB monitors. Analog RGB monitors still have three video input signals, but don't have the intensity input. Because the video signals are analog signals instead of two-level TTL signals, they are any voltage level between 0.0 V and 0.7 V. This allows an infinite number of colors to be displayed. This is because an infinite number of voltage levels between the minimum and maximum could be generated. In practice, a finite number of levels are generated. This is usually either 256K, 16M, or 24M colors depending on the standard.

Figure 11–36 illustrates the connector used for an analog RGB or analog monochrome monitor. Notice that the connector has 15 pins and supports both RGB and monochrome analog displays. The way data are displayed on an analog RGB monitor depends on the interface standard used with the monitor. Pin 9 is a key which means that no hole exists on the female connector for this pin.

Most analog displays use a *digital-to-analog converter* (DAC) to generate each color video voltage. A common standard uses a 6-bit DAC for each video signal to generate 64 different voltage levels between 0 V and 0.7 V. There are 64 different red

FIGURE 11–35 The 9-pin connector found on a TTL monitor.

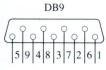

DB9

Pin	Function
1	Ground
2	Ground
3	Red video
4	Green video
5	Blue video
6	Intensity
7	Normal video
8	Horizontal retrace
9	Vertical retrace

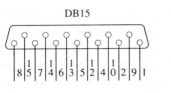

DB15	Pin	Function
	1	Red video
	2	Green video (monochrome video)
	3	Blue video
	4	Ground
	5	Ground
	6	Red ground
	7	Green ground (monochrome ground)
	8	Blue ground
	9	Blocked as a key
	10	Ground
	11	Color detect (ground on a color monitor)
	12	Monochrome detect (ground on a monochrome monitor)
	13	Horizontal retrace
	14	Vertical retrace
	15	Ground

FIGURE 11–36 The 15-pin connector found on an analog monitor.

video levels, 64 different green video levels, and 64 different blue video levels. This allows 64 × 64 × 64 different colors to be displayed or 262,144 (256K) colors.

Other arrangements are possible, but the speed of the DAC is critical. Most modern displays require an operating conversion time of 25 ns to 40 ns maximum. When converter technology advances, additional resolution at a reasonable price will become available. If 7-bit converters are used for generating video, 128 × 128 × 128 or 2,097,152 (2M) colors are displayed. In this system a 21-bit color code is needed so that a 7-bit code is applied to each DAC. Eight-bit converters also find applications and allow 256 × 256 × 256 or 16,777,216 (16M) colors.

Figure 11–37 illustrates the video generation circuit employed in many common video standards such as *EGA* (enhanced graphics adaptor) and *VGA* (variable graphics array) as used with an IBM-PC. This circuit is used to generate VGA video. Notice that each color is generated with an 18-bit digital code. Six of the 18 bits are used to generate each video color voltage when applied to the inputs of a 6-bit DAC.

A high-speed palette SRAM (access time of less than 40 ns) is used to store 256 different 18-bit codes that represent 256 different hues. This 18-bit code is applied to the digital-to-analog converters. The address input to the SRAM selects one of the 256 colors stored as 18-bit binary codes. This system allows 256 colors out of a possible 256K colors to be displayed at one time. In order to select any of 256 colors, an 8-bit code that is stored in the computer's video display RAM is used to specify the color of a picture element. If more colors are used in a system, the code must be wider. For example, a system that displays 1,024 colors out of 256K colors requires a 10-bit code to address the SRAM which contains 1,024 locations, each containing an 18-bit color code.

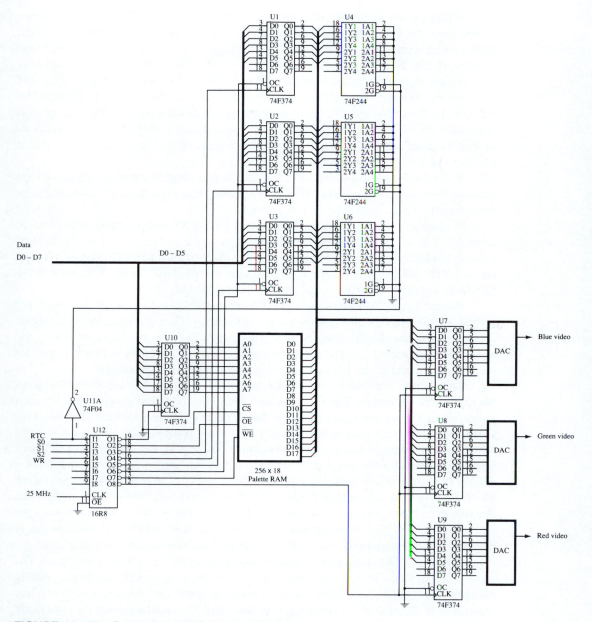

FIGURE 11–37   Generation of VGA video signals

The Apple Macintosh IIci uses a 24-bit binary code to specify each color in its color video adapter. Each DAC is 8 bits wide. This means that each converter can generate 256 different video voltage levels. There are $256 \times 256 \times 256$ or 16,777,216 different possible colors. As with the IBM VGA standard, only 256 colors are displayed at a time. The SRAM in the Apple interface is 256×24 instead of 256×18.

Whenever a color is placed on the video display, provided RTC is a logic zero, the system sends the 8-bit code that represents a color to the D0–D7 connections. The PAL 16R8 then generates a clock pulse for U10 which latches the color code. After 40 ns (one 25 MHz clock), the PAL generates a clock pulse for the DAC latches (U7, U8, and U9). This amount of time is required for the palette SRAM to look up the 18-bit contents of the memory location selected by U10. Once the color code (18-bit) is latched into U7–U9, the three DACs convert it to three video voltages for the monitor. This process is repeated for each 40 ns wide picture element (*pixel*) that is displayed. The pixel is 40 ns wide because a 25 MHz clock is used in this system. Higher resolution is attainable if a higher clock frequency is used with the system.

If the color codes (18 bits) stored in the SRAM must be changed, this is always accomplished during retrace when RTC is a logic one. This prevents any video noise from disrupting the image displayed on the monitor.

In order to change a color, the system uses the S0, S1, and S2 inputs of the PAL to select U1, U2, U3, or U10. First the address of the color to be changed is sent to latch U10. This addresses a location in the palette SRAM. Next each new video color is loaded into U1, U2, and U3. Finally, the PAL generates a write pulse for the $\overline{WE}$ input to the SRAM to write the new color code into the palette SRAM.

Retrace occurs 70.1 times per second in the vertical direction and 31,500 times per second in the horizontal direction for a 640 × 480 display. During retrace, the video signal voltage sent to the display must be 0 V. This causes black to be displayed during the retrace. Retrace itself is used to move the electron beam to the upper left-hand corner for vertical retrace and to the left margin of the screen for horizontal retrace.

The circuit illustrated causes U4–U6 buffers to enable so they apply 00000 each to the DAC latch for retrace. The DAC latches capture this code and generate 0 V for each video color signal to blank the screen. By definition, 0 V is considered the black level for video and 0.7 V is considered full intensity on a video color signal.

The resolution of the display, for example 640 × 400, determines the amount of memory required for the video interface card. If this resolution is used with a 256 color display (8 bits per pixel), then 640 × 400 bytes of memory (256,000) are required to store all of the pixels for the display. Higher resolution displays are possible, but as you can imagine even more memory is required. A 640 × 400 display has 400 video raster lines and 640 pixels per line. A **raster line** is the horizontal line of video information that is displayed on the monitor. A pixel is the smallest subdivision of this horizontal line.

Figure 11–38 illustrates the video display showing the video lines, and retrace. The slant of each video line in this illustration is greatly exaggerated, as is the spacing between lines. This illustration shows retrace in both the vertical and horizontal directions. In the case of a VGA display, as described, the vertical retrace occurs exactly 70.1 times per second and the horizontal retrace occurs exactly 31,500 times per second. (The Apple Macintosh IIci uses a vertical rate of 66.67 Hz and a horizontal rate of 35 KHz to generate a 640 × 480 color display.)

In order to generate 640 pixels across one line, it takes 40 ns × 640 or 25.6 μs. A horizontal time of 31,500 Hz allows a horizontal line time of 1/31,500 or 31.746 μs. The difference between these two times is the retrace time allowed to the monitor. (The Apple Macintosh IIci has a horizontal line time of 28.57 μs.)

Because the vertical retrace repetition rate is 70.1 Hz, the number of lines generated is determined by dividing the vertical time into the horizontal time. [In the case of a VGA

FIGURE 11–38 A video
screen illustrating the raster
lines and retrace.

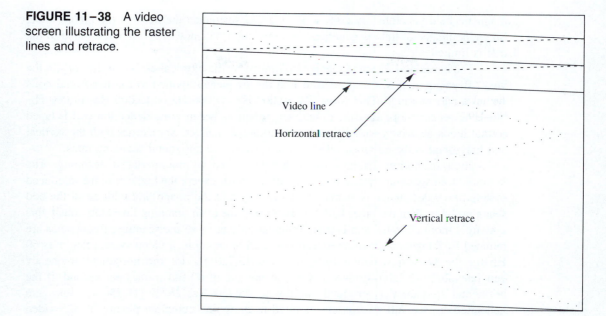

Video line

Horizontal retrace

Vertical retrace

640 × 400 display this is 449.358 lines.] Only 400 of these lines are used to display information, the rest are lost during the retrace. Since 49.358 lines are lost during the retrace, the retrace time is 49.358 × 31.766 μs or 1568 μs. It is during this relatively large amount of time that the color palette SRAM is changed or the display memory system is updated for a new video display. In the Apple Macintosh IIci computer (640 × 480) the number of lines generated is 525 lines. Of these total number of lines, 45 are lost during vertical retrace.

Other display resolutions are 800 × 600 and 1024 × 768. The 800 × 600 SVGA (super VGA) display is ideal for a 14" color monitor, while the 1024 × 768 EVGA or XVGA (extended VGA) is ideal for a 21" or 25" monitor used in CAD systems. These resolutions sound like just another set of numbers, but realize that an average home television receiver has a resolution of approximately 400 × 300. The high resolution display available on computer systems is much clearer than that available as home television. A resolution of 1024 × 768 approaches that found in 35 mm film. The only disadvantage of the video display on a computer screen is the number of colors displayed at a time, but as time passes this will surely improve. Additional colors allow the image to appear more realistic because of subtle shadings that are required for a true high-quality life-like image.

If a display system operates with a 60 Hz vertical time and a 15,600 Hz horizontal time, the number of lines generated is 15,600/60 or 260 lines. The number of usable lines in this system is most likely 240 where 20 are lost during vertical retrace. It is clear that the number of scanning lines is adjustable by changing the vertical and horizontal scanning rates.

The vertical scanning rate must be greater than or equal to 50 Hz or flickering will occur. The vertical rate must not be higher than about 75 Hz or problems with the vertical deflection coil may occur. The electron beam in a monitor is positioned by an electrical magnetic field generated by coils in a yoke that surrounds the neck of the picture tube. Since the magnetic field is generated by coils, the frequency of the signal applied to the coil is limited.

The horizontal scanning rate is also limited by the physical design of the coils in the yoke. Because of this it is normal to find the frequency applied to the horizontal coils within a narrow range. This is usually 30,000 Hz–37,000 Hz or 15,000 Hz–17,000 Hz. Some newer monitors are called multisync monitors because the deflection coil is taped so that it can be driven with different deflection frequencies. Sometimes both the vertical and horizontal coils are taped for different vertical and horizontal scanning rates.

High resolution displays use either interlaced or noninterlaced scanning. The noninterlaced scanning system is used in all standards except the highest. In the interlaced system, the video image is displayed by drawing half the image first with all of the odd scanning lines, then the other half is drawn using the even scanning lines. Obviously this system is more complex and is more efficient only because the scanning frequencies are reduced by 50 percent in an interlaced system. For example, a video system that uses 60 Hz for the vertical scanning frequency and 15,720 Hz for the horizontal frequency generates 262 (15,720/60) lines of video at the rate of 60 full frames per second. If the horizontal frequency is changed slightly to 15,750 Hz, 262.5 (15,750/60) lines are generated so two full sweeps are required to draw one complete picture of 525 video lines. Notice how just a slight change in horizontal frequency doubled the number of raster lines.

11–6   SUMMARY

1. The HOLD input is used to request a DMA action and the HLDA output signals that the hold is in effect. When a logic 1 is placed on the HOLD input, the microprocessor (1) stops executing the program, (2) places its address, data, and control bus at their high-impedance state, and (3) signals the hold is in effect by placing a logic 1 on the HLDA pin.

2. A DMA read operation transfers data from a memory location to an external I/O device. A DMA write operation transfers data from an I/O device into the memory. Also available is a memory-to-memory transfer that allows data to be transferred between two memory locations using DMA techniques.

3. The 8237 direct memory access (DMA) controller is a four-channel device that can be expanded to include additional channels of DMA.

4. Disk memory comes in the form of floppy disk storage that is found as either the 5¼″ minifloppy disk or 3½″ microfloppy disk. Both disks are found as double-sided, double-density (DSDD) or as high-density (HD) storage devices. The DSDD 5¼″ disk stores 360K bytes of data and the HD 5¼″ disk stores 1.2M bytes of data. The DSDD 3½″ disk stores 720K bytes of data and the HD 3½″ disk stores 1.44M bytes of data.

5. Floppy disk memory data are stored using NRZ (nonreturn to zero) recording. This method saturates the disk with one polarity of magnetic energy for a logic one and the

opposite polarity for a logic zero. In either case, the magnetic field never returns to zero. This technique eliminates the need for a separate erase head.

6. Data are recorded on disks by using either modified frequency modulation (MFM) or by run-length limited (RLL) encoding schemes. The MFM scheme records a data pulse for a logic 1, no data or clock for the first logic zero of a string of zeros, and a clock pulse for the second and subsequent logic zero in a string of zeros. The RLL scheme encodes data so 50 percent more information can be packed onto the same disk area. Most modern disk memory systems use the RLL encoding scheme.

7. Video monitors are either TTL or analog. The TTL monitor uses two discrete voltage levels of 0 V and 5.0 V. The analog monitor uses an infinite number of voltage levels between 0.0 V and 0.7 V. The analog monitor can display an infinite number of video levels, while the TTL monitor is limited to two video levels.

8. The color TTL monitor displays 16 different colors. This is accomplished through three video signals (red, green, and blue) and an intensity input. The analog color monitor can display an infinite number of colors through its three video inputs. In practice, the most common form of color analog display system (VGA) can display 256K different colors.

9. The video standards found today include: VGA (640 × 480), SVGA (800 × 600), and EVGA or XVGA (1024 × 768). In all three cases, the video information can be 256 colors out of a total possible 256K colors.

11-7   QUESTIONS AND PROBLEMS

1. What microprocessor pins are used to request and acknowledge a DMA transfer?
2. Explain what happens whenever a logic 1 is placed on the HOLD input pin.
3. A DMA read transfers data from _____ to _____ .
4. A DMA write transfers data from _____ to _____ .
5. The DMA controller selects the memory location used for a DMA transfer through what bus signals?
6. The DMA controller selects the I/O device used during a DMA transfer by which pin?
7. What is a memory-to-memory DMA transfer?
8. Describe the effect on the microprocessor and DMA controller when the HOLD and HLDA pins are at their logic 1 levels.
9. Describe the effect on the microprocessor and DMA controller when the HOLD and HLDA pins are at their logic 0 levels.
10. The 8237 DMA controller is a _____ channel DMA controller.
11. If the 8237 DMA controller is decoded at I/O ports 2000H–200FH, what ports are used to program channel 1?
12. Which 8237 DMA controller register is programmed to initialize the controller?
13. How many bytes can be transferred by the 8237 DMA controller?
14. Write a sequence of instructions that transfer data from memory location 21000H–210FFH to 20000H–200FFH using channel 2 of the 8237 DMA controller. You must initialize the 8237 and use the latch described in section 11–1 to hold A19–A16.

15. Write a sequence of instructions that transfers data from memory to an external I/O device using channel 3 of the 8237. The memory area to be transferred is at location 20000H–20FFFH.
16. The 5¼″ disk is known as a _____ floppy disk.
17. The 3½″ disk is known as a _____ floppy disk.
18. Data are recorded in concentric rings on the surface of a disk known as a _____ .
19. A track is divided into sections of data called _____ .
20. On a double-sided disk, the upper and lower tracks together are called a _____ .
21. Why is NRZ recording used on a disk memory system?
22. Draw the timing diagram generated to write a 1001010000 using MFM encoding.
23. Draw the timing diagram generated to write a 1001010000 using RLL encoding.
24. What is a flying head?
25. Why must the heads on a hard disk be parked?
26. What is the difference between a voice coil head position mechanism and a stepper motor head positioning mechanism?
27. What is a WORM?
28. What is a CDROM?
29. What is the difference between a TTL monitor and an analog monitor?
30. What are the three primary colors of light?
31. What are the three secondary colors of light?
32. What is a pixel?
33. A video display with a resolution of 800 × 600 contains _____ lines of video information with each line divided into _____ pixels.
34. Explain how a TTL RGB monitor can display 16 different colors.
35. Explain how an analog RGB monitor can display an infinite number of colors.
36. If an analog RGB video system uses 7-bit DACs, it can generate _____ different colors.
37. Why does standard VGA only allow 256 different colors out of 256K colors to be displayed at one time?
38. If a video system uses a vertical frequency of 60 Hz and a horizontal frequency of 32,400 Hz, how many raster lines are generated?

CHAPTER 12

The Family
of Arithmetic Coprocessors

INTRODUCTION

The Intel family of arithmetic coprocessors includes the 8087, 80287, 80387SX, 80387DX, 80487SX, and the 80486DX microprocessor, which contains its own built-in arithmetic coprocessor. The instruction sets and programming for these devices are almost identical; the difference is that each coprocessor is designed to function with a different Intel microprocessor. This chapter provides detail on the entire family generically.

The family of coprocessor, which we will label the 80X87, is able to multiply, divide, add, subtract, find the square root, partial tangent, partial arctangent, and logarithms. Data types include: 16-, 32-, and 64-bit signed integers; 18-digit BCD data; and 32-, 64-, and 80-bit floating-point numbers. The operations performed by the 80X87 generally execute at about 100 times faster than equivalent operations written with the most efficient programs.

CHAPTER OBJECTIVES

Upon completion of this chapter, you will be able to:

1. Convert data between decimal and the data type allowed for the arithmetic coprocessor.
2. Explain the operation of the 80X87 arithmetic coprocessor when interfaced to the microprocessor.
3. Explain the operation and addressing modes for each arithmetic coprocessor instruction.
4. Develop software solving complex arithmetic problems using the arithmetic coprocessor.

12–1   DATA FORMATS FOR THE ARITHMETIC COPROCESSOR

This section of the text presents the types of data used with all family members (8087, 80287, 80387SX, 80387DX, 80487SX, and the 80486DX). These types include signed-integer, BCD, and floating-point. Each has a specific use in a system, and many systems require all three data types.

Signed Integers

The signed integers used with the coprocessor are basically the same as those described in Chapter 1. When used with the arithmetic coprocessor, signed integers are 16 (word), 32 (short integer), or 64 bits (long integer) in width. Conversion between decimal and signed-integer format is handled in exactly the same manner as for the 8-bit signed integers described in Chapter 1. As you will recall, positive numbers are stored in true form with a leftmost sign-bit of 0, and negative numbers are stored in two's complement form with a leftmost sign-bit of 1.

The word integers range in value from −32,768 to +32,767, the short integer from $-2 \times 10^{+9}$ to $+2 \times 10^{-9}$, and the long integer from $-9 \times 10^{+18}$ to $+9 \times 10^{-18}$. Integer data types are found in applications that use the arithmetic coprocessor. Refer to Figure 12–1, which shows these three forms of signed-integer data.

Data are stored in memory using the same assembler directives described and used in earlier chapters. We use the DW directive to define words, DD to define short integers, and DQ to define long integers. Example 12–1 shows how several different sizes of signed integers are defined for use by the assembler.

EXAMPLE 12–1

```
0000  0002                     DATA1   DW   +2        ;16-bit integer
0002  FFDE                     DATA2   DW   -34       ;16-bit integer
0004  000004D2                 DATA3   DD   +1234     ;short integer
0008  FFFFFF9C                 DATA4   DD   -100      ;short integer
000C  0000000000005BA0         DATA5   DQ   +23456    ;long integer
0014  FFFFFFFFFFFFFF86         DATA6   DQ   -122      ;long integer
```

FIGURE 12–1 Integer forms of data for the 8087 family of numeric coprocessors. (a) Word, (b) short, and (c) long.

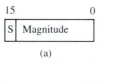

(a)

(b)

(c)

Binary-Coded Decimal (BCD)

The binary-coded decimal (BCD) form requires 80 bits of memory. Each number is stored as an 18-digit packed integer in 9 bytes of memory as two digits per byte. The tenth byte contains only a sign bit for the 18-digit signed BCD number. Figure 12–2 shows the format of the BCD number used with the arithmetic coprocessor. Note that both positive and negative numbers are stored in true form and never in 10's complement form. The DT directive stores BCD data in the memory.

Floating-Point

Floating-point numbers are often called *real numbers* because they hold integers, fractions, or mixed numbers. A floating-point number has three parts: a *sign-bit*, a *biased exponent*, and a *significand*. Floating-point numbers are written in *scientific binary notation*. The Intel family of arithmetic coprocessors supports three types of floating-point numbers: short (32 bits), long (64 bits), and temporary (80 bits). Refer to Figure 12–3 for the three forms of the floating-point number. Please note that we also call the short form a *single-precision* number and the long form a *double-precision* number. Sometimes the 80-bit temporary form is called an *extended-precision* number. The floating-point numbers, and the operations performed by the arithmetic coprocessor, conform to the IEEE-754 standard as adopted by all major software producers. This includes Microsoft, which recently stopped supporting the Microsoft floating-point format.

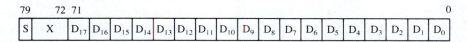

FIGURE 12–2   BCD data format for the 8087 family of numeric coprocessors.

FIGURE 12–3   Floating-point (real) numbers. (a) Short with a bias of 127 (7FH) and an implicit 1, (b) long with a bias of 1023 (3FFH) and an implicit 1, and (c) temporary with a bias of 16,383 (3FFFH) and a non-implicit 1.

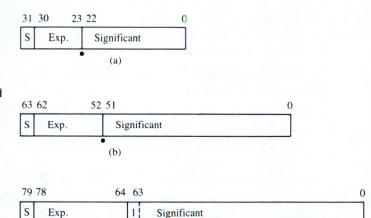

Converting to Floating-Point Form.   Converting from decimal to floating-point form is a simple task that is accomplished by the following steps:

1. Convert the decimal number into binary.
2. Normalize the binary number.
3. Calculate the biased exponent.
4. Store the number in floating-point form.

These four steps are illustrated for the decimal number 100.25 in Example 12–2. Here the decimal number is converted to a single-precision floating-point number.

EXAMPLE 12–2

```
Step            Result

1          100.25 = 1100100.01

2          1100100.01 = 1.10010001 × 2⁶

3          110 = 110 + 0111111 = 10000101

           S Exponent Significand

4          0 10000101 10010001000000000000000
```

In step three, the biased exponent is the exponent, a +6 (110), plus a bias of 01111111 (7FH). All single-precision numbers use a bias of 7FH, double-precision numbers use a bias of 3FFH, and extended-precision numbers use a bias of 3FFFH.

Step 4 is where the information is combined to generate the floating-point number. The leftmost bit is the sign-bit of the number. In this case it is a 0 because the number is +100.25. The biased exponent follows the sign-bit. The significand is a 23-bit number with an implied one-bit. Note that the significand of a number 1.XXXX is the XXXX portion. The 1. is an implied one-bit that is only stored in the extended-precision form of the floating-point number as an explicit one-bit.

Some special rules apply to a few numbers. The number 0, for example, is stored as all zeros except for the sign-bit, which can be a logic 1 to represent a negative zero. We also store plus and minus infinity as logic 1's in the exponent with a significand of all zeros and the sign-bit that represents plus or minus. A NAN (not-a-number) is an invalid floating-point result that has all ones in the exponent with a significand that is *not* all zeros.

Converting from Floating-Point Form.   Conversion to a decimal number from a floating-point number is summarized in the following steps:

1. Separate the sign-bit, biased exponent, and significand.
2. Convert the biased exponent into a true exponent by subtracting the bias.
3. Write the number as a normalized binary number.
4. Convert it to a denormalized binary number.
5. Convert the denormalized binary number into decimal.

These five steps convert a single-precision floating-point number to decimal in Example 12–3. Notice how the sign-bit of 1 makes the decimal result negative. Also notice that the implied 1 bit is added to the normalized binary result in step 3.

EXAMPLE 12-3

```
Step                 Result
1                    1 100000011 10010010000000000000000

2                    10000011 = 1000011 - 01111111 = 100

3                    1.1001001 × 2⁴

4                    11001.001

5                    -25.125
```

Storing Floating-Point Data in Memory. Floating-point numbers are stored with the assembler using the DD directive for single-precision, DQ for double-precision, and DT for extended-precision. Some examples of floating-point data storage are shown in Example 12–4. The Microsoft version 6.0 assembler contains an error that does not allow a plus sign to be used with positive floating-point numbers. A +92.45 must be defined as 92.45 for the assembler to function correctly.

EXAMPLE 12-4

```
0000 C377999A               DATA7    DD    -247.6      ;define single-precision
0004 40000000               DATA8    DD    2.0         ;define single-precision
0008 486F4200               DATA9    DD    2.45E+5     ;define single-precision
000C 4059100000000000       DATA10   DQ    100.25      ;define double-precision
0014 3F543BF727136A40       DATA11   DQ    0.001235    ;define double-precision
001C 400487F34D6A161E4F76   DATA12   DT    33.9876     ;define extended-precision
```

12-2   THE 80X87 ARCHITECTURE

The 80X87 is designed to operate concurrently with the microprocessor. Note that the 80486 microprocessor contains its own *internal* and fully compatible version of the 80387. With other family members, the coprocessor is an external integrated circuit that parallels most of the connections on the microprocessor. The 80X87 executes 68 different instructions with the microprocessor. The microprocessor executes all normal instructions and the 80X87 executes arithmetic coprocessor instructions. To illustrate one of the coprocessors, Figure 12–4 shows the pinout of the 80287 arithmetic coprocessor, sometimes called a *numeric coprocessor.*

80287 Pin Definitions

The following list describes all the pins on the 80287 arithmetic coprocessor:

1. CLK—Clock Input: provides the 80287 with its basic timing signal.
2. CLM—Clock Mode: selects whether the CLK input is divided by 3 or used directly. A logic 1 on this pin will cause the CLK input to be used as the internal clock signal.
3. CLK286—80286 Clock Input: connected to the 80286 CLK pin in most systems.
4. RESET—Reset Input: used to initialize the 80287.

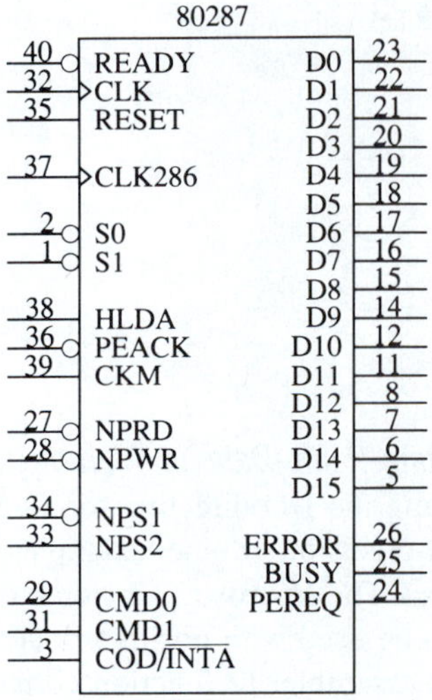

FIGURE 12–4 The 80827
arithmetic coprocessor.

5. D15–D0—Data Bus: used to capture data and commands from the system data bus and to transfer information to the system data bus.

6. $\overline{BUSY}$—Busy Output: a signal that indicates the 80287 is busy executing an arithmetic coprocessor instruction. This pin is connected to the $\overline{BUSY}$ pin on the 80286 microprocessor. The $\overline{TEST}$ on the 8086/8088 is the same as the $\overline{BUSY}$ pin.

7. $\overline{ERROR}$—Error Output: a signal that indicates an unmasked error condition and is a direct reflection of the ES status bit.

8. PEREQ—Coprocessor Operand Data Transfer Request: signals that the 80287 is ready to transfer data through its data bus connection.

9. $\overline{PEACK}$—Coprocessor Operand Data Transfer Acknowledge: an input that indicates that the PEREQ signal has been recognized by the 80286 microprocessor.

10. $\overline{NPRD}$—Coprocessor Read: this input enables a data transfer from the 80287.

11. $\overline{NPWR}$—Coprocessor Write: this input writes data to the 80287.

12. $\overline{NPS1}$, NPS2—Coprocessor Select: these lines select the 80287 so it can perform arithmetic coprocessor operations.

13. CMD1, CMD0—Command Lines: direct the operation of the 80287. These pins normally connect to A2 and A1 respectively.

14. HLDA—Hold Acknowledge: connects directly to the HLDA pin on the 80286.

15. COD/$\overline{INTA}$—Code/Interrupt Acknowledge: connects to the same pin on the 80286.

16. Vcc—Power Supply: connected to the system +5.0 V power supply bus.

17. Vss—Ground: connected to the system ground.

Internal Structure of the 80287

Figure 12–5 shows the internal structure of the arithmetic coprocessor. Notice that this device is divided into two major sections: the *control unit* and the *numeric execution unit.*

The control unit interfaces the coprocessor to the microprocessor system data bus. Both the devices monitor the instruction stream. If the instruction is an ESC

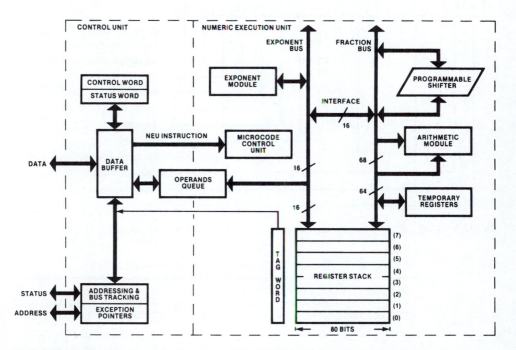

FIGURE 12-5 The internal structure of the 80X87. (Courtesy of Intel Corporation)

(coprocessor) instruction, the coprocessor executes it and if not, the microprocessor executes it.

The numeric execution unit (NEU) is responsible for executing all 68 instructions. The NEU has an eight-register stack that holds operands for arithmetic instructions and for results of arithmetic instructions. Instructions either address data in specific stack data registers or use a push and pop mechanism to store and retrieve data. Other registers in the NEU are status, control, tag, and exception pointers.

The stack within the coprocessor contains eight registers that are each 80 bits in width. These stack registers always contain an 80-bit extended-precision floating-point number. The only time data appear as any other form is when they are transferred between the coprocessor and the memory system.

Status Register.   The status register (see Figure 12-6) reflects the overall operation of the coprocessor. The status register is accessed by executing the instruction (FSTSW) that stores the contents of the status register into a word of memory. The FSTSWAX instruction copies the status register directly to the AX register. Once status is stored in memory or AX, the bit positions of the status register can be examined by normal software.

Following is a list of the status bits and their application:

1. B—Busy: indicates that the coprocessor is busy executing a task.
2. C3–C0—Condition Code Bits: refer to Table 12–1 for a complete listing of each combination of these bits and their function. Note that these bits have different meanings for different instructions.

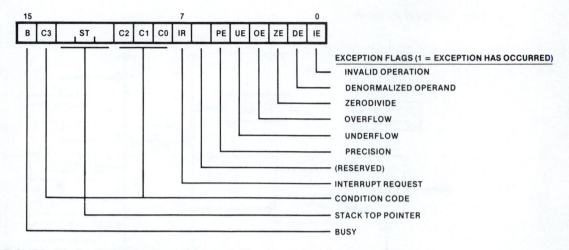

FIGURE 12-6 80X87 family status word. (Courtesy of Intel Corporation)

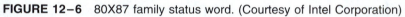

TABLE 12-1 The 80287 status register condition code bits

Instruction	C3	C2	C1	C0	Function
FTST,FCOM	0	0	X	0	ST > Source or (0 FTST)
	0	0	X	1	ST < Source or (0 FTST)
	1	0	X	0	ST = Source or (0 FTST)
	1	1	X	1	ST is not comparable
FPREM	Q1	0	Q0	Q2	rightmost 3 bits of quotient
	?	1	?	?	incomplete
FXAM	0	0	0	0	+ unnormal
	0	0	0	1	+ NAN
	0	0	1	0	− unnormal
	0	0	1	1	− NAN
	0	1	0	0	+ normal
	0	1	0	1	+ ∞
	0	1	1	0	− normal
	0	1	1	1	− ∞
	1	0	0	0	+ 0
	1	0	0	1	empty
	1	0	1	0	− 0
	1	0	1	1	empty
	1	1	0	0	+ denormal
	1	1	0	1	empty
	1	1	1	0	− denormal
	1	1	1	1	empty

Notes: unnormal = leading bits of the significand are zero, denormal = exponent at its most negative value, normal = standard floating-point form, and NAN (not-a-number) = an exponent of all ones and a significand not equal to zero.

3. TOP—Top-of-Stack: indicates the current register addressed as the top-of-the-stack.
4. ES—Error Summary: is set if any unmasked error bit (PE, UE, OE, ZE, DE, or IE) is set.
5. PE—Precision Error: result or operands exceed selected precision.
6. UE—Underflow Error: indicates a nonzero result that is too small to represent.
7. OE—Overflow Error: indicates a result that is too large to be represented. If this error is masked, the coprocessor generates infinity.
8. ZE—Zero Error: indicates the divisor was zero while the dividend is a noninfinity, nonzero number.
9. DE—Denormalized Error: indicates at least one of the operands is denormalized.
10. IE—Invalid Error: indicates a stack overflow or underflow, indeterminate form (0/0, ∞, −∞, etc.) or the use of a NAN as an operand. This flag indicates errors such as those produced by taking the square root of a negative number, etc.

Control Register.   The control register is pictured in Figure 12–7. The control word selects precision, rounding control, and infinity control. It also masks and unmasks the exception bits that correspond to the rightmost 6 bits of the status register. The FLDCW instruction is used to load a value into the control register.

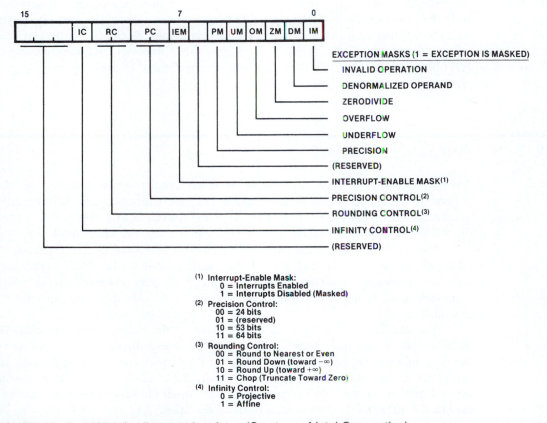

FIGURE 12–7   80X87 family control register. (Courtesy of Intel Corporation)

FIGURE 12–8 The TAG register and conditions helc in each TAG. (Courtesy of Intel Corporation)

TAG (7)	TAG (6)	TAG (5)	TAG (4)	TAG (3)	TAG (2)	TAG (1)	TAG (0)

15 0

NOTE:
The index i of tag(i) is not top–relative. A program typically uses the "top" field of Status Word to determine which tag(i) field refers to logical top of stack.

TAG VALUES:
00 = VALID
01 = ZERO
10 = INVALID or INFINITY
11 = EMPTY

Following is a description of each bit or grouping of bits found in the control register:

1. IC—Infinity Control: selects either affine or projective infinity. Affine allows positive and negative affinity, while projective assumes infinity is unsigned.
2. RC—Rounding Control: selects the type of rounding as defined in Figure 12–7.
3. PC—Precision Control: selects the precision of the result as defined in Figure 12–7.
4. Exception Masks: determine whether the error indicated by the exception affects the error bit in the status register. If a logic 1 is placed in one of the exception control bits, the corresponding status register bit is masked off.

Tag Register.   The tag register indicates the contents of each location in the coprocessor stack. Figure 12–8 illustrates the tag register and the status indicated by each tag. The tag indicates whether a register is: valid; zero; invalid or infinity; or empty. The only way that a program can view the tag register is by storing the coprocessor environment using the FSTENV, FSAVE, or FRSTOR instructions. Each of these instructions stores the tag register along with other coprocessor data.

12–3   PROCESSOR INTERFACE

The interface of the 80287 and 80286 is much simpler when compared to most peripherals. This also applies to other coprocessor family members and their respective microprocessors. Figure 12–9 illustrates the 80287 interfaced to a system that contains the 80286 microprocessor, 82288 system bus controller, and the 82284 clock generator.

The interface to the 80286 system requires one additional circuit to decode I/O addresses 00F8H, 00FAH, and 00FCH that are dedicated to the 80287 coprocessor. The microprocessor automatically generates these I/O port addresses during normal communications to the 80287. Note that only the 80287 uses these I/O ports for this communication.

The RESET pin initializes the 80287 whenever the microprocessor is reset. The 80287 responds to a reset input or to the software reset instruction, FINIT, in almost the same manner. The hardware reset forces the 80287 to operate in the real mode, and the FINIT instruction does not change the mode. Table 12–2 shows how the various internal sections of the 80287 respond to a reset. In all but special cases we normally operate the 80287 in the default reset mode of operation.

FIGURE 12-9 The 80287 interfaced to the 80286, 82288, and 82284.

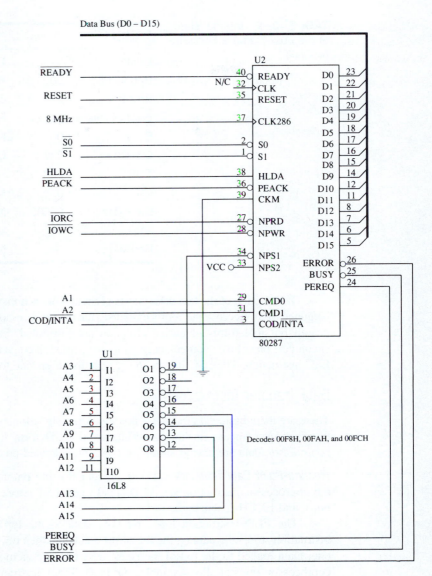

Data Bus (D0 – D15)

12-4 INSTRUCTION SET

The arithmetic coprocessor executes 68 different instructions. Whenever a coprocessor instruction references memory, the microprocessor automatically generates the memory address for the instruction. The coprocessor uses the data bus for data transfers during coprocessor instructions and the microprocessor uses it during normal instructions.

TABLE 12–2 Internal state of the 80287 after a RESET or FINIT

Field	Value	Condition
Infinity	0	Projective
Rounding	00	Round-to-nearest
Precision	11	64-bit
Error Masks	11111	Error bits disabled
Busy	0	Not busy
C3–C0	????	Unknown
TOP	000	Register 000
ES	0	No error
Error Bits	00000	No errors
Tags	11	Empty
Registers	—	Not changed

This section of the text describes the function of each instruction and lists its assembly language form. Because the coprocessor uses the microprocessor memory-addressing modes, not all possible forms of each instruction are illustrated. Each time that the assembler encounters one of the coprocessor mnemonic opcodes, it converts it into a machine language ESC instruction. The ESC instruction represents an opcode to the coprocessor.

Data Transfer Instructions

There are three basic data transfers: floating-point, signed-integer, and BCD. The only time that data ever appear in the signed-integer or BCD form is in the memory. Inside the coprocessor, data are always stored as an 80-bit extended-precision floating-point number.

Floating-Point Data Transfers.   There are four floating-point data transfer instructions in the coprocessor instruction set: FLD (load real), FST (store real), FSTP (store real and pop), and FXCH (exchange).

The FLD instruction loads memory data to the top of the internal stack. This instruction stores the data on the top of the stack and then decrements the stack pointer by one. Data loaded to the top of the stack are from any memory location or from another coprocessor register. For example, an FLD ST(2) instruction copies the contents of register 2 to the stack top, which is ST. The top of the stack is register 0 when the coprocessor is reset or initialized. Another example is the FLD DATA7 instruction, which copies the contents of memory location DATA7 to the top of the stack. The size of the transfer is automatically determined by the assembler through the directives DD for single-precision, DQ for double-precision, and DT for extended-precision.

The FST instruction stores a copy of the top of the stack into the memory location or coprocessor register indicated by the operand. At the time of storage, the internal, extended-precision floating-point number is rounded to the size of the floating-point number indicated by the control register.

The FSTP (floating-point store and pop) instruction stores a copy of the top of the stack into memory or any coprocessor register and then pops the data from the top of the stack. You might think of FST as a *copy* instruction and FSTP as a *removal* instruction.

The FXCH instruction exchanges the register indicated by the operand with the top of the stack. For example, the FXCH ST(2) instruction exchanges the top of the stack with register 2.

Integer Data Transfer Instructions. The coprocessor supports three integer data transfer instructions: FILD (load integer), FIST (store integer), and FISTP (store integer and pop). These three instructions function as did FLD, FST, and FSTP except the data transferred are integer data. The coprocessor automatically converts the internal extended-precision data to integer data. The size of the data is determined by the way that the label is defined with DW, DD, or DQ.

BCD Data Transfer Instructions. Two instructions load or store BCD data. The FBLD instruction loads the top of the stack with BCD memory data and the FBSTP stores the top of the stack and does a pop.

Example 12–5 shows how the assembler automatically adjusts the FLD, FILD, and FBLD instructions for different size operands. (Look closely at the machine coded forms of the instructions.) Note in this example that it begins with the .286 and .287 directives that identify the microprocessor as an 80286 and the coprocessor as an 80287. Note that if the 80386 microprocessor is in use with its coprocessor, the directives .386 and .387 appear. The assembler by default assumes that the software is assembled for an 8086/8088 with an 8087 coprocessor.

EXAMPLE 12–5

```
                                    .286
                                    .287

0000                        DATAS   SEGMENT

0000 41F00000               DATA1   DD    30.0            ;single-precision
0004 0000000000003E40       DATA2   DQ    30.0            ;double-precision
000C 00000000000000F00340   DATA3   DT    30.0            ;extended-precision

0016 001E                   DATA4   DW    30              ;16-bit integer
0018 0000001E               DATA5   DD    30              ;32-bit integer
001C 1E00000000000000       DATA6   DQ    30              ;64-bit integer

0024 30000000000000000000   DATA7   DT    30H             ;BCD 30

002E                        DATAS   ENDS

0000                        CODE    SEGMENT

                                    ASSUME CS:CODE,DS:DATAS

0000 D9 06 0000 R                   FLD    DATA1
0004 DD 06 0004 R                   FLD    DATA2
0008 DB 2E 000C R                   FLD    DATA3

000C DF 06 0016 R                   FILD DATA4
0010 DB 06 0018 R                   FILD DATA5
0014 DF 2E 001C R                   FILD DATA6

0018 DF 26 0024 R                   FBLD DATA7

001C                        CODE    ENDS
                                    END
```

Arithmetic Instructions

Arithmetic instructions for the coprocessor include addition, subtraction, multiplication, division, and square root. The arithmetic-related instructions are scaling, rounding, absolute value, and changing the sign.

Table 12–3 shows the basic addressing modes allowed for the arithmetic operations. Each addressing mode is shown with an example using the FADD (real addition) instruction. All arithmetic operations are floating-point except in some cases when memory data are referenced as an operand.

The classic stack form of addressing operand data (stack addressing) uses the top of the stack as the source operand and the next to the top of the stack as the destination operand. Afterward, the two original data are removed from the stack and only the result remains at the top of the stack. (Internally the coprocessor pops the source from the top of the stack.) To use this addressing mode, the instruction is placed in the program without any operands such as FADD or FSUB. The FADD instruction adds ST to ST(1) and stores the answer at the top of the stack; it also removes the original two data from the stack by popping.

The register-addressing mode uses ST for the top of the stack and ST(n) for another location where n is the register number. With this form, one operand must be ST and the other is ST(n). Note that to double the top of the stack we use the FADD ST,ST(0) instruction where ST(0) addresses the top of the stack. One of the two operands in the register-addressing mode must be ST, while the other must be in the form ST(n), where n is a stack register 0–7.

The memory-addressing mode always uses a destination of the top of the stack because the coprocessor is a stack-oriented machine. For example, the FADD DATA instruction adds the real number contents of memory location data to the top of the stack.

Arithmetic Operations. The letter P in an opcode specifies a register pop after the operation (FADDP compared to FADD). The letter R in an opcode (subtraction and division only) indicates reverse mode. The reverse mode is useful for memory data because normally memory data subtracts from the top of the stack. A reversed subtract instruction subtracts the top of the stack from memory and stores the result in the top of the stack. For example, if the top of the stack contains a 10 and memory location DATA1

TABLE 12–3 Arithmetic addressing modes

Mode	Form	Examples
Stack	ST,ST(1)	FADD
Register	ST,ST(n)	FADD ST,ST(2)
	ST(n),ST	FADD ST(6),ST
Register pop	ST(n),ST	FADDP ST(3),ST
Memory	operand	FADD DATA

Note: Stack addressing is fixed as ST,ST(1) and n = register number 0–7.

contains a 1, then the FSUB DATA1 instruction results in a +9 on the stack top and the FSUBR instruction results in a −9.

The letter I as a second letter in an opcode indicates that the memory operand is an integer. For example, the FADD DATA instruction is a floating-point addition, while the FIADD DATA is an integer addition that adds the integer at memory location DATA to the floating-point number at the top of the stack. The same rules apply to FADD, FSUB, FMUL, and FDIV instructions.

Arithmetic-related Operations.   Other operations that are arithmetic in nature include: FSQRT (square root), FSCALE (scale a number), FPREM (find partial remainder), FRNDINT (round to integer), FXTRACT (extract exponent and significand), FABS (find absolute value), and FCHG (change sign). These instructions and the functions they perform follow:

1. FSQRT—finds the square root of the top of the stack and leaves the resultant square root at the top of the stack. An invalid error occurs for the square root of a negative number. For this reason, the IE bit of the status register should be tested whenever an invalid result can occur.
2. FSCALE—adds the contents of ST(1) (interpreted as an integer) to the exponent at the top of the stack. FSCALE can multiply or divide rapidly by powers of two. The value in ST(1) must be between 2^{-15} and 2^{+15}.
3. FPREM—performs modulo division of ST by ST(1). The resultant remainder is found in the top of the stack and has the same sign as the original dividend.
4. FRNDINT—rounds the top of the stack to an integer.
5. FXTRACT—decomposes the number at the top of the stack into two separate numbers that represent the value of the exponent and the value of the significand. The extracted significand is found at the top of the stack and the exponent at ST(1). We often use this instruction in converting a floating-point number into a form that can be printed.
6. FABS—changes the sign of the top of the stack to positive.
7. FCHS—changes the sign from positive to negative or negative to positive.

Comparison Instructions

The comparison instructions all examine data at the top of the stack in relation to another element and return the result of the comparison in the status register condition code bits C3–C0. Comparisons that are allowed by the coprocessor are: FCOM (floating-point compare), FCOMP (floating-point compare with a pop), FCOMPP (floating-point compare with 2 pops), FICOM (integer compare), FICOMP (integer compare and pop), FSTS (test), and FXAM (examine). Following is a list of these instructions with a description of their function:

1. FCOM—compares the floating-point data at the top of the stack with an operand, which may be any register or any memory operand. If the operand is not coded with the instruction, the next stack element ST(1) is compared with the stack top ST.

2. FCOMP and FCOMPP—both instructions perform as FCOM, but they also pop one or two registers from the stack.
3. FICOM and FICOMP—the top of the stack is compared with the integer stored at a memory operand. In addition to the compare, FICOMP also pops the top of the stack.
4. FTST—test the contents of the top of the stack against a zero. The result of the comparison is coded in the status register condition code bits as illustrated in Table 12–1 with the status register.
5. FXAM—examines the stack top and modifies the condition code bits to indicate whether the contents are positive, negative, normalized, etc. Refer back to the status register in Table 12–1.

Transcendental Operations

The transcendental instructions include: FPTAN (partial tangent), FPATAM (partial arctangent), F2XM1 ($2^x - 1$), FYL2X (Y $\log_2$ X), and FYL2XP1 (Y $\log_2$(X + 1)). A list of these operations follows with a description of each transcendental operation:

1. FPTAN—finds the partial tangent of Y/X = tan θ. The value of θ is at the top of the stack and must be between 0 and $\pi/4$. The result is a ratio found as ST = X and ST(1) = Y. If the value is outside of the allowable range, an invalid error occurs as indicated by the status register.
2. FPATAN—finds the partial tangent as θ = ARCTAN X/Y. The value of X is at the top of the stack and Y is at ST(1). The values of X and Y must be as follows: $0 \leq Y < X < \infty$. The instruction pops the stack and leaves θ at the top of the stack.
3. F2AM1—finds the function $2^x - 1$. The value of X is taken from the top of the stack and the result is returned to the top of the stack. To obtain 2^x, add one to the result at the top of the stack. This function can be used to derive the function listed in Table 12–4. Note that the constants $\log_2{}^{10}$ and $\log_2 e$ are built in as standard values for the coprocessor.
4. FYL2X—finds Y $\log_2$X. The value X is taken from the stack top and Y is taken from ST(1). The result is found at the top of the stack after a pop. The value of X must range between 0 and ∞ and the value of Y must be between $-\infty$ and $+\infty$.
5. FYL2XP1—finds Y $\log_2$(X + 1). The value of X is taken from the stack top and Y is taken from ST(1). The result is found at the top of the stack after a pop. The value of X must range between 0 and $1 - \sqrt{2}/2$ and the value of Y must be between $-\infty$ and $+\infty$.

Constant Operations

The coprocessor instruction set includes opcodes that return constants to the top of the stack. A list of these instructions appears in Table 12–5.

TABLE 12–4 Exponential functions

Function	Equation
10^x	$2^x \log 2^{10}$
e^x	$2^x \log 2^e$
Y^x	$2^x \log 2^y$

TABLE 12-5 Constant operations

Instruction	Constant Pushed to ST
FLDZ	+0.0
FLD1	+1.0
FLDPI	π
FLDL2T	$\log_2 10$
FLDL2E	$\log_2 e$
FLDLG2	$\log_{10} 2$
FLDLN2	$\log_e 2$

Coprocessor Control Instructions

The coprocessor has control instructions for initialization, exception handling, and task switching. The control instructions have two forms. For example, FINIT initializes the coprocessor and so does FNINIT. The difference is that FNINIT does not cause any wait states, while FINIT does cause waits. The microprocessor waits for the FINIT instruction by testing the $\overline{\text{BUSY}}$ pin on the coprocessor. All control instructions have these two forms. Following is a list of each control instruction with its function:

1. FINIT/FNINIT—this instruction performs the same basic function as reset as described in section 12–3. The coprocessor operates with a closure of projective, rounds to the nearest, and uses a precision of 64 bits when reset or initialized.
2. FSETPM—changes the addressing mode of the coprocessor to the protected addressing mode. This mode is used when the microprocessor is also operated in the protected mode. As with the microprocessor, protected mode can only be exited by a hardware reset or in the case of the 80386/80486 with a change to the control register.
3. FLDCW—loads the control register with the word addressed by the operand.
4. FSTCW/FNSTCW—stores the control register into the word-sized memory operand.
5. FSTSW AX/FNSTSW AX—copies the contents of the control register to the AX register.
6. FCLEX/FNCLEX—clears the error flags in the status register and also the busy flag.
7. FSAVE/FNSAVE—writes the entire state of the machine to memory. Figure 12–10 shows the memory layout for this instruction.
8. FRSTOR—restores the state of the machine from memory. This instruction is used to restore the information saved by FSAVE/FNSAVE.
9. FSTENV/FNSTENV—stores the environment of the coprocessor as shown in Figure 12–11.
10. FLDENV—reloads the environment saved by FSTENV/FNSTENV.
11. FINCST—increments the stack pointer.
12. FDECSTP—decrements the stack pointer.
13. FFREE—frees a register by changing the destination register's tag to empty. It does not affect the contents of the register.

FIGURE 12–10 Memory format when the 8087 registers are stored by the FSAVE instruction. (Courtesy of Intel Corporation)

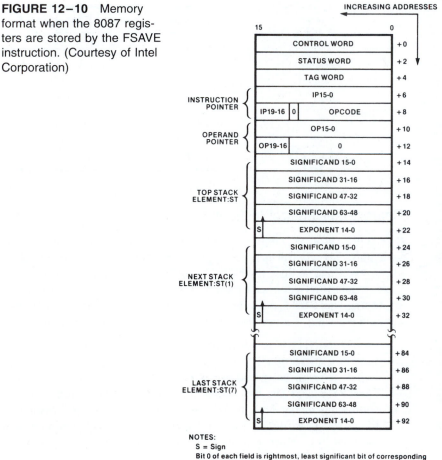

NOTES:
S = Sign
Bit 0 of each field is rightmost, least significant bit of corresponding register field.
Bit 63 of significand is integer bit (assumed binary point is immediately to the right).

14. FNOP—floating-point coprocessor NOP.
15. FWAIT—causes the microprocessor to wait for the coprocessor to finish an operation. FWAIT should be used before the microprocessor accesses memory data that are affected by the coprocessor.

80387/80487 Instructions

Although we have yet to talk about the 80386 microprocessor and its companion coprocessor the 80387, 80486DX and its built-in coprocessor, or the 80486SX and its companion coprocessor the 80487SX, we can discuss the instruction sets of these coprocessors and their differences with the other versions of the coprocessor. These newer coprocessors contain the same basic instruction provided by the earlier versions, with a few additional instructions.

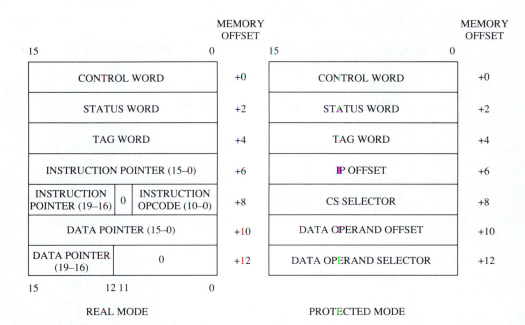

FIGURE 12-11 The memory format for the FSTENV instruction. (Courtesy of Intel Corporation.

The 80387, 80486, and 80486SX contain the following additional instructions: FCOS (cosine), FPREM1 (partial remainder), FSIN (sine), FSINCOS (sine and cosine), and FUCOM/FUCOMP/FUCOMPP (unordered compare). The sine and cosine instructions are the most significant addition to the instruction set. In the earlier versions of the coprocessor we must calculate sine and cosine from the tangent.

Table 12-6 lists the instruction sets for all versions of the coprocessor. It also lists the number of clocking periods required to execute each instruction. Execution times are listed for the 8087, 80287, 80387, and 80486 or 80487. To determine the execution time of an instruction, the clock time is multiplied times the listed execution time. The FADD instruction requires 70-143 clocks for the 80287. Suppose that we use an 8 Mhz clock for the 80287 that has a clock period of 1/8 MHz or 125 ns per clock. The FADD instruction requires between 8.75 µs and 17.875 gms to execute. Using a 25 Mhz (40 ns) 80486, this instruction requires between 0.32 µs and 0.8 µs to execute.

Table 12-6 uses some shorthand notations to represent the displacement that may or may not be required for an instruction that uses a memory-addressing mode. It also uses the abbreviation to represent the mode, mmm, to represent a register/memory addressing mode, and rrr to represent one of the floating-point coprocessor registers ST(0)–ST(7). The d bit that appears in some instruction opcodes defines the direction of the data flow as in FADD ST,ST(2) or FADD ST(2),ST. The d-bit is a logic 0 for flow toward ST as in FADD ST,ST(2) and a logic 1 for FADD ST(2),ST.

TABLE 12–6 The instruction set of the arithmetic coprocessor

F2XM1 $2^{ST} - 1$

11011001 11110000

Example		Clocks
F2XM1	8087	310—630
	80287	310—630
	80387	211—476
	80486/7	140—279

FABS   Absolute value of ST

11011001 11100001

Example		Clocks
FABS	8087	10—17
	80287	10—17
	80387	22
	80486/7	3

FADD/FADDP/FIADD   Addition

```
11011000  oo000mmm  disp      32-bit memory (FADD)
11011100  oo000mmm  disp      64-bit memory (FADD)
11011d00  11000rrr            FADD ST,ST(rrr)
11011110  11000rrr            FADDP ST,ST(rrr)
11011110  oo000mmm  disp      16-bit memory (FIADD)
11011010  oo000mmm  disp      32-bit memory (FIADD)
```

Format	Examples		Clocks
FADD	FADD DATA	8087	70—143
FADDP	FADD ST,ST(1)		
FIADD	FADDP	80287	70—143
	FIADD NUMBER		
	FADD ST,ST(3)	80387	23—72
	FADDP ST,ST(2)		
	FADD ST(2),ST	80486/7	8—20

FCLEX/FNCLEX   Clear errors

11011011 11100010

Example		Clocks
FCLEX	8087	2—8
FNCLEX		
	80287	2—8
	80387	11
	80486/7	7

530

FCOM/FCOMP/FCOMPP/FICOM/FICOMP   Compare

```
11011000  oo010mmm  disp        32-bit memory (FCOM)
11011100  oo010mmm  disp        64-bit memory (FCOM)
11011000  11010rrr              FCOM ST(rrr)
11011000  oo011mmm  disp        32-bit memory (FCOMP)
11011100  oo011mmm  disp        64-bit memory (FCOMP)
11011000  11011rrr              FCOMP ST(rrr)
11011110  11011001             FCOMPP
11011110  oo010mmm  disp        16-bit memory (FICOM)
11011010  oo010mmm  disp        32-bit memory (FICOM)
11011110  oo011mmm  disp        16-bit memory (FICOMP)
11011010  oo011mmm  disp        32-bit memory (FICOMP)
```

Format	Examples		Clocks
FCOM	FCOM ST(2)	8087	40—93
FCOMP	FCOMP DATA		
FCOMPP	FCOMPP	80287	40—93
FICOM	FICOM NUMBER		
FICOMP	FICOMP DATA3	80387	24—63
		80486/7	15—20

FCOS   Cosine of ST

```
11011001  11111111
```

Example		Clocks
FCOS	8087	—
	80287	—
	80387	123—772
	80486/7	193—279

FDECSTP   Decrement stack pointer

```
11011001  11110110
```

Example		Clocks
FDECSTP	8087	6—12
	80287	6—12
	80387	22
	80486/7	3

FDISI/FNDISI   Disable interrupts

```
11011011  11100001
```

(ignored on the 80287, 80387, and 80486/7)

TABLE 12–6   (continued)

Example		Clocks
FDISI FNDISI	8087	2—8
	80287	—
	80387	—
	80486/7	—

FDIV/FDIVP/FIDIV   Divison

```
11011000  oo110mmm  disp      32-bit memory (FDIV)
11011100  oo100mmm  disp      64-bit memory (FDIV)
11011d00  11111rrr            FDIV ST,ST(rrr)
11011110  11111rrr            FDIVP ST,ST(rrr)
11011110  oo110mmm  disp      16-bit memory (FIDIV)
11011010  oo110mmm  disp      32-bit memory (FIDIV)
```

Format	Examples		Clocks
FDIV FDIVP FIDIV	FDIV DATA FDIV ST,ST(3) FDIVP FIDIV NUMBER FDIV ST,ST(5) FDIVP ST,ST(2) FDIV ST(2),ST	8087	191—243
		80287	191—243
		80387	88—140
		80486/7	8—89

FDIVR/FDIVRP/FIDIVR   Divison reversed

```
11011000  oo111mmm  disp      32-bit memory (FDIVR)
11011100  oo111mmm  disp      64-bit memory (FDIVR)
11011d00  11110rrr            FDIVR ST,ST(rrr)
11011110  11110rrr            FDIVRP ST,ST(rrr)
11011110  oo111mmm  disp      16-bit memory (FIDIVR)
11011010  oo111mmm  disp      32-bit memory (FIDIVR)
```

Format	Examples		Clocks
FDIVR FDIVRP FIDIVR	FDIVR DATA FDIVR ST,ST(3) FDIVRP FIDIVR NUMBER FDIVR ST,ST(5) FDIVRP ST,ST(2) FDIVR ST(2),ST	8087	191—243
		80287	191—243
		80387	88—140
		80486/7	8—89

FENI/FNENI   Disable interrupts

```
11011011  11100000
```

(ignored on the 80287, 80387, and 80486/7)

Example		Clocks
FENI FNENI	8087	2—8
	80287	—
	80387	—
	80486/7	—

FFREE   Free register

11011101 11000rrr

Format	Examples		Clocks
FFREE	FFREE FFREE ST(1) FFREE ST(2)	8087	9—16
		80287	9—16
		80387	18
		80486/7	3

FINCSTP   Increment stack pointer

11011001 11110111

Example		Clocks
FINCSTP	8087	6—12
	80287	6—12
	80387	21
	80486/7	3

FINIT/FNINIT   Initialize coprocessor

11011001 11110110

Example		Clocks
FINIT FNINIT	8087	2—8
	80287	2—8
	80387	33
	80486/7	17

FLD/FILD/FBLD   Load data to ST(0)

```
11011001  oo000mmm  disp      32-bit memory (FLD)
11011101  oo000mmm  disp      64-bit memory (FLD)
11011011  oo101mmm  disp      80-bit memory (FLD)
11011111  oo000mmm  disp      16-bit memory (FILD)
11011011  oo000mmm  disp      32-bit memory (FILD)
11011111  oo101mmm  disp      64-bit memory (FILD)
11011111  oo100mmm  disp      80-bit memory (FBLD)
```

Format	Examples		Clocks
FLD FILD FBLD	FLD DATA FILD DATA1 FBLD DEC_DATA	8087	17—310
		80287	17—310
		80387	14—275
		80486/7	3—103

TABLE 12–6 (continued)

FLD1 Load + 1.0 to ST(0)

11011001 11101000		
Example		Clocks
FLD1	8087	15—21
	80287	15—21
	80387	24
	80486/7	4

FLDZ Load + 0.0 to ST(0)

11011001 11101110		
Example		Clocks
FLDZ	8087	11—17
	80287	11—17
	80387	20
	80486/7	4

FLDPI Load π to ST(0)

11011001 11101011		
Example		Clocks
FLDPI	8087	16—22
	80287	16—22
	80387	40
	80486/7	8

FLDL2E Load $\log_2$ e to ST(0)

11011001 11101010		
Example		Clocks
FLDL2E	8087	15—21
	80287	15—21
	80387	40
	80486/7	8

FLDL2T   Load $\log_2 10$ to ST(0)

11011001 11101001

Example		Clocks
FLDL2T	8087	16—22
	80287	16—22
	80387	40
	80486/7	8

FLDLG2   Load $\log_{10} 2$ to ST(0)

11011001 11101000

Example		Clocks
FLDLG2	8087	18—24
	80287	18—24
	80387	41
	80486/7	8

FLDLN2   Load $\log_e 2$ to ST(0)

11011001 11101101

Example		Clocks
FLDLN2	8087	17—23
	80287	17—23
	80387	41
	80486/7	8

FLDCW   Load control register

11011001 oo101mmm disp

Format	Examples		Clocks
FLDCW	FLDCW DATA FLDCW STATUS	8087	7—14
		80287	7—14
		80387	19
		80486/7	4

TABLE 12-6 (continued)

FLDENV Load environment

11011001 oo100mmm disp

Format	Examples	Clocks	
FLDENV	FLDENV ENVIRON FLDENV DATA	8087	35—45
		80287	25—45
		80387	71
		80486/7	34—44

FMUL/FMULP/FIMUL Multiplication

11011000 oo001mmm disp	32-bit memory (FMUL)	
11011100 oo001mmm disp	64-bit memory (FMUL)	
11011d00 11001rrr	FMUL ST,ST(rrr)	
11011110 11001rrr	FMULP ST,ST(rrr)	
11011110 oo001mmm disp	16-bit memory (FIMUL)	
11011010 oo001mmm disp	32-bit memory (FIMUL)	

Format	Examples	Clocks	
FMUL FMULP FIMUL	FMUL DATA FMUL ST,ST(2) FMUL ST(2),ST FMULP FIMUL DATA3	8087	110—168
		80287	110—168
		80387	29—82
		80486/7	11—27

FNOP No operation

11011001 11010000

Example	Clocks	
FNOP	8087	10—16
	80287	10—16
	80387	12
	80486/7	3

FPATAN Partial arctangent of ST(0)

11011001 11110011

Example	Clocks	
FPATAN	8087	250—800
	80287	250—800
	80387	314—487
	80486/7	218—303

FPREM   Partial remainder

11011001 11111000

Example		Clocks
FPREM	8087	15—190
	80287	15—190
	80387	74—155
	80486/7	70—138

FPREM1   Partial remainder (IEEE)

11011001 11110101

Example		Clocks
FPREM1	8087	—
	80287	—
	80387	95—185
	80486/7	72—167

FPTAN   Partial tangent of ST(0)

11011001 11110010

Example		Clocks
FPTAN	8087	30—450
	80287	30—450
	80387	191—497
	80486/7	200—273

FRNDINT   Round ST(0) to an integer

11011001 11111100

Example		Clocks
FRNDINT	8087	16—50
	80287	16—50
	80387	66—80
	80486/7	21—30

TABLE 12–6 (continued)

FRSTOR   Restore state

11011101 oo110mmm disp

Format	Examples	Clocks	
FRSTOR	FRSTOR DATA FRSTOR STATE FRSTOR NACHINE	8087	197—207
		80287	197—207
		80387	308
		80486/7	120—131

FSAVE/FNSAVE   Save machine state

11011101 oo110mmm disp

Format	Examples	Clocks	
FSAVE FNSAVE ◄	FSAVE STATE FNSAVE STATUS FSAVE MACHINE	8087	197—207
		80287	197—207
		80387	375
		80486/7	143—154

FSCALE   Scale ST(0) by ST(1)

11011001 11111101

Example	Clocks	
FSCALE	8087	32—38
	80287	32—38
	80387	67—86
	80486/7	30—32

FSETPM   Set protected mode

11011011 11100100

Example	Clocks	
FSETPM	8087	—
	80287	2—18
	80387	12
	80486/7	—

FSIN   Sine of ST(0)

11011001 11111110

Example		Clocks
FSIN	8087	—
	80287	—
	80387	122—771
	80486/7	193—279

FSINCOS   Find sine and cosine of ST(0)

11011001 11111011

Example		Clocks
FSINCOS	8087	—
	80287	—
	80387	194—809
	80486/7	243—329

FSQRT   Square root of ST(0)

11011001 11111010

Example		Clocks
FSQRT	8087	180—186
	80287	180—186
	80387	122—129
	80486/7	83—87

FST/FSTP/FIST/FISTP/FBSTP   Store

```
11011001  oo010mmm  disp     32-bit memory (FST)
11011101  oo010mmm  disp     64-bit memory (FST)
11011101  11010rrr           FST ST(rrr)
11011011  oo011mmm  disp     32-bit memory (FSTP)
11011101  oo011mmm  disp     64-bit memory (FSTP)
11011011  oo111mmm  disp     80-bit memory (FSTP)
11011101  11001rrr           FSTP ST(rrr)
11011111  oo010mmm  disp     16-bit memory (FIST)
11011011  oo010mmm  disp     32-bit memory (FIST)
11011111  oo011mmm  disp     16-bit memory (FISTP)
11011011  oo011mmm  disp     32-bit memory (FISTP)
11011111  oo111mmm  disp     64-bit memory (FISTP)
11011111  oo110mmm  disp     80-bit memory (FBSTP)
```

TABLE 12–6   (continued)

Format	Examples		Clocks
FST FSTP FIST FISTP FBSTP	FST DATA FST ST(3) FST FSTP FIST DATA2 FBSTP DATA6 FISTP DATA9	8087	15—540
		80287	15—540
		80387	11—534
		80486/7	3—176

FSTCW/FNSTCW   Store control register

11011001 oo111mmm disp

Format	Examples		Clocks
FSTCW FNSTCW	FSTCW CONTROL FNSTCW STATUS FSTCW MACHINE	8087	12—18
		80287	12—18
		80387	15
		80486/7	3

FSTENV/FNSTENV   Store environment

11011001 oo110mmm disp

Format	Examples		Clocks
FSTENV FNSTENV	FSTENV CONTROL FNSTENV STATUS FSTENV MACHINE	8087	40—50
		80287	40—50
		80387	103—104
		80486/7	58—67

FSTSW/FNSTSW   Store status register

11011101 oo111mmm disp

Format	Examples		Clocks
FSTSW FNSTSW	FSTSW CONTROL FNSTSW STATUS FSTSW MACHINE	8087	12—18
		80287	12—18
		80387	15
		80486/7	3

FSUB/FSUBP/FISUB   Subtraction

11011000	oo100mmm disp	32-bit memory (FSUB)
11011100	oo100mmm disp	64-bit memory (FSUB)
11011d00	11101rrr	FSUB ST,ST(rrr)
11011110	11101rrr	FSUBP ST,ST(rrr)
11011110	oo100mmm disp	16-bit memory (FISUB)
11011010	oo100mmm disp	32-bit memory (FISUB)

Format	Examples	Clocks	
FSUB FSUBP FISUB	FSUB DATA FSUB ST,ST(2) FSUB ST(2),ST FSUBP FISUB DATA3	8087	70—143
		80287	70—143
		80387	29—82
		80486/7	8—35

FSUBR/FSUBRP/FISUBR   Reverse subtraction

```
11011000  oo101mmm  disp      32-bit memory (FSUBR)
11011100  oo101mmm  disp      64-bit memory (FSUBR)
11011d00  11100rrr            FSUBR ST,ST(rrr)
11011110  11100rrr            FSUBRP ST,ST(rrr)
11011110  oo101mmm  disp      16-bit memory (FISUBR)
11011010  oo101mmm  disp      32-bit memory (FISUBR)
```

Format	Examples	Clocks	
FSUBR FSUBRP FISUBR	FSUBR DATA FSUBR ST,ST(2) FSUBR ST(2),ST FSUBRP FISUBR DATA3	8087	70—143
		80287	70—143
		80387	29—82
		80486/7	8—35

FTST   Compare ST(0) with + 0.0

```
11011001  11100100
```

Example	Clocks	
FTST	8087	38—48
	80287	38—48
	80387	28
	80486/7	4

FUCOM/FUCOMP/FUCOMPP   Unordered compare

```
11011101  11100rrr        FUCOM ST,ST(rrr)
11011101  11101rrr        FUCOMP ST,ST(rrr)
11011101  11101001        FUCOMPP
```

Format	Examples	Clocks	
FUCOM FUCOMP FUCOMPP	FUCOM ST,ST(2) FUCOM FUCOMP ST,ST(3) FUCOMP FUCOMPP	8087	—
		80287	—
		80387	24—26
		80486/7	4—5

TABLE 12–6 (continued)

FWAIT Wait

10011011

Example	Clocks	
FWAIT	8087	4
	80287	3
	80387	6
	80486/7	1—3

FXAM Examine ST(0)

11011001 11100101

Example	Clocks	
FXAM	8087	12—23
	80287	12—23
	80387	30—38
	80486/7	8

FXCH Exchange ST(0) with another register

11011001 11001rrr   FXCH ST,ST(rrr)

Format	Examples	Clocks	
FXCH	FXCH ST,ST(1) FXCH FXCH ST,ST(4)	8087	10—15
		80287	10—15
		80387	18
		80486/7	4

FXTRACT Extract components of ST(0)

11011001 11110100

Example	Clocks	
FXTRACT	8087	27—55
	80287	27—55
	80387	70—76
	80486/7	16—20

FYL2X ST(1) x $\log_2$ ST(0)

11011001 11110001		
Example		Clocks
FYL2X	8087	900—1100
	80287	900—1100
	80387	120—538
	80486/7	196—329

FXL2XP1 $ST(1) \times \log_2 [ST(0) + 1.0]$

11011001 11111001		
Example		Clocks
FXL2XP1	8087	700—1000
	80287	700—1000
	80387	257—547
	80486/7	171—326

Note: d = direction where d = 0 for ST as the destination and d = 1 for ST as the source, rrr = floating-point register number, oo = mode, mmm = r/m field, and disp = displacement.

12-5 PROGRAMMING WITH THE ARITHMETIC COPROCESSOR

This section of the chapter provides programming examples for the arithmetic coprocessor. Each example is chosen to illustrate a programming technique for the coprocessor.

Calculating the Area of a Circle

This programming example provides a simple illustration of a method of addressing the coprocessor stack. First recall that the equation for calculating the area of a circle is $A = \pi R^2$. A procedure that performs this calculation is listed in Example 12-6.

EXAMPLE 12-6

```
;Procedure that calculates the area of a circle.
;
;The radius must be stored at memory location RADIUS
;before calling this procedure. The result is found
;in memory location AREA after the procedure.
;
```

```
0000                    AREAS   PROC    FAR

0000 D9 06 0004 R               FLD     RADIUS          ;radius to ST
0004 D8 C8                      FMUL    ST,ST(0)        ;sqaure radius
0006 D9 EB                      FLDPI                   ;π to ST
0008 DE C9                      FMUL                    ;multiply ST = ST × ST(1)
000A D9 1E 0000 R               FSTP    AREA            ;save area
000E 9B                         FWAIT                   ;wait for coprocessor
000F CB                         RET

0010                    AREAS   ENDP
```

This is a rather simple procedure, bit it does illustrate the operation of the stack. To provide a better understanding of the operation of the stack, Figure 12–12 shows the contents of the stack after each instruction of Example 12–6 executes.

The first instruction loads the contents of memory location RADIUS to the top of the stack. Next the FMUL ST,ST(0) instruction squares the radius on the top of the stack. The FLDPI instruction loads π to the stack top. The FMUL instructions use the classic stack addressing mode to multiply ST by ST(1). After the multiplication, both prior values are removed from the stack and the product replaces them at the top of the stack. Finally the FSTP instruction copies the top of the stack, the area, to memory location AREA and clears the stack.

FIGURE 12–12 Operation of the 80287 stack with the procedure of Example 12–6. Note: Stack shown after the execution of the indicated instruction.

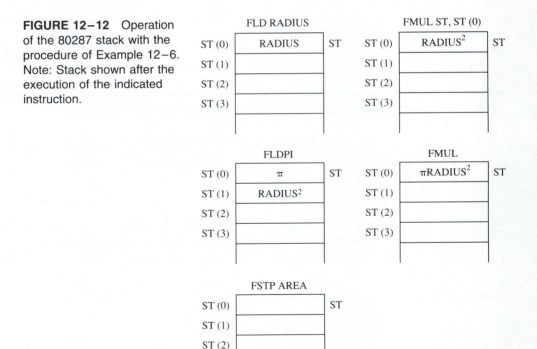

The FWAIT instruction appears just before the return instruction in this example. The reason that we use the FWAIT instruction is to wait for the coprocessor to finish finding the area before returning. If we were not to wait, the main program might access memory location AREA before the coprocessor stores the result into location AREA.

Finding the Resonant Frequency

An equation commonly used in electronics is the formula for determining the resonant frequency of an LC circuit. The equation solved by the procedure illustrated in Example 12–7 is $Fr = 1/(2\pi\sqrt{LC})$.

EXAMPLE 12–7

```
0000                    DATAS   SEGMENT

0000 00000000           RESO    DD      ?               ;resonant frequency
0004 358637BD           L       DD      .000001         ;inductance
0008 358637BD           C       DD      .000001         ;capacitance
000C 40000000           TWO     DD      2.0             ;constant

0010                    DATAS   ENDS

0000                    CODE    SEGMENT

                        ASSUME  CS:Code,DS:DATAS

                ;Procedure that finds the resonant frequency.

0000                    FREQ    PROC    FAR

0000 D9 06 0004 R               FLD     L               ;get L
0004 D8 0E 0008 R               FMUL    C               ;find LC

0008 D9 FA                      FSQRT                   ;find √LC

000A D8 0E 000C R               FMUL    TWO             ;find 2√LC

000E D9 EB                      FLDPI                   ;get π
0010 DE C9                      FMUL                    ;get 2π√LC

0012 D9 E8                      FLD1                    ;get 1
0014 DE F1                      FDIVR                   ;form 1/(2π√LC)

0016 D9 1E 0000 R               FSTP    RESO            ;save frequency

001A 9B                         FWAIT
001B CB                         RET

001C                    FREQ    ENDP

001C                    CODE    ENDS

                        END
```

Notice the straightforward manner in which the procedure solves this equation. Very little extra data manipulation is required because of the stack inside the coprocessor.

Also notice how the constant TWO is defined for the program and how the DIVRP, using classic stack addressing, is used to form the reciprocal.

Finding the Roots Using the Quadratic Equation

This example illustrates how to find the roots of a polynomial expression $(ax^2 + bx + c = 0)$ using the quadratic equation. The quadratic equation is $(b \pm \sqrt{\sqrt{b^2 - 4ac}})/2a$. Example illustrates a procedure that finds the roots (R1 and R2) for the quadratic equation. The constants are stored in memory locations A, B, and C.

EXAMPLE 12–8

```
                       .286
                       .287
0000                   DATAS   SEGMENT
0000  40000000         TWO     DD      2.0
0004  40800000         FOUR    DD      4.0
0008  3F800000         A       DD      1.0
000C  C1800000         B       DD      -16.0
0010  421C0000         C       DD      +39.0
0014  00000000         R1      DD      ?
0018  00000000         R2      DD      ?
001C                   DATAS   ENDS

0000                   CODE    SEGMENT

                       ASSUME  CS:CODE,DS:DATAS

                       ;Procedure that solves the quadratic equation.

0000                   ROOTS   PROC    FAR

0000  D9 06 0000 R             FLD     TWO
0004  D8 0E 0008 R             FMUL    A           ;form 2a
0008  D9 06 0004 R             FLD     FOUR
000C  D8 0E 0008 R             FMUL    A
0010  D8 0E 0010 R             FMUL    C           ;form 4ac
0014  D9 06 000C R             FLD     B
0018  D8 0E 000C R             FMUL    B           ;form b²
001C  DE E1                    FSUBR               ;form b² - 4ac
001E  D9 FA                    FSQRT               ;form square root of b² - 4ac

0020  D9 06 000C R             FLD     B
0024  D8 E1                    FSUB    ST,ST(1)
0026  D8 F2                    FDIV    ST,ST(2)
0028  D9 1E 0014 R             FSTP    R1          ;save root1

002C  D9 06 000C R             FLD     B
0030  DE C1                    FADD
0032  DE F1                    FDIVR
0034  D9 1E 0018 R             FSTP    R2          ;save root2

0038  9B                       FWAIT
0039  CB                       RET

003A                   ROOTS   ENDP

003A                   CODE    ENDS

                               END
```

Displaying a Single-Precision Floating-Point Number

This section of the text shows how to take the floating-point contents of a 32-bit single-precision floating-point number and display it on the video display. The procedure displays the floating-point number as a mixed number with an integer part and a fractional part separated by a decimal point. In order to simplify the procedure, we have placed a limit on the display size of the mixed number so the integer portion is a 32-bit binary number and the fraction is a 24-bit binary number. The procedure will not function properly for larger or smaller numbers.

EXAMPLE 12–9

```
                        .286
                        .287
0000                    DATAS    SEGMENT

0000 C50B0C00           NUMB     DD      -2224.75
0004 0000               TEMP     DW      ?
0006 0000               WHOLE    DW      ?
0008 00000000           FRACT    DD      ?

000C                    DATAS    ENDS

0000                    CODE     SEGMENT

                        ASSUME CS:CODE,DS:DATAS

                        ;Main program that displays NUMB
                        ;
0000                    MAIN     PROC    FAR

0000 B8 ---- R                   MOV     AX,DATAS
0003 8E D8                       MOV     DS,AX
0005 E8 0013 R                   CALL    DISP            ;display NUMB
0008 B4 4C                       MOV     AH,4CH          ;exit to DOS
000A CD 21                       INT     21H

000C                    MAIN     ENDP

000C                    DISPS    PROC    NEAR

000C B4 06                       MOV     AH,6            ;display AL
000E 8A D0                       MOV     DL,AL
0010 CD 21                       INT     21H
0012 C3                          RET

0013                    DISPS    ENDP

0013                    DISP     PROC    NEAR

0013 9B D9 3E 0004 R             FSTCW   TEMP            ;set rounding to chop
0018 81 0E 0004 R 0C00           OR      TEMP,0C00H
001E 9B D9 2E 0004 R             FLDCW   TEMP

0023 D9 06 0000 R                FLD     NUMB            ;get NUMB
0027 D9 E4                       FTST                    ;test NUMB
0029 9B DF E0                    FSTSW   AX              ;status to AX
002C 25 4500                     AND     AX,4500H        ;get C3,C2, and C0
002F 3D 0100                     CMP     AX,0100H        ;test for -
```

```
0032 75 05                       JNE     DISP1              ;if positive
0034 B0 2D                       MOV     AL,'-'
0036 E8 000C R                   CALL    DISPS              ;display minus

0039                  DISP1:

0039 D9 E1                       FABS                       ;make ST positive
003B D9 FC                       FRNDINT                    ;get integer
003D DF 16 0006 R                FIST    WHOLE              ;store integer
0041 D9 06 0000 R                FLD     NUMB
0045 D9 E1                       FABS
0047 DE E9                       FSUB                       ;get fraction
0049 D9 E1                       FABS
004B D9 1E 0008 R                FSTP    FRACT              ;save fraction
004F 9B                          FWAIT

                     ;display integer part

0050 A1 0006 R                   MOV     AX,WHOLE
0053 B9 0000                     MOV     CX,0
0056 BB 000A                     MOV     BX,10

0059                  DISP2:

0059 41                          INC     CX
005A 33 D2                       XOR     DX,DX
005C F7 F3                       DIV     BX
005E 83 C2 30                    ADD     DX,'0'             ;convert to ASCII
0061 52                          PUSH    DX
0062 0B C0                       OR      AX,AX
0064 75 F3                       JNE     DISP2              ;if not zero

0066                  DISP3:

0066 58                          POP     AX
0067 E8 000C R                   CALL    DISPS              ;display it
006A E2 FA                       LOOP    DISP3
006C B0 2E                       MOV     AL,'.'             ;display decimal point
006E E8 000C R                   CALL    DISPS

                     ;display fractional part

0071 A1 0008 R                   MOV     AX,WORD PTR FRACT
0074 8B 16 000A R                MOV     DX,WORD PTR FRACT+2
0078 B9 0008                     MOV     CX,8

007B                  DISP4:

007B D1 E0                       SHL     AX,1
007D D1 D2                       RCL     DX,1
007F E2 FA                       LOOP    DISP4
0081 81 CA 8000                  OR      DX,8000H           ;set implied bit
0085 92                          XCHG    AX,DX
0086 BB 000A                     MOV     BX,10

0089                  DISP5:

0089 F7 E3                       MUL     BX
008B 50                          PUSH    AX
008C 92                          XCHG    DX,AX
008D 04 30                       ADD     AL,'0'
```

```
008F E8 000C R                 CALL    DISPS              ;display digit
0092 58                        POP     AX
0093 0B C0                     OR      AX,AX
0095 75 F2                     JNZ     DISP5
0097 C3                        RET

0098               DISP        ENDP

0098               CODE        ENDS

                   END         MAIN
```

Example 12–9 lists the procedure for displaying the contents of memory location NUMB on the video display at the current cursor position. The procedure first tests the sign of the number and displays a space for positive and a minus sign for a negative number. After displaying the sign, the number is made positive by the FABS instruction. Next we divide it into integer and fractional parts and store them at WHOLE and FRACT.

The last part of the procedure displays the whole number part followed by the fractional part. Note that the fractional part may contain a rounding error for certain values. We have not adjusted the number to remove the rounding error that is inherent in floating-point fractional numbers.

Reading a Mixed-Number from the Keyboard

If floating-point arithmetic is used in a program, we must have a method of reading the number from the keyboard and converting it to floating-point. The procedure listed in Example 12–10 reads a signed mixed number from the keyboard and converts it to a floating-point number located at the top of the stack inside the coprocessor.

EXAMPLE 12–10

```
                               .286
                               .287
0000               DATA        SEGMENT

0000 00            SIGN        DB      ?
0001 0000          TEMP1       DW      ?
0003 41200000      TEN         DD      10.0

0007               DATA        ENDS

0000               CODE        SEGMENT

                   ASSUME CS:CODE,DS:DATA

                   ;procedure that reads a mixed number from the keyboard
                   ;and leaves it at the top of the coprocessor stack.

0000               READ        PROC    FAR

0000 B8 ---- R                 MOV     AX,DATA            ;address data segment
0003 8E D8                     MOV     DS,AX
0005 9B D9 EE                  FLDZ                       ;clear ST
0008 C6 06 0000 R 00           MOV     SIGN,0             ;clear sign
000D E8 007C                   CALL    GET                ;read a character
0010 3C 2D                     CMP     AL,'-'             ;test for minus
```

```
0012 75 07                      JNE      READ1              ;if not minus
0014 C6 06 0000 R FF            MOV      SIGN,0FFH          ;set sign for minus
0019 EB 0F                      JMP      READ3              ;Get integer part

001B                READ1:

001B 3C 2B                      CMP      AL,'+'             ;test for plus
001D 74 0B                      JE       READ3              ;get integer part
001F 3C 30                      CMP      AL,'0'             ;test for number
0021 72 06                      JB       READ2
0023 3C 39                      CMP      AL,'9'
0025 77 02                      JA       READ2
0027 EB 04                      JMP      READ4              ;if a number

0029                READ2:

0029 CB                         RET

002A                READ3:

002A E8 005F                    CALL     GET                ;read integer part

002D                READ4:

002D 3C 2E                      CMP      AL,'.'             ;test for fraction
002F 74 27                      JE       READ7              ;if fraction
0031 3C 30                      CMP      AL,'0'             ;test for number
0033 72 17                      JB       READ5
0035 3C 39                      CMP      AL,'9'
0037 77 13                      JA       READ5
0039 9B D8 0E 0003 R           FMUL     TEN                ;form integer
003E 32 E4                      XOR      AH,AH
0040 2C 30                      SUB      AL,'0'
0042 A3 0001 R                  MOV      TEMP1,AX
0045 9B DE 06 0001 R           FIADD    TEMP1
004A EB DE                      JMP      READ3

004C                READ5:

004C 80 3E 0000 R 00           CMP      SIGN,0             ;adjust sign
0051 75 01                      JNE      READ6
0053 CB                         RET

0054                READ6:

0054 9B D9 E0                   FCHS
0057 CB                         RET

0058                READ7:

0058 9B D9 E8                   FLD1                        ;from fraction
005B 9B D8 36 0003 R           FDIV     TEN

0060                READ8:

0060 E8 0029                    CALL     GET                ;read character
0063 3C 30                      CMP      AL,'0'             ;test for number
0065 72 20                      JB       READ9
0067 3C 39                      CMP      AL,'9'
0069 77 1C                      JA       READ9
```

```
006B 32 E4                    XOR      AH,AH
006D 2C 30                    SUB      AL,'0'
006F A3 0001 R                MOV      TEMP1,AX
0072 9B DF 06 0001 R          FILD     TEMP1              ;load number
0077 9B D8 C9                 FMUL     ST,ST(1)           ;form fraction
007A 9B DC C2                 FADD     ST(2),ST
007D 9B D8 D9                 FCOMP
0080 9B D8 36 0003 R          FDIV     TEN
0085 EB D9                    JMP      READ8

0087                  READ9:

0087 9B D8 D9                 FCOMP                       ;clear stack
008A EB C0                    JMP      READ5

008C                  READ     ENDP

008C                  GET      PROC     NEAR

008C B4 06                    MOV      AH,6               ;read character
008E B2 FF                    MOV      DL,0FFH
0090 CD 21                    INT      21H
0092 74 F8                    JZ       GET
0094 C3                       RET

0095                  GET      ENDP

0095                  CODE     ENDS

                              END
```

Here the sign is first read from the keyboard, if present, and saved for later use in adjusting the sign of the resultant floating-point number. Next, the integer portion of the number is read. This portion terminates with a period, space, or carriage return. If a period is typed, then the procedure continues and reads a fractional part. If a space or carriage return is entered, the number is converted to floating-point form.

12-6 SUMMARY

1. The arithmetic coprocessor functions in parallel with the microprocessor.
2. The data types manipulated by the coprocessor include signed-integer, floating-point, and binary-coded decimal (BCD).
3. There are three forms of integers for the coprocessor: word (16 bits), short (32 bits), and long (64 bits). Each integer contains a signed number in true magnitude for positive numbers and two's complement form for negative numbers.
4. A BCD number is stored as an 18-digit number in 10 bytes of memory. The most significant byte contains the sign-bit, and the remaining 9 bytes contain an 18-digit packed BCD number.
5. The coprocessor supports three types of floating-point numbers: single-precision (32 bits), double-precision (64 bits), and extended-precision (80 bits). A floating-point num-

ber is formed of three parts: the sign, biased exponent, and significand. In the copro-cessor, the exponent is biased with a constant and the integer bit of the normalized number is not stored in the significand except in the extended-precision form.

6. Decimal numbers are converted to floating-point numbers by converting the number to binary, normalizing the binary number, adding the bias to the exponent, and storing the number in floating-point form.

7. Floating-point numbers are converted to decimal by subtracting the bias from the exponent, unnormalizing the number, and then converting it to decimal.

8. The 80287 uses I/O space for the execution of some of its instructions. This space is invisible to the program and is used internally by the 80286/80287 system. These 16-bit I/O addresses are 00F8H, 00FAH, and 00FCH that must not be used for I/O data transfers in a system that contains an 80287.

9. The coprocessor contains a status register that indicates busy, what conditions follow a compare or test, the location of the top of the stack, and the state of the error bits.

10. The control register of the coprocessor contains control bits that select infinity, rounding, precision, and error masks.

11. The following directives are often used with the coprocessor for storing data: DW (define word), DD (define doubleword), DQ (define quad_word) and DT (define 10 bytes).

12. The coprocessor uses a stack to transfer data between itself and the memory system. Generally data are loaded to the top of the stack or removed from the top of the stack for storage.

13. All internal coprocessor data are always in the 80-bit extended-precision form. The only time that data are in any other form is when they are stored or loaded from the memory.

14. The coprocessor addressing modes include: the classic stack mode, register, register with a pop, and memory. Stack addressing is implied and the data at ST becomes the source, ST(1) the destination, and the result is found in ST after a pop. The other addressing modes are self-explanatory.

15. The coprocessor's arithmetic operations include addition, subtraction, multiplication, division, and square root.

16. There are transcendental functions in the coprocessor's instruction set. These functions find the partial tangent or arctangent, $2^x - 1$, Y log $_2$X, and Y log $_2$(X + 1).

17. Constants are stored inside the coprocessor that provide: +0.0, +1.0, π, $\log_2 10$, $\log_2 e$, $\log_{10} 2$, and $\log_e 2$.

18. The 80387 functions with the 80386 microprocessor and the 80487SX functions with the 80486SX microprocessor, but the 80486DX contains its own internal arithmetic coprocessor. The instructions performed by the earlier versions are available on these coprocessors. In addition to these instructions, the 80387 and 80486/7 also can find the sine and cosine.

12-7   QUESTIONS AND PROBLEMS

1. List the three types of data that are loaded or stored in memory by the coprocessor.

2. List the three integer data types, the range of the integers stored in them, and the number of bits allotted to each.

3. Explain how a BCD number is stored in memory by the coprocessor.
4. List the three types of floating-point numbers used with the coprocessor and the number of binary bits assigned to each.
5. Convert the following decimal numbers into single-precision floating-point numbers:
   a. 28.75   b. 624   c. −0.615   d. + 0.0   e. −1000.5
6. Convert the following single-precision floating-point number into decimal:
   a. 11000000 11110000 00000000 00000000
   b. 00111111 00010000 00000000 00000000
   c. 01000011 10011001 00000000 00000000
   d. 01000000 00000000 00000000 00000000
   e. 01000001 00100000 00000000 00000000
   f. 00000000 00000000 00000000 00000000
7. What is the purpose of the CLM pin on the 80287?
8. Where is the $\overline{BUSY}$ pin on the 80287 connected?
9. What is the purpose of $\overline{NPRD}$ and where does it connect?
10. Explain what the 80287 does when a normal 80286 instruction executes.
11. Explain what the 80286 does when an 80287 instruction executes.
12. What is the purpose of the C3–C0 bits in the status register?
13. How is the rounding mode selected in the 80287?
14. What coprocessor instruction uses the microprocessor's AX register?
15. How are data stored inside the coprocessor?
16. Whenever the coprocessor is reset, the top of the stack register is register number _____ .
17. What does the term chop mean in the rounding control bits of the control register?
18. What is the difference between affine and projective infinity control?
19. What microprocessor instruction forms the opcodes for the coprocessor?
20. Using assembler pseudo-opcodes, form statements that accomplish the following:
   a. Store a 23.44 into a double-precision floating-point memory location named FROG.
   b. Store a −123 into a 32-bit signed integer location named DATA3.
   c. Store a −23.8 into a single-precision floating-point memory location named DATA1.
   d. Reserve a double-precision memory location named DATA2.
21. Describe how the FST DATA instruction functions. Assume that DATA is defined as a 64-bit memory location.
22. What does the FILD DATA instruction accomplish?
23. Form an instruction that adds the contents of register 3 to the top of the stack.
24. Describe the operation of the FADD instruction.
25. Choose an instruction that subtracts the contents of register 2 from the top of the stack and store the result in register 2.
26. What is the function of the FBSTP DATA instruction?
27. What is the difference between a forward and a reverse division?
28. What is the difference between the FTST instruction and FXAM?
29. Explain what the F2XM1 instruction calculates.
30. What instruction pushes π onto the top of the stack?
31. What will FFREE ST(2) accomplish when executed?

32. What instruction stores the environment?
33. What does the FSAVE instruction save?
34. Develop a procedure that finds the area of a rectangle (A = L × W). Memory locations for this procedure are single-precision A, L, and W.
35. Write a procedure that finds the inductive reactance (XL = 2πFL). Memory locations for this procedure are single-precision XL, F, and L.
36. Develop a procedure that generates a table of square roots for the integers 2 through 10.
37. When is the FWAIT instruction used in a program?
38. Given the series/parallel circuit and equation illustrated in Figure 12–13, develop a program using single-precision values for R1, R2, R3, and R4 that finds the total resistance and stores the result at single-precision location RT.

FIGURE 12–13

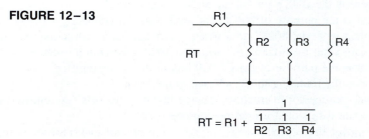

CHAPTER 13

The 80186/80188 and 80286 Microprocessor

INTRODUCTION

The Intel 80186/80188 and the 80286 are enhanced versions of the earlier 8086/8088 microprocessor. The 80186/80188 and 80286 are all 16-bit microprocessors that are upward compatible to the 8086/8088. Even the hardware of these microprocessors is similar to the earlier versions. This chapter presents an overview of each microprocessor and points out the differences or enhancements that are present in each version. The first part of the chapter describes the 80186/80188 microprocessor, and the last part shows the 80286 microprocessor.

CHAPTER OBJECTIVES

Upon completion of this chapter, you will be able to:

1. Describe the hardware and software enhancements of the 80186/80188 and the 80286 microprocessors as compared to the 8086/8088.
2. Interface the 80186/80188 and the 80286 to memory and I/O.
3. Develop software using the enhancements provided in these microprocessors.
4. Describe the operation of the memory management unit (MMU) within the 80286 microprocessor.

13–1   80186/80188 ARCHITECTURE

The 80186 and 80188, like the 8086 and 8088, are nearly identical. The only difference between the 80186 and 80188 is the width of their data buses. The 80186 (like the 8086) contains a 16-bit data bus, while the 80188 (like the 8088) contains an 8-bit data bus. The internal register structure of the 80186/80188 is virtually identical to the 8086/8088. About the only difference is that the 80186/80188 contain additional reserved interrupt vectors and some very powerful built-in I/O features. The 80186/80188 are often called embedded controllers because of their application, not as a microprocessor-based computer, but as a controller.

80186 Block Diagram

Figure 13–1 provides the block diagram of the 80186 microprocessor. Notice that this microprocessor has a great deal more internal circuitry than the 8086. The block diagram of the 80186 and 80188 are identical except for the prefetch queue, which is 4 bytes in the 80188 and 6 bytes in the 80186. Like the 8086, the 80186 contains a bus interface unit (BIU) and an execution unit (EU).

In addition to the BIU and EU, the 80186 contains a clock generator, a programmable interrupt controller, programmable timers, a programmable DMA controller, and a programmable chip selection unit. These enhancements greatly

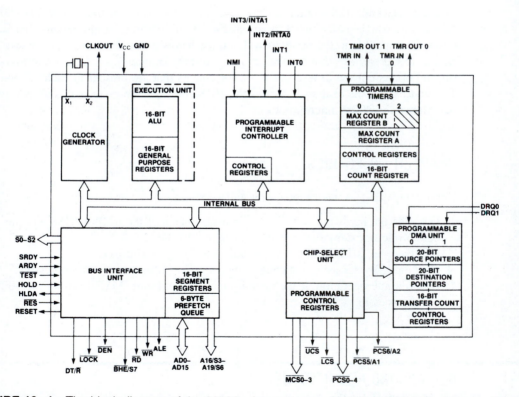

FIGURE 13–1   The block diagram of the 80186 microprocessor. Note that the block diagram of the 80188 is identical except $\overline{\text{BHE}}$/S7 is missing and AD15–AD8 are relabeled A15–A8. (Courtesy of Intel Corporation)

increase the utility of the 80186 and reduce the number of peripheral components required to implement a system. Many popular subsystems for the personal computer use the 80186 microprocessor as caching disk controllers, local area network (LAN) controllers, etc. The 80186 also finds application in the cellular telephone network as a switcher.

Software for the 80186/80188 is identical to the 80286 microprocessor without the memory management instructions. This means that immediate multiplication, immediate shift counts, string I/O, PUSHA, POPA, BOUND, and ENTER, and LEAVE all function on the 80186/80188 microprocessor.

80186/80188 Enhancements

In this segment of the text, we introduce the enhancements of the 80186/80188 microprocessor or embedded controller, but do not provide an exclusive coverage. More details on the operation of each enhancement are provided later in the chapter.

Clock Generator. The internal clock generator replaces the external 8284A clock generator used with the 8086/8088 microprocessor. This reduces the component count in a system.

The internal clock generator has three pin connections: X_1, X_2, and CLKOUT. The X_1 and X_2 pins are connected to a crystal that resonates at twice the operating frequency of the microprocessor. In the 8 MHz version of the 80186/80188, a 16 MHz crystal is attached to X_1 and X_2. The 80186/80188 is available as a 6 MHz, 8 MHz, 12 MHz, or 16 MHz version and also in CMOS as the 80C186 and 80C188.

The CLKOUT pin provides a system clock signal that is one half the crystal frequency with a 50 percent duty cycle. The CLKOUT pin drives other devices in a system and provides a timing source to additional microprocessors in the system.

In addition to these external pins, the clock generator provides the internal timing for synchronizing the READY input pin, whereas in the 8086/8088 system, READY synchronization is provided by the 8284A clock generator.

Programmable Interrupt Controller. The programmable interrupt controller (PIC) arbitrates all internal and external interrupts and controls up to two external 8259A PICs. When an external 8259 is attached, the 80186/80188 functions as the master and the 8259 functions as the slave.

If the PIC is operated without an 8259, it has five interrupt inputs: INT_0–INT_3 and NMI. This is an expansion from the two interrupt inputs available on the 8086/8088 microprocessor. In many systems, the five interrupt inputs are adequate.

Timers. The timer section contains three fully programmable 16-bit timers. Timers 0 and 1 generate waveforms for external use and are driven by either the master clock of the 80186/80188 or by an external clock. They are also used to count external events. The third timer, timer 2, is internal and clocked by the master clock. The output of timer 2 generates an interrupt after a specified number of clocks and also can provide a clock to the other timers. Timer 2 can also be used as a watchdog timer, because it can be programmed to interrupt the microprocessor after a certain length of time.

Programmable DMA Unit.   The programmable DMA unit contains two DMA channels. Each channel can transfer data between memory locations, between memory and I/O, or between I/O devices. This DMA controller is similar to the 8237 DMA controller discussed in Chapter 12. The main difference is that the 8237 has 4 channels.

Programmable Chip Selection Unit.   The chip selection is a built-in programmable memory and I/O decoder. It has six output lines to select memory and seven lines to select I/O.

The memory selection lines are divided into three groups that select memory for the major sections of the 80186/80188 memory map. The lower memory select signal enables memory for the interrupt vectors, the upper memory select signal enables memory for reset, and the middle memory select signals enable up to four middle memory devices. The boundary of the lower memory begins at location 00000H, and the boundary of the upper memory ends at location FFFFFH. The size of the memory areas are programmable, and wait states (0–3 waits) can be automatically inserted with the selection of an area of memory.

Each programmable I/O selection signal addresses a 128-byte block of I/O space. The programmable I/O area starts at a base I/O address programmed by the user and all seven 128 byte blocks are contiguous.

Pinout

Figure 13–2 illustrates the pinout of the 80186 microprocessor. Notice that the 80186 is packaged in either a 68-pin leadless chip carrier (LCC) as shown, or in a pin grid array (PGA). The LCC package is illustrated in Figure 13–3.

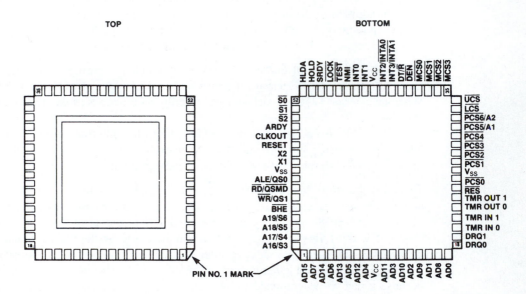

FIGURE 13–2   Pinout of the 80186 microprocessor. (Courtesy of Intel Corporation)

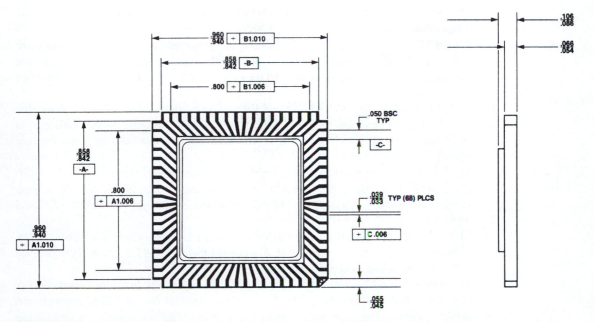

FIGURE 13-3 Leadless chip carrier (LCC) for the 80186/80188 microprocessor. (Courtesy of Intel Corporation)

Pin Definitions. The following list defines each 80186 pin and notes any differences between the 80186 and 80188 microprocessors.

1. Vcc is the system power supply connection for ±10%, +5.0 V.
2. Vss is the system ground connection.
3. X_1 and X_2 are generally connected to a fundamental mode parallel resonant crystal that operates an internal crystal oscillator. An external clock signal may be connected to the X_1 pin. The internal master clock operates at one half the external crystal or clock input signal.
4. CLKOUT provides a timing signal to system peripherals at one-half the clock frequency with a 50 percent duty cycle.
5. $\overline{\text{RES}}$ resets the 80186/80188. For a proper reset, the $\overline{\text{RES}}$ must be held low for at least 50 ms after power is applied. This pin is often connected to an RC circuit that generates a reset signal after power is applied. The reset location is identical to that of the 8086/8088 microprocessor—FFFF0H.
6. $\overline{\text{TEST}}$ is normally connected to the BUSY output of the 80187 numeric coprocessor. The $\overline{\text{TEST}}$ pin is interrogated with the WAIT instruction.
7. TMRIN 0, TMRIN 1 are used as external clocking sources to timers 0 and 1.
8. TMROUT 0 and TMROUT 1 provide the output signals from timers 0 and 1, which can be programmed to provide square waves or pulses.
9. DRQ_0 and DRQ_1 are active-high level triggered DMA request lines for DMA channels 0 and 1.

10. NMI is a nonmaskable interrupt input. It is positive edge-triggered and always active. When NMI is activated, it uses interrupt vector 2.

11. INT_0, INT_1, $INT_2/\overline{INTA_0}$, and $INT_3/\overline{INTA_1}$ are maskable interrupt inputs. They are active-high and are programmed as either level- or edge-triggered. These pins are configured as four interrupt inputs if no external 8259 is present or as 2 interrupt inputs if 8259s are present.

12. A19/S6, A18/S5, A17/S4, A16/S3 are multiplexed address status connections that provide the address (A19–A16) and status (S6–S3). Status bit S6 indicates a processor cycle when low or a DMA cycle when high. The remaining status bits are always a logic 0.

13. AD15–AD0 are multiplexed address/data bus connections. During T1, the 80186 places A15–A0 on these pins, and during T2, T3, and T4, the 80186 uses these pins as the data bus for signals D15–D0. Note that the 80188 has pins AD7–AD0 and A15–A8.

14. $\overline{BHE}$/S7 indicates (when a logic 0) that valid data are transferred through data bus connections D15–D8. On the 80188, this pin is labeled S7. S7 is always a logic 1 so no latch is required to demultiplex S7.

15. ALE/QS_0 is a multiplexed output pin that contains ALE one-half clock cycle earlier than in the 8086. QS_0 is the queue status signal required for the 80187 coprocessor.

16. $\overline{WR}$/QS_1 causes data to be written to memory or I/O. The $\overline{WR}$ signal is active during T3, TW, and T4, and QS_1 is active during the queue status mode and is provided for the 80187.

17. $\overline{RD}$/QSMD causes data to be read from memory or I/O. The $\overline{RD}$ signal is active during T2, TW, and T4, and QSMD is selected if this input/output pin is grounded by the 80187. The only time that QS_0 and QS_1 are available is during the queue status mode.

18. ARDY (asynchronous READY input) informs the 80186/80188 that the memory or I/O is ready for the 80186/80188 to read or write data. If this pin is tied to +5.0 V, the microprocessor functions normally; if it is grounded the microprocessor enters wait states.

19. SRDY (synchronous READY input) is synchronized with the system clock to provide a relaxed timing for the ready input. As with ARDY, SRDY is tied to +5.0 V for no wait states.

20. $\overline{LOCK}$ is an output controlled by the LOCK prefix. If an instruction is prefixed with LOCK, the $\overline{LOCK}$ pin becomes a logic 0 for the duration of the locked instruction.

21. $\overline{S2}$, $\overline{S1}$, and $\overline{S0}$ are status bits that provide the system with the type of bus transfer in effect. $\overline{S2}$ is used as the M/$\overline{IO}$ signal and $\overline{S1}$ is used as DT/$\overline{R}$. The 80188 uses the $\overline{S2}$ signal as M/$\overline{IO}$ and not IO/$\overline{M}$ as on the 8088.

22. HOLD and HLDA are pins used with external DMA devices. HOLD is an input that requests a DMA action and HLDA is a signal that acknowledges that the DMA action is in effect. During the DMA, the microprocessor floats its address, data, and control buses.

23. $\overline{UCS}$ (upper-memory-chip select) selects memory on the upper portion of the memory map. This output is programmable to enable memory sizes of 1K–256K bytes ending at location FFFFFH.

24. $\overline{\text{LCS}}$ (lower-memory-chip select) enables memory beginning at location 00000H. This pin is programmed to select memory sizes from 1K to 256K bytes.
25. $\overline{\text{MCS}_0}$–$\overline{\text{MCS}_3}$ (middle-memory-chip select) enables four middle memory devices. These pins are programmable to select an 8K–512K byte block of memory containing four devices.
26. $\overline{\text{PCS}_0}$–$\overline{\text{PCS}_4}$ are five different peripheral selection lines.
27. $\overline{\text{PCS}_5}$/A1 and $\overline{\text{PCS}_6}$/A2 are programmed as peripheral selection lines or as internally latched address bits A2 and A1.
28. DT/$\overline{\text{R}}$ controls the direction of data bus buffers if attached to the system.
29. $\overline{\text{DEN}}$ enables the external data bus buffers.

DC Operating Characteristics

It is necessary to know the DC operating characteristics before attempting to interface or operate the microprocessor. The 80186/80188 microprocessor requires between 450 and 550 mA of power supply current and the 80C186/80C188 require about 10 mA. Each output pin provides 2.0 mA or logic 0 current and 400 μA of logic 1 current except the CLKOUT pin that provides 4.0 mA of logic 0 current and the status bits that provide 2.5 mA.

80186/80188 Timing

The timing diagram for the 80186 is provided in Figure 13–4. Timing for the 80188 is identical except for the multiplexed address connections, which are AD7–AD0 instead of AD15–AD0, and the $\overline{\text{BHE}}$, which does not exist on the 80188.

The basic timing for the 80186/80188 is composed of four clocking periods just as in the 8086/8088. A bus cycle for the 6 MHz version requires 667 ns, while the 16 MHz version requires 250 ns.

There are very few differences between the timing for the 80186/80188 and the 8086/8088. The most noticeable difference is that ALE appears one-half clock cycle earlier in the 80186/80188.

Memory Access Time. One of the more important points in any microprocessor's timing diagram is the memory access time. Access time calculations for the 80186/80188 are identical to that of the 8086/8088. Recall that the access time is the time allotted to the memory and I/O to provide data to the microprocessor after the microprocessor sends the memory or I/O its address.

A close examination of the timing diagram reveals that the address appears on the address bus T_{CLAV} time after the start of T1. T_{CLAV} is listed as 63 ns for the 6 MHz version and 44 ns for the 8 MHz version (see Figure 13–5). Data are sampled from the data bus at the end of T3, but a setup time is required before the clock defined as T_{DVCL}. The time listed for T_{DVCL} is 20 ns for both versions of the microprocessor. Access time is therefore equal to three clocking periods minus both T_{CLAV} and T_{DVCL}. Access time for the 6 MHz microprocessor is 500 ns – 63 ns – 20 ns or 417 ns.

FIGURE 13–4   80186/
80188 timing. (a) Read cycle
timing and (b) write cycle timing. (Courtesy of Intel Corporation)

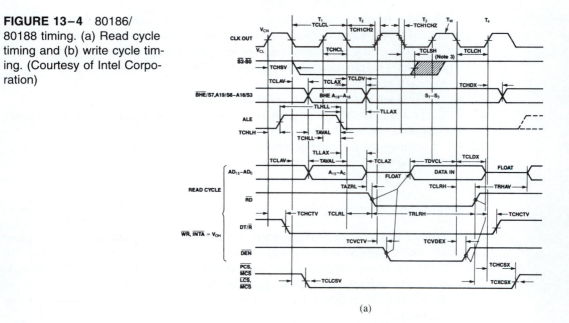

(a)

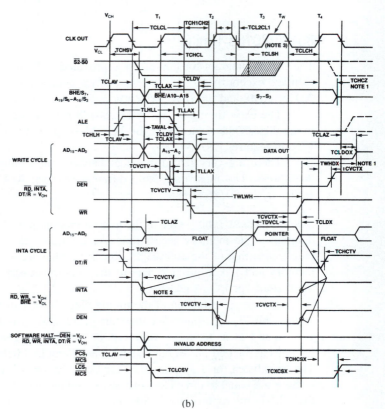

(b)

80186 Master Interface Timing Responses

Symbol	Parameters	80188 (8 MHz) Min.	80188 (8 MHz) Max.	80188-6 (6 MHz) Min.	80188-6 (6 MHz) Max.	Units	Test Conditions
T_{CLAV}	Address Valid Delay	5	44	5	63	ns	C_L = 20-200 pF all outputs
T_{CLAX}	Address Hold	10		10		ns	
T_{CLAZ}	Address Float Delay	T_{CLAX}	35	T_{CLAX}	44	ns	
T_{CHCZ}	Command Lines Float Delay		45		56	ns	
T_{CHCV}	Command Lines Valid Delay (after float)		55		76	ns	
T_{LHLL}	ALE Width	$T_{CLCL-35}$		$T_{CLCL-35}$		ns	
T_{CHLH}	ALE Active Delay		35		44	ns	
T_{CHLL}	ALE Inactive Delay		35		44	ns	
T_{LLAX}	Address Hold to ALE Inactive	$T_{CHCL-25}$		$T_{CHCL-30}$		ns	
T_{CLDV}	Data Valid Delay	10	44	10	55	ns	
T_{CLDOX}	Data Hold Time	10		10		ns	
T_{WHDX}	Data Hold after WR	$T_{CLCL-40}$		$T_{CLCL-50}$		ns	
T_{CVCTV}	Control Active Delay 1	5	70	5	87	ns	
T_{CHCTV}	Control Active Delay 2	10	55	10	76	ns	
T_{CVCTX}	Control Inactive Delay	5	55	5	76	ns	
T_{CVDEX}	DEN Inactive Delay (Non-Write Cycle)		70		87	ns	
T_{AZRL}	Address Float to RD Active	0		0		ns	
T_{CLRL}	RD Active Delay	10	70	10	87	ns	
T_{CLRH}	RD Inactive Delay	10	55	10	76	ns	
T_{RHAV}	RD Inactive to Address Active	$T_{CLCL-40}$		$T_{CLCL-50}$		ns	
T_{CLHAV}	HLDA Valid Delay	10	50	10	67	ns	
T_{RLRH}	RD Width	$2T_{CLCL-50}$		$2T_{CLCL-50}$		ns	
T_{WLWH}	WR Width	$2T_{CLCL-40}$		$2T_{CLCL-40}$		ns	
T_{AVAL}	Address Valid to ALE Low	$T_{CLCH-25}$		$T_{CLCH-45}$		ns	
T_{CHSV}	Status Active Delay	10	55	10	76	ns	
T_{CLSH}	Status Inactive Delay	10	55	10	76	ns	
T_{CLTMV}	Timer Output Delay		60		75	ns	100 pF max
T_{CLRO}	Reset Delay		60		75	ns	
T_{CHQSV}	Queue Status Delay		35		44	ns	

80186 Chip-Select Timing Responses

Symbol	Parameter	Min.	Max.	Min.	Max.	Units	Test Conditions
T_{CLCSV}	Chip-Select Active Delay		66		80	ns	
T_{CXCSX}	Chip-Selct Hold from Command Inactive	35		35		ns	
T_{CHCSX}	Chip-Select Inactive Delay	5	35	5	47	ns	

Symbol	Parameter	Min.	Max.	Units	Test Conditions
TDVCL	Data in Setup (A/D)	20		ns	
TCLDX	Data in Hold (A/D)	10		ns	
TARYHCH	Asynchronous Ready (AREADY) active setup time*	20		ns	
TARYLCL	AREADY inactive setup time	35		ns	
TCHARYX	AREADY hold time	15		ns	
TSRYCL	Synchronous Ready (SREADY) transition setup time	35		ns	
TCLSRY	SREADY transition hold time	15		ns	
THVCL	HOLD Setup*	25		ns	
TINVCH	INTR, NMI, TEST, TIMERIN, Setup*	25		ns	
TINVCL	DRQ0, DRQ1, Setup*	25		ns	

*To guarantee recognition at next clock.

FIGURE 13–5 80186 AC characteristics. (Courtesy of Intel Corporation)

563

13–2 PROGRAMMING THE 80186/80188 ENHANCEMENTS

This section provides detail on the programming and operation of the 80186/80188 enhancements. The next section details the use of the 80186/80188 in a system that uses many of the enhancements discussed here. The only new feature not discussed here is the clock generator that is completely described in the previous section on architecture.

Peripheral Control Block

All internal peripherals are controlled by a set of registers located in the peripheral control block (PCB). The PCB (see Figure 13–6) is a set of 256 registers located in the I/O or memory space.

Whenever the 80186/80188 is reset, the peripheral control block is automatically located at the top of the I/O map (I/O addresses FF00H–FFFFH). The PCB may be relocated at any time to any other area of memory or I/O. Relocation is accomplished by changing the contents of the relocation register (see Figure 13–7) located at offset addresses FEH and FFH.

FIGURE 13–6 Peripheral control block (PCB) of the 80186/80188. (Courtesy of Intel Corporation)

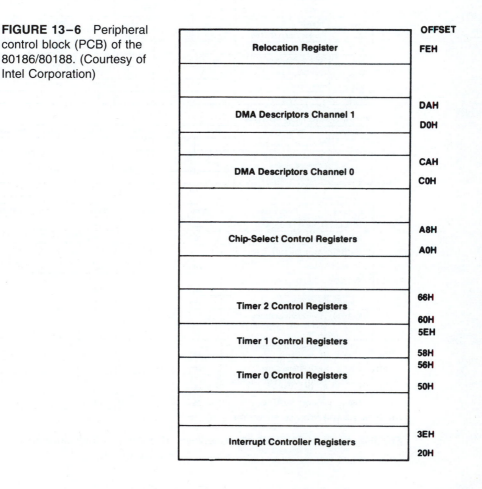

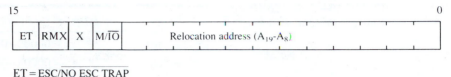

ET = ESC/NO ESC TRAP
RMX = iRM × 86 mode/master mode
M/IO = Memory/IO space
X = Unused

FIGURE 13-7 Peripheral control register.

The relocation register is set to a 20FFH when the 80186/80188 is reset. This locates the PCB at I/O addresses FF00H–FFFFH afterward. To relocate the PCB, the user need only send a word OUT to I/O address FFFEH with a new bit pattern. For example, to relocate the PCB to memory locations 20000H–200FFH, a 1200H is sent to I/O address FFFEH. Notice that M/IO is a logic 1 selecting memory and that a 200H selects memory address 20000H as the base address of the PCB. Note that all accesses to the PCB must be word accesses because it is organized as 16-bit-wide registers.

Interrupts in the 80186/80188

The interrupts in the 80186/80188 are identical to the 8086/8088 except there are additional interrupt vectors defined for some of the internal devices. A complete listing of the reserved interrupt vectors appears in Table 13–1. The first five are identical to the 8086/8088.

The array BOUNDs interrupt is requested if the boundary of an index register is outside the values set up in the memory.

The unused opcode interrupt occurs whenever the 80186/80188 executes any undefined opcode. This is important if a program begins to run awry.

The ESC opcode interrupt occurs if ESC opcodes D8H–DFH are executed. This occurs only if the ET (escape trap) bit of the relocation register is set. If an ESC interrupt occurs, the address stored on the stack by the interrupt points to the ESC instruction or to its segment override prefix if one is used.

The internal hardware interrupts must be enabled by the I flag bit and must be unmasked to function. The I flag bit is set (enabled) with STI and cleared (disabled) with CLI. The remaining internally decoded interrupts are discussed with the timers and DMA controller later in this section.

Interrupt Controller

The interrupt controller inside the 80186/80188 is a fairly sophisticated device. It has many interrupt inputs that arrive from the five external interrupt inputs, the DMA controller, and the three timers. Figure 13–8 provides a block diagram of the interrupt structure of the 80186/80188 interrupt controller.

The interrupt controller operates in two modes: master and iRMX86[1] or slave mode. The mode is selected by a bit in the peripheral control register by the RMX bit. If

---

[1]iRMX86 is a trademark of Intel Corporation.

TABLE 13-1   80186/80188
interrupt vectors

Name	Type	Address	Priority
Divide error	0	00000–00003	1
Single-step	1	00004–00007	1A
NMI	2	00008–0000B	1
Breakpoint	3	0000C–0000F	1
INTO	4	00010–00013	1
Array BOUNDs	5	00014–00017	1
Unused opcode	6	00018–0001B	1
ESC opcode	7	0001C–0001F	1
Timer 0	8	00020–00023	2A
Timer 1	18	00048–0004B	2B
Timer 2	19	0004C–0004F	2C
Reserved	9	00024–00027	3
DMA 0	10	00028–0002C	4
DMA 1	11	0002C–0002F	5
INT0	12	00030–00033	6
INT1	13	00034–00037	7
INT2	14	00038–0003B	8
INT3	15	0003C–0003F	9
80187	16	00040–00043	1

Note: Interrupt priority level 1 is the highest and 9 is the lowest. Some interrupts have the same priority.

FIGURE 13-8   80186/
80188 programmable inter-
rupt controller. (Courtesy of
Intel Corporation)

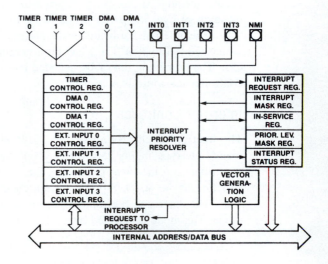

RMX is a logic 1, the interrupt controller connects to external 8259A programmable interrupt controllers, and if RMX is a logic 0, the internal interrupt controller is selected.

This portion of the text does not detail the programming of the interrupt controller. Instead, it is limited to a discussion of the internal structure of the interrupt controller. The programming and application of the interrupt controller are discussed in the sections that describe the timer and DMA controller.

Interrupt Controller Registers. Figure 13–9 illustrates the interrupt controller registers, which are located in the peripheral control block beginning at offset address 20H. Notice that two completely different sets of registers exist—one for the internal master mode and the other for the iRMX86 external slave (8259A) mode.

iRMX86 Slave Mode. When the interrupt controller operates in the slave mode, it uses up to two external 8259A programmable interrupt controllers for interrupt input expansion. Figure 13–10 shows how the external interrupt controllers connect to the 80186/80188 interrupt input pins for slave operation. Here the INT0 and INT1 inputs are used as external connections to the interrupt request outputs of the 8259s and $\overline{INTA_0}$ ($INT_2/\overline{TA_0}$) and $\overline{INTA_1}$ ($INT_3/\overline{TA_1}$) are used as interrupt acknowledge signals to the external controllers.

Interrupt Control Registers. There are interrupt control registers in both modes of operation that each control a single interrupt source. The master mode contains seven interrupt control registers and the iRMX86 slave mode contains five. Figure 13–11

Master mode registers	Offset	iRMX86 Slave mode registers
INT3 Control register	3EH	
INT2 Control register	3CH	iRMX86 Slave mode registers
INT1 Control register	3AH	Level 5 Control register (Timer 2)
INT0 Control register	38H	Level 4 Control register (Timer 1)
DMA 1 Control register	36H	Level 3 Control register (DMA 1)
DMA 0 Control register	34H	Level 2 Control register (DMA 0)
Timer Control register	32H	Level 0 Control register (Timer 0)
Interrupt status register	30H	Interrupt status register
Interrupt request register	2EH	Interrupt request register
In-service register	2CH	In-service register
Priority mask register	2AH	Priority mask register
Mask register	28H	Mask register
Poll status register	26H	
Poll register	24H	
EOI register	22H	EOI register
	20H	Interrupt vector register

FIGURE 13–9 80186/80188 programmable interrupt controller registers.

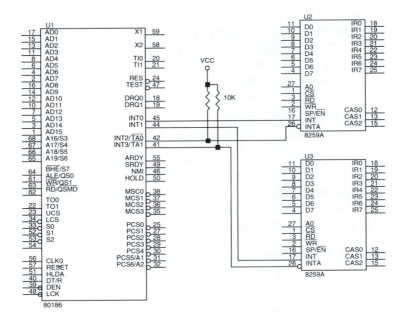

FIGURE 13–10   Two 8259A interrupt controllers interfaced to the 80186 microprocessor. Note that only the interrupt control connections are illustrated.

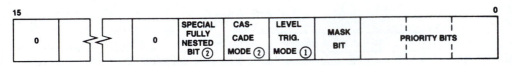

1. This bit present only in INT0-INT3 control registers
2. These bits present only in INT0-INT1 control register

FIGURE 13–11   Interrupt control register. (Courtesy of Intel Corporation)

depicts the binary bit pattern of each of these interrupt control registers. The mask bit enables (0) or disables (1) the interrupt input represented by the control word, and the priority bits set the priority level of the interrupt source. The highest priority level is 000 and the lowest is 111. The three remaining bits are used only in the master mode to select various modes of operation that are similar to the modes found in the 8259A.

Interrupt Request Register.   The interrupt request register contains an image of the interrupt sources in each mode of operation. Whenever an interrupt is requested, the corresponding interrupt request bit becomes a logic 1 even if the interrupt is masked. The request is cleared whenever the 80186/80188 acknowledges the interrupt. Figure 13–12 illustrates the binary bit pattern of the interrupt request register for both the master and iRMX86 slave modes.

Mask and Priority Mask Registers.   The interrupt mask register has the same format as the interrupt register illustrated in Figure 13–12. If a source is masked (disabled), the

15	MASTER MODE							0
X X X	I3	I2	I1	I0	D1	D0	X	TMR

15	iRMX™ 86 MODE						0
X X X	TMR 2	TMR 1	D0	D1	X	TMR 0

FIGURE 13–12   Interrupt request register shown for both modes of operation. (Courtesy of Intel Corporation)

corresponding bit of the interrupt mask register contains a logic 1, and if enabled it contains a logic 0. The interrupt mask register is read to determine which interrupt sources are masked and which are enabled. A source is masked by setting the source's mask bit in its interrupt control register.

The priority mask register, illustrated in Figure 13–13, shows the priority of the interrupt currently being serviced by the 80186/80188. The level of the interrupt is indicated by priority bits P2–P0. Internally, these bits prevent an interrupt by a lower priority source. These bits are automatically set to the next lower level at the end of an interrupt as issued by the 80186/80188. If no other interrupts are pending, these bits are set (111) to enable all priority levels.

In-Service Register.   The in-service register has the same binary bit pattern as the request register of Figure 13–12. The bit that corresponds to the interrupt source is set if the 80186/80188 is currently acknowledging the interrupt. The bit is reset at the end of an interrupt.

Poll and Poll Status Registers.   Both the interrupt poll and interrupt poll status registers share the same binary bit patterns as those illustrated in Figure 13–14. These registers have a bit (INT REQ) that indicates an interrupt is pending. This bit is set if an interrupt is received with sufficient priority and cleared when an interrupt is acknowledged. The S bits indicate the interrupt vector type number of the highest priority pending interrupt.

These two registers may appear to be identical because they contain the same information; however, they differ in function. When the interrupt poll register is read, the interrupt is acknowledged. When the interrupt poll status register is read, no acknowledge is sent. These registers are used only in the master mode and not the iRMX86 slave mode.

End-Of-Interrupt Register.   The end-of-interrupt (EOI) register causes the termination of an interrupt when written by a program. Figure 13–15 shows the contents of the EOI register for both the master and iRMX86 slave mode.

In the master mode, writing to the EOI register ends either a specific interrupt level or whatever level is currently active (nonspecific). In the nonspecific mode, the SPEC/NSPEC bit must be set before the EOI register is written to end a nonspecific

FIGURE 13–13   Interrupt priority mask register. (Courtesy of Intel Corporation)

15							0
X	X	X	X	X	P2	P1	P0

FIGURE 13–14   Interrupt poll and poll status registers (Courtesy of Intel Corporation)

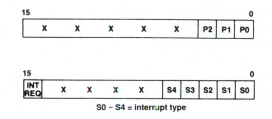

15									0
INT REQ	X	X	X	X	S4	S3	S2	S1	S0

S0 – S4 = interrupt type

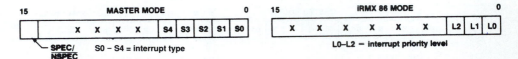

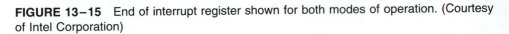

FIGURE 13-15 End of interrupt register shown for both modes of operation. (Courtesy of Intel Corporation)

interrupt. The nonspecific EOI clears the highest level interrupt bit in the in-service register. The specific EOI clears the selected bit in the in-service register.

In the iRMX86 slave mode, the level of the interrupt to be terminated is written to the EOI register. The slave mode does not allow a nonspecific EOI.

Interrupt Status Register. The format of the interrupt status register is depicted in Figure 13–16. In the master mode, T2–T0 indicate which timer (timer 0, timer 1, or timer 2) is causing an interrupt. This is necessary because all three timers have the same interrupt priority level. These bits are set when the timer requests an interrupt and cleared when the interrupt is acknowledged. The DHLT (DMA halt) bit is only used in the master mode and when set, it stops a DMA action.

Interrupt Vector Register. The interrupt vector register is present only in the iRMX86 slave mode and is used to specify the most significant five bits of the interrupt vector type number. Figure 13–17 illustrates the format of this register. The lower three bits of the vector number are determined by the priority level of the interrupt.

Timers

The 80186/80188 contains three fully programmable 16-bit timers. Each is totally independent of the others. Two of the timers (timer 0 and timer 1) have input and output pins that allow them to count external events or generate waveforms. The third timer (timer 2) connects to the 80186/80188 clock and is used as a DMA request source, a prescaler for other timers, or as a watchdog timer.

Figure 13–18 shows the internal structure of the timer unit. Notice that the timer unit contains one counting element that is responsible for updating all three counters. Each timer is actually a register that is rewritten from the counting element (a circuit that reads a value from a timer register and increments it before returning it). The counter element is also responsible for generating the outputs through pins T_0OUT and T_1OUT,

FIGURE 13-16 Interrupt status register. (Courtesy of Intel Corporation)

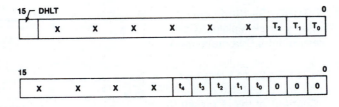

FIGURE 13-17 Interrupt vector register. (Courtesy of Intel Corporation)

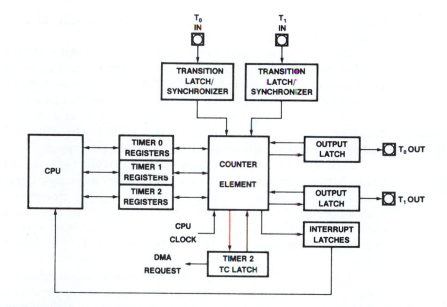

FIGURE 13–18 Internal structure of the 80186/80188 timers. (Courtesy of Intel Corporation)

reading the T_0IN and T_1IN pins, and causing a DMA request from the terminal count (TC) of timer 2 if timer 2 is programmed to request a DMA action.

Timer Register Operation. The timers are controlled by a block of registers in the peripheral control block (see Figure 13–19). Each timer has a count register, maximum-count register or registers, and a control register. These registers may all be read or

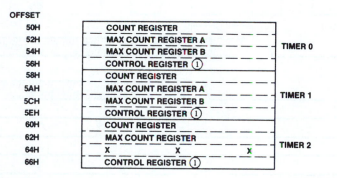

FIGURE 13–19 The timer registers. (Courtesy of Intel Corporation)

written at any time because the 80186/80188 ensures that the contents never change during a read or write.

The timer count register contains a 16-bit number that is incremented whenever an input to the timer occurs. Timers 0 and 1 are incremented at the positive edge on an external input pin, every fourth 80186/80188 clock, or by the output of timer 2. Timer 2 is clocked on every fourth 80186/80188 clock pulse and has no other timing source. This means that in the 8 MHz version of the 80186/80188, timer 2 operates at 2 MHz and the maximum counting frequency of timers 0 and 1 is 2 MHz. Figure 13–20 depicts these four clocking periods, which are not related to the bus timing.

Each timer has at least one maximum-count register (register A for timers 0 and 1) that is controlled with the counts of the count register to generate an output. Whenever the count register is equal to the maximum-count register, it is cleared to 0. With a maximum count of 0000H, the counter counts 65,536 times. For any other value, the timer counts the true value of the count. For example, if the maximum count is 0002H, then the counter will count from 0 to 1 and then be cleared to 0—a modulus 2 counter having 2 states.

Timers 0 and 1 each have a second maximum-count register (register B) that is selected by the control register for the timer. Either maximum-count register A or both maximum counts A and B are used with these timers as programmed by the ALT bit in the control register for the timer. When both maximum-count registers are used, the timer counts up to the value in maximum-count register A, clears to 0, and then counts up to the count in maximum-count register B. This process is then repeated. Using both maximum-count registers allows the timer to count up to 131,072.

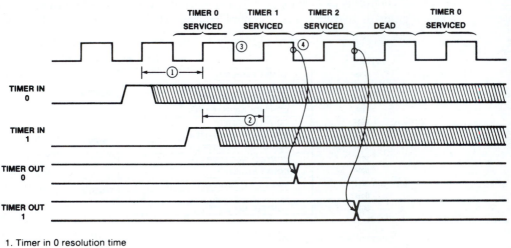

1. Timer in 0 resolution time
2. Timer in 1 resolution time
3. Modified count value written into 80186 timer 0 count register
4. Modified count value written into 80186 time

FIGURE 13–20   Timing for the 80186/80188 timers. (Courtesy of Intel Corporation)

The control register (refer again to Figure 13–19) of each timer is 10 bits wide and specifies the operation of the timer. A definition of each control bit follows:

1. EN (enable) allows the timer to start counting. If EN is cleared, the timer will not count. If it is set, the timer counts.
2. $\overline{INH}$ (inhibit) allows a write to the timer control register to affect the enable bit (EN). If $\overline{INH}$ is set, then the EN bit can be set or cleared to control the counting. If $\overline{INH}$ is cleared, EN is not affected by a write to the timer control register. This allows other features of the timer to be modified without enabling or disabling the timer.
3. INT (interrupt) allows an interrupt to be generated by the timer. If INT is set, an interrupt will occur each time that the maximum count is reached in either maximum-count register. If this bit is cleared, no interrupt is generated. When the interrupt request is generated, it remains in force even if the EN bit is cleared after the interrupt request.
4. RIU (register in use) indicates which maximum-count register is currently in use by the timer. If RIU is a logic 0, then maximum-count register A is in use. This bit is a read-only bit, and writes do not affect it.
5. MC (maximum count) indicates that the timer has reached its maximum count. This bit becomes a logic 1 when the timer reaches its maximum count and remains a logic 1 until the MC bit is cleared by writing a logic 0. This allows the maximum count to be detected by software.
6. RTG (retrigger) is active only for external clocking (EXT = 0). The RTG bit is used only with timers 0 and 1 to select the operation of the timer input pins (T_0IN and T_1IN). If RTG is a logic 0, the external input will cause the timer to count if it is a logic 1 and to hold its count (stop counting) if it is a logic 0. If RTG is a logic 1, the external input pin clears the timer count to 0000H each time a positive edge occurs.
7. P (prescaler) selects the clocking source for timers 0 and 1. If EXT = 0 and P = 0, the source is one fourth the system clock frequency. If P = 1, the source is timer 2.
8. EXT (external) selects internal timing (EXT = 0) or external timing (EXT = 1). If EXT = 1, the timing source is applied to the T_0IN or T_1IN pins. In this mode the timer increments after each positive edge on the timer input pin. If EXT = 0, the clocking source is from one of the internal sources.
9. ALT (alternate) selects single maximum-count mode (maximum-count register A) if a logic 0 or alternate maximum-count mode (maximum-count registers A and B) if a logic 1.
10. CONT (continuous) selects continuous operation if a logic 1. In continuous operation, the counter automatically continues counting after it reaches its maximum count. If CONT is a logic 0, the timer will automatically stop counting and clear the EN bit. Note that whenever the 80186/80188 is reset, the timers are automatically disabled.

Timer Output Pin.   Timers 0 and 1 have an output pin used to generate either square waves or pulses. To produce pulses, the timer is operated in single maximum-count mode

(ALT = 0). In this mode, the output pin goes low for one clock period when the counter reaches its maximum count. By controlling the CONT bit in the control register, either a single pulse or continuous pulses can be generated.

To produce square waves or varying duty cycles, the alternate mode (ALT = 1) is selected. In this mode, the output pin is a logic 1 while maximum-count register A controls the timer and a logic 0 while maximum-count register B controls the timer. As with the single maximum-count mode, the timer can generate either a single square wave or continuous square waves. Refer to Table 13–2 for the function of the ALT and CONT control bits.

Almost any duty cycle can be generated in the alternate mode. For example, suppose that a 10 percent duty cycle is required at a timer output pin. Maximum-count register A is loaded with a 10 and maximum-count register B with a 90 to produce an output that is a logic 1 for 10 clocks and a logic 0 for 90 clocks. This also divides the frequency of the timing source by a factor of 100.

Real-Time Clock Example.   Many systems require the time of day. This is often called a *real-time clock*. A timer within the 80186/80188 can provide the timing source for software that maintains the time of day.

The hardware required for this application is illustrated in Figure 13–21. Notice that the only connection required to implement a real-time clock is a single resistor connected from the T_1IN pin to +5.0 V to enable timer 1. In the example, timers 1 and 2 are used to generate a 1-second interrupt that provides the software with a timing source.

TABLE 13–2 Function of ALT and CONT in the timer control register

ALT	CONT	Mode
0	0	single pulse
0	1	continuous pulses
1	0	single square wave
1	1	continuous square waves

FIGURE 13–21 Timer hardward for a real-time clock.

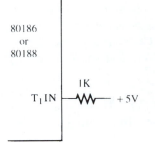

EXAMPLE 13–1

```
            ;Software to control the timers for a real-time clock.
            ;
            ;It is assumed that the peripheral control block (PCB)
            ;is as it is set after a reset at I/O ports FF00H -- FFFFH.
            ;
= FF62          TIM2_MCOUNT     EQU    0FF62H          ;max count Timer 2
= FF66          TIM2_CONTR      EQU    0FF66H          ;control Timer 2
= FF5A          TIM1_MCOUNT     EQU    0FF5AH          ;max count Timer 1
= FF5E          TIM1_CONTR      EQU    0FF5EH          ;control Timer 1

0000            SET_UP          PROC   NEAR

0000    B8 07D0                 MOV    AX,2000         ;load count Timer 2
0003    BA FF62                 MOV    DX,TIM2_MCOUNT
0006    EF                      OUT    DX,AX

0007    B8 C001                 MOV    AX,0C001H       ;enable timer 2
000A    BA FF66                 MOV    DX,TIM2_CONTR
000D    EF                      OUT    DX,AX

000E    B8 0064                 MOV    AX,100          ;load count Timer 1
0011    BA FF5A                 MOV    DX,TIM1_MCOUNT
0014    EF                      OUT    DX,AX

0015    B8 E009                 MOV    AX,0E009H       ;enable Timer 1
0018    BA FF5E                 MOV    DX,TIM1_CONTR
001B    EF                      OUT    DX,AX
001C    C3                      RET

001D            SET_UP          ENDP


001D            INTERRUPT       PROC   FAR

001D    56                      PUSH   SI
001E    50                      PUSH   AX

001F    BE 0000 R               MOV    SI,OFFSET SECONDS
0022    B4 60                   MOV    AH,60H

0024    E8 0038 R               CALL   UP_COUNT        ;increment seconds
0027    75 0C                   JNZ    ENDI
0029    46                      INC    SI

002A    E8 0038 R               CALL   UP_COUNT        ;increment minutes
002D    75 06                   JNZ    ENDI
002F    46                      INC    SI
0030    B4 24                   MOV    AH,24H
0032    E8 0038 R               CALL   UP_COUNT        ;increment hours

0035            ENDI:

0035    58                      POP    AX
0036    5E                      POP    SI
0037    CF                      IRET

0038            INTERRUPT ENDP

0038            UP_COUNT PROC   NEAR
```

```
0038 8A 04                    MOV    AL,[SI]
003A 04 01                    ADD    AL,1
003C 27                       DAA
003D 88 04                    MOV    [SI],AL
003F 2A C4                    SUB    AL,AH
0041 75 02                    JNZ    UP_END
0043 88 04                    MOV    [SI],AL

0045                          UP_END:

0045 C3                       RET

0046          UP_COUNT        ENDP
```

The software required to implement a real-time clock is listed in Example 13–1. Here there are two procedures: one program timer 1 and 2 and the other, an interrupt service procedure, to keep time. This is the third procedure that increments a BCD modulus counter. None of the software required to install the interrupt vector and time of day is illustrated here.

Timer 3 is programmed to divide by a factor of 20,000. This causes the clock (2 MHz on the 8 MHz version of the 80186/80188) to be divided down to one pulse every 10 ms. The clock for timer 1 is derived from the timer 2 output. Timer 1 is programmed to divide by 100 and generates a pulse once per second. The control register of timer 1 is programmed so it generates an interrupt once per second.

The interrupt service procedure is called once per second to keep time. This procedure increments the contents of memory location SECONDS. Once every 60 seconds, the contents of next memory location (SECONDS + 1) is incremented. Finally, once per hour, the contents of memory location SECONDS + 2 is incremented. The time is stored in these three consecutive memory locations in BCD so the system software can easily access the time.

DMA Controller

The DMA controller within the 80186/80188 has two fully independent DMA channels. Each has its own set of 20-bit address registers so any memory or I/O location is accessible for a DMA transfer. In addition, each channel is programmable for auto-increment or auto-decrement to either source or destination registers.

Figure 13–22 illustrates the internal register structure of the DMA controller. These registers are located in the peripheral control block at offset addresses C0H–DFH.

Notice that both DMA channel register sets are identical. Each channel contains a control word, a source and destination pointer, and a transfer count. The transfer count is 16 bits and allows unattended DMA transfers of bytes (80188/80186) and words (80186 only). Each time that a byte or word is transferred, the count is decremented by 1 until it reaches 0000H—the terminal count.

The source and destination pointers are each 20 bits wide so DMA transfers can occur to any memory location or I/O address without concern for segment and offset addresses. If the source or destination address is an I/O port, bits A19–A16 must be 0000 or a malfunction may occur.

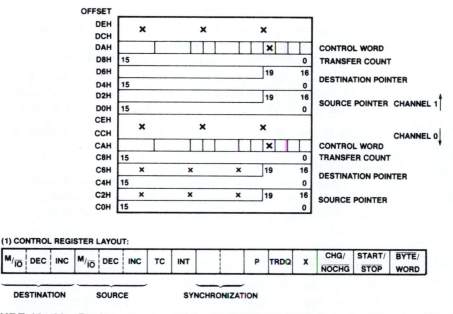

(1) CONTROL REGISTER LAYOUT:

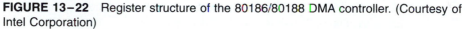

M/$\overline{\text{IO}}$	DEC	INC	M/$\overline{\text{IO}}$	DEC	INC	TC	INT			P	TRDQ	X	CHG/ NOCHG	START/ STOP	BYTE/ WORD

DESTINATION   SOURCE   SYNCHRONIZATION

FIGURE 13–22   Register structure of the 80186/80188 DMA controller. (Courtesy of Intel Corporation)

Channel Control Register.   Each DMA channel contains its own channel control register (refer to Figure 13–22), which defines its operation. The leftmost 6 bits specify the operation of the source and destination registers. The M/$\overline{\text{IO}}$ bit indicates a memory or I/O location, DEC causes the pointer to be decremented, and INC causes the pointer to be incremented. If both the INC and DEC bits are 1, then the pointer is unchanged after each DMA transfer. Notice that memory-to-memory transfers are possible with this DMA controller.

The TC (terminal count) bit causes the DMA channel to stop transfers when the channel count register is decremented to 0000H. If this bit is a logic 0, the DMA controller continues to transfer data even after the terminal count is reached.

The INT bit enables interrupts to the interrupt controller. If set, this bit causes an interrupt to be issued when the terminal count of the channel is reached.

The SYN bit selects the type of synchronization for the channel: 00 = no synchronization, 01 = source synchronization, and 10 = destination synchronization. When either unsynchronized or source synchronization is selected, data are transferred at the rate of 2 M bytes per second. These two types of synchronization allow transfers to occur without interruption. If destination synchronization is selected, the transfer rate is slower (1.3 M bytes per second), and the controller relinquishes control to the 80186/80188 after each DMA transfer.

The P bit selects the channel priority. If P = 1, the channel has the highest priority. If both channels have the same priority, the controller alternates transfers between channels.

The TRDQ bit enables DMA transfers from timer 2. If this bit is a logic 1, the DMA request originates from timer 2. This can prevent the DMA transfers from using all of the microprocessor's time for the transfer.

The CHG/$\overline{\text{NOCHG}}$ bit determines whether START/$\overline{\text{STOP}}$ changes for a write to the control register. The START/$\overline{\text{STOP}}$ bit starts or stops the DMA transfer. To start a DMA transfer, both CHG/$\overline{\text{NOCHG}}$ and START/$\overline{\text{STOP}}$ are placed at a logic 1 level.

The $\overline{\text{BYTE}}$/WORD selects whether the transfer is byte- or word-sized.

Sample Memory-to-Memory Transfer.   The built-in DMA controller is capable of performing memory-to-memory transfers. The procedure used to program the controller and start the transfer is listed in Example 13–2.

This procedure transfers data from the data segment location addressed by SI into the extra segment location addressed by DI. The number of bytes transferred is held in register CX. This operation is identical to the REP MOVSB instruction, but execution occurs at a much higher speed.

Chip Selection Unit

The chip selection unit simplifies the interface of memory and I/O to the 80186/80188. This unit contains programmable chip selection logic. In small- and medium-sized systems no external decoder is required to select memory and I/O. Large systems, however, may still require external decoders.

Memory Chip Selects.   Six pins are used to select different external memory components in a small- or medium-sized 80186/80188-based system. The $\overline{\text{UCS}}$ (upper chip select) pin enables the memory device located in the upper portion of the memory map most often populated with ROM. This programmable pin allows the size of the ROM to be specified and also the number of wait states required. Note that the ending address of the ROM is FFFFFH.

EXAMPLE 13–2

```
        ;Memory-to-memory DMA transfer procedure
        ;
        ;Source address is DS:SI
        ;Destination address is ES:DI
        ;Count is CX
        ;
        ;Peripheral control block (PCB) is at FF00H -- FFFFH
        ;
0000              MOVE_BYTES    PROC FAR

0000 8C D8              MOV     AX,DS       ;form source
0002 C1 E0 04           SHL     AX,4
0005 03 C6              ADD     AX,SI
0007 BA FFC0            MOV     DX,0FFC0H
000A EF                 OUT     DX,AX
000B 9C                 PUSHF
000C 8C D8              MOV     AX,DS
000E C1 E8 0C           SHR     AX,12
0011 9D                 POPF
0012 05 0000            ADD     AX,0
```

```
0015  83 C2 02                          ADD       DX,2
0018  EF                                OUT       DX,AX

0019  8C C0                             MOV       AX,ES      ;form destination
001B  C1 E0 04                          SHL       AX,4
001E  83 C2 02                          ADD       DX,2
0021  03 C7                             ADD       AX,DI
0023  EF                                OUT       DX,AX
0024  9C                                PUSHF
0025  8C C0                             MOV       AX,ES
0027  C1 E8 0C                          SHR       AX,12
002A  9D                                POPF
002B  05 0000                           ADD       AX,0
002E  83 C2 02                          ADD       DX,2
0031  EF                                OUT       DX,AX

0032  8B C1                             MOV       AX,CX      ;program count
0034  83 C2 02                          ADD       DX,2
0037  EF                                OUT       DX,AX

0038  B8 B606                           MOV       AX,0B606H ;program control
003B  83 C2 02                          ADD       DX,2
003E  EF                                OUT       DX,AX      ;start transfer

003F  CB                                RET

0040              MOV_BYTES             ENDP
```

The $\overline{\text{LCS}}$ (lower chip select) pin selects the memory device (usually a RAM) that begins at memory location 00000H. As with the $\overline{\text{UCS}}$ pin, the memory size and number of wait states are programmable.

The remaining four pins select middle memory devices. These four pins ($\overline{\text{MCS3}}$–$\overline{\text{MCS0}}$) are programmed for both the starting (base) address and memory size. Note that all devices must be of the same size.

Peripheral Chip Selects. The 80186/80188 addresses up to seven external peripheral devices with pins $\overline{\text{PCS6}}$–$\overline{\text{PCS0}}$. The base I/O address is programmed at any 1K-byte interval with port address block sizes of 128 bytes.

Programming the Chip Selection Unit. The number of wait states in each section of the memory and the I/O are programmable. The 80186/80188 has a built-in wait state generator that can introduce between 0 and 3 wait states. Table 13–3 lists the logic levels required on bits R2–R0 in each programmable register to select various numbers of wait states. These three lines also select if an external READY signal is required to generate wait states. If READY is selected, the external READY signal is in parallel with the internal wait state generator. For example, if READY is a logic 0 for three clocking periods, but the internal wait state generator is programmed to insert 2 wait states, three are inserted.

Suppose that a 64K byte EPROM is located at the top of the memory system and requires 2 wait states for proper operation. To select this device for this section of memory, the $\overline{\text{UCS}}$ pin is programmed for a memory range of F0000H–FFFFFH with 2 wait states. Figure 13–23 lists the control registers for all memory and I/O selection in the peripheral control block at offset addresses A0–A9H. Notice that the rightmost 3 bits of these control registers are from Table 13–3. The control register for the upper memory

TABLE 13–3 Wait state control bits R2, R1, and R0

R2	R1	R0	Number of Waits	READY Required
0	0	0	0	Yes
0	0	1	1	Yes
0	1	0	2	Yes
0	1	1	3	Yes
1	0	0	0	No
1	0	1	1	No
1	1	0	2	No
1	1	1	3	No

area is located at PCB offset address A0H. This 16-bit register is programmed with the starting address of the memory area (F0000H in this case) and the number of wait states. Refer to Table 13–4 for example codings for various memory sizes illustrated with no wait states. Because our example requires 2 wait states, the basic address is the same as in the table for a 64K device, except the rightmost three bits are 110 instead of 000. The data sent to the upper memory control register are F03EH.

Suppose that a 32K byte SRAM that requires no waits and no READY input is located at the bottom of the memory system. To program the $\overline{LCS}$ pin to select this device, register A2 is loaded in exactly the same manner as register A0H. In this example, a 07FCH is sent to register A2H. Table 13–5 lists the programming values for the lower chip selection output.

The central part of the memory is programmed via two registers: A6H and A8H. Register A6H programs the beginning or base address of the middle memory select lines ($\overline{MCS3}$–$\overline{MCS0}$) and number of waits. Register A8H defines the size of the block of memory and the individual memory device size (refer to Table 13–6). In addition to

FIGURE 13–23 Register structure for the 80186/80188 chip select unit. (Courtesy of Intel Corporation)

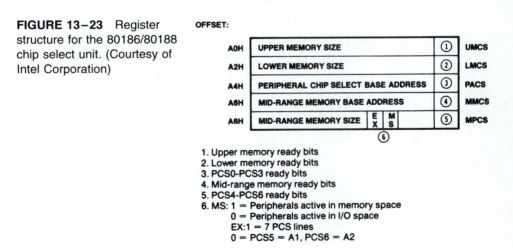

Not all bits of every field are used

TABLE 13-4 Upper memory programming for register A0H

Start Address	Block Size	Value for No Waits, No READY
FFC00H	1K	FFF8H
FF800H	2K	FFB8H
FF000H	4K	FF38H
FE000H	8K	FE38H
FC000H	16K	FC38H
F8000H	32K	F838H
F0000H	64K	F038H
E0000H	128K	E038H
C0000H	256K	C038H

TABLE 13-5 Lower memory programming for register A2H

Ending Address	Block Size	Value for No Waits, No READY
003FFH	1K	0038H
007FFH	2K	0078H
00FFFH	4K	00F8H
01FFFH	8K	01F8H
03FFFH	16K	03F8H
07FFFH	32K	07F8H
0FFFFH	64K	0FF8H
1FFFFH	128K	1FF8H
3FFFFH	256K	3FF8H

TABLE 13-6 Middle memory programming for register A8H

Block Size	Chip Size	Value for No Waits, No READY, and EX = MS = 0
8K	2K	8138H
16K	4K	8238H
32K	8K	8438H
64K	16K	8838H
128K	32K	9038H
256K	64K	A038H
512K	128K	C038H

block size, the number of peripheral wait states are programmed as with other areas of memory. The EX (bit 7) and MS (bit 6) specify the peripheral selection lines and will be discussed shortly.

For example, suppose that four 32K byte SRAMs are added to the middle memory area beginning at location 80000H and ending at location 9FFFFH with no wait states. To program the middle memory selection lines for this area of memory, we place the leftmost seven address bits in register A6H with bits 8 through 3 containing logic ones and the rightmost three bits containing the ready control bits. For this example register A6H is loaded with 81FCH. Register A8H is programmed with a 903CH assuming that EX = MS = 0 and no wait states and no READY are required for the peripherals.

Register A4H programs the peripheral chip selection pins ($\overline{PCS0}$–$\overline{PCS6}$) along with the EX and MS bits of register A8H. Register A4H holds the beginning or base address of the peripheral selection lines. The peripherals may be placed in memory or I/O map. If they are placed in the I/O map, A19–A16 of the port number must be 0000. Once the starting address is programmed on any 1K byte boundary, the $\overline{PCS}$ pins are spaced at 128-byte intervals.

For example, if register A4H is programmed with a 00FCH, with no waits and no READY synchronization, the memory address begins at 00C00H or the I/O port begins at 0C00H. In this case, the I/O ports are: $\overline{PCS0}$ = 0C00H, $\overline{PCS1}$ = 0C80H, $\overline{PCS2}$ = 0D00H, $\overline{PCS3}$ = 0D80H, $\overline{PCS4}$ = 0E00H, $\overline{PCS5}$ = 0E80H, and $\overline{PCS6}$ = 0F00H.

The MS bit of register A8H selects memory mapping or I/O mapping for the peripheral select pins. If MS is a logic 1, then the $\overline{PCS}$ lines are decoded in the memory map. If it is a logic 0, then the $\overline{PCS}$ lines are in the I/O map.

The EX bit selects the function of the $\overline{PCS5}$ and $\overline{PCS6}$ pins. If EX = 1, these $\overline{PCS}$ pins select I/O devices. If EX = 0, these pins provide the system with latched address lines A1 and A2. The A1 and A2 pins are used by some I/O devices to select internal registers and are provided for this purpose.

13–3   80188 EXAMPLE INTERFACE

Because the 80186/80188 is designed as an embedded controller, this section of the text provides an example of such an application. The example illustrates simple memory and I/O attached to the 80188 microprocessor. It also lists the software required to program the 80188 and its internal registers after a system reset. The software to control the system itself is not provided.

The 80188 can be interfaced with a small system designed to be used as a microprocessor trainer. The trainer itself uses a 2764 EPROM for program storage, three 62256 SRAMs for data storage, an 8279 programmable keyboard/display interface, and an 8251A USART. Figure 13–24 illustrates a small microprocessor trainer based on the 80188 microprocessor.

Memory is selected by the $\overline{\text{UCS}}$ pin for the 2764 EPROM, the $\overline{\text{LCS}}$ pin for one of the SRAMs, and the $\overline{\text{MCS0}}$ and $\overline{\text{MCS1}}$ pins select the remaining SRAM devices. Peripherals are selected by $\overline{\text{PCS0}}$ and $\overline{\text{PCS1}}$ where $\overline{\text{PCS0}}$ enables the 8279 and $\overline{\text{PCS1}}$ enables the 8251A. Note that two wait states are programmed for the EPROM, 8251A, and 8279 because they require more access time than the SRAM, which functions without any wait states.

The system places the EPROM at memory addresses FE000H–FFFFFH; the SRAM at 00000H–07FFFH, 80000H–87FFFH, and 88000H–8FFFFH; the 8279 at I/O ports 1000H–107FH; and the 8251A at I/O ports 1080H–108FH. In this example we do not modify the address of the peripheral control block, which resides at I/O ports FF00H–FFFFH.

EXAMPLE 13–3

```
                    ;Initialization software for the 80188 microprocessor trainer
FFF0                    ORG   0FFF0H

FFF0 EB 8E              JMP   SETUP

FF80                    ORG   0FF80H

FF80         SETUP:
FF80 B8 FF3E            MOV   AX,0FE3EH      ;2 waits, 8K block
FF83 BA FFA0            MOV   DX,0FFA0H      ;address A0H
FF86 EF                 OUT   DX,AX          ;program upper memroy

FF87 B8 07FC            MOV   AX,07FCH       ;0 waits, 32K block
FF8A 83 C2 02           ADD   DX,2           ;address A2H
FF8D EF                 OUT   DX,AX          ;program lower memory

FF8E B8 103E            MOV   AX,103EH       ;2 waits, address 1000H
FF91 83 C2 02           ADD   DX,2           ;address A4H
FF94 EF                 OUT   DX,AX          ;program I/0

FF95 B8 81FC            MOV   AX,81FCH       ;no waits, address 80000H
FF98 83 C2 02           ADD   DX,2           ;address A6H
FF9B EF                 OUT   DX,AX          ;program middle memory base

FF9C B8 903C            MOV   AX,903CH       ;no waits, 32K devices
FF9F 83 C2 02           ADD   DX,2           ;address A8H
FFA2 EF                 OUT   DX,AX          ;program middle memory size

FFA3 E9 F000 R          JMP   SYSTEM         ;go to system program

F000                    ORG   0F000H

F000         SYSTEM:                         ;system program
```

Example 13–3 lists the software required to initialize the 80188 microprocessor. It does not list any of the software required to program the 8251A or 8279, nor does it show the software required to operate the system as a microprocessor-based trainer.

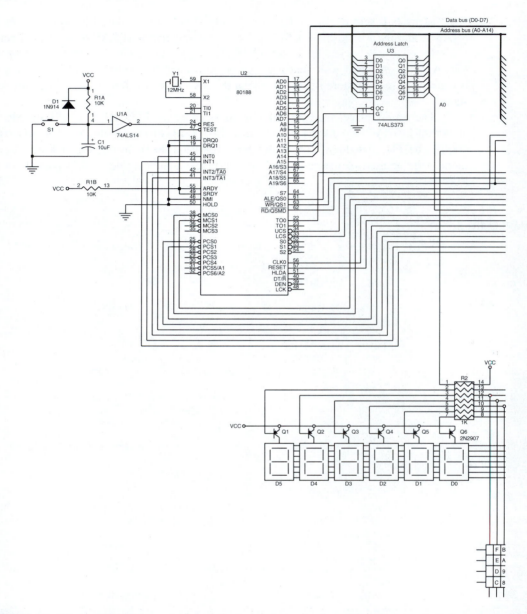

FIGURE 13–24   An 80188-based system that contains a keyboard interface, a 6-digit numeric display, and a serial interface.

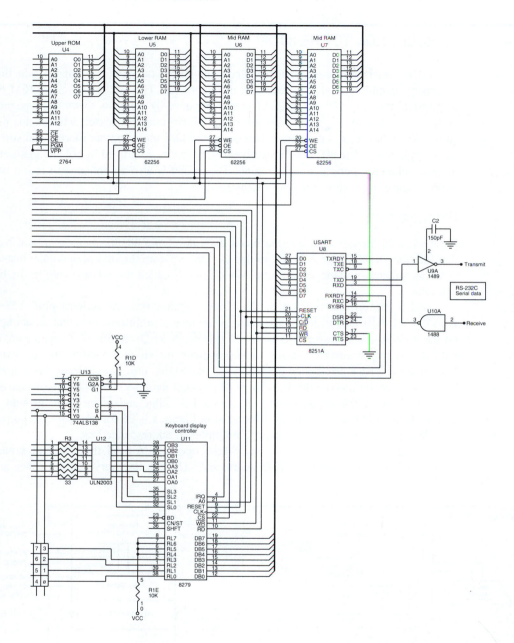

13–4   INTRODUCTION TO THE 80286

The 80286 microprocessor is an advanced version of the 8086 microprocessor that is designed for multiuser and multitasking environments. The 80286 addresses 16M bytes of physical memory and 1G bytes of virtual memory by using its memory-management system. This section of the text introduces the 80286 microprocessor, which finds use in earlier AT-style personal computers that once pervaded the computer market and still find some application. The 80286 is basically an 8086 that is optimized to execute instructions in fewer clocking periods than the 8086. The 80286 is also an enhanced version of the 8086 because it contains a memory manager.

Hardware Features

Figure 13–25 provides the internal block diagram of the 80286 microprocessor. Notice that like the 80186/80188, the 80286 does not incorporate internal peripherals; instead it contains a memory-management unit (MMU) that is called the *address unit* in the block diagram.

As a careful examination of the block diagram reveals, address pins A23–A0, $\overline{BUSY}$, CAP, $\overline{ERROR}$, $\overline{PEREQ}$, and $\overline{PEACK}$ are new or additional pins that do not appear on the 8086 microprocessor. The $\overline{BUSY}$, $\overline{ERROR}$, $\overline{PEREQ}$, and $\overline{PEACK}$ signals are used with the microprocessor extension or coprocessor, of which the 80287 is an example. Note that the $\overline{TEST}$ pin is now referred to as the $\overline{BUSY}$ pin. The address bus is now 24 bits wide to accommodate the 16M bytes of physical memory. The CAP pin is connected to a 0.047 μF, ±20% capacitor that acts as a 12V filter and connects to ground. The pinouts of the 8086 and 80286 are illustrated in Figure 13–26 for comparative purposes. Note that the 80286 does not contain a multiplexed address/data bus.

As mentioned in Chapter 1, the 80286 operates in both the real and protected modes. In the real mode, the 80286 addresses a 1M-byte memory address space and is

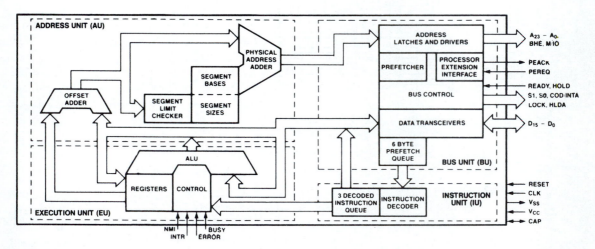

FIGURE 13–25   The block diagram of the 80286 microprocessor. (Courtesy of Intel Corporation)

FIGURE 13-26 The 8086 and 80286 microprocessor pinouts. Notice that the 80286 does not have a multiplexed address/data bus.

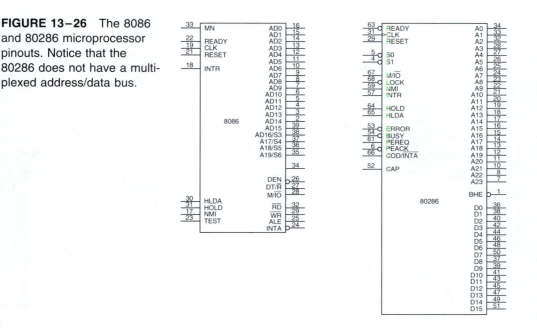

virtually identical to the 8086. In the protected mode, the 80286 addresses a 16M-byte memory space.

Figure 13-27 illustrates the basic 80286 microprocessor system. Notice that the clock is provided by the 82284 clock generator (similar to the 8284A) and the system control signals are provided by the 82288 system bus controller (similar to the 8288). Also notice the absence of the latch circuits used to demultiplex the 8086 address/data bus.

Additional Instructions

The 80286 has even more instructions than its predecessors. These extra instructions control the virtual memory system through the memory manager of the 80286. Table 13-7 lists the additional 80286 with a comment about the purpose of each instruction. These instructions are the only new instructions added to the 80286. Note that the 80286 also contains the new instructions added to the 80186/80188 such as INS, OUTS, BOUND, ENTER, LEAVE, PUSHA, POPA, and the immediate multiplication and immediate shift and rotate counts.

Following are descriptions of instructions not explained under the memory-management section. The instructions described here are special in nature and only used for the conditions indicated.

CLTS.   The clear task-switched flag instruction (CLTS) clears the TS (task-switched) flag bit to a logic 0. If the TS flag bit is a logic 1, and the 80287 numeric coprocessor is used by the task, an interrupt occurs (vector type 7). This allows the function of the coprocessor to be emulated with software. The CLTS instruction is used in a system and is considered a privileged instruction because it can only be executed in the protected

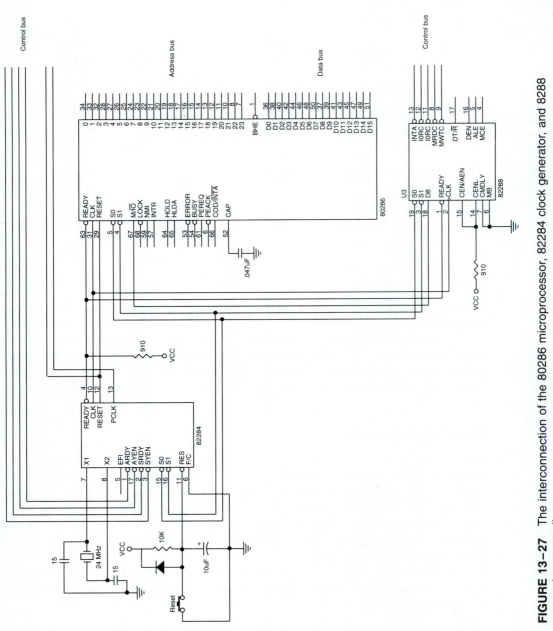

FIGURE 13–27 The interconnection of the 80286 microprocessor, 82284 clock generator, and 8288 system bus controller.

TABLE 13–7 Additional 80286 instructions

Instruction	Comment
CLTS	Clears the task-switched flag
LDGT	Loads the global descriptor table register
SGDT	Stores the global descriptor table register
LIDT	Loads the interrupt descriptor table register
SIDT	Stores the interrupt descriptor table register
LLDT	Loads the local descriptor table register
SLDT	Stores the local descriptor table register
LMSW	Loads the machine status word
SMSW	Stores the machine status word
LAR	Loads the access rights
LSL	Loads the segment limit
SAR	Stores the access rights
ARPL	Adjusts the requested privilege level
VERR	Verifies a read access
VERW	Verifies a write access

mode at privilege level 0. There is no set TS flag instruction. This is accomplished by writing a logic 1 to bit position 3 (TS) of the machine status word (MSW) by using the LMSW instruction.

LAR. The load access rights (LAR) reads the segment descriptor and places a copy of the access rights byte into a 16-bit register. An example is the LAR AX,BX instruction that loads AX with the access rights byte from the descriptor selected by the selector value found in BX. This instruction is used to get the access rights so it can be checked before a program uses the segment of memory described by the descriptor.

LSL. The load segment limit instruction (LSL) loads a user-specified register with the segment limit. For example, the LSL AX,BX instruction loads AX with the limit of the segment described by the descriptor selected by the selector in BX. This instruction is used to test the limit of a segment.

ARPL. The adjust requested privilege level (ARPL) instruction is used to test a selector so the privilege level of the requested selector is not violated. An example is ARPL AX,CX where AX contains the requested privilege level and CX contains the selector value to be used to access a descriptor. If the requested privilege level is of a lower priority than the descriptor under test, the zero flag is set. This may require that a program adjust the requested privilege level or indicate a privilege violation.

VERR. The verify for read access instruction (VERR) verifies that a segment can be read. Recall from Chapter 1 that a code segment can be read protected. If the code segment can be read, the zero flag bit is set. The VERR AX instruction tests the descriptor selected by the AX register.

VERW.   The verify for write access (VERW) instruction is used to verify that a segment can be written. Recall from Chapter 1 that a data segment can be write protected. If the data segment can be written, the zero flag bit is set.

The Virtual Memory Machine

A *virtual memory machine* is a machine that maps a larger memory space (1G bytes for the 80286) into a much smaller physical memory space (16M bytes for the 80286). This allows a very large system to execute in smaller physical memory systems. This is accomplished by spooling the data and programs between the fixed disk memory system and the physical memory. Addressing a 1G byte memory system is accomplished by the descriptors in the 80286 microprocessor. Each 80286 descriptor describes a 64K byte memory segment and the 80286 allows 16K descriptors. This (64K × 16K) allows a maximum of 1G bytes of memory to be described for the system.

As mentioned in Chapter 1, descriptors describe the memory segment in the protected mode. The 80286 has descriptors that define code, data, and stack segment, interrupts, procedures, and tasks. Descriptor accesses are performed by loading a segment register with a selector in the protected mode. The selector accesses a descriptor that describes an area of the memory. Additional details on descriptors and their application are defined in Chapter 1 and also Chapter 14. Please refer to these sections of the text for a much more detailed view of the protected mode memory-management system.

13–5   SUMMARY

1. The 80186/80188 contains the same basic instruction set as the 8086/8088 microprocessor, except that a few additional instructions are added. It is thus an enhanced version of the 8086/8088 microprocessor. The new instructions include PUSHA, POPA, INS, OUTS, BOUND, ENTER, LEAVE, and immediate multiplication and shift/rotate counts.
2. Hardware enhancements to the 80186/80188 include a clock generator, programmable interrupt controller, three programmable timers, programmable DMA controller, and programmable chip selection logic unit.
3. The clock generator allows the 80186/80188 to operate from an external TTL level clock source or from a crystal attached to the X1 and X2 pins. The frequency of the crystal is twice the operating frequency of the microprocessor. The 80186/80188 is available in speeds of 6–12 MHz.
4. The programmable interrupt controller arbitrates all internal and external interrupt requests. It is also capable of operating with two external 8259A interrupt controllers.
5. There are three programmable timers located within the 80186/80188. Each timer is a fully programmable 16-bit counter used to generate waveforms or count events. Two of the timers, timer 0 and 1, have external inputs and outputs. The third timer, timer 2, is clocked from the system clock and is either used to provide a clock for another timer or to request a DMA action.

6. The programmable DMA controller is a fully programmable two-channel controller. DMA transfers are made between memory and I/O, I/O and I/O, or between memory locations. DMA requests occur from software, hardware, or the output of timer 2.

7. The programmable chip selection unit is an internal decoder that provides up to 13 output pins to select memory (6 pins) and I/O (7 pins). It also inserts 0–3 wait states with or without external READY synchronization.

8. The only difference between the timing of the 80186/80188 and the 8086/8088 is that ALE appears one half clock pulse earlier. Otherwise the timing is identical.

9. The 6 MHz version of the 80186/80188 allows 417 ns of access time for the memory, and the 8 MHz version allows 309 ns.

10. The internal 80186/80188 peripherals are programmed via a peripheral control block (PCB) initialized at I/O ports FF00H–FFFFH. The PCB may be moved to any area of memory or I/O by changing the contents of the PCB relocation register at initial I/O location FFFEH and FFFFH.

11. The 80286 is an 8086 that has been enhanced to include a memory-management unit (MMU). The 80286 is capable of addressing a 16M byte physical memory space because of the management unit.

12. The 80286 contains the same instructions as the 80186/80188 except for a handful of additional instructions that control the memory-management unit.

13. Through the memory-management unit, the 80286 microprocessor addresses a virtual memory space of 1G bytes as specified by the 16K descriptors stored in two descriptor tables.

13-6   QUESTIONS AND PROBLEMS

1. List the differences between the 8086/8088 and the 80186/80188 microprocessor.

2. What hardware enhancements are added to the 80186/80188 that are not present in the 8086/8088?

3. The 80186/80188 is packaged in what types of integrated circuit?

4. If the 20 MHz crystal is connected to X1 and X2, what frequency signal is found at CLKOUT?

5. How is the queue status made available to the 80187 numeric coprocessor on the ALE and $\overline{WR}$ pins?

6. The fanout from any 80186/80188 pin except for CLKOUT and $\overline{S2}/\overline{S0}$ is _____ for a logic 0.

7. How many clocking periods are found in an 80186/80188 bus cycle?

8. What is the main difference between the 8086/8088 and 80186/80188 timing?

9. What is the importance of memory access time?

10. How much memory access time is allowed by the 80186/80188 if operated with a 6 MHz clock?

11. Where is the peripheral control block located after the 80186/80188 is reset?

12. Write the software required to move the peripheral control block to memory locations 10000H–100FFH.

13. What interrupt vector is used by the INTO pin on the 80186/80188 microprocessor?

14. How many interrupt vectors are available to the interrupt controller located within the 80186/80188 microprocessor?
15. What two modes of operation are available to the interrupt controller?
16. What is the purpose of the interrupt control register?
17. Whenever an interrupt source is masked, the mask bit in the interrupt mask register is a logic _____ .
18. What is the difference between the interrupt poll and interrupt poll status registers?
19. What is the purpose of the end-of-interrupt (EOI) register?
20. How many 16-bit timers are found within the 80186/80188?
21. Which timers have input and output pin connections?
22. Which timer connects to the system clock?
23. If two maximum-count registers are used with a timer, explain the operation of the timer.
24. What is the purpose of the $\overline{\text{INH}}$ timer control register bit?
25. What is the purpose of the P timer control register bit?
26. The timer control register bit ALT selects what type of operation for timers 0 and 1?
27. Explain how the timer output pins are used.
28. Develop a program that causes timer 1 to generate a continuous signal that is a logic 1 for 123 counts and a logic 1 for 23 counts.
29. Develop a program that causes timer 0 to generate a single pulse after 345 clock pulses on its input pin have occurred.
30. How many DMA channels are controlled by the DMA controller?
31. The DMA controller's source and destination registers are each _____ bits wide.
32. How is the DMA channel started with software?
33. The chip selection unit has _____ pins to select memory devices.
34. The chip selection unit has _____ pins to select peripheral devices.
35. The last location of the upper memory block as selected by the $\overline{\text{UCS}}$ pin is location _____ .
36. The middle memory chip selection pins are programmed for a _____ address and a block size.
37. The lower memory area as selected by $\overline{\text{LCS}}$ begins at address _____ .
38. The internal wait state generator is capable of inserting between _____ and _____ wait states.
39. Program register A8H so the midrange memory block size is 128K bytes.
40. What is the purpose of the EX bit in register A8H?
41. The 80286 microprocessor addresses _____ bytes of physical memory.
42. When the memory manager is in use, the 80286 addresses _____ bytes of virtual memory.
43. The instruction set of the 80286 is identical to the _____ , except for the memory-management instructions.
44. What is the purpose of the VERR instruction?
45. What is the purpose of the LSL instruction?

CHAPTER 14

The 80386 and 80486 Microprocessors

INTRODUCTION

The 80386 microprocessor is a full 32-bit version of the 80286 microprocessor. Along with a larger word size (double word), there are many improvements and additional features. The 80386 microprocessor features multitasking, memory management, virtual memory with or without paging, software protection, and a large memory system. All software written for the early 8086/8088, 80186/80188, and the 80286 are upward compatible to the 80386 microprocessor. The amount of memory addressable by the 80386 is increased from the 1M bytes found in the 8086/8088/80186/80188 and the 16M bytes found in the 80286 to 4G bytes in the 80386. The 80386 can switch between protected mode and real mode without resetting the microprocessor. Switching from protected mode to real mode is a problem on the 80286 microprocessor.

The 80486 microprocessor is an enhanced version of the 80386 microprocessor that executes many of its instructions in one clocking period instead of the two required on the 80386. The 80486 microprocessor also contains an 8K-byte cache memory and improved version of the 80387 numeric coprocessor. When the 80486 is operated at the same clock frequency as an 80386, it performs with about a 50 percent speed improvement.

CHAPTER OBJECTIVES

Upon completion of this chapter, you will be able to:

1. Contrast the 80386 microprocessor with the earlier family members.
2. Describe the organization and interface of the 32-bit 80386 memory system.
3. Describe the operation of the 80386 memory-management unit and paging unit.
4. Switch between protected mode and real mode.
5. Define the operation of additional 80386 instructions and addressing modes.

6. Explain the operation of a cache memory system and an interleaved memory system.
7. Detail the interrupt structure and direct memory access structure of the 80386.
8. Contrast the 80486 with the 80386 and 80286 microprocessors.
9. Detail the operation of new 80486 instructions.
10. Explain the operation of the 80486 cache memory.

14-1 INTRODUCTION TO THE 80386 MICROPROCESSOR

Before this microprocessor can be used in a system, the function of each pin must be understood. This section of the chapter details the operation of each pin along with the internal register structure and external memory system and I/O structures of the 80386 microprocessor.

Figure 14-1 illustrates the pinout of the 80386DX microprocessor that is packaged in a 132-pin PGA (pin grid array) and the 80386SX microprocessor. These microprocessors are also available in the smaller surface mount package. Two versions of the 80386 are commonly available: the 80386DX, illustrated and described in this chapter, is the full version and the 80386SX is a reduced bus version of the 80386. A new version of the 80386—the 80386SL—which incorporates much of the AT bus system, is also available. The 80386DX addresses 4G bytes of memory through its 32-bit data bus and

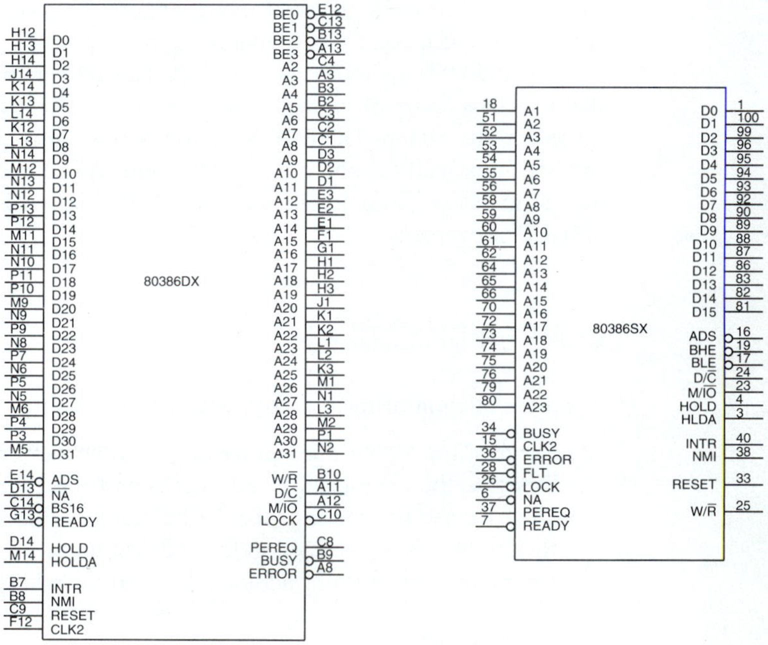

FIGURE 14-1 The pinouts of the 80386DX and 80486SX microprocessor.

32-bit address. The 80386SX, more like the 80286, addresses 16M bytes of memory with its 24-bit address bus via its 16-bit data bus. The 80386SX was developed after the 80386DX for applications that didn't require the full 32-bit bus version. The 80386SX is found in many personal computers that use the same basic mother-board design as the 80286. At this time, most applications require less than 16M bytes of memory, so the 80386SX is a fairly popular and less costly version of the 80386 microprocessor.

The prior family members require a +5.0 V power supply as does the 80386 microprocessor. (Note that some of the newer microprocessors for notebook computers use a +3.0 V power supply.) The power supply current averages 550 mA for the 25 MHz version of the 80386, 500 mA for the 20 MHz version, and 450 mA for the 16 MHz version. Also available is a 33 MHz version that requires 600 mA of power supply current. Note that during some modes of normal operation, power supply current can surge to over 1.0 A. This means that the power supply and power distribution network must be capable of supplying these surges. This device contains multiple Vcc and Vss connections that must all be connected to +5.0 V and ground for proper operation. Some of the pins are labeled N/C (no connection) and must not be connected.

Each 80386 output pin is capable of sinking (logic 0) 4.0 mA (address and data connections) or 5.0 mA (other connections). This represents an increase in drive current compared to the 2.0 mA available on earlier family member output pins. Each input pin represents a small load requiring only ± 10 μA of current. In most systems, except the smallest, these current levels require bus buffers.

The function of each 80386 group of pins follows:

1. A31–A2—Address Bus Connections: are used to address any of the 1G × 32 memory locations found in the 80386 memory system. Note that A0 and A1 are encoded in the bus enable ($\overline{BE3}$–$\overline{BE0}$) described elsewhere. (Note that the 80386SX contains address connections A23–A1.)

2. D31–D0—Data Bus Connections: are used to transfer data between the micropro-cessor and its memory and I/O system. (Note that the 80386SX contains data bus connections D15–D0.)

3. $\overline{BE3}$–$\overline{BE0}$—Bank Enable Signals: are used to access a byte, word, or double word of data. These signals are generated internally by the microprocessor from address bits A1 and A0. (Note the 80386SX contains $\overline{BHE}$ and $\overline{BLE}$ for bank selection.)

4. M/$\overline{IO}$—Memory/IO: selects a memory device when a logic 1 or an I/O device when a logic 0. During the I/O operation the address bus contains a 16-bit I/O address.

5. W/$\overline{R}$—Write/Read: indicates that the current bus cycle is a write when a logic 1 or a read when a logic 0.

6. $\overline{ADS}$—Address Data Strobe: becomes active whenever the 80386 has issued a valid memory or I/O address. This signal is combined with the W/$\overline{R}$ signal to generate the separate read and write signals present in the earlier 8086/8088 system.

7. RESET—Reset: initializes the 80386 causing it to begin executing software from memory location FFFFFFF0H. The 80386 is reset to the real mode and the leftmost 12 address connections remain logic 1's (FFFH) until a far jump or far call is executed when they are cleared to logic 0's (000H).

8. CLK2—Clock Times 2: is driven by a clock signal that is twice the operating frequency of the 80386. For example, to operate the 80386 at 16 MHz, we apply a 32 MHz clock to this pin.

9. $\overline{\text{READY}}$—Ready: controls the number of wait states inserted into the timing to control memory accesses.
10. $\overline{\text{LOCK}}$—Lock: becomes a logic 0 whenever an instruction is prefixed with the LOCK: prefix. This is most often used during DMA accesses.
11. D/$\overline{\text{C}}$—Data/Control: indicates the data bus contains data for or from memory or I/O when a logic 1. If D/$\overline{\text{C}}$ is a logic 0, the microprocessor is halted or executing an interrupt acknowledge.
12. $\overline{\text{BS16}}$—Bus Size 16 Bits: selects either a 32-bit data bus ($\overline{\text{BS16}}$ = 1) or a 16-bit data bus ($\overline{\text{BS16}}$ = 0). In most cases if an 80386 is operated on a 16-bit data bus, we use the 80386SX that has a 16-bit data bus.
13. $\overline{\text{NA}}$—Next Address: causes the 80386 to output the address of the next instruction or data in the current bus cycle. This pin is often used for pipelining the address.
14. HOLD—Hold: requests a DMA action as it did on the 8086/8088.
15. HLDA—Hold Acknowledge: indicates that the 80386 is currently in a hold condition.
16. $\overline{\text{PEREQ}}$—Coprocessor Request: asks the 80386 to relinquish control and is a direct connection to the 80387 arithmetic coprocessor.
17. $\overline{\text{BUSY}}$—Busy: an input used by the WAIT or FWAIT instruction that waits for the coprocessor to become not busy. This is also a direct connection to the 80387 from the 80386. This pin functions as the $\overline{\text{TEST}}$ pin on the 8086/8088.
18. $\overline{\text{ERROR}}$—Error: indicates to the microprocessor that an error is detected by the coprocessor.
19. INTR—Interrupt Request: is used by external circuitry to request an interrupt.
20. NMI—Nonmaskable Interrupt: requests a nonmaskable interrupt as it did on the 8086 microprocessor.

The Memory System

The physical memory system of the 80386DX is 4G bytes in size and can be addressed as such, or if virtual addressing is used, 64T bytes are mapped into the 4G bytes of physical space by the memory management unit. Figure 14–2 shows the organization of the 80386DX physical memory system.

The memory is divided into four 8-bit-wide memory banks with each containing up to 1G bytes of memory. This 32-bit-wide memory organization allows bytes, words, or double words of memory data to be accessed directly. The 80386DX transfers up to a 32-bit-wide number in a single memory cycle, where the early 8088 requires 4 cycles to accomplish the same transfer and the 80286 requires 2 cycles. Today, this data width is important, especially for single-precision floating-point numbers that are 32 bits in width that are used with graphics programs. High-level software normally uses floating-point numbers for data storage, so 32-bit memory locations speed the execution of high-level software if it is written to take advantage of this wider memory.

Each memory byte is numbered in hexadecimal as in the prior versions of the family. The difference is that the 80386DX uses a 32-bit-wide memory address with memory bytes numbered from location 00000000H through FFFFFFFFH.

The two memory banks in the 8086 system are accessed via A0 and $\overline{\text{BHE}}$. In the 80386DX, the memory banks are accessed via four bank enable signals $\overline{\text{BE0}}$–$\overline{\text{BE3}}$. This arrangement allows a single byte to be accessed when one bank enable signal is activated by the microprocessor. It also allows a word to be addressed when two bank enable

FIGURE 14–2 The memory system for the 80386 micro- processor. Notice that the memory is organized as 4 banks with each containing 1G bytes. Memory is ac- cessed as 8-, 16-, or 32-bit data.

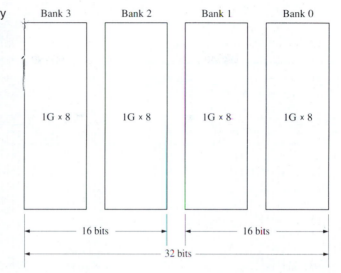

signals are activated. In most cases, a word is addressed in bank 0 and 1 or in bank 2 and 3. Memory location 00000000H is in bank 0, memory location 00000001H is in bank 1, 00000002H is in bank 2, and location 00000003H is in bank 3. The 80386DX does not contain address connections A0 and A1 because these have been encoded as the bank enable signals.

Buffered System. Figure 14–3 shows the 80386DX connected to buffers that increase fanout from its address, data, and control connections. This microprocessor is operated at 25 MHz using a 50 MHz clock input signal that is generated by a integrated oscillator module. Oscillator modules are almost always used to provide a clock in modern microprocessor-based equipment. The HLDA signal connects to the buffer enable control input of buffers in a system that uses direct memory access. Otherwise, the buffer enable pins are connected to ground in a non-DMA system.

Pipelines, Interleaves, and Caches. The cache memory is a buffer that allows the 80386 to function more efficiently with lower DRAM speeds. A pipeline is a special way of handling memory accesses so the memory has additional time to access data. A 16 MHz 80386 allows memory devices with access times of 50 ns or less to operate at full speed. Obviously there are no DRAMs currently available with these access times. In fact, the fastest DRAMs currently in production have access time of 55 ns or longer. This means that some technique must be found to interface these, slower than the microprocessor, memory devices. Three techniques are available: interleaved memory, caching, and a pipeline. The 16 MHz 80386 operates using 100 ns DRAM in a system that uses interleaved memory.

The pipeline is the preferred means of interfacing memory because the micropro- cessor supports pipelined memory accesses. Pipelining in the 80386 allows memory an extra clocking period to access data. The extra clock extends the access time from 50 ns to 81 ns on an 80386 operating with a 16 MHz clock. The *pipe,* as it is often called, is set up by the microprocessor. When an instruction is fetched from memory, the micropro-

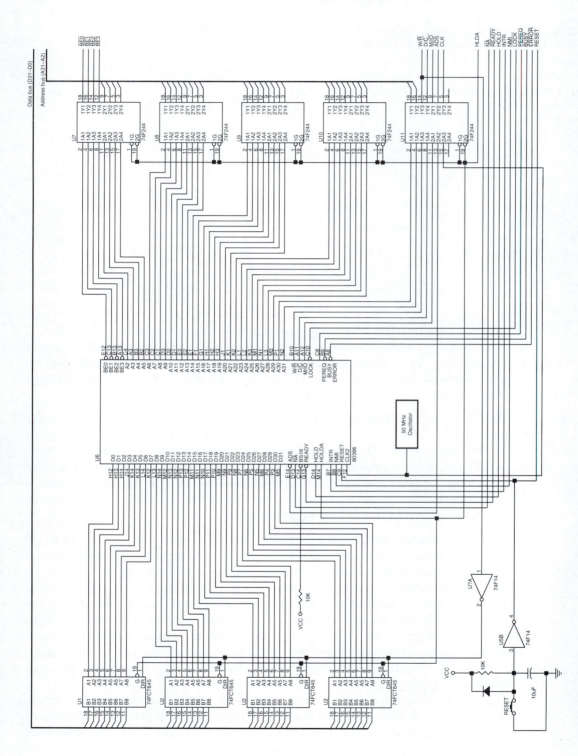

FIGURE 14–3 A fully buffered 25MHz 80386DX.

cessor has extra time before the next instruction is fetched. During this extra time, the address of the next instruction is sent out of the address bus ahead of time. This extra time (one clock period) is used to allow additional access time to slower memory components.

Not all memory references can take advantage of the pipe, which means that some memory cycles are not pipelined. These nonpipelined memory cycles request one wait state if the normal pipeline cycle requires no wait states. Overall, pipes are a cost-saving feature that reduces the access time required by the memory system in low-speed systems.

Not all systems can take advantage of the pipe. Those systems are typically ones that operate at 25 or 33 MHz. In these higher speed systems, another technique must be used to increase the memory system speed. The *cache* memory system improves overall performance of the memory systems for data that are accessed more than once.

A cache is a high-speed memory system that is placed between the microprocessor and the DRAM memory system. Cache memory devices are usually TTL memory components with access times of less than 25 ns. In many cases we see cache memory systems of sizes between 32K bytes and 256K bytes. The size of the cache memory is determined more by the application than by the microprocessor. If a program is small and refers to little memory data, a small cache is beneficial. If a program is large and references large blocks of memory, the largest cache size possible is recommended. In many cases a 64K improves speed sufficiently.

The cache memory operates in the following fashion. Whenever the microprocessor accesses memory, the cache is first tested to see if the data are stored in the cache. If the data are in the cache, we have a cache *hit*. Whenever a hit occurs the data are fetched from the cache without any wait states. If the data are not in the cache we have a cache *miss*. When a miss occurs, the data are read from the DRAM and stored in the cache and read into the microprocessor. This of course requires wait states to slow the microprocessor to match speeds with the slow speed DRAM memory.

When writing data to the memory, we also write it to the cache. Although this causes normal DRAM wait states, if the data are read later, it is already in the cache meaning zero wait state operation on subsequent reads of the same data. This method of writing is called *cache write through* operation.

In a cache memory system, data are organized into blocks of bytes. Blocks are from 2 bytes to 16 bytes in length. Each time there is a cache miss, the microprocessor reads from 2 to 16 bytes of data from the memory into the cache. In the case of the 80386 microprocessor, we use a block size of 16 bytes or four 32-bit memory locations. When data are fetched from memory as four 32-bit memory locations, we call the transfer a *burst transfer*. The reason that the cache is organized this way is because most programs and data are sequential. By transferring four 32-bit double words from the memory into the cache for each miss, we are actually storing the next data or instructions used by the microprocessor in the cache. This method of filling the cache is called *cache lookahead*.

Figure 14-4 depicts a typical 32K byte cache memory system. The cache is organized as an 8K × 49 memory. This means that there are 8K locations with each location containing 49 bits. The 49-bit-wide memory is divided into two sections: one section is 32 bits wide and stores data, the other is 17 bits wide and stores a tag. The tag is a portion of the memory address (A32–A15). This means that there are 32K bytes (8K × 32) for data storage and 8K x 17 for tag information. Tag information is

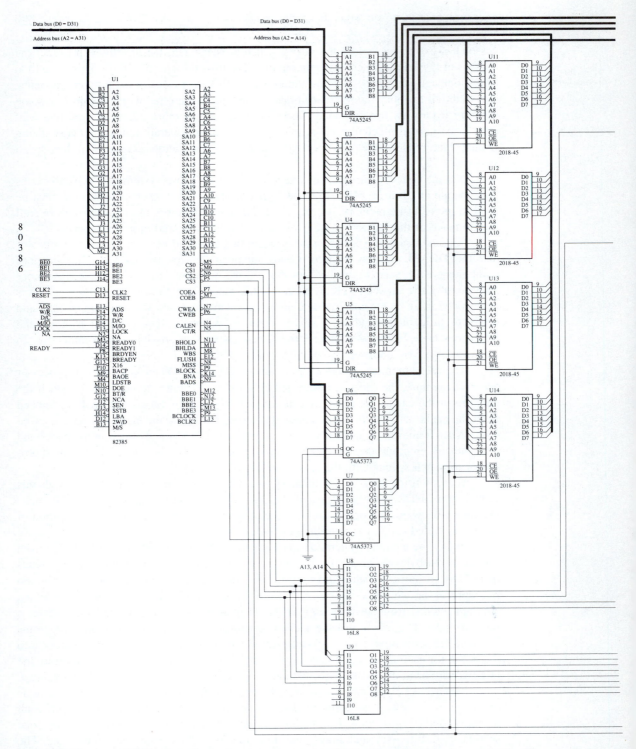

FIGURE 14–4 A 32K-byte cache memory system controlled by the 82385 cache controller. The memory consists of 2K × 8 high-speed stack RAM that has an access time of 45 ns.

600

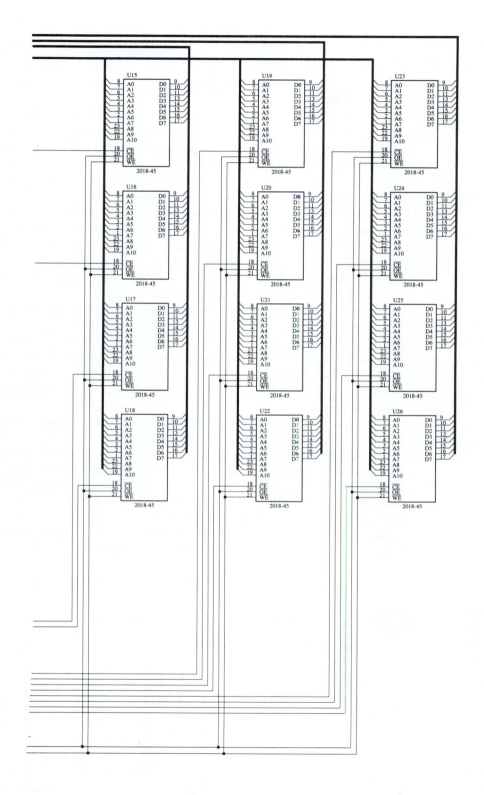

601

never included in the cache memory size, so this is a 32K byte cache. The tags are stored inside the cache controller and therefore no external memory is required for tag storage.

This is a direct mapped cache because only the leftmost 17 bits of the address are stored in the tag field. The remaining 13 bits of the address (A14–A2) are used to address one of the 8K data locations (4 bytes) and a location in the 8K tag memory. (See Figure 14–5 for the cache memory organization.)

Each time that the microprocessor sends an address to the memory system, the cache controller checks the tag (A31–A15) to determine whether the location addressed by A14–A2 is stored in the cache. The comparison tests the address stored in the tag field against address bits A31–A15 to check for a match or hit. If the tag matches, the microprocessor fetches the data from the cache memory. If it doesn't match, the microprocessor reads the data from the main memory, stores it in the cache, and also stores the tag in the tag memory. To read data from the main memory may require up to four wait states, while a read from the cache requires no waits.

If data are written to the memory, the cache controller writes the data to a cache location and also to the tag memory, A write typically takes 1 wait state.

Suppose the microprocessor has just read data from memory location 01007FF0H. The data from this location are stored in the cache memory at location 111 1111 1111 00XX (least-significant 13 address bits). The tag that is stored in the tag memory for this access is 0000 0001 0000 0000 0. If this is the same address currently stored in the tag memory location, we have a hit.

If we have a hit in this example for location 01007FF0H and the microprocessor now attempts to read location 02007FF0H, we address the same location in the cache and also the same tag location. Because the leftmost 17 address bits do not match, we have a miss. Luckily, memory accesses are normally sequential so this type of miss rarely happens. More commonly the next miss would occur when address 0100FFF0H is accessed. (Note that 0100FFF0H is 32K bytes above 01007FF0H.)

Interleaved memory systems are found so memory access times can be lengthened without the need for wait states. An interleaved memory system requires two complete sets of buses and a controller that provides addresses for each bus.

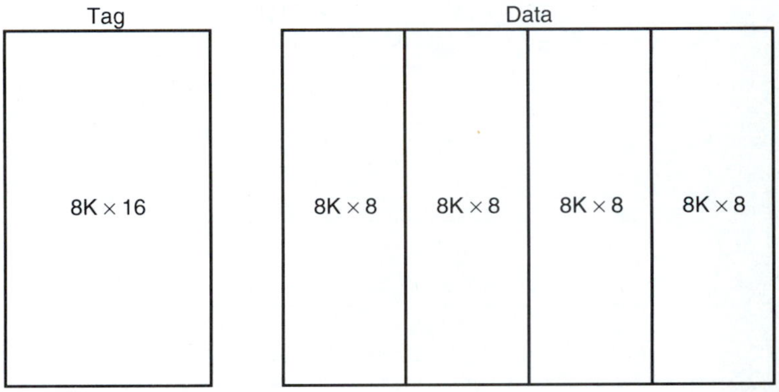

FIGURE 14–5 Organization of the direct-mapped 32K byte cache memory.

An interleaved memory is divided into two parts. For the 80386 microprocessor, one part contains 32-bit addresses 000000H–000003H, 000008H–00000BH, etc., while the other part contains addresses 000004–000007, 00000CH–00000FH, etc. While the microprocessor accesses locations 000000H–000003H, the interleave control logic generates the address strobe signal for locations 000004H–000007H. This process is continued as the microprocessor addresses consecutive memory locations. This process of addressing alternate banks of memory lengthens the amount of access time provided to the memory because the address is generated before the microprocessor requires the data. This is because the microprocessor pipelines memory addresses, sending the next address out before the data are read from the last address.

The problem with interleaving, although not major, is the memory addresses must be accessed so each section is addressed alternately. This does not always happen as a program executes. Under normal program execution, the microprocessor alternately addresses memory approximately 93 percent of the time. The remaining 7 percent, the microprocessor addresses data in the same memory section, which means that in these 7 percent of the memory accesses, the memory system must cause wait states because of the reduced access time. The access time is reduced because the memory must wait until the previous data are transferred before it can obtain its address. This leaves it with less access time; therefore a wait state is required for accesses in the same memory bank.

Refer to Figure 14–6 for the timing diagram of the address as it appears at the microprocessor address pins. This timing diagram shows how the next address is output before the current data are accessed. It also shows how access time is increased using interleaved memory addresses for each section of memory compared to a noninterleaved access, which requires a wait state.

Figure 14–7 pictures the interleave controller. Admittedly this is a fairly complex logic circuit that needs some explanation. First, if the SEL input (used to select this section of the memory) is inactive (logic 0), then the $\overline{\text{WAIT}}$ signal is a logic 1. Also, both $\overline{\text{ADS0}}$ and $\overline{\text{ADS1}}$, used to strobe the address to the memory sections, are both logic 1's causing the latches connected to them to become transparent.

As soon as the SEL input becomes a logic 1, this circuit begins to function. The A3 input is used to determine which latch (U2B or U5A) becomes a logic 0 selecting a section of the memory. Also the $\overline{\text{ADS}}$ pin that becomes a logic 0 is compared with the previous state of the $\overline{\text{ADS}}$ pins. If the same section of memory is accessed a second time, the $\overline{\text{WAIT}}$ signal becomes a logic 0 requesting a wait state.

Figure 14–8 illustrates an interleaved memory system that uses the circuit of Figure 14–7. Notice how the $\overline{\text{ADS0}}$ and $\overline{\text{ADS1}}$ signals are used to capture the address for either section of memory. The memory in each bank is 16 bits wide. If accesses to memory require 8-bit data, then in most cases the system causes wait states. As a program executes, the 80386 fetches instructions 16 bits at a time from normally sequential memory locations. Program execution uses interleaving in most cases. If a system is going to access mostly 8-bit data, it is doubtful that memory interleaving will reduce the number of wait states.

The access time allowed by an interleaved system such as the one shown in Figure 14–8 is increased to 145.5 ns from 78 ns using a 16 MHz system clock. (If a wait state is inserted, access time with an 8 MHz clock is 140.5 ns, which means an interleaved system performs at about the same rate as a system with one wait state.) If the clock is

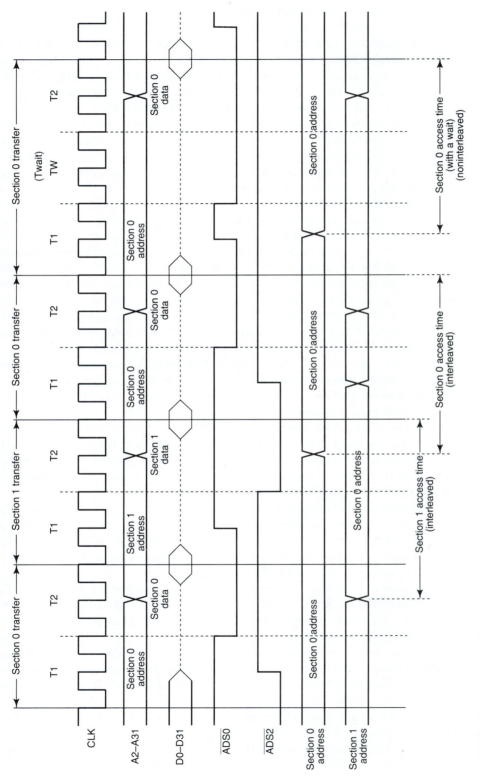

FIGURE 14–6 The timing diagram of an interleaved memory system showing the access times and address signals for both sections of memory.

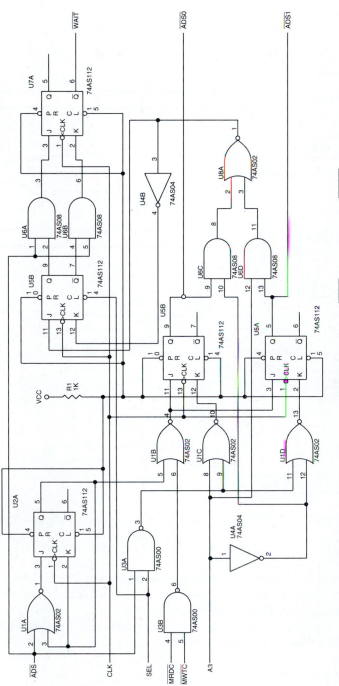

FIGURE 14–7 The interleave control logic which generates separate $\overline{\text{ADS}}$ signals and a $\overline{\text{WAIT}}$ signal used to control interleaved memory.

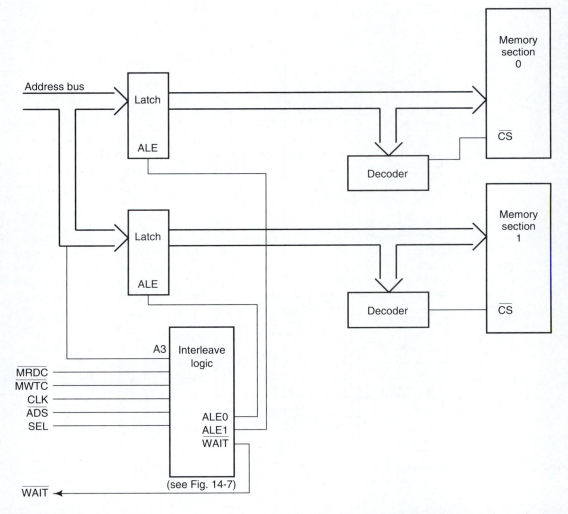

FIGURE 14–8   An interleaved memory system showing the address latches and the interleave logic circuit.

increased to 33 MHz, the interleaved memory requires 72.75 ns while standard memory interfaces allow 46 ns for memory access. At this higher clock rate a 55 ns DRAM functions properly, without wait states when the memory addresses are interleaved. If an access to the same section occurs, then a wait state is inserted because the microprocessor only allows 39 ns without any wait states in this case.

The I/O System

The I/O system of the 80386 is basically the same as that found in the earlier versions of the microprocessor. There are 64K different bytes of I/O space available if isolated I/O is implemented. The I/O port address appears on address bus connections A15–A2, with $\overline{BE3}$–$\overline{BE0}$ used to select a byte, word, or double word of I/O data. If memory-mapped I/O is implemented, then the number of I/O locations can be any amount up to 4G bytes. Almost all 80386 systems use isolated I/O because of the I/O protection scheme used by the 80386 in protected mode.

Figure 14–9 shows the I/O map for the 80386 microprocessor. Unlike the I/O map for the 8086, the 80386 uses a full 32-bit-wide I/O system divided into four banks as the memory system is divided into four banks. Most I/O transfers are 8 bits wide because we often use ASCII code (a 7-bit code) for transferring alphanumeric data between the microprocessor and printers and keyboards. Recently, I/O devices that are 16 and even 32 bits wide (EISA or local bus) have appeared for systems such as disk memory and video display interfaces. These wider I/O paths increase the data transfer rate between the microprocessor and the I/O device when compared to 8-bit transfers.

The I/O locations are numbered from 0000H through FFFFH. A portion of the I/O map is designated for the 80387 arithmetic coprocessor. Although the port numbers for the coprocessor are well above the normal I/O map, it is important that they be taken into account when decoding I/O space (overlaps). The coprocessor uses I/O location 800000F8H–800000FFH for communications between the 80387 and 80386. (Recall that the 80287 used I/O addresses 00F8H–00FFH for the same purpose.) Because we often only decode address connections A15–A2 to select an I/O device, be aware that the coprocessor will activate devices 00F8H–00FFH unless address line A31 is also decoded.

The only new feature added to the 80386 with respect to I/O is the I/O privilege information added to the tail end of the TSS when the 80386 is operated in protected mode. In the protected mode, as described in the section on 80386 memory management, an I/O location can be blocked or inhibited. If the blocked I/O location is addressed, an interrupt (type 13) is generated. This scheme is added so I/O access can be prohibited in a multiuser environment. Blocking is an extension of the protected mode operation, as are privilege levels.

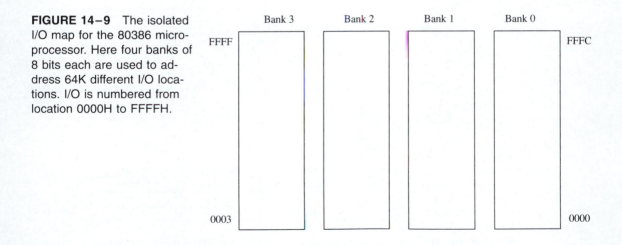

FIGURE 14–9 The isolated I/O map for the 80386 microprocessor. Here four banks of 8 bits each are used to address 64K different I/O locations. I/O is numbered from location 0000H to FFFFH.

Memory and I/O Control Signals

As with the 8086, the memory and I/O are controlled with separate signals. The M/$\overline{\text{IO}}$ signal indicates whether the transfer is memory or I/O. In addition to M/$\overline{\text{IO}}$, the memory and I/O systems must read or write data. The W/$\overline{\text{R}}$ signal is a logic 0 for a read operation, and a logic 1 for a write operation. The $\overline{\text{ADS}}$ signal is used to qualify these two control signals. This is a deviation from the 8086 system that used separate signals for memory read and write and I/O read and write.

Timing.   Timing is important in understanding how to interface memory and I/O to the 80386 microprocessor. Figure 14–10 shows the timing diagram of a nonpipelined memory read cycle. Notice that the timing is referenced to the CLK2 input signal and that a bus cycle consists of four clocking periods.

Each bus cycle contains 2 clocking states with each state (T1 and T2) containing 2 clocking periods. Notice in Figure 14–10 that the access time is listed as time number 3. The 16 MHz version allows memory an access time of 78 ns before wait states are inserted in this nonpipelined mode of operation. To select the nonpipelined mode, we place a logic 1 on the $\overline{\text{NA}}$ pin.

Figure 14–11 illustrates the read timing when the 80386 is operated in the pipelined mode. Notice that additional time is allowed the memory for accessing data because the address is sent out early. Pipelined mode is selected by placing a logic 0 on

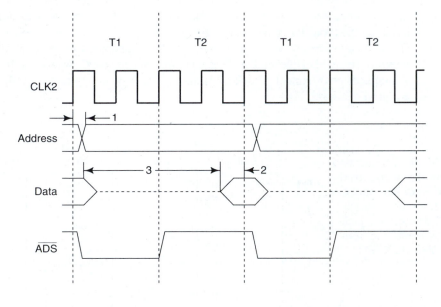

	33 MHz	25 MHz	20 MHz	16 MHz
Time 1:	4–15 ns	4–21 ns	4–30 ns	4–36 ns
Time 2:	5 ns	7 ns	11 ns	11 ns
Time 3:	46 ns	52 ns	59 ns	78 ns

FIGURE 14–10   The nonpipelined read timing for the 80386 microprocessor.

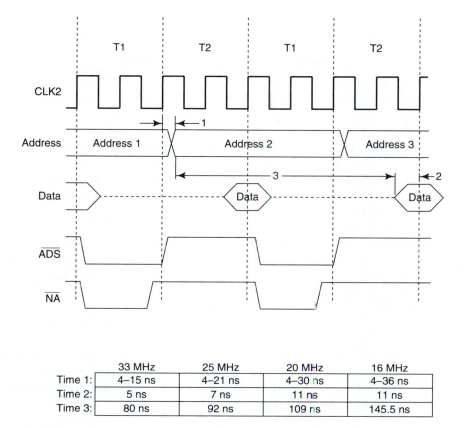

	33 MHz	25 MHz	20 MHz	16 MHz
Time 1:	4–15 ns	4–21 ns	4–30 ns	4–36 ns
Time 2:	5 ns	7 ns	11 ns	11 ns
Time 3:	80 ns	92 ns	109 ns	145.5 ns

FIGURE 14–11   The pipelined read timing for the 80386 microprocessor.

the $\overline{\text{NA}}$ pin and using address latches to capture the pipelined address. The clock pulse applied to the address latches is the $\overline{\text{ADS}}$ signal. Address latches must be used with a pipelined system as well as interleaved memory banks. The minimum number of interleaved banks is two, and four have been successfully used in some applications.

Notice that the pipelined address appears one complete clocking state before it normally appears with nonpipelined addressing. In the 16 MHz version of the 80386, this allows an additional 67.5 ns for memory access. In the nonpipelined system, we had a memory access time of 78 ns and in the pipelined system we have 145.5 ns. The advantages of the pipelined system are that no wait states (in many, but not all bus cycles) are required and much lower speed memory devices may be connected to the micropro- cessor. The disadvantage is that we need to interleave memory to use a pipe, which requires additional circuitry and occasional wait states.

Wait States

Just as with the 8086, we need to introduce wait states if memory access times are long compared with the time allowed by the 80386 for memory access. In a nonpipelined 33

MHz system, access time is only 46 ns. No DRAM memory exists that has an access time of 46 ns. This means that wait states must be introduced to access the DRAM (1 wait for 60 ns DRAM) or an EPROM that has an access time of 100 ns (2 waits).

The $\overline{\text{READY}}$ input controls whether or not waits states are inserted into the timing. The $\overline{\text{READY}}$ input on the 80386 is a dynamic input that must be activated during each bus cycle. Figure 14–12 shows a few bus cycles with one normal (0 wait) cycle and one that contains a single wait state. Notice how the $\overline{\text{READY}}$ is controlled to cause 0 or 1 wait.

The $\overline{\text{READY}}$ signal is sampled at the end of a bus cycle to determine if the clock cycle is T2 or TW. If $\overline{\text{READY}}$ = 0 at this time, it is the end of the bus cycle or T2. If $\overline{\text{READY}}$ is 1 at the end of a clock cycle, the cycle is a TW and the microprocessor continues to test $\overline{\text{READY}}$ searching for a logic 0 and the end of the bus cycle.

In the nonpipelined system, whenever $\overline{\text{ADS}}$ becomes a logic zero, $\overline{\text{READY}}$ = 1. After $\overline{\text{ADS}}$ returns to a logic 1, the positive edges of the clock are counted to generate the $\overline{\text{READY}}$ signal. The $\overline{\text{READY}}$ signal becomes a logic 0 after the first clock to insert 0 waits states. If 1 wait state is inserted, the READY line must remain a logic 1 until at least two clocks have elapsed. If additional wait states are desired, then additional time must elapse before $\overline{\text{READY}}$ is cleared.

Figure 14–13 shows a circuit that inserts 0 through 3 wait states for various memory addresses. In the example, 1 wait state is produced for a DRAM access and 2 waits for an EPROM access. The 74F164 clears whenever $\overline{\text{ADS}}$ is low and D/$\overline{\text{C}}$ is high. It begins to shift after $\overline{\text{ADS}}$ returns to a logic 1 level. As it shifts, the 00000000 in the shift register begins to fill with logic 1's from the QA connection toward the QH connection. The 4 different outputs are connected to an inverting multiplexer that generates the active low $\overline{\text{READY}}$ signal.

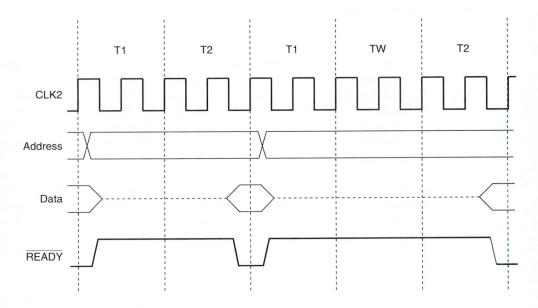

FIGURE 14–12   A nonpipelined 80386 shown with 0 and 1 wait states.

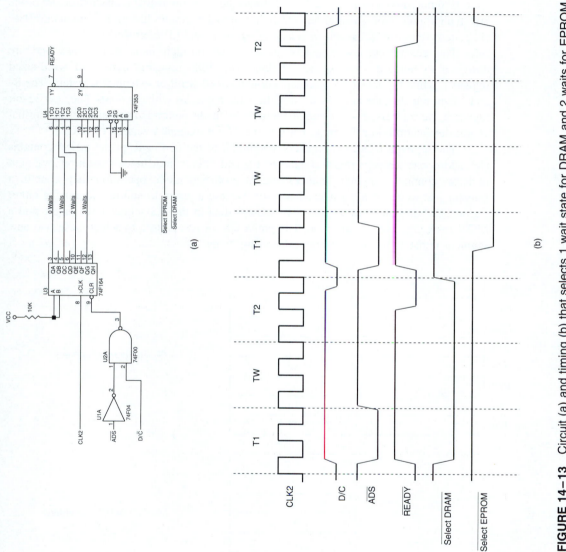

FIGURE 14–13 Circuit (a) and timing (b) that selects 1 wait state for DRAM and 2 waits for EPROM.

14-2   THE 80386 REGISTER STRUCTURE

The register structure of the 80386 is a much expanded version of the registers found in the 80286 microprocessor. Figure 14-14 shows the program visible register structure of the 80386 microprocessor. The registers are divided into the sections just as they are in the 8086: (1) *general-purpose,* (2) *segment (selector) registers,* and (3) *housekeeping.*

The general-purpose registers are accessed through most instructions and are designed to hold, 8-, 16- or 32-bit data. The 8086 contains byte- and word-sized registers, while the 80386 also contains double-word-sized or extended registers. The 8- and 16-bit registers are addressed using the same names as with the 8086. The new 32-bit registers are addressed as extended registers with the letter E augmenting the normal 16-bit designation. For example, EAX is the 32-bit extended version of AX.

The segment (selector) registers are similar to the 8086 except the 80386 contains two additional segment registers labeled FS and GS. In real mode operation, segment registers contain a segment address and in protected mode operation they contain a selector just as in the 8086 microprocessor. We use a prefix to address data using either FS or GS. For example, to use GS to address data in the GS segment we might find a MOV EAX,GS:DATA instruction. The prefix GS: or FS: is used to select these two new segment registers for any memory addressing mode.

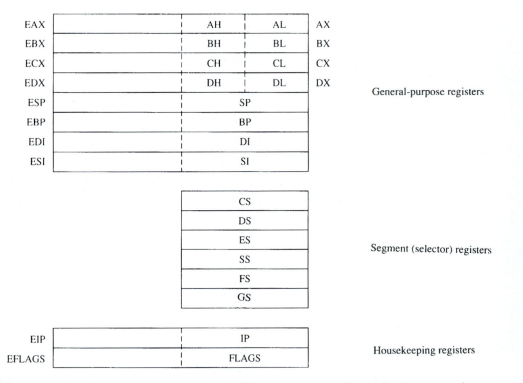

FIGURE 14-14 The internal structure of the 80386 microprocessor illustrating the general, segment, and housekeeping registers.

The housekeeping registers consist of a 32-bit instruction pointer (EIP) and a 32-bit flag register (EFLAGS). During real mode operation, only the rightmost 16 bits of EIP contain the offset address of the next instruction executed in a program. In protected mode operation, all 32 bits of EIP are used to address segments that may contain a program or data that is up to 4G bytes in length. This is a significant improvement over the 64K byte segments available in the 80286.

EXAMPLE 14-1

```
                             .386

                             ;example 80386 instructions using a variety of
                             ;addressing modes

0000                         PROGRAM  SEGMENT   USE16

0000 66| B8 22223333                  MOV   EAX,22223333H
0006 66| BB 44445555                  MOV   EBX,44445555H
000C BF 1000                          MOV   DI,1000H
000F BD 2000                          MOV   BP,2000H
0012 8A 0D                            MOV   CL,[DI]
0014 3E: 8A 6E 00                     MOV   CH,DS:[BP]
0018 66| 03 D8                        ADD   EBX,EAX
001B 66| 8B F3                        MOV   ESI,EBX
001E 66| F7 E6                        MUL   ESI
0021 67| 66| 89 01                    MOV   [ECX],EAX
0025 64: 67| 88 0403                  MOV   FS:[EBX+EAX],AL
002A 65: 67| 8B 07                    MOV   AX,GS:[EDI]


002E                         PROGRAM  ENDS

                                      END
```

Example 14-1 lists a variety of instructions that use the 32-bit registers. Any instruction operating in real or protected mode can use any 32-bit register. The example begins with a .386 that designates to the assembler that the program is an 80386 program. The USE 16 directive tells the assembler to use standard 16-bit offset addresses for real mode operation. In protected mode we often include a USE 32 directive that tells the assembler to use 32-bit offset addresses. More about the USE 16 or USE 32 directives appears in Appendix A.

The EFLAG register is pictured in Figure 14-15. Notice that the rightmost 16 bits are identical to the 80286 flag register. The RF and VM flag bits are new to the 80386. The RF (resume flag) is used with debugging to temporarily disable debugging for the next instruction. The VM (virtual mode) flag bit selects virtual 8086 mode while the 80386 is operated in the protected mode. This special mode is discussed in a later section of this chapter.

System Address Registers

The system address registers are: GDTR (global descriptor table register), LDTR (local descriptor table register), IDTR (interrupt descriptor table register), and TR (task register). All system address registers are program-invisible registers that are not directly accessed, except for loading or storing. The first three are used to address areas of

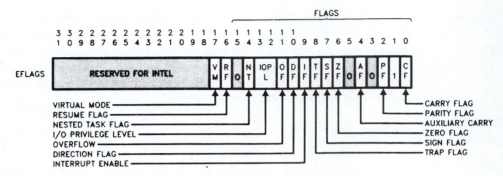

FIGURE 14–15   The EFLAG register. (Courtesy of Intel Corporation)

memory that contain the global, local, and interrupt descriptor tables used during protected mode operation. The task register (TR) is used to address a selector that defines the current task in the form of the TSS (task state segment). These registers perform the same functions as they did in the 80286 microprocessor except the base address is 32 bits wide instead of 24 bits and the limit is 20 bits instead of 16 bits.

Control Registers

In addition to the EFLAGS and EIP as described earlier, there are other control registers found in the 80386. Control register 0 (CR0) is identical to the MSW (machine status word) found in the 80286 microprocessor except it is 32 bits wide instead of 16 bits. Additional control registers are CR1, CR2, and CR3.

Figure 14–16 illustrates the control register of the 80386. Control register CR1 is not used in the 80386, but is reserved for future products. Control register CR2 holds the linear page address of the last page accessed before a page fault interrupt. Finally, control register CR3 holds the base address of the page directory. The rightmost 12 bits of the 32-bit page table address contain zeros and combine with the remainder of the register to locate the start of the 4K long page table.

Register CR0 contains a number of special control bits that are defined as follows in the 80386:

1. PG—selects page table translation of linear addresses into physical addresses when PG = 1. Page table translation allows any linear address to be assigned any physical memory location.
2. ET—selects the 80287 coprocessor when ET = 0 or the 80387 coprocessor when ET = 1. This bit was installed because when the 80386 first appeared, there was no 80387 available. In most systems, ET is set to indicate that an 80387 is present in the system.
3. TS—indicates that the 80386 has switched tasks. If TS = 1, a numeric coprocessor instruction causes a type 7 (coprocessor not available) interrupt.
4. EM—is set to cause a type 7 interrupt for each ESC instruction. (ESCape instructions are used to encode instructions for the 80387 coprocessor.) We often use this interrupt to emulate, with software, the function of the coprocessor. Emulation reduces the system cost, but requires at least 100 times longer to execute the emulated coprocessor instructions.

FIGURE 14-16 The control-register structure of the 80386 microprocessor.

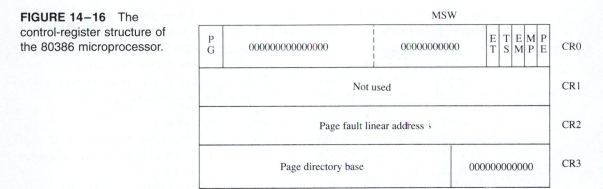

5. MP—is set to indicate that the arithmetic coprocessor is present in the system.
6. PE—is set to select the protected mode of operation for the 80386. It may also be cleared to reenter the real mode. This bit can only be set in the 80286. The 80286 could not return to real mode without a hardware reset, which precludes its use in most systems that use protected mode.

Debug and Test Registers

A new series of registers not found in the 8086 appear in the 80386 as debug and test registers. Registers DR0–DR7 facilitate debugging and registers TR6 and TR7 are used to test paging and caching.

Figure 14–17 shows the sets of debug and test registers. The first four debug registers contain 32-bit linear breakpoint addresses. (A *linear address* is a 32-bit address

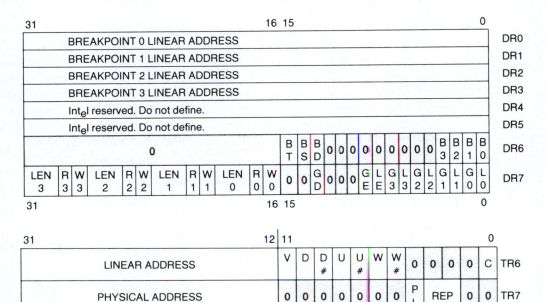

FIGURE 14-17 The debug and test registers of the 80386. (Courtesy of Intel Corporation)

generated by a microprocessor instruction that may or may not be the same as the physical address.) The breakpoint addresses, which may locate an instruction or datum, are constantly compared with the addresses generated by the program. If a match occurs, the 80386 will, if directed by DR6 and DR7, cause a type 1 interrupt (TRAP or debug interrupt) to occur. These breakpoint addresses are very useful in debugging faulty software. The control bits in DR6 and DR7 are defined as follows:

1. BT—if set, the debug interrupt was caused by a task switch.
2. BS—if set, the debug interrupt was caused by the TF bit in the flag register.
3. BD—if set, the debug interrupt was caused by an attempt to read the debug register with the GD bit set. The GD bit protects access to the debug registers.
4. B3–B0—indicate which of the four debug breakpoint addresses caused the debug interrupt.
5. LEN—each of the four length fields pertains to each of the four breakpoint addresses stored in DR0–DR3. These bits further define the size of access at the breakpoint address as 00 (byte), 01 (word), or 11 (double word).
6. RW—each of the four read/write fields pertains to each of the four breakpoint addresses stored in DR0–DR3. The RW field selects the cause of action that enabled a breakpoint address as 00 (instruction access), 01 (data write), and 11 (data read and write).
7. GD—if set, GD prevents any read or write of a debug register by generating the debug interrupt. This bit is automatically cleared during the debug interrupt so the debug registers can be read or changed if needed.
8. GE—if set, selects a global breakpoint address for any of the four breakpoint address registers.
9. LE—if set, selects a local breakpoint address for any of the four breakpoint address registers.

The test registers, TR6 and TR7, test the translation lookaside buffer (TLB). The TLB is used with the paging unit within the 80386. The TLB holds the most commonly used page table address translations. The TLB reduces the number of memory reads required for looking up page translation table entries. The TLB holds the most common 32 entries from the page table, and it is tested with the TR6 and TR7 test registers.

Test register TR6 holds the tag field (linear address) of the TLB, and TR7 holds the physical address of the TLB. To write a TLB entry, perform the following steps:

1. Write TR7 for the desired physical address, PL, and REP values.
2. Write TR6 with the linear address making sure that C = 0.

To read a TLB entry:

1. Write TR6 with the linear address making sure that C = 1.
2. Read both TR6 and TR7. If the PL bit indicates a hit, then the desired values of TR6 and TR7 indicate the contents of the TLB.

The bits found in TR6 and TR7 indicate the following conditions:

1. V—shows the entry in the TLB is valid.
2. D—indicates the entry in the TLB is invalid or dirty.
3. U—a user bit for the TLB.

4. W—indicates that the area addressed by the TLB entry is writable.

5. C—selects a write (0) or immediate lookup (1) for the TLB.

6. PL—indicates a hit if a logic 1.

7. REP—selects which block of the RLB is written.

Refer to the section on memory management and the paging unit for more detail on the function of the TLB.

14–3 THE 80386 INSTRUCTION SET

The instruction set of the 80386 contains all of the instructions discussed for the 8086 plus a vast number of additional instructions and addressing modes that are new to the 80386 as introduced in earlier chapters on the microprocessor instruction set. Many of the new variations are due to the 32-bit extended registers found in the 80386 microprocessor. In addition to the 8- and 16-bit registers found in the 8086, we also have the following 32-bit extended registers: EAX, EBX, ECX, EDX, ESP, EBP, EDI, and ESI, along with two new segment (selector) registers: FS and GS. These additional registers increase the number of valid instructions for the 80386.

These new registers are used with instructions just as the 8- and 16-bit registers are used with the 8086 instruction set. The 32-bit registers may be accessed in either the real or protected mode of operation. Appendix B, which describes the entire instruction set of all variations of the Intel family, lists many examples of 80386 instructions. In addition to the new 32-bit registers and new segment registers, there are also 14 new instructions (see Table 14–1) and many new addressing modes. Note that all of these instructions are explained in earlier chapters.

TABLE 14–1 New 80386 instructions

Instruction	Comment	Example
BSF	Bit scan forward	BSF EAX,DATA
BSR	Bit scan reverse	BSR EAX,LIST
BT	Bit test	BT DATA,EAX
BTC	Bit test and complement	BTC AX,WATER
BTR	Bit test and reset	BTR EBX,4
BTS	Bit test and set	BTS BX,2
LFS	Load FS	LFS DI,DATA
LGS	Load GS	LGS SI,FIELD
LSS	Load SS	LSS SP,STACK
MOVZX	Move with zero-extend	MOVZX EAX,CX
MOVSX	Move with sign-extend	MOVSX ECX,DL
SETcd	Set byte on condition	SETNC AL
SHLD	Double-precision shift left	SHLD AX,BX,8
SHRD	Double-precision shift right	SHRD AX,BX,4

Notes on Older Instructions

In the 80286 microprocessor, the LMSW instruction loads the machine status word (MSW). On the 80386 the MSW is CR0. If you plan to modify the contents of CR0, don't use the LMSW instruction. Use the MOV EAX,CR0 instruction to move CR0 into EAX and then change it with the AND or OR instruction. After changing the image of CR0 in EAX, move it back into CR0 with the MOV CR0,EAX instruction. Likewise, the SMSW instruction should never be used in 80386 programs.

In general, most of the 8086 instructions can be adjusted for use with 32-bit registers on the 80386 microprocessor. For example, if you need to load EAX with a 12H, use the MOV EAX,12H instruction. Refer to Appendix B for a multitude of examples of instruction usage. Almost any instruction that uses an 8- or 16-bit register or pointer can use a 32-bit register or pointer.

New Addressing Modes

The number of addressing modes has been increased from the modes allowed by the 8086 microprocessor. The additional modes found in the 80386 microprocessor include using extended (32-bit) registers as 32-bit offset addresses and pointers. Also, some additional forms of indexing have been added, called *scaling*.

The most obvious of the new addressing modes use the new segment registers with the segment override prefix (FS: or GS:). The MOV AL,FS:[DI] instruction loads AL with the data stored in segment FS at offset address DI. Any instruction that can be prefixed can use either FS or GS to address these two additional memory segments.

In addition to the indirect memory addressing modes used with the 8086 microprocessor, the 80386 contains additional modes as illustrated in Table 14–2. Notice that quite a few additional indirect addressing modes are added to the 80386 instruction set. The 8086 allowed memory to be indirectly addressed through only DI, SI, BX, or BP. These are still allowed in the 80386, but we may also use any of the new modes listed in Table 14–2. If these new addressing modes are used in the real mode, they may only access the first 1M byte of memory.

Notice that memory can be indirectly addressed using a 32-bit register or directly using a 32-bit displacement. This increases the possible number of instructions available to the 80386 by a tremendous factor.

In the 8086 microprocessor, we can combine only certain pointers to indirectly address memory: [BX + DI], [BX + SI], [BP + DI], and [BP + SI]. In the 80386 any two 32-bit registers (except ESP) can be combined to address memory data. These additional addressing modes (see Table 14–3) use the following form [E?? + scaled index], where E?? is any 32-bit register except ESP and scaled index is any scaled 32-bit register except ESP. The MOV EAX,[EBX + ECX] instruction is an example of this new addressing mode. This instruction loads EAX with memory data stored in the data segment at the location address by the sum of EBX and ECX.

The term **scaled index** means that the second 32-bit register can be scaled (multiplied) by a factor of 1X, 2X, 4X, or 8X. A scaling factor of 1X is never used and is implied as in the MOV EAX,[EBX + ECX] instruction. The scaling factor multiplies the second register by 1, 2, 4, or 8, but it does not change the value in the register.

The scaling factor is used to address elements within arrays of data. Suppose that ECX addresses an array called ARRAY and that the element number is located in EDX.

TABLE 14–2 Additional indirect addressing modes for the 80386 microprocessor

Mode	Default Segment	Example
[EAX]	DS	ADD ECX,[EAX]
[EBX]	DS	SUB [EBX],AL
[ECX]	DS	MOV AX,[ECX]
[EDX]	DS	MOV AL,[EDX]
[EBP]	SS	MOV CL,[EBP]
[EDI]	DS	MOV [EDI],ECX
[ESI]	DS	MOV [ESI],EDI
d32	DS	MOV AL,DATA
[EAX + d8]	DS	ADD ECX,[EAX + 9]
[EBX + d8]	DS	SUB [EBX + 10H],AL
[ECX + d8]	DS	MOV AX,[ECX – 2]
[EDX + d8]	DS	MOV AL,[EDX – 12H]
[EBP + d8]	SS	MOV CL,[EBP + 1]
[EDI + d8]	DS	MOV [EDI – 33],ECX
[ESI + d8]	DS	MOV [ESI + 9],EDI
[EAX + d32]	DS	ADD ECX,TABLE[EAX]
[EBX + d32]	DS	SUB [EBX + 10000H],AL
[ECX + d32]	DS	MOV AX,ARRAY[ECX]
[EDX + d32]	DS	MOV AL,[EDX – 200000H]
[EBP + d32]	SS	MOV CL,[EBP + 1]
[EDI + d32]	DS	MOV TABLE[EDI],ECX
[ESI + d32]	DS	MOV TABLE[ESI + 92],EDI

Notes: d8 = 8-bit signed displacement and d32 = 32-bit signed displacement.

If the ARRAY is a byte-sized array, then EDX addresses the array element. If the ARRAY is word-sized, EDX must be multiplied by a factor (scale) of 2 to address the correct memory location for the array element. In a word-sized array, element 0 is at offset address 0 and 1; element 2 is at offset address 2 and 3; and so forth. Scaling factors of 4X and 8X are used to index array elements in double-word and quad-word arrays.

Example 14–2 lists a short procedure that adds floating-point single-precision numbers in LIST1 and LIST2 and stores the result in LIST3. Each array contains 100H double words of data in this example procedure that uses scaled indexed addressing to access the array elements. If the scaling factor is changed from 4X to 8X, double-precision floating-point data are added. Also notice that a 4 is subtracted inside of each indirect addressing mode because the last count in CX is a 1, not a zero. Note this software is written assuming real mode operation in a DOS-based system and no attempt is made to place numbers inside of the two source arrays LIST1 and LIST2.

TABLE 14-3   Scaled index addressing mode for the 80386 microprocessor

Mode	Default Segment	Example
[EAX + scaled index]	DS	MOV BH,[EAX + 2*ECX]
[EBX + scaled index]	DS	ADD AL,[EBX + EAX]
[ECX + scaled index]	DS	INC BYTE PTR [ECX + 4*EAX]
[EDX + scaled index]	DS	MOV [EDX + 8*EAX],SP
[EBP + scaled index]	SS	MOV AL,[EBP + ECX]
[EDI + scaled index]	DS	MOV BL,[EDI + ESI]
[ESI + scaled index]	DS	SUB BYTE PTR [ESI + EBX],22H
[EAX + scaled index + d8]	DS	MOV BH,[EAX + 2*ECX + 3]
[EBX + scaled index + d8]	DS	ADD AL,[EBX + EAX – 2]
[ECX + scaled index + d8]	DS	INC BYTE PTR [ECX + 4*EAX – 9]
[EDX + scaled index + d8]	DS	MOV [EDX + 8*EAX – 10H],SP
[EBP + scaled index + d8]	SS	MOV AL,[EBP + ECX + 1AH]
[EDI + scaled index + d8]	DS	MOV BL,[EDI + ESI – 2]
[ESI + scaled index + d8]	DS	SUB BYTE PTR [ESI + EBX – 4],22H
[EAX + scaled index + d32]	DS	MOV BH,[EAX + 2*ECX + 200000H]
[EBX + scaled index + d32]	DS	ADD AL,TABLE[EBX + EAX]
[ECX + scaled index + d32]	DS	INC BYTE PTR ARRAY[ECX + 4*EAX]
[EDX + scaled index + d32]	DS	MOV ARRAY[EDX + 8*EAX + 100H],SP
[EBP + scaled index + d32]	SS	MOV AL,LIST[EBP + ECX]
[EDI + scaled index + d32]	DS	MOV BL,LIST[EDI + ESI + 10000H]
[ESI + scaled index + d32]	DS	SUB BYTE PTR ARRAY[ESI + EBX],22H

Notes: d8 = 8-bit signed displacement, d32 = 32-bit signed displacement, and scaled index = EAX, EBX, ECX, EDX, EBP, EDI, or ESI with a scaling factor of 1X, 2X, 4X, or 8X.

EXAMPLE 14-2

```
                        .386
                        .387
                        ; Procedure that adds groups of floating-point data

0000                    CODE    SEGMENT USE16

                                ASSUME   CS:CODE,DS:CODE

0000 0100 [             LIST1   DD    100H DUP (?)
          00000000
                 ]
0400 0100 [             LIST2   DD    100H DUP (?)
          00000000
                 ]
0800 0100 [             LIST3   DD    100H DUP (?)
          00000000
                 ]
```

```
0C00                          ADDS      PROC FAR

0C00 1E                                 PUSH  DS
0C01 8C C8                              MOV   AX,CS
0C03 8E D8                              MOV   DS,AX

0C05 66| 33 C0                          XOR   EAX,EAX               ;clear registers
0C08 66| 33 DB                          XOR   EBX,EBX
0C0B 66| 33 C9                          XOR   ECX,ECX
0C0E 66| 33 D2                          XOR   EDX,EDX

0C11 B8 0000 R                          MOV   AX,OFFSET LIST1       ;address data
0C14 BB 0400 R                          MOV   BX,OFFSET LIST2
0C17 BA 0800 R                          MOV   DX,OFFSET LIST3

0C1A B9 0100                            MOV   CX,100H               ;load count

0C1D                          REPS:
0C1D 67& D9 44 88 FC                    FLD   DWORD PTR [EAX+4*ECX-4]
0C22 67& D8 44 8B FC                    FADD  DWORD PTR [EBX+4*ECX-4]
0C27 67& D9 5C 8A FC                    FSTP  DWORD PTR [EDX+4*ECS-4]
0C2C E2 EF                              LOOP  REPS

0C2E 1F                                 POP   DS
0C2F CB                                 RET

0C30                          ADDS      ENDP

0C30                          CODE      ENDS

                                        END   ADDS
```

Interrupts

Although this topic contains hardware interfacing information, it also contains instructions so it is presented with the instruction set. Figure 14–18 shows the predefined interrupts for the 80386. These should be compared to the interrupts found in the 8086 in Chapter 10. The 80386 contains interrupt type number 14 and 16 that are not defined for earlier versions of the microprocessor. Type 14 occurs for a page mechanism fault and type 16 for a coprocessor error.

We often call interrupts generated by the INTR and NMI inputs *hardware interrupts* and any other type is called an *exception*. Exceptions are generated by internal events, while interrupts are generated by external events. An **exception** is an exception to the normal progress of a program. The predefined interrupts and exceptions above level 5 are defined in the following list:

1. Type 6—any illegal instruction causes a type 6 interrupt.
2. Type 7—if the EM bit in the CR0 is set, the type 7 interrupt occurs for any arithmetic coprocessor instruction. If the MP bit of CR0 is set and TS is set by a task switch, the WAIT instruction will also cause a type 7 interrupt.
3. Type 8—a double fault or abort exception occurs whenever the 80386 detects a type 10, 11, 12, or 13 interrupt at the same time an interrupt other than a type 14 occurs.
4. Type 9—this exception occurs if the operand address for an arithmetic coprocessor instruction wraps around from location FFFFH to 0000H or 0000H to FFFFH on the real mode. In the protected mode, this exception occurs if the address wraps around from FFFFFFFFH to 00000000H or from 00000000H to FFFFFFFFH.

Function	Interrupt Number	Instruction Which Can Cause Exception	Return Address Points to Faulting Instruction	Type
Divide Error	0	DIV, IDIV	YES	FAULT
Debug Exception	1	any instruction	YES	TRAP*
NMI Interrupt	2	INT 2 or NMI	NO	NMI
One Byte Interrupt	3	INT	NO	TRAP
Interrupt on Overflow	4	INTO	NO	TRAP
Array Bounds Check	5	BOUND	YES	FAULT
Invalid OP-Code	6	Any Illegal Instruction	YES	FAULT
Device Not Available	7	ESC, WAIT	YES	FAULT
Double Fault	8	Any Instruction That Can Generate an Exception		ABORT
Coprocessor Segment Overrun	9	ESC	NO	ABORT
Invalid TSS	10	JMP, CALL, IRET, INT	YES	FAULT
Segment Not Present	11	Segment Register Instructions	YES	FAULT
Stack Fault	12	Stack References	YES	FAULT
General Protection Fault	13	Any Memory Reference	YES	FAULT
Page Fault	14	Any Memory Access or Code Fetch	YES	FAULT
Coprocessor Error	16	ESC, WAIT	YES	FAULT
Intel Reserved	17–32			
Two Byte Interrupt	0–255	INT n	NO	TRAP

* Some debug exceptions may report both traps on the previous instruction, and faults on the next instruction.

FIGURE 14–18   The predefined interrupt vectors for the 80386 microprocessor. (Courtesy of Intel Corporation)

5. Type 10—if an invalid TSS is accessed, the type 10 exception occurs. An invalid TSS occurs whenever the selector is outside the table limit, if a code in the stack segment is outside the table limit, if a stack is not writable, or if the requested privilege level is not equal to the current privilege level of the accessed TSS.

6. Type 11—occurs if the P-bit of the descriptor indicates that the segment is not present (P = 0).

7. Type 12—occurs if the SS descriptor accesses a segment that is not present or if any stack operation causes a limit violation.

8. Type 13—occurs for any of the following reasons: exceeding segment limit, writing to a read-only data segment or code segment, loading a selector with a system descriptor, reading an execute-only code segment, switching to a busy task, violating privilege level for a data segment, or loading CR0 with PG = 1 and PE = 0.

9. Type 14—a page fault exception occurs if PG = 1 and the privilege level is incorrect or the page table or directory contains a zero.

10. Type 16—the $\overline{ERROR}$ pin on the 80387 causes a type 16 exception.

Hardware interrupts for the 80386 are the same as for the 8086. To refresh your understanding of the INTR and NMI inputs, refer to Chapter 10 for a complete discussion of these interrupt inputs.

14–4   80386 MEMORY MANAGEMENT

The memory-management unit (MMU) within the 80386 is similar to the MMU inside the 80286, except the 80386 has a paging unit not found in the 80286. The MMU performs the task of converting logical addresses as they appear as outputs from a program, into physical addresses that access a physical memory location located anywhere within the memory system. The 80386 can use a paging mechanism to allocate any physical address to any logical address. What this means is that even though the program is accessing memory location A0000H with an instruction, the actual physical address could be memory location 100000H, or any other location if paging is enabled. Paging allows virtually any software, written to operate at any memory location, to function in an 80386 because any physical location can become any logical location. The 80286 did not have this flexibility. Paging is used in newer versions of DOS to relocate the 80386 and 80486 memory at addresses above FFFFFH into spaces between ROM at locations D0000–DFFFFH and other areas as they are available.

Descriptors and Selectors

Before the memory paging unit is discussed, the descriptor and selector are discussed for the 80386 microprocessor. The 80386 uses descriptors in much the same fashion as the 80286 (see Chapter 1). In both microprocessors, a **descriptor** is a series of 8 bytes that describe and locate a memory segment. A **selector** (segment register) is used to index a descriptor from a table of descriptors. The main difference between the 80286 and 80386 is that there are two additional selectors (FS and GS). The 80386 descriptors also use a 32-bit base address and a 20-bit limit instead of a 24-bit base address and a 16-bit limit as found on the 80286.

The 80286 addresses a 16M byte memory space with its 24-bit base address and has a segment length limit of 64K bytes due to the 16-bit limit. The 80386 addresses a 4G byte memory space with its 32-bit base address and has a segment length limit of 1M bytes or 4G bytes due to a 20-bit limit that is used in two different ways. The 20-bit limit can access a segment with a length of 1M byte if the granularity bit (G) = 0. If G = 1, the 20-bit limit allows a segment length of 4G bytes.

The granularity bit is found in the 80386 descriptor. If G = 0, the number stored in the limit is interpreted directly as a limit allowing it to contain any limit between 00000H and FFFFFH for a segment size up to 1M bytes. If G = 1, the number stored in the limit is interpreted as 00000XXXH through FFFFFXXXH, where the XXX is 000H. This allows the limit of the segment to range from 0 bytes to 4G bytes in steps of 4K bytes. A limit of 00001H indicates that the limit is 4K bytes when G = 1, and 1 byte when G = 0.

Figure 14–19 shows the way that the 80386 addresses a memory segment in the protected mode using a selector and a descriptor. Notice that this is identical to the way

FIGURE 14–19 Protected mode addressing using a segment register as a selector. (Courtesy of Intel Corporation)

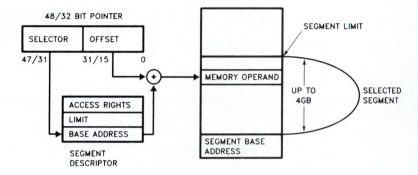

that a segment is addressed by the 80286. The difference is the size of the segment accessed by the 80386. The selector uses its leftmost 13 bits to access a descriptor from a descriptor table. The TI bit indicates either the local (TI = 1) or global (TI = 0) descriptor table. The rightmost 2 bits of the selector define the requested privilege level of the access.

Because the selector uses a 13-bit code to access a descriptor, there are at most 8,192 descriptors in each table, local or global. Since each segment, in an 80386, can be 4G bytes in length, we can access 16,384 segments at a time with the two descriptor tables. This allows the 80386 to access a virtual memory size of 64T bytes. Of course, only 4G bytes of memory actually exist in the memory system (1T byte = 1,024G bytes). If a program requires more than 4G bytes of memory at a time, it can be swapped between the memory system and a disk drive or other form of large volume storage. Disk swapping is routine in operating systems such as windows or OS/2.

As with the 80286, the 80386 uses tables for both global (GDT) and local (LDT) descriptors. Both machines also use a third table for interrupts (IDT) descriptors or gates. The descriptors for the 80386 are different from the 80286 as illustrated in the comparison of these descriptors in Figure 14–20. Notice how both descriptors use the same data for the first 6 bytes. This allows 80286 software to be upward compatible with the 80386. (Recall that an 80286 descriptor used 00H for its most significant two bytes.) The base address is 32-bits in the 80386, the limit is 20 bits, and a G bit selects the limit multiplier (1 time or 4K times). The fields in the descriptor for the 80386 are defined as follows:

1. Base (B0–B31)—defines the starting 32-bit address of the segment within the 4G byte physical address space of the 80386 microprocessor.
2. Limit (L0–L19)—defines the limit of the segment in units of bytes if the G bit = 0, or in units of 4K bytes if G = 1. This allows a segment to be of any length from 1 byte to 1M bytes if G = 0 and from 4K bytes to 4G bytes in steps of 4K bytes if G = 1. Recall that the limit indicates the last byte in a segment.
3. Access Rights—determines privilege level, and other information about the segment. This byte varies with different types of descriptors and is elaborated with each descriptor type.
4. G—the granularity bit selects a multiplier of 1 or 4K times for the limit field. If G = 0, the multiplier is 1 and if G = 1, the multiplier is 4K.

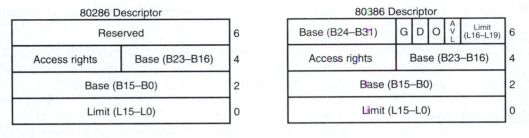

FIGURE 14–20   The descriptors for the 80286 and 80386 microprocessors.

5. D—selects the default register size. If D = 0, the registers are 16 bits wide as in the 80286 and if D = 1, they are 32 bits wide as in the 80386. This bit determines whether prefixes are required for 32-bit data and index registers. If D = 0, then a prefix is required to access 32-bit registers and to use 32-bit pointers. If D = 1, then a prefix is required to access 16-bit registers and 16-bit pointers. The USE16 and USE32 directives appended to the SEGMENT statement in assembly language control the setting of the D bit. In the real mode, it is always assumed that the registers are 16 bits wide, so any instruction that references a 32-bit register or pointer must be prefixed. Note that current versions of DOS, Windows,[1] and OS/2[2] assume that D = 0.

6. AVL—this bit is available to the operating system to use in any way that it sees fit. It often indicates that the segment described by the descriptor is available.

Descriptors appear in two forms in the 80386 microprocessor: the segment descriptor and the system descriptor. The segment descriptor defines data, stack, and code segments and the system descriptor defines information about the system's tables, tasks, and gates.

Segment Descriptors.   Figure 14–21 shows the segment descriptor. This descriptor fits the general form as dictated in Figure 14–20, but the access rights bits are defined to indicate how the data, stack, or code segment described by the descriptor functions. Bit position 4 of the access rights byte determines if the descriptor is a data or code segment descriptor (S = 1) or a system segment descriptor (S = 0).

FIGURE 14–21   The format of the 80386 segment descriptor.

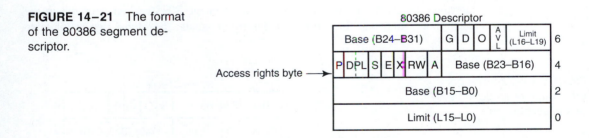

Access rights byte ⟶

[1]Windows is a tradmark of Microsoft Corporation.
[2]OS/2 is a trademark of International Business Machines Incorporated.

Following is a description of the access rights bits and their function in the segment descriptor:

1. P—Present: is a logic 1 to indicate that the segment is present. If P = 0 and the segment is accessed through the descriptor, a type 11 interrupt occurs. This interrupt indicates that a segment was accessed that is not present in the system.

2. DPL—Descriptor Privilege Level: sets the privilege level of the descriptor where 00 has the highest privilege and 11 has the lowest. This is used to protect access to segments. If a segment is accessed with a privilege level that is lower (higher in number) than the DPL, a privilege violation interrupt occurs. Privilege levels are used in multiuser systems to prevent access to an area of the system memory.

3. S—Segment: indicates a data or code segment descriptor (S = 1) or a system segment descriptor (S = 0).

4. E—Executable: selects a data (stack) segment (E = 0) or a code segment (E = 1). E also defines the function of the next two bits (X and RW).

5. X—if E = 0 then X indicates the direction of expansion for the data segment. If X = 0 the segment expands upward as in a data segment and if X = 1, the segment expands downward as in a stack segment. If E = 1, then X indicates if the privilege level of the code segment is ignored (X = 0) or observed (X = 1).

6. RW—Read/Write: if E = 0 then RW indicates that the data segment may be written (RW = 1) or not written (RW = 0). If E = 1 then RW indicates that the code segment may be read (RW = 1) or not read (RW = 0).

7. A—Accessed: this bit is set each time that the microprocessor accesses the segment. It is sometimes used by the operating system to keep track of which segments have been accessed.

System Descriptor.   The system descriptor is illustrated in Figure 14–22. There are 16 possible system descriptor types (see Table 14–4 for the different descriptor types), but not all are used in the 80386 microprocessor. Some of these types are defined for the 80286 so the 80286 software is compatible with the 80386. Some of the types are new and unique to the 80386. Some have yet to be defined and are reserved for future Intel products.

Descriptor Tables

The descriptor tables define all the segments used in the 80386 when operated in the protected mode. There are three types of descriptor tables: the global descriptor table

FIGURE 14–22 The general format of an 80386 system descriptor.

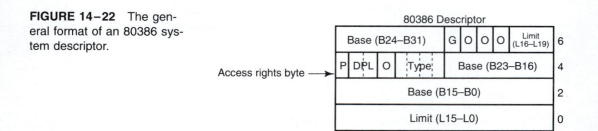

TABLE 14-4 80386 system descriptor types

Type	Description
0000	Invalid
0001	Available 80286 TSS
0010	LDT
0011	Busy 80286 TSS
0100	80286 call gate
0101	Task gate (80286 or 80386)
0110	80286 interrupt gate
0111	80286 trap gate
1000	Invalid
1001	Available 80386 TSS
1010	Reserved for future Intel products
1011	Busy 80386 TSS
1100	80386 call gate
1101	Reserved for future Intel products
1110	80386 interrupt gate
1111	80386 trap gate

(GDT), the local descriptor table (LDT), and the interrupt descriptor table (IDT). The registers used by the 80386 to address these three tables are called the global descriptor table register (GDTR), the local descriptor table register (LDTR), and the interrupt descriptor table register (IDTR). These registers are loaded respectively with the LGDT, LLDT, and LIDT instructions.

The **descriptor table** is a variable-length array of data with each entry holding an 8-byte-long descriptor. The local and global descriptor tables hold 8,192 entries each and the interrupt descriptor table holds 256 entries. A descriptor is indexed from either the local or global descriptor table by the selector that appears in a segment register. Figure 14-23 shows a segment register and the selector that it holds in the protected mode. The leftmost 13 bits index a descriptor, the TI bit selects either the local (TI = 1) or global (TI = 0) descriptor table, and the RPL bits indicate the requested privilege level.

Whenever a new selector is placed into one of the segment registers, the 80386 accesses one of the descriptor tables and automatically loads the descriptor into the invisible cache portion of the segment register. As long as the selector remains the same in the segment register, no additional accesses are required to the descriptor table. The operation of fetching a new descriptor from the descriptor table is program invisible

FIGURE 14-23 Any segment register showing the selector, TI bit, and requested privilege level (RPL) bits.

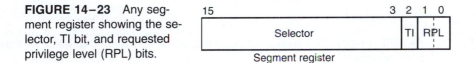

because the microprocessor automatically accomplishes this each time that the segment register contents are changed in the protected mode.

Figure 14–24 shows how a sample global descriptor table (GDT), which is stored at memory address 00010000H, is accessed through the segment register and its selector. This table contains four entries. The first is a null (0) descriptor. Descriptor 0 must always be a null descriptor. The other entries address various segments in the 80386 protected mode memory system. In this illustration, the data segment register contains a 0008H. This means that the selector is indexing descriptor location 1 in the global descriptor table (TI = 0), with a requested privilege level of 00. Descriptor 1 is located 8 bytes above the base descriptor table address at location 00010008H. The descriptor located in this memory location accesses a base address of 00200000H and a limit of 100H. This means that this descriptor addresses memory locations 00200000H–00200100H. Because this is the DS (data segment) register, this means that the data segment is located at these locations in the memory system. If data are accessed outside of these boundaries, an interrupt occurs.

The local descriptor table (LDT) is accessed in the same manner as the global descriptor table (GDT). The only difference in access is the TI bit is cleared for a global access and set for a local access. Another difference exists if the local and global descriptor table registers are examined. The global descriptor table register (GDTR) contains the base address of the global descriptor table and the limit. The local descriptor table register (LDTR) only contains a selector and is 16 bits wide. The contents of the LDTR addresses

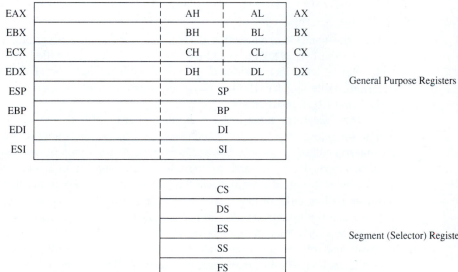

FIGURE 14–24 The data segment used to hold a selector that addresses global descriptor entry 1.

a type 0010 system descriptor that contains the base address and limit of the LDT. This scheme allows one global table for all tasks, but many local tables, one or more for each task, if necessary. Global descriptors describe memory for the system, while local descriptors describe memory for applications or tasks.

The interrupt descriptor table (IDT) is addressed as is the GDT by storing the base address and limit in the interrupt descriptor table register (IDTR). The main difference between the GDT and IDT is that the IDT contains only interrupt gates rather than segment and system descriptors as do the GDT and LDT.

Figure 14–25 shows the gate descriptor, a special form of the system descriptor described earlier. (Refer back to Table 14–4 for the different gate descriptor types.) Notice that the gate descriptor contains a 32-bit offset address, a word count, and a selector. The 32-bit offset address points to the location of the interrupt service procedure or other procedure. The word count indicates how many words are transferred from the caller's stack to the stack of the procedure accessed by a call gate. The word count field is not used with an interrupt gate. The selector is used to indicate the location of the task state segment (TSS) in the GDT or LDT if it is a local procedure.

When a gate is accessed, the contents of the selector are loaded into the task register (TR). The acceptance of the gate depends on the privilege and priority levels. A return instruction (RET) ends a call gate procedure and a return from interrupt instruction (IRET) ends an interrupt gate procedure. Tasks are usually accessed with a CALL or an INT instruction.

The difference between real mode interrupts and protected mode interrupts is that the interrupt vector table is an IDT in the protected mode. The IDT still contains up to 256 interrupt levels, but each level is accessed through an interrupt gate instead of an interrupt vector. Thus, interrupt type number 2 is located at IDT descriptor number 2 at 16 locations above the base address of the IDT. This also means that the first 1K byte of memory no longer must contain interrupt vectors as in the real mode. The IDT can be located at any location in the memory system.

The Task State Segment (TSS)

The task state segment (TSS) descriptor contains information about the location, size, and privilege level of the task state segment, just as any other descriptor. The difference is that the TSS described by the TSS descriptor does not contain data or code. It contains the state of the task and linkage so tasks can be nested, that is, one task can call a second which can call a third and so forth. The TSS descriptor is addressed by the task register (TR). The contents of the TR are changed by the LTR instruction or whenever the protected mode program executes a far JMP or CALL instruction. The LTR instruction is used to initially

FIGURE 14–25 The gate descriptor for the 80386 microprocessor.

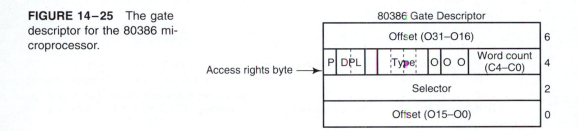

access a task during system initialization. After initialization, the CALL or JUMP instructions normally switch tasks. In most cases we use the CALL instructions to initiate a new task.

The TSS is illustrated in Figure 14–26. As can be seen, the TSS is quite a formidable section of memory containing many different types of information. The first word of the TSS is labeled back-link. This is the selector that is used on a return (RET or IRET) to link back to the prior TSS by loading the back-link selector into the TR. The following word must contain a 0. The second through the seventh double words contain the ESP and ESS values for privilege levels 0–2. These are required in case the current task is interrupted so these privilege level (PL) stacks can be addressed. The eighth word (offset 1CH) contains the contents of CR3 that stores the base address of the prior state's page directory register. This must be restored if paging is in effect. The contents of the next 17 double words are loaded into the registers indicated. Whenever a task is accessed, the entire state of the machine is stored in these memory locations and then reloaded from the same locations in the new TSS. The last word (offset 66H) contains the I/O permission bit map base address.

The I/O permission bit map allows the TSS to block I/O operations to inhibit I/O port addresses via an I/O permission denial interrupt. The permission denial interrupt is type number 13, the general protection fault interrupt. The I/O permission bit map base address is the offset address from the start of the TSS. This allows the same permission map to be used by many TSSs.

Each I/O permission bit map is 64K bits (8K bytes) in length beginning at the offset address indicated by the I/O permission bit map base address. The first byte of the I/O permission bit map contains I/O permission for I/O ports 0000H–0007H. The rightmost bit contains permission for port number 0000H and the leftmost for port number 0007H. This sequence continues for the very last port address (FFFFH) stored in the leftmost bit of the last byte of the I/O permission bit map. A logic 0 placed in an I/O permission bit map bit enables the I/O port address, while a logic 1 inhibits or blocks the I/O port address.

In review of the operation of a task switch, which requires only 17 μs to execute, we list the following steps:

1. The gate contains the address of the procedure or location jumped to by the task switch. It also contains the selector number of the TSS descriptor and the number of words transferred from the caller to the user stack area for parameter passing.
2. The selector is loaded into TR from the gate. (This step is accomplished by a CALL or JMP that refers to a valid TSS descriptor.)
3. The TR selects the TSS.
4. The current state is saved in the current TSS and the new TSS is accessed with the state of the new task (all the registers) loaded into the microprocessor. The current state is saved at the TSS selector currently found in the TR. Once the current state is saved, a new value (by the JMP or CALL) for the TSS selector is loaded into TR and the new state is loaded from the new TSS.

The return from a task is accomplished by the following steps:

1. The current state of the microprocessor is saved in the current TSS.
2. The back-link selector is loaded to the TR to access the prior TSS so the prior state of the machine can be returned to and be restored to the microprocessor. The return for a called TSS is accomplished by the IRET instruction.

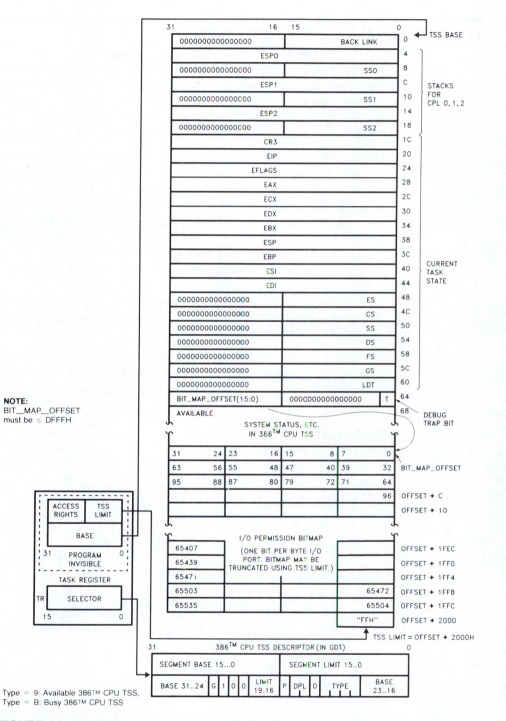

FIGURE 14-26 The task state segment (TSS) descriptor. (Courtesy of Intel Corporation)

14–5   MOVING TO PROTECTED MODE

In order to change the operation of the 80386 from the real mode to the protected mode, several steps must be followed. Real mode operation is accessed after a hardware reset or by changing the PE bit to a logic 0 in CR0. Protected mode is accessed by placing a logic 1 into the PE bit of CR0, but before this is done some other things must be initialized. The following steps accomplish the switch from the real mode to the protected mode:

1. Initialize the interrupt descriptor table so it contains valid interrupt gates for at least the first 32 interrupt type numbers. The IDT may contain up to 256, eight-byte interrupt gates defining all 256 interrupt types, and often does.
2. Initialize the global descriptor table (GDT) so it contains a null descriptor at descriptor 0, and valid descriptors for at least a one code, one stack, and one data segment.
3. Switch to protected mode by setting the PE bit in CR0.
4. Perform an intrasegment (near) JMP to flush the internal instruction queue and load the TR with the base TSS descriptor.
5. Load all the data selectors (segment registers) with their initial selector values.
6. The 80386 is now operating in the protected mode using the segment descriptors that are defined in GDT and IDT.

Figure 14–27 shows the protected system memory map set up using steps 1–5. The software for this task is listed in Example 14–3. This system contains one data segment descriptor and one code segment descriptor with each segment set to 4G bytes in length.

FIGURE 14–27 The memory map for Example 14–3.

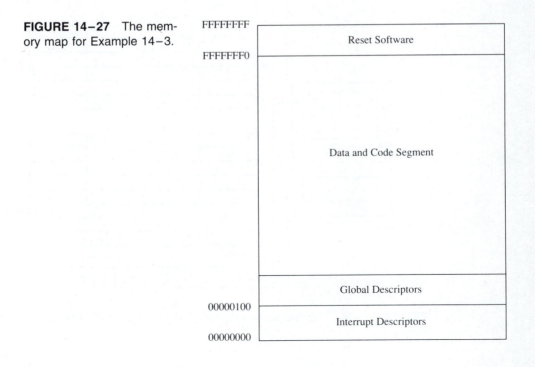

This is the simplest protected mode system possible loading all the segment registers, except code, with the same data segment descriptor from the GDT. The privilege level is initialized to 00, the highest level. This system is most often used where one user has access to the microprocessor and requires the entire memory space.

EXAMPLE 14-3

```
                              .386p
                              ;This software causes the 80386 to enter the protected mode.
                              ;It does not illustrate the interrupt descriptors or any
                              ;software that will be executed in the protected mode.

0000                          DATA    SEGMENT AT 0000H    ;segment address = 0000H

0000                                  ORG   0000H

                              ;first 32 interrupt vectors placed here

                                      ORG   0100H

                              ;Global Descriptor Table

0100 0000000000000000         DES0    DQ    0                    ;null descriptor

                              ;Code Segment Descriptor

0108 FFFF                     DES1    DW    0FFFFH               ;limit 4 G
010A 0000                             DW    0                    ;base address = 00000000H
010C 00                               DB    0
010D 9E                               DB    9EH                  ;code segment
010E 8F                               DB    8FH                  ;G = 1
010F 00                               DB    0

                              ;Data Segment Descriptor

0110 FFFF                     DES2    DW    0FFFFH               ;limit 4 G
0112 0000                             DW    0                    ;base address = 00000000H
0114 00                               DB    0
0115 92                               DB    92H                  ;data segment
0116 8F                               DB    8FH                  ;G = 1
0117 00                               DB    0

                              ;IDT table data

0118 00FF                     IDT     DW    0FFH                 ;set limit to FFH
011A 00000000                         DD    0                    ;base address 0H

                              ;GDT table data

011E 0017                     GDT     DW    17H                  ;set limit to 17H
0120 00000100                         DD    100H                 ;base address 100H

0124                          DATA    ENDS

0000                          CODE    SEGMENT USE16

                                      ASSUME CS:CODE,DS:DATA

0000 B8 ---- R                START:  MOV   AX,DATA              ;load DS
0003 8E D8                             MOV   DS,AX
```

```
0005 67| 0F 01 1D 00000118 R          LIDT FWORD PTR IDT ;load IDTR
000D 67| 0F 01 15 0000011E R          LGDT FWORD PTR GDT ;load GDTR

0015 0F 20 C0                         MOV   EAX,CR0        ;set PE
0018 0C 01                            OR    AL,1
001A 0F 22 C0                         MOV   CR0,EAX

001D EB 01 90                         JMP   START1         ;near jump

0020                        START1:
0020 B8 0010                          MOV   AX,10H         ;selector 2
0023 8E D8                            MOV   DS,AX
0025 8E C0                            MOV   ES,AX
0027 8E D0                            MOV   SS,AX
0029 8E E8                            MOV   GS,AX
002B 8E E0                            MOV   FS,AX
002D 66| BC FFFFFFFF                  MOV   ESP,0FFFFFFFFH

                     ;at this point we are in the protected mode


0033                        CODE   ENDS

                            END    START
```

In more complex systems, the steps required to initialize the system in the protected mode are more involved. For complex systems that are often multiuser systems, the registers are loaded using the task state segment (TSS). The steps required to place the 80386 into protected mode operation for a more complex system using a task switch follow:

1. Initialize the interrupt descriptor table so it refers to valid interrupt descriptors with at least 32 descriptors in the IDT.
2. Initialize the global descriptor table so it contains at least two task state segment (TSS) descriptors and the initial code and data segments required for the initial task.
3. Initialize the task register (TR) so it points to a valid TSS because when the initial task switch occurs and accesses the new TSS, the current registers are stored in the initial TSS.
4. Switch to protected mode using an intrasegment (near) jump to flush the internal instruction queue. Load TR with the current TSS selector.
5. Load the TR with a far jump instruction to access the new TSS and save the current state.
6. The 80386 is now operating in the protected mode under control of the first task.

Example 14–4 illustrates the software required to initialize the system and switch to protected mode using a task switch. The initial system task operates at the highest level of protection (00) and controls the entire operating environment for the 80386. In many cases, it is used to boot (load) software that allows many users to access the system in a multiuser environment.

EXAMPLE 14–4 (page 1 of 5)

```
0008                        DESC    STRUC                       ;define descriptor structure

0000 0000                   LIMIT_L DW       0
0002 0000                   BASE_L  DW       0
0004 00                     BASE_M  DB       0
```

EXAMPLE 14–4 (page 2 of 5)

```
0005 00                    ACCESS   DB      0
0006 00                    LIMIT_H  DB      0
0007 00                    BASE_H   DB      0

                           DESC     ENDS

0068                       TSS      STRUC                    ;define TSS structure

0000 0000                  BACK_L   DW      0
0002 0000                           DW      0
0004 00000000              ESP0     DD      0
0008 0000                  SS0      DW      0
000A 0000                           DW      0
000C 00000000              ESP1     DD      0
0010 0000                  SS1      DW      0
0012 0000                           DW      0
0014 00000000              ESP2     DD      0
0018 0000                  SS2      DW      0
001A 0000                           DW      0
001C 00000000              CCR3     DD      0
0020 00000000              EIP      DD      0
0024 00000000              TFLAGS   DD      0
0028 00000000              EEAX     DD      0
002C 00000000              EECX     DD      0
0030 00000000              EEDX     DD      0
0034 00000000              EEBX     DD      0
0038 00000000              EESP     DD      0
003C 00000000              EEBP     DD      0
0040 00000000              EESI     DD      0
0044 00000000              EEDI     DD      0
0048 0020                  EES      DW      20H
004A 0000                           DW      0
004C 0018                  ECS      DW      18H
004E 0000                           DW      0
0050 0020                  ESS      DW      20H
0052 0000                           DW      0
0054 0020                  EDS      DW      20H
0056 0000                           DW      0
0058 0020                  EFS      DW      20H
005A 0000                           DW      0
005C 0020                  EGS      DW      20H
005E 0000                           DW      0
0060 0000                  ELDT     DW      0
0062 0000                           DW      0
0064 0000                           DW      0
0066 0000                  BIT_MAP  DW      0

                           TSS      ENDS

0000                       STACK    SEGMENT STACK

0000 0400 [                         DW      400H DUP (?)
          0000
                ]

0800                       STACK    ENDS

                           .386P
0000                       CODE     SEGMENT USE16
                           ASSUME   CS:CODE,SS:STACK
```

EXAMPLE 14–4 (page 3 of 5)

```
0000 0000  0000 00000000              TSS1   TSS  <>                 ;task state segment 1
           0000 0000 00000000
           0000 0000 00000000
           0000 0000 00000000
           00000000 00000000
           00000000 00000000
           00000000 00000000
           00000000 00000000
           00000000 00000000
           0020 0000 0018
           0000 0020 0000
           0020 0000 0020
           0000 0020 0000
           0000 0000 0000
           0000

0068 0000 0000 00000000              TSS2   TSS  <>                 ;task state segment 2
           0000 0000 00000000
           0000 0000 00000000
           0000 0000 00000000
           00000000 00000000
           00000000 00000000
           00000000 00000000
           00000000 00000000
           00000000 00000000
           0020 0000 0018
           0000 0020 0000
           0020 0000 0020
           0000 0020 0000
           0000 0000 0000
           0000

00D0 0800 [              IDT     DB      8*256 DUP (?)             ;interrupt descriptor table
         00
             ]

08D0 0000 0000 00 00   GDT     DESC    <>                       ;null descriptor
     00 00
08D8 0000 0028 00 85   TGI     DESC    <0,28H,0,85H,0,0>        ;task gate 1
     00 00
08E0 0000 0030 00 85   TG2     DESC    <0,30H,0,85H,0,0>        ;task gate 2
     00 00
08E8 FFFF 0000 00 9A   CS      DESC    <-1,0,0,9AH,0CFH,0>      ;code segment (4G)
     CF 00
08F0 FFFF 0000 00 92   DS1     DESC    <-1,0,0,92H,0CFH,0>      ;data segment (4G)
     CF 00
08F8 FFFF 0000 00 89   TSS1    DESC    <-1,0,0,89H,0CFH,0>      ;TSS1 available
     CF 00
0900 FFFF 0000 00 89   TSS2    DESC    <-1,0,0,89H,0CFH,0>      ;TSS2 available
     CF 00
0908 2000 [            IOBP    DB      2000H DUP (0)            ;enable all I/O
         00
             ]
2908 FF                        DB      0FFH                     ;end of I/O bit map

0006                   GDT_A   STRUC

0000 0000              A       DW      0
0002 0000              B       DW      0
```

EXAMPLE 14–4 (page 4 of 5)

```
0004 0000                    CC      DW      0

                             GDT_A   ENDS

2909 0000 0000 0000   GDT_A  GDT_A   <>                          ;address of GDT

290F                         MAIN    PROC    FAR

290F 8C C8                   MOV     AX,CS
2911 8E D8                   MOV     DS,AX
2913 E8 0098                 CALL    DO_IDT                      ;set up IDT
2916 B8 0908 R               MOV     AX,OFFSET IOBP              ;set up I/0 bit maps
2919 2E: A3 0066 R           MOV     TSS1.BIT_MAP,AX
291D 2E: A3 00CE R           MOV     TSS2.BIT_MAP,AX

2921 66| 33 C0               XOR     EAX,EAX                     ;get linear start address
2924 8C C8                   MOV     AX,CS
2926 66| C1 E0 04            SHL     EAX,4
292A 66| 33 DB               XOR     EBX,EBX
292D BB 29AE R               MOV     BX,OFFSET TASK1
2930 66| 50                  PUSH    EAX
2932 66| 03 C3               ADD     EAX,EBX
2935 66| 2E: A3 0088 R       MOV     TSS2.EIP,EAX                ;setup TASK1 as start address
293A 66| 58                  POP     EAX
293C 66| 50                  PUSH    EAX
293E BB 0000 R               MOV     BX,OFFSET TSS1              ;load TSS1 address
2941 66| 03 C3               ADD     EAX,EBX
2944 2E: A3 0002 R           MOV     TSS1.BASE_L,AX
2948 66| C1 E8 10            SHR     EAX,16
294C 2E: A2 0004 R           MOV     TSS1.BASE_M,AL
2950 2E: 88 26 0007 R        MOV     TSS1.BASE_H,AH
2955 66| 58                  POP     EAX
2957 66| 50                  PUSH    EAX
2959 BB 0068 R               MOV     BX,OFFSET TSS2              ;load TSS2 address
295C 66| 03 C3               ADD     EAX,EBX
295F 2E: A3 006A R           MOV     TSS2.BASE_L,AX
2963 66| C1 E8 10            SHR     EAX,16
2967 2E: A2 006C R           MOV     TSS2.BASE_M,AL
296B 2E: 88 26 006F R        MOV     TSS2.BASE_H,AH

2970 66| 58                  POP     EAX
2972 B8 FFFF                 MOV     AX,-1
2975 2E: A3 290B R           MOV     GDT_AD.B,AX
2979 66| 58                  POP     EAX
297B 66| C1 E0 04            SHL     EAX,4
297F BB 08D0 R               MOV     BX,OFFSET GDT
2982 66| 03 C3               ADD     EAX,EBX
2985 2E: A3 2909 R           MOV     GDT_AD.A,AX
2989 66| C1 E8 10            SHR     EAX,16
298D 2E: A3 290D R           MOV     GDT_AD.CC,AX               ;set up GDT address
2991 2E: 0F 01 16 2909 R     LGDT    GDT_AD                     ;load GDT register
2997 0F 20 C0                MOV     EAX,CR0                    ;set PM
299A 66| 83 C8 01            OR      EAX,1
299E 0F 22 C0                MOV     CR0,EAX                    ;protected mode
29A1 EB 00                   JMP     NEXT

29A3                  NEXT:

29A3 B8 0008                 MOV     AX,8
```

EXAMPLE 14–4 (page 5 of 5)

```
29A6 0F 00 D8              LTR    AX                      ;address TSS1
29A9 B8 0010              MOV    AX,10H
29AC FF E0               JMP    AX                       ;jump to TSS2

29AE             MAIN    ENDP

29AE             DO_IDT  PROC    NEAR

                 ;set up interrupts (now shown here)

29AE             DO_IDT  ENDP

29AE             TASK1:                                   ;main program starts here

29AE             CODE    ENDS
                 END     MAIN
```

14–6   VIRTUAL 8086 MODE

One special mode of operation not discussed thus far is the virtual 8086 mode. This special mode is designed so multiple 8086 real mode software applications can execute at

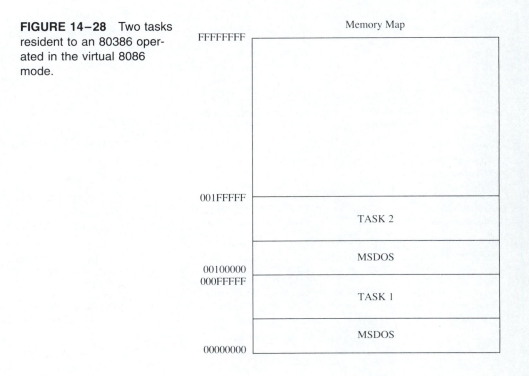

FIGURE 14–28 Two tasks resident to an 80386 operated in the virtual 8086 mode.

one time. Figure 14–28 illustrates two 8086 applications mapped into the 80386 using the virtual mode. If the operating system allows multiple applications to execute, it is usually done through a technique called *time-slicing*. The operating system allocates a set amount of time to each task. For example, if three tasks are executing, the operating system can allocate 1 ms to each task. This means that after each millisecond, a task switch occurs to the next task. In this manner all tasks receive a portion of the 80386 execution time, resulting in a system that appears to execute more than one task at a time. The task times can be adjusted to give any task any percentage of the microprocessor execution time.

A system that can use this technique is a print spooler. The print spooler can function in one DOS partition and be accessed 10 percent of the time. This allows the system to print using the print spooler, but it doesn't detract from the system because it only uses 10 percent of the system time.

The main difference between 80386 protected mode operation and the virtual 8086 mode is the way the segment registers are interpreted by the microprocessor. In the virtual 8086 mode, the segment registers are used as they are in the real mode. That is as a segment address and offset address capable of accessing a 1M byte memory space from location 00000H–FFFFFH. Access to many virtual 8086 mode systems is made possible by the paging unit that is explained in the next section. Through paging, the program still accesses memory below the 1M byte boundary, yet the microprocessor can access a physical memory space at any location in the 4G byte range of the memory system.

Virtual 8086 mode is entered by changing the VM bit in the EFLAG register to a logic 1. This mode is entered via an IRET instruction if the privilege level is 00. This bit cannot be set in any other manner. An attempt to access a memory address above the 1M byte boundary will cause a type-13 interrupt to occur.

The virtual 8086 mode could be used to share one microprocessor with many users by partitioning the memory so each user has its own DOS partition. User 1 could be allocated memory locations 00100000H–001FFFFFH, user 2 locations 0020000H–002FFFFFH, and so forth. The system software located at memory locations 00000000H–000FFFFFH could then share the microprocessor between users by switching from one to another to execute software. In this manner, one microprocessor is shared by many users.

14-7   THE MEMORY PAGING MECHANISM

The paging mechanism allows any linear (logical) address, as it is generated by a program, to be placed into any physical memory page, as generated by the paging mechanism. A **linear memory page** is a page that is addressed with a selector and an offset in either the real or protected mode. A **physical memory page** is a page that exists at some actual physical memory location. For example, linear memory location 20000H could be mapped into physical memory location 30000H, or any other location, with the paging unit. This means that an instruction that accesses location 20000H actually accesses location 30000H.

Each 80386 memory page is 4K bytes in length. Paging allows the system software to be placed at any physical address with the paging mechanism. Three components are used in page address translation: the page directory, the page table, and the actual physical memory page.

The Page Directory

The page directory contains the location of up to 1,024 page translation tables. Each page translation table translates a logic address into a physical address. The page directory is stored in the memory and accessed by the page descriptor address register (CR3). Control register CR3 holds the base address of the page directory, which starts at any 4K byte boundary in the memory system. The MOV CR3,reg instruction is used to initialize CR3 for paging. In a virtual 8086 mode system, each 8086 DOS partition would have its own page directory.

The page directory contains up to 1,024 entries that are each 4 bytes in length. The page directory itself occupies one 4K byte memory page. Each entry in the page directory (refer to Figure 14–29) translates the leftmost 10 bits of the memory address. This 10-bit portion of the linear address is used to locate different page tables for different page table entries. The page table address (A32–A12), stored in a page directory entry, accesses a 4K byte long page translation table. To completely translate any linear address into any physical address requires 1,024 page tables that are each 4K bytes in length plus the page table directory, which is 4K bytes in length. This translation scheme requires up to 4M plus 4K bytes of memory for a full address translation. Only the largest operating systems support this size address translation. Many commonly found operating systems translate only the first 16M or 32M bytes of the memory system if paging is enabled. This includes programs such as Windows 3.1.[3]

The page table directory entry control bits, as illustrated in Figure 14–29, perform the following functions:

1. D—Dirty: is undefined for page table directory entries by the 80386 microprocessor and is provided for use by the operating system.
2. A—Accessed: is set to a logic 1 whenever the microprocessor accesses the page directory entry.
3. R/W and U/S—Read/Write and User/Supervisor: are both used in the protection scheme as listed in Table 14–5. Both bits combine to develop paging priority level protection for level 3, the lowest user level.
4. P—Present: if a logic 1, indicates that the entry can be used in address translation. If P = 0, the entry cannot be used for translation. A not present entry can be used for other purposes, such as indicating that the page is currently stored on the disk. If P = 0, the remaining bits of the entry can be used to indicate the location of the page on the disk memory system.

---

[3]Windows is a program produced by Microsoft Corporation.

FIGURE 14–29 The page table directory entry.

| | 31 | 12 11 10 9 8 7 6 5 4 3 2 1 0 |

| Page Table Address (A31—A12) | Reserved 0 0 D A 0 0 U/S R/W P |

TABLE 14–5 Protection for level 3 using U/S and R/W

U/S	R/W	Access Level 3
0	0	None
0	1	None
1	0	Read-only
1	1	Read/write

Page Table

The page table contains 1,024 physical page addresses accessed to translate a linear address into a physical address. The format for the page table entry is exactly the same as for the page directory entry (refer to Figure 14–29). The main difference is that the page directory entry contains the physical address of a page table, while the page table entry contains the physical address of a 4K byte physical page of memory. The other difference is the D (dirty bit), which has no function in the page directory entry, but indicates that a page has been written to in a page table entry.

Figure 14–30 illustrates the paging mechanism in the 80386 microprocessor. Here, the linear address 00C03FFCH, as generated by a program, is converted to physical address XXXXX3FCH, as translated by the paging mechanism. (Note: XXXXX is any 4K byte physical page address.) The paging mechanism functions in the following manner:

1. The 4K byte long page directory is stored as the physical address located by CR3. This address is often called the *root address*. One page directory exists in a system at a time. In the 8086 virtual mode, each task has its own page directory allowing different areas of physical memory to be assigned to different 8086 virtual tasks.
2. The upper 10 bits of the linear address (bits 31–22), as determined by the descriptors described earlier in this chapter or by a real address, are applied to the paging mechanism to select an entry in the page directory. This maps the page directory entry to the leftmost 10 bits of the linear address.
3. The page table is addressed by the entry stored in the page directory. This allows up to 4K page tables in a fully populated and translated system.
4. An entry in the page table is addressed by the next 10 bits of the linear address (bits 21–12).
5. The page table entry contains the actual physical address of the 4K byte memory page.
6. The rightmost 12 bits of the linear address (bits 11–0) select a location in the memory page.

The paging mechanism allows the physical memory to be assigned to any linear address through the paging mechanism. For example, suppose that linear address 20000000H is selected by a program, but this memory location does not exist in the physical memory system. The 4K byte linear page is referenced as locations

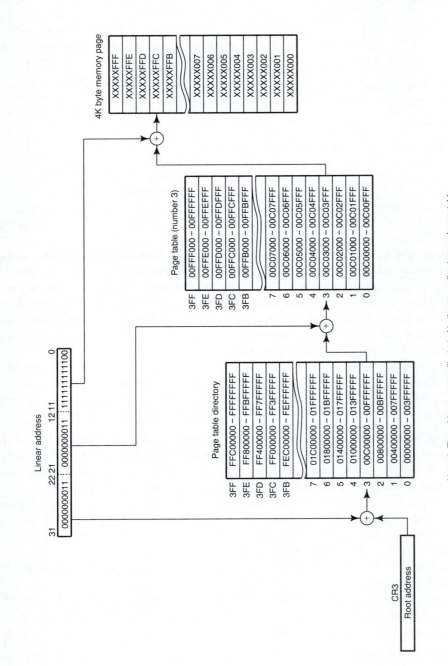

FIGURE 14–30 The translation of linear address 00C03FFC to physical memory address XXXXXFFC. The value of XXXXX is determined by the page table entry (not shown here).

20000000H–20000FFFH by the program. Because this section of physical memory does not exist, the operating system might assign an existing physical memory page such as 12000000H–12000FFFH to this linear address range.

In the address translation process, the leftmost 10 bits of the linear address select page directory entry 200H are located at offset address 800H in the page directory. This page directory entry contains the address of the page table for linear addresses 20000000H–203FFFFFH. Linear address bits (21–12) select an entry in this page table that corresponds to a 4K byte memory page. For linear addresses 2000000H–20000FFFH, the first entry (entry 0) in the page table is selected. This first entry contains the physical address of the actual memory page or 12000000H–12000FFFH in this example.

Take, for example, a typical DOS-based computer system. The memory map for the system appears in Figure 14–31. Notice from the map that there are unused areas of memory that could be paged to a different location, giving a DOS real mode application program more memory. The normal DOS memory system begins at location 00000H and extends to location 9FFFFH, which is 640K bytes of memory. Above location 9FFFFH we find sections devoted to video cards, disk cards, and the system BIOS ROM. In this

FIGURE 14–31 Memory map for an AT-style clone.

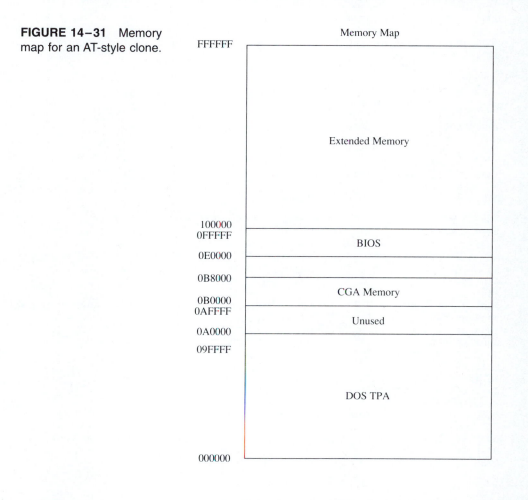

example an area of memory just above 9FFFFH is unused (A0000–AFFFFH). This section of the memory could be used by DOS so that the total applications memory area is 704K instead of 640K.

This section of memory can be used by mapping it into extended memory at locations 102000H–11FFFFH. Software to accomplish this translation and initialize the page table directory and page tables required to set up memory are illustrated in Example 14–5. Note that this procedure initializes the page table directory, a page table, and loads CR3. It does not switch to protected mode and it does enable paging. Note that paging functions in real mode memory operation.

EXAMPLE 14–5

```
                        .386P
                        ;Software that sets up a paged memory system
                        ;that accesses memory above location FFFFFH.
                        ;
                        ;Page Directory

0000                    DATA    SEGMENT

0000 = 0000             PG_DIR  EQU     $

0000 00001000 R         TAB0PT  DD      TAB0
0004 03FF [             DD      1023 DUP (?)
            00000000
                 ]

                        ;Page Table

1000 0400 [             TAB0    DD      1024 DUP (?)
            00000000
                 ]

2000                    DATA    ENDS

0000                    CODE    SEGMENT USE16

                        ASSUME  CS:CODE,DS:DATA

0000                    PAGES   PROC    FAR

0000 1E                         PUSH    DS
0001 06                         PUSH    ES
0002 FC                         CLD
0003 B8 ---- R                  MOV     AX,DATA         ;load segment registers
0006 8E D8                      MOV     DS,AX
0008 8E C0                      MOV     ES,AX
000A BF 0000 R                  MOV     DI,OFFSET PG_DIR  ;address page table
000D 66| 83 05 07               ADD     DWORD PTR [DI] ,7
0011 B9 0100                    MOV     CX,256
0014 BF 1000 R                  MOV     DI,OFFSET TAB0
0017 66| B8 00000007            MOV     EAX,7

001D                    PAGES1:

001D 66| AB                     STOSD                   ;fill page table
001F 66| 05 00001000            ADD     EAX,4096
0025 E2 F6                      LOOP    PAGES1
```

```
0027 BF 1280 R            MOV      DI,OFFSET TAB0+4*0A0H
002A 66| B8 00102007      MOV      EAX,00102007H
0030 B9 0010              MOV      CX,16

0033                PAGES2:

0033 66| AB               STOSD                        ;remap A0000H-AFFFFH
0035 66| 05 00001000      ADD      EAX,4096            ;to 102000H-11FFFFH
003B E2 F6               LOOP     PAGES2

003D 66| 33 C0            XOR      EAX,EAX
0040 8C D8               MOV      AX,DS
0042 66| C1 E0 04         SHL      EAX,4
0046 0F 22 D8             MOV      C3,EAX;address page directory

0049 07                  POP      ES
004A 1F                  POP      DS
004B CB                  RET

004C              PAGES   ENDP

004C              CODE    ENDS

                         END
```

14-8   INTRODUCTION TO THE 80486 MICROPROCESSOR

The 80486 microprocessor is a highly integrated device containing well over 1,200,000 transistors. Located within this powerful integrated circuit are a memory-management unit (MMU); a complete numeric coprocessor that is compatible with the 80387; a high-speed cache memory that contains 8K bytes of space; and a full 32-bit microprocessor that is upward compatible with the 80386 microprocessor. The 80486 is currently available as a 25 MHz, 33 MHz, and 50 MHz version. Intel has demonstrated a 100 MHz version of the 80486, but it has yet to be released. The 80486 comes as an 80486DX or an 80486SX. The only difference between these devices is that the 80486SX does not contain the numeric coprocessor, which reduces its price. The 80487SX numeric coprocessor is available as a separate component for the 80486SX microprocessor. Also available are the double-clocked versions such as the 80486DX2 (50 MHz and 66 MHz versions). The double-clocked versions operate internally at 50 MHz or 66 MHz, yet use a bus speed of 25 MHz or 33 MHz to ease requirements on the memory system. The double-clocked 50 MHz version executes software at an average speed between the 33 MHz and 50 MHz versions. The double-clocked 66 MHz version operates at a slightly better rate than the 50 MHz version. Note that no system change is usually required to upgrade to a double-clocked version in most mother boards. Also available are the Overdrive[4] versions which are extra circuits that plug into a socket next to the microprocessor to increase the performance to about that of the double-clocked version.

---

[4]Overdrive is a trademark of Intel Corporation.

The Overdrive processor is an efficient way to upgrade from an 80486SX microprocessor as it is supported by the mother board.

This section details the differences between the 80486 and 80386 microprocessors. These differences are few; the most notable differences apply to the cache memory system and parity generator.

Pinout of the 80486DX and 80486SX Microprocessors

Figure 14–32 illustrate the pinout of the 80486DX microprocessor, a 168-pin PGA. The 80486SX, also packaged in a 168-pin PGA, is not illustrated because few differences exist. Note pin B15 is NMI on the 80486DX and pin A15 is NMI on the 80486SX. The only other differences are that pin A15 is $\overline{\text{IGNNE}}$ on the 80486DX (not present on the 80486SX), pin C14 is $\overline{\text{FERR}}$ on the 80486DX, and pins B15 and C14 on the 80486SX are not connected.

When connecting the 80486 microprocessor, all VCC and VSS pins must be connected to the power supply for proper operation. The power supply must be capable of

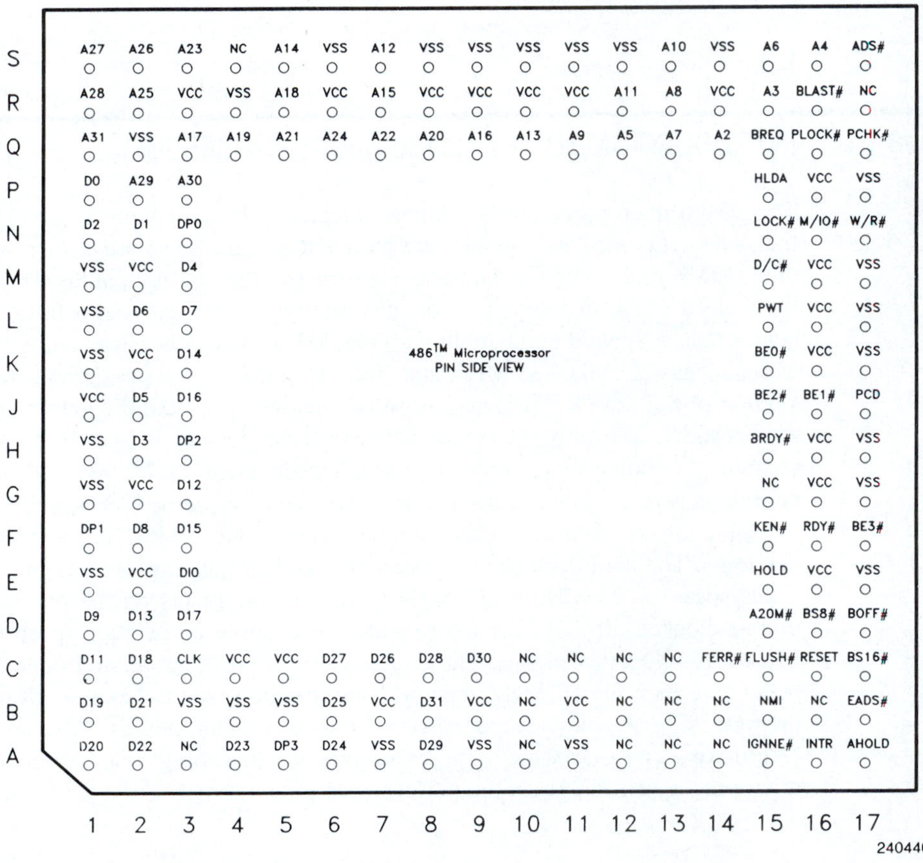

FIGURE 14–32   The pinout of the 80486. (Courtesy of Intel Corporation)

supplying 5.0 V ±10%, with up to 1.2 A of surge current for the 33 MHz version. The average supply current is 650 mA for the 33 MHz version. Logic 0 outputs allow up to 4.0 mA of current and logic 1 outputs allow up to 1.0 mA. If larger currents are required, as they often are, then the 80486 must be buffered. Figure 14–33 shows a buffered 80486DX system. In the circuit shown, only the address, data, and parity signals are buffered.

Pin Definitions.

1. A31–A2 (Address Outputs): provide the memory and I/O with the address during normal operation and during a cache line invalidation, A31–A4 are used to drive the microprocessor.
2. $\overline{A20M}$ (Address Bit 20 Mask): used to cause the 80486 to wrap its address around from location 000FFFFFH to 00000000H as does the 8086 microprocessor. This provides a memory system that functions as does the 1M byte memory in the 8086 microprocessor. Most systems do not use the address system mask because the HIMEM.SYS program cannot access the additional memory located at address 100000H–10FFEFH.
3. ADS (Address Data Strobe): becomes a logic zero to indicate that the address bus contains a valid memory address.
4. AHOLD (Address Hold Input): causes the microprocessor to place its address bus connections at their high-impedance state, with the remainder of the buses staying active. Often used by another bus master to gain access for a cache invalidation cycle.
5. $\overline{BE3}$–$\overline{BE1}$ (Byte Enable Outputs): select a bank of the memory system when information is transferred between the microprocessor and its memory and I/O space. The $\overline{BE3}$ signal enables D31–D24, $\overline{BE2}$ enables D23–D16, $\overline{BE1}$ enables D15–D8, and $\overline{BE0}$ enables D7–D0.
6. $\overline{BLAST}$ (Burst Last Output): shows that the burst bus cycle is complete on the next activation of the $\overline{BRDY}$ signal.
7. $\overline{BOFF}$ (Backoff Input): causes the microprocessor to place its buses at their high-impedance state during the next clock cycle. The microprocessor remains in the bus hold state until the $\overline{BOFF}$ pin is placed at a logic 1 level.
8. $\overline{BRDY}$ (Burst Ready Input): used to signal the microprocessor that a burst cycle is complete.
9. BREQ (Bus Request Output): indicates that the 80486 has generated an internal bus request.
10. $\overline{BS8}$ (Bus Size 8 Input): causes the 80486 to structure itself with an 8-bit data bus to access bytewide memory and I/O components.
11. $\overline{BS16}$ (Bus Size 16 Input): causes the 80486 to structure itself with a 16-bit data bus to access wordwide memory and I/O components.
12. CLK (Clock Input): provides the 80486 with its basic timing signal. The clock input is a TTL compatible input that is 25 MHz to operate the 80486 at 25 MHz.
13. D31–D0 (Data Bus): transfers data between the microprocessor and its memory and I/O system. Data bus connections D7–D0 are also used to accept the interrupt vector type number during an interrupt acknowledge cycle.
14. $D/\overline{C}$ (Data/Control): indicates whether the current operation is a data transfer or control cycle. Refer to Table 14–6 for the function of $D/\overline{C}$, $M/\overline{IO}$, and $W/\overline{R}$.

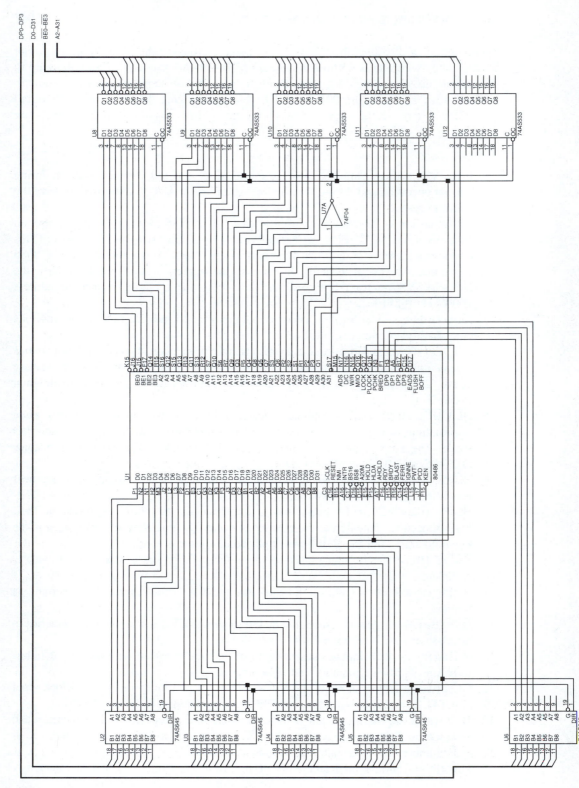

FIGURE 14–33 An 80486 microprocessor showing the buffered address, data, and parity buses.

TABLE 14–6 Bus cycle identification

M/$\overline{\text{IO}}$	D/$\overline{\text{C}}$	W/$\overline{\text{R}}$	Bus Cycle Type
0	0	0	Interrupt acknowledge
0	0	1	Halt/special
0	1	0	I/O read
0	1	1	I/O write
1	0	0	Code cycle (opcode fetch)
1	0	1	Reserved
1	1	0	Memory read
1	1	1	Memory write

15. DP3–DP0 (Data Parity I/O): provide even parity for a write operation and check parity for a read operation. If a parity error is detected during a read, the $\overline{\text{PCHK}}$ output becomes a logic 0 to indicate a parity error. If parity is not used in a system, these lines must be pulled-high to +5.0 V.
16. $\overline{\text{EADS}}$ (External Address Strobe Input): used with AHOLD to signal that an external address is used to perform a cache invalidation cycle.
17. $\overline{\text{FERR}}$ (Floating-Point Error Output): indicates the floating-point coprocessor has detected an error condition. Used to maintain compatibility with DOS software.
18. $\overline{\text{FLUSH}}$ (Cache Flush Input): forces the microprocessor to erase the contents of its 8K byte internal cache.
19. HLDA (Hold Acknowledge Output): indicates that the HOLD input is active and that the microprocessor has placed its buses at their high-impedance state.
20. HOLD (Hold Input): used to request a DMA action. It causes the address, data, and control buses to be placed at their high-impedance state and also, once recognized, causes HLDA to become a logic 0.
21. $\overline{\text{IGNNE}}$ (Ignore Numeric Error Input): causes the coprocessor to ignore floating-point errors and to continue processing data. This signal does not affect the state of the $\overline{\text{FERR}}$ pin.
22. INTR (Interrupt Request Input): requests a maskable interrupt as it does on all other family members.
23. $\overline{\text{KEN}}$ (Cache Enable Input): causes the current bus to be stored in the internal cache.
24. $\overline{\text{LOCK}}$ (Lock Output): becomes a logic 0 for any instruction that is prefixed with the lock prefix.
25. M/$\overline{\text{IO}}$ (Memory/$\overline{\text{IO}}$): defines whether the address bus contains a memory address or an I/O port number. It is also combined with the W/$\overline{\text{R}}$ signal to generate memory and I/O read and write control signals.
26. NMI (Non-Maskable Interrupt Input): requests a type 2 interrupt.
27. PCD (page Cache Disable Output): reflects the state of the PCD attribute bit in the page table entry or the page directory entry.
28. $\overline{\text{PCHK}}$ (Parity Check Output): indicates that a parity error was detected during a read operation on the DP3–DP0 pins.

29. $\overline{\text{PLOCK}}$ (Pseudo-Lock Output): indicates that the current operation requires more than one bus cycle to perform. This signal becomes a logic 0 for arithmetic coprocessor operations that access 64- or 80-bit memory data.

30. PWT (page Write Through Output): indicates the state of the PWT attribute bit in the page table entry or the page directory entry.

31. $\overline{\text{RDY}}$ (Ready Input): indicates that a nonburst bus cycle is complete. The $\overline{\text{RDY}}$ signal must be returned or the microprocessor places wait states into its timing until $\overline{\text{RDY}}$ is asserted.

32. RESET (Reset Input): initializes the 80486 as it does in other family members. Table 14–7 shows the effect of the RESET input on the 80486 microprocessor.

33. W/$\overline{\text{R}}$ (Write/$\overline{\text{Read}}$): signals that the current bus cycle is either a read or a write.

Basic 80486 Architecture

The architecture of the 80486DX is almost identical to the 80386 plus the 80387 math coprocessor and an internal 8K byte cache. The 80486SX is almost identical to an 80386 with an 8K byte cache. Figure 14–34 illustrates the basic internal structure of the 80486 microprocessor. If this is compared to the architecture of the 80386, no differences are observed. The most prominent difference between the 80386 and the 80486 is that almost half of the 80486 instructions execute in 1 clocking period instead of the 2 clocking periods for the 80386 to execute like instructions.

As with the 80386, the 80486 contains eight general-purpose 32-bit registers: EAX, EBX, ECX, EDX, EBP, EDI, ESI, and ESP. These registers may be used as 8-, 16-, or 32-bit data registers or to address a location in the memory system. The 16-bit registers

TABLE 14–7 The effect of the RESET signal

Register	Initial Value with Self-Test	Initial Value without Self-Test
EAX	00000000H	?
EDX	00000400H+ID[1]	00000400H+ID
EFLAGS	00000002H	00000002H
EIP	0000FFF0H	0000FFF0H
ES	0000H	0000H
CS	F000H	F000H
DS	0000H	0000H
SS	0000H	0000H
FS	0000H	0000H
GS	0000H	0000H
IDTR	Base = 0, limit 3FFH	Base = 0, limit = 3FFH
CR0	60000010H	60000010H
DR7	00000000H	00000000H

[1]Revision ID number supplied by Intel for revisions to the microprocessor.

FIGURE 14–34 The internal programming model of the 80486. (Courtesy of Intel Corporation)

General-Purpose Registers

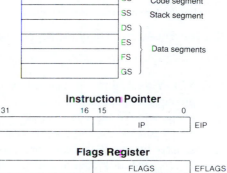

Segment Registers

CS	Code segment
SS	Stack segment
DS	
ES	Data segments
FS	
GS	

Instruction Pointer

Flags Register

are the same set as found in the 80286 and are assigned: AX, BX, CX, DX, BP, DI, SI, and SP. The 8-bit registers are: AH, AL, BH, BL, CH, CL, DH, and DL.

In addition to the general-purpose registers, the 80486 also contains the same segment registers as the 80386 which are: CS, DS, ES, SS, FS, and GS. Each are 16 bits wide as in all earlier versions of the family.

The IP (instruction pointer) addresses the program located within the 1M byte of memory in combination with CS, or as EIP (extended instruction pointer) to address a program at any location within the 4G byte memory system. In protected mode operation, the segment registers function to hold selectors as they did in the 80286 and 80386 microprocessors.

The 80486 also contains the global, local, and interrupt descriptor table registers and memory-management unit as the 80386. These registers are not illustrated in Figure 14–34, but are present as in the 80386. The function of the MMU and its paging unit is described with the 80386 earlier in this chapter.

The extended flag register (EFLAGS) is illustrated in Figure 14–35. As with other family members, the rightmost flag bits perform the same functions for compatibility. Following is a list of each flag bit with a description of its function:

1. AC (Alignment Check): new to the 80486 microprocessor, used to indicate that the microprocessor has accessed a word at an odd address or a double word stored at a non-double-word boundary. Efficient software and execution require that data are stored at word or double-word boundaries.

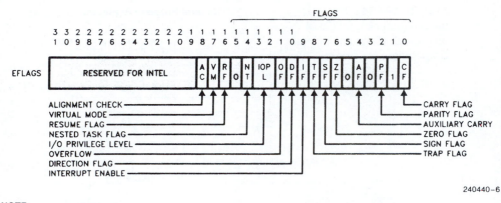

NOTE:
0 indicates Intel Reserved: do not define; see Section 2.1.6.

FIGURE 14-35   The EFLAG register of the 80486. (Courtesy of Intel Corporation)

2. VM (Virtual Mode): is entered by setting this bit while the 80486 is operated in the protected mode. This bit is always cleared by a PUSHF instruction, even if the 80486 is operating in the virtual mode.

3. RF (Resume): used in conjunction with the debug registers as defined earlier in the chapter for the 80386 microprocessor.

4. NT (Nested Task): set to indicate that the 80486 is performing a task that is nested within another task.

5. IOPL (I/O Privilege Level): indicates the current maximum privilege level assigned to the I/O system.

6. OF (Overflow): indicates the result of a signed arithmetic operation has overflowed the capacity of the destination. It is also used with the multiply instruction.

7. DF (Direction): selects auto-increment (DF = 0) or auto-decrement (DF = 1) operation for the string instructions.

8. IF (Interrupt Enable): enables the INTR pin if this bit is set.

9. TF (Trap): set to enable debugging as described by the debug registers.

10. SF (Sign): indicates that the sign of the result is set or cleared.

11. ZF (Zero): indicates that the result of an arithmetic or logic operation is zero (ZF = 1) or nonzero (ZF = 0).

12. AF (Auxiliary): used with the DAA and DAS instructions to adjust the result of a BCD addition or subtraction.

13. PF (Parity): indicates the parity of the result of an arithmetic or logic operation. If the parity is odd, PF = 0, and if the parity is even, PF = 1.

14. CF (Carry): shows if a carry has occurred after an addition or a borrow after a subtraction.

80486 Memory System

The memory system for the 80486 is identical to the 80386 microprocessor. The 80486 contains 4G bytes of memory beginning at location 00000000H and ending at location

FFFFFFFFH. The major change to the memory system is internal to the 80486 in the form of an 8K byte cache memory which speeds the execution of instructions and the acquisition of data. Another addition is the parity checker/generator built into the 80486 microprocessor.

Parity Checker/Generator. *Parity* is often used to determine if data are correctly read from a memory location. To facilitate this, Intel has incorporated an internal *parity generator/detector.* Parity is generated by the 80486 during each write cycle. Parity is generated as *even parity* and a parity bit is provided for each byte of memory. The parity check bits appear on pins DP0–DP3, which are also parity inputs as well as outputs. These are typically stored in memory during each write cycle and read from memory during each read cycle.

On a read, the microprocessor checks parity and generates a parity check error, *if it occurs,* on the $\overline{\text{PCHK}}$ pin. A parity error causes no change in processing unless the user applies the $\overline{\text{PCHK}}$ signal to an interrupt input. Interrupts are often used to signal a parity error in DOS-based computer systems. Figure 14–36 shows the organization of the 80486 memory system that includes parity storage. Note that this is the same as for the 80386, except for the parity bit storage. If parity is not used, Intel recommends that the DP0–DP3 pins are pulled-up to +5.0 V.

Cache Memory. The cache memory system caches (stores) both data used by a program and also the instructions of the program. The *cache* is organized as a four-way set associative cache with each location (line) containing 16 bytes or four double words of data. The cache operates as a *write-through* cache. Note that the cache only changes if a miss occurs. This means that data written to memory location not already cached are not written to the cache. In many cases, much of the active portion of a program is found completely inside the cache memory. This causes execution to occur at the rate of 1 clock cycle for many of the instructions that are commonly used in a program. About the only way that these efficient instructions are slowed is when the microprocessor must fill a line in the cache. Data are also stored in the cache, but they have less of an impact on the

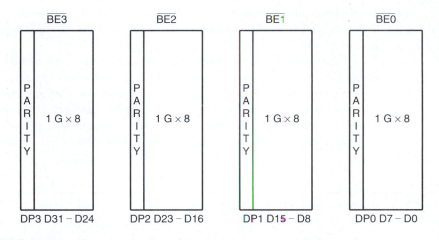

FIGURE 14–36 The organization of the 80486 memory showing parity.

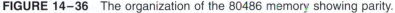

execution speed of a program because data are not referenced repeatedly as many portions of a program are.

Control register 0 (CR0) is used to control the cache with two new control bits not present in the 80386 microprocessor. (Refer to Figure 14–37 for CR0 in the 80486 microprocessor.) The CD (*cache disable*) and NW (*noncache write-through*) bits are new to the 80486 and are used to control the 8K byte cache. If the CD bit is a logic 1, all cache operations are inhibited. This setting is only used for debugging software and normally remains cleared. The NW bit is used to inhibit cache write-through operation. As with CD, cache write-through is only inhibited for testing. For normal program operation, CD = 0 and NW = 0.

Because the cache is new to the 80486 microprocessor and the cache is filled using burst cycles not present on the 80386, some detail is required to understand bus filling cycles. When a bus line is filled, the 80486 must acquire four 32-bit numbers from the memory system to fill a line in the cache. Filling is accomplished with a *burst cycle*. The burst cycle is a special memory where four 32-bit numbers are fetched from the memory system in 5 clocking periods. This assumes that the speed of the memory is sufficient and that no wait states are required. If the clock frequency of the 80486 is 33 MHz we can fill a cache line in 167 ns, which is very efficient considering a normal, nonburst 32-bit memory read operation requires 2 clocking periods.

Memory Read Timing. Figure 14–38 illustrates the read timing for the 80486 for a nonburst memory operation. Note that two clocking periods are used to transfer data. Clocking period T1 provides the memory address and control signals and clocking period T2 is where the data are transferred between the memory and the microprocessor. Note that the $\overline{\text{RDY}}$ must become a logic zero to cause data to be transferred and to terminate the bus cycle. Access time for a nonburst access is determined by taking 2 clocking periods minus the time required for the address to appear on the address bus connection minus a setup time for the data bus connections. For the 20 MHz version of the 80486, two clocking periods require 100 ns minus 28 ns for address setup time and 3 ns for data setup time. This yields a nonburst access time of 100 ns − 31 ns or 69 ns. Of course if decoder time and delay times are included, the access time allowed the memory is even less for no wait state operation. Also if a higher frequency version of the 80486 is used in a system, memory access time is still less.

Figure 14–39 illustrates the timing diagram for filling a cache line with four 32-bit numbers using a burst. Notice that the addresses (A31–A4) appear during T1 and remain constant throughout the burst cycle. Also notice that A2 and A3 change during each T2 after the first to address four consecutive 32-bit numbers in the memory system. As mentioned, cache fills using bursts require only five clocking periods (one T1 and 4 T2) to fill a cache line with four double words of data. Access time using a 20 MHz version

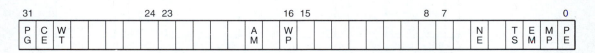

FIGURE 14–37   Control register zero (CR0) for the 80486 microprocessor.

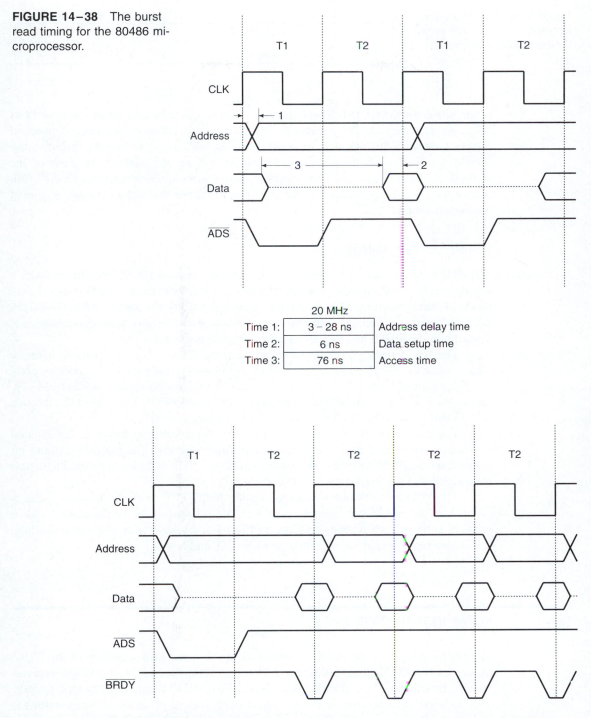

FIGURE 14-38 The burst read timing for the 80486 microprocessor.

	20 MHz	
Time 1:	3 – 28 ns	Address delay time
Time 2:	6 ns	Data setup time
Time 3:	76 ns	Access time

FIGURE 14-39 A burst cycle that reads 4 double words in 5 clocking periods in the 80486 system.

FIGURE 14–40 The page directory or page table entry for the 80486 microprocessor.

31		12	11 10 9	8	7	6	5	4	3	2	1	0
Page Table or Page frame			0S Bits	O	O	D	A	P C D	P W T	U S	R W	P

of the 80486 for the second and subsequent double words is 50 ns − 28 ns − 3 ns or 19 ns assuming no delays in the system. To use burst mode transfers, we need high-speed memory. Because DRAM memory access times at best are 55 ns, we are forced to use SRAM for burst cycle transfers. Even with SRAM we are pushing the limit of the technology for even a 20 MHz 80486 microprocessor. Note that the $\overline{\text{BRDY}}$ pin acknowledges a burst transfer rather than the $\overline{\text{RDY}}$ pin that acknowledges a normal memory transfer.

80486 Memory Management

The 80486 contains the same memory-management system as the 80386. This includes a paging unit to allow any 4K byte block of physical memory to be assigned to any 4K byte block of linear memory. The descriptor types are exactly the same as for the 80386 microprocessor. In fact, the only difference between the 80386 memory-management system and the 80486 memory-management system is paging.

The 80486 paging system can disable caching for sections of translated memory pages, while the 80386 could not. Figure 14–40 illustrates the page table directory entry and the page table entry. If these are compared with the 80386 entries in Figure 14–29, the addition of 2 new control bits is observed (PWT and PCD). The page write-through (PWT) and page cache disable (PCD) control caching.

The PWT controls how the cache functions for a write operation of the external cache memory. It does not control writing to the internal cache. The logic level of this bit is found on the PWT pin of the 80486 microprocessor. Externally it can be used to dictate the write-through policy of the external cache.

The PCD bit controls the on-chip cache. If the PCD = 0, the on-chip cache is enabled for the current page of memory. Note that 80386 page table entries place a logic 0 in the PCD bit position enabling caching. If PCD = 1, it disables the on-chip cache. Caching is disabled regardless of the condition of $\overline{\text{KEN}}$, CD, and NW.

14–9   80486 INSTRUCTION SET

The instruction set of the 80486 is almost identical to the instruction set of the 80386 except for a few additional instructions. The main difference is that the 80486 executes many instructions in one clocking period where the 80386 required 2 clocking periods. This increase accounts for an overall speed improvement of about 50 percent for the 80486 when compared to the 80386 microprocessor. Table 14–8 lists the instructions that are new to the 80486 microprocessor. Note that since the 80486 also includes an

TABLE 14–8 New instructions for the 80486 microprocessor

Instruction	Function
BSWAP	Swaps the bytes in a register
CMPXCHG	Compare and exchange
INVD	Flushes the internal cache memory
INVLPG	Invalidates a TLB entry
WBINVD	Flushes the internal cache memory after writing dirty lines to the memory
XADD	Exchange and add

integrated 80387 numeric coprocessor, the coprocessor instructions listed in Chapter 12 also apply to the 80486 instruction set.

The BSWAP instruction allows bytes to be swapped in any 32-bit extended register. When the BSWAP instruction executes, it exchanges the rightmost byte with the leftmost byte and also exchanges the two middle bytes. For example, if EAX = 01234567H and the BSWAP EAX instruction executes, the result is 67452301H.

The CMPXCHG compares the destination operand to the contents of the accumulator (EAX, AX, or AL). If the destination operand is equal to the accumulator, the source operand is copied to the destination operand. If the destination operand is not equal to the accumulator, the destination operand is copied to the accumulator. An example is a CMPXCHG CX,DX, which copies DX into CX if DX = AX; otherwise it copies CX into AX. In all cases the CMPXCHG instruction changes the flag bits to indicate the outcome of the comparison. Another example is CMPXCHG CL,DATA, which copies the contents of memory location DATA into CL if CL = AL; otherwise it copies CL into AL.

The INVD (invalidate data cache) instruction empties the contents of the current data cache without writing changes to the memory system. Care must be exercised when using this instruction because data can be lost if INVD is executed before data are written to the memory system from the cache. This instruction is primarily used at the system software level.

The INVLPG (invalidate TLB entry) instruction invalidates an entry in the translation lookaside buffer (TLB) used by the demand-paging system in a virtual memory system. The instruction calculates the address of the operand and removes it from the TLB if the entry has been mapped into the TLB. As with the INVD instruction, this instruction is used at the operating system level instead of the application level.

The WBINVD (write before invalidating data cache) instruction functions as the INVD instruction except the contents of any dirty location in the data cache is first written to memory before the cache is flushed. This instruction is normally found at the system level.

The XADD instruction exchanges and adds data in two registers or between memory and a register. For example, the XADD EAX,EBX instruction adds EBX to EAX and stores the sum in EAX, just as an add instruction. The difference is that the original value in EAX is moved into EBX. Just as addition affects the flags, so does the XADD instruction.

Cache Test Registers

Although not instructions, the cache test registers are placed in this section to illustrate the use of the cache test registers and some software for the 80486 microprocessor. The 80486 cache test registers are TR3 (cache data register), TR4 (cache status test register), and TR5 (cache control test register) that are undefined for the 80386 microprocessor. These three registers are illustrated in Figure 14–41.

The cache data register (TR3) is used to access either the cache fill buffer for a write test operation or the cache read buffer for a cache read test operation. This register is a window into the 8K byte cache memory located within the 80486 and is used for testing the cache. In order to fill or read a cache line (128 bits wide), TR3 must be written or read four times.

The contents of the set select field in TR5 determine which internal cache line is written or read through TR3. The 7-bit test field selects one of the 128 different 16 bytewide cache lines. The entry select bits of TR5 select an entry in the set or the 32-bit location in the fill/read buffer. The control bits in TR5 enable the fill buffer or read buffer operation (00), perform a cache write (01), a cache read (10), or flush the cache (11).

The cache status register (TR4) holds the cache tag, LRU bits, and a valid bit. This register is loaded with the tag and valid bit before a cache write operation and contains the tag, valid bit, LRU bits, and four valid bits on a cache test read.

The cache is tested each time that the microprocessor is reset if the AHOLD pin is high for 2 clocks prior to the RESET pin going low. This causes the 80486 to completely test itself with a built-in self-test or BIST. The BIST uses TR3, TR4, and TR5 to completely test the internal cache. Its outcome is reported in register EAX. If EAX is a zero, the microprocessor, coprocessor, and cache have passed the self-test. The value of EAX can be tested after a reset to determine if an error is detected. In most cases we do not directly access the test registers unless we wish to perform our own tests on the cache or TLB.

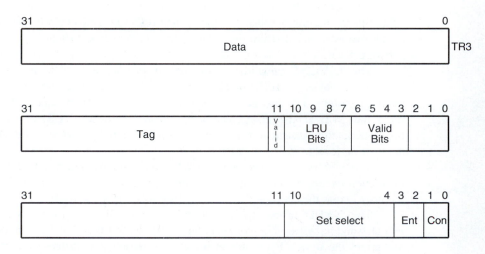

FIGURE 14–41   Cache test register of the 80486 microprocessor.

14–10 SUMMARY

1. The 80386 microprocessor is an enhanced version of the 80286 microprocessor that includes a memory-management unit that is enhanced to provide memory paging. The 80386 also includes 32-bit extended registers and a 32-bit address and data bus. A scaled-down version of the 80386DX with a 16-bit data and 24-bit address bus is available as the 80386SX microprocessor.

2. The 80386 has a physical memory size of 4G bytes that can be addressed as a virtual memory with up to 64T bytes. The 80386 memory is 32 bits in width and is addressed as bytes, words, or double words.

3. When the 80386 is operated in the pipelined mode, it sends the address of the next instruction or memory data to the memory system prior to completing the execution of the current instruction. This allows the memory system to begin fetching the next instruction or data before the current one is completed. This increases access time, thus reducing the speed of the memory.

4. A cache memory system allows data that are frequently read to be accessed in less time because they are stored in high-speed semiconductor memory. If data are written to memory, they are also written to the cache so the most current data are always present in the cache.

5. The I/O structure of the 80386 is almost identical to the 80286, except that I/O can be inhibited when the 80386 is operated in the protected mode through the I/O bit protection map stored with the TSS.

6. The register set of the 80386 contains extended versions of the registers introduced on the 80286 microprocessor. These extended registers include: EAX, EBX, ECX, EDX, EBP, ESP, EDI, ESI, EIP, and EFLAGS. In addition to the extended registers, two supplemental segment registers (FS and GS) are added. Debug registers and control registers handle system debugging tasks and memory management in the protected mode.

7. The instruction set of the 80386 is enhanced to include instructions that address the 32-bit extended register set. The enhancements also include additional addressing modes that allow any extended register to address memory data. Scaling has been added so an index register can be multiplied by 1, 2, 4, or 8. New instruction types include bit scan, string moves with sign- or zero-extension, set byte upon condition, and double-precision shifts.

8. Interrupts, in the 80386 microprocessor, have been expanded to include additional predefined interrupts in the interrupt vector table. These additional interrupts are used with the memory-management system.

9. The 80386 memory manager is similar to the 80286, except the physical addresses generated by the MMU are 32 bits wide instead of 24 bits. The 80386 MMU is also capable of paging.

10. The 80386 is operated in the real mode (8086 mode) when it is reset. The real mode allows the microprocessor to address data in the first 1M byte of memory. In the protected mode, the 80386 addresses any location in its 4G byte physical address range.

11. A descriptor is a series of 8 bytes that specify how a code or data segment is used by the 80386. The descriptor is selected by a selector that is stored in one of the segment registers. Descriptors are only used in the protected mode.

12. Memory management is accomplished through a series of descriptors stored in descriptor tables. To facilitate memory management, the 80386 uses three descriptor tables: the global descriptor table (GDT), the local descriptor table (LDT), and the interrupt descriptor table (IDT). The GDT and LDT each hold up to 8,192 descriptors, while the IDT holds up to 256 descriptors. The GDT and LDT describe code and data segments and also tasks. The IDT describes the 256 different interrupt levels through interrupt gate descriptors.

13. The TSS (task state segment) contains information about the current task and also the previous task. Appended to the end of the TSS is an I/O bit protection map that inhibits selected I/O port addresses.

14. The memory paging mechanism allows any 4K byte physical memory page to be mapped to any 4K byte linear memory page. For example, memory location 00A00000H can be assigned memory location A0000000H through the paging mechanism. A page directory and page tables are used to assign any physical address to any linear address. The paging mechanism can be used in the protected mode or the virtual mode.

15. The 80486 microprocessor is an improved version of the 80386 microprocessor that contains an 8K byte cache, an 80387 arithmetic coprocessor, and executes many instructions in one clocking period.

16. The 80486 microprocessor executes a few new instructions that control the internal cache memory and allow addition (XADD) and comparison (CMPXCHG) with an exchange and a byte swap (BSWAP) operation. Other than these few additional instructions, the 80486 is 100 percent upward compatible with the 80386 and 80387.

17. A new feature found in the 80486 is the BIST (built-in self-test) that tests the microprocessor, coprocessor, and cache at reset time. If the 80486 passes the test, EAX contains a zero.

18. Additional test registers are added to the 80486 to allow the cache memory to be tested. These new test registers are TR3 (cache data), TR4 (cache status), and TR5 (cache control). Although we seldom use these registers, they are used by BIST each time that a BIST is performed after a reset operation.

14–11   QUESTIONS AND PROBLEMS

1. The 80386 microprocessor addresses _____ bytes of physical memory when operated in the protected mode.

2. The 80386 microprocessor addresses _____ bytes of virtual memory through its memory-management unit.

3. Describe the differences between the 80386DX and the 80386SX.

4. Draw the memory map of the 80386 when operated in the
   (a) protected mode
   (b) real mode

5. How much current is available on various 80386 output pin connections? Compare these currents with the currents available at the output pin connection of an 8086 microprocessor.

6. Describe the 80386 memory system and explain the purpose and operation of the bank selection signals.

7. Explain the action of a hardware reset on the address bus connections of the 80386.

8. Explain how pipelining lengthens the access time for many memory references in the 80386 microprocessor-based system.

9. Briefly describe how the cache memory system functions.

10. I/O ports in the 80386 start at I/O address _____ and extend to I/O address _____ .

11. What I/O ports communicate data between the 80386 and its companion 80387 coprocesssor?

12. Compare and contrast the memory and I/O connections found on the 80386 with those found on the 8086.

13. If the 80386 operates at 20 MHz, what clocking frequency is applied to the CLK2 pin?

14. What is the purpose of the $\overline{BS16}$ pin on the 80386 microprocessor?

15. What two additional segment registers are found in the 80386 programming model that are not present in the 8086?

16. List the extended registers found in the 80386 microprocessor.

17. List each 80386 flag register bit and describe its purpose.

18. Define the purpose of each of the control registers (CR0, CR1, CR2, and CR3) found within the 80386.

19. Define the purpose of each 80386 debug register.

20. The debug registers cause which level of interrupt?

21. Describe the operation of the bit scan forward instruction.

22. Describe the operation of the bit scan reverse instruction.

23. Describe the operation of the SHRD instruction.

24. Form an instruction that accesses data in the FS segment at the location indirectly addressed by the DI register. The instruction should store the contents of EAX into this memory location.

25. What is scaled index addressing?

26. Is the following instruction legal? MOV AX,[EBX+ECX]

27. Explain how the following instructions calculate the memory address:
    (a) ADD [EBX+8*ECX],AL
    (b) MOV DATA[EAX+EBX],CX
    (c) SUB EAX,DATA
    (d) MOV ECX,[EBX]

28. What is the purpose of interrupt type number 7?

29. Which interrupt vector type number is activated for a protection privilege violation?

30. What is a double interrupt fault?

31. If an interrupt occurs in the protected mode, what defines the interrupt vectors?

32. What is a descriptor?

33. What is a selector?

34. How does the selector choose the local descriptor table?
35. What register is used to address the global descriptor table?
36. How many global descriptors can be stored in the GDT?
37. Explain how the 80386 can address a virtual memory space of 64T bytes when the physical memory contains only 4G bytes of memory.
38. What is the difference between a segment descriptor and a system descriptor?
39. What is the task state segment (TSS)?
40. How is the TSS addressed?
41. Describe how the 80386 switches from the real mode to the protected mode.
42. Describe how the 80386 switches from the protected mode to the real mode.
43. What is virtual 8086 mode operation of the 80386 microprocessor?
44. How is the paging directory located by the 80386?
45. How many bytes are found in a page of memory?
46. Explain how linear memory address D0000000H can be assigned to physical memory address C0000000H with the paging unit of the 80386.
47. What are the differences between an 80386 and 80486 microprocessor?
48. What is the purpose of the $\overline{\text{FLUSH}}$ input pin on the 80486 microprocessor?
49. Compare the register set of the 80386 with the 80486 microprocessor.
50. What differences exist in the flags of the 80486 when compared to the 80386 microprocessor?
51. What pins are used for parity checking on the 80486 microprocessor?
52. The 80486 microprocessor uses _____ parity.
53. The cache inside the 80486 microprocessor is _____ K bytes.
54. A cache line is filled by reading _____ bytes from the memory system.
55. What is an 80486 burst?
56. Define the term cache-write through?
57. What is a BIST?
58. Can 80486 caching be disabled by software? (Explain your answer.)
59. Explain how the XADD EBX,EDX instruction operates.
60. The CMPXCHG CL,AL instruction compares CL with AL. What else occurs when this instruction executes?
61. Compare the INVD instruction with the WBINVD instruction.
62. What is the purpose of the PCD bit in the page table directory or page table entry?
63. Does the PWT bit in the page table directory or page table entry affect the on-chip cache?

APPENDIX A

The Assembler and Disk Operating System

This appendix is provided so the use of the assembler can be understood and also to show the DOS (disk operating system) and BIOS (basic I/O system) function calls that are used by assembly language to control the IBM-PC or its clone. The function calls control everything from reading and writing disk data to managing the keyboard and displays. The assembler represented in this text is the Microsoft ML (Version 6.0) and MASM (version 5.10) macro assembler programs.

ASSEMBLER USAGE

The assembler program requires that a symbolic program be first written, using a word processor, text editor, or the workbench program provided with the assembler package. The editor provided with version 5.10 is M.EXE and it is strictly a full-screen editor. The editor provided with version 6.0 is PWB.EXE and is a fully integrated development system that contains extensive help. Refer to the documentation that accompanies your assembler package for details on the operation of the editor program. If at all possible use version 6.0 of the assembler because it contains a detailed help file that guides the user through assembly language statements, directives, and even the DOS and BIOS interrupt function calls.

If you are using a word processor to develop your software, make sure that it is initialized to generate a pure ASCII file. The source file that you generate must use the extension .ASM that is required for the assembler to properly identify your source program.

Once your source file is prepared, it must now be assembled. If you are using the workbench provided with version 6.0, this is accomplished by selecting the compile feature with your mouse. If you are using a word processor and DOS command lines with version 5.10, then see Example A–1 for the dialog for version 5.10 to assemble a file called FROG.ASM. Note that this example shows the portions typed by the user in italics.

EXAMPLE A–1

```
A>MASM

Microsoft (R) Macro Assembler Version 5.10
Copyright (C) Microsoft Corp 1981, 1989. All rights reserved.

Source filename [.ASM]:FILE
Object filename [FILE.OBJ]:FILE
Source filename [NUL.LST]:FILE
Cross reference [NUL.CRF]:FILE
```

Once a program is assembled, it must be linked before it can be executed. The linker converts the object file into an executable file (.EXE). Example A–2 shows the dialog required for the linker using a MASM version 5.10 object file. If the ML version 6.0 assembler is in use, it automatically assembles and links a program using the COMPILE or BUILD command from workbench. After compiling with ML, workbench allows the program to be debugged with a debugging tool called code view. Code view is also available with MASM, but CV must be typed at the DOS command line to access it.

EXAMPLE A–2

```
A>LINK

Microsoft (R) Overlay Linker Version 3.64
Copyright (C) Microsoft Corp 1983-1988. All rights reserved.

Object Modules [.OBJ]:TEST
Run File [TEST.EXE]:TEST
List File [NUL.MAP]:TEST
Libraries [.LIB]:SUBR
```

Version 6.0 of the Microsoft MASM program contains the programmer's workbench program. This program allows an assembly language program to be developed with its full-screen editor and tool bar. Figure A–1 illustrates the display found with programmer's workbench. To access this program type PWB at the DOS prompt. The make option allows a program to be automatically assembled and linked, making these tasks simple in comparison to version 5.10 of the assembler.

ASSEMBLER MEMORY MODELS

Memory models and the .MODEL statement are introduced in Chapter 6. Here we completely define the memory models available for software development. Each model defines the way that a program is stored in the memory system. Table A–1 describes the different models available with MASM and also ML.

Note that the tiny model is used to create a .COM file instead of an execute file. The .COM file is different because all data and code fit into one code segment. A .COM file must have the program originated to start at offset address 0100H. A .COM file loads from the disk and executes faster than the normal execute (.EXE) file. For most applications we normally use the execute file (.EXE) and the small memory model.

```
 File   Edit   View   Search   Make   Run   Options   Browse          Help
                            C:\ASSM\SLOT.ASM
 DATA   SEGMENT
                    33H                ;position
 POS    DB

 DATA   ENDS

 CODE   SEGMENT  'CODE'
        ASSUME   CS:CODE,DS:DATA

 PORTA  EQU      40H                ;port number

 STEP   PROC     FAR

        MOV      AL,POS             ;get position
        CMP      CX,8000H
        JA       RH                 ;if right-hand direction
        CMP      CX,0
        JE       STEP_OUT           ;if no steps
 STEP1:
        ROL      AL,1               ;step left
        OUT      PORTA,AL

 <General Help>  <F1=Help>  <Alt=Menu>              macro       N  00001.001
```

FIGURE A–1 The edit screen from programmer's workbench used to develop assembly language programs.

TABLE A–1 Memory models for the assembler

Type	Description
Tiny	All data and code fit into one segment, the code segment. Tiny model programs are written in the .COM file format, which means that the program must be originated at memory location 0100H. This model is most often used with small programs.
Small	All data fit into a single 64K byte data segment and all code fits into another single 64K byte code segment. This allows all code to be accessed with near jumps and calls.
Medium	All data fit into a single 64K byte data segment, and code fits into more than one code segment. This allows code to exist in multiple segments.
Compact	All code fits into a single 64K byte code segment, and data fit into more than one data segment.
Large	Both code and data fit into multiple code and data segments.
Huge	Same as large, but allows data segments that are larger than 64K bytes.
Flat	Not available in MASM version 5.10. The flat memory model uses one segment with a maximum length of 512M bytes to store data and code.

TABLE A–2   Defaults for the .MODEL directive

Model	Directive	Name	Align	Combine	Class	Group
Tiny	.CODE	_TEXT	Word	PUBLIC	'CODE'	DGROUP
	.FARDATA	FAR_DATA	Para	Private	'FAR_DATA'	
	.FARDATA?	FAR_BSS	Para	Private	'FAR_BSS'	
	.DATA	_DATA	Word	PUBLIC	'DATA'	DGROUP
	.CONST	CONST	Word	PUBLIC	'CONST'	DGROUP
	.DATA?	_BSS	Word	PUBLIC	'BSS'	DGROUP
Small	.CODE	_TEXT	Word	PUBLIC	'CODE'	
	.FARDATA	FAR_DATA	Para	Private	'FAR_DATA'	
	.FARDATA?	FAR_BSS	Para	Private	'FAR_BSS'	
	.DATA	_DATA	Word	PUBLIC	'DATA'	DGROUP
	.CONST	CONST	Word	PUBLIC	'CONST'	DGROUP
	.DATA?	_BSS	Word	PUBLIC	'BSS'	DGROUP
	.STACK	STACK	Para	STACK	'STACK'	DGROUP
Medium	.CODE	name_TEXT	Word	PUBLIC	'CODE'	
	.FARDATA	FAR_DATA	Para	Private	'FAR_DATA'	
	.FARDATA?	FAR_BSS	Para	Private	'FAR_BSS'	
	.DATA	_DATA	Word	PUBLIC	'DATA'	DGROUP
	.CONST	CONST	Word	PUBLIC	'CONST'	DGROUP
	.DATA?	_BSS	Word	PUBLIC	'BSS'	DGROUP
	.STACK	STACK	Para	STACK	'STACK'	DGROUP
Compact	.CODE	_TEXT	Word	PUBLIC	'CODE'	
	.FARDATA	FAR_DATA	Para	Private	'FAR_DATA'	
	.FARDATA?	FAR_BSS	Para	Private	'FAR_BSS'	
	.DATA	_DATA	Word	PUBLIC	'DATA'	DGROUP
	.CONST	CONST	Word	PUBLIC	'CONST'	DGROUP
	.DATA?	_BSS	Word	PUBLIC	'BSS'	DGROUP
	.STACK	STACK	Para	STACK	'STACK'	DGROUP
Large	.CODE	name_TEXT	Word	PUBLIC	'CODE'	
or	.FARDATA	FAR_DATA	Para	Private	'FAR_DATA'	
huge	.FARDATA?	FAR_BSS	Para	Private	'FAR_BSS'	
	.DATA	_DATA	Word	PUBLIC	'DATA'	DGROUP
	.CONST	CONST	Word	PUBLIC	'CONST'	DGROUP
	.DATA?	_BSS	Word	PUBLIC	'BSS'	DGROUP
	.STACK	STACK	Para	STACK	'STACK'	DGROUP
Flat	.CODE	_TEXT	Dword	PUBLIC	'CODE'	
	.FARDATA	_DATA	Dword	PUBLIC	'DATA'	
	.FARDATA?	_BSS	Dword	PUBLIC	'BSS'	
	.DATA	_DATA	Dword	PUBLIC	'DATA'	
	.CONST	CONST	Dword	PUBLIC	'CONST'	
	.DATA?	_BSS	Dword	PUBLIC	'BSS'	
	.STACK	STACK	Dword	PUBLIC	'STACK	

When models are used to create a program, certain defaults apply as illustrated in Table A–2. The directive in this table is used to start a particular type of segment for the models listed in the table. If the .CODE directive is placed in a program, it indicates the beginning of the code segment. Likewise, .DATA indicates the start of a data segment. The name column indicates the name of the segment. Align indicates whether the segment is aligned on a word, double word, or a 16-byte paragraph. Combine indicates the type of segment created. The class indicates the class of the segment, such as 'CODE' or 'DATA'. The group indicates the group type of the segment.

Example A–3 shows a program that uses the small model. The small model is used for programs that contain one DATA and one CODE segment. This applies to many programs that are developed. Notice that not only is the program listed, but so is all the information generated by the assembler. Here the .DATA directive and .CODE directive indicate the start of segments. Also notice how the DS register is loaded in this program.

EXAMPLE A–3

```
Microsoft (R) Macro Assembler Version 6.00

                              .MODEL SMALL
                              .STACK 100H
0000                          .DATA

0000 0A               FROG      DB        10
0001 0064 [           DATA1     DB        100 DUP (2)
          02
     ]

0000                          .CODE

0000 B8 ---- R        BEGIN:  MOV       AX,DGROUP          ;set up DS
0003 8E D8                    MOV       DS,AX
                             .
                             .
                             .
                             END       BEGIN
```

Segments and Groups:

N a m e	Size	Length	Align	Combine	Class
DGROUP	GROUP				
_DATA	16 Bit	0065	Word	Public	'DATA'
STACK	16 Bit	0100	Para	Stack	'STACK'
_TEXT	16 Bit	0005	Word	Public	'CODE'

Symbols:

N a m e	Type	Value	Attr
@CodeSize	Number	0000h	
@DataSize	Number	0000h	
@Interface	Number	0000h	
@Model	Number	0002h	
@code	Text		_TEXT
@data	Text		DGROUP
@fardata?	Text		FAR_BSS
@fardata	Text		FAR_DATA

```
@stack ............ Text            DGROUP
BEGIN ............. L Near  0000    _TEXT
DATA1 ............. Byte    0001    _DATA
FROG .............. Byte    0000    _DATA


         0 Warnings
         0 Errors
```

Example A–4 lists a program that uses the large model. Notice how it differs from the small model program of Example A–3. Models can be very useful in developing software, but often we use full segment descriptions as depicted in Chapter 6.

EXAMPLE A–4 (page 1 of 2)

```
Microsoft (R) Macro Assembler Version 6.00              07/30/91 22:38:58

                        .MODEL LARGE
                        .STACK 1000H
0000                    .FARDATA?

0000 00                 FROG    DB      ?
0001 0064 [             DATA1   DW      100 DUP (?)
       0000
            ]

0000                    .CONST

0000 54 68 69 73 20 69  MES1    DB      'This is a character string'
     73 20 61 20 63 68
     61 72 61 63 74 65
     72 20 73 74 72 69
     6E 67
001A 53 6F 20 69 73 20  MES2    DB      'So is this!'
     74 68 69 73 21

0000                    .DATA

0000 0000C              DATA2   DW      12
0002 00C8 [             DATA3   DB      200 DUP (1)
       01
          ]

0000                    .CODE

0000                    FUNC    PROC    FAR
                                .
                                .
                                .
                                .
0000 CB                         RET

0001                    FUNC    ENDP

                        END     FUNC

Segments and Groups:

     N a m e       Size       Length   Align   Combine Class

D GROUP............GROUP
_DATA ............ 16 Bit     00CA     Word            Public 'DATA'
```

EXAMPLE A–4 (page 2 of 2)

```
STACK ............ 16 Bit      1000      Para      Stack 'STACK'
CONST ............ 16 Bit      0025      Word                Public 'CONST'        ReadOnly
EXA_TEXT ......... 16 Bit      0001      Word                Public 'CODE'
FAR_BSS .......... 16 Bit      00C9      Para Private 'FAR_BSS'
_TEXT ............ 16 Bit      0000      Word Public 'CODE'
```

Procedures, parameters and locals:

```
     N a m e        Type       Value      Attr

FUNC ............. P Far       0000       EXA_TEXT         Length=0001 Public
```

Symbols:

```
     N a m e        Type       Value      Attr

@CodeSize ........ Number      0001h
@DataSize ........ Number      0001h
@Interface ....... Number      0000h
@Model ........... Number      0005h
@code ............ Text                   EXA_TEXT
@data ............ Text                   DGROUP
@fardata? ........ Text                   FAR_BSS
@fardata ......... Text                   FAR_DATA
@stack ........... Text                   DGROUP
DATA1 ............ Word        0001       FAR_BSS
DATA2 ............ Word        0000       _DATA
DATA3 ............ Byte        0002       _DATA
FROG ............. Byte        0000       FAR_BSS
MES1 ............. Byte        0000       CONST
MES2 ............. Byte        001A       CONST

         0 Warnings
         0 Errors
```

DOS FUNCTION CALLS

EXAMPLE A–5

```
0000 B4 06                     MOV      AH,6
0002 B2 41                     MOV      DL,'A'
0004 CD 21                     INT      21H
```

In order to use DOS function calls, place the function number into register AH and load all other pertinent information into registers as described in the table. Once this is accomplished, follow with an INT 21H to execute the DOS function. Example A–5 shows how to display an ASCII A on the CRT screen at the current cursor position with a DOS function call. Following is a complete listing of the DOS function calls. Note that some function calls require a segment and offset address, indicated as DS:DI, for example. This means the data segment is the segment address and DI is the offset address. All of the function calls use INT 21H and AH contains the function call number. Note that functions marked with an @ should not be used unless DOS version 2.XX is in use. As a rule, DOS function calls save all registers not used as exit data, but in certain cases some registers may change. In order to prevent problems, it is advisable to save registers where problems occur.

00H	TERMINATE A PROGRAM
Entry	AH = 00H CS = program segment prefix address
Exit	DOS is entered

01H	READ THE KEYBOARD
Entry	AH = 01H
Exit	AL = ASCII character
Notes	If AL = 00H the function call must be invoked again to read an extended ASCII character. Refer to Chapter 6, Table 6-1, for a listing of the extended ASCII keyboard codes. This function call automatically echoes whatever is typed to the video screen.

02H	WRITE TO STANDARD OUTPUT DEVICE
Entry	AH = 02H AL = ASCII character to be displayed
Notes	This function call normally displays data on the video display.

03H	READ CHARACTER FROM COM1
Entry	AH = 03H
Exit	AL = ASCII character read from the communications port
Notes	This function call reads data from the serial communications port.

04H	WRITE TO COM1
Entry	AH = 04H DL = character to be sent out of COM1
Notes	This function transmits data through the serial communications port.

05H	WRITE TO LPT1
Entry	AH = 05H DL = ASCII character to be printed
Notes	Prints DL on the line printer attached to LPT1

06H	DIRECT CONSOLE READ/WRITE
Entry	AH = 06H DL = 0FFH or DL = ASCII character
Exit	AL = ASCII character
Notes	If DL = 0FFH on entry, then this function reads the console. If DL = ASCII character, then this function displays the ASCII character on the console video screen. If a character is read from the console keyboard, the zero flag (ZF) indicates whether a character was typed. A zero condition indicates no key is typed and a not-zero condition indicates that AL contains the ASCII code of the key or a 00H. If AL = 00H, the function must again be invoked to read an extended ASCII character from the keyboard. Note that the key does not echo to the video screen.

07H	DIRECT CONSOLE INPUT WITHOUT ECHO
Entry	AH = 07H
Exit	AL = ASCII character
Notes	This functions exactly as function number 06H with DL = 0FFH, but it will not return from the function until the key is typed.

08H	READ STANDARD INPUT WITHOUT ECHO
Entry	AH = 08H
Exit	AL = ASCII character
Notes	Performs as function 07H, except it reads the standard input device. The standard input device can be assigned as either the keyboard or the COM port. This function also responds to a control-break, where function 06H and 07H do not. A control-break causes INT 23H to execute.

09H	DISPLAY A CHARACTER STRING
Entry	AH = 09H DS:DX = address of the character string
Notes	The character string must end with an ASCII $ (24H). The character string can be of any length and may contain control characters such as carriage return (0DH) and line feed (0AH).

0AH	BUFFERED KEYBOARD INPUT
Entry	AH = 0AH DS:DX = address of keyboard input buffer
Notes	The first byte of the buffer contains the size of the buffer (up to 255). The second byte is filled with the number of characters typed upon return. The third byte through the end of the buffer contains the character string typed followed by a carriage return (0DH). This function continues to read the keyboard (displaying data as typed) until either the specified number of characters are typed or until a carriage return (enter) key is typed.

0BH	TEST STATUS OF THE STANDARD INPUT DEVICE
Entry	AH = 0BH
Exit	AL = status of the input device
Notes	This function tests the standard input device to determine if data are available. If AL = 00, no data are available. If AL = 0FFH, then data are available that must be input using function number 08H.

0CH	CLEAR KEYBOARD BUFFER AND INVOKE KEYBOARD FUNCTION
Entry	AH = 0CH AL = 01H, 06H, 07H, or 0AH
Exit	see exit for functions 01H, 06H, 07H, or 0AH
Notes	The keyboard buffer holds keystrokes while programs execute other tasks. This function empties or clears the buffer and then invokes the keyboard function located in register AL.

0DH	FLUSH DISK BUFFERS
Entry	AH = 0DH
Notes	Erases all file names stored in disk buffers. This function does not close the files specified by the disk buffers, so care must be exercised in its usage.

0EH	SELECT DEFAULT DISK DRIVE
Entry	AH = 0DH DL = desired default disk drive number
Exit	AL = the total number of drives present in the system
Notes	Drive A = 00H, drive B = 01H, drive C = 02H, and so forth.

0FH	@OPEN FILE WITH FCB
Entry	AH = 0FH DS:DX = address of the unopened file control block (FCB)
Exit	AL = 00H if file found AL = 0FFH if file not found
Notes	The file control block (FCB) is only used with early DOS software and should never be used with new programs. File control blocks do not allow path names as do the newer file access function codes presented later. Figure A-2 illustrates the structure of the FCB. To open a file, the file must either be present on the disk or be created with function call 16H.
10H	@CLOSE FILE WITH FCB
Entry	AH = 10H DS:DX = address of the opened file control block (FCB)
Exit	AL = 00H if file closed AL = 0FFH if error found
Notes	Errors that occurs usually indicate that either the disk is full or the media is bad.
11H	@SEARCH FOR FIRST MATCH (FCB)
Entry	AH = 11H DS:DX = address of the file control block to be searched
Exit	AL = 00H if file found AL = 0FFH if file not found

FIGURE A-2 Contents of the file control block (FCB).

Offset	Contents
00H	Drive
01H	8-character filename
09H	3-character file extension
0CH	Current block number
0EH	Record size
10H	File size
14H	Creation date
16H	Reserved space
20H	Current record number
21H	Relative record number

Notes	Wild card characters (? or *) may be used to search for a file name. The ? wild card character matches any character and the * matches any name or extension.
12H	@SEARCH FOR NEXT MATCH (FCB)
Entry	AH = 12H DS:DX = address of the file control block to be searched
Exit	AL = 00H if file found AL = 0FFH if file not found
Notes	This function is used after function 11H finds the first matching file name.
13H	@DELETE FILE USING FCB
Entry	AH = 13H DS:DX = address of the file control block to be deleted
Exit	AL = 00H if file deleted AL = 0FFH if error occurred
Notes	Errors that most often occur are defective media errors.
14H	@SEQUENTIAL READ (FCB)
Entry	AH = 14H DS:DX = address of the file control block to be read
Exit	AL = 00H if read successful AL = 01H if end of file reached AL = 02H if DTA had a segment wrap AL = 03H if less than 128 bytes were read
15H	@SEQUENTIAL WRITE (FCB)
Entry	AH = 15H DS:DX = address of the file control block to be written
Exit	AL = 00H if write successful AL = 01H if disk is full AL = 02H if DTA had a segment wrap
16H	@CREATE A FILE (FCB)
Entry	AH = 16H DS:DX = address of an unopened file control block
Exit	AL = 00H if file created AL = 01H if disk is full

17H	@RENAME A FILE (FCB)
Entry	AH = 17H DS:DX = address of a modified file control block
Exit	AL = 00H if file renamed AL = 01H if error occurred
Notes	Refer to Figure A-3 for the modified FCB used to rename a file.

18H	NOT ASSIGNED

19H	RETURN CURRENT DRIVE
Entry	AH = 19H
Exit	AL = current drive
Notes	AL = 00H for drive A, 01H for drive B, and so forth.

1AH	SET DISK TRANSFER AREA
Entry	AH = 1AH DS:DX = address of new DTA
Notes	The disk transfer area is normally located within the program segment prefix at offset address 80H. The DTA is used by DOS for all disk data transfers using file control blocks.

1BH	GET DEFAULT DRIVE FILE ALLOCATION TABLE (FAT)
Entry	AH = 1BH

FIGURE A-3 Contents of the modified file control block (FCB).

Offset	Content
00H	Drive
01H	8-character filename
09H	3-character extension
0CH	Current block number
0EH	Record Size
10H	File size
14H	Creation date
16H	Second file name

Exit	AL = number of sectors per cluster DS:BX = address of the media-descriptor CX = size of a sector in bytes DX = number of clusters on drive
Notes	Refer to Figure A-4 for the format of the media-descriptor byte. The DS register is changed by this function so make sure to save it before using this function.
1CH	GET ANY DRIVE FILE ALLOCATION TABLE (FAT)
Entry	AH = 1CH DL = disk drive number
Exit	AL = number of sectors per cluster DS:BX = address of the media-descriptor CX = size of a sector in bytes DX = number of clusters on drive
1DH	NOT ASSIGNED
1EH	NOT ASSIGNED
1FH	NOT ASSIGNED
20H	NOT ASSIGNED
21H	@RANDOM READ USING FCB
Entry	AH = 21H DS:DX = address of opened FCB

FIGURE A–4 Contents of the media-descriptor byte.

7	6	5	4	3	2	1	0
?	?	?	?	?	?	?	?

Bit 0 = 0 if not two-sided
      = 1 if two-sided

Bit 1 = 0 if not eight sectors per track
      = 1 if eight sectors per track

Bit 2 = 0 if nonremovable
      = 1 if removable

Exit	AL = 00H if read successful AL = 01H if end of file reached AL = 02H if the segment wrapped AL = 03H if less than 128 bytes read
22H	@RANDOM WRITE USING FCB
Entry	AH = 22H DS:DX = address of opened FCB
Exit	AL = 00H if write successful AL = 01H if disk full AL = 02H if the segment wrapped
23H	@RETURN NUMBER OF RECORDS (FCB)
Entry	AH = 23H DS:DX = address of FCB
Exit	AL = 00H number of records AL = 0FFH if file not found
24H	@SET RELATIVE RECORD SIZE (FCB)
Entry	AH = 24H DS:DX = address of FCB
Notes	Sets the record field to the value contained in the FCB.
25H	SET INTERRUPT VECTOR
Entry	AH = 25H AL = interrupt vector number DS:DX = address of new interrupt procedure
Notes	Before changing the interrupt vector, it is suggested that the current interrupt vector is first saved using DOS function 35H. This allows a back-link so the original vector can later be restored.
26H	CREATE NEW PROGRAM SEGMENT PREFIX
Entry	AH = 26H DX = segment address of new PSP
Notes	Figure A-5 illustrates the structure of the program segment prefix.

FIGURE A–5 Contents of the program-segment prefix (PSP).

Offset	Content
00H	INT 20H
02H	Top of memory
04H	Reserved
05H	Opcode
06H	Number of bytes in segment
0AH	Terminate address (offset)
0CH	Terminate address (segment)
0EH	Control break address (offset)
10H	Control break address (segment)
12H	Critical error address (offset)
14H	Critical error address (segment)
16H	Reserved
2CH	Environment address (segment)
2EH	Reserved
50H	DOS call
52H	Reserved
5CH	File control block 1
6CH	File control block 2
80H	Command line length
81H	Command line

27H	@RANDOM FILE BLOCK READ (FCB)
Entry	AH = 27H CX = the number of records DS:DX = address of opened FCB
Exit	AL = 00H if read successful AL = 01H if end of file reached AL = 02H if the segment wrapped AL = 03H if less than 128 bytes read CX = the number of records read

28H	@RANDOM FILE BLOCK WRITE (FCB)
Entry	AH = 28H CX = the number of records DS:DX = address of opened FCB
Exit	AL = 00H if write successful AL = 01H if disk full AL = 02H if the segment wrapped CX = the number of records written

29H	@PARSE COMMAND LINE (FCB)
Entry	AH = 29H AL = parse mask DS:SI = address of FCB DS:DI = address of command line
Exit	AL = 00H if no file name characters found AL = 01H if file name characters found AL = 0FFH if drive specifier incorrect DS:SI = address of character after name DS:DI = address first byte of FCB

2AH	READ SYSTEM DATE
Entry	AH = 2AH
Exit	AL = day of the week CX = the year (1980—2099) DH = the month DL = day of the month
Notes	The day of the week is encoded as Sunday = 00H through Saturday = 06H. The year is a binary number equal to 1980 through 2099.

2BH	SET SYSTEM DATE
Entry	AH = 2BH CX = the year (1980—2099) DH = the month DL = day of the month

2CH	READ SYSTEM TIME
Entry	AH = 2CH
Exit	CH = hours (0—23) CL = minutes DH = seconds DL = hundredths of seconds

2DH	SET SYSTEM TIME
Entry	AH = 2DH CH = hours CL = minutes DH = seconds DL = hundredths of seconds

2EH	DISK VERIFY WRITE
Entry	AH = 2EH AL = 00H to disable verify on write AL = 01H to enable verify on write

2FH	READ DISK TRANSFER AREA
Entry	AH = 2FH
Exit	ES:BX = contains DTA address

30H	READ DOS VERSION NUMBER
Entry	AH = 30H
Exit	AH = fractional version number AL = whole number version number
Notes	For example, DOS version number 3.2 is returned as a 3 in AL and a 14H in AH.

31H	TERMINATE AND STAY RESIDENT (TSR)
Entry	AH = 31H AL = the DOS return code DX = number of paragraphs to reserve
Notes	A paragraph is 16 bytes and the DOS return code is read at the batch file level with ERRORCODE.

32H	NOT ASSIGNED

33H	TEST CONTROL-BREAK

Entry	AH = 33H AL = 00H to request current control-break AL = 01H to change control-break DL = 00H to disable control-break DL = 01H to enable control-break
Exit	DL = current control-break state

34H	GET ADDRESS OF InDOS FLAG
Entry	AH = 34H
Exit	ES:BX = address of InDOS flag
Notes	The InDOS flag is available in DOS versions 3.2 or newer and indicates DOS activity. If InDOS = 00H, DOS is inactive or 0FFH if DOS is active.

35H	READ INTERRUPT VECTOR
Entry	AH = 35H AL = interrupt vector number
Exit	ES:BX = address stored at vector
Notes	This DOS function is used with function 25H to install/remove interrupt handlers.

36H	DETERMINE FREE DISK SPACE
Entry	AH = 36H DL = drive number
Exit	AX = FFFFH if drive invalid AX = number of sectors per cluster BX = number of free clusters CX = bytes per sector DX = number of clusters on drive
Notes	The default disk drive is DL = 00H, drive A = 01H, drive B = 02H, and so forth.

37H	NOT ASSIGNED

38H	RETURN COUNTRY CODE
Entry	AH = 38H AL = 00H for current country code BX = 16-bit country code DS:DX = data buffer address

Exit	AX = error code if carry set BX = counter code DS:DX = data buffer address
39H	**CREATE SUBDIRECTORY**
Entry	AH = 39H DS:DX = address of ASCII-Z string subdirectory name
Exit	AX = error code if carry set
Notes	The ASCII-Z string is the name of the subdirectory in ASCII code ended with a 00H instead of a carriage return/line feed.
3AH	**ERASE SUBDIRECTORY**
Entry	AH = 3AH DS:DX = address of ASCII-Z string subdirectory name
Exit	AX = error code if carry set
3BH	**CHANGE SUBDIRECTORY**
Entry	AH = 3BH DS:DX = address of new ASCII-Z string subdirectory name
Exit	AX = error code if carry set
3CH	**CREATE A NEW FILE**
Entry	AH = 3CH CX = attribute word DS:DX = address of ASCII-Z string file name
Exit	AX = error code if carry set AX = file handle if carry cleared
Notes	The attribute word can contain any of the following (added together): 01H read-only access, 02H = hidden file or directory, 04H = system file, 08H = volume label, 10H = subdirectory, and 20H = archive bit. In most cases a file is created with 0000H.
3DH	**OPEN A FILE**
Entry	AH = 3DH AL = access code DS:DX = address of ASCII-Z string file name
Exit	AX = error code if carry set AX = file handle if carry cleared

Notes	The access code in AL = 00H for a read-only access, AL = 01H for a write-only access, and AL = 02H for a read/write access. For shared files in a network environment, bit 4 of AL = 1 will deny read/write access, bit 5 of AL = 1 will deny a write access, bits 4 and 5 of AL = 1 will deny read access, bit 6 of AL = 1 denies none, bit 7 of AL = 0 causes the file to be inherited by child, and if bit 7 of AL = 1 file is restricted to current process.
3EH	CLOSE A FILE
Entry	AH = 3EH BX = file handle
Exit	AX = error code if carry set
3FH	READ A FILE
Entry	AH = 3FH BX = file handle CX = number of bytes to be read DS:DX = address of file buffer to hold data read
Exit	AX = error code if carry set AX = number of bytes read if carry cleared
40H	WRITE A FILE
Entry	AH = 40H BX = file handle CX = number of bytes to write DS:DX = address of file buffer that holds write data
Exit	AX = error code if carry set AX = number of bytes written if carry cleared
41H	DELETE A FILE
Entry	AH = 41H DS:DX = address of ASCII-Z string file name
Exit	AX = error code if carry set
42H	MOVE FILE POINTER
Entry	AH = 42H AL = move technique BX = file handle CX:DX = number of bytes pointer moved

Exit	AX = error code if carry set AX:DX = bytes pointer moved
Notes	The move technique causes the pointer to move from the start of the file if AL = 00H, from the current location if AL = 01H and from the end of the file if AL = 02H. The count is stored so DX contains the least significant 16-bits and either CX or AX contains the most significant 16 bits.

43H	READ/WRITE FILE ATTRIBUTES
Entry	AH = 43H AL = 00H to read attributes AL = 01H to write attributes CX = attribute word (see function 3CH) DS:DX = address of ASCII-Z string file name
Exit	AX = error code if carry set CX = attribute word of carry cleared

44H	I/O DEVICE CONTROL (IOTCL)
Entry	AH = 44H AL = code (see notes) AL = 01H to write attributes BX = file handle or device number CX = number of bytes DS:DX = data or address
Exit	AX = error code if carry set AX and DX = parameters
Notes	The codes found in AL are as follows: 00H = read device status (DX = status) 01H = write device status (DX = status written) 02H = read data from device (DS:DX = buffer address) 03H = write data to device (DS:DX = buffer address) 04H = read data from disk drive 05H = write data to disk drive 06H = read input status (AL = 00H ready or 0FH not ready) 07H = read output status (AL = 00H ready or 0FH not ready) 08H = removable media? (AL = 00H removable, 01H fixed) 09H = local or remote device? (bit 12 of DX set for remote) 0AH = local or remote handle? (bit 15 of DX set for remote) 0BH = change entry count 0CH = generic I/O control for character devices 0DH = generic I/O control for block devices 0EH = return number of logical devices (AL = number) 0FH = change number of logical devices

45H	DUPLICATE FILE HANDLE
Entry	AH = 45H BX = current file handle

Exit	AX = error code if carry set AX = duplicate file handle

46H	FORCE DUPLICATE FILE HANDLE
Entry	AH = 46H BX = current file handle CX = new file handle
Exit	AX = error code if carry set
Notes	This function works like function 45H except function 45H allows DOS to select the new handle while this function allows the user to select the new handle.

47H	READ CURRENT DIRECTORY
Entry	AH = 47H DL = drive number DS:SI = address of a 64 byte buffer for directory name
Exit	DS:SI addresses current directory name if carry cleared

48H	ALLOCATE MEMORY BLOCK
Entry	AH = 48H BX = number of paragraphs to allocate CX = new file handle
Exit	BX = largest block available if carry cleared

49H	RELEASE ALLOCATED MEMORY BLOCK
Entry	AH = 49H ES = segment address of block to be released CX = new file handle
Exit	Carry indicates an error if set

4AH	MODIFY ALLOCATED MEMORY BLOCK
Entry	AH = 4AH BX = new block size in paragraphs ES = segment address of block to be modified
Exit	BX = largest block available if carry cleared

4BH	LOAD OR EXECUTE A PROGRAM
Entry	AH = 4BH AL = function code ES:BX = address of parameter block DS:DX = address ASCII-Z string command
Exit	Carry indicates an error if set
Notes	The function codes are: AL = 00H to load and execute a program and AL = 03H to load a program but not execute it. Figure A-6 shows the parameter block used with this function.
4CH	TERMINATE A PROCESS
Entry	AH = 4CH AL = error code
Exit	Returns control to DOS
Notes	This function returns control to DOS with the error code saved so it can be obtained using DOS ERROR LEVEL batch processing system. We normally use this function with an error code of 00H to return to DOS.
4DH	READ RETURN CODE
Entry	AH = 4DH

FIGURE A–6   The parameter blocks used with function 4BH (EXEC). (a) For function code 00H. (b) For function code 03H.

(a)

Offset	Contents
00H	Environment address (segment)
02H	Command line address (offset)
04H	Command line address (segment)
06H	File control block 1 address (offset)
08H	File control block 1 address (segment)
0AH	File control block 2 address (segment)
0CH	File control block 2 address (offset)

(b)

Offset	Contents
00H	Overlay destination segment address
02H	Relocation factor

Exit	AX = return error code
Notes	This function is used to obtain the return status code created by executing a program with DOS function 4BH. The return codes are: AX = 0000H for a normal—no error—termination, AX = 0001H for a control-break termination, AX = 0002H for a critical device error, and AX = 0003H for a termination by an INT 31H.

4EH	FIND FIRST MATCHING FILE
Entry	AH = 4EH CX = file attributes DS:DX = address ASCII-Z string file name
Exit	Carry is set for file not found
Notes	This function searches the current or named directory for the first matching file. Upon exit, the DTA contains the file information. See Figure A-7 for the disk transfer area (DTA).

4FH	FIND NEXT MATCHING FILE
Entry	AH = 4FH
Exit	Carry is set for file not found
Notes	This function is used after the first file is found with function 4EH

50H	SET PROGRAM SEGMENT PREFIX (PSP) ADDRESS
Entry	AH = 50H BX = offset address of the new PSP
Notes	Extreme care must be used with this function because no error recovery is possible.

FIGURE A–7 Data transfer area (DTA) used to find a file.

Offset	Contents
15H	Attributes
16H	Creation time
18H	Creation date
1AH	Low word file size
1CH	High word file size
1EH	Search file name

51H	GET PSP ADDRESS
Entry	AH = 51H
Exit	BX = current PSP segment address

52H	NOT ASSIGNED

53H	NOT ASSIGNED

54H	READ DISK VERIFY STATUS
Entry	AH = 54H
Exit	AL = 00H if verify off AL = 01H if verify on

55H	NOT ASSIGNED

56H	RENAME FILE
Entry	AH = 56H ES:DI = address of ASCII-Z string containing new file name DS:DX = address of ASCII-Z string containing file to be renamed
Exit	Carry is set for error condition

57H	READ FILE'S DATE AND TIME STAMP
Entry	AH = 57H AL = function code BX = file handle CX = new time DX = new date
Exit	Carry is set for error condition CX = time if carry cleared DX = date if carry cleared
Notes	AL = 00H to read date and time or 01H to write date and time.

58H	NOT ASSIGNED

59H	GET EXTENDED ERROR INFORMATION
Entry	AH = 59H BX = 0000H for DOS version 3.X
Exit	AX = extended error code BH = error class BL = recommended action CH = locus
Notes	Following are the error codes found in AX: 0001H = invalid function number 0002H = file not found 0003H = path not found 0004H = no file handles available 0005H = access denied 0006H = file handle invalid 0007H = memory control block failure 0008H = insufficient memory 0009H = memory block address invalid 000AH = environment failure 000BH = format invalid 000CH = access code invalid 000DH = data invalid 000EH = unknown unit 000FH = disk drive invalid 0010H = attempted to remove current directory 0011H = not same device 0012H = no more files 0013H = disk write-protected 0014H = unknown unit 0015H = drive not ready 0016H = unknown command 0017H = data error (CRC check error) 0018H = bad request structure length 0019H = seek error 001AH = unknown media type 001BH = sector not found 001CH = printer out of paper 001DH = write fault 001EH = read fault 001FH = general failure 0020H = sharing violation 0021H = lock violation 0022H = disk change invalid 0023H = FCB unavailable 0024H = sharing buffer exceeded 0025H = code page mismatch 0026H = handle end of file operation not completed 0027H = disk full 0028H — 0031H reserved 0032H = unsupported network request 0033H = remote machine not listed 0034H = duplicate name on network 0035H = network name not found 0036H = network busy 0037H = device no longer exists on network

```
0038H = netBIOS command limit exceeded
0039H = error in network adapter hardware
003AH = incorrect response from network
003BH = unexpected network error
003CH = remote adapter is incompatible
003DH = print queue is full
003EH = not enough room for print file
003FH = print file was deleted
0040H = network name deleted
0041H = network access denied
0042H = incorrect network device type
0043H = network name not found
0044H = network name exceeded limit
0045H = netBIOS session limit exceeded
0046H = temporary pause
0047H = network request not accepted
0048H = print or disk redirection pause
0049H — 004FH reserved
0050H = file already exists
0051H = duplicate FCB
0052H = cannot make directory
0053H = failure in INT 24H (critical error)
0054H = too many redirections
0055H = duplicate redirection
0056H = invalid password
0057H = invalid parameter
0058H = network write failure
0059H = function not supported by network
005AH = required system component not installed
0065H = device not selected
```

Following are the error class codes as found in BH:

```
01H = no resources available
02H = temporary error
03H = authorization error
04H = internal software error
05H = hardware error
06H = system failure
07H = application software error
08H = item not found
09H = invalid format
0AH = item blocked
0BH = media error
0CH = item already exists
0DH = unknown error
```

Following is the recommended action as found in BL:

```
01H = retry operation
02H = delay and retry operation
03H = user retry
04H = abort processing
05H = immediate exit
06H = ignore error
07H = retry with user intervention
```

Following is a list of locus in CH:

```
01H = unknown source
02H = block device error
```

	03H = network area 04H = serial device error 05H = memory error
5AH	CREATE UNIQUE FILE NAME
Entry	AH = 5AH CX = attribute code DS:DX = address of the ASCII-Z string directory path
Exit	Carry is set for error condition AX = file handle if carry cleared DS:DX = address of the appended directory name
Notes	The ASCII-Z file directory path must end with a backslash (\). On exit the directory name is appended with a unique file name.
5BH	CREATE A DOS FILE
Entry	AH = 5BH CX = attribute code DS:DX = address of the ASCII-Z string contain the file name
Exit	Carry is set for error condition AX = file handle if carry cleared
Notes	The function only works in DOS version 3.X or higher.
5CH	LOCK/UNLOCK FILE CONTENTS
Entry	AH = 5CH BX = file handle CX:DX = offset address of locked/unlocked area SI:DI = number of bytes to lock or unlock beginning at offset
Exit	Carry is set for error condition
5DH	SET EXTENDED ERROR INFORMATION
Entry	AH = 5DH AL = 0AH DS:DX = address of the extended error data structure
Notes	This function is used by DOS version 3.1 or higher to store extended error information.
5EH	NETWORK/PRINTER
Entry	AH = 5EH AL = 00H (get network name) DS:DX = address of the ASCII-Z string containing network name

Exit	Carry is set for error condition CL = netBIOS number if carry cleared
Entry	AH = 5EH AL = 02H (define network printer) BX = redirection list CX = length of setup string DS:DX = address of printer setup buffer
Exit	Carry is set for error condition
Entry	AH = 5EH AL = 03H (read network printer setup string) BX = redirection list DS:DX = address of printer setup buffer
Exit	Carry is set for error condition CX = length of setup string if carry cleared ES:DI = address of printer setup buffer

62H	GET PSP ADDRESS
Entry	AH = 62H
Exit	BX = segment address of the current program
Notes	The function only works in DOS version 3.0 or higher.

65H	GET EXTENDED COUNTRY INFORMATION
Entry	AH = 65H AL = function code ES:DI = address of buffer to receive information
Exit	Carry is set for error condition CX = length of country information
Notes	The function only works in DOS version 3.3 or higher.

66H	GET/SET CODE PAGE
Entry	AH = 66H AL = function code BX = code page number
Exit	Carry is set for error condition BX = active code page number DX = default code page number
Notes	A function code in AL of 01H gets the code page number and a code of 02H sets the code page number

67H	SET HANDLE COUNT
Entry	AH = 67H BX = number of handles desired
Exit	Carry is set for error condition
Notes	This function is available for DOS version 3.3 or higher

68H	COMMIT FILE
Entry	AH = 68H BX = handle number
Exit	Carry is set for error condition Else, the date and time stamp is written to directory
Notes	This function is available for DOS version 3.3 or higher

6CH	EXTENDED OPEN FILE
Entry	AH = 6CH AL = 00H BX = open mode CX = attributes DX = open flag DS:SI = address of ASCII-Z string file name
Exit	AX = error code if carry is set AX = handle if carry is cleared CX = 0001H file existed and was opened CX = 0002H file did not exist and was created
Notes	This function is available for DOS version 4.0 or higher

BIOS FUNCTION CALLS

In addition to DOS function call INT 21H, some other BIOS function calls prove useful in controlling the I/O environment of the computer. Unlike INT 21H, which exists in the DOS program, the BIOS function calls are found stored in the BIOS ROM. These BIOS functions directly control the I/O devices with or without DOS loaded into a system.

INT 10H

The INT 10H BIOS interrupt is often called the video services interrupt because it directly controls the video display in a system. The INT 10H instruction uses register AH to select the video service provided by this interrupt.

Video Mode Selection.   The mode of operation for the video display is selected by placing a 00H into AH followed by one of many mode numbers in AL. Table A–3 lists the modes of operation found in video display systems using standard video modes. The VGA can use any mode listed, while the other displays are more restrictive in use. Additional higher resolution modes are explained later in this section.

Example A–6 lists a short sequence of instructions that place the video display in mode 03H. This mode is available on CGA, EGA, and VGA displays. This mode allows the display to draw test with 16 colors at various resolutions dependent upon the display adapter.

EXAMPLE A–6

```
0000 B4 00              MOV     AH,0            ;select mode
0002 B0 03              MOV     AL,3            ;mode is 03H
0004 CD 10              INT     10H
```

TABLE A–3   Video display modes

Mode	Type	Columns	Rows	Resolution	Standard	Colors
00H	Text	40	25	320 × 200	CGA	2
00H	Text	40	25	320 × 350	EGA	2
00H	Text	40	25	360 × 400	VGA	2
01H	Text	40	25	320 × 200	CGA	16
01H	Text	40	25	320 × 350	EGA	16
01H	Text	40	25	360 × 400	VGA	16
02H	Text	80	25	640 × 200	CGA	2
02H	Text	80	25	640 × 350	EGA	2
02H	Text	80	25	720 × 400	VGA	2
03H	Text	80	25	640 × 200	CGA	16
03H	Text	80	25	640 × 350	EGA	16
03H	Text	80	25	720 × 400	VGA	16
04H	Graphics	40	25	320 × 200	CGA	4
05H	Graphics	40	25	320 × 200	CGA	2
06H	Graphics	80	25	640 × 200	CGA	2
07H	Text	80	25	720 × 350	EGA	4
07H	Text	80	25	720 × 400	VGA	4
0DH	Graphics	80	25	320 × 200	CGA	16
0EH	Graphics	80	25	640 × 200	CGA	16
0FH	Graphics	80	25	640 × 350	EGA	4
10H	Graphics	80	25	640 × 350	EGA	16
11H	Graphics	80	30	640 × 480	VGA	2
12H	Graphics	80	30	640 × 480	VGA	16
13H	Graphics	40	25	320 × 200	VGA	256

Cursor control.   Table A–4 shows the function codes used to control the cursor on the video display. These cursor control function will work on any video display from the CGA display to the latest super VGA display.

   If an SVGA (super VGA) EVGA (extended VGA), or XVGA (also extended VGA) adapter is available, the super VGA mode is set by using INT 10H function call AX = 4F02H with BX = to the VGA mode for these advanced display adapters. This conforms to the VESA standard for VGA adapters. Table A–5 shows the modes selected by register BX for this INT 10H function call.

TABLE A–4   Video BIOS (INT 10H) functions

00H	SELECT VIDEO MODE
Entry	AH = 00H AL = mode number
Exit	Mode changed and screen cleared
01H	SELECT CURSOR TYPE
Entry	AH = 01H CH = starting line number CL = ending line number
Exit	Cursor size changed
02H	SELECT CURSOR POSITION
Entry	AH = 02H BH = page number (usually 0) DH = row number (beginning with 0) DL = column number (beginning with 0)
Exit	Changes cursor to new position
03H	READ CURSOR POSITION
Entry	AH = 03H BH = page number
Exit	CH = starting line (cursor size) CL = ending line (cursor size) DH = current row DL = current column
04H	READ LIGHT PEN
Entry	AH = 04H (not supported in VGA)

TABLE A–4   (continued)

Exit	AH = 0, light pen triggered BX = pixel column CX = pixel row DH = character row DL = character column

05H	SELECT DISPLAY PAGE
Entry	AH = 05H AL = page number
Exit	Page number selected. Following are the valid page numbers. Mode 0 and 1 support pages 0—7 Mode 2 and 3 support pages 0—7 Mode 4, 5, and 6 support page 0 Mode 7 and D support pages 0—7 Mode E supports pages 0—3 Mode F and 10 support pages 0—1 Mode 11, 12, and 13 support page 0

06H	SCROLL PAGE UP
Entry	AH = 06H AL = number of lines to scroll (0 clears window) BH = character attribute for new lines CH = top row of scroll window CL = left column of scroll window DH = bottom row of scroll window DL = right column of scroll window
Exit	Scrolls window from the bottom toward the top of the screen. Blank lines fill the bottom using the character attribute in BH.

07H	SCROLL PAGE DOWN
Entry	AH = 07H AL = number of lines to scroll (0 clears window) BH = character attribute for new lines CH = top row of scroll window CL = left column of scroll window DH = bottom row of scroll window DL = right column of scroll window
Exit	Scrolls window from the top toward the bottom of the screen. Blank lines fill from the top using the character attribute in BH.

08H	READ ATTRIBUTE/CHARACTER AT CURRENT CURSOR POSITION
Entry	AH = 08H BH = page number

Exit	AL = ASCII character code AH = character attribute Note: This function does not advance the cursor.
09H	WRITE ATTRIBUTE/CHARACTER AT CURRENT CURSOR POSITION
Entry	AH = 09H AL = ASCII character code BH = page number BL = character attribute CX = number of characters to write
Exit	Note: This function does not advance the cursor.
0AH	WRITE CHARACTER AT CURRENT CURSOR POSITION
Entry	AH = 0AH AL = ASCII character code BH = page number CX = number of characters to write
Exit	Note: This function does not advance the cursor.
0FH	READ VIDEO MODE
Entry	AH = 0FH
Exit	AL = current video mode AH = number of character columns BH = page number
10H	SET VGA PALETTE REGISTER
Entry	AH = 10H AL = 10H BX = color number (0—255) CH = green (0—63) CL = blue (0—63) DH = red (0—63)
Exit	Palette register color is changed. Note: the first 16 colors (0—15) are used in the 16-color, VGA text mode and other modes.
10H	READ VGA PALETTE REGISTER
Entry	AH = 10H AL = 15H BX = color number (0—255)

TABLE A–4   (continued)

Exit	CH = green CL = blue DH = red
11H	**GET ROM CHARACTER SET**
Entry	AH = 11H AL = 30H BH = 2 = ROM 8 x 14 character set BH = 3 = ROM 8 x 8 character set BH = 4 = ROM 8 x 8 extended character set BH = 5 = ROM 9 x 14 character set BH = 6 = ROM 8 x 16 character set BH = 7 = ROM 9 x 16 character set
Exit	CX = bytes per character DL = rows per character ES:BP = address of character set

TABLE A–5   Extended VGA functions

BX	Function
100H	640 × 400 with 256 colors
101H	640 × 480 with 256 colors
102H	800 × 600 with 16 colors
103H	800 × 600 with 256 colors
104H	1,024 × 768 with 16 colors
105H	1,024 × 768 with 256 colors
106H	1,280 × 1,024 with 16 colors
107H	1,280 × 1,024 with 256 colors
108H	80 × 60 in text mode
109H	132 × 25 in text mode
10AH	132 × 43 in text mode
10BH	132 × 50 in text mode
10CH	132 × 60 in text mode

INT 11H

This function is used to determine the type of equipment installed in the system. To use this call, the AX register is loaded with an FFFFH and then the INT 11H instruction is executed. In return, an INT 11H provides information as listed in Figure A–8.

INT 12H

The memory size is returned by the INT 12H instruction. After executing the INT 12H instruction, the AX register contains the number of 1K byte blocks of

FIGURE A–8 The contents of AX as it indicates the equipment attached to the computer.

P1, P0 = number of parallel ports
G = 1 if game I/O attached
S2, S1, S0 = number of serial ports
D2, D1 = number of disk drives

memory (conventional memory in the first 1M bytes of address space) installed in the computer.

INT 13H

This call controls the diskettes (5¼" or 3½") and also fixed or hard disk drives attached to the system. Table A–6 lists the functions available to this interrupt via register AH. The direct control of a floppy disk or hard disk can lead to problems. Therefore, we only provide a listing of the functions without detail on their usage. Before using these functions, refer to the BIOS literature available from the company that produced your version of the BIOS ROM.

INT 14H

Interrupt 14H controls the serial COM (communications) ports attached to the computer. The computer system contains two COM ports, COM1 and COM2, unless you have a newer AT-style machine where the number of communications ports are extended to COM3 and COM4. Communications ports are normally controlled with software packages that allow data transfer through a modem and the telephone lines. The INT 14H instruction controls these ports as illustrated in Table A–7.

INT 15H

The INT 15H instruction controls many of the various I/O devices interfaced to the computer. It also allows access to protected mode operation and the extended memory system on an 80286, 80386, or 80486 system. Table A–8 lists the functions supported by INT 15H.

INT 16H

The INT 16H instruction is used as a keyboard interrupt. This interrupt is accessed by DOS interrupt INT 21H, but can be accessed directly. Table A–9 shows the functions performed by INT 16H.

TABLE A–6 Disk I/O function via INT 13H

AH	Function
00H	Reset disk system
01H	Get disk system status into AL
02H	Read sector
03H	Write sector
04H	Verify sector
05H	Format track
06H	Format bad track
07H	Format drive
08H	Get drive parameters
09H	Initialize fixed disk characteristics
0AH	Read long sector
0BH	Write long sector
0CH	Seek
0DH	Reset fixed disk system
0EH	Read sector buffer
0FH	Write sector buffer
10H	Get drive status
11H	Recalibrate drive
12H	Controller RAM diagnostics
13H	Controller drive diagnostics
14H	Controller internal diagnostics
15H	Get disk type
16H	Get disk change status
17H	Set disk type
18H	Set media type
19H	Park heads
1AH	Format ESDI drive

TABLE A–7 COM port interrupt INT 14H

AH	Function
00H	Initialize communications port
01H	Send character
02H	Receive character
03H	Get COM port status
04H	Extended initialize communications port
05H	Extended communications port control

TABLE A-8 The I/O subsystem interrupt INT 15H

AH	Function
00H	Cassette motor on
01H	Cassette motor off
02H	Read cassette
03H	Write cassette
0FH	Format ESDI drive periodic interrupt
21H	Keyboard intercept
80H	Device open
81H	Device closed
82H	Process termination
83H	Event wait
84H	Read joystick
85H	System request key
86H	Delay
87H	Move extended block of memory
88H	Get extended memory size
89H	Enter protected mode
90H	Device wait
91H	Device power on self test (POST)
C0H	Get system environment
C1H	Get address of extended BIOS data area
C2H	Mouse pointer
C3H	Set watch-dog timer
C4H	Programmable option select

TABLE A-9 Keyboard interrupt INT 16H

AH	Function
00H	Read keyboard character
01H	Get keyboard status
02H	Get keyboard flags
03H	Set repeat rate
04H	Set keyclick
05H	Push character and scan code

TABLE A–10   Parallel
printer interrupt INT 17H

AH	Function
00H	Print character
01H	Initialize printer
02H	Get printer status

INT 17H

The INT 17H instruction accesses the parallel printer port usually labeled LPT1 in most systems. Table A–10 lists the three functions available for the INT 17H instruction.

DOS SYSTEM MEMORY MAP

Figure A–9 illustrates the memory map used by a DOS computer system. The first 1M byte of memory is listed with all the areas containing different devices and programs used with DOS. The transient program area (TPA) is where DOS applications programs are loaded and executed. The size of the TPA is usually slightly over 500K bytes unless many TSR programs and drivers fill memory before the TPA.

DOS LOW MEMORY ASSIGNMENTS

Table A–11 shows the low memory assignments (00000H–005FFH) for the DOS-based microprocessor system. This area of memory contains the interrupt vectors, BIOS data area, and the DOS/BIOS data area illustrated in Figure A–9.

FIGURE A–9   Memory map
of DOS illustrating the first
1M bytes of memory.

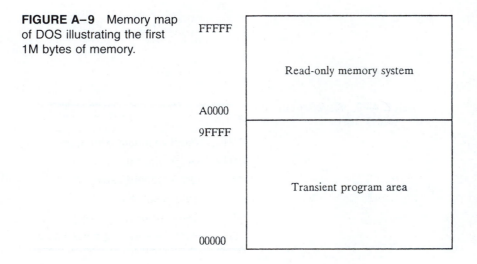

TABLE A-11 DOS low memory assignments

Location	Purpose	
00000H–002FFH	System interrupt vectors	
00300H–003FFH	System interrupt vectors, power on, and bootstrap area	
00400H–00407H	COM1–COM4 I/O port base addresses	
00408H–0040FH	LPT1–LPT4 I/O port base addresses	
00410H–00411H	Equipment flag word, returned in AX by an INT 11H	
	Bit	Purpose
	15–14	Number of parallel printers (LPT1–LPT4)
	13	Internal MODEM installed
	12	Joystick installed
	11–9	Number of serial ports (COM1–COM4)
	8	Unused
	7–6	Number of disk drives
	5–4	Video mode
	3–2	Unused
	1	Math coprocessor installed
	0	Disk installed
00412H	Reserved	
00413H–00414H	Memory size in K bytes (0–640K)	
00415H–00416H	Reserved	
00417H	Keyboard control byte	
	Bit	Purpose
	7	Insert locked
	6	Caps locked
	5	Numbers locked
	4	Scroll locked
	3	Alternate key pressed
	2	Control key pressed
	1	Left shift key pressed
	0	Right shift key pressed
00418H	Keyboard control byte	
	Bit	Purpose
	7	Insert key pressed
	6	Caps lock key pressed
	5	Numbers lock key pressed
	4	Scroll lock key pressed
	3	Pause locked
	2	System request key pressed
	1	Left alternate key pressed

Location	Purpose
	0 Right control key pressed
00419H	Alternate keyboard entry
0041AH–0041BH	Keyboard buffer header pointer
0041CH–0041DH	Keyboard buffer tail pointer
0041EH–0043DH	32 byte keyboard buffer area
0043EH–00448H	Disk drive control area
00449H–00466H	Video control data area
00467H–0046BH	Reserved
0046CH–0046FH	Timer counter
00470H	Timer overflow
00471H	Break key state
00472H–00473H	Reset flag
00474H–00477H	Hard disk drive data area
00478H–0047BH	LPT1–LPT4 timeout area
0047CH–0047FH	COM1–COM4 timeout area
00480H–00481H	Keyboard buffer start offset pointer
00482H–00483H	Keyboard buffer end offset pointer
00484H–0048AH	Video control data area
0048BH–00495H	Hard drive control area
00496H	Keyboard mode, state, and type flag
00497H	Keyboard LED flags
00498H–00499H	Offset address of user wait complete flag
0049AH–0049BH	Segment address of user wait complete flag
0049CH–0049DH	User wait count (low word)
0049EH–0049FH	User wait count (high word)
004A0H	Wait active flag
004A1H–004A7H	Reserved
004A8H–004ABH	Pointer to video parameters
004ACH–004EFH	Reserved
004F0H–004FFH	Applications program communications area
00500H	Print screen status
00501H–00503H	Reserved
00504H	Single drive mode status
00505H–0050FH	Reserved
00510H–00521H	Used by ROM BASIC
00522H–0052FH	Used by DOS for disk initialization
00530H–00533H	Used by MODE command
00534H–005FFH	Reserved

DOS VERSION 5.0 MEMORY MAP

Microsoft DOS version 5.0 has a slightly different memory map than earlier versions of DOS because of its ability to load drivers and programs in the system area. If the microprocessor is an 80386 or 80486, memory between the ROM memory located between addresses A0000H and FFFFFH can be backfilled with extended memory for drivers and programs. In many systems memory area D0000H–DFFFFH is unused as is E0000H–EFFFFH. These areas can be filled with extended memory through memory paging found in the 80386 and 80486 microprocessors. This new memory area can then be filled with and addressed by normal real mode memory programs extending the memory available to DOS applications.

The drivers HIMEM.SYS and EMM386.SYS are used to accomplish the backfilling. If you want to use memory area E0000H–EFFFFH, you must load EMM386.SYS as EMM386.SYS I=E000=EFFF. Using these drivers increases the DOS TPA to more than 600K bytes. A typical CONFIG.SYS file for DOS 5.0 appears in Example A–7. Notice that drivers after EMM386.SYS are loaded in high memory with the DEVICEHIGH directive instead of the DEVICE directive. Programs are loaded using the LOADHIGH or LH directive in front of the program name.

EXAMPLE A–7

```
(CONFIG.SYS file)

FILES=30
BUFFERS=30
STACKS=64,128
FCBS=48
SHELL=C:\DOS\COMMAND.COM C:\DOS\/E:256 /P
DEVICE=C:\DOS\HIMEM.SYS
DOS=HIGH,UMB
DEVICE=C:\DOS\EMM386.EXE I=C800-EFFF NOEMS
DEVICEHIGH SIZE=1EB0 C:\LASERLIB\SONY_CDU.SYS /D:SONY_001 /B:340 /Q:* /T:* /M:H
DEVICEHIGH SIZE=0910 C:\DOS\SETVER.EXE
DEVICEHIGH SIZE=3150 C:\MOUSE1\MOUSE.SYS
LASTDRIVE = F


(AUTOEXEC.BAT file)

PATH C:\DOS;C:\;C:\MASM\BIN;C:\MASM\BINB\;C:\UTILITY;C:\WS;C:\LASERLIB
SET BLASTER=A220 I7 D1 T3
SET INCLUDE=C:\MASM\INCLUDE\
SET HELPFILES=C:\MASM\HELP\*.HLP
SET INIT=C:\MASM\INIT\
SET ASMEX=C:\MASM\SAMPLES\
SET TMP=C:\MASM\TMP
SET SOUND=C:\SB
LOADHIGH C:\LASERLIB\MSCDEX.EXE /D:SONY_001 /L:F /M:8
LOADHIGH C:\LASERLIB\LLTSR.EXE ALT-Q
LOADHIGH C:\DOS\FASTOPEN C:=256
LOADHIGH C:\DOS\DOSKEY /BUFSIZE=1024
LOADHIGH C:\LASERLIB\PRINTF.COM
DOSKEY GO=DOSSHELL
DOSSHELL
```

APPENDIX B

Instruction Set Summary

The instruction set summary, which follows this introduction, contains a complete listing of all instructions for the 8086, 8088, 80286, 80386, and 80486 microprocessors. Note that numeric coprocessor instructions for the 80486 appear in Chapter 12.

Each instruction entry lists the mnemonic opcode plus a brief description of the purpose of the instruction. Also listed is the binary machine language coding for each instruction plus any other data required to form the instruction such as displacement or immediate data. Next to the binary machine language version of the instruction appears the flag register bits and any change that might occur for a given instruction. In this listing, a blank indicates no change, a ? indicates a change with an unpredictable outcome, a * indicates a predictable change, a 1 indicates the flag is set, and a 0 indicates the flag is cleared.

Before the instruction listing begins, some information about the bit settings in the binary machine language versions of the instructions is required. Table B–1 shows the modifier bits, coded as oo in the instruction listings, so instructions can be formed with a register, displacement, or no displacement.

Table B–2 lists the memory-addressing modes available with the register/memory field, coded as mmm. This table applies to all versions of the microprocessor.

Table B–3 lists the register options (rrr) when encoded for either an 8-bit or a 16-bit register. This table also lists the 32-bit registers used with the 80386 and 80486 microprocessors.

TABLE B–1 The modifier bits, coded as oo in the instruction listing

oo	Function
00	If mmm = 110, then a displacement follows the opcode; otherwise, no displacement is used
01	An 8-bit signed displacement follows the opcode
10	A 16-bit signed displacement follows the opcode
11	mmm specifies a register, instead of an addressing mode

TABLE B-2 Register/memory field (mmm) description

mmm	Function
000	DS:[BX+SI]
001	DS:[BX+DI]
010	SS:[BP+SI]
011	SS:[BP+DI]
100	DS:[SI]
101	DS:[DI]
110	SS:[BP]
111	DS:[BX]

TABLE B-3 Register field (rrr) options

rrr	W=0	W=1	reg32
000	AL	AX	EAX
001	CL	CX	ECX
010	DL	DX	EDX
011	BL	BX	EBX
100	AH	SP	ESP
101	CH	BP	EBP
110	DH	SI	ESI
111	BH	DI	EDI

Table B-4 lists the segment register bit assignments (rrr) for the MOV, PUSH, and POP instructions, which use these segment registers.

When the 80386 and 80486 microprocessors are used, some of the definitions provided in the prior tables will change. Refer to Tables B-5 and B-6 for these changes as they apply to the 80386 and 80486 microprocessors.

The instruction set summary that follows lists all of the instructions, with examples, for the 8086, 8088, 80286, 80386, and 80486 microprocessors. Missing are the segment override prefixes: CS (2EH), SS (36H), DS (3EH), ES (26H), FS (64H), and GS (65H). These prefixes are one byte in length and placed in memory before the instruction that is prefixed.

Table B-7 lists the effective address calculations that apply only to the 8086 and 8088 microprocessors as ea or a in the instruction set summary. For example, the 8086 ADD DATA,AL instruction 16 + ea clocks. Because the table lists displacement addressing as requiring 6 clocks, this instruction requires 22 clocks to execute. Note that all times listed are maximum times and that in some cases the microprocessor may execute the instruction in less time.

The D-bit, in the code segment descriptor, indicates the default size of the operand and the addresses for the 80386 and 80486 microprocessors. If D = 1, then all addresses and operands are 32 bits and if D = 0, all addresses and operands are 16 bits. In the real mode, the D-bit is set to zero by the 80386 and 80486 microprocessors, so operands and addresses are 16-bits.

TABLE B–4   Register field assignments (rrr) that are used to represent the segment registers

rrr	Register
000	ES
001	CS
010	SS
011	DS

TABLE B–5   Index registers are specified with rrr in the 80386 and 80486 microprocessor

rrr	Index register
000	EAX
001	ECX
010	EDX
011	EBX
100	No index
101	EBP
110	ESI
111	EDI

Table B–6   Possible combinations of oo, mmm, and rrr for the 80386 and 80486 instruction set using the 32-bit addressing mode

oo	mmm	rrr	Function
00	000	—	DS:[EAX]
00	001	—	DS:[ECX]
00	010	—	DS:[EDX]
00	011	—	DS:[EBX]
00	100	000	DS:[EAX+scaled-index]
00	100	001	DS:[ECX+scaled-index]
00	100	010	DS:[EDX+scaled-index]
00	100	011	DS:[EBX+scaled-index]
00	100	100	SS:[ESP+scaled-index]
00	100	101	DS:[disp32+scaled-index]
00	100	110	DS:[ESI+scaled-index]
00	100	111	DS:[EDI+scaled-index]
00	101	—	DS:disp32
00	110	—	DS:[ESI]
00	111	—	DS:[EDI]
01	000	—	DS:[EAX+disp8]

Table B–6   *continued*

oo	mmm	rrr	Function
01	001	—	DS:[ECX+disp8]
01	010	—	DS:[EDX+disp8]
01	011	—	DS:[EBX+disp8]
01	100	000	DS:[EAX+scaled-index+disp8]
01	100	001	DS:[ECX+scaled-index+disp8]
01	100	010	DS:[EDX+scaled-index+disp8]
01	100	011	DS:[EBX+scaled-index+disp8]
01	100	100	SS:[ESP+scaled-index+disp8]
01	100	101	SS:[EBP+scaled-index+disp8]
01	100	110	DS:[ESI+scaled-index+disp8]
01	100	111	DS:[EDI+scaled-index+disp8]
01	101	—	SS:[EBP+disp8]
01	110	—	DS:[ESI+disp8]
01	111	—	DS:[EDI+disp8]
10	000	—	DS:[EAX+disp32]
10	001	—	DS:[ECX+disp32]
10	010	—	DS:[EDX+disp32]
10	011	—	DS:[EBX+disp32]
10	100	000	DS:[EAX+scaled-index+disp32]
10	100	001	DS:[ECX+scaled-index+disp32]
10	100	010	DS:[EDX+scaled-index+disp32]
10	100	011	DS:[EBX+scaled-index+disp32]
10	100	100	SS:[ESP+scaled-index+disp32]
10	100	101	SS:[EBP+scaled-index+disp32]
10	100	110	DS:[ESI+scaled-index+disp32]
10	100	111	DS:[EDI+scaled-index+disp32]
01	101	—	SS:[EBP+disp32]
01	110	—	DS:[ESI+disp32]
01	111	—	DS:[EDI+disp32]

Notes: disp8 = 8-bit displacement, disp32 = 32-bit displacement

TABLE B–7   Effective address calculations for the 8086 and 8088 microprocessors

Type	Clocks	Example
Base or index	5	MOV CL,[DI]
Displacement	3	MOV AL,DATA
Base plus index [BP+DI] or [BX+SI]	7	MOV BL,[BP+DI]
Base plus index [BP+SI] of [BX+DI]	8	MOV CL,[BP+SI]
Displacement plus base or index	9	MOV DH,[DI+20H]
Base plus index plus displacement [BP+DI+disp] or [BX+SI+disp]	11	MOV CX,DATA[BX+SI]
Base plus index plus displacement [BP+SI+disp] or [BX+DI+disp]	12	MOV CX,[BX+DI+2]
Segment override prefix	ea+2	MOV AL,ES:DATA

The address-size prefix (67H) must be placed before instructions in the 80386 and 80486 to change the default size as selected by the D-bit. For example, the MOV AX,[ECX] instruction must have the address-size prefix placed before it in machine code if the default size is 16 bits. If the default size is 32 bits, the address prefix is not needed with this instruction. The operand-override prefix (66H) functions in much the same manner as the address-size prefix. In the previous example, the operand size is 16 bits. If the D-bit selects 32-bit operands and addresses, this instruction requires the operand-size prefix.

INSTRUCTION SET SUMMARY

AAA	ASCII adjust after addition		
00110111		O D I T S Z A P C	
		? ? ? * ? *	
Example			Clocks
AAA		8086	8
		8088	8
		80286	3
		80386	4
		80486	3

AAD	ASCII adjust before division		
11010101 00001010		O D I T S Z A P C	
		? * * ? * ?	
Example			Clocks

AAD		
	8086	60
	8088	60
	80286	14
	80386	19
	80486	14

AAM   ASCII adjust after multiplication

11010100 00001010	O D I T S Z A P C	
	? * * ? * ?	
Example		Clocks
AAM	8086	83
	8088	83
	80286	16
	80386	17
	80486	15

AAS   ASCII adjust after subtraction

00111111	O D I T S Z A P C	
	? ? ? * ? *	
Example		Clocks
AAS	8086	8
	8088	8
	80286	3
	80386	4
	80486	3

ADC   Addition with carry

000100dw oorrrmmm disp		O D I T S Z A P C	
		* * * * * *	
Format	Examples		Clocks
ADC reg,reg	ADC AX,BX ADC AL,BL ADC EAX,EBX ADC CX,SI ADC ESI,EDI	8086	3
		8088	3
		80286	2
		80386	2
		80486	1

ADC mem,reg	ADC DATA,AL ADC LIST,SI ADC DATA [DI],CL ADC [EAX],BL ADC [EBX+2*ECX],EDX	8086	16+ea
		8088	24+ea
		80286	7
		80386	7
		80486	3
ADC reg,mem	ADC BL,DATA ADC SI,LIST ADC CL,DATA [DI] ADC CL,[EAX] ADC EDX,[EBX+100H]	8086	9+ea
		8088	13+ea
		80286	7
		80386	6
		80486	2

100000sw oo010mmm disp data

Format	Examples		Clocks
ADC reg,imm	ADC CX,3 ADC DI,1AH ADC DL,34H ADC EAX,12345 ADC CX,1234H	8086	4
		8088	4
		80286	3
		80386	2
		80486	1
ADC mem,imm	ADC DATA,33 ADC LIST,'A' ADC DATA [DI],2 ADC BYTE PTR [EAX],3 ADC WORD PTR [DI],669H	8086	17+ea
		8088	23+ea
		80286	7
		80386	7
		80486	3

0001010w data

Format	Examples		Clocks
ADC acc,imm	ADC AX,3 ADC AL,1AH ADC AH,34 ADC EAX,3 ADC AL,'Z'	8086	4
		8088	4
		80286	3
		80386	2
		80486	1

ADD   Addition

000000dw oorrrmmm disp		O D I T S Z A P C
		* * * * * *

Format	Examples		Clocks

ADD reg,reg	ADD AX,BX
	ADD AL,BL
	ADD EAX,EBX
	ADD CX,SI
	ADD ESI,EDI
		8086	3

		8088	3
		80286	2
		80386	2
		80486	1

ADD mem,reg	ADD DATA,AL
	ADD LIST,SI
	ADD DATA [DI],CL
	ADD [EAX],CL
	ADD [EBX+4*EDX],EBX
		8086	16+ea

		8088	24+ea
		80286	7
		80386	7
		80486	3

ADD reg,mem	ADD BL,DATA
	ADD SI,LIST
	ADD CL,DATA [DI]
	ADD CL,[EAX]
	ADD EDX,[EBX+200H]
		80286	9+ea

		8088	13+ea
		80286	7
		80386	6
		80486	2

100000sw oo000mmm disp data		
Format	Examples		Clocks

ADD reg,imm	ADD CX,3
	ADD DI,1AH
	ADD DL,34H
	ADD EAX,123456
	ADD CX,18AFH
		80286	4

		8088	4
		80286	3
		80386	2
		80486	1

ADD mem,imm	ADD DATA,33
	ADD LIST,'A'
	ADD DATA [DI],2
	ADD BYTE PTR [EAX],3
	ADD WORD PTR [DI],6A8H
		8086	17+ea

		8088	23+ea
		80286	7
		80386	7
		80486	3

0000010w data

Format	Examples		

ADD acc,imm	ADD AX,3
	ADD AL,1AH
	ADD AH,56
	ADD EAX,3
	ADD AL,'D'
			Clocks

		8086	4
		8088	4
		80286	3
		80386	2
		80486	1

AND   Logical AND

001000dw oorrrmmm disp

O	D	I	T	S	Z	A	P	C
0				*	*	?	*	0

Format	Examples		Clocks
AND reg,reg	AND CX,BX AND DL,BL AND ECX,EBX AND BP,SI AND EDX,EDI	8086	3
		8088	3
		80286	2
		80386	2
		80486	1
AND mem,reg	AND BIT,CH AND LIST,DI AND DATA [BX],CL AND [ECX],AL AND [EDX+8*ECX],EDI	8086	16+ea
		8088	24+ea
		80286	7
		80386	7
		80486	3
AND reg,mem	AND BL,DATA AND SI,LIST AND CL,DATA [DI] AND CL,[EAX] AND EDX,[EBX+34AH]	8086	9+ea
		8088	13+ea
		80286	7
		80386	6
		80486	2

100000sw oo100mmm disp data

Format	Examples		Clocks
AND reg,imm	AND BP,1 AND DI,10H AND DL,34H AND EBP,12345 AND SP,1234H	8086	4
		8088	4
		80286	3
		80386	2
		80486	1

AND mem,imm	AND DATA,33 AND LIST,4 AND DATA [SI],2 AND BYTE PTR [EAX],3 AND DWORD PTR [DI],32	8086	17+ea
		8088	23+ea
		80286	7
		80386	7
		80486	3

0010010w data			
Format	Examples		Clocks
AND acc,imm	AND AX,15 AND AL,1FH AND AH,34 AND EAX,3 AND AL,'R'	8086	4
		8088	4
		80286	3
		80386	2
		80486	1

ARPL   Adjust requested privilege level

01100011 oorrrmmm disp		O D I T S Z A P C *	
Format	Examples		Clocks
ARPL reg,reg	ARPL AX,BX ARPL BX,SI ARPL CX,DX ARPL BX,AX ARPL DI,SI	8086	—
		8088	—
		80286	10
		80386	20
		80486	9
ARPL mem,reg	ARPL NUMB,AX ARPL LIST,DI ARPL DATA [BX],CX ARPL [ECX],AX ARPL [EDX+4*ECX],DI	8086	—
		8088	—
		80286	11
		80386	21
		80486	9

BOUND   Check array bounds

01100010 oorrrmmm disp		O D I T S Z A P C	
Format	Examples		Clocks
BOUND	BOUND AX,BETS	8086	—

reg,mem	BOUND BX,SAID BOUND CX,DATA BOUND BX,[DI] BOUND DI,[BX+2]	8088	—
		80286	13
		80386	10
		80486	7

BSF   Bit scan forward

00001111 10111100 oorrmmm disp		O D I T S Z A P C *
Format	Examples	Clocks

BSF reg,reg	BSF AX,BX BSF BX,SI BSF ECX,EBX BSF EBX,EAX BSF DI,SI	8086	—
		8088	—
		80286	—
		80386	10+3n
		80486	6—42
BSF reg,mem	BSF AX,DATA BSF BP,LISTG BSF ECX,MEMORY BSF EAX,DATA6 BSF DI,[ECX]	8086	—
		8088	—
		80286	—
		80386	10+3n
		80486	7—43

BSR   Bit scan reverse

00001111 10111101 oorrmmm disp		O D I T S Z A P C *
Format	Examples	Clocks

BSR reg,reg	BSR AX,BX BSR BX,SI BSR ECX,EBX BSR EBX,EAX BSR DI,SP	8086	—
		8088	—
		80286	—
		80386	10+3n
		80486	6—103
BSR reg,mem	BSR AX,DATA BSR BP,LISTG BSR ECX,MEMORY BSR EAX,DATA6 BSR DI,[EBX]	8086	—
		8088	—
		80286	—
		80386	10+3n
		80486	7—104

BSWAP   Byte swap

00001111 11001rrr		O D I T S Z A P C	
Format	**Examples**		**Clocks**
BSWAP reg	BSWAP EAX	8086	—
	BSWAP EBX		
	BSWAP ECX	8088	—
	BSWAP EDX		
	BSWAP EDI	80286	—
		80386	—
		80486	1

BT   Bit test

00001111 10111010 oo100mmm disp data		O D I T S Z A P C *	
Format	**Examples**		**Clocks**
BT reg,imm8	BT AX,2	8086	—
	BT CX,4		
	BT BP,10H	8088	—
	BT CX,8		
	BT BX,2	80286	—
		80386	3
		80486	3
BT mem,imm8	BT DATA1,2	8086	—
	BT LIST,2		
	BT DATA [DI],2	8088	—
	BT [BX],1		
	BT FROG,3	80286	—
		80386	6
		80486	3

00001111 10100011 disp			
Format	**Examples**		**Clocks**
BT reg,reg	BT AX,CX	8086	—
	BT CX,DX		
	BT BP,AX	8088	—
	BT SI,CX		
	BT CX,BP	80286	—
		80386	3
		80486	3

BT mem,reg	BT DATA1,AX BT LIST,DX BT DATA3,CX BT DATA9,BX BT DATA[[DI],AX	8086	—
		8088	—
		80286	—
		80386	12
		80486	8

BTC   Bit test and complement

00001111 10111010 oo111mmm disp data		O D I T S Z A P C *
Format	Examples	Clocks

BTC reg,imm8	BTC AX,2 BTC CX,4 BTC BP,10H BTC CX,8 BTC BX,2	8086	—
		8088	—
		80286	—
		80386	6
		80486	6
BTC mem,imm8	DATA1,2 BTC LIST,2 BTC DATA [DI],3 BTC [BX],1 BTC TOAD,5	8086	—
		8088	—
		80286	—
		80386	8
		80486	8

00001111 10111011 disp		
Format	Examples	Clocks

BTC reg,reg	BTC AX,CX BTC CX,DX BTC BP,AX BTC SI,CX BTC CX,BX	8086	—
		8088	—
		80286	—
		80386	6
		80486	6
BTC mem,reg	BTC DATA1,AX BTC LIST,DX BTC DATA3,CX BTC DATA9,BX BTC DATA [DI],AX	8086	—
		8088	—
		80286	—
		80386	13
		80486	13

BTR   Bit test and reset

| 00001111 10111010 oo110mmm disp data | | O D I T S Z A P C
* | |
Format	Examples		Clocks
BTR reg,imm8	BTR AX,2 BTR CX,4 BTR BP,10H BTR CX,8 BTR BX,2	8086	—
		8088	—
		80286	—
		80386	6
		80486	6
BTR mem,imm8	BTR DATA1,2 BTR LIST,2 BTR DATA [DI],4 BTR [BX],1 BTR SLED,6	8086	—
		8088	—
		80286	—
		80386	8
		80486	8

| 00001111 10110011 disp | | | |
Format	Examples		Clocks
BTR reg,reg	BTR AX,CX BTR CX,DX BTR BP,AX BTR SI,CX BTR BP,CX	8086	—
		8088	—
		80286	—
		80386	6
		80486	6
BTR mem,reg	BTR DATA1,AX BTR LIST,DX BTR DATA3,CX BTR DATA9,BX BTR DATA [BX],AX	8086	—
		8088	—
		80286	—
		80386	13
		80486	13

BTS   Bit test and set

| 00001111 10111010 oo101mmm disp data | | O D I T S Z A P C
* | |
Format	Examples		Clocks
BTS reg,imm8	BTS AX,2 BTS CX,4 BTS BP,10H BTS CX,8 BTS BX,3	8086	—
		8088	—
		80286	—
		80386	6
		80486	6

BTS mem,imm8	BTS DATA1,2 BTS LIST,2 BTS DATA [BP],7 BTS [BX],1 BTS FROG,3	8086	—
		8088	—
		80286	—
		80386	8
		80486	8

00001111 10101011 disp

Format	Examples		Clocks
BTS reg,reg	BTS AX,CX BTS CX,DX BTS BP,AX BTS SI,CX BTS CX,BP	8086	—
		8088	—
		80286	—
		80386	6
		80486	6
BTS mem,reg	BTS DATA1,AX BTS LIST,DX BTS DATA3,CX BTS DATA9,BX BTS DATA [BP],AX	8086	—
		8088	—
		80286	—
		80386	13
		80486	13

CALL   Call procedure (subroutine)

11101000 disp   O D I T S Z A P C

Format	Examples		Clocks
CALL label (near)	CALL FOR FUN CALL HOME CALL ET CALL WAITING CALL SOMEONE	8086	19
		8088	23
		80286	7
		80386	3
		80486	3

10011010 disp

Format	Examples		Clocks
CALL label (far)	CALL FAR PTR DATES CALL WHAT CALL WHERE CALL FARCE CALL WHOM	8086	28
		8088	36
		80286	13
		80386	17
		80486	18

11111111 oo010mmm

Format	Examples		Clocks
CALL reg (near)	CALL AX CALL BX CALL CX CALL DI CALL SI	8086	16
		8088	20
		80286	7
		80386	7
		80486	5
CALL mem (near)	CALL ADDRESS CALL NEAR PTR [DI] CALL DATA CALL FROG CALL HERO	8086	21+ea
		8088	29+ea
		80286	11
		80386	10
		80486	5

11111111 oo011mmm

Format	Examples		Clocks
CALL mem (far)	CALL FAR_LIST [SI] CALL FROM_HERE CALL TO_THERE CALL SIXX CALL OCT	8086	37+ea
		8088	53+ea
		80286	16
		80386	22
		80486	17

CBW   Convert byte to word

10011000		O D I T S Z A P C
Example		Clocks
CBW	8086	2
	8088	2
	80286	2
	80386	3
	80486	3

CDQ   Convert double word to quad word

10011001		O D I T S Z A P C
Example		Clocks

CDQ	8086	—
	8088	—
	80286	—
	80386	2
	80486	2

CLC   Clear carry flag

11111000		O D I T S Z A P C 0
Example		Clocks

CLC	8086	2
	8088	2
	80286	2
	80386	2
	80486	2

CLD   Clear direction flag

11111100		O D I T S Z A P C 0
Example		Clocks

CLD	8086	2
	8088	2
	80286	2
	80386	2
	80486	2

CLI   Clear interrupt flag

11111010		O D I T S Z A P C 0
Example		Clocks

CLI	8086	2
	8088	2
	80286	3
	80386	3
	80486	5

CLTS   Clear task switched flag

00001111 00000110		O D I T S Z A P C
Example		**Clocks**
CLTS	8086	—
	8088	—
	80286	2
	80386	5
	80486	7

CMC   Complement carry flag

10011000		O D I T S Z A P C*
Example		**Clocks**
CMC	8086	2
	8088	2
	80286	2
	80386	2
	80486	2

CMP   Compare operands

001110dw oorrrmmm disp		O* D I T S* Z* A* P* C*
Format	**Examples**	**Clocks**

CMP reg,reg	CMP AX,BX
	CMP AL,BL
	CMP EAX,EBX
	CMP CX,SI
	CMP ESI,EDI
		8086	3

		8088	3
		80286	2
		80386	2
		80486	1

CMP mem,reg	CMP DATA,AL
	CMP LIST,SI
	CMP DATA [BX],CL
	CMP [EAX],AL
	CMP [EBX+2*ECX],EBX
		8086	9+ea

		8088	13+ea
		80286	7
		80386	5
		80486	2

CMP reg,mem	CMP BL,DATA
	CMP SI,LIST
	CMP CL,DATA [DI]
	CMP CL,[EAX]
	CMP EDX,[EBX+200H]
		8086	9+ea

		8088	13+ea
		80286	6
		80386	6
		80486	2

100000sw oo111mmm disp data			
Format	Examples		Clocks

CMP reg,imm	CMP CX,3
	CMP DI,1AH
	CMP DL,34H
	CMP EBX,12345
	CMP CX,123AH
		8086	4

		8088	4
		80286	3
		80386	2
		80486	1

CMP mem,imm	CMP DATA,33
	CMP LIST,'A'
	CMP DATA [DI],87H
	CMP BYTE PTR [EAX],3
	CMP WORD PTR [SI],7
		8086	10+ea

		8088	14+ea
		80286	6
		80386	5
		80486	2

0011110w data			
Format	Examples		Clocks

CMP acc,imm	CMP AX,3
	CMP AL,1AH
	CMP AH,34
	CMP EAX,3
	CMP AL,'I'
		8086	4

		8088	4
		80286	3
		80386	2
		80486	1

CMPS   Compare strings

1010011w		O D I T S Z A P C * * * * * *	
Format	Examples		Clocks
CMPSB CMPSW CMPSD	CMPSB CMPSW CMPSD CMPS DATA1 REPE CMPSB REPNE CMPSW	8086	22
		8088	30
		80286	8
		80386	10
		80486	8

CMPXCHG   Compare and exchange

00001111 1011000w 11rrrrrr		O D I T S Z A P C
		* * * * * *
Format	**Examples**	**Clocks**

Format	Examples		
CMPXCHG reg,reg	CMPXCHG EAX,EBX CMPXCHG ECX,EDX	8086	—
		8088	—
		80286	—
		80386	—
		80486	6

00001111 1011000w oorrrmmm		
Format	**Examples**	**Clocks**

Format	Examples		
CMPXCHG mem,reg	CMPXCHG DATA,EAX CMPXCHG DATA2,EBX	8086	—
		8088	—
		80286	—
		80386	—
		80486	7

CWD   Convert word to double word

10011001	O D I T S Z A P C
Example	**Clocks**

Example		
CWD	8086	5
	8088	5
	80286	2
	80386	2
	80486	3

CWDE   Convert word to extended double word

10011000	O D I T S Z A P C
Example	**Clocks**

Example		
CWDE	8086	—
	8088	—
	80286	—
	80386	3
	80486	3

DAA   Decimal adjust after addition

00100111		O D I T S Z A P C ? * * * * *	
Example			**Clocks**
DAA		8086	4
		8088	4
		80286	3
		80386	4
		80486	2

DAS   Decimal adjust after subtraction

00101111		O D I T S Z A P C ? * * * * *	
Example			**Clocks**
DAS		8086	4
		8088	4
		80286	3
		80386	4
		80486	2

DEC   Decrement

1111111w oo001mmm disp		O D I T S Z A P C * * * * *	
Format	**Examples**		**Clocks**
DEC reg8	DEC BL DEC BH DEC CL DEC DH DEC AH	8086	3
		8088	3
		80286	2
		80386	2
		80486	1
DEC mem	DEC DATA DEC LIST DEC DATA [SI] DEC BYTE PTR [EAX] DEC WORD PTR [DI]	8086	15+ea
		8088	23+ea
		80286	7
		80386	6
		80486	3

01001rrr

Format	Examples		Clocks
DEC reg16 DEC reg32	DEC AX DEC EAX DEC CX DEC EBX DEC DI	8086	3
		8088	3
		80286	2
		80386	2
		80486	1

DIV   Unsigned division

1111011w oo110mmm disp

O D I T S Z A P C
?   ? ? ? ? ?

Format	Examples		Clocks
DIV reg	DIV BL DIV BH DIV ECX DIV BH DIV CH	8086	162
		8088	162
		80286	22
		80386	38
		80486	40
DIV mem	DIV DATA DIV LIST DIV DATA [DI] DIV BYTE PTR [EAX] DIV WORD PTR [DI]	8086	168
		8088	176
		80286	25
		80386	41
		80486	40

ENTER   Create a stack frame

11001000 data

O D I T S Z A P C

Format	Examples		Clocks
ENTER imm,0	ENTER 4,0 ENTER 8,0 ENTER 100,0 ENTER 200,0 ENTER 1024,0	8086	—
		8088	—
		80286	11
		80386	10
		80486	14

ENTER imm,1	ENTER 4,1 ENTER 10,1	8086	—
		8088	—
		80286	15
		80386	12
		80486	17
ENTER imm,imm	ENTER 3,6 ENTER 100,3	8086	—
		8088	—
		80286	12
		80386	15
		80486	17

ESC   Escape

11011nnn oonnnmmm		O D I T S Z A P C	
nnnnnn = opcode for coprocessor			
Format	Examples		Clocks
ESC imm,reg	ESC 5,AL ESC 5,BH ESC 6,CH FADD ST,ST(3)	8086	2
		8088	2
		80286	20
		80386	var
		80486	var
ESC imm,mem	ESC 2,DATA ESC 3,FROG FADD DATA FMUL FROG	8086	8+ea
		8088	12+ea
		80286	20
		80386	var
		80486	var

HLT   Halt

11110100		O D I T S Z A P C	
Example			Clocks
HLT		8086	2
		8088	2
		80286	2
		80386	5
		80486	4

IDIV
Signed division

1111011w oo111mmm disp		O D I T S Z A P C ? ? ? ? ?	
Format	Examples		Clocks
IDIV reg	IDIV BL IDIV BH IDIV ECX IDIV BH IDIV CX	8086	184
		8088	184
		80286	25
		80386	43
		80486	43
IDIV mem	IDIV DATA IDIV LIST IDIV DATA [DI] IDIV BYTE PTR [EAX] IDIV WORD PTR [DI]	8086	190
		8088	194
		80286	28
		80386	46
		80486	44

IMUL
Signed multiplication

1111011w oo101mmm disp		O D I T S Z A P C * ? ? ? ? *	
Format	Examples		Clocks
IMUL reg	IMUL BL IMUL CL IMUL CX IMUL ECX IMUL EBX	8086	154
		8088	154
		80286	21
		80386	38
		80486	42
IMUL mem	IMUL DATA IMUL LIST IMUL DATA [SI] IMUL BYTE PTR [EAX] IMUL WORD PTR [DI]	8086	160
		8088	164
		80286	24
		80386	41
		80486	42

011010sl oorrrmmm disp data			
Format	**Examples**		**Clocks**
IMUL reg,imm	IMUL CX,16 IMUL DX,100 IMUL EAX,20	8086	—
		8088	—
		80286	21
		80386	38
		80486	42
IMUL reg,reg,imm	IMUL DX,AX,2 IMUL CX,DX,3 IMUL BX,AX,33	8086	—
		8088	—
		80286	21
		80386	38
		80486	42
IMUL reg,mem,imm	IMUL CX,DATA,4	8086	—
		8088	—
		80286	24
		80386	38
		80486	42

00001111 10101111 oorrrmmm disp			
Format	**Examples**		**Clocks**
IMUL reg,reg	IMUL CX,DX IMUL DX,BX IMUL EAX,ECX	8086	—
		8088	—
		80286	—
		80386	38
		80486	42
IMUL reg,mem	IMUL DX,DATA IMUL CX,FROG IMUL BX,LISTS	8086	—
		8088	—
		80286	—
		80386	41
		80486	42

IN   Input data from port

1110010w port number		O D I T S Z A P C
Format	**Examples**	**Clocks**

IN acc,pt	IN AL,12H IN AX,12H IN AL,0FFH IN AX,0FFH IN EAX,10H	8086	10
		8088	14
		80286	5
		80386	12
		80486	14

1110110w

Format	Examples		Clocks
IN acc,DX	IN AL,DX IN AX,DX IN EAX,DX	8086	8
		8088	12
		80286	5
		80386	13
		80486	14

INC   Increment

1111111w oo000mmm disp

O	D	I	T	S	Z	A	P	C
*				*	*	*	*	

Format	Examples		Clocks
INC reg8	INC BL INC BH INC CL INC DH INC AH	8086	3
		8088	3
		80286	2
		80386	2
		80486	1
INC mem	INC DATA INC LIST INC DATA [BX] INC BYTE PTR [EAX] INC WORD PTR [BX] INC DWORD PTR [ECX]	8086	15+ea
		8088	23+ea
		80286	7
		80386	6
		80486	3

01000rrr

Format	Examples		Clocks
INC reg16 INC reg32	INC AX INC EAX INC CX INC EBX INC DI	8086	3
		8088	3
		80286	2
		80386	2
		80486	1

INS   Input string from port

0110110w		O D I T S Z A P C	
Format	Examples		Clocks
INSB INSW INSD	INSB INSW INSD INS DATA REP INSB	8086	—
		8088	—
		80286	5
		80386	15
		80486	17

INT   Interrupt

11001101 type		O D I T S Z A P C	
Format	Examples		Clocks
INT type	INT 10H INT 255 INT 21H INT 20H INT 15H	8086	51
		8088	71
		80286	23
		80386	37
		80486	30

11001100			
Example			Clocks
INT 3		8086	52
		8088	72
		80286	23
		80386	33
		80486	26

INTO   Interrupt on overflow

11001110		O D I T S Z A P C	
Example			Clocks
INTO		8086	53
		8088	73
		80286	24
		80386	35
		80486	28

INVD   Invalidate data cache

00001111 00001000		O D I T S Z A P C
Example		Clocks
INVD	8086	—
	8088	—
	80286	—
	80386	—
	80486	4

INVLPG   Invalidate TLB entry

00001111 00000001 oo111mmm			O D I T S Z A P C
Format	Examples		Clocks
INVLPG mem	INVLPG DATA INVLPG LIST	8086	—
		8088	—
		80286	—
		80386	—
		80486	12

IRET   Interrupt return

11001101 data			O D I T S Z A P C * * * * * * * * *
Format	Examples		Clocks
IRET IRETD	IRET IRETD IRET 10H	8086	32
		8088	44
		80286	17
		80386	22
		80486	15

Jconditional   Conditional jump

0111cccc disp				O D I T S Z A P C	
Format	Examples			Clocks	
Jcc label (8-bit disp)	JA BELOW JB ABOVE JG GREATER JE EQUAL JZ ZERO			8086	16/4
				8088	16/4
				80286	7/3
				80386	7/3
				80486	3/1

00001111 1000cccc disp			
Format	Examples	Clocks	
Jcc label (16-bit disp)	JNE NOT_MORE JLE LESS_THAN	8086	—
		8088	—
		80286	—
		80386	7/3
		80486	3/1

Condition Codes	Mnemonic	Flag	Description
0000	JO	O = 1	Jump if overflow
0001	JNO	O = 0	Jump if no overflow
0010	JB/JNAE	C = 1	Jump if below
0011	JAE/JNB	C = 0	Jump if above or equal
0100	JE/JZ	Z = 1	Jump if equal/zero
0101	JNE/JNZ	Z = 0	Jump if not equal/not zero
0110	JBE/JNA	C = 1 + Z = 1	Jump if below or equal
0111	JA/JNBE	C = 0 • Z = 0	Jump if above
1000	JS	S = 1	Jump if sign
1001	JNS	S = 0	Jump if no sign
1010	JP/JPE	P = 1	Jump if parity even
1011	JNP/JPO	P = 0	Jump if parity odd
1100	JL/JNGE	S • O	Jump if less than
1101	JGE/JNL	S = O	Jump greater or equal
1110	JLE/JNG	Z = 1 + S • O	Jump if less than or equal
1111	JG/JNLE	Z = 0 + S = O	Jump if greater

JCXZ/JECXZ   Jump if CX (ECX) equals zero

11100011		O D I T S Z A P C	
Format	Examples	Clocks	
JCXZ label JECXZ label	JCXZ LOTSA JCXZ OVER	8086	18/6
	JECXZ UPPER	8088	18/6
	JECXZ UNDER JCXZ NEXT	80286	8/4
		80386	9/5
		80486	8/5

JMP   Unconditional jump

11101011 disp		O D I T S Z A P C	
Format	Examples	Clocks	
JMP label (short)	JMP SHORT UP JMP SHORT DOWN	8086	15
	JMP SHORT OVER	8088	15
	JMP SHORT CIRCUIT JMP SHORT ARM	80286	7
		80386	7
		80486	3

11101001 disp			
Format	Examples	Clocks	
JMP label (near)	JMP VER JMP FROG	8086	15
	JMP UNDER	8088	15
	JMP NEAR PTR OVER	80286	7
		80386	7
		80486	3

11101010 disp			
Format	Examples	Clocks	
JMP label (far)	JMP VER JMP FROG	8086	15
	JMP UNDER	8088	15
	JMP FAR PTR THERE	80286	11
		80386	12
		80486	17

11111111 oo100mmm

Format	Examples		Clocks
JMP reg (near)	JMP AX JMP EAX JMP CX JMP DX	8086	11
		8088	11
		80286	7
		80386	7
		80486	3
JMP mem (near)	JMP DATA JMP LIST JMP DATA [DI+2]	8086	18+ea
		8088	18+ea
		80286	11
		80386	10
		80486	5

11111111 oo101mmm

Format	Examples		Clocks
JMP mem (far)	JMP WAY_OFF JMP TABLE JMP UP	8086	24+ea
		8088	24+ea
		80286	15
		80386	12
		80486	13

LAHF   Load AH from flags

10011111   O D I T S Z A P C

Example		Clocks
LAHF	8086	4
	8088	4
	80286	2
	80386	2
	80486	3

LAR   Load access rights

00001111 00000010 oorrrmmm disp		O D I T S Z A P C *
Format	Examples	Clocks
LAR reg,reg	LAR AX,BX LAR CX,DX LAR EAX,ECX	8086	—
		8088	—
		80286	14
		80386	15
		80486	11
LAR reg,mem	LAR CX,DATA LAR AX,LIST LAR ECX,FROG	8086	—
		8088	—
		80286	16
		80386	16
		80486	11

LDS   Load far pointer

11000101 oorrrmmm		O D I T S Z A P C
Format	Examples	Clocks

LDS reg,mem	LDS DI,DATA
	LDS SI,LIST
	LDS BX,ARRAY
	LDS CX,PNTR
		8086	16+ea

		8088	24+ea
		80286	7
		80386	7
		80486	6

LES   Load far pointer

11000100 oorrrmmm		O D I T S Z A P C
Format	Examples	Clocks
LES reg,mem	LES DI,DATA LES SI,LIST LES BX,ARRAY LES CX,PNTR	8086	16+ea
		8088	24+ea
		80286	7
		80386	7
		80486	6

LFS   Load far pointer

00001111 10110100 oorrrmmm disp	O D I T S Z A P C
Format **Examples**	**Clocks**

Format	Examples		
LFS reg,mem	LFS DI,DATA LFS SI,LIST LFS BX,ARRAY LFS CX,PNTR	8086	—
		8088	—
		80286	—
		80386	7
		80486	6

LGS   Load far pointer

00001111 10110101 oorrrmmm disp	O D I T S Z A P C
Format **Examples**	**Clocks**

Format	Examples		
LGS reg,mem	LGS DI,DATA LGS SI,LIST LGS BX,ARRAY LGS CX,PNTR	8086	—
		8088	—
		80286	—
		80386	7
		80486	6

LSS   Load far pointer

00001111 10110010 oorrrmmm disp	O D I T S Z A P C
Format **Examples**	**Clocks**

Format	Examples		
LSS reg,mem	LSS DI,DATA LSS SI,LIST LSS BX,ARRAY LSS CX,PNTR	8086	—
		8088	—
		80286	—
		80386	7
		80486	6

LEA   Load effective address

10001101 oorrrmmm disp		O D I T S Z A P C	
Format	Examples		Clocks
LEA reg,mem	LEA DI,DATA LEA SI,LIST LEA BX,ARRAY LEA CX,PNTR LEA BP,ADDR	8086	2+ea
		8088	2+ea
		80286	3
		80386	2
		80486	2

LEAVE   Leave high-level procedure

11001001	O D I T S Z A P C	
Example		Clocks
LEAVE	8086	—
	8088	—
	80286	5
	80386	4
	80486	5

LGDT   Load global descriptor table

00001111 00000001 oo010mmm disp		O D I T S Z A P C	
Format	Examples		Clocks
LGDT mem64	LGDT DESCRIP LGDT TABLE	8086	—
		8088	—
		80286	11
		80386	11
		80486	11

LIDT   Load interrupt descriptor table

00001111 00000001 oo011mmm disp		O D I T S Z A P C	
Format	Examples		Clocks
LIGT mem64	LIDT DATA LIDT DESCRIP	8086	—
		8088	—
		80286	12
		80386	11
		80486	11

LLDT   Load local descriptor table

00001111 00000000 oo010mmm disp		O D I T S Z A P C
Format	Examples	Clocks

LLDT reg	LLDT AX / LLDT CX	8086	—
		8088	—
		80286	17
		80386	20
		80486	11
LLDT mem	LLDT DATA / LLDT LIST	8086	—
		8088	—
		80286	19
		80386	24
		80486	11

LMSW   Load machine status word

00001111 00000001 oo110mmm disp		O D I T S Z A P C

should only be used with the 80286

Format	Examples	Clocks

LMSW reg	LMSW AX / LMSW CX	8086	—
		8088	—
		80286	3
		80386	10
		80486	2
LMSW mem	LMSW DATA / LMSW LIST	8086	—
		8088	—
		80286	6
		80386	13
		80486	3

LOCK   Lock the bus

11110000		O D I T S Z A P C	
Format	Examples		Clocks
LOCK inst	LOCK:XCHG AX,BX LOCK:MOV AL,AH	8086	2
		8088	2
		80286	0
		80386	0
		80486	1

LODS   Load string operand

1010110w		O D I T S Z A P C	
Format	Examples		Clocks
LODSB LODSW LODSD	LODSB LODSW LODSD LODS DATA LODS ES:DATA	8086	12
		8088	16
		80286	5
		80386	5
		80486	5

LOOP   Loop until CX = 0

11100010 disp		O D I T S Z A P C	
Format	Examples		Clocks
LOOP label	LOOP DATA LOOP BACK	8086	17/5
		8088	17/5
		80286	8/4
		80386	11
		80486	7/6

LOOPE   Loop while equal

11100001 disp		O D I T S Z A P C	
Format	Examples		Clocks
LOOPE label LOOPZ label	LOOPE NEXT LOOPE AGAIN LOOPZ REPEAT	8086	18/6
		8088	18/6
		80286	8/4
		80386	11
		80486	9/6

LOOPNE   Loop while not equal

11100000 disp		O D I T S Z A P C	
Format	**Examples**		**Clocks**
LOOPNE label LOOPNZ label	LOOPNE AGAIN LOOPNE BACK LOOPNZ REPL	8086	19/5
		8088	19/5
		80286	8/4
		80386	11
		80486	9/6

LSL   Load segment limit

00001111 00000011 oorrrmmm disp		O D I T S Z A P C *	
Format	**Examples**		**Clocks**
LSL reg,reg	LSL AX,BX LSL CX,BX LSL DX,AX	8086	—
		8088	—
		80286	14
		80386	25
		80486	10
LSL reg,mem	LSL AX,LIMIT LSL EAX,NUMB	8086	—
		8088	—
		80286	16
		80386	26
		80486	10

LTR   Load task register

00001111 00000000 oo001mmm disp		O D I T S Z A P C	
Format	**Examples**		**Clocks**
LTR reg	LTR AX LTR CX LTR DX	8086	—
		8088	—
		80286	17
		80386	23
		80486	20

LTR mem	LTR TASK LTR EDGE	8086	—
		8088	—
		80286	19
		80386	27
		80486	20

MOV   Move data

100010dw oorrrmmm disp		O D I T S Z A P C	
Format	Examples		Clocks

MOV reg,reg	MOV CL,CH
	MOV BH,CL
	MOV CX,DX
	MOV EAX,ECX
	MOV EBP,ESI
		8086	2

		8088	2
		80286	2
		80386	2
		80486	1

MOV mem,reg	MOV DATA,DL
	MOV NUMB,CX
	MOV TEMP,EBX
	MOV TEMP1,CH
	MOV DATA2,CL
		8086	9+ea

		8088	13+ea
		80286	3
		80386	2
		80486	1

MOV reg,mem	MOV DL,DATA
	MOV DX,NUMB
	MOV EBX,TEMP
	MOV CH,TEMP1
	MOV CL,DATA2
		8086	10+ea

		8088	12+ea
		80286	5
		80386	4
		80486	1

1100011w oo000mmm disp data			
Format	Examples		Clocks

MOV mem,imm	MOV DATA,23H
	MOV LIST,12H
	MOV BYTE PTR [DI],2
	MOV NUMB,234H
	MOV DWORD PTR [SI],100
		8086	10+ea

		8088	14+ea
		80286	3
		80386	2
		80486	1

1011wrrr data

Format	Examples		Clocks

MOV reg,imm	MOV BX,23H
	MOV CX,12H
	MOV CL,2
	MOV ECX,123423H
	MOV DI,100
		8086	4

		8088	4
		80286	3
		80386	2
		80486	1

101000dw disp

Format	Examples		Clocks

MOV mem,acc	MOV DATA,AL
	MOV NUMB,AX
	MOV NUMB1,EAX
		8086	10

		8088	14
		80286	3
		80386	2
		80486	1

MOV acc,mem	MOV AL,DATA
	MOV AX,NUMB
	MOV EAX,TEMP
		8086	10

		8088	14
		80286	5
		80386	4
		80486	1

100011d0 oosssmmm disp

Format	Examples		Clocks

MOV seg,reg	MOV SS,AX
	MOV DS,DX
	MOV ES,CX
		8086	2

		8088	2
		80286	2
		80386	2
		80486	1

MOV seg,mem	MOV SS,DATA
	MOV DS,NUMB
	MOV ES,TEMP1
		8086	8+ea

		8088	12+ea
		80286	2
		80386	2
		80486	1

MOV reg,seg	MOV AX,DS
	MOV DX,ES
	MOV CX,CS
		8086	2

		8088	2
		80286	2
		80386	2
		80486	1

MOV mem,seg	MOV DATA,SS
	MOV NUMB,ES
	MOV TEMP1,DS
		8086	9+ea

		8088	13+ea
		80286	3
		80386	2
		80486	1

00001111 001000d0 11rrrmmm

Format	Examples		Clocks

MOV reg,cr	MOV EAX,CR0
	MOV EBX,CR2
	MOV ECX,CR3
		8086	—

		8088	—
		80286	—
		80386	6
		80486	4

MOV cr,reg	MOV CR0,EAX
	MOV CR2,EBX
	MOV CR3,ECX
		8086	—

		8088	—
		80286	—
		80386	10
		80486	4

00001111 001000d1 11rrrmmm

Format	Examples		Clocks

MOV reg,dr	MOV EBX,DR6
	MOV EAX,DR6
	MOV EDX,DR1
		8086	—

		8088	—
		80286	—
		80386	22
		80486	10

MOV dr,reg	MOV DR1,ECX
	MOV DR2,ESI
	MOV DR6,EBP
		8086	—

		8088	—
		80286	—
		80386	22
		80486	11

00001111 001001d0 11rrrmmm

Format	Examples		Clocks
MOV reg,tr	MOV EAX,TR6 MOV EDX,TR7	8086	—
		8088	—
		80286	—
		80386	12
		80486	4
MOV tr,seg	MOV TR6,EDX MOV TR7,ESI	8086	—
		8088	—
		80286	—
		80386	12
		80486	6

MOVS   Move string data

1010010w   O D I T S Z A P C

Format	Examples		Clocks
MOVSB MOVSW MOVSD	MOVSB MOVSW MOVSD MOVS DAT1,DAT2 REP MOVSB	8086	18
		8088	26
		80286	5
		80386	7
		80486	7

MOVSX   Move with sign extend

00001111 1011111w oorrrmmm disp		O D I T S Z A P C
Format	**Examples**	**Clocks**

MOVSX reg,reg	MOVSX BX,AL MOVSX EAX,DX	8086	—
		8088	—
		80286	—
		80386	3
		80486	3
MOVSX reg,mem	MOVSX AX,DATA MOVSX EAX,NUMB	8086	
		8088	—
		80286	—
		80386	6
		80486	3

MOVZX   Move with zero extend

00001111 1011011w oorrrmmm disp		O D I T S Z A P C
Format	**Examples**	**Clocks**

MOVZX reg,reg	MOVZX BX,AL MOVZX EAX,DX	8086	—
		8088	—
		80286	—
		80386	3
		80486	3
MOVZX reg,mem	MOVZX AX,DATA MOVZX EAX,NUMB	8086	—
		8088	—
		80286	—
		80386	6
		80486	3

MUL   Unsigned multiplication

1111011w oo100mmm disp			O D I T S Z A P C * ? ? ? ? *	
Format	Examples		Clocks	
MUL reg	MUL BL MUL CX MUL ECX	8086	118	
		8088	143	
		80286	21	
		80386	38	
		80486	42	
MUL mem	MUL DATA MUL BYTE PTR [SI] MUL WORD PTR [SI] MUL DWORD PTR [ECX]	8086	139	
		8088	143	
		80286	24	
		80386	41	
		80486	42	

NEG   Negate

1111011w oo011mmm disp			O D I T S Z A P C * * * * * *	
Format	Examples		Clocks	
NEG reg	NEG AX NEG CX NEG EDX	8086	3	
		8088	3	
		80286	2	
		80386	2	
		80486	1	
NEG mem	NEG DATA NEG NUMB NEG WORD PTR [DI]	8086	16+ea	
		8088	24+ea	
		80286	7	
		80386	6	
		80486	3	

NOP   No operation

10010000		O D I T S Z A P C
Example		**Clocks**
NOP		8086	3
		8088	3
		80286	3
		80386	3
		80486	3

NOT   One's complement

1111011w oo010mmm disp		O D I T S Z A P C
Format	**Examples**	**Clocks**
NOT reg	NOT AX NOT CX NOT EDX	8086	3
		8088	3
		80286	2
		80386	2
		80486	1
NOT mem	NOT DATA NOT NUMB NOT WORD PTR [DI]	8086	16+ea
		8088	24+ea
		80286	7
		80386	6
		80486	3

OR   Inclusive-OR

000010dw oorrrmmm disp		O D I T S Z A P C 0 * * ? * 0
Format	**Examples**	**Clocks**
OR reg,reg	OR CL,BL OR CX,DX OR ECX,EBX	8086	3
		8088	3
		80286	2
		80386	2
		80486	1

OR mem,reg	OR DATA,CL OR NUMB,CX OR [DI],CX	8086	16+ea
		8088	24+ea
		80286	7
		80386	7
		80486	3
OR reg,mem	OR CL,DATA OR CX,NUMB OR CX,[SI]	8086	9+ea
		8088	13+ea
		80286	7
		80386	6
		80486	2

100000sw oo001mmm disp data

Format	Examples		Clocks
OR reg,imm	OR CL,3 OR DX,1000H OR EBX,100000H	8086	4
		8088	4
		80286	3
		80386	2
		80486	1
OR mem,imm	OR DATA,33 OR NUMB,4AH OR NUMS,123498H OR BYTE PTR [ECX],2	8086	17+ea
		8088	25+ea
		80286	7
		80386	7
		80486	3

0000110w data

Format	Examples		Clocks
OR acc,imm	OR AL,3 OR AX,1000H OR EAX,100000H	8086	4
		8088	4
		80286	3
		80386	2
		80486	1

OUT   Output data to port

1110011w port number			O D I T S Z A P C	
Format	Examples			Clocks
OUT pt,acc	OUT 12H,AL OUT 12H,AX OUT 0FFH,AL OUT 0FEH,AX OUT 10H,EAX		8086	10
			8088	14
			80286	3
			80386	10
			80486	10

1110111w				
Format	Examples			Clocks
OUT DX,acc	OUT DX,AL OUT DX,AX OUT DX,EAX		8086	8
			8088	12
			80286	3
			80386	11
			80486	10

OUTS   Output string data to port

1110011w port number			O D I T S Z A P C	
Format	Examples			Clocks
OUTSB OUTSW OUTSD	OUTSB OUTSW OUTSD OUTS DATA REP OUTSB		8086	—
			8088	—
			80286	5
			80386	14
			80486	10

POP   Pop data from stack

01011rrr			O D I T S Z A P C	
Format	Examples			Clocks
POP reg	POP CX POP AX POP EBX		8086	8
			8088	12
			80286	5
			80386	4
			80486	1

10001111 oo000mmm disp

Format	Examples		Clocks
POP mem	POP DATA POP LISTS POP NUMBS	8086	17+ea
		8088	25+ea
		80286	5
		80386	5
		80486	4

00sss111

Format	Examples		Clocks
POP seg	POP DS POP ES POP SS	8086	8
		8088	12
		80286	5
		80386	7
		80486	3

00001111 10sss001

Format	Examples		Clocks
POP seg	POP FS POP GS	8086	—
		8088	—
		80286	—
		80386	7
		80486	3

POPA/POPAD   Pop all registers from stack

01100001		O D I T S Z A P C
Example		Clocks
POPA POPAD	8086	—
	8088	—
	80286	19
	80386	24
	80486	9

POPF/POPFD   Pop flags from stack

10011101		O D I T S Z A P C * * * * * * * * *
Example		Clocks
POPF POPFD	8086	—
	8088	—
	80286	5
	80386	5
	80486	6

PUSH   Push data onto stack

01010rrr			O D I T S Z A P C
Format	Examples		Clocks
PUSH reg	PUSH CX PUSH AX PUSH ECX	8086	11
		8088	15
		80286	3
		80386	2
		80486	1

11111111 oo110mmm disp			
Format	Examples		Clocks
PUSH mem	PUSH DATA PUSH LISTS PUSH NUMB PUSH DWORD PTR [ECX]	8086	16+ea
		8088	24+ea
		80286	5
		80386	5
		80486	4

00sss110			
Format	Examples		Clocks
PUSH seg	PUSH DS PUSH CS PUSH ES	8086	10
		8088	14
		80286	3
		80386	2
		80486	3

00001111 10sss000

Format	Examples	Clocks	
PUSH seg	PUSH FS PUSH GS	8086	—
		8088	—
		80286	—
		80386	2
		80486	3

011010s0 data

Format	Examples	Clocks	
PUSH imm	PUSH 2000H PUSH 5322H PUSHW 10H PUSHD 100000H	8086	—
		8088	—
		80286	3
		80386	2
		80486	1

PUSHA/PUSHAD   Push all registers

01100000   O D I T S Z A P C

Example	Clocks	
PUSHA PUSHAD	8086	—
	8088	—
	80286	17
	80386	18
	80486	11

PUSHF/PUSHFD   Push flags onto stack

10011100   O D I T S Z A P C

Example	Clocks	
PUSHF PUSHFD	8086	10
	8088	14
	80286	3
	80386	4
	80486	3

RCL/RCR/ROL/ROR   Rotate

1101000w ooTTTmmm disp		O D I T S Z A P C
		* *

TTT = 000 = ROL
TTT = 001 = ROR
TTT = 010 = RCL
TTT = 011 = RCR

Format	Examples		Clocks
ROL reg,1 ROR reg,1	ROL CL,1 ROL DX,1 ROR CH,1 ROL SI,1	8086	2
		8088	2
		80286	2
		80386	3
		80486	3
RCL reg,1 RCR reg,1	RCL CL,1 RCL SI,1 RCR AH,1 RCR EBX,1	8086	2
		8088	2
		80286	2
		80386	9
		80486	3
ROL mem,1 ROR mem,1	ROL DATA,1 ROL BYTE PTR [DI],1 ROR NUMB,1 ROR DWORD PTR [ECX],1	8086	15+ea
		8088	23+ea
		80286	7
		80386	7
		80486	4
RCL mem,1 RCR mem,1	RCL DATA,1 RCL BYTE PTR [DI],1 RCR NUMB,1 RCR WORD PTR [ECX],1	8086	15+ea
		8088	23+ea
		80286	7
		80386	10
		80486	4

1101001w ooTTTmmm disp		
Format	Examples		Clocks
---	---	---	---
ROL reg,CL ROR reg,CL	ROL CH,CL ROL DX,CL ROR CH,CL ROL SI,CL	8086	8+4n
		8088	8+4n
		80286	5+n
		80386	3
		80486	3

RCL reg,CL RCR reg,CL	RCL DL,CL RCL SI,CL RCR AH,CL RCR BX,CL	8086	8+4n
		8088	8+4n
		80286	5+n
		80386	9
		80486	8
ROL mem,CL ROR mem,CL	ROL DATA,CL ROL BYTE PTR [DI],CL ROR NUMB,CL ROR WORD PTR [ECX],CL	8086	20+a+4n
		8088	28+a+4n
		80286	8+n
		80386	7
		80486	4
RCL mem,CL RCR mem,CL	RCL DATA,CL RCL BYTE PTR [DI],CL RCR NUMB,CL RCR WORD PTR [ECX],CL	8086	20+a+4n
		8088	28+a+4n
		80286	8+n
		80386	10
		80486	9

1100000w ooTTTmmm disp data

Format	Examples		Clocks
ROL reg,imm ROR reg,imm	ROL CL,4 ROL DX,5 ROR CH,12 ROL SI,9	8086	—
		8088	—
		80286	5+n
		80386	3
		80486	2
RCL reg,imm RCR reg,imm	RCL CL,2 RCL SI,3 RCR AH,5 RCR BX,13	8086	—
		8088	—
		80286	5+n
		80386	9
		80486	8
ROL mem,imm ROR mem,imm	ROL DATA,4 ROL BYTE PTR [DI],2 ROR NUMB,2 ROR WORD PTR [ECX],3	8086	—
		8088	—
		80286	8+n
		80386	7
		80486	4

RCL mem,imm RCR mem,imm	RCL DATA,6 RCL BYTE PTR [DI],7 RCR NUMB,6 RCR WORD PTR [ECX],5	8086	—
		8088	—
		80286	8+n
		80386	10
		80486	9

REP   Repeat prefix

11110010 1010010w   O D I T S Z A P C

Format	Examples		Clocks
REP MOVS	REP MOVSB REP MOVSW REP MOVSD REP MOVS DATA1,DATA2	8086	9+17n
		8088	9+25n
		80286	5+4n
		80386	8+4n
		80486	12+3n

11110010 1010101w

Format	Examples		Clocks
REP STOS	REP STOSB REP STOSW REP STOSD REP STOS DATA3	8086	9+10n
		8088	9+14n
		80286	4+3n
		80386	5+5n
		80486	7+4n

11110010 0110110w

Format	Examples		Clocks
REP INS	REP INSB REP INSW REP INSD REP INS DATA4	8086	—
		8088	—
		80286	5+4n
		80386	13+6n
		80486	16+8n

11110010 0110111w

Format	Examples		Clocks
REP OUTS	REP OUTSB REP OUTSW REP OUTSD REP OUTS DATA5	8086	—
		8088	—
		80286	5+4n
		80386	12+5n
		80486	17+5n

REPE/REPNE   Repeat conditional

11110011 1010011w

			O D I T S Z A P C *
Format	Examples		Clocks
REPE CMPS	REPE CMPSB REPE CMPSW REPE CMPSD REPE CMPS DATA6,DATA7	8086	9+22n
		8088	9+30n
		80286	5+9n
		80386	5+9n
		80486	7+7n

11110011 1010111w

Format	Examples		Clocks
REPE SCAS	REPE SCASB REPE SCASW REPE SCASD REPE SCAS DATA8	8086	9+15n
		8088	9+19n
		80286	5+8n
		80386	5+8n
		80486	7+5n

11110010 1010011w

Format	Examples		Clocks
REPNE CMPS	REPNE CMPSB REPNE CMPSW REPNE CMPSD REPNE CMPS DATA9,DATA10	8086	9+22n
		8088	9+30n
		80286	5+9n
		80386	5+9n
		80486	7+7n

11110010 1010111w

Format	Examples		Clocks
REPNE SCAS	REPNE SCASB REPNE SCASW REPNE SCASD REPNE SCAS DATA11	8086	9+15n
		8088	9+19n
		80286	5+8n
		80386	5+8n
		80486	7+5n

RET   Return from procedure

11000011		O D I T S Z A P C
Example		**Clocks**
RET (near)	8086	16
	8088	20
	80286	11
	80386	10
	80486	5

11000010 data			
Format	Examples		Clocks
RET imm (near)	RET 4 RET 100H	8086	20
		8088	24
		80286	11
		80386	10
		80486	5

11001011		
Example		**Clocks**
RET (far)	8086	26
	8088	34
	80286	15
	80386	18
	80486	13

11001010 data

Format	Examples		Clocks
RET imm (far)	RET 4 RET 100H	8086	25
		8088	33
		80286	11
		80386	10
		80486	5

SAHF   Store AH into flags

10011110		O D I T S Z A P C * * * * *

Example		Clocks
SAHF	8086	4
	8088	4
	80286	2
	80386	3
	80486	2

SAL/SAR/SHL/SHR   Shift

1101000w ooTTTmmm disp   O D I T S Z A P C
                                 *   * * ? * *

TTT = 100 = SHL/SAL
TTT = 101 = SHR
TTT = 111 = SAR

Format	Examples		Clocks
SAL reg,1 SHL reg,1 SHR reg,1 SAR reg 1	SAL CL,1 SHL DX,1 SHR CH,1 SAR SI,1	8086	2
		8088	2
		80286	2
		80386	3
		80486	3
SAL mem,1 SHL mem,1 SHR mem,1 SAR mem,1	SAL DATA,1 SHL BYTE PTR [DI],1 SHR NUMB,1 SAR WORD PTR [ECX],1	8086	15+ea
		8088	23+ea
		80286	7
		80386	7
		80486	4

1101001w ooTTTmmm disp

Format	Examples		Clocks
SAL reg,CL SHL reg,CL SHR reg,CL SAR reg,CL	SAL CH,CL SHL DX,CL SHR CH,CL SAR SI,CL	8086	8+4n
		8088	8+4n
		80286	5+n
		80386	3
		80486	3
SAL mem,CL SHL mem,CL SHR mem,CL SAR mem,CL	SAL DATA,CL SHL BYTE PTR [DI],CL SHR NUMB,CL SAR WORD PTR [ECX],CL	8086	20+a+4n
		8088	28+a+4n
		80286	8+n
		80386	7
		80486	4

1100000w ooTTTmmm disp data

Format	Examples		Clocks
SAL reg,imm SHL reg,imm SHR reg,imm SAR reg,imm	SAL CL,4 SHL DX,5 SHR CH,12 SAR SI,9	8086	—
		8088	—
		80286	5+n
		80386	3
		80486	2
SAL mem,imm SHL mem,imm SHR mem,imm SAR mem,imm	SAL DATA,6 SHL BYTE PTR [DI],7 SHR NUMB,6 SAR WORD PTR [ECX],5	8086	—
		8088	—
		80286	8+n
		80386	7
		80486	4

SBB   Subtract with borrow

000110dw oorrrmmm disp

	O D I T S Z A P C
	* * * * * *

Format	Examples		Clocks
SBB reg,reg	SBB CL,DL SBB AX,DX SBB CH,CL SBB EAX,EBX	8086	3
		8088	3
		80286	2
		80386	2
		80486	1

SBB mem,reg	SBB DATA,CL SBB BYTES,CX SBB NUMBS,ECX SBB [EAX],CX	8086	16+ea
		8088	24+ea
		80286	7
		80386	6
		80486	3
SBB reg,mem	SBB CL,DATA SBB CX,BYTES SBB ECX,NUMBS SBB CX,[EDX]	8086	9+ea
		8088	13+ea
		80286	7
		80386	7
		80486	2

100000sw oo011mmm disp data

Format	Examples		Clocks
SBB reg,imm	SBB CL,4 SBB DX,5 SBB CH,12 SBB SI,9	8086	4
		8088	4
		80286	3
		80386	2
		80486	1
SBB mem,imm	SBB DATA,6 SBB BYTE PTR [DI],7 SBB NUMB,6 SBB WORD PTR [ECX],5	8086	17+ea
		8088	25+ea
		80286	7
		80386	7
		80486	3

0001110w data

Format	Examples		Clocks
SBB acc,imm	SBB AL,4 SBB AX,5 SBB AH,12 SBB AX,9	8086	4
		8088	4
		80286	3
		80386	2
		80486	1

SCAS   Scan string

1010111w			O D I T S Z A P C * * * * * *
Format	Examples		Clocks
SCASB SCASW SCASD	SCASB SCASW SCASD SCAS DATA REP SCASB	8086	15
		8088	19
		80286	7
		80386	7
		80486	6

SET   Set on condition

00001111 1001cccc oo000mmm			O D I T S Z A P C
Format	Examples		Clocks
SETcd reg8	SETA BL SETB CH SETG DL SETE BH SETZ AL	8086	—
		8088	—
		80286	—
		80386	4
		80486	3
SETcd mem8	SETE DATA SETLE BYTES	8086	—
		8088	—
		80286	—
		80386	5
		80486	3

Condition Codes	Mnemonic	Flag	Description
0000	SETO	$O = 1$	Set if overflow
0001	SETNO	$O = 0$	Set if no overflow
0010	SETB/SETNAE	$C = 1$	Set if below
0011	SETAE/SETNB	$C = 0$	Set if above or equal
0100	SETE/SETZ	$Z = 1$	Set if equal/zero
0101	SETNE/SETNZ	$Z = 0$	Set if not equal/not zero
0110	SETBE/SETNA	$C = 1 + Z = 1$	Set if below or equal
0111	SETA/SETNBE	$C = 0 \cdot Z = 0$	Set if above
1000	SETS	$S = 1$	Set if sign
1001	SETNS	$S = 0$	Set if no sign
1010	SETP/SETPE	$P = 1$	Set if parity even
1011	SETNP/SETPO	$P = 0$	Set if parity odd
1100	SETL/SETNGE	$S \cdot O$	Set if less than
1101	SETGE/SETNL	$S = O$	Set greater or equal
1110	SETLE/SETNG	$Z = 1 + S \cdot O$	Set if less than or equal
1111	SETG/SETNLE	$Z = 0 + S = O$	Set if greater

SGDT/SIDT/SLDT   Store descriptor table

00001111 00000001 oo000mmm disp		O D I T S Z A P C
Format	Examples	Clocks

SGDT mem	SGDT MEMORY SGDT GLOBAL	8086	—
		8088	—
		80286	11
		80386	9
		80486	10

00001111 00000001 oo001mmm disp		
Format	Examples	Clocks

SIDT mem	SIDT DATAS SIDT INTERRUPT	8086	—
		8088	—
		80286	12
		80386	9
		80486	10

00001111 00000000 oo000mmm disp		
Format	Examples	Clocks

SLDT reg	SLDT CX SLDT DX	8086	—
		8088	—
		80286	2
		80386	2
		80486	2
SLDT mem	SLDT NUMBS SLDT LOCALS	8086	—
		8088	—
		80286	3
		80386	2
		80486	3

SHLD/SHRD   Double-precision shift

00001111 10100100 oorrrmmm disp data		O D I T S Z A P C
		? * * ? * *
Format	Examples	Clocks

Format	Examples		Clocks
SHLD reg,reg,imm	SHLD AX,CX,10 SHLD DX,BX,8 SHLD CX,DX,2	8086	—
		8088	—
		80286	—
		80386	3
		80486	2
SHLD mem,reg,imm	SHLD DATA,CX,8	8086	—
		8088	—
		80286	—
		80386	7
		80486	3

00001111 10101100 oorrrmmm disp data		
Format	Examples	Clocks

Format	Examples		Clocks
SHRD reg,reg,imm	SHRD CX,DX,2	8086	—
		8088	—
		80286	—
		80386	3
		80486	2
SHRD mem,reg,imm	SHRD DATA,CX,3	8086	—
		8088	—
		80286	—
		80386	7
		80486	3

00001111 10100101 oorrrmmm disp		
Format	Examples	Clocks

Format	Examples		Clocks
SHLD reg,reg,CL	SHLD DX,BX,CL	8086	—
		8088	—
		80286	—
		80386	3
		80486	3

SHLD mem,reg,CL	SHLD DATA,AX,CL	8086	—
		8088	—
		80286	—
		80386	7
		80486	3

00001111 10100101 oorrrmmm disp

Format	Examples		Clocks
SHRD reg,reg,CL	SHRD DX,BX,CL	8086	—
		8088	—
		80286	—
		80386	3
		80486	3
SHRD mem,reg,CL	SHRD DATA,AX,CL	8086	—
		8088	—
		80286	—
		80386	7
		80486	3

SMSW   Store machine status word

00001111 00000001 oo100mmm disp

O D I T S Z A P C

(should only be used by the 80286)

Format	Examples		Clocks
SMSW reg	SMSW AX SMSW DX SMSW CX	8086	—
		8088	—
		80286	2
		80386	10
		80486	2
SMSW mem	SMSW DATA	8086	—
		8088	—
		80286	3
		80386	3
		80486	3

STC   Set carry flag

11111001		O D I T S Z A P C
Example		1
		Clocks
STC	8086	2
	8088	2
	80286	2
	80386	2
	80486	2

STD   Set direction flag

11111101		O D I T S Z A P C
Example		1
		Clocks
STD	8086	2
	8088	2
	80286	2
	80386	2
	80486	2

STI   Set interrupt flag

11111011		O D I T S Z A P C
Example		1
		Clocks
STI	8086	2
	8088	2
	80286	2
	80386	3
	80486	5

STOS   Store string data

1010101w			O D I T S Z A P C
Format	Examples		Clocks
STOSB STOSW STOSD	STOSB STOSW STOSD STOS DATA REP STOSB	8086	11
		8088	15
		80286	3
		80386	4
		80486	5

STR — Store task register

00001111 00000000 oo001mmm disp		O D I T S Z A P C	
Format	**Examples**		**Clocks**
STR reg	STR DX STR CX STR AX	8086	—
		8088	—
		80286	2
		80386	2
		80486	2
STR mem	STR DATA	8086	—
		8088	—
		80286	3
		80386	2
		80486	3

SUB — Subtract

001010dw oorrrmmm disp		O D I T S Z A P C * * * * * *	
Format	**Examples**		**Clocks**

SUB reg,reg	SUB CL,DL
	SUB AX,DX
	SUB CH,CL
	SUB EAX,EBX
		8086	3

		8088	3
		80286	2
		80386	2
		80486	1

SUB mem,reg	SUB DATA,CL
	SUB BYTES,CX
	SUB NUMBS,ECX
	SUB [EAX],CX
		8086	16+ea

		8088	24+ea
		80286	7
		80386	6
		80486	3

SUB reg,mem	SUB CL,DATA
	SUB CX,BYTES
	SUB ECX,NUMBS
	SUB CX,[EDX]
		8086	9+ea

		8088	13+ea
		80286	7
		80386	7
		80486	2

100000sw oo101mmm disp data

Format	Examples		Clocks

SUB reg,imm	SUB CL,4
	SUB DX,5
	SUB CH,12
	SUB SI,9
		8086	4

		8088	4
		80286	3
		80386	2
		80486	1

SUB mem,imm	SUB DATA,6
	SUB BYTE PTR [DI],7
	SUB NUMB,6
	SUB WORD PTR [ECX],5
		8086	17+ea

		8088	25+ea
		80286	7
		80386	7
		80486	3

0010110w data

Format	Examples		Clocks

SUB acc,imm	SUB AL,4
	SUB AX,5
	SUB AH,12
	SUB AX,9
		8086	4

		8088	4
		80286	3
		80386	2
		80486	1

TEST   Test operands (logical compare)

1000011w oorrrmmm disp

			O D I T S Z A P C 0 * * ? * 0
Format	Examples		Clocks
TEST reg,reg	TEST CL,DL TEST CX,DX TEST CL,CH TEST ECX,EBX	8086	5
		8088	5
		80286	2
		80386	2
		80486	1
TEST reg,mem mem,reg	TEST DATA,CL TEST CL,DATA	8086	9+ea
		8088	13+ea
		80286	6
		80386	5
		80486	2

1111011w oo000mmm disp data

Format	Examples		Clocks
TEST reg,imm	TEST CL,4 TEST DX,5 TEST CH,12H TEST SI,256	8086	4
		8088	4
		80286	3
		80386	2
		80486	1
TEST mem,imm	TEST DATA,6	8086	11+ea
		8088	11+ea
		80286	6
		80386	5
		80486	2

1010100w data

Format	Examples		Clocks
TEST acc,imm	TEST AL,4 TEST AX,5 TEST AH,12 TEST AX,9 TEST EAX,2	8086	4
		8088	4
		80286	3
		80386	2
		80486	1

VERR/VERW   Verify read or write

00001111 00000000 oo100mmm disp		O D I T S Z A P C ⠀⠀⠀⠀⠀⠀⠀*	
Format	Examples		Clocks
VERR reg	VERR BX VERR CX VERR DX	8086	—
		8088	—
		80286	14
		80386	10
		80486	11
VERR mem	VERR DATA	8086	—
		8088	—
		80286	16
		80386	11
		80486	11

00001111 00000000 oo101mmm disp

Format	Examples	Clocks	
VERW reg	VERW AX VERW CX VERW DX	8086	—
		8088	—
		80286	14
		80386	15
		80486	11
VERW mem	VERW DATA	8086	—
		8088	—
		80286	16
		80386	16
		80486	11

WAIT   Wait for coprocessor

10011011		O D I T S Z A P C	
Examples			Clocks
WAIT FWAIT		8086	4
		8088	4
		80286	3
		80386	6
		80486	6

WBINVD   Write back and invalidate data cache

00001111 00001001	O D I T S Z A P C	
Example		Clocks
WBINVD	8086	—
	8088	—
	80286	—
	80386	—
	80486	5

XADD   Exchange and add

0000111p ?!100000w 11rrrrrr

		O D I T S Z A P C
		* * * * * *
Format	Examples	Clocks
XADD reg,reg	XADD EBX,ECX XADD EDX,EAX XADD EDI,EBP	8086	—

Format	Examples		Clocks
XADD reg,reg	XADD EBX,ECX XADD EDX,EAX XADD EDI,EBP	8086	—
		8088	—
		80286	—
		80386	—
		80486	3

00001111 1100000w oorrrmmm disp

Format	Examples		Clocks
XADD mem,reg	XADD DATA,EAX XADD [DI],EAX XADD [ECX],EDX	8086	—
		8088	—
		80286	—
		80386	—
		80486	4

XCHG   Exchange

1000011w 1oorrrmmm   O D I T S Z A P C

Format	Examples		Clocks
XCHG reg,reg	XCHG BL,CL XCHG AX,DX XCHG EDI,EBP	8086	4
		8088	4
		80286	3
		80386	3
		80486	3
XCHG reg,mem mem,reg	XCHG CL,DATA XCHG DATA,CL XCHG DX,[DI] XCHG ECX,[EBP]	8086	17+ea
		8088	25+ea
		80286	5
		80386	5
		80486	5

10010reg			
Format	**Examples**		**Clocks**
XCHG acc,reg XCHG reg,acc	XCHG DATA,AL XCHG AX,FRIED	8086	3
		8088	3
		80286	3
		80386	3
		80486	3

XLAT   Translate

11010111		O D I T S Z A P C	
Example			**Clocks**
XLAT		8086	11
		8088	11
		80286	5
		80386	3
		80486	4

XOR   Exclusive-OR

001100dw oorrrmmm disp		O D I T S Z A P C 0 * * ? * 0	
Format	**Examples**		**Clocks**
XOR reg,reg	XOR BL,CL XOR CX,DX XOR CH,CL XOR EAX,EBX	8086	3
		8088	3
		80286	2
		80386	2
		80486	1
XOR mem,reg	XOR DATA,CL XOR BYTES,CX XOR NUMBS,ECX XOR [EAX],CX	8086	16+ea
		8088	24+ea
		80286	7
		80386	6
		80486	3

XOR reg,mem	XOR CL,DATA XOR CX,BYTES XOR ECX,NUMBS XOR CX,[EDX]	8086	9+ea
		8088	13+ea
		80286	7
		80386	7
		80486	2

100000sw oo110mmm disp data

Format	Examples		Clocks
XOR reg,imm	XOR BL,33 XOR CX,234H XOR CH,'A' XOR EAX,123445	8086	4
		8088	4
		80286	3
		80386	2
		80486	1
XOR mem,imm	XOR DATA,34 XOR BYTES,1234 XOR NUMBS,123 XOR [EAX],11	8086	17+ea
		8088	25+ea
		80286	7
		80386	7
		80486	3

0011010w data

Format	Examples		Clocks
XOR acc,imm	XOR AL,33 XOR AX,234H XOR AL,'A' XOR EAX,123445	8086	4
		8088	4
		80286	3
		80386	2
		80486	1

APPENDIX C

Flag Bit Changes

This appendix shows only the instructions that actually change the flag bits. Any instruction not listed does not affect any of the flag bits.

Instruction	O	D	I	T	S	Z	A	P	C
AAA	?				?	?	*	?	*
AAD	?				*	*	?	*	?
AAM	?				*	*	?	*	?
AAS	?				?	?	*	?	*
ADC	*				*	*	*	*	*
ADD	*				*	*	*	*	*
AND	0				*	*	?	*	0
ARPL						*			
BSF						*			
BSR						*			
BT									*
BTC									*
BTR									*
BTS									*
CLC									0
CLD		0							
CLI			0						
CMC									*

Instruction	Flags								
	O	D	I	T	S	Z	A	P	C
CMP	*				*	*	*	*	*
CMPS	*				*	*	*	*	*
CMPXCHG	*				*	*	*	*	*
DAA	?				*	*	*	*	*
DAS	?				*	*	*	*	*
DEC	*				*	*	*	*	
DIV	?				?	?	?	?	?
IDIV	?				?	?	?	?	?
IMUL	*				?	?	?	?	*
INC	*				*	*	*	*	
IRET	*	*	*	*	*	*	*	*	*
LAR					*				
LSL					*				
MUL	*				?	?	?	?	*
NEG	*				*	*	*	*	*
OR	0				*	*	?	*	0
POPF/POPFD	*	*	*	*	*	*	*	*	*
RCL/RCR	*								*
REPE/REPNE						*			
ROL/ROR	*								*
SAHF					*	*	*	*	*
SAL/SAR	*				*	*	?	*	*
SHL/SHR	*				*	*	?	*	*
SBB	*				*	*	*	*	*
SCAS	*				*	*	*	*	*
SHLD/SHRD	?				*	*	?	*	*
STC									1
STD		1							
STI			1						
SUB	*				*	*	*	*	*
TEST	0				*	*	?	*	0
VERR/VERW					*				
XADD	*				*	*	*	*	*
XOR	0				*	*	?	*	0

APPENDIX D

Bus Standards

This appendix illustrates the bus standards found in most clone and IBM-PC systems. These buses are usually called ISA (IBM standard architecture). Although other bus standards exist, these represent the two that are most often found in computer systems.

Figure D–1 illustrates the 8-bit ISA standard found in the XT computer. Figure D–2 illustrates the 16-bit ISA standard found in the AT computer. Notice that the top connector in the AT standard is identical to the XT standard. This allows older 8-bit boards to be plugged into any 16-bit AT slot in an AT style computer system.

FIGURE D–1 The 8-bit XT-style edge connector.

Rear of computer

GND	B1	A1	$\overline{\text{IO CHCK}}$
RESET DRV	B2	A2	SD7
+5VDC	B3	A3	SD6
IRQ9	B4	A4	SD5
-5VDC	B5	A5	SD4
DRQ2	B6	A6	SD3
-12VDC	B7	A7	SD2
$\overline{\text{OWS}}$	B8	A8	SD1
+12VDC	B9	A9	SD0
GND	B10	A10	$\overline{\text{IO CHRDY}}$
$\overline{\text{SMEMW}}$	B11	A11	AEN
$\overline{\text{SMEMR}}$	B12	A12	SA19
$\overline{\text{IOW}}$	B13	A13	SA18
$\overline{\text{IOR}}$	B14	A14	SA17
$\overline{\text{DACK3}}$	B15	A15	SA16
DRQ3	B16	A16	SA15
$\overline{\text{DACK1}}$	B17	A17	SA14
DRQ1	B18	A18	SA13
$\overline{\text{REFRESH}}$	B19	A19	SA12
CLK	B20	A20	SA11
IRQ7	B21	A21	SA10
IRQ6	B22	A22	SA9
IRQ5	B23	A23	SA8
IRQ4	B24	A24	SA7
IRQ3	B25	A25	SA6
$\overline{\text{DACK2}}$	B26	A26	SA5
T/C	B27	A27	SA4
BALE	B28	A28	SA3
+5VDC	B29	A29	SA2
OSC	B30	A30	SA1
GND	B31	A31	SA0

Component side edge connector

FIGURE D–2   The 16-bit
AT-style bus connector.

Rear of computer

GND	B1	A1	IO CHCK
RESET DRV	B2	A2	SD7
+5VDC	B3	A3	SD6
IRQ9	B4	A4	SD5
-5VDC	B5	A5	SD4
DRQ2	B6	A6	SD3
-12VDC	B7	A7	SD2
OWS	B8	A8	SD1
+12VDC	B9	A9	SD0
GND	B10	A10	IO CHRDY
SMEMW	B11	A11	AEN
SMEMR	B12	A12	SA19
IOW	B13	A13	SA18
IOR	B14	A14	SA17
DACK3	B15	A15	SA16
DRQ3	B16	A16	SA15
DACK1	B17	A17	SA14
DRQ1	B18	A18	SA13
REFRESH	B19	A19	SA12
CLK	B20	A20	SA11
IRQ7	B21	A21	SA10
IRQ6	B22	A22	SA9
IRQ5	B23	A23	SA8
IRQ4	B24	A24	SA7
IRQ3	B25	A25	SA6
DACK2	B26	A26	SA5
T/C	B27	A27	SA4
BALE	B28	A28	SA3
+5VDC	B29	A29	SA2
OSC	B30	A30	SA1
GND	B31	A31	SA0

MEMCS16	D1	C1	SBHE
IOCS16	D2	C2	LA23
IRQ10	D3	C3	LA22
IRQ11	D4	C4	LA21
IRQ12	D5	C5	LA20
IRQ15	D6	C6	LA19
IRQ14	D7	C7	LA18
DACK0	D8	C8	LA17
DRQ0	D9	C9	MEMR
DACK5	D10	C10	MEMW
DRQ5	D11	C11	SD08
DACK6	D12	C12	SD09
DRQ6	D13	C13	SD10
DACK7	D14	C14	SD11
DRQ7	D15	C15	SD12
+5VDC	D16	C16	SD13
MASTER	D17	C17	SD14
GND	D18	C18	SD15

Component side edge connector

APPENDIX E

Answers to Even-Numbered Questions and Problems

CHAPTER 1

2. Video games, microwave ovens, and simple control systems.
4. Execution speeds of the 4-bit microprocessor were 20 KIPS, with the latest 32-bit microprocessor approaching 60 MIPs.
6. 4G bytes.
8. A pipeline is a term used to describe the data flow through the microprocessor. The microprocessor executes software more efficiently because the pipeline feeds various units within the microprocessor with instructions at various phases of execution.
10. 1M
12. 32 bits
14. 16 bits
16. No difference exists between the memory maps.
18. 512K bytes
20. 100000H
22. 8. AL, AH, BL, BH, CL, CH, DL, and DH.
24. 4. EAX, EBX, ECX, and EDX.
26. It is used with certain instructions to hold data for the execution of the instruction.
28. The rightmost side of the segment register is appended with a 0000_2 or 0H.
30. Yes, 16 bytes.
32. 12440H
34. Data segment. Extra segment.
36. Z = zero flag indicates if the result is zero
    S = sign flag holds the sign (+ or −)
    C = holds the carry after addition or borrow after subtraction
    A = holds the half-carry or half-borrow
    P = holds the parity (even or odd)
38. The D flag selects auto-increment or auto-decrement for the string instructions.
40. 8-bit, 16-bit, and 32-bits.

42. Word: 10000H = 34H and 10001H = 12H
    Double word: 10000H = 34H, 10001H = 12H, 10002H = 00H, and 10003 = 00H
44. A any segment register.
46. (a) 1111111110010111, (b) 0000000100101110, (c) 1111111111110100, (d) 0000000010000110, and (e) 1111000101000101.
48. (a) 0 10000010 01000000000000000000000
    (b) 1 10000010 01100000000000000000000
    (c) 0 10000101 10010000100000000000000
    (d) 1 10000101 00000100001000000000000
    (e) 0 10000111 00101100000110000000000

CHAPTER 2

2. AL, AH, BL, BH, CL, CH, DL, and DH.
4. EAX, EBX, ECX, EDX, ESP, EBP, ESI, and EDI.
6. You may not use register of mixed sizes.
8. (a) MOV EDX,EBX
   (b) MOV CL,BL
   (c) MOV BX,SI
   (d) MOV AX,DS
   (e) MOV AH,AL
10. #
12. An indicate mode of addressing memory data.
14. (a) 03234H, (b) 02300H, and (c) 02400H
16. MOV BYTE PTR [DI],3
18. MOV DWORD PTR [BX],23456H
20. (a) 21100H, (b) 10100H, and (c) 21000H
22. (a) 11750H, (b) 11950H, and (c) 11700H
24. BP
26. Direct, relative, and indirect.
28. The intersegment jump allows the program to jump to any memory location, while the intrasegment jump allows it to jump to any location within the current code segment.
30. A far jump allows the program to jump to any memory location.
32. (a) short, (b) near, (c) short, and (d) far.
34. JMP NEAR PTR [BX] assuming that BX contains offset address TABLE.
36. The PUSH [DI] instruction obtains a word from the data segment memory location addressed by DI and pushes onto the stack.
38. The PUSHAD instruction pushes EAX, EBX, ECX, EDX, ESP, EBP, EDI, and ESI onto the stack.

CHAPTER 3

2. D = the direction of the data flow and W indicates a word or double word.
4. DL

6. [BX+DI]

8. MOV AX,BX

10. 8B77

12. You may not change the code segment register.

14. CS

16. EAX, ECX, EDX, EBX, ESP, EBP, ESI, and EDI.

18. The PUSH BX instruction copies the contents of BX to the stack. 020FFH = BH and 020FEH = BL.

20. 2

22. The MOV DI,NUMB instruction loads DI with the 16-bit data stored at memory location NUMB. The LEA DI,NUMB instruction stores the address of NUMB in DI.

24. MOV with OFFSET is more efficient.

26. Both instructions are identical except LDS loads the DS register and LSS loads the SS register.

28. It selects auto-increment or auto-decrement mode for the string instructions.

30. DI address data in the extra segment and SI addresses data in the data segment.

32. The STOSW instruction copies AX into the extra segment memory location addressed by DI and the increments or decrements DI by 2.

34. The REP (repeat) prefix repeats a string instruction the number of times loaded into register CX.

36. In the DX register.

38. In software translated from an 8085 microprocessor.

40. (see Example E–1)

EXAMPLE E–1

```
TABLE   DB    30H,31H,32H,33H
        DB    33H,35H,36H,37H
        DB    38H,39H
        MOV   BX,OFFSET TABLE
        XLAT
```

42. The OUT DX,AX instruction sends the contents of AX to an I/O device addressed by DX.

44. MOV ES:[BX],AH

46. A command to the assembler that may or may not generate data.

48. LIST1 DB 30 DUP (?)

50. The ,386 directive selects the 80386 instruction set for the assembler.

52. Memory models.

54. Ends a program and returns control to DOS.

56. Allows selected register to be automatically pushed onto the stack and popped off the stack within a procedure.

58. (see Example E–2)

EXAMPLE E–2

```
COPY    PROC FAR

        MOV   AX,CS:DATA1
        MOV   BX,AX
```

```
        MOV   CX,AX
        MOV   DX,AX
        MOV   SI,AX
        RET

COPY    ENDP
```

CHAPTER 4

2. You may not use mixed register/data sizes.
4. Sum = 2100H. Z = 0, C = 0, AC = 1, P = 1, S = 0, and O = 0.
6. (see Example E–3)

EXAMPLE E–3

```
ADD   AX,BX
ADD   AX,CX
ADD   AX,DX
ADD   AX,SP
MOV   DI,AX
```

8. ADC DX,BX
10. The assembler has no way to identify the memory data as a byte, word, or double word.
12. Difference = 81H. Z = 0, C = 0, AC = 0, P = 1, S = 1, O = 0.
14. DEC EBX
16. Both SUB and CMP perform subtraction and the flags change for each instruction, but CMP discards the result.
18. DX and AX.
20. EDX and EAX.
22. (see Example E–4)

EXAMPLE E–4

```
MOV   AL,DL
MUL   DL
MUL   DL
MOV   DX,AX
```

24. AX
26. Division by zero and overflow.
28. AH
30. DAA and DAS.
32. AAM divides the contents of AX by 10 and leaves the quotient in AH and the remainder in AL.
34. (a) AND BX,DX, (b) AND DH,0EAH, (c) AND DI,BP, (d) AND EAX,1122H, (e) AND [BP],CX, and (f) AND DX,[SI-8].
36. (a) OR AH,BL, (b) OR ECX,88H, (c) OR SI,DX, (d) OR BP,1122H, (e) OR [BX],CX (f) OR AL,[BP+40], and (g) OR WHEN,AH.

38. (a) XOR AH,BH, (b) XOR CL,99H, (c) XOR DX,DI, (d) XOR ESP,1A23H, (e) XOR [EBX],DX, (f) XOR DI,[BP+60], and (g) XOR DI,WELL.

40. Both AND and TEST perform the AND operation and change the flags, but the result is discarded by the TEST instruction.

42. The NOT instruction performs the 1's complement, while the NEG instruction performs the 2's complement.

44. The SCASB instruction compares AL with the extra segment memory location addressed by the DI register.

46. The D flag = 0 to select auto-increment and D flag = 1 to select auto-decrement for the string instruction pointers SI and/or DI.

48. The REPNE SCASB instruction terminates if CX = 0 or if AL = the contents of the extra segment memory location addressed by DI.

50. (see Example E–5)

EXAMPLE E–5

```
MOV    DI,OFFSET LIST
MOV    CX,300H
MOV    AL,66H
REPNE SCASB
```

CHAPTER 5

2. The near jump.
4. The far jump.
6. It is a near label.
8. The IP register or the IP and CS registers.
10. The JMP DI instruction jumps to the memory location addressed by DI and the JMP [DI] goes to the data segment memory location addressed by DI and fetches the jump address from that location.
12. Z (JNZ/JNE or JZ/JE), S (JS or JNS), C (JC or JNC), P (JP or JNP), O (JO or JNO).
14. Whenever the overflow flag-bit is set.
16. JZ, JNZ, JA, JAE, JB, or JBE.
18. JCXZ jumps if CX = 0000H.
20. CX
22. The LOOPE instruction decrements CX and then tests the zero-flag bit and jumps if the condition is zero. Note that the decrement does not affect the flag bits.
24. (see Example E–6)

EXAMPLE E–6

```
LOOK    PROC NEAR

        MOV SI,OFFSET BLOCK
        MOV CX,100H
        MOV UP,0
        MOV DOWN,0
REPS:
        CMP BYTE PTR [SI],42H
```

```
             JA    REPS1
             JB    REPS2
             LOOP  REPS
             RET
REPS1:
             INC   UP
             LOOP  REPS
             RET
REPS2:
             INC   DOWN
             LOOP  REPS
             RET

LOOK         ENDP
```

26. The near CALL calls a procedure within the current code segment, while the far CALL calls a procedure at any memory location.
28. RET
30. A procedure is identified as near or far by using NEAR and FAR with the PROC statement.
32. (see Example E–7)

EXAMPLE E–7

```
CUBE         PROC  NEAR
             XOR   DX,DX
             MOV   AX,CX
             MUL   CX
             MUL   CX
             RET

CUBE         ENDP
```

34. (see Example E–8)

EXAMPLE E–8

```
SUMS         PROC  NEAR

             XOR   EDI,EDI
             ADD   EAX,EBX
             JNC   SUMS1
             INC   EDI
SUMS1:
             ADD   EAX,ECX
             JNC   SUMS2
             INC   EDI
SUMS2:
             ADD   EAX,EDX
             JNC   SUMS3
             INC   EDI
SUMS3:
             RET

SUMS         ENDP
```

36. INT or INTO

38. Division error.
40. The IRET instruction pops the flags from the stack in addition to returning.
42. When overflow is set.
44. STI and CLI.
46. Interrupt vector 9.
48. When the value of the register is not within the upper and lower boundary.
50. BP

CHAPTER 6

2. TEST.OBJ, TEST.LST, and TEST.CRF
4. It indicates that the label may be used by other programming modules.
6. BYTE PTR, WORD PTR, DWORD PTR, NEAR PTR, and FAR PTR.
8. MACRO
10. Parameters are transferred to the macro either in register or as special data that follow the MACRO statement.
12. The LOCAL macro must immediately follow the MACRO statement and it identifies local variables.
14. (see Example E–9)

EXAMPLE E–9

```
ADDM     MACRO  LIST,LENGTH
         LOCAL  ADM1,ADM2
         CLD
         MOV    CX,LENGTH
         MOV    SI,OFFSET LIST
         XOR    AX,AX
ADM1:
         ADD    AL,[SI]
         JNC    ADM2
         INC    AH
ADM2:
         INC    SI
         LOOP   ADM1
         ENDM
```

16. (see Example E–10)

EXAMPLE E–10

```
RANDOM   PROC NEAR

         INC   CL
         MOV   AH,6
         MOV   DL,0FFH
         INT   21H
         JZ    RANDOM
         RET

RANDOM   ENDP
```

18. (see Example E–11)

EXAMPLE E–11

```
READ_E  PROC NEAR

        MOV   AH,6
        MOV   DL,0FFH
        INT   21H
        JE    READ_E
        OR    AL,AL
        JNE   READ_E
        INT   21H
        CALL  DISP
        ROR   AL,1
        ROR   AL,1
        ROR   AL,1
        ROR   AL,1
        CALL  DISP
        RET

READ_E  ENDP

DISP    PROC NEAR

        PUSH  AX
        AND   AL,0FH
        ADD   AL,30H
        CMP   AL,39
        JBE   DISP1
        ADD   AL,7
DISP1:
        MOV   DL,AL
        INT   21H
        POP   AX
        RET

DISP    ENDP
```

20. AAM
22. 30H
24. (see Example E–12)

EXAMPLE E–12

```
READ    PROC  NEAR

        MOV   DI,OFFSET DATA
READ1:
        MOV   AH,6
        MOV   DL,0FFH
        INT   21H
        JZ    READ1
        CMP   AL,30H
        JB    READ2
        CMP   AL,39H
        JA    READ2
        SUB   AL,30H
        STOSB
        JMP   READ1
```

```
READ2:
                RET

        READ    ENDP
```

26. (see Example E–13)

EXAMPLE E–13

```
CONVERT PROC NEAR

        CMP   AL,'a'
        JB    CONVERT1
        CMP   AL,'z'
        JA    CONVERT1
        SUB   AL,20H
CONVERT1:
        RET

CONVERT ENDP
```

28. (see Example E–14)

EXAMPLE E–14

```
CMP   AL,6
JE    ONE
CMP   AL,7
JE    TWO
CMP   AL,8
JE    THREE
```

30. The boot sector contains a program that loads DOS into the system memory. The FAT allocates disk clusters to various program files. The root directory contains 128 file or subdirectory names.
32. The bootstrap loader loads DOS into memory and is found in the boot sector.
34. If it is read-only, a volume label, etc.
36. 4,294,967,295 bytes.
38. (see Example E–15)

EXAMPLE E–15

```
RENAME  PROC NEAR

        PUSH ES
        MOV  AX,DS
        MOV  ES,AX
        MOV  DI,OFFSET TEST_LST
        MOV  EI,OFFSET TEST_LIS
        MOV  AH,56H
        INT  21H
        POP  ES
        RET

RENAME  ENDP
```

40. (see Example E–16)

EXAMPLE E–16

```
DATA1    DB,  13,10,'2 = $'
DATA2    DB   13,10,'$'
POWERS   PROC NEAR
         MOV  CX,8
POWERS1:
         MOV  AH,9
         MOV  DX,OFFSET DATA1
         INT  21H
         PUSH CX
         MOV  AX,CX
         SUB  AX,8
         MOV  CX,AX
         MOV  AL,1
         ROR  AL,CL
         CALL DISP
         POP  CX
         MOV  AH,9
         MOV  DX,OFFSET DATA2
         INT  21H
         MOV  AX,CX
         SUB  8
         CALL DISP
         LOOP POWERS1
POWERS   ENDP
DISP     PROC NEAR
         XOR  AH,AH
         AAM
         CMP  AH,0
         JZ   DISP1
         PUSH AX
         ADD  AH,30H
         MOV  DL,AH
         MOV  AH,6
         INT  21H
         POP  AX
DISP1:
         ADD  AL,30H
         MOV  DL,AL
         MOV  AH,6
         INT  21H
         RET
DISP     ENDP
```

42. (see Example E–17)

EXAMPLE E–17 (page 1 of 4)

```
PROG     SEGMENT
         ASSUME CS:PROG

MAIN     PROC FAR

         CALL GET_ADR
         CALL NEW
         CALL DISP
```

EXAMPLE E–17 (page 2 of 4)

```
          MOV  AH,4CH
          INT  21H

MAIN      ENDP

MES1      DB   13,10,'Enter the starting address: $'

GET_ADR PROC NEAR

          PUSH DS
          MOV  AX,CS
          MOV  DS,AX
          MOV  DX,OFFSET MES1
          MOV  AH,9
          INT  21H
          POP  DS
          CALL READ
          RET

GET_ADR ENDP

READ      PROC NEAR

          XOR  CX,CX
READ1:
          CALL GET
          CMP  AL,13                    ;enter key
          JE   READ3
          CMP  AL,'0'
          JB   READ1
          CMP  AL,'9'
          JBE  READ2
          SUB  AL,7
          CMP  AL,'A-7'
          JB   READ1
          CMP  AL,'F-7'
          JA   READ1
READ2:
          SUB  AL,'0'
          PUSH AX
          INC  CX
          JMP  READ1
READ3:
          XOR  DX,DX
          XOR  BX,BX
          OR   CX,CX
          JE   READ5
READ4:
          POP  AX
          SHL  BX,1
          RCL  DX,1
          SHL  BX,1
          RCL  DX,1
          SHL  BX,1
          RCL  DX,1
          SHL  BX,1
          RCL  DX,1
          ADD  BL,AL
          LOOP READ4
          SHR  DX,1
```

EXAMPLE E–17 (page 3 of 4)

```
              RCR   BX,1
              SHR   DX,1
              RCR   BX,1
              SHR   DX,1
              RCR   BX,1
              SHR   DX,1
              RCR   BX,1
READ5:
              MOV   DS,BX
              XOR   SI,0
              RET

READ    ENDP

NEW     PROC  NEAR

              MOV   AL,13
              CALL  DIP
              MOV   AL,10
              CALL  DIP
              RET

NEW     ENDP

DIP     PROC  NEAR

              MOV   AH,6
              MOV   DL,AL
              INT   21H
              RET

DIP     ENDP

GET     PROC  NEAR

              MOV   AH,6
              MOV   DL,0FFH
              INT   21H
              JE    GET
              RET

GET     ENDP

DISP    PROC  NEAR

              MOV   CX,256
DISP1:
              MOV   AX,SI
              AND   AX,0FH
              JNZ   DISP2
              CALL  ADDR
DISP2:
              LODSB
              CALL  DIPS
              MOV   AL,20H
              INT   21H
              LOOP  DISP1
              RET

DISP    ENDP
```

EXAMPLE E–17 (page 4 of 4)

```
DIPS      PROC NEAR

          PUSH AX
          SHR  AX,4
          ADD  AL,30H
          CMP  AL,'9'
          JBE  DIPS1
          ADD  AL,7
DIPS1:
          CALL DIP
          POP  AX
          ADD  AL,30H
          CMP  AL,'9'
          JBE  DIPS2
          ADD  AL,7
DIPS2:
          CALL DIP
          RET

DIPS      ENDP

ADDR      PROC NEAR

          CALL NEW
          MOV  AX,DS
          PUSH AX
          MOV  AL,AH
          CALL DIPS
          POP  AX
          CALL DIPS
          MOV  AL,':'
          CALL DIPS
          MOV  AX,SI
          MOV  AL,AH
          CALL DIPS
          MOV  AX,SI
          CALL DIPS
          MOV  AL,20H
          CALL DIPS
          RET

ADDR      ENDP

PROG      ENDS

          END  MAIN
```

CHAPTER 7

2. The 8086/8088 is TTL compatible as long as the load current is limited to no more than 2.0 mA.

4. A7–A0

6. That the microprocessor is about to read data through the data bus connections.

8. The signal applied to the CLK input must be a TTL compatible square wave that has a frequency of between 500 KHz and 5.0 MHz for the standard version.

10. The $\overline{WR}$ indicates that the microprocessor is about to write data through its data bus to either the I/O or memory system.

12. The DT/$\overline{R}$ signal is a logic one to redirect the bus buffers to transmit data from the microprocessor toward the memory and I/O system.

14. IO/$\overline{M}$, DT/$\overline{R}$, and $\overline{SSO}$.

16. The queue status bits indicate the condition of the internal queue for the external numeric coprocessor.

18. 3

20. 2.333 MHz

22. AD15–AD0, A19/S6–A16/S3, and $\overline{BHE}$/S7.

24. The 74LS373 latch.

26. Because the 8086/8088 only sink 2.0 mA of current, we often need to buffer the microprocessor to increase the drive current.

28. 4

30. A read or a write.

32. (a) used to provide the memory or I/O with the address

   (b) allows time for the memory or I/O to access data

   (c) issues the read or write control signals

   (d) reads or writes the data

34. The $\overline{DEN}$ is 580 ns wide.

36. It selects one stage of synchronization.

38. Minimum mode operation is similar to the early 8-bit microprocessors, where maximum mode operation is provided to interface the microprocessor to its coprocessor.

CHAPTER 8

2. (a) 256, (b) 2K, (c) 4K, and (d) 8K.

4. These pins enable or select the memory device.

6. The $\overline{WE}$ is used to enable a write operation if the $\overline{CS}$ pin is also activated.

8. The 8088 allows 460 ns of access time for the memory, if you include the time it takes to decode the memory address, less than 450 ns are left for memory access. This prevents the 450 ns EPROM from working correctly.

10. The $\overline{S}$ pin selects the memory device so it can read or write data, the $\overline{G}$ pin causes a read if the $\overline{S}$ pin is active, and the $\overline{W}$ pin causes a write if the $\overline{S}$ pin is active.

12. Dynamic random access memory.

14. The $\overline{CAS}$ sends the column address into the multiplexed address pins of the DRAM and the $\overline{RAS}$ sends the row address the pins.

16. Memory address decoders allow more than one memory device to function in the memory system.

18. (see Figure E–1)

20. (see Figure E–2)

22. The 74LS139 decoder is a dual 2-to-4 lines decoder.

FIGURE E-1

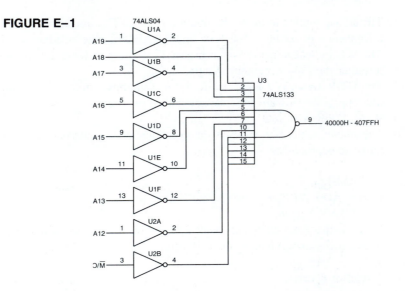

FIGURE E-2

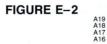

24.

Inputs										Outputs							
$\overline{OE}$	A8	A7	A6	A5	A4	A3	A2	A1	A0	O0	O1	O2	O3	O4	O5	O6	O7
0	0	0	1	0	0	0	0	0	0	0	1	1	1	1	1	1	1
0	0	0	1	0	0	0	0	0	1	1	0	1	1	1	1	1	1
0	0	0	1	0	0	0	0	1	0	1	1	0	1	1	1	1	1
0	0	0	1	0	0	0	0	1	1	1	1	1	0	1	1	1	1
0	0	0	1	0	0	0	1	0	0	1	1	1	1	0	1	1	1
0	0	0	1	0	0	0	1	0	1	1	1	1	1	1	0	1	1
0	0	0	1	0	0	0	1	1	0	1	1	1	1	1	1	0	1
0	0	0	1	0	0	0	1	1	1	1	1	1	1	1	1	1	0
all other address combinations										1	1	1	1	1	1	1	1

26. $\overline{MRDC}$ and $\overline{MWTC}$
28. (see Figure E-3)
30. (see Figure E-4)

FIGURE E–3

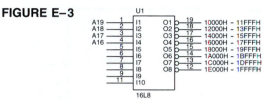

32. 5
34. 1
36. The $\overline{BHE}$ indicates that the microprocessor will use D15–D8 for a read or write and A0 indicates it will use A7–A0.
38. high
40. The microprocessor may not read part of the bus, but this will not cause any damage if data are presented to that part of the bus with the $\overline{RD}$ strobe.
42. (see Figure E–5)
44. An $\overline{RAS}$-only cycle is used to refresh the DRAM without reading or writing data.
46. 15.625 μs.
48. This selects a memory bank.
50. TWST inserts a wait state.
52. (see Example E–18)

EXAMPLE E–18

```
TITLE        Address Decoder
PATTERN      Test 1U4 (PAL U4)
REVISION     A
AUTHOR       Barry B. Brey
COMPANY      Symbiotic Systems
DATE         6/27/93
CHIP         Decoder1U4 PAL16L8


;pins 1     2   3   4   5   6   7   8   9   10
      MWTC  BE0 BE1 BE2 BE3 A22 A23 A24 A25 GND

;pins 11  12 13 14  15  16  17  18  19  20
      A26 NC U2 MB1 WR0 WR1 WR2 WR3 MB0 VCC
EQUATIONS
/WRO = /MWTC * /BE0
/WR1 = /MWTC * /BE1
/WR2 = /MWTC * /BE2
/WR3 = /MWTC * /BE3
/MBO = /A26 * /A25 * /A24 * /A23 * /A22 * /U2
/MB1 = /A26 * /A25 * /A24 * /A23 *  A22 * /U2


TITLE        Address Decoder
PATTERN      Test 1U5 (PAL U5)
REVISION     A
AUTHOR       Barry B. Brey
COMPANY      Symbiotic Systems
DATE         6/27/93
CHIP         Decoder1U5 PAL16L8
```

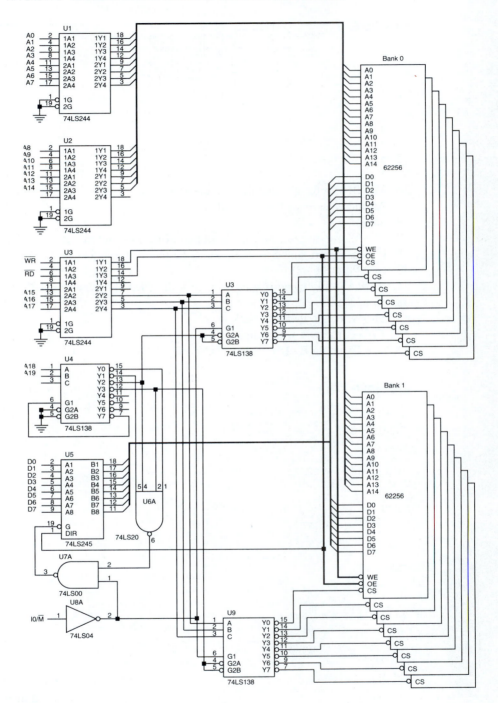

FIGURE E–4

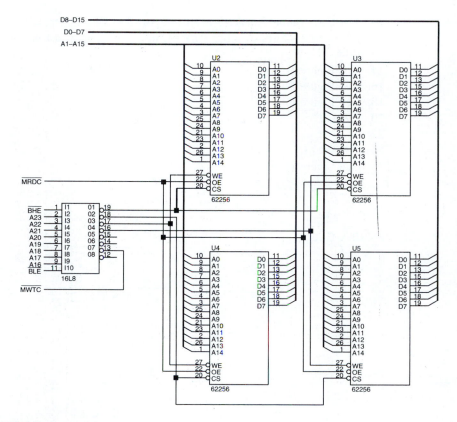

FIGURE E–5

```
;pins 1     2    3    4    5    6    7   8   9   10
      A27  A28  A29  A30  A31  CAS  NC  NC  NC  GND

;pins 11  12  13  14  15  16  17  18  19   20
      NC  NC  NC  NC  NC  NC  NC  NC  U2   VCC

EQUATIONS

/U2 = A31 * /A30 * A29 * /A28 * /A27 * /CAS
```

CHAPTER 9

2. The byte following the opcode holds the port number.

4. DX

6. The OUTSB instruction copies the contents of the data segment memory location addressed by SI to the I/O port addressed by DX. After the transfer, SI is either incremented by one or decremented by one.

8. Isolated I/O uses the I/O ports located in a separate map called an *I/O map* at I/O address 0000H–FFFFH to access I/O. Memory-mapped I/O uses a portion of the memory system to access I/O devices.

10. The basic output interface is an I/O port decoder connected to the clock input of a latch that captures data bus data whenever the output instruction is executed.

12. Low.

14. (see Figure E–6)

16. (see Figure E–7)

18. (see Figure E–8)

20. D7–D0.

22. 24.

24. A1 and A0.

26. (see Figure E–9)

FIGURE E–6

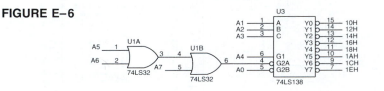

FIGURE E–7

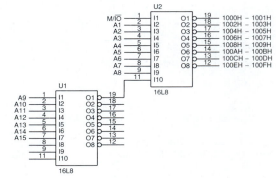

FIGURE E–8

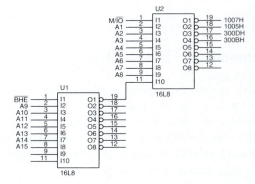

FIGURE E–9

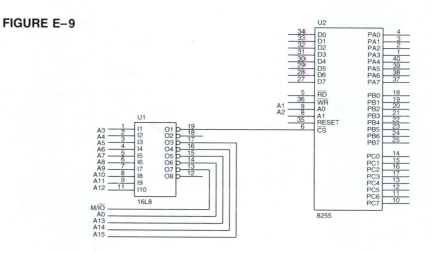

28. Latched I/O, strobed I/O, and bidirectional I/O
30. The armature rotates each time current flows through a pair of coils.
32. (see Example E–19)

EXAMPLE E–19

```
MOV   AL,0FH
OUT   COMMAND,AL
```

34. The $\overline{\text{ACK}}$ signal clears the output buffer full flag to indicate that the data have been removed from the I/O port.
36. (see Example E–20)

EXAMPLE E–20

```
IN    AL,PORTC
TEST  AL,10H
JNZ   PC4_IS_ONE
```

38. PC0–PC2.
40. 2
42. An overrun error occurs if the software fails to remove data from the keyboard FIFO when it becomes full.
44. (see Figure E–10)
46. 10 MHz
48. (see Figure E–11)
50. Low order byte.
52. (see Example E–21)

EXAMPLE E–21

```
;This software assumes a 1 MHz clock
;
MOV   AL,74H
```

FIGURE E–10

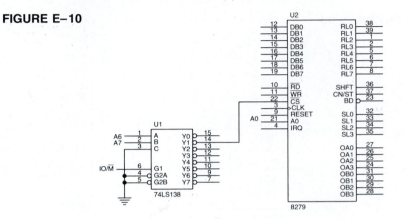

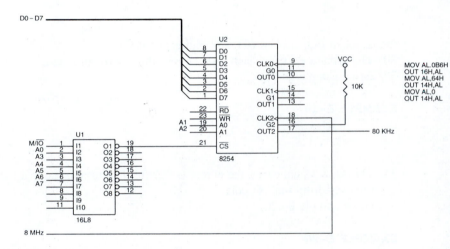

FIGURE E–11

```
OUT   COMMAND,AL        ;select mode 2
MOV   AL,65H            ;count is 101
OUT   TIMER1,AL
XOR   AL,AL
OUT   TIMER1,AL
```

54. Data that are transmitted without a clock signal.

56. The number of bits transmitted per second including the start and stop bits.

58. 36,000 Hz.

60. By sending three 00Hs to the command register followed by the reset command 40H.

62. +.01 V

64. (see Example E–22)

EXAMPLE E–22

```
MOV   DX,400H          ;address port 400H
XOR   AL,AL            ;start data at 00H
```

FIGURE E–12

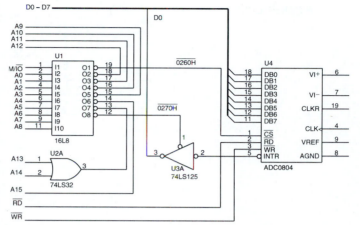

```
REPS:
        OUT   DX,AL              ;send data
        CALL  DELAY             ;wait 17.7 µs
        INC   AL
        JNZ   REPS
        DEC   AL
REPS1:
        DEC   AL
        JZ    REPS
        OUT   DX,AL
        CALL  DELAY
        JMP   REPS1
```

66. This pin signals the end of the conversion.
68. (see Figure E–12)

CHAPTER 10

2. An interrupt is a hardware initiated CALL to a procedure that services the interrupt. This CALL interrupts the currently executing program until the interrupt service procedure is complete.

4. The I/O devices do not require attention until they activate the interrupt request input to the microprocessor. This uses the least amount of execution time.

6. INT nn (including INT 3), INTO, IRET, STI, and CLI.

8. 00000H–003FFH

10. Vectors 0–31 (0H–1FH).

12. The BOUND instruction compares a register with the contents of two words of memory, one contains a lower limit and the other the upper limit. If the number in the register is outside of these "bounds," an interrupt occurs.

14. 00110H–00113H.

16. This interrupt is used to emulate the numeric coprocessor in the 80286–80486.

FIGURE E–13

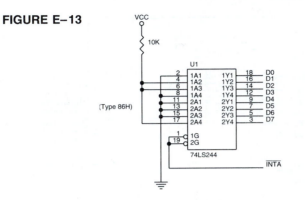

18. The interrupt flag controls the INTR pin. If the I flag = 0, the INTR is masked off and if the I flag = 1, the INTR pin is active.
20. The interrupt flag is cleared and set with the CLI and STI instructions.
22. 2
24. Positive
26. Vector
28. (see Figure E–13)
30. When the microprocessor inputs these data bus connections to determine the interrupt vector number, it sees an FFH because the bus is pulled high.
32. The daisy-chain does not indicate which device caused the interrupt; this is the responsibility of the software, which must poll the devices to determine which device caused the interrupt.
34. 9
36. The cascade pins are used when more than one 8259 is present in the system.
38. The ICW is an initialization command word used to program the 8259.
40. ICW1, ICW2, and ICW4.
42. ICW1
44. A command that ends the currently active interrupt as determined by the 8259A.
46. The IRR indicates which interrupt levels are masked.

CHAPTER 11

2. The microprocessor suspends execution of the current instruction and floats its address, data, and control buses.
4. I/O to memory.
6. DACK
8. The microprocessor is idle and the DMA controller governs the system.
10. 4
12. Command register.
14. (see Example E–23)

EXAMPLE E-23

```
MOV   AL,2H
OUT   LATCH,AL              ;set A19-A16 to 2
OUT   FL,AL                 ;clear F/L FF
XOR   AL,AL                 ;source of 21000H
OUT   CHO_ADD
MOV   AL,10H
OUT   CHO_ADD
XOR   AL,AL                 ;destination of 20000H
OUT   CH1_ADD,AL
OUT   CH1_ADD,AL
MOV   AL,0FFH               ;program count
OUT   CH1_CNT,AL
XOR   AL,AL
OUT   CH1_CNT,AL
MOV   AL,88H                ;program mode
OUT   MODE,AL
MOV   AL,85H
OUT   MODE,AL
MOV   AL,1
OUT   CMD,AL                ;enable block move
MOV   AL,0EH
OUT   MASKS,AL              ;unmask channel 0
MOV   AL,4
OUT   REQ,AL                ;request DMA
```

16. Mini
18. Tracks
20. Cylinder
22. (see Figure E-14)
24. The head assembly on a fixed disk is aerodynamically designed to glide on a thin cushion of air over the surface of the disk. It is called a flying head.
26. The voice coil is much more accurate than the stepper motor because its position can be finely adjusted while the disk system operates.
28. A CDROM is very similar to the audio CD in that it stores data in the form of music or digital codes for the computer.
30. Red, green, and blue.
32. The smallest displayed unit in a video display system.
34. The TTL RGB monitor displays 16 colors because it controls the three primary colors of light at two intensities.
36. 2,097,152 colors.
38. 32,400/60 = 540.

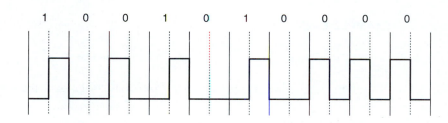

FIGURE E-14

CHAPTER 12

2. The word integers range in value from −32,768 to +32,767, the short integer from −2 × 10^{+9} to +2 × 10^{−9}, and the long integer from −9 × 10^{+18} to +9 × 10^{−18}.

4. Single-precision (32 bits), double-precision (64 bits), and extended-precision (80 bits).

6. (a) − 15, (b) + .5625, (c) + 306, (d) + 1, (e) + 10, (f) = + 0.0

8. To the $\overline{\text{BUSY}}$ pin on the 80286.

10. The 80287 is idle or executing a coprocessor instruction while the 80286 executes normal instructions.

12. After an FXAM instruction they indicate if the top of the stack is positive, negative, invalid, normalized, unnormalized, 0, or empty.

14. FLDCW

16. ST(0).

18. Affine selects signed infinity and projected selects unsigned infinity.

20. (a) FROG DQ 23.44, (b) DATA3 DD −123, (c) DATA1 DD −23.8, and (d) DATA2 DQ ?.

22. Loads an integer from memory location DATA to the top of the stack.

24. The FADD instruction adds the top of the stack—ST—to the next to the top of the stack—ST(1)—and removes both numbers from the stack. The result is placed at the top of the stack.

26. Stores the ST as a BCD number in the 80 bits of memory beginning at DATA and then pops the top of the stack.

28. Both test the top of the stack, the FTST compares the ST with 0, while the FXAM instruction reports what is at the top of the stack. The status register bits contain (C0–C3) this information.

30. FLDPI

32. FSTENV

34. (see Example E−24)

EXAMPLE E−24

```
FLD   L
FLD   W
FMUL
FSTP  A
```

36. (see Example E−25)

EXAMPLE E−25

```
        MOV   SI,OFFSET TABLE        ;table
        MOV   NUMB,2                 ;16-bi integer
REPS:
        FILD NUMB                    ;get number
        FSQRT
        FSTP DWORD PTR [SI]          ;save square root
        ADD   SI,4
        INC   NUMB
        CMP   NUMB,11
        JNE   REPS
```

38. (see Example E–26)

EXAMPLE E–26

```
FLD1
FDIV   R2                        ;1/R2
FLD1
FDIV   R3                        ;1/R3
FLD1
FDIV   R4                        ;1/R4
FADD                             ;1/R3 + 1/R4
FADD                             ;1/R2 + 1/R3 + 1/R4
FLD1
FDIV
FADD   R1
FSTP   RT
```

CHAPTER 13

2. Clock generator, three timers, programmable interrupt controller, programmable DMA controller, and a memory/peripheral chip selection unit.
4. 10 MHz
6. 2.0 mA
8. The ALE signal appears one half clocking period early.
10. 417 ns
12. (see Example E–27)

EXAMPLE E–27

```
MOV   AX,3100H                   ;new relocation value
MOV   DX,0FFFEH
OUT   DX,AX
```

14. 9
16. The control register selects priority, trigger level, mask, and type of operation for the device.
18. If the interrupt poll status is read, the interrupt is acknowledged; if the interrupt poll register is read, the interrupt is not acknowledged.
20. 3
22. Timer 2
24. Controls whether EN can change or not change.
26. Selects single maximum-count register (A) or dual maximum-count register operation (A plus B).
28. (see Example E–28)

EXAMPLE E–28

```
MOV   AX,123
MOV   DX,0FF5AH
OUT   DX,AX                      ;program A
MOV   AX,23
```

```
ADD    DX,2
OUT    DX,AX                    ;program B
MOV    DX,0FF58H
MOV    AX,8007H
OUT    DX,AX                    ;start Timer 1
```

30. 2
32. The channel is started by software (control register) or by hardware (timer 2 or the DRQ input).
34. 7
36. Base
38. 0 and 3
40. Selects the operation of $\overline{PCS5}$/A0 and $\overline{PCS6}$/A1.
42. 1G
44. Verifies if a read operation can be performed on a memory segment.

CHAPTER 14

2. 64T
4. (see Figure E–15)
6. The memory system is 32 bits wide containing four banks that are each 8 bits wide. The bank selection signals ($\overline{BE0}$-$\overline{BE3}$) select all four banks for a 32-bit operation, two banks for a 16-bit operation, and a single bank for an 8-bit operation.

FIGURE E–15

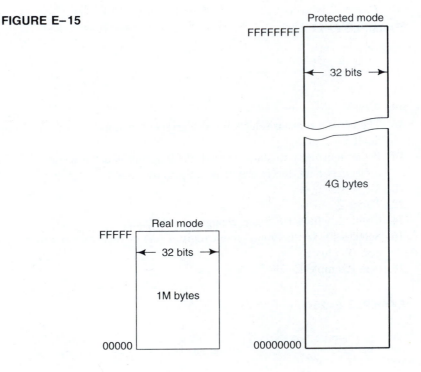

8. The pipeline lengthens access time because the microprocessor sends the address a clock pulse earlier.

10. 0000H–FFFFH

12. The 80386 I/O space is identical, but the memory contains 4,096M bytes instead of 1M byte in the 8086/8088.

14. This structures the 80386 so it has a 16-bit data bus.

16. EAX, EBX, ECX, EDX, ESP, EBP, ESI, EDI, EIP, and EFLAGS.

18. CRO controls the protected mode environment and selects paging, CR1 is not used, CR2 holds the page fault address when paging is active, and CR3 holds the base address of the page directory.

20. Type 1

22. The bit scan reverse instruction scans a register searching for a logic one from the left toward the right; if a one is found, its bit position bit is reported.

24. MOV FS:[DI],EAX

26. Yes

28. It acts as a coprocessor emulation interrupt.

30. A double interrupt fault occurs when a type 10, 11, 12, or 13 interrupt occurs at the same time as a type 14.

32. A descriptor describes the location, size, and access rights of a memory segment, an interrupt, procedure, or a task.

34. The TI bit in the segment register is a logic 1.

36. 8,192

38. A segment descriptor describes a code, data, or stack segment and a system descriptor describes an interrupt, call, or jump.

40. The TSS is addressed by loading a new value to the TR (task register).

42. The 80386 switches from protected mode to real mode by placing a logic 0 in the PE bit of CR0.

44. With the base address in CR3.

46. The paging unit reassigns memory address D0000000H to location C0000000H as an instruction executes.

48. The $\overline{\text{FLUSH}}$ erases the contents of the internal 80486 cache.

50. The 80486 flag register contains an AC flag bit for use with the 80487 coprocessor.

52. Even

54. 16 bytes

56. The term indicates that a write occurs to both the cache and the memory simultaneously.

58. Yes, the cache is disabled by a bit in CR0.

60. It either copies AL into AL or CL into CL.

62. It disables the cache.

INDEX